Karl Baedeker

Southern Germany, Including Wurtemberg and Bavaria

Handbook for Travellers. Eighth Edition

Karl Baedeker

Southern Germany, Including Wurtemberg and Bavaria
Handbook for Travellers. Eighth Edition

ISBN/EAN: 9783337209797

Printed in Europe, USA, Canada, Australia, Japan

Cover: Foto ©Andreas Hilbeck / pixelio.de

More available books at **www.hansebooks.com**

MONEY TABLE.

(Comp. p. xi.)

Approximate Equivalents.

American Money		English Money			French Money		German Money		Austrian Money	
Doll.	Cts.	L.	S.	D.	Fr.	Cts.	ℳ	Pf.	Fl.	Kr.
—	1¼	—	—	⅝	—	6¼	—	5	—	3
—	2½	—	—	1¼	—	12½	—	10	—	6
—	5	—	—	2½	—	25	—	20	—	12
—	10	—	—	5	—	50	—	40	—	24
—	12½	—	—	6	—	62½	—	50	—	30
—	20	—	—	10	1	—	—	80	—	48
—	25	—	1	—	1	25	1	—	—	60
—	50	—	2	—	2	50	2	—	1	20
—	75	—	3	—	3	75	3	—	1	75
1	—	—	4	—	5	—	4	—	2	40
1	25	—	5	—	6	25	5	—	3	—
1	50	—	6	—	7	50	6	—	3	50
1	75	—	7	—	8	75	7	—	4	10
2	—	—	8	—	10	—	8	—	4	80
2	25	—	9	—	11	25	9	—	5	40
2	50	—	10	—	12	50	10	—	6	—
3	—	—	12	—	15	—	12	—	7	20
4	—	—	16	—	20	—	16	—	9	60
5	—	1	—	—	25	—	20	—	12	25
25	—	5	—	—	125	—	100	—	60	—
125	—	25	—	—	625	—	500	—	300	—

SOUTHERN GERMANY,

INCLUDING

WURTEMBERG AND BAVARIA

HANDBOOK FOR TRAVELLERS

BY

KARL BAEDEKER

With 16 Maps and 15 Plans

EIGHTH REVISED EDITION

LEIPSIC: KARL BAEDEKER, PUBLISHER.
LONDON: DULAU & CO., 37 SOHO SQUARE W.
1895

'Go, little book, God send thee good passage,
And specially let this be thy prayere,
Unto them all that thee will read or hear,
Where thou art wrong, after their help to call,
Thee to correct in any part or all.'

PREFACE.

The HANDBOOK FOR SOUTHERN GERMANY, which is now issued for the eighth time, and corresponds with the twenty-fifth German edition, is designed to assist the traveller in planning his tour and disposing of his time to the best advantage, to render him as far as possible independent of the services of hotel-keepers, commissionnaires, and guides, and thus to enable him the more thoroughly to enjoy and appreciate the objects of interest he meets with on his tour.

The Handbook has been compiled almost entirely from the personal observation of the Editor, and most of the country described has been repeatedly explored by him with a view to procure the latest possible information; but, as many of the data in the Handbook relate to matters which are constantly undergoing alteration, he will highly appreciate any corrections or suggestions with which travellers may favour him. Those already received, which in many instances have proved most useful, he gratefully acknowledges.

In previous issues of the Handbook, Southern Germany was combined in one volume with Austria, but the two countries will henceforth appear separately. In the present volume special attention has been devoted to the art-treasures of Munich and other large cities; and it is believed that the introductory article upon South German art, by the late *Professor Anton Springer*, will be welcome to many travellers. The Alpine tourist will find the mountainous districts more fully described in the Handbook to the Eastern Alps. For Baden, Alsace, Lorraine, and Rhenish Bavaria the traveller is referred to the Handbook to the Rhine.

The MAPS and PLANS, on which special care has been bestowed, will, it is hoped, render material service to the traveller in planning his tour.

TIME TABLES. Information as to the departure of trains, steamboats, and diligences is seldom to be relied upon unless obtained from local sources. Full and accurate timetables are contained in the '*Reichs-Kursbuch*', published at Berlin, and in '*Hendschel's Telegraph*', published at Frankfort on the Main, both of which are issued monthly in summer.

DISTANCES by road are given approximately in English miles; but in the case of mountain-excursions they are expressed by the time in which they can be accomplished by average walkers. HEIGHTS are given in English feet (1 Engl. ft. = 0,3048 mètre = 0,938 Parisian ft. = 0,971 Prussian ft.), and the POPULATIONS from data furnished by the most recent census.

HOTELS. The Editor has endeavoured to enumerate, not only the first-class hotels, but others of a less pretending kind, which may be safely selected by the 'voyageur en garçon', with little sacrifice of comfort, and great saving of expenditure. Hotel-charges, as well as carriage-fares and fees to guides, are liable to frequent variation, and generally have a strong upward tendency; but these items, as stated in the Handbook either from the personal experience of the Editor or from data furnished by numerous correspondents, will at least afford the traveller an approximate idea of his expenditure. Those hotels which the Editor has reason to believe good of their class are distinguished by an asterisk, but he does not doubt that equal excellence may often be found in hotels that are unstarred and even unmentioned.

To hotel-keepers, tradesmen, and others the Editor begs to intimate that a character for fair dealing towards travellers forms the sole passport to his commendation, and that advertisements of every kind are strictly excluded from his Handbooks. Hotel-keepers are also warned against persons representing themselves as agents for Baedeker's Handbooks.

CONTENTS.

	Page.
I. Language. Money	xi
II. Passports. Custom Houses	xii
III. Conveyances	xii
IV. Excursions on Foot	xiii
V. Hotels	xiii
South German Art, by *Professor* Anton *Springer*	xv

Wurtemberg.

Route.
1. Stuttgart and Environs 1
2. From Heidelberg to Stuttgart by Bruchsal 14
   Maulbronn, 15. — From Zuffenhausen to Calw and Horb, 16.
3. From Stuttgart to Wildbad 17
   From Pforzheim to Calw, 17. — From Pforzheim to Durlach, 18. — Excursions from Wildbad, 19.
4. From Stuttgart to Hanau 19
   From Jagstfeld to Osterburken and to Heidelberg, 22.
5. From Heilbronn to Schwäbisch-Hall (Nuremberg) . . . 23
6. From Stuttgart to Crailsheim and Nuremberg viâ Backnang . 24
   From Backnang to Bietigheim, 25. — From Crailsheim to Mergentheim and to Nördlingen, 26.
7. From Stuttgart to Nördlingen and Nuremberg 27
   From Aalen to Ulm, 28.
8. From Stuttgart to Friedrichshafen 29
   From Geislingen to the Swabian Alb, 31. — From Ulm to Kempten, 33. — Veitsburg. Waldburg, 35.
9. From Stuttgart to Tübingen and Horb 35
   Bebenhausen. Wurmlinger Capelle. The Baths of Imnau. Haigerloch, 38.
10. From Stuttgart to Böblingen and Schaffhausen . . . 39
    From Eutingen to Hausach, 39. — From Rottweil to Villingen, 40. — Hohentwiel, 41.
11. The Swabian Alb 42
12. From Tübingen to Hechingen and Sigmaringen 48
    Hohenzollern, 48. — The Upper Valley of the Danube, 52.
13. From Ulm to Radolfzell and Constance 52
    Schmiechthal. Grosse Lauterthal, 53. — Zwiefalten. From Herbertingen to Memmingen. From Mengen to Sigmaringen, 54. — From Schwakenreute to Aulendorf, 55. — Mainau. Meersburg. Ueberlingen, 57, 58.

CONTENTS.

Bavaria.

Route. | Page.

14. From Frankfort to Nuremberg by Würzburg 59
From Frankfort to Hanau viâ Offenbach, 59. — Kahlgrund, 59. — From Aschaffenburg to Mayence direct. From Aschaffenburg to Amorbach, 61. — From Miltenberg and from Lohr to Wertheim, 62. — The Spessart. From Gemünden to Elm, to Hammelburg, and to Schweinfurt, 63, 64. — Windsheim, 69. — From Fürth to Cadolzburg, 70.

15. From Würzburg to Heidelberg 70
From Lauda to Wertheim and to Mergentheim, 70. — From Osterburken to Jagstfeld. From Neckarelz to Meckesheim, 71.

16. From Leipsic to Nuremberg by Bamberg 72
From Plauen to Eger, 72. — The Baths of Steben. From Hof to Eger, 73. — From Hochstadt to Saalfeld, 74. — Banz. Vierzehnheiligen, 75. — From Erlangen to Gräfenberg, 81.

17. From Würzburg to Bamberg. Kissingen 81
The Ludwigsbad Wipfeld, 82. — Excursions from Bocklet and from Brückenau, 85. — From Kissingen to Meiningen, 85.

18. From Neuenmarkt to Weiden. The Fichtelgebirge ... 86

19. Franconian Switzerland 92

20. Nuremberg 95

21. From Nuremberg to Eger by Schnabelwaid 109
The Nuremberg Switzerland. From Schnabelwaid to Baireuth, 110.

22. From Nuremberg to Augsburg 111
From Nördlingen to Dombühl, 112. — From Donauwörth to Neu-Offingen, 113.

23. From Nuremberg to Ratisbon 118
The Walhalla, 124.

24. From Ratisbon to Donauwörth (and Augsburg) 125
Kelheim and the Befreiungshalle. The Altmühl-Thal. The Danube from Kelheim to Weltenburg, 125, 126. — From Abensberg to Eining (Abusina). The Teufelsmauer, 127. — From Ingolstadt to Augsburg, 127.

25. From Frankfort to Munich by Ansbach and Ingolstadt .. 128
Rothenburg on the Tauber, 128.

26. From Stuttgart to Munich 133

27. From Leipsic to Munich viâ Hof and Ratisbon 134
Burg Landshut, 135. — From Landshut to Landau, 136.

28. Munich 137
Environs of Munich. Grosshesselohe. Nymphenburg. Schleissheim. 193, 194. — From Munich to Wolfratshausen (Isarthal Railway), 194. — The Churches of Pipping and Blutenburg, 195.

29. The Starnberger See and Ammersee. The Hohe Peissenberg 195
Schloss Berg. Rottmannshöhe, 196. — From Peissenberg to Ober-Ammergau, 197.

30. From Munich to Lindau 198
From Kaufering to Schongau and to Bobingen. From Augsburg to Buchloe. From Buchloe to Memmingen, 198. — The Stuiben, 199. — From Immenstadt to Oberstdorf. Grünten, 200. — Excursions from Lindau. The Lake of Constance, 201.

CONTENTS.

Route. Page.
31. **From Munich to Füssen (Hohenschwangau) and Reutte** . 202
    From Kempten to Füssen, 202. — Excursions from Hohenschwangau. Marienbrücke. Jugend. Schützensteig. Tegelberg Alp, 205. — Stuiben Falls. From Reutte to Imst viâ Lermoos and Nassereit, 206.
32. **From Munich to Partenkirchen and Mittenwald.** 207
    Kohlgrub, 207. — Excursions from Partenkirchen and Garmisch. Faukenschlucht. Riesserbauer. Partnachklamm and Vorder-Graseck. Eckbauer. Schlattan and Gschwandner Bauer. Badersee. Eibsee. Krottenkopf. Schachen, 208-210. — From Partenkirchen to Lermoos. Barmsee, 210. — From Mittenwald viâ Seefeld to Zirl, 211.
33. **From Munich to Ober-Ammergau and viâ Linderhof to Reutte-Hohenschwangau** 211
    From Ober-Ammergau to Peissenberg through the Ammer-Thal. From the Plansee to Partenkirchen, 212.
34. **From Munich to Mittenwald viâ Benediktbeuern** 213
    Schlehdorf. Herzogstand. Heimgarten, 214.
35. **From Munich to Tölz and Mittenwald** 215
    From Tölz to the Walchensee. From Hinter-Riss to the Achensee over the Plumser Joch, 216.
36. **From Munich to Tegernsee, Wildbad Kreuth, and the Achensee** 217
    Excursions from Tegernsee. Kaltenbrunn. Parapluie. Falls of the Rottach. Neureut. Hirschberg, 217, 218. — The Unnütz. From the Achensee to the Inn Valley, 219.
37. **From Munich to Kufstein viâ Schliersee and Bairisch-Zell** 220
    From Neuhaus to Falepp, 220. — The Wendelstein. From Bairisch-Zell to Oberandorf viâ the Tatzelwurm, 221.
38. **From Munich to Salzburg and Reichenhall.** 221
    From Grafing to Glonn, 221. — From Munich to Rosenheim viâ Holzkirchen, 222. — The Chiemsee, 222. — From Prien to Niederaschau. The Baths of Adelholzen. Hochfelln. From Traunstein to Reichenhall viâ Inzell, 223. — From Traunstein to Trostberg, 224. — Excursions from Reichenhall. Gross-Gmain. Zwiesel. Thumsee. Mauthhäusl, 225, 226. — From Reichenhall to Lofer, 226.
39. **From Reichenhall to Berchtesgaden. Königs-See** . . . 226
    From Salzburg to Berchtesgaden, 227. — Excursions from Berchtesgaden. Lockstein. Bischofswiesen. Gern. Schönau. Upper Salzberg. Almbach-Klamm. Vorderbrand. Scharitzkehl-Alp, etc., 228-30. — Gotzen-Alp. From Berchtesgaden to Reichenhall. Ramsau. Wimbach-Klamm, 231. — Watzmann, 232. — From Berchtesgaden to Ober-Weissbach. Hintersee. Kammerlinghorn. Seisenberg-Klamm, 232, 233.
40. **From Munich to Linz by Simbach** 233
    Alt-Oetting, 233.
41. **From Nuremberg to Furth (and Prague)** 234
    From Neukirchen to Weiden. From Cham to Lam, 235. — The Hohe Bogen, 236.
42. **From Ratisbon to Passau and Linz** 236
    Excursions from Passau, 210, 211. — From Passau to Freyung in the Bavarian Forest. The Dreisesselstein, 241. — The Bohemian Forest. The Danube from Passau to Linz, 242.

MAPS AND PLANS.

Route. Page.
43. From Rosenheim **to Eisenstein by Mühldorf and Plattling.**
The Bavarian Forest 243
From Neumarkt to Passau, 244. — The Rusel. Hirschenstein. From Gotteszell to Viechtach, 245. — From Zwiesel to Grafenau. Rachel. Bodenmais. Arber, 247. — Excursions from Eisenstein. Osser. From Eisenstein to Pilsen, 248.

Maps.

1. The ENVIRONS OF STUTTGART: R. 2; p. 12.
2. The SWABIAN ALB: RR. 8, 9, 11-12; p. 42.
3. The SPESSART: R. 14; p. 62.
4. The FRANCONIAN SWITZERLAND: R. 19; p. 77.
5. The FICHTELGEBIRGE: RR. 18, 21; p. 89.
6. The STARNBERGER SEE AND AMMERSEE: RR. 29, 32; p. 196.
7. The ENVIRONS OF FÜSSEN, REUTTE, NASSEREIT, PARTENKIRCHEN, MITTENWALD, AND WALCHENSEE: RR. 31-35; p. 202.
8. The ENVIRONS OF HOHENSCHWANGAU: R. 31; p. 204.
9. The ENVIRONS OF PARTENKIRCHEN: R. 32; p. 208.
10. The ENVIRONS OF TÖLZ, TEGERNSEE, AND SCHLIERSEE: RR. 34-38; p. 214.
11. The ENVIRONS OF THE ACHENSEE: RR. 35, 36; p. 218.
12. The ENVIRONS OF ROSENHEIM, KUFSTEIN, TRAUNSTEIN, AND LOFER (the CHIEMSEE and ACHENTHAL): R. 38; p. 222.
13. The ENVIRONS OF SALZBURG, REICHENHALL, AND BERCHTESGADEN: RR. 38, 39; p. 224.
14. The BAVARIAN FOREST: RR. 42, 43; p. 244.
15. SOUTHERN GERMANY: after the Index.
16. RAILWAY MAP OF GERMANY: at the end of the book.

Plans.

Aschaffenburg (p. 64); Augsburg (p. 112); Bamberg (p. 76); Bayreuth (p. 88); Constance (p. 55); Heilbronn (p. 13); Hohenzollern (p. 49); Kissingen (p. 83); Munich (p. 136); Nuremberg (p. 96); Passau (p. 237); Ratisbon (p. 118); Stuttgart (p. 1); Ulm (p. 42); Würzburg (p. 65).

INTRODUCTION.

I. Language. Money.

LANGUAGE. A slight acquaintance with German is very desirable for travellers who purpose exploring the more remote districts of Southern Germany. Those who do not deviate from the beaten track will generally find that English or French is spoken at the principal hotels and the usual resorts of strangers. But those who are entirely ignorant of the language must be prepared frequently to submit to the extortions practised by commissionnaires, waiters, cab-drivers, etc., which even the data furnished by the Handbook will not always enable them to avoid.

MONEY. The German mark ($\mathcal{M}$), which is nearly equivalent to the English shilling, is divided into 100 pfennigs. Banknotes of 5, 20, and 50 $\mathcal{M}$ are issued by the German Imperial Bank ('Deutsche Reichsbank'), and others of 100, 500, and 1000 $\mathcal{M}$ by the Imperial Bank and by twelve other banks which possess the privilege. The current gold coins are pieces of 10 ('Krone') and of 20 marks ('Doppelkrone'), the intrinsic value of which is slightly lower than that of the English half-sovereign and sovereign (1 l. being worth about 20 $\mathcal{M}$ 43 pf.). The paper currency is of the same value as the precious metals. The silver coins are pieces of 5, 3 (the old thaler or dollar), 2, 1, $1/2$ (50 pf.), and $1/5$ mark (20 pf.). In nickel there are coins of 10 and 5 pfennigs (groschen and half-groschen), and in copper there are pieces of 2 and 1 pfennig.

English sovereigns and banknotes may be exchanged at all the principal towns in Germany, and Napoleons are also favourably received (20 fr. = 16s. = 16 $\mathcal{M}$ 20 pf., and often a few pfennigs more). Those who travel with large sums should carry them in the form of circular notes (issued by the chief British and American banks), rather than in banknotes or gold, as the value of circular notes, if lost or stolen, is recoverable.

The expense of a tour in Southern Germany depends, of course, on a great variety of circumstances. It may, however, be stated generally that travelling in this region is less expensive than in most other European countries. The modest pedestrian, who knows something of the language, and avoids the beaten track of ordinary tourists as much as possible, may succeed in limiting his expenditure to 8-10s. per diem. Those, on the other hand, who prefer driving to walking, frequent hotels of the highest class, and employ guides, commissionnaires, etc., must be prepared to expend 25-30s. daily.

II. Passports and Custom Houses.

PASSPORTS are now unnecessary in Germany, as in most of the other countries of Europe, but they are frequently serviceable in proving the identity of the traveller, procuring admission to collections, and obtaining delivery of registered letters. The following are the principal passport-agents in London: Lee and Carter, 440 West Strand; E. Stanford, 55 Charing Cross; W. J. Adams, 59 Fleet Street; C. Smith & Son, 63 Charing Cross (charge 2s.; agent's fee 1s. 6d.).

CUSTOM HOUSE formalities are now almost everywhere lenient. As a rule, however, articles purchased during the journey, which are not destined for personal use, should be declared at the frontier.

III. Conveyances.

RAILWAY TRAVELLING in Germany is less expensive than in most other parts of Europe, and the carriages are generally clean and comfortable. The second-class carriages, furnished with spring-seats, are sometimes as good as those of the first class in England. The first-class carriages, lined with velvet, are comparatively little used, but are recommended to the lover of fresh air, as he will be more likely to secure a seat next to the window. The third-class travelling community is generally quiet and respectable, but the carriages are generally very poor. On a few railways there is even a fourth class, unprovided with seats. Smoking is allowed in all the carriages, except those 'Für Nichtraucher' and the coupés for ladies. The average fares for the different classes in S. Germany are $1^3/_5 d.$, $1^1/_5 d.$, and $^4/_5 d.$ per Engl. M. respectively. The speed seldom exceeds 25 M. per hour, and as the railways are generally well organised and under the immediate supervision of government, accidents are very rare. On many lines 20-50 lbs. of luggage are free, in addition to smaller articles carried in the hand. Over-weight is charged for at moderate rates. In all cases the heavier luggage must be booked, and a ticket procured for it. This being done, the traveller need not look after his luggage till he arrives at his final destination, where it will be kept in safe custody, generally gratis for the first day or two, until he presents his ticket. When a frontier has to be crossed, the traveller is strongly recommended to take his luggage with him, and to superintend the custom-house examination in person. If luggage be sent across a frontier by goods-train or diligence, the keys must be sent along with it, as otherwise it will be detained at the custom-house; but the pecuniary saving effected by such a course is far outweighed by the risk of vexatious delays, pilferage, and damage, for which it is difficult or impossible to obtain redress.

The enormous **weight of the trunks used by some travellers** not unfrequently inflicts serious injury **on the hotel and railway porters who have to handle them.** Travellers are **therefore urged to place their heavy articles in the** smaller packages and **thus minimize the evil as far as possible.**

DILIGENCES generally carry three passengers only, two in the *intérieur*, and one in the *coupé*. As the latter alone affords a tolerable survey of the scenery, it should if possible be secured in good time. In much-frequented districts it is frequently engaged several days beforehand. The guards, who are often retired non-commissioned officers, are generally well-informed and obliging. The usual amount of luggage carried free by the diligence does not exceed 20-30 lbs., over-weight being charged for by tariff. Passengers are required to book their luggage two hours before the time of starting, and sometimes even on the previous evening; but these rules are seldom rigidly enforced. An 'extra-post' conveyance for one or more persons may generally be obtained on application at the post-offices. The average tariff is 50 pf. (6*d.*) per mile for 1-2, and 1 ℳ (1*s.*) per mile for 3-4 persons. Private conveyances may be hired at the rate of 10-15 ℳ for a one-horse, 12-25 ℳ for a two-horse carriage per diem.

IV. Excursions on Foot.

The pedestrian is unquestionably the most independent of travellers, and to him alone the beautiful scenery of some of the more remote districts is accessible. For a short tour a couple of flannel shirts, a pair of worsted stockings, slippers, the articles of the toilette, a light waterproof, and a stout umbrella will generally be found a sufficient equipment. Strong and well-tried boots are essential to comfort. Heavy and complicated knapsacks should be avoided; a light pouch or game-bag is far less irksome, and its position may be shifted at pleasure. A more extensive reserve of clothing should not exceed the limits of a small portmanteau, which can be easily wielded, and may be forwarded from town to town by post.

Southern Germany comprises many attractive and picturesque districts, such as the Swabian Alb (R. 11), the Fichtelgebirge (R. 18), Franconian Switzerland (R. 19), and the Bavarian Forest (R. 43). The student of art is strongly recommended to visit Munich, Nuremberg, and Stuttgart. By consulting the Handbook the traveller will discover many other interesting places, whether the object of his tour be amusement or instruction.

V. Hotels.

Little variation occurs in the accommodation and charges of first-class hotels in the principal towns and watering-places throughout Germany; but it frequently happens that in old-fashioned hotels of unassuming exterior the traveller finds as much real comfort as in the modern establishments, while the charges are lower. The best houses of both descriptions are therefore enumerated.

HOTELS.

Where the traveller remains for a week or more at a hotel, it is advisable to pay, or at least call for, his account every two or three days, in order that errors may be at once detected. Verbal reckonings are objectionable. A waiter's arithmetic is faulty, and his mistakes are seldom in favour of the traveller. It is also objectionable to delay paying one's bill till the last moment, when errors or wilful impositions must be submitted to for want of time to investigate them. Those who intend starting early in the morning will do well to ask for their bills on the previous evening.

Pedestrians and travellers of moderate requirements will find the country inns in Southern Germany very reasonable, 5-6s. a day being generally sufficient to include every item.

Hotel-keepers who wish to commend their houses to British and American travellers are reminded of the desirability of providing the bedrooms with *large* basins, foot-baths, plenty of water, and an adequate supply of towels. Great care should be taken to ensure that the sanitary arrangements are in proper order, including a strong flush of water and proper toilette-paper; and no house that is deficient in this respect can rank as first-class or receive a star of commendation, whatever may be its excellencies in other departments.

The word *Pension* is used in the Handbook as including board, lodging, and attendance.

English travellers often give trouble by ordering things almost unknown in German usage; and they are apt to become involved in disputes owing to their ignorance of the language. They should therefore endeavour to acquire enough of the language to render them intelligible to the servants, and should try to conform as far as possible to the habits of the country. For this purpose *Baedeker's* 'Conversation Dictionary' (in four languages; 3 ℳ) and 'Traveller's Manual of Conversation' (3 ℳ) will be found useful.

Valets-de-place generally charge 2-3 ℳ for half-a-day, and 3½-5 ℳ for a whole day.

Abbreviations.

R. = Room; also Route.	N. = North, northern, etc.
B. = Breakfast.	S. = South, etc.
D. = Dinner.	E. = East, etc.
A. = Attendance.	W. = West, etc.
L. = Light.	ℳ = mark.
M. = English mile.	pf. = pfennig.
R., L. = right, left.	fl. = florin.
ft. = English foot.	kr. = kreuzer.
omn. = omnibus.	pens. = pension.

Objects of special interest, and hotels which are believed worthy of special commendation are denoted by asterisks.

The number prefixed to the name of a place on a railway or high-road indicates its distance in English miles from the starting-point of the route or sub-route. The number of feet given after the name of a place shows its height above the sea-level. The letter *d*, with a date, after the name of a person, indicates the year of his death.

South German Art.

A Historical Sketch by *Professor Anton Springer.*

It is neither the function nor the intention of the following sketch to divert the traveller's attention from the beauties of nature and to direct it instead to the study of art. But the great cities of Southern Germany, whether they be the express object of the traveller's journey or his temporary resting-places on his way elsewhere, cannot fail of themselves to inspire him with some interest in the art both of the present and of the past; while at numerous other points his glance is arrested and his attention excited by ancient or modern monuments of art. Interest in such things has widened and deepened to a surprizing extent within recent times. A few decades ago old-fashioned German furniture was ignored, and German buildings of the 16th and 17th centuries were for the most part passed with a contemptuous shrug. Now the 'German Renaissance' is a theme of admiration and an object for eager imitation. Then only a few mediæval cathedrals received the meed of general admiration or passed muster as true works of artistic genius, while the overwhelming majority of mediæval works remained unknown and unregarded. Now hardly anyone is either wholly indifferent to or wholly ignorant of the development of art in the middle ages. The cultivation of the historic sense has largely affected the æsthetic attitude in this direction, swelling the aggregate of artistic interest and bringing the more remote periods within the limits of intelligent comprehension. It is the object of the following lines to support and extend this historic sense.

The civilization and art of Southern Germany reach back to a very early period; they antedate by a thousand years the entrance of the North German lands into the light of authentic history. Numerous excavations have yielded traces of an early intercourse with Italy, carried on to some extent before the Christian era; and not less numerous traces have been found of the Roman settlements that were established along the great trade-routes and waterways, though these Roman discoveries are far inferior both in extent and importance to those in the valley of the Moselle and elsewhere on the left bank of the Rhine. The Roman remains at Trèves appeal to the imagination of the ordinary traveller, while the Roman remains in Noricum and Rhætia arrest the attention of the archæologist only. Christianity early made its way into Southern Germany (St. Severinus; 5th cent.), and Frank and Irish missionaries reaped a rich harvest. Convent after convent was founded; and there is probably no other district where monastic establishments were so thickly planted about the close of the 10th cent., as the banks of the Danube, at the foot of the Alps. Most of these preserved their celebrity and their wealth almost down to the present century, though their importance as art-monuments has in many instances disappeared with the substitution of new buildings for old ones. No considerable art-monuments have come down to us even from the Carlovingian period, which saw the beginning of Ratisbon's importance, except in the domains of the goldsmith's craft and miniature-painting. The Reiche Capelle at Munich contains the finest specimens of the former, the libraries at Munich and Vienna of the latter.

The unbroken chain of artistic activity begins for us about the 10th century. The art-style which prevailed from the 10th to the 13th cent. is generally known as the ROMANESQUE. Its characteristics find their most distinct expression in ecclesiastical architecture. The plan of the Romanesque church was suggested by the Roman basilica of early-Christian times, the essence of which consisted in an oblong hall, divided into three aisles by two rows of columns. At one end of the basilica was a semicircular vaulted recess, known as the Apsis; at the other end was a fore-court (Atrium), enclosed by a portico. Occasionally a transept was interposed between the three-aisled nave and the apse, and thus the whole building gradually assumed the clearly marked form of a cross. In the course of centuries and in different countries this early-Christian nucleus underwent numerous modifications, some due to the use of new building materials, some to peculiarities of national customs, but most to the at first slowly growing improvement in technical skill. It is apparent from the earliest Romanesque edifices, that their builders had difficulty in rising to the demands of their task, and that they had but scanty notions of measure and proportion. Romanesque architecture did not attain an artistic perfection until the 12th century.

It is not difficult to identify a Romanesque building and at the same time to decide with some certainty whether it belongs to the earlier or later period (*i.e.* 11th or 12th cent.). The characteristic forms of the Romanesque style are everywhere essentially the same. The round arch is used to unite the interior pillars or columns, to finish off windows and portals, and to form a continuous frieze on the exterior wall; the columns have either cubical capitals or foliage-capitals modelled on the antique; the ornamentation is predominantly either in the geometric style (lozenges; zigzags; checker-work) or of conventionalized foliage. In the earlier churches vaulting is used only for the crypt, the burial vaults, and the apse, while the nave has a flat roof; but by the 12th cent. we find the vault-principle triumphant, while the supporting pillars are also more richly articulated. At the foot of the columns appears the base-ornament, uniting the plinth with the torus of the base.

Though it is thus easy to recognize the general Romanesque character of a building, there are no sufficiently distinctive peculiarities to differentiate the style prevailing in Southern Germany from that prevailing elsewhere. Even when we confine ourselves to narrowed limits and enquire whether the Romanesque buildings in Southern Germany could be classified into Alemannic, Swabian, Bavarian, and Austrian groups, we arrive at no satisfactory result. All that we can say is that columns are frequently used to support the upper walls (this form being known as the columned basilica) and that there is a frequent tendency towards a richly decorative, and even fantastic arrangement of the interior fittings. No traveller in the neighbourhood of the Lake of Constance should omit to visit the three churches on the island of *Reichenau* (p. 55); that at Oberzell, a small columned basilica, dates back to the 10th cent.; while the larger church at Mittelzell is probably one of the oldest pillar-basilicas in the district. The church of the former Benedictine abbey of *Alpirsbach* (p. 39) in the Kinzig-Thal, founded in the 11th cent., surprizes us by its stately proportions and the perspicuous development of the ground-plan; while another Swabian church, at *Maulbronn* (p. 15), is an excellent specimen of a large, mediæval conventual edifice. *Ratisbon* (p. 119) is rich in Romanesque buildings, including the Cathedral, the Obermünster, the Schottenkirche, and the church of St. Emmeram. Several of these have been sadly disfigured by later decorations; and, indeed, the true Romanesque nucleus of many churches can only with difficulty be disentangled from later alterations. The meaning of the chaotic plastic embellishments on the portal of the Schottenkirche will probably excite the curiosity of the ordinary traveller even less than the sculptures in the spacious crypt of *Freising Cathedral* (p. 136), which are, at any rate, decorative in their general effect.

The churches above mentioned, some of which lie quite off the main lines of communication, appeal on the whole mainly to the professional archæologist or architect. There is, however, at least one Romanesque church in Southern Germany which will excite the warm admiration of the tourist and yield him unqualified delight — viz. the *Cathedral of Bamberg* (p. 77). The plan of this church includes a nave and aisles, an elevated choir at each end with a crypt below, and a transept between the W. choir and the nave. In comparison with other buildings in the same style it takes a preëminent place by its imposing dimensions, by its spacious, airy, and harmonious proportions, by the elaborate ornamentation of its portals (Fürstenthor), and by the number and variety of its towers. The occurrence of the pointed arch must not mislead the visitor into the error of taking it as a sign of the admixture of Gothic elements. The Gothic style is not characterized by the pointed arch, which was also used in earlier times, but by its system of buttresses to counteract the thrust of the vaulting, by its abundant use of articulation, and by the rich ornamentation applied to wall-surfaces and other non-constructive portions of the building.

SOUTH GERMAN ART.

The early-Gothic period is but scantily represented in Southern Germany, and it is not till the second half of the 13th century that the GOTHIC STYLE appears here in a developed and victorious form, while the building activity of the two following centuries brought it to a pitch of great perfection. The number of Gothic edifices on South German soil is very large, and the variety they show is very remarkable. An imposing series of cathedrals, accompanied by at least as many parochial city-churches and conventual churches, extends all the way from Alsace to the borders of Hungary. The *Cathedral of Freiburg* (see *Baedeker's Rhine*) may be coupled with Strassburg Cathedral, as among the finest structures of its class, if not in unity of style, yet by the completeness of its execution and by its imposing tower and airy pyramid of perforated masonry. With the exception of Prague Cathedral, the choir of which shows the influence of French models, the South German cathedrals testify to considerable independence on the part of their architects. The French masters were probably not unknown to them, but they did not allow themselves to be dominated by foreign ideas. The *Cathedral of Ratisbon* (p. 120), begun in 1275 and completed after a long interval in our own days, shows neither the marked development of the transept nor the rich elaboration of the choir which were customary in the cathedrals of Western Europe. The transept does not project beyond the aisles, and the nave and aisles each end in a separate apse instead of the aisles extending in the form of an ambulatory round the choir. Another peculiarity in German cathedrals is that the nave and aisles are occasionally of the same height — a peculiarity found nowhere else in cathedral-architecture, the beginning and early development of which must be attributed to the architects of Northern France. Thus the choir of the *Cathedral of St. Stephen*, at Vienna, a work of the 14th century, has its nave and aisles of the same height, while the main nave of the church, of a little later date, is but slightly higher than the aisles and is united under the same roof with them. The *Minster of Ulm* (p. 32) is only a parish-church, and thus lacks the extensive choir necessary for the numerous clergy of a cathedral, while it has only one tower on the façade; the ambition of the citizens, however, made it one of the largest and loftiest Gothic churches in Germany, and it ranks worthily with the cathedrals of Freiburg, Ratisbon, and Vienna. The interior originally consisted of a nave and two aisles, all of equal breadth; but at a later period the latter were subdivided by rows of slender round pillars.

The number of the notable Gothic churches in Southern Germany is by no means exhausted by the foregoing list of cathedrals and minsters. The towns of Swabia were marked by great zeal and activity in building during the later middle ages. In the Liebfrauenkirche *Esslingen* (p. 29) possesses a masterpiece, which, though of small dimensions, is rich in ornamentation of every kind, culminating in the graceful open-work tower. Similar small towers of openwork are found at *Bebenhausen*, near Tübingen, at *Thann*, in Alsace, and at *Maria-Strassengel*, in Styria. Among the other fine Gothic churches of Swabia are the minster of *Ueberlingen*, on the Lake of Constance (p. 58), **the** church of *Gmünd* (p. 28), the chief church of *Nördlingen* (p. 111), the church of St. George at *Dinkelsbühl* (p. 112), and the abbey-church of *Tübingen* (p. 36). The churches of *Nuremberg* (p. **95**) form a well-known group. It is true that neither St. Sebaldus **nor St. Lawrence has** been finished on a uniform plan, choir and nave in each case showing different styles of architecture; but the impression produced by the choir and richly decorated bridal door of St. Sebaldus and by the façade of St. Lawrence is a very striking one. The small importance attached to tradition **even** in the 14th century is illustrated by the way in which **the façade of the** *Frauenkirche* (p. 99) differs from earlier ecclesiastical fronts. In Bavaria our attention and interest are mainly excited by a few huge brick edifices, like the Frauenkirche at *Munich* (p. 189) and St. Martin's Church at *Landshut* (p. 135), which served as the model of a whole series of churches. The Gothic style was also sedulously cultivated in *Bohemia* from the time of Charles IV. onwards. In Prague there are the Cathedral, the Teynkirche, and the Synagogue, while the bold vaulting of the Karlshof Church also **excites the** interest of the architect; and there are other handsome **edifices, some** of which recall the earlier cathedral-style, in such provincial towns as Kolin, Kuttenberg, Pilsen, and Eger.

Towards Italy the limits of the spread of **the** Gothic style is marked by the parish-church of *Botzen*, towards the East by the church of St. Elizabeth at *Kaschau*. Few of the **parochial and** monastic churches of the towns are remarkable for their structural forms, which are generally of great simplicity, while the original kernel is often wholly lost amid alterations and additions. The richness and artistic merit of the decoration of their individual parts is, however, perhaps all the more striking on this account. The architect is thrown into the shade by the sculptor and the stone-carver. The mouldings on the walls, the tracery of the windows, the details of the buttresses, and the carvings of the doorways are all executed with the most admirable care and in the richest and most delicate manner, while the interior of the church is filled with works of art in metal, stone, and wood.

SCULPTURE and PAINTING both find a favourable soil in Southern **Germany in** the 15th century. The former, in particular, is indebted for its solid foundation and its admirable command of technical skill to its diligent practitioners of the Gothic period. It thus does not break abruptly with tradition, but gradually fits the new realistic features into the frame-work of the old forms. For centuries the tasks of the sculptor remain the same; he has to chisel tombstones of stone, to carve altars in wood, to cast fonts in metal. **The ap-**

plication of metal to **monumental works is** of comparatively late introduction; hence **in this sphere the** deviation from the mediæval style is most striking, **while in works of** marble, stone, and wood suggestions of Gothic art **may be traced even in** the 16th century. Sculptures in stone **and wood continue to be decidedly the** most popular branches of art. Wood-carving was diligently practised from the earliest **times in such** Alpine districts as Ammergau, while the **woodcarvers of the great towns** of Southern Germany **also found** ample **employment in the** preparation of large altars, choir-stalls, and the **like. The sculptures on** the altars were usually painted. **This polychrome** decoration was rendered necessary, partly by the nature of **the material,** which possessed no rich colouring of **its own, and partly by** the immediate neighbourhood of the pictures, **which were generally** added as wings **to the carved** centre of **the altar. Altars of this kind** may be studied **either in** museums (Bavarian National Museum at Munich, Germanic Museum at Nuremberg), **or in their original** positions at *Rothenburg, Blaubeuren, Gmünd, St. Wolfgang,* **and many other** places. A few of their **artists are still known by name.** The two most important **are** *Jörg Syrlin,* **first heard of in** 1458 and the **creator of the** choir-stalls **of the Minster of Ulm, and** *Veit Stoss* of Cracow (? 1438-1532), who **is known to us by his works** in Nuremberg, produced almost wholly **towards the close of a long life.** *Ulm* and *Nuremberg,* and next to them *Augsburg,* **are the chief centres of** South German **art in the 15th and 16th centuries. But this by no means implies that the other free towns of the empire neglected the pursuit of art. On the contrary, local research is** constantly **adding new names to the artistic roll of honour. It is, however, only in the three towns named that we find anything like schools of art or an artistic activity of more than local interest. The chief painter at Ulm was** *Bartholomäus* Zeitblom, the son-in-law of **the venerable Hans Schuelein. He** flourished in 1484-1517, **and his works, which may be** seen in the galleries of Stuttgart and Augsburg **and the Pinakothek** of Munich, **are distinguished by the clearness and vigour of their** colouring, though the drawing is hard **and the** types **of his** heads unpleasing **and** deficient in variety. **Of his pictures,** as of early-German paintings **in general, it may be asserted that the** colouring is their strongest **point, even though lacking in a delicate** graduation of tone. **They also succeed better with individual figures and quiet groups than with** dramatic situations, **the representation of which often led to exaggerated effects and** the admixture **of coarsely realistic traits.**

The Augsburg **school is best** represented **by** *Hans Burgkmair* (1473-1531), a master gifted **with a** fine sense for landscape beauty, **and by** *Holbein the Elder* (1460-1524). **The latter in especial, now that** a number **of** works formerly ascribed to his son have been accredited **to** him, ranks among the most interesting of early-German painters. His professional activity may be traced from the last decade of the 15th century onwards. For a considerable time his personal gifts do not help him to transcend the limits of the prevailing style. Eeven his Madonnas and women are lacking in charm; in emotional scenes, such as the Passion, a tendency to the coarse and common is apparent. [This early manner of the painter is best studied at the Augsburg gallery.] It was not till towards the end of his career — and so far we have not material enough to trace the intermediate development — that the elder Holbein produced in the Altar of St. Sebastian (Munich Pinakothek) a work that placed him far above all his contemporaries. He has learned to use the new graces borrowed from Italy, he endues his women's heads with elegance and charm, he models the nude with surprizing accuracy, he exhibits a vigorous realism restrained within due bounds. With the completion of this work in 1516 he disappears from the scene; and the only later information that we possess about him is the news of his death in Alsace some time before 1526. The works of his son *Hans Holbein the Younger* (1497-1543) cannot be effectively studied except at Bâle, to which he migrated at an early age, and in England, where he spent the latter part of his life. The South German galleries, however, contain a few fine examples of his talent. Thus, at Darmstadt is the Madonna of Burgomaster Meyer, the original of the celebrated picture at Dresden; and in the Pinakothek of Munich are two fine portraits.

The picture presented by the old, art-loving city of *Nuremberg* is one that takes by storm the fancy of all. Poets and romance-writers have celebrated the life and activity of the town in trade and industry, science and art, and the spirit of its people, easily moved to love or hate; and they, perhaps, exaggerated its importance as the *beau idéal* of a mediæval city. As a matter of fact its artistic activity began at the close of the mediæval period, and it was in the 16th century that it reached its zenith. The Nuremberg artists are known far and wide. The names of Michael Wohlgemut, Veit Stoss, Adam Krafft, and Peter Vischer are authoritative even with those who know nothing more of early-German art. *Wohlgemut* (1434-1519) generally passes as the type of the respectable and conscientious painter, who practises his art with honest simplicity. Later researches have, however, somewhat modified this view and credited Wohlgemut with a more important personality; but this revised judgment applies to him rather in his capacity as engraver than as painter. *Adam Krafft*, the stone-cutter (ca. 1450-1507), also stands to some extent on the footing of the handicraftsman and follows the tracks of the old tradition. His religious representations (such as the Schreyer Tomb on the outside of St. Sebald's, and the Seven Stations on the way to the Cemetery of St. John) show the regular 15th century mixture of pictorial and plastic elements in the composition, and the usual realistic hardness in the individual figures and in the drapery. A few of the heads only (such as those of the Dead Christ and of the Virgin in the relief of the Seventh Station) are permeated by a finer.

personal feeling. He shows himself at his highest degree of freedom from the traditional limitations in the fresh and true relief of the Stadtwage (p. 102) and in the three small and lifelike statuettes that adorn the large late-Gothic ciborium in the church of St. Lawrence. Krafft's works are superior to most of the productions of the other Nuremberg sculptors and their congeners, even to those of the diligent *Tilman Riemenschneider* (d. 1531) of Würzburg, whose masterpiece is in Bamberg Cathedral (p. 77). The nameless sculptor of the wooden figure of the Praying Virgin (now in the Germanic Museum, p. 106), of whom we know no other work, is, however, superior to Krafft and to all contemporary sculptors. Krafft's art may be thoroughly studied in his native city; and Nuremberg also possesses at least the masterpiece of *Peter Vischer* (1455-1529), the celebrated bronze-founder (St. Sebald's Monument). The architectural frame-work enshrining the silver coffin of the saint still shows traces of the conflict between Gothic and Renaissance forms. The small figures of children, Prophets, and Apostles, on the other hand, are creations of a free play of fancy, aiming not merely at truth to nature but also at grace and charm or at dignified and measured seriousness. Peter Vischer was afterwards joined in his foundry by his sons; but Nuremberg does not afford adequate examples of his later development or of the ever stronger infusion of the Italian Renaissance in the native style. The Little Goose-Man of *Pancraz Labenwolf* (1492-1563) is an almost solitary instance of the continued lifelike conception of nature coupled with freshness and naïveté. A visit to Nuremberg is still less satisfactory for a full appreciation of *Albrecht Dürer* (1471-1528), the greatest of German painters, though the imagination cannot but be pleasantly stimulated by lingering on the spot where he lived and worked. In order to form an adequate judgment of this many-sided master, remarkable alike for the profundity and the richness of his artistic conceptions, we must study not only his wood-cuts and engravings, but also his drawings. The best collection of these last is found in the Albertina at Vienna, a visit to which will intensely interest the serious student of art. The drawings also afford the only means of uninterruptedly tracing Dürer's artistic evolution from his early boyish efforts to the products of his closing years. This cannot be said of his paintings, which are distributed very unequally among the different periods of his life. It is really only twice in his career that his activity in painting is so great as to form the main ground of our judgment of him; the first of these periods was during and immediately after his visit to Venice (1505-09), the second was at the end of his life. From the Venetians he borrowed certain details of composition and learned the secret of his clear, warm, vigorous, and harmonious colouring; in the evening of his days he reached a complete plastic command of the pithy power of characterization visible in all his figures. The South German galleries still contain the most important products of his art. Munich possesses the Paumgärtner Altar, one of his earliest pictures; the portrait of himself, unfortunately retouched, and probably painted somewhat later than the date (1500) on the work itself; and, finally, his masterpiece, the double-panels **known as** the Four Temperaments (p. 162), with the heads of SS. Peter and John, SS. Paul and Mark. In this work he has, in allusion to the religious disorders of his environment, created four permanent types of Christian character, the corner-stones of the Reform movement; he has given pure and lifelike artistic form to the test and the defence of truth. Of the numerous Dürer treasures once preserved in Nuremberg scarcely **one remains. The** portrait of Hieronymus Holzschuher (1526), the most perfect portrait we possess from Dürer's hand, formerly in the Germanic Museum, is now at Berlin.

The South German galleries afford abundant opportunity for a study of the painters, who were grouped round Dürer and to some extent influenced by him, such as *Hans Schäuffelein* (d. 1540), *Sebald Beham* (ca. 1450), *Barthel Beham* (d. 1540), *Alb. Altdorfer* (d. 1538), *Hans Baldung Grien* (d. 1545), and *Christoph* **Amberger** (d. 1562). Numerous specimens of these masters will be found in the Munich Pinakothek and in the galleries of Augsburg, Donaueschingen, and Sigmaringen. **Those** who have not the leisure or the inclination to study their religious and historical pictures should at least spare a glance for their efforts in portraiture. In this field these masters show to the **best advantage** their fresh and vigorous observation of nature, unhampered by the prevalent custom of obscuring the main subject by a multiplicity of detail, or by the attempt to create ideal forms without the requisite powers.

A revolution in artistic tendencies is already obvious among the masters last named. **The traditional** style no longer sufficed. The knowledge of Italian art, fostered by the custom, which grew up towards the end of the **15th** century**, of the** visiting of Italy by northern artists, broke through the **old** barriers and encouraged the imitation of the new models. This Italian influence, however, did not bring any very desirable fruit **to** maturity. The German masters, like those of the Netherlands, remained essentially Northerners; they studied Italian art but could not assimilate the Italian nature. Though the Italian painters did homage to the ideal in their works, they never disguised their nationality. Even their most idealized creations reveal a direct life which smacks of the soil and the atmosphere. Foreigners could not inspire their paintings with this national trait, and thus, in spite of their personal talents, never advanced beyond the out-works of the Italian style. The race of artists that flourished in the second half of the 16th century stamped the Italian manner still more strongly on their works, aided and abetted in this by the gradual change in the patronage of art. While the earlier form of art was most at home in middle-class circles, various princely patrons of art, such as the Emp. Rudolph II. and the

Dukes of Bavaria, now step into the foreground. **Wood-cuts still remained popular and were widely circulated in the homes of the people; engravings were chiefly sought as patterns for the metalworker and other artistic handicraftsmen; but painting now solicited the favour of the art-loving courts. In these Italian art, like Italian culture generally, was strongly in the ascendant.** Italian artists and **Italian works of art began to migrate** across the **Alps; and** thus the **native artists, already attracted by the** forms of the Renaissance, **received a new inducement to perfect** themselves in the schools of Rome, Florence, and Venice. It **would be** unjust to eliminate entirely **from the lists of northern artists the names of** the Dutch and German masters who followed **this course** (such as *Bartholomäus Spranger, Georg Hufnagel, Christoph Schwarz, Johann van Aken,* and *Johann Rottenhammer*); **and some** of them have produced works of **considerable value, especially as** regards technical qualities. **But it remains true that, however great may be our desire to make 'historical rescues' by emphasizing** their merits, **it** certainly **has not yet gone far enough to induce us** to profess unqualified pleasure in **the works of** these mannerists. Those who take an interest in **the subject will find innumerable** examples of their art in **Vienna and** in other Austrian galleries.

The corresponding movement in architecture **and the decorative arts** has, on the other hand, become of late astonishingly popular. **For the last** quarter-of-a-century the GERMAN RENAISSANCE **has** obtained almost **universal favour and plays a most important rôle in the national art. Even the layman now shows lively interest in the** once **unregarded and despised buildings of the** German Renaissance, and **considers a visitation of them a worthy** object **for a** tour. The **name German Renaissance of itself indicates** the double root from **which the style springs. The German Renaissance could not have come into being without a** knowledge of the architecture, which **became predominant in** Italy through the revived interest in the **antique in the 15th** century. It borrowed **from it** the columnar **orders, the pilasters,** the varieties of cornice, innumerable ornamental **motives, and many other** details. It seldom, however, sank to a slavish imitation of its Italian models, **but remained faithful in many points to its** native traditions and tried to **combine these harmoniously with the new forms. It is true that** the Gothic **tracery,** mullions, mouldings, **and geometrical patterns** had to be given up, **and** that the pointed arch lost its importance. In the constructive **parts, however, in the** articulation and ground-plan old usages still **generally held their ground.** The genesis of the German Renaissance **is also** the best explanation of it. Even in **the early years of the 16th century the German** painters and engravers had begun to **use the graceful schemes of** foliage and branches that were characteristic **of the** Renaissance ornamentation of Italy; **and a knowledge of the different orders of architecture,** the rules of which were sought in

Vitruvius, also quickly penetrated to the N. side of the Alps. The masters of decorative sculpture were the next to adapt themselves to the new Italian style, which we meet on tombstones, screens, fountains, and works in wood and metal. Its latest conquest was in the sphere of architecture, where it at first appears only in the ornamental parts such as doors, windows, and the articulation of wall-surfaces. If the builder wished the work to be erected in a pure Italian style, he had to send for an Italian architect; and many Italians crossed the Alps and made plans, which they left to be executed by native workmen. The traces of this intercourse are distinctly recognizable in the German buildings. It was in the sphere of the handicraftsman that the new movement and the artistic advance found their greatest strength; no wonder that the forms here created attained a universal application and were adopted also by architecture and the monumental arts. As a matter of fact we meet numerous suggestions of metal-work in architectural ornamentation. The lower parts of the shafts of columns appear as if adorned with mountings of metal; in other cases hammered iron-work is imitated or the stone is treated as if it were a soft and elastic material. The lofty gable is a distinct reminiscence of the mediæval house, while the Italian Renaissance is practically destitute of roof-structures; the richly decorated balcony or oriel is also a northern peculiarity. The manner in which the German Renaissance came into existence explains the want of a uniform type or a normal style. It assumes a different character in each different district. The Renaissance in Northern Germany, so brilliantly developed in timber and brick architecture, differs widely from the Renaissance in Southern Germany, where the greater proximity of Italy exercised a stronger influence. This is especially marked in such imposing ecclesiastical edifices as *St. Michael's* in *Munich* (p. 190). These buildings, erected under the influence of the order of the Jesuits, bear the stamp impressed by the Jesuits on their buildings in all countries. But the secular buildings also show the influence of the neighbourhood of Italy and of the Italian culture predominant in courts and in aristocratic circles generally. Some buildings are German only through the soil on which they stand, while in style they belong exclusively to the Italian Renaissance; of this number are the so-called Belvedere of Emperor Ferdinand I. at *Prague* and the Fugger Bath Rooms at *Augsburg* (p. 116).

The preference for the Italian style is revealed more strongly in the châteaux of the noblesse than in the private buildings of the towns, the free towns of the empire clinging especially to the older traditions. Southern Germany contains a stately series of châteaux, which, in giving up the character of castles and assuming that of palaces, illustrate in the most signal manner the difference between the Middle Ages and the Renaissance. At the head of these stands the *Otto-Heinrichs-Bau* at *Heidelberg*, the gem of German castle-architecture, which is remarkable for its harmonious proportions and architectonic articulation and still more for its rich and well thought-out plastic decoration. When the *Friedrichsbau* was taken in hand a few generations later (1601), the native workmen had already become entirely accustomed to the new style. The ornamentation of the younger building shows clear traces of its Germanic origin. Few of the other princely châteaux can at all compare with that of Heidelberg. The *Schloss of Tübingen* (p. 37) still suggests the old style of castle-building, while the fresh and somewhat coarse strength of the Renaissance is most strikingly illustrated in the portals. In the *Old Palace of Stuttgart* (p. 4), the most attractive part is the inner court, with its arcades; but our fancy must lend the colours for a picture of the fitting-up of the now somewhat neglected state-rooms. The constantly increasing power of the Bavarian dukes is mirrored in the magnificence of their *Palace* at *Munich* (p. 145).

It was not always possible to proceed according to a uniform plan. The famous *Castle of Landshut* (p. 135), for instance, is wholly irregular in plan and shows clear traces of the different periods in which it was built. The decoration of the rooms is mainly entrusted to the painter, — a fact that alone shows the growth of Italian influence. The same tendency is seen more clearly in the *New Palace of Landshut* (p. 135), the court of which is articulated and decorated exactly in the taste of Italian palaces. A building of great interest is the *Old Palace of Munich*, erected by Elector Maximilian in 1602-19, planned on an extensive scale, and elaborately adorned with plastic and pictorial ornamentation (the latter now sadly faded). The group of buildings at *Prague* is, perhaps, the most interesting of the kind on Austrian soil. The new style established itself in the Bohemian capital at an astonishingly early date and maintained itself in comparative purity down to the 17th century. The large loggia on the garden-side of the Wallenstein Palace is the final link of a chain of building activity extending across the whole of the country. In order to give an adequate idea of the German Renaissance, it would be necessary to attempt a full enumeration of the individual buildings, for not only every district, but often each monument in each district, shows peculiarities, the study of which affords genuine pleasure and reveals the wealth of Renaissance art. Now it is a portal, now a balcony, or, again, the arrangement of a court or the fitting-up of a room that especially calls for our admiration.

The lover of the Renaissance is advised not to confine his wanderings to the great cities and the chief lines of communication. The keen eye will discover interesting buildings in almost every parish. Thus the towns and villages of Tyrol contain many, hitherto neglected, examples of the Renaissance. A similar remark may be made about many other buildings, not merely with regard to châteaux and manorhouses but also, and in a still higher degree, with regard to the residences of the ordinary citizen. In most cases, indeed, it will be the bare architecture alone that the **connoisseur will have a** chance to enjoy; the **interior fittings, which add so much** to the charm of a Renaissance house and contribute not a little to its comprehension, have **invariably disappeared** — perhaps to satisfy the recent craving of museums **and collectors.** The contents of the older industrial museums were **mainly drawn from** the treasures **of the** princely collections that came into vogue in the 16th century. **The** predominant objects were works of the goldsmith and furniture of costly woods, inlaid with ivory and metal. The equipment of the private house of the Renaissance period was, naturally, much more simple. The panelling of the walls found a counterpart in the well-carved **cabinets** and coffers; the metal **utensils were often made of brass, the** general appearance of which harmonized admirably with the wooden fittings; the coarse nature of the pottery was disguised by colour, plastic ornamentation, and variety of form. Where the original furnishing is still in place, the eye will easily recognize the perfect harmony subsisting between the interior fittings and the architectural plan, and will see how the **house** has, as it were, grown from **within** outwards. A mere sight of the façades is **not** enough, **especially when** the Renaissance houses occur sporadically among modern edifices. A better **idea is** gained from rows of houses, **streets, or squares not yet invaded by the** modern builder. *Nuremberg* **formerly stood** unquestionably at the head of all German **Renaissance towns. A number** of patrician **houses** of **the** 16th and **the beginning of** the 17th century can, it is true, still be cited; but the general appearance of the town has begun to alter. On the other hand *Rothenburg on the Tauber* (p. 128), with its Rathhaus, **towers, fountains,** and well-preserved houses, still presents an almost **unimpaired picture of a German** town of the Renaissance period. Here, **as in most of** the free towns of the empire, the details of construction and ornamentation borrowed from **the native traditions or directly** due **to the** national spirit **are seen** in great **force, while the Italian influence is much** slighter than in the case of palaces and châteaux. It is not till the 17th century that the Italian style becomes predominant in municipal architecture, as in the façade of the Nuremberg Rathhaus and the splendid interior (Goldner Saal) of the Augsburg Rathhaus. Owing, however, to its lively intercourse with Venice, the Italian style found comparatively ready acceptance at Augsburg and had *(e.g.)* familiarized the Augsburgers with the fashion of painted façades.

The period of the Thirty Years' War sadly interrupted the evolution of German art and broke off many bleeding branches from **the** tree of German culture. Some departments of art did not recover for two centuries; the once so popular work of the wood-carver was forgotten; **painting was but** scantily cultivated and **sank to a greater dependence on foreign models than** ever before. **From this calamitous period dates the predominance** of the foreigner **in all** matters of taste. **Thus the contemplation of the art-life** of Germany **in** the second half **of the 17th and the first half of the** 18th **century gives but** little satisfaction. The greatest activity took place in Southern Germany and Austria, and those who can overcome their dislike on general grounds to the BAROQUE STYLE will find here many and varied proofs of a renewed interest in art. In Italy a decided revolution in architecture had taken place towards the close of the 16th century. While the individual Renaissance forms were retained, a new spirit was apparent in their embodiment and combination. The old and genuine Renaissance style seemed too cold and too simple, and not sufficiently effective. The architectural members were made coarser and more massive, the straight line was replaced by curves, the help of light and shade was appealed to. The façade assumes a curved form; columns are moved towards the front and draw the entire entablature with them; gables and cornices are made to project strongly; the profiles are more accentuated; ornamentation is used to an exaggerated extent, almost obscuring the constructive elements. This baroque style, which is at bottom closely akin to the contemporary mannerism and the increased realism in painting and sculpture, soon found acceptance in Southern Germany. We see it in the numerous churches and convents that were rebuilt with increased magnificence after the close of the Thirty Years' War; and we likewise see it in all its pomp, but also with all its weaknesses, in the numerous palaces built between 1680 and 1740. The Palace of Versailles is imitated in a few cases only *(Nymphenburg, Mannheim)*; the predominant style is the Italian baroque, especially as it had been developed by Borromini. Excellent examples of the baroque style are found in *Würzburg, Munich, Vienna*, and especially at *Prague*, where the traveller may go through a complete course in baroque architecture and become familiar with all its peculiarities.

Architecture became practically paralysed about the middle of last century in consequence of the wars between Prussia and Austria. On the other hand an attempt was made, without much success, to revive the art of painting by the foundation of academies at Vienna and Stuttgart (Karlsschule). At the beginning of the present century the young artists of Germany had still to make the pilgrimage to Rome in order to train their eye and taste and to enkindle their imagination before the works of classical and old Italian art. More recent events must be passed over with a word. In the reign of King Lewis I. Munich won a European reputation as a school of art through the creations of Cornelius and his associates; and after a period of stagnation about the middle of the century it has again reached a position of great importance. Vienna has been specially distinguished for its successes in architecture, while Stuttgart enjoys a well-merited renown in the domain of industrial art.

WURTEMBERG.

1. Stuttgart and Environs.

Railway Stations. 1. *Haupt-Bahnhof*, or *Central Station* (Pl. E, 3), at the corner of the Schloss-Str. and the Friedrichs-Str. — 2. *West Station* (the former Hasenberg Station), at the W. extremity of the town (see p. 12). — 3. *Zahnrad-Bahnhof* or *Mountain Railway Station* (Pl. D, 7), Filder-Str., for the trains to Degerloch, Möhringen, and Hohenheim.

Hotels. °MARQUARDT (Pl. a; E, 3), conveniently situated **near the station**, with electric lighting and steam-heat, R., L., & A. 2¹/₂-6, B. **1, D.** at 1 o'clock 3, at 5 o'clock 4 ℳ, pens. for a prolonged stay at lower charges. — °HÔTEL DIERLAMM (Pl. e; E, 3), Friedrichs-Str. 30, near the station, R. 2¹/₂ ℳ; °HÔTEL ROYAL (Pl. b; E, 3), Schloss-Str. 5, opposite the station, R., L., & A. 2-3, B. 1, D. 2¹/₂ ℳ; °SILBER (Pl. d; F, 4), Dorotheen-Str. 2, R., L., & A. 2-3 ℳ, B. 80 pf., D. 2¹/₂, omn. ¹/₂ ℳ, good cuisine; WEBER (Pl. f; E, 3), Schloss-Str. 7, opposite the station, R. 2-2¹/₂ ℳ, B. 70 pf.; °TEXTOR (Pl. h; E, 3), R. 1 ℳ 80 pf., B. 1. D. 2¹/₂ ℳ; OBERPOLLINGER (Pl. g; E, 3), ZÄCH (Pl. i; E, 3), BILFINGER, DREI MOHREN, all in the Friedrichs-**Str.**, **near the station**, **moderate** and unpretending; KÖNIG VON WÜRTEMBERG (Pl. c; E, 4), Kronprinz-Str. 26; HÔT. IHLE (Pl. k; E, 3), Schelling-Str.; GOLDNER BÄR (Pl. l; F, 5), Esslinger-Str. 19; BERTRAND, Calwer-Str. 7, R., L., & A. 1¹/₂-2, B. ¹/₂, D. 2 ℳ; HILLER, Leder-Str. 6, unpretending; HERZOG CHRISTOPH (Evangelischer Verein), Christoph-Str. 16, R. 1¹/₄-2 ℳ; EUROPÄISCHER HOF (Katholischer Verein), Friedrichs-Str. 10. — **Pensions.** *Sigle*, Moser-Str. 28; *Gobert*, Schloss-Str. 57; *Strich*, Blumen-Str. 27; *Erpf*, Neckar-Str. 48 B; *Bunzel*, Olga-Str. 10; *Rüthling*, Olga-Str. 31; *Stütz*, Wera-Str. 6.

Cafés-Restaurants. °*Bechtel*, Schloss-Str. 14; °*Wiener Café Königsbau*, **in the** Königsbau (p. **3**), **with** ladies' room; *Bachner*, Charlotten-Str. 26; *Residenz-Café*, Friedrichs-Str. 62; *Wiener Café*, Königs-Str. 62; *König Karl*, Schul-Str. 20, overlooking the Königs-Str.; *Krug*, Charlotten-Str. 8; *Murschel*, Post-Str. 1. — **Restaurants.** °*Railway Restaurant*; °*Dierlamm*, °*Hôt. Royal*, with garden (see above); °*Kaiserhof*, Marien-Str. 10; *Weber* (see above), near the station; °*Zäch* (see above), Friedrichs-Str. 54; *Feil*, Kronprinz-Str. 1a; *Michoud*, Linden-Str. 5; *Rauh*, Sophien-Str. 35; *Adler*, Marktplatz 18; Old German Beer-Room in the *Hôt. Hiller*, Leder-Str. 6; *Friedel* (Munich beer), Linden-Str. 14. — **Beer Gardens.** °*Stadt-Garten* (p. 10), adm. 50 pf.; *Nill's Thiergarten* (p. 2); *Englischer Garten*, Ludwigsburger-Str. 16, above the horse-groups in the Anlagen, with fine view; *Schützenhaus-Garten*, Kanonenweg, with fine view; *Dinkelacker*, Tübinger-Str. 46; *Wulle*, Neckar-Str. 60; *Liederhalle-Garten* (p. 10), free except on Sun. afternoon and Tues. evening; *Hôt. Royal*, *Dierlamm*, *Textor*, see above. — **Wine Rooms.** °*Weber & Fromm* (in the old-German style). Kanzlei-Str. 3; *Gutscher*, Rothebuhl-Str. 1; *Klug*, Esslinger-Str. 10; *Zur Schule*, Schul-Str. 11; *Treiber*, Calwer-Str. 2.

Cabs. Per drive of 10 min. for 1-2 pers. 60 pf., 3-4 pers. 80 pf.; ¹/₄ hr. 80 pf. or 1 ℳ; 20 min. 1 ℳ or 1 ℳ 20; 20-30 min. 1 ℳ. 20 or 1 ℳ 60; 30-40 min. 1 ℳ 50 or 2 ℳ; 40-50 min. 1 ℳ 80 or 2 ℳ 40; 50-60 min. 2 ℳ 10 or 2 ℳ 80; each additional 10 min. 30 or 40 pf. — In driving to the railway station, theatre, concerts, or at night, the driver may demand the fare in advance. For drives in the environs a bargain should be struck beforehand.

Tramway. Chief station in the *Schlossplatz*, by the Königsbau. Thence every 6 min. through the Neckar-Strasse to Berg and the König-Karl-Brücke at Cannstatt; through the Königs-Str., Tübinger-Str., Marien-Platz (Mountain Railway Station, p. 11), Böblinger-Str., Esslinger-Str., Hauptstätter-

Str., and Tübinger-Str.; Charlotten-Str., Olga-Str., and Wilhelm-Str.; through the Olga-Str. to the Wilhelm-Str., Schloss-Str., Liederhalle, Militär-Str., and Silberburg; Calwer-Str., Rothebühl-Str., and Schwab-Str.; Friedrichs-Str., Bahnhof-Str., and Prag Cemetery. A branch-line, beginning at the Eugen-Str. (Pl. G, 3), runs through the Neckar-Str., Hauptstätter-Str., Tübinger-Str., Marien-Platz (see above), and Böblinger-Str. Fare in the town 10, beyond it 15-30 pf.

Post Office (Pl. E, 3), Fürsten-Str. 2, adjoining the railway-station. Branch-offices: Paulinen-Str. 35, Wilhelms-Platz 13a, Neckar-Str. 121, Johannes-Str. 35, Olga-Str. 32, Rothebühl-Str. 102a. — **Telegraph Offices** at the Post Office, Fürsten-Str. 2.

Enquiry Office of the 'Verein für Fremdenverkehr' at *H. Wildt's* bookshop, Königs-Str. 38 (information of all kinds gratis).

Baths. °*Stuttgart Swimming Baths* (Pl. C, D, 3; p. 10), Büchsen-Str. 53½, with two large swimming basins (for summer and winter), and Turkish and other baths; *Charlotten-Bad*, Charlotten-Str. 15; *Johannes-Bad*, Rothebühl-Str. 55; *Wilhelmsbad*, Schlosser-Str. 9 (Turkish baths at all three).

Theatres. *Royal Theatre* (Pl. F, 3), daily (box-office open 11-1 and 3-4); closed in July and August. — *Summer Theatre* at *Berg*, see p. 12. — *Theatre of Varieties* in the Reichshallen, Karl-Str. 3 (Pl. F, 4).

Military Concerts at the *Stadt-Garten* (p. 10) daily in summer and on Wed. & Sat. in winter; at the *Liederhalle Garden*, *Kaiserhof*, and *Bachner's Restaurant* (see p. 1); also at *Nill's Thiergarten* on Sun. & Wed. (see below). — A band plays every Sun. at noon in the Schlossplatz, except during the autumn manœuvres.

Sights and Collections:

Antiquities, Collection of (p. 5), daily 11-1 & 2-4 (from Nov. to March 11-2 & 2-3); closed on Monday.
Art Union, Exhibition of the (p. 9), week-days 9-5, Sun. 11-4, holidays 11-1; adm. 50 pf.; closed on Saturday.
Engravings, Cabinet of, see *Museum of Art*.
Industrial Museum (p. 10), week-days 10-12 & 2-6; Collection of Models also on Sun., 10.30-12.30.
Kunstgewerbeverein, Exhibition of the (p. 3), week-days 9-6, Sun. 11-4; adm. 20 pf.
Kunstverein, see *Art Union*.
Landesgewerbe-Museum, see *Industrial Museum*.
Lapidarium, see *Museum of Art*.
Library (p. 5), week-days 10-12 & 2-5; closed on Saturday.
°*Museum of Art* (p. 6), Tues., Wed., & Frid. 10-3 (Nov. to April, 11-3), Sun. 11-3; at other times, fee. *Engravings*, Tues., Wed., Thurs., & Frid. 2-4. *Lapidarium* (Roman Stone Monuments), Sun. 11-12.
Natural History, Cabinet of (p. 5), week-days 11-12 & 2-4, Sun. 11-1 & 2-4 (Nov. to March, daily 11-12 & 2-3); closed on the great festivals.
Nill's Thiergarten (p. 10), open all day; adm. 50 pf.
Panorama (p. 10), open all day; adm. 1 *M*.
Royal Palace (Residenz; p. 4), week-days 9-6, Sun. & holidays 11-6; gratuity ½-1 *M*.

Rosenstein (p. 13) ⎫
Villa Berg (p. 12) ⎬ These three are shown in summer (15th April-15th Oct.) daily, 9-12 (Sun. and holidays 11-12) and 2-6. Tickets (1-6 pers. 25 pf.) in the Enquiry Office mentioned above. Tickets for Villa Berg also at Olga-Str. 33, for Rosenstein and Wilhelma at the office of the Oberhofmeister in the Old Palace (p. 4). Fees forbidden.
°*Wilhelma* (p. 13) ⎭

Principal Attractions (for a visit of two days). First Day. In the morning, °*Schlossplatz* (p. 3), *Stiftskirche* (p. 4), *Industrial Museum* (p. 10), *Stadt-Garten* (p. 10); afternoon, *Schloss-Garten* (p. 9), *Rosenstein* (p. 13), °*Wilhelma* (p. 13). — Second Day. In the morning, *Museum of Art* (p. 6), *Cabinet of Natural History* (p. 5); afternoon, by °Railway to the *West Station* (p. 12), °*Jägerhaus*. — Any additional time may be devoted to the *Uhlandshöhe* (p. 11), *Villa Berg* (p. 12), and a trip by mountain-railway to

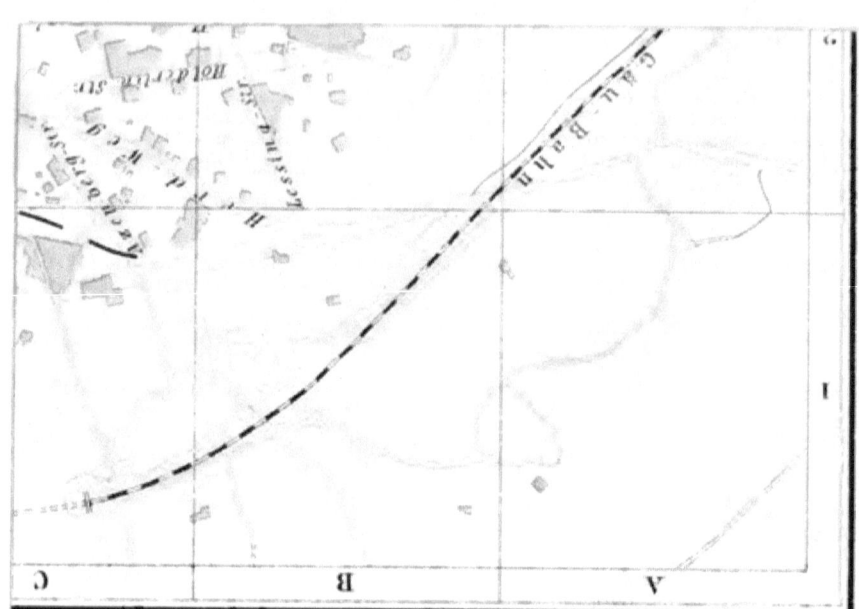

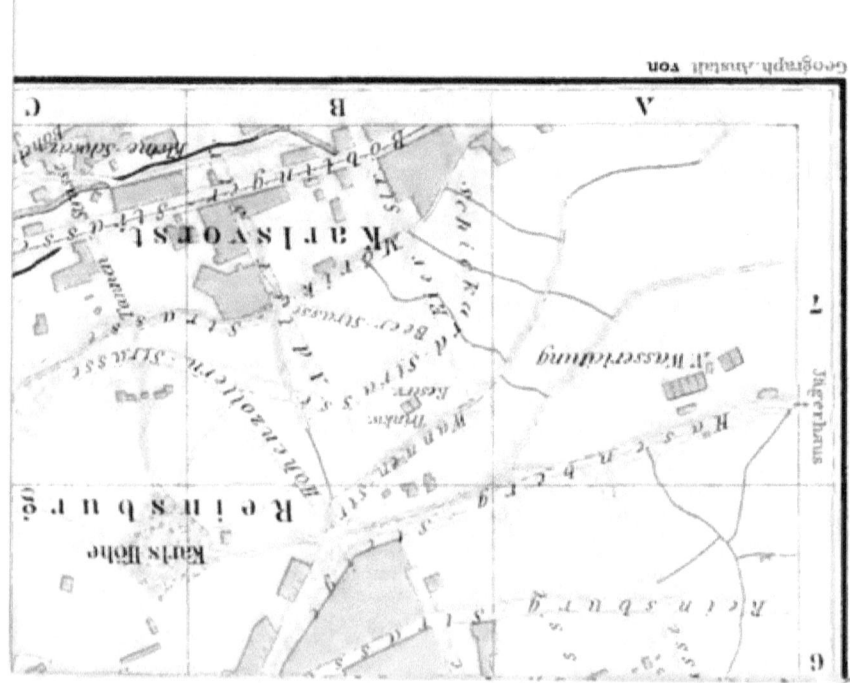

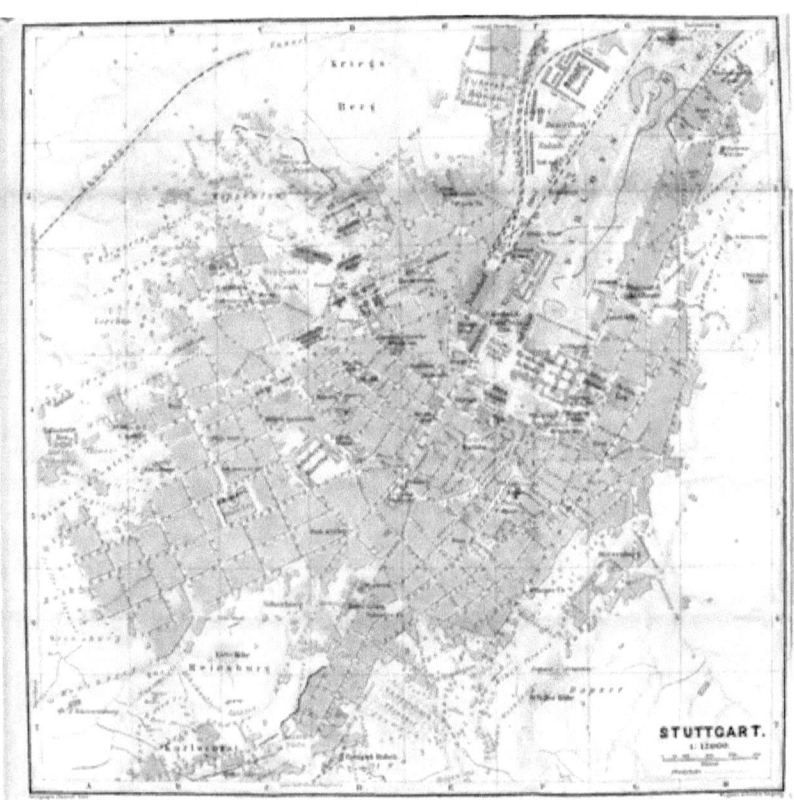

Degerloch (p. 11), returning viâ the *Schillerhöhe* (p. 11) and the *Neue Weinsteige*. — Excursion to the *Solitude*, **see** p. 14; to *Ludwigsburg*, see p. 15. — **British Consul,** *A. v. Kaulla, Esq.*, Schloss-Str. 47. — **United States Consul,** *Alfred C. Johnson, Esq.*, Herdweg **11 B**.

English Church (Pl. 13; F, 6) in the Olga-Strasse; services on Sun. at 8 a. m., 10.30 a. m., and 6 p. m.; on Frid. and Saints' Days at 10.30. a. m. — **Wesleyan Church,** Sophien-Str.; service at 10.45 a. m. — *Methodist Chapel* at Cannstatt (p. 11).

Stuttgart (892 ft.), the capital of Wurtemberg, with 139,660 inhab. (mainly Protestants, and including a garrison of 3200 men), a city of comparatively modern origin, is beautifully situated $2-2^{1}/_{2}$ M. from the Neckar, and surrounded by picturesque vine-clad and wooded heights. The name first occurs in a charter of 1229; from 1265 to 1325 it was the favourite residence of the counts of Wurtemberg; it became the capital of the country in 1482; and at length, in the reigns of Kings Frederick (1797-1816), William I. (1816-64), and Charles (1864-91), it attained its present dimensions and appearance. In the modern revival of Renaissance forms of art, Stuttgart has taken a prominent part through its numerous talented architects.

The inner town is intersected from S.W. to N.E. by the handsome *Königs-Strasse*, $^{3}/_{4}$ M. in length, formed in part by filling up the old moat. In this street, opposite the Schloss-Platz, rise the *Königin-Olga-Bau* (Pl. F, 3), erected in 1893-95, and the imposing Königsbau (Pl. E, 3), 440 ft. long and 135 ft. wide, erected by *Leins* in 1856-60. In front is an Ionic colonnade, broken by two projecting Corinthian porticoes. The lower story contains a café-restaurant (p. 1) and the permanent exhibition of the *Kunstgewerbeverein*, with the latest achievements of the industrial arts (adm., see p. 2); on the first floor are large concert and ball rooms. — Adjoining the Königsbau is the *Palace of the Crown Prince* (Pl. E, 4). On the right, farther on, are the *Bazaar*, the *Kanzlei* (government-offices), and the '*Ministerium*' of the Exterior, or Foreign Office (Pl. E, 4).

The extensive *Schloss-Platz (Pl. E, F, 3, 4) is adorned with a **Column**, 93 ft. high, erected in 1841 to the memory of King William, and crowned with a *Concordia* in bronze, 15 ft. high, from a design by *Hofer*. At the corners of the pedestal are represented the 'Lehrstand', 'Nährstand', 'Wehrstand' (*i.e.* the teachers, the bread-winners, and the defenders of the country), and Commerce, also by *Hofer*. The reliefs on the pedestal represent the confirmation of the constitution, the battles of La Fère-Champenoise and Brienne, and the storming of Sens, and are cast in bronze from designs by *Wagner*. The genii at the base of the two neighbouring fountains, representing the rivers of Wurtemberg, are by *Kopp*. Opposite rises the **Monument of Duke Christopher of Wurtemberg** (d. 1568), erected in 1889, adorned with reliefs from his life on the pedestal by *Paul Müller*. In the grounds to the right is a *Marble Bust of Dannecker*, by Kurfess (1888), crowned by a genius in bronze. Band on Sun. (see p. 2).

The new **Palace** (Pl. E, 3, 4), built in 1746-1807 and unoc-

1 *

cupied since the death of the **Queen Dowager** Olga in 1892, consists of a central building, adorned with a gilded crown, and of **two wings, and** contains about 360 apartments. The hall, the staircase, and the 'marble', the 'blue', the 'white', and the 'dining' rooms **are best** worth seeing (adm., see p. 2; **entrance in the** S.W. wing).

The groundfloor **and first floor contain a** series **of** large frescoes by *Gegenbaur*, executed in 1843-45, chiefly **from the** history of Count Eberhard im Bart (see below). Among the numerous pictures may **be** mentioned: *Pollak*, Oriental woman with carrier-pigeon; *E. Stöckler*, Lady of the 18th cent. (water-colour). Sculptures: *Dannecker*, Bacchus, Venus. Few of the others are original works. Then china from the factories of Ludwigsburg and Meissen, Sèvres porcelain presented by Napoleon I., Pompeian antiques, etc. A collection of upwards of 500 Majolica vases of the 16th **cent.** (from **Faenza and** Urbino), purchased at Venice in **the** 18th cent. by Duke Charles **Eugene, is not** usually **shown to** visitors.

The N. wing of the palace adjoins **the** *Royal Theatre* (*Hoftheater*; Pl. E, 3). On the E. side **of the palace are the** *Private Royal Stables* (**Pl. E, 4**), and at the end of the Königs-Strasse are the *Royal Mews* (Pl. F, 3).

The Old Palace (Pl. E, F, 4), on the S. side of the Schloss-Platz, erected by *Tretsch* in 1553-70, forms an irregular quadrangle, with round towers at the corners and a court surrounded by arcades in the middle. On **the S. side is the** entrance to the tasteful Gothic *Chapel* (restored). **In the court rises** the equestrian **Statue of Count Eberhard im Bart (d. 1496), a Count of Wurtemberg who** was created a duke **by the Emp. Max, by** *Hofer* (1859). **This palace contains the office of the** *Obersthofmeister*, or chief intendant of **the palace (see p. 2; open on week-days 8-9 a.m.).** In the E. **tower the second floor is reached by an inclined** plane instead of a **staircase.**

In the Schiller-Platz, which adjoins the Old Palace on the **W.,** rises the *Statue of Schiller (Pl. E, 4), designed by *Thorwaldsen*, and erected in 1839 by subscriptions from all parts of Germany.

On the S. **side** of the Schiller-Platz is the *Stiftskirche (Pl. E, 4; **bell at** the S. Portal), **Protestant** since 1534, **in the** Gothic style, **erected** in 1436-95. Towers unfinished. Reliefs **on the S. Portal: Christ bearing** the Cross, Christ and the Apostles.

The interior, restored by Heideloff in 1839-43, contains *Stained Glass* of 1848-51, from drawings by Neher: in the choir the Nativity, Crucifixion, Resurrection, Pentecost, and the Last Judgment; in the organ-choir King David. By the N. wall of the choir, eleven *Stone Figures* of Counts of Wurtemberg, dating from the close of the 16th century. The chapels to the left **and** right of the choir contain many old monuments, including the painted stone monument of Count Albert von Hohenlohe (d. 1575) in the Urbankapelle (left). Adjacent, at the end of the N. aisle, is an old votive relief in stone, representing Christ as the Judge of the World (above), and the Wise and Foolish Virgins (below). Gothic pulpit in stone, of the beginning of **the** 16th cent., with reliefs, disfigured by bronzing.

A few paces to the S. lies the MARKET PLACE (Pl. **E,** 4), the centre **of** old Stuttgart, with **a** few patrician dwelling-houses of the 16th **cent. and the insignificant** *Town Hall*. The latter **is** to be replaced by **a new structure.** — The Markt-Strasse leads to the S.E.

to the *St. Leonhards-Platz*, with the late-Gothic church of *St. Leonhard* (Pl. F, 5). By the choir is a 'Calvary' of 1501, recently restored by Donndorf.

The *Olga-Strasse*, which runs hence to the E., and in which is the new **English Church** (Pl. F, 5), built by Wagner, and the *Neckar-Strasse*, which begins at the Charlotten-Platz, are among the finest of the new streets.

At the beginning of the NECKAR-STRASSE (through which runs the tramway to Berg and Cannstatt, p. 12), on the right, is the *Palace of King William II.* (Pl. F, 4). In the Charlotten-Platz opposite are *Marble Busts of Bismarck* and *Moltke*, by Donndorf (1889). To the right, at the other corner of the Charlotten-Str., is the *Kriegsministerium* or war-office.

No. 4, adjoining the palace, is occupied by the *State Archives* (Pl. F, 4). On the middle and upper floors and in the N. wing (Neckar-Str. 6) of this building is the extensive and valuable *Cabinet of Natural History (adm., see p. 2).

The collections are divided into two sections, the one general, the other relating to Wurtemberg only. On the groundfloor is the *Mineralogical-Geognostic-Palaeontological Collection* relating to Wurtemberg: minerals from the old Black Forest mines; specimens of the geological formations from the earliest to the latest periods; and prehistoric antiquities down to the lake-dwelling era. Observe the numerous saurians (labyrinthodon, etc.), the pentacrinites, the group with thirteen mammoth's teeth, and the twenty-four lizards from the white sandstone of Stuttgart. — The second floor contains the *Zoological Museum*: in the wing to the right are mammalia; in the chief hall to the left are birds (Elliot's collection of Himalaya pheasants), fishes, reptiles; also corals and insects, particularly from S. Africa. — The upper floor, in the wing to the right, contains the *Zoological and Botanical Collections* of Wurtemberg (admirably arranged, chronologically, topographically, etc.). The main hall on the left is devoted to the general *Palaeontological, Mineralogical, and Geognostic Collections*, an *Osteological Collection*, and the general *Botanical Collection*, with herbarium, fruits, woods, etc.

The large building opposite, with four wings and three courts, is the Academy (Pl. F, 4), the seat in 1775-1794 of the *Karls-Schule* (p. 14), founded by Duke Charles, where Schiller received his education as a student of medicine, and where he surreptitiously wrote his 'Robbers'. The dining-hall contains the *King's Private Library*. On the groundfloor are guard-rooms.

The royal Library (Pl. F, G, 4), Neckar-Str. 8, a massive building by Landauer (1883), contains 500,000 vols., 3800 MSS., 7200 Bibles in more than 100 different languages, and 2400 specimens of early printing (adm., see p. 2).

The groundfloor of this building is occupied by the **Collection of Wurtemberg** Antiquities (adm., see p. 2).

To the right of the entrance-hall are objects from *Lake Dwellings* and *Pre-Roman Tumuli*, chiefly found in Wurtemberg. The second compartment to the right contains articles of special interest in gold, bronze, and iron from the royal tombs at Hundersingen (on the Danube), Klein-Aspergle, and Belle-Remise (Ludwigsburg), proving a commercial intercourse with Italy in the 4th cent. B. C. — Roman *Anticagliae*. — Objects from *Tumuli* of the Pre-Carlovingian and the Carlovingian periods, including many gold ornaments, curious silver **damaskeened work**, and weapons. — Stove-plates of the 16th cent., in **cast and forged iron**; objects in tin, bronze, and copper. — Gold and silver **ornaments, weapons**, and armour, including a curious jousting helmet. The '**Red Room**', in the S. wing, contains the *Royal Cabinet of Art and Antiquities*, founded by the Dukes of Wurtemberg and specially rich in vessels and weapons of the Renaissance. Italian bronzes of the 17th century. In one of the long cases is a pack of cards, painted in the 15th century. On both sides of this room are reproductions of Renaissance apartments.

To the left of the entrance-hall we first reach the *Ceramic Collection*, including numerous tile-stoves of various periods and styles (late-Gothic stove from Ravensburg). The *Murschel Collection of Porcelain* contains objects chiefly of Ludwigsburg manufacture. The Rococo Room is adjoined by one fitted up in the style of the 17th cent., with guild-vessels and household gear. Opposite is the collection of *Glass, Articles in Wood and Leather, Instruments, Textile Fabrics*, and *Costumes*. The S. Room contains the collection of ecclesiastical art, including paintings by *Zeitblom* (altar-piece from Hausen of 1488, another from the church of Heerberg of 1497), *Schaffner, B. Strigel, Amberger* (portraits of Heinrich März and Afra Rehm), and other Swabian masters of the 15-16th centuries. Fine stained glass. Byzantine and Roman vessels. Carpets and embroideries.

Beyond the library are the extensive **Law Courts** (Pl. G, 4), built by Landauer in 1880, with a fine vestibule and jury court. The colossal groups of Law and Justice on the attic-story are by Kopp.

Farther down the Neckar-Strasse (No. 32), opposite the Mint, is the ***Museum of Art** (Pl. G, 3), including the Lapidarium (Roman stone monuments), a Cabinet of Engravings, and Collections of Paintings and Sculptures (adm., see p. 2). In the court-yard rises an *Equestrian Statue of King William I.* (d. 1864), by Hofer, erected in 1884.

On the groundfloor are **Casts**, the rooms to the left containing those after ancient, the rooms to the right those after modern works. Among the latter are numerous models and casts of *Thorwaldsen's* works, presented by himself (d. 1844). — Among the **Original Works** in the principal room to the right are *Dannecker's* celebrated bust of Schiller in marble (hair partially mutilated by the master himself in a fit of mental aberration; 1st section to the right); marble busts of Uhland by *Rau* and King Charles by *Federlein* (1st section, left); Bathsheba by *Kopf* and Girl bathing (bronze) by *Falconnet* (2nd sec., left); *Venus by *Bissen* and Boy in danger by *Rösch* (3rd sec., right); Rape of Proserpine by *Hofer* (4th sec., right).

The Picture Gallery is on the upper floor (more than 800 pictures, each furnished with the name of its subject and painter; catalogue 80 pf.; director, Prof. Rustige).

Room I. Italian Masters. To the right: 8. *Tintoretto*, Portrait of a Venetian Senator; 10. *Bonifacio II.*, Adoration of the Shepherds; °16. *Giov. Bellini*, Pietà; 14. *Lor. Lotto*, Christ on the Cross; 23. *Carlo Dolci*, The Virgin; 33. *Titian*, Mary Magdalen; 34. *Venetian School*, Madonna with SS. Rosalie and Jerome (injured); 64. *Franc. Torbido*, Adoration of the Shepherds; 4. *L. Giordano*, Rinaldo and Armida; 1. *Paolo Veronese*, Lady in Venetian costume.

Cabinets: I. (left) 68. *School of Caravaggio*, Soldiers playing dice; (right) 77. *Ant. Canale (Canaletto)*, Venetian scene. — II. (left) 93. *Giov. Bellini*, Madonna enthroned with saints and worshipping donor; (right) 109. *Canaletto*, Piazza of San Marco in Venice. — III. (right) 128, 131. *P Mignard*, Madonnas. — IV. (left) 140. *Fr. Vanni*, Madonna and saints; (right) 150. *Tiepolo*, Apollo (sketch). — V. (left) *Tiepolo*, Finding of Moses; 163. *C. J. Vernet*, Sea-piece; (right) 173. *Canaletto*, Piazza of San Marco. — VI. (right) 197. *Le Sueur*, Entombment (in grisaille).

Room II. (Right) 259. *Cl. Lorrain*, Landscape; 267. *Le Brun*, Wild-boar hunt; 268, 272, *Kupetzky* (d. 1740), Portraits of himself and his wife; 271.

Canaletto, Canal Grande at Venice; 250. *G. F. Penni*, Holy Family; 248. *Guido Reni*, Martyrdom of St. Sebastian; 245. *Zurbaran*, Holy Family; 239. *After Leonardo da Vinci*, Portrait of Mona Lisa; 238. *Cesare da Sesto*, Madonna and Child with St. Jerome; 233. *Phil. de Champaigne*, Christ on the Mt. of Olives; 230, 224, 215, 217, 209, 212. *Canaletto*, Views of Venice. — We now return to the corridor and proceed in a straight direction to —

Room III. Netherlands School. To the left: 284. *A. van der Werff*, Mary Magdalen; 287. *C. Netscher*, Portrait of a man; 288. *A. Brouwer*, Old man counting money; 291. *Jan van der Baen*, Portrait of a man; 292. *C. Netscher*, Portrait of a woman. — 293. *Brouwer*, Operation on a peasant's foot; 302. *Ph. Wouwerman*, Two peasants bringing a horse to a gentleman; 305. *Van Dyck*, De Crayer, the painter; 307. *Rubens* (?), Repentant Magdalen; 308. *Rembrandt* (?), Old woman; 309. *Ph. Wouwerman*, Peasants with horses; 310. *J. van Ruysdael*, Forest-scene; 314. *Fr. Pourbus the Younger*, Portrait of a man; 315. *Hobbema*, Landscape. — 321. *Lierens*, Portrait of an elderly man; 322. *Weenix the Elder*, Shepherd reposing; 325. *Hobbema*, Landscape; 327. *M. J. Mierevelt*, Dutch Burgomaster; 328. *Rembrandt*, St. Paul in prison, an early work (1627); 329. *Metsu*, Portrait of a young lady; 331. *Moucheron*, Forest-scene; 332. *A. van Everdingen*, Northern landscape; 333. *Mierevelt*. Portrait of a man; 336. *Jordaens*, Vertumnus and Pomona. — 338. *G. Flinck*, Portrait of a boy; 341. *Ph. Wouwerman*, Wagoner; 344. *Wybrandt van Geest*, Dutch family; 346. *Ph. Wouwerman*, Horses by a village-tavern; 348. *Teniers the Younger*, Alchemist. — 356, 364. *M. d'Hondecoeter*, Poultry; 359. *Frans Hals*, Man with falcon; 358. *P. Brueghel*, Christ entering Jerusalem; 355. *Unknown Master*, Portrait of a woman

Corridor. Chiefly small Dutch pictures: 393, 396, 406, 409. *Jan Brueghel*, Allegorical representations of the elements; 447. *Roos*, Evening-scene, with herd of cattle; 453. *S. Koninck*, A scholar; 454. *A. Cuyp*, Landscape with cattle; 455. *Bakhuysen*, Rough sea, with vessels.

Room to the Right (adjoining the Corridor). Continuation of small Dutch and German pictures. 574, 564. *Rugendas*, Battle, Encampment; 566, 579. *Frank*, Adoration of the Magi; 581, 589. *Rugendas*, Battle-pieces; 585. *Frank the Elder*, Adoration of the Magi.

Room IV. Old German Masters, particularly of the Swabian School. *Barth. Zeitblom* is well represented (465, 466, 471, 472. Wings of an altar-piece from Eschach, etc.). 464. *Mabuse*, Crucifixion; 526. *School of Ulm*, Portrait of a woman; 524. *B. Strigel*, Coronation of the Virgin; 522. *Memling* (?), Bathsheba; 513. *Barthel Beham*, St. Benedict. — 494. *Amberger*, Portrait. — 488. *Herlin*, The Magi on the way to Bethlehem; 483, 481. *C. Vos*, Scenes from the life of St. George; 477. *Herlin*, Entombment; 479, 475. *B. Strigel*, Entombment, Flight into Egypt.

Room adjoining the 4th Saloon. Also old German pictures. (Right) 527. *Old Flemish School*, Madonna; 528. *School of Holbein the Younger*, Portrait; 529, 532. *Lucas Cranach*, Judith, Portrait of a woman.

Adjoining Room III is the new South Wing, in the five rooms of which the *Modern Pictures* are arranged.

Room V. Several works by the Stuttgart artists *Schick* (d. 1812) and *Wächter* (d. 1852). 596. *Leybold*, Portrait of Dannecker; 595. *Reinhardt*, Landscape during a storm; 598. *J. A. Koch*, Landscape after a thunderstorm (accessories by *Heydeck*); 617. *Angelica Kauffmann*, Portrait of a lady; 617. *J. A. Koch*, Landscape.

Room VI. To the left: °653. *O. Achenbach*, Posilipo; 735. *Nahl*, Wallenstein and Seni; 655. *K. von Piloty*, Nero (study of a head); 654. *Laupheimer*, A bashful adorer; °656. *Bleibtreu*, Battle of Wörth; 657. *Barison*, Venetian family; 784. *Kauffmann*, 'Dog Latin'; 788. *Höcker*, Twilight; 659. *Dill*, Canal Grande; °789. *Chierici*, A surprise; 696. *Funk*, The Kaiser-Gebirge; 713. *Irmer*, Scene in the Hartz Mts.; 652. *H. Baisch*, Curiosity; 797. *W. von Kaulbach*, Battle of the Huns (sketch); 678. *Majer*, Monk asleep; 662. *Zügel*, Autumn; °733. *Morgenstern*, The Elbe by moonlight; 668. *Häberlin*, Prince Alexander of Wurtemberg at the battle of Peterwardein; 663. *Adam*, Hungarian market-scene; °672. *Peters*, Flowers; 673. *Friedr. Keller*, Entombment; °675. *Aiwasowsky*. Sea-piece; °661. *Lier*, View on the Scottish coast; °674. *Braith*, Flock of sheep returning home.

8 *Route 1.* STUTTGART. *Museum of Art.*

Room VII. To the left: 660. *K. von Piloty*, Three sketches for the frescoes on the Maximilianeum in Munich (p. 156); 711. *Neher*, The Widow's Son at Nain; °681. *A. Zimmermann*, The Obersee; 686. *Neher*, Descent from the Cross; 687. *Kleyen*, Madonna; 780. *Preller*, Tumulus; °690. *Gude*, Calm; 691. *Bauerle*, Orphans; 697 *Ebert*, Amper-Thal; no number, °*O. Achenbach*, Storm on the Roman Campagna; °792. *Haug*, The Prussians at Möckern; 651. *Ludwig*, Landscape; 695. *Gudin*, After the storm; 701. *Lange*, Château of Kolowrat; 702. *Heck*, Itinerant preacher; °703. *Tiesenhausen*, On the Baltic; 705. *Heck*, In church; 707. *Kurzbauer*, The first picture-book; 709. *Kappis*, Black Forest village in winter; 710. *Reiniger*, Landscape; °796. *Ekenaes*, Preparing for the fishing; 791. *Mali*, Flock of sheep in winter; 712. *A. von Werner*, Luther at the Diet of Worms; 800. *Bredt*, Street letter-writer in Algiers.

Room VIII. To the left: 714. *Rottmann*, Epidaurus; 715. *Closs*, Hadrian's Villa at Tivoli; °716. *Dietz*, Scene outside the gates of Leipsic in 1813; no number, *Russ*, Market-place at Friesach; 719. *Schaumann*, Popular fête at Cannstatt; °717. *Bürkel*, Tyrolese pass; 722. *Rustige*, Emp. Otho I. after the conquest of the Danes; °723. *Schönleber*, Evening at Dort; °725. *Bokelmann*, At the pawnbroker's; 727. *Lessing*, Franconian mountain-scene; 730. *Loltz*, Alpine herd-girls; °729. *R. Jordan*, Shipwreck; 732. *Braekeleer*, Peasants drinking; no number, *Van Hove*, Dutch interior; no number, *Eggel*, Odin's Hunt; 801. *Lenbach*, William I.; no number, *Bossuet*, Mauresco-Spanish gate; 740. *Funk*. Scene in the Eifel; *C. von Müller*, 741 Judgment of Paris, 745. Romeo and Juliet; 742. *Löfftz*, Erasmus; 743. *O. Baisch*, Rendezvous; °744. *Ludwig*, The St. Gotthard.

Room IX. To the left: °746. *Jos. Brandt*, Cavalry-skirmish; 747. *Mali*, North Italian mountain-scene; °748. *W. von Kaulbach*, Battle of Salamis, a sketch in colours; 750. *Schendel*, Vegetable-seller; 749. *Ed. Schleich*, Landscape; °751. *Defregger*, The wounded huntsman; 753. *Faber du Faur*, Battle of Cœuilly, 1870; 754. *Rethel*, Finding of the body of Gustavus Adolphus at Lützen; 755. *Rottmann*, The Hintersee; 756. *Grünewald*, Hail-storm in harvest; 757. *Hummel*, Mountain-scene; °758. *O. Achenbach*, The strangers' cemetery at Rome; °759. *Feuerbach*, Iphigeneia; °760. *Makart*, Cleopatra; 761. *Löffler*, Jerusalem; 762. *Bohn*, Serenade; 763. *Peters*, Hunting-seat in winter; 765. *Riedel*, Medea; °764. *A. Achenbach*, Dutch landscape; 766. *Brion*, Marriage-procession in Alsace; 767. *Ebert*, Forest-scene; 768. *Schrader*, Shakespeare brought before the justice for poaching; °769. *Braith*, Cattle in a thunder-storm; 770. *Faber du Faur*, Battle of Champigny; 771. *Häberlin*. Suppression of the Wurtemberg monastery of Alpirsbach in 1648; 772. *Mali*, The shepherd's morning-greeting; 773. *Ed. Schleich*, Landscape; 774. *Gegenbaur*, Hercules and Omphale; 775. *Rustige*, The Duke of Alva in the castle of Rudolstadt; 776 *Schütz*, Midday-rest in harvest; 777. *Leu*, The Hohe Göll near Berchtesgaden.

The corridor of the new N. Wing contains seven cartoons for *Gegenbaur's* frescoes in the Palace (p. 4). Adjacent, in —

Room I, is the continuation of the modern pictures (the most recent acquisitions). To the left, 790. *Chierici*. Portrait of himself; 808. *Fouace*, At the buffet; 807. *De Bock*, Scene on the Dunes; 805. *De Haas*, Cattle on the Dunes; no number, *Courtens*, Boats by morning light; *Buttersack*, Village-pond; 802. *Lenbach*, Prince Bismarck (chalk drawing); 834. *José Villegas*, In church; no number, *Zügel*, Cattle pasturing; *Lautenschlager*, Lost in thought; *Igler*, Knitting-school; *Windmaier*, Winter-scene.

Room II contains the collection left to the Museum by Queen Olga (1893), consisting of water-colour copies of celebrated pictures by the old masters and also of a few original works. Among the latter are: to the left, *Rizzoni*, Polish Tavern; *Spitzweg*, The Alchemist; *Böcklin*. Castle on the sea; *Giov. Bellini* (?), Madonna; *Perugino* (?), Holy Family with angels; *Franc. Francia*, Madonna; *Buchner*, Portrait of Queen Olga; *Gabriel Max*, Study of a head; *Perugino*, Madonna; *Igler*. Singing lesson; *Domenichino*, St. Sebastian; *Vervloet*, The Pope washing the feet of twelve poor men.

On a height to the right of the museum is the *Kunstschule* (Pl. G, 3), adorned externally with frescoes and with statues of Phidias,

Polygnotus, Michael Angelo, and Raphael on the eastern façade in the Urban-Str. — Near the **Museum**, in a niche on a house at the corner of the Eugen-Str. and the Moser-Str. (Pl. G, 3, 4), is a bronze bust of the jurist *Joh. Jac. Moser* (1701-85), by Kopp, erected in 1885. A flight of steps ascends hence to the *Eugen-Platz* (Pl. G, H, 4), which is adorned with a handsome fountain (Galatea) by Rieth and affords a fine view of the town. Below is a bronze bust of *Duke Eugene of Wurtemberg* (d. 1857), by Pelargus. To the *Uhlandshöhe*, see p. 11. — About ½ M. beyond the Museum the Neckar-Str. expands into the so-called Neckarthor, an open space embellished with a *Water Nymph* by Dannecker. To the right, above, is the Romanesque *Friedenskirche* (Pl. H, 2), built by Dollinger in 1893.

On the W. side of the Neckar-Strasse is the *****Schloss-Garten** or *Anlagen* (Pl. F, G, 3-1), laid out in the English style in 1808. These charming pleasure-grounds, with their fine groups of trees, flower-beds, and sheets of water, 200 acres in area and extending to a length of 2 M. (nearly to Cannstatt), are adorned with modern sculptures in marble (chiefly copies from the antique), especially in the so-called *Botanic Garden* to the E. of the upper pond. Above the conduit which feeds the pond, on the side next the palace, is a colossal group by *Dannecker*, representing water and meadow nymphs. In the 'Rondel' of the main avenue on the front: Count Eberhard and the Shepherd (from Uhland), a colossal group by *Paul Müller* (1881). On an island at the end of this avenue is the Abduction of Hylas, by *Hofer* (1850), and a little farther on, at the beginning of the chestnut avenue leading to (1¼ M.) *Rosenstein* (p. 13), are two Horse-tamers, also by *Hofer* (1848).

We now enter the N.W. quarter of the town, and note the fine buildings of the *Württembergische Vereinsbank* and the *Reichsbank*, both in the *Friedrichs-Strasse* (Nos. 48, 22). The *Kriegsberg-Strasse* and the *Goethe-Strasse* contain, perhaps, the handsomest new buildings in this quarter.

In the Schelling-Str. (No. 5) is the building of the *Wurtemberg Art Union* (*Kunstverein;* Pl. E, 3), with a permanent exhibition of modern works of art (adm., see p. 2).

The **Polytechnic School** (Pl. E, 3), in the Stadtgarten-Platz (Alleen-Platz), erected in the Italian Renaissance style by *Egle* in 1860-65, and enlarged by *Tritschler* in 1879, is adorned to the right and left of the door with statues of Dürer and Kepler. Between the Corinthian columns on the upper story are ten allegorical statues representing the professions for which a technical education prepares the student; to the right and left of these are two admirable allegorical representations of Art and Science, by *Th. Bechlar* of Munich. The N. façade bears medallion-portraits of celebrated architects and mathematicians. The garden in front was adorned in 1889 with marble busts of *Friedrich Vischer* (1807-87), the writer on æsthetics, by Donndorf, and of *Rob. Mayer* (1814-78), the physicist, by Kopf.

The *Stadt-Garten (Pl. D, E, 3; adm. 50 pf.; concerts, see p. 2) is a favourite pleasure-resort, with a restaurant.

On the W. side, at the angle of the Kanzlei-Str. and Schelling-Str., is the handsome *Architectural School* (*Baugewerkschule;* Pl. D, 3), with a Mansard roof and fine courts, by Egle (1870). In the Kriegsberg-Str. is the *Gewerbehalle* (Pl. D, 3), the building of the Industrial Exhibition of 1881, now containing the *Exchange* (business-hour 2-3 p. m.) and an exhibition of *Export-Products*.

About 1/2 M. to the N.W., in the Herdweg (No. 10 D), is *Nill's Thiergarten* (Pl. C, 2), with a restaurant (beer) and a large concert-garden. Adm., see p. 2.

In the Linden-Strasse (Pl. D, 2) are the *Panorama* (p. 2; Crucifixion, with view of Jerusalem, by Frosch, Krüger, and Leigh), the *Gymnastic Hall*, and the *Garrison Church*, a brick edifice in the Romanesque style by Dollinger, with a dome and corner-towers. These three are on the right; to the left are the handsome *Realgymnasium* and the *Chemical Laboratory*, the latter a Renaissance edifice completed in 1894.

Near this, in the Hoppenlau-Str., is the *Hoppenlau Cemetery* (Pl. C, D, 3), with the graves of the sculptor Dannecker (d. 1841) and the authors Wilhelm Hauff (d. 1827) and Gustav Schwab (d. 1850). — In the Büchsen-Str. are the large *Stuttgart Swimming Baths* (Pl. D, 3), erected in the Moorish style in 1888-89 (adm., see p. 2). Adjacent is the **Liederhalle** (Pl. C, D, 3), the property of a vocal society, with large concert-rooms. The new hall, built by *Leins* in 1875, is the largest in Germany, having an area of 1600 sq. yds. In the garden-veranda are plaster models of the statues of Schiller at Marbach and Uhland at Tübingen. The garden (restaurant and concerts, see pp. 1, 2) contains a colossal bust of *Uhland* in bronze, and marble busts of *G. Schwab* and *Franz Schubert*.

To the N.E., between the Linden-Str., Kanzlei-Str., and Schloss-Str., is the handsome new *Landesgewerbe-Museum (Pl. D, E, 3), or *Industrial Museum*, erected by *Neckelmann* in an elaborate late-Renaissance style. The principal façade is turned towards the Schloss-Str. The lower story is of rustic masonry; the upper is articulated by six pairs of Corinthian columns. The attic is adorned with figures, and domed turrets rise at the angles. The whole of the building is embellished with medallions of famous Swabians and other plastic decoration. The chief features of the interior are the grand staircase and the King Charles Exhibition Gallery, the latter adorned with a painted frieze by *Ferd. Keller* and sculptures by *Hundrieser* and *Eberlein*. This museum (to be opened in Oct., 1895) will contain the collections previously exhibited in the Legionskaserne (Pl. D, E, 5), including *Models*, an *Educational Exhibition*, and an *Art Library* (adm., see p. 2).

In the late-Gothic **Spitalkirche** (Pl. D, 4), erected in 1471-93, and restored in 1841, is a model of Dannecker's large marble statue of Christ (p. 123). The cloisters contain the tomb of Reuchlin (d. 1522), the erudite friend of Melanchthon. — A few hundred paces distant (Hospital-Strasse 38) is the **Synagogue** (Pl. D, 4), in the Moorish style, with two handsome domes, erected in 1861. Between the Schloss-Strasse, Kasernen-Strasse, and Lange-Strasse (Pl. C, 4) rise the imposing new *Municipal School Buildings*. Farther to the W., in the Lindenspür-Strasse, is the *Ludwig Hospital* ('Charlottenhilfe'; Pl. B, 3), founded and admirably fitted up by the late Staatsrath von Ludwig.

On the *Feuersee* (Pl. C, 5), in the S.W. quarter of the city, is the handsome Gothic *Church of St. John, by *Leins* (1866-76), finely situated, with richly painted interior. — To the S.E. of this point is the *Silberburg-Garten* (Pl. C, D, 6), belonging to the Museum-Gesellschaft, the leading club of Stuttgart (tickets for strangers at Kanzlei-Str. 14). In the grounds below the garden, between the Marienthor and the Silberburgthor, is a marble bust of *E. Mörike*, the poet (d. 1875), by Rösch. — In the Tübinger-Str. is the Roman Catholic *Marienkirche (Pl. D, 6), early-Gothic, with two towers, by *Egle* (1872-75). — Among the handsome houses of the Reinsburg-Strasse, which connects these two churches, are the *Villa Siegle* by Gnauth, and the houses of Hr. Bohnenberger by Beisbarth, and Prof. Rustige by Leins. — The suburb of *Heslach* has a Romanesque church by *Wolff* (1881).

In the *Fangelsbach Cemetery*, to the S.E. of the town, stands the *War Memorial*, designed by Gnauth, representing Germania dispensing wreaths. — The Central Cemetery, to the N.W., beyond the *Eisenbahndörfchen* (cottages of railway employees) and the new *Municipal Hospital*, contains a Gothic burial-chapel and several handsome mausoleums; it commands a fine view. About ³/₄ M. higher up, at the N.E. end of the *Feuerbacher Heide*, is the *Weissenhof*, a popular garden-restaurant (view).

Charming walk on the E. side of Stuttgart, from the Neckar-Str. through the Eugen-Str. to the *Eugen-Platz* (p. 9), and past the *Schiesshaus* to the (¹/₂ br.) *Uhlandshöhe (Pl. H, 3), with a series of charming views of Stuttgart and the valley of the Neckar, the finest points being the pavilion at the top and 'Uhland's Lime-tree'. A similar point is the Schillerhöhe, on the *Bopser*, to the S.E., reached by the Neue Weinsteige (Pl. E, F, 7), commanding varied views during its winding ascent from the Olga-Str. We may return via the Hohenheimer-Str. (Pl. F, G, 6, 5; to the left, below, the *Stitzenburg Restaurant*, with a good view of the city); or we may continue the excursion through the *Bopserwald* to *Degerloch*.

The MOUNTAIN RAILWAY (*Zahnradbahn*, 'rack-and-pinion line') to Degerloch (*Curhaus; Schweizerhaus*, by the station; *Wilhelmshöhe Inn*, with garden) starts from the Filder-Str. (Pl. D, 7). At least 6 or 8 trains daily each way (12-14 min.; up 30, down 20 pf.); views on the left. Splendid view from the tower (1585 ft.), 5 min. from the station at the top (20 pf.). Tramway from the Schloss-Str. every 36 min.; see p. 1. — From Degerloch a steam-tramway runs in ³/₄ hr. to *Hohenheim* (p. 14), via *Möhringen*, *Echterdingen*, and *Garbe* (*Plieningen*).

An *EXCURSION TO THE WEST STATION BY THE GÄU RAILWAY will be found interesting (views to the left). On quitting the station, the line (for Böblingen, Freudenstadt, etc.; see R. 10) describes a sharp curve round the brick-works on the *Prag-Aecker*, and then runs southward in the direction of the vine-clad *Kriegsberg*, which juts far into the valley. On the top of the latter (to the right) is the *Feuerbacher Heide*, with the *Weissenhof* (see p. 11). The gradient is very steep (1:52). Beyond a tunnel, 500 yds. long, we obtain to the left a striking *VIEW of the town, with the dome of the new garrison-church in the foreground and the picturesque hills opposite. The train continues to ascend the slopes of the valley, through gardens and vineyards, and describes a wide circle round the town. The view increases in attraction. After 20 min. we cross the *Vogelsang-Thal* by a viaduct 130 ft. in height, and stop at the West Station (the former *Hasenberg Station*; 1210 ft. above the sea, 394 ft. above the station at Stuttgart), which lies at the corner of the wood. This point, which commands the whole town and the valley of the Neckar, may also be reached by the new and winding Rothebühl-Strasse (Pl. A, 7). Still finer views are obtained from the *Jägerhaus (*Restaurant*), near which a bust of the novelist *Hauff* was erected in 1882, and from the (¼ hr.) stone *Belvedere Tower, 130 ft. in height, erected in 1879 (cross the rails and enter the wood): the view extends as far as the Wartberg at Heilbronn and the Melibocus; to the S. the entire chain of the Swabian Alb, with the Hohenstaufen, Rechberg, Neuffen, Achalm, and Hohenzollern. — From the Jägerhaus to the N.W. through the woods to the *Gais-Eiche*, ¼ hr.; to the W. to the deer-park (p. 14), ½ hr. — The direct path from the Jägerhaus to Stuttgart descends abruptly in 20-25 min., passing on the right the reservoir of the new aqueduct and the *Reinsburg*, with the *Karls-Linde* (Pl. C, 6), a hill affording a fine view, immediately to the S. of Stuttgart. Tramway from the Schwab-Strasse, see p. 1.

FROM STUTTGART TO CANNSTATT, 2½ M. The RAILWAY (R. 8; 8-11 min.) penetrates the *Rosenstein* (see below) by a tunnel 450 yds. long, crosses the *Neckar*, and reaches the station of *Cannstatt*, on the left bank.

The TRAMWAY (p. 1; 2½ M. from the Palace at Stuttgart, in 20 min.) traverses first the *Neckar-Strasse* (p. 5), and then the *Untere Neckar-Strasse* (view of the Royal Villa, see below), which extends to Berg; from Berg it crosses the *König-Karl-Brücke* (p. 13) direct to *Cannstatt* (terminus near the rail. station). The old high-road runs from Berg along the E. slope of the *Rosenstein*, passes the lower entrance of the *Wilhelma* (p. 13), and sweeps round to Cannstatt on the right bank.

Berg, the N.E. suburb of Stuttgart, sharing its rapid growth, lies on the left bank of the Neckar and, like Cannstatt, is frequented as a health-resort. *Neuner's Mineralbad*, near the tramway office at the beginning of the town, possesses a swimming-bath (open in winter also), an aquarium, a garden-restaurant, and a favourite open-air theatre (p. 2). On a slight eminence above the town rises the Gothic church, built by Gaab in 1855, with open tower. — The *Sprudel*, which bursts from the earth like that of Carlsbad, and other mineral springs on the *Neckar-Insel*, an island which extends from Berg almost to Cannstatt, has given rise to a number of bath-houses (**Leuze's Inselbad*, with pension; band plays at 6 a.m.; closed in winter).

The Royal Villa, on the top of the hill to the S. of Berg, a modern Renaissance edifice, built by *Leins* in 1846-53, and sur-

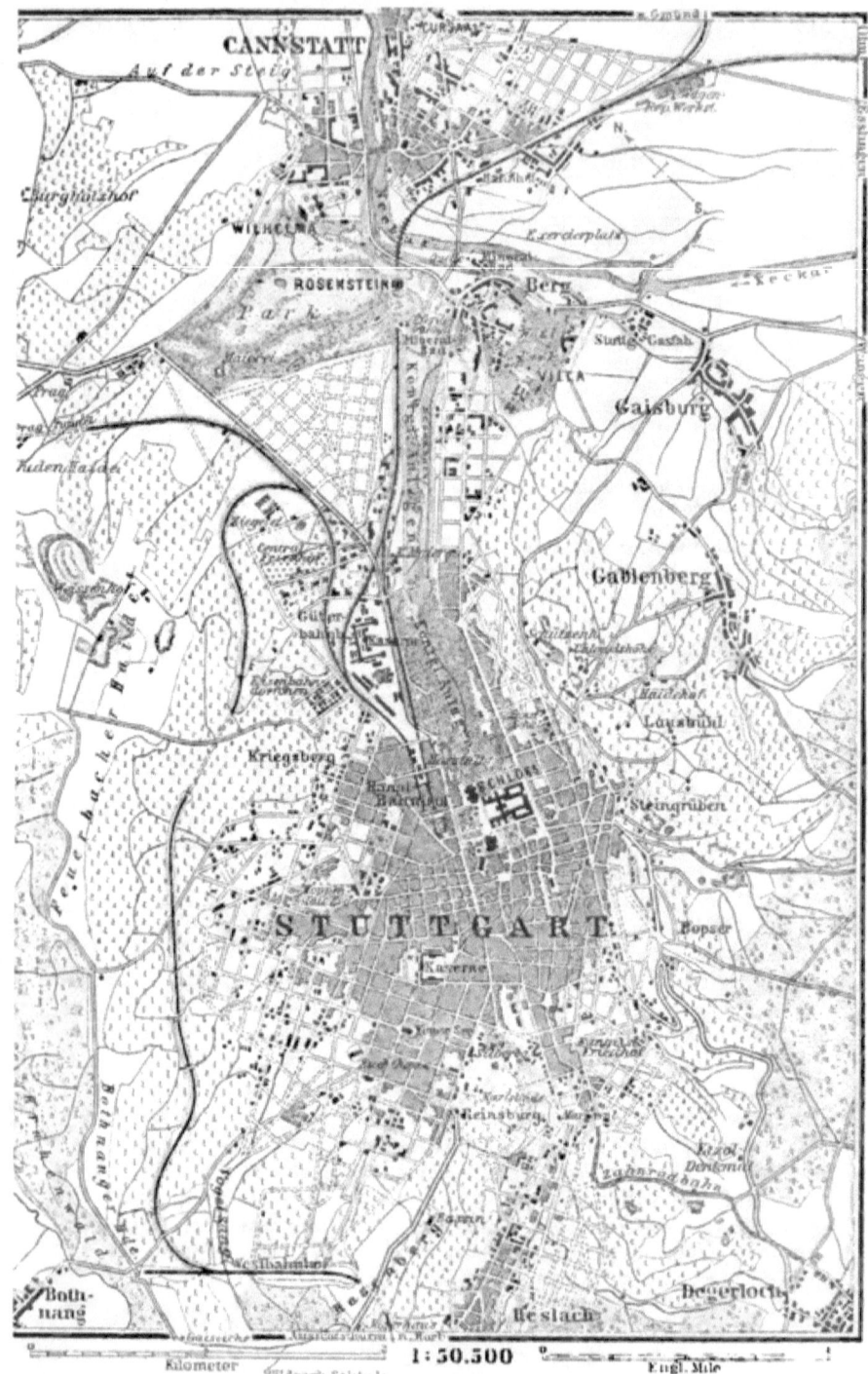

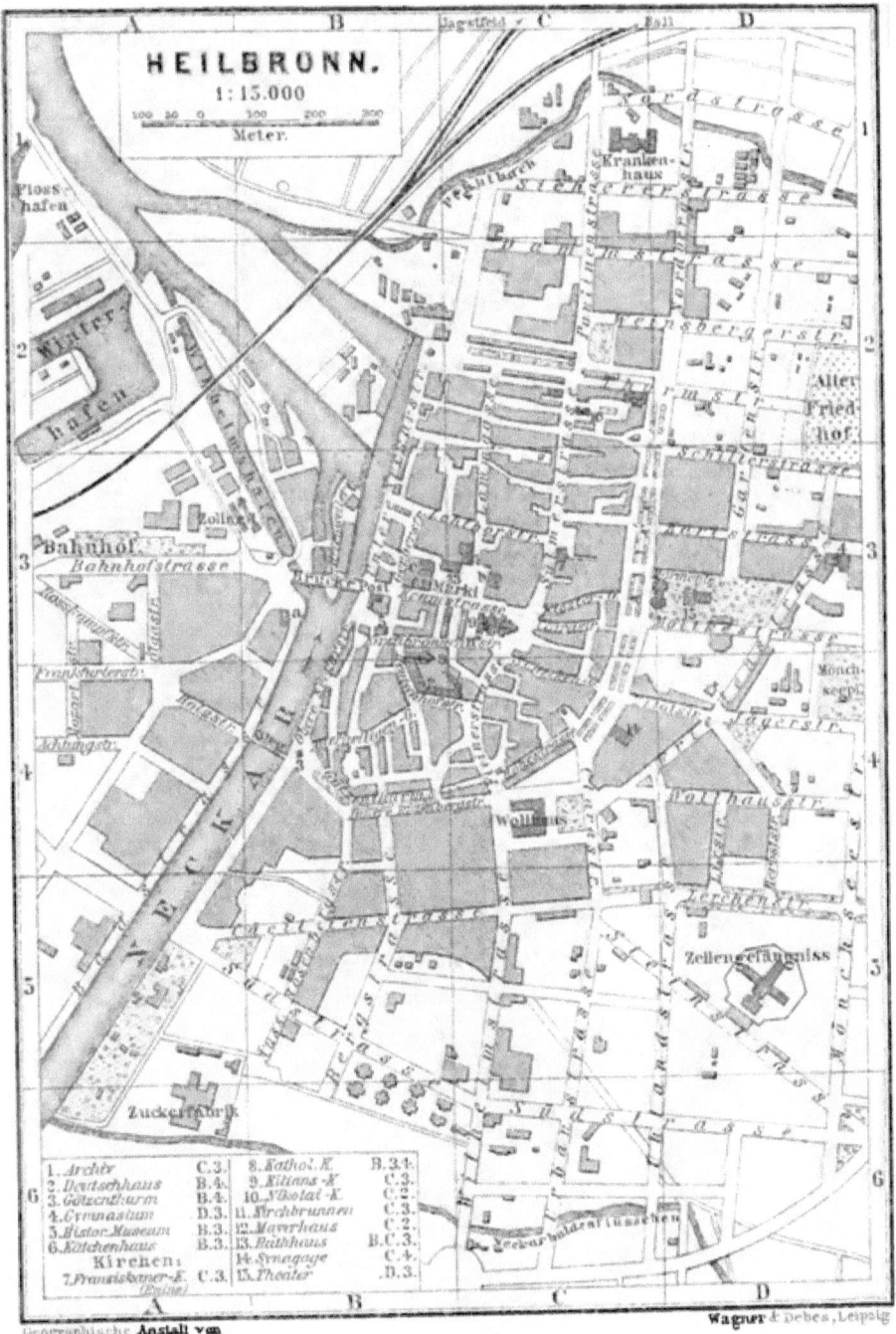

rounded with gardens and hot-houses, commands a charming view. In the interior are pictures by *Nic. de Keyser*, *Kaminski*, *Bohn*, *Karl Müller*, etc., and sculptures by *Tenerani* and other masters. In the garden are statues of the four seasons by *Kopf*, and busts in bronze of Nicholas, Emperor of Russia, and his consort, by *Rauch*. The villa belongs to the Duchess Wera (adm., see p. 2).

The **Rosenstein**, a villa in the Romanesque style on the hill to the N. of Berg, with colonnades, built by *Salucci* in 1823-29, contains numerous sculptures (by *Wagner*, *Wolf*, *Hoyer*, *Tenerani*, *Hofer*, etc.) and an extensive collection of pictures (catalogue from the steward). Admission, see p. 2; the main entrance is on the S.W. side of the park, opposite the chestnut avenue mentioned at p. 9. — From the back of the château walks descend through the grounds to the Wilhelma.

The *Wilhelma, an edifice in the Moorish style, in the midst of well-kept grounds, was erected for King William I. in 1842-51 (adm., see p. 2).

The *Festsaalbau* contains a single saloon sumptuously fitted up. It is connected by means of circular colonnades with two *Pavilions* (that to the right contains a *Picture Gallery*, of Oriental subjects only) and with the *Château* itself on the upper terrace. In the centre of the latter is the audience-chamber, on the right a drawing-room, on the left the king's study. There are also bedrooms, dressing-rooms, and a bath-room (with a fine **stalactite** ceiling). At the back of the château several other terraces rise to the plateau of the hill, on the summit of which is a *Belvedere*, also in the Moorish style, commanding a charming view. The lower terraces within the colonnades are embellished with flower-beds, fountains, and groups of animals in marble and bronze by Güldenstein.

Cannstatt. — **Hotels:** STÄDTISCHES LOGIERHAUS, at the Cursaal, for patients; VIER JAHRESZEITEN, SANNWALD'S BAHNHOF-HÔTEL, GASTHOF & RESTAURANT ZUM BAHNHOF, at the station, second-class; BÄR, in the market-place. *PENSION LIEB, König-Str. 13. — **Restaurants:** *Cursaal*; *Sannwald*; *Krauss*; *Krone*.

Sanatory Establishments: Dr. *Veiel's*, for cutaneous diseases; Dr. *Bilfinger's*, for the 'Kneipp Cure'; *Wilhelmsbad*, the property of the town, open in winter also. Baths also in the *Russischer Hof* and the *Neues Cannstatter Mineralbad*, Badgasse (also open in winter).

Popular Festival, with exhibitions, races, etc., every alternate year, beginning on 28th Sept. and lasting 3-7 days.

Cannstatt, a town with 20,267 inhab., is connected with Berg by the *König-Karl-Brücke*, a railway-bridge with five arches, 1000 ft. long, erected in 1891-93 by K. von Leibbrand. It possesses warm saline and chalybeate springs which attract a number of patients, but is rapidly becoming a manufacturing place. The *Cursaal*, with the *Wilhelmsbrunnen* (62-66° Fahr.), the chief mineral spring, lies on the *Sulzerain* (view), on the N. side of the town. Adjacent are a whey-cure establishment, a restaurant, a reading-room, and a Trinkhalle. In front of the Cursaal is a bronze *Equestrian Statue of King William I.* (d. 1864), by Halbig, erected in 1875. — In the Uffkirchhof is the grave of *Ferdinand Freiligrath*, the poet (d. 1876), with a bronze bust by Donndorf.

The *Burgholz* (1175 ft.; view-tower), 4 M. from Stuttgart and 2 M. from Cannstatt (refreshments at the Burgholzhof), affords a fine view of Stuttgart and up the valley of the Neckar.

About 6 M. to the S. of Stuttgart (railway viâ *Degerloch* and *Möhringen* in 55 min.) lies **Hohenheim**, a château built by Duke Charles in 1768, now an agricultural school. Fine view from the top. — *Klein-Hohenheim, Scharnhausen*, and *Weil*, with their model-farms and the horse-breeding establishment at Weil, may be visited on the same day as Hohenheim. Permission obtained at the offices of the Hofdomäne, Friedrichs-Str. 26. Weil is 1½ M. from Esslingen (p. 29).

Unter- and *Ober-Türkheim* and the *Rothenberg*, see p. 29.

The Solitude (1540 ft.), 6 M. to the W. of Stuttgart, built in 1763-67 by Duke Charles, was in 1770-75 the seat of the Karls-Schule, where Schiller received part of his education, before its transference to Stuttgart (p. 5). Schiller's father was inspector of the gardens here. The grounds and park command a fine view (best from the dome of the Schloss). A whey-cure establishment here attracts visitors in summer. A little to the S. is a well-stocked deer-park, with the 'Bärenschlösschen' and the *Bären-See*. Deer fed at 11 a.m., wild boars at 6 p.m. (cards of adm. at the office of the royal chasse, in the Academy, p. 4). From the deer-park to the *Jägerhaus*, see p. 12.

2. From Heidelberg to Stuttgart by Bruchsal.

69 M. Railway in 2½-4½ hrs. (fares 9 ℳ 60, 6 ℳ 30, 4 ℳ 10 pf.; express 10 ℳ 95, 7 ℳ 65, 5 ℳ 45 pf.). — Route viâ *Heilbronn*, see R. 4.

The line traverses a fertile plain, within a short distance of the mountains. Stations *Kirchheim, St. Ilgen, Wiesloch*. Nearing (15 M.) *Langenbrücken* (Ochs; Sonne), a small place with sulphur-baths, we notice *Kislau*, once a château of the prince-bishops of Speyer, now a penitentiary for women, on the right.

20½ M. **Bruchsal** *(*Hôtel Keller*, near the station; *Railway Restaurant)* is the junction of the Bâle line (see *Baedeker's Rhine*). The town (11,900 inhab.) was formerly the residence of the Bishops of Speyer, whose *Schloss*, a fine rococo edifice, handsomely fitted up, and adorned with frescoes by Zick, is worthy of a visit. The castellated building on the left as the station is approached is a prison, erected in 1845.

Beyond Bruchsal a short tunnel. 24½ M. *Heidelsheim*. 27 M. *Gondelsheim*, with the ruined castle and modern château of Count Langenstein.

30 M. **Bretten** (540 ft.; *Krone*, ¼ M. from the station; *Rail. Restaurant*), a small town commanded by an ancient watch-tower. In the Bahnhof-Strasse is a block of granite with a bronze medallion of Grand-Duke Frederick of Baden, erected to commemorate the jubilee of his reign (1891). In the market-place, opposite the post-office, is a fountain, surmounted by the figure of a tailless dog. Adjacent is the house in which Philip Melanchthon (1497-1560), the 'Præceptor Germaniæ', was born; a monument was erected to him in 1864 in front of the school-house, at the end of the

town. Branch-lines to *Durlach* and *Heilbronn*, p. 18. — 36 M. *Maulbronn*.

Maulbronn (2 M. **from the** station; *Post*, high charges; *Brewery*, good beer, also beds; post-omnibus to the village thrice daily in 25 min.) possesses a Protestant theological seminary, which was once a celebrated Cistercian abbey, and afterwards the seat of the 'monastery school' founded by Duke Christopher in 1556. The *Abbey Church, consecrated in 1187, **is a** fine Romanesque basilica with aisles. The late-Gothic chapels **on the** S. side **were** subsequent additions. A **Romanesque screen** with **two doors** separates the choir of the **monks from the** nave; in front **of the** central niche are **a** richly-decorated throne and an altar with **a colossal** crucifix dating from 1473. The choir, adorned with two **handsome Gothic** windows, contains 92 well-carved stalls in the late-Gothic style. Each of the transepts, on the N. and S. side of the choir respectively, **contains** three rectangular chapels. At the W. **end of the** church is a ***Vestibule** ('Paradies') **with** elegant late-Romanesque arcade-windows and **fine** vaulting. The *Cloisters on the N. side of the church are interesting. **The** S. passage, in the transition style (1303), **is the** richest; the others, **in** the Gothic style, are simpler. In front of the **N. wing of** the cloisters **is a** tastefully-constructed well-house. Beyond it **is the** summer-refectory ('Rebenthal'), with fine vaulting. Other apartments (chamber of flagellation, chapter-house, **audience** saloon, residence **of** the superior) adjoin the E. side of the cloisters. **On** the W. **side is** the winter or lay-refectory, divided into two parts by seven double columns. The entire structure, one of the best preserved of the **older** monasteries of Germany, has been restored under the superintendence of Landauer. — A pleasant road, partly through wood, leads by (3 M.; diligence twice daily in $^3/_4$ hr.) the small town of *Knittlingen* **(Kanne)**, the traditional birthplace of **Dr. Faust**, to *Bretten* (see above).

The train now passes through a tunnel of 357 yds., under the watershed between the Neckar and the Rhine. 40 M. *Mühlacker*, junction for *Pforzheim* (p. 17); 44 M. *Illingen*; 47 M. *Vaihingen*, with a large château, now an asylum; 50 M. *Gross-Sachsenheim*. On the left rise the *Stromberg* and the *Heuchelberg*, two low, wooded chains of hills. The train traverses the old *Kraichgau* and *Salzgau*, a fertile, hilly district, and crosses the deep valley of the *Enz* by a *Viaduct, 115 ft. high, and 357 yds. long, supported by 21 arches, in two series, one above the other (well seen from the Bietigheim station). At (54$^1/_2$ M.) **Bietigheim** the line to Heilbronn and Hall diverges to the N. (see R. 4). Beyond Bietigheim the line presents few attractions. 56$^1/_2$ M. *Thamm*. Farther on, to the right, near (57$^1/_2$ M.) *Asperg*, rises a vine-clad hill (1165 ft.) crowned by the small fortress of *Hohenasperg* (still a prison), where Duke Charles confined the poet Schubart from 1777 to 1787 for having composed a satirical epigram on him; fine *View from the view-tower (10 pf.).

60 M. **Ludwigsburg** (*Railway Hotel, opposite the station, with a concert-hall; *Kanne*, *Sonne*, in the town), a town with 17,673 inhab., the military depôt of Wurtemberg, contains an arsenal, cannon-foundry, barracks, military schools, &c. It was founded at the beginning of last century by Duke Eberhard Ludwig (d. 1733; whose statue adorns the market-place), as a rival of Stuttgart, and was extended by Duke Charles, who resided here in 1764-85. The streets are broad and regular. The *Marble Statue of Schiller* in the

Wilhelms-Platz, by Hofer, was erected in 1882; the poet lived in 1793-94 in the house at the corner of the Post-Str. (now a wine-shop). Ludwigsburg was the birthplace of *David Strauss* (1808-74), the theologian, *Justinus Kerner* (1786-1862) and *Edw. Mörike* (1804-75), the poets, and *F. T. Vischer* (1807-87), the philosopher.

The *Palace* (uninhabited), a handsome rococo building, containing 460 rooms and a gallery of the portraits of sovereigns of Wurtemberg, was erected by Duke Eberhard Ludwig in 1710-20 and is surrounded by extensive, well-kept grounds. The balcony of the *Emichsburg*, an artificial ruin, commands a fine view. A subterranean vault contains a representation in wax of Count Emich, an ancestor of the royal House of Wurtemberg, carousing with a Capuchin. In the cellar is a *Cask* with a capacity of 20,000 gallons. — At the S.E. extremity of the Schloss-Garten is the *Churchyard*, containing Dannecker's monument to Count Zeppelin (d. 1801), the minister of King Frederick, erected by order of the latter. — The N. prolongation of the grounds is the *Favoriten-Park*, with the tasteful little *Favorite Château*, containing a splendid collection of antlers (tickets of admission at the office of the Royal Chasse, in Stuttgart). An avenue of poplars leads hence to (1½ M.) *Monrepos*, a royal château with a model farm, pretty grounds, and a lake. We may now return to Ludwigsburg viâ *Eglosheim* and the *Villa Marienwahl*, the summer-residence of King William II.

Among the chief boasts of Ludwigsburg are the magnificent avenues of limes and chestnuts leading from the palace to the *Salonwald*, a large park commanding admirable views. Adjacent is the *Karlshöhe*, a refuge and school for children. Near the beginning of the straight road to (12 M.) the Solitude (p. 14) are the *Römerhügel* and the *Kaiserstein* (views).

Ludwigsburg is connected by a branch-railway with (3 M.) *Beihingen* (p. 25), on the railway from Backnang to Bietigheim. — *Marbach* (p. 25; railway in 25 min., carr. viâ *Benningen* in 1 hr.) and *Hohenasperg* (p. 15; railway in 6 min.) are best visited from Ludwigsburg.

63 M. *Kornwestheim*. — 64½ M. **Zuffenhausen**.

To CALW AND HORB, 55½ M., railway in 3¼-4 hrs. — 2 M. Kornthal (°*Gemeinde-Gasthof*, wine of Jerusalem) is the seat of a sect resembling the Moravians, with several good schools. — 4½ M. *Ditzingen*. — 9 M. *Leonberg* (Lamm or Post; Löwe), the birthplace of the philosopher Schelling (p. 152), possesses an early-Gothic church of the 15th cent., and is noted for a fine breed of large dogs resembling the now extinct St. Bernard race. — Then past (12½ M.) *Renningen* to (16 M.) *Weilderstadt* (*Krone*; *Löwe*), with the late-Gothic Church of St. Peter & St. Paul (end of 15th cent.), the birthplace of the astronomer Kepler (d. 1630), a bronze °Statue of whom, by Kreling, adorns the market-place. — 18½ M. *Schafhausen*; 21 M. *Althengstett*. — At (30 M.) Calw (1095 ft.; *Waldhorn*; *Badischer Hof*), a town with 4700 inhab. and a considerable timber-trade, the line enters the picturesque *Nagold-Thal*. — Railway to *Pforzheim* in ½-¾ hr., see p. 17.

The line then leads through the Nagold-Thal (several tunnels), past *Kentheim*, to (32 M.) *Teinach*, at the union of the Teinach and Nagold. About 1½ M. up the valley of the Teinach (omnibus in 25 min.) are the charmingly-situated baths of **Teinach** (°*Bad-Hôtel zur Krone*, with rooms for 300 visitors, D. 2 ℳ 80, S. 1 ℳ 20, B. 70 pf., pension 50-80 ℳ per week; *Hirsch*; *Zum Kühlen Brunnen*). On the hill above is *Zavelstein* (°Lamm), a summer-resort, with a ruined castle, **the tower** of which **is a fine** point of view.

34 M. *Thalmühle* (*Inn*); in the woods near it is *Burg* **Waldeck**. 36½ M. *Wildberg* (Adler; Schwan), a small and ancient town, is prettily situated on a rock washed by the Nagold. 42 M. *Nagold* (1295 ft.; *Post; Hirsch*), a busy place, commanded by the ruined castle of *Hohennagold*, which was destroyed during the Thirty Years' War. Handsome modern Gothic church. — The train quits the Nagold-Thal, which here turns to the W., ascends the *Steinach-Thal* to *Gündringen*, and passes through the *Hochdorfer Tunnel*, **1360 yds.** long, **to** (48½ M.) *Hochdorf* (1650 ft.; °Inn, plain), the culminating **point** of the line, with a fine **view** of the distant chain of the Swabian **Jura.** — Beyond (51 M.) *Eutingen*, the junction for the Gäubahn and the line to Hausach (p. 39), the train descends the narrow valley of Mühlen to the Neckar-Thal and (56½ M.) *Horb* (p. 39).

66 M. *Feuerbach*, beyond which the **train passes through a tunnel of 1000** yds. under the *Prag*.

69 M. Stuttgart, see p. 1.

From *Carlsruhe* to *Stuttgart by Pforzheim*, see **below**.

3. From Stuttgart to Wildbad.

52 M. RAILWAY viâ Pforzheim in 3-4 hrs.; fares 6 *M* 80, 4 *M* 50, 2 *M* 85 pf. (viâ *Calw* in 4½ hrs., see above).

From Stuttgart to (29 M.) *Mühlacker*, see R. 2. Beyond (31½ M.) *Enzberg* the line enters the Duchy of Baden, and crosses the *Enz*. 33 M. *Niefern*; 35 M. *Eutingen*, near which is a Roman castrum.

37½ M. **Pforzheim** (810 ft.; *Hôtel Nusser or *Post; Schwarzer Adler; Victoria, Zur Eisenbahn*, both at the station; wine at the *Rappen*, Karl-Friedrich-Str.; *Hydropathic*, pens. 3-6 *M*), a busy, manufacturing town (30,000 inhab.), lies at the confluence of the *Enz*, the *Würm*, and the *Nagold*. The staple commodities, gold and silver wares, employ 10,000 workmen.

Near the station is the Romanesque and Gothic *Schlosskirche, erected in the 12-15th centuries.

In the choir are the statues of the Margraves **Ernest** (d. 1604), **James** (d. 1590), and **Charles II.** (d. 1577). Charles II. **was the first** prince of **this line** who **embraced the** Reformed faith. **Then the** statue of his wife **Kuni**gunde, Margravine of Brandenburg (d. 1558); **Countess** Palatine Anna (d. 1587); Albert Alcibiades of Brandenburg-Bayreuth, celebrated for his numerous campaigns, who died here (in 1557) under the imperial ban; also Margr. Bernhard (d. 1553). On a large sarcophagus are the recumbent figures of Margr. **Ernest** (d. 1558) and his wife Ursula (d. 1538). Beneath a Gothic covering is the bust of the Grand-Duke Charles Frederick (d. 1811). A monument on the **wall** commemorates the supposed death of 400 citizens of Pforzheim in the **battle of Wimpffen (1622)**, but this event lacks historical evidence.

In the market-place rises a *Warriors' Monument*. In the Leopold-Platz is a fountain with a *Statue of Margrave Ernest* (d. 1558), founder of the extinct Baden-Durlach-Ernestine family.

About 6 M. to the S.E. of Pforzheim, in the pleasant *Würmthal*, lies Tiefenbronn (*Löwe*), with an interesting *Abbey Church*. This contains a fine high-altar by Hans Schühlein of Ulm (1409), and four other well-preserved altars of the 15-16th cent., the best of which is the Magdalen Altar, with paintings **by Lucas** Moser (1432).

FROM PFORZHEIM TO CALW, 17 M. (railway in ½-¾ hr.). The train diverges to the left from the Wildbad line at *Brötzingen* (p. 18), crosses the *Enz*, penetrates the watershed between the Enz and the *Nagold* by means of a tunnel, 490 yds. long, and enters the beautiful wooded *Nagold-Thal*. Beyond another tunnel is (3½ M.) *Weissenstein* (*Sonne), with a picturesque ruined castle. Then the *Zelgenberg Tunnel*, 560 yds. in length. At (7 M.) *Unter-Reichenbach* we cross the Nagold. — 12 M. **Liebenzell** (*Unteres Bad; Oberes Bad; *Ochs*), a watering-place with warm springs of old repute, pleasantly situated, and overlooked by a ruined castle. — 14½ M. **Hirsau** (*Rössle Schwan, Kloster Hirsau* etc.), with a celebrated ruined monastery (Benedictine, founded in 830, destroyed by Melac in 1692). — 17 M. *Calw*. — From Calw to *Stuttgart*, see p. 16; to *Horb*, see p. 16.

From Pforzheim to Durlach *(Carlsruhe)*, 16 M., railway in 1 hr. The line skirts the N. slopes of the Black Forest Mts. and traverses the fertile valley of the *Pfinz*. Stations *Ispringen, Ersingen, Königsbach, Wilferdingen* (Krone), *Söllingen, Berghausen, Grötzingen* (junction for *Bretten* and *Heilbronn*, p. 20). At Durlach *(Carlsruhg)*, a town of 7474 inhab., the train reaches the Baden main line; see *Baedeker's Rhine*.

The railway to Wildbad continues to follow the picturesque green valley of the *Enz*. 39 M. *Brötzingen;* 40½ M. *Birkenfeld*.

43½ M. **Neuenbürg** *(Post; Bär)* is a picturesquely situated town, overlooked by the *Schloss*, erected on a wooded **eminence above the** Enz by Duke Christopher in 1658 **on the site of an older building (now** government offices). Adjacent **is the** so-called *Fruchtspeicher*, **the ruins of** a castle on Roman **foundations.**

The **train** crosses the Enz, passes through **a tunnel under the** Schlossberg, and recrosses the river. 46 M. *Röthenbach;* 48 M. *Höfen* (*Ochse), a favourite summer-resort, with pretty villas; 49 M. *Calmbach* (Sonne, poor), **a thriving place, with a neat modern church,** and also a summer-resort.

52 M. **Wildbad.** — Hotels. *Royal Bad-Hôtel, R. from 2½, D. 3 *M*; *Klumpp, or Bär, **R.** from 3, B. 1¼, D. at 1 p.m. 3½, at 5 p.m. 4½ *M;* *Bellevue, R. from 3, B. 1¼, D. 3½ *M;* *Post, R. 2-5, B. 1, D. 2½, pens. 6½-10 *M*; Hôtel Garni Keim; Hôtel de Russie, R. from 2, D. 2½ *M;* *Goldnes Lamm, Curplatz, R., L., & A. 2-2½, D. 2, B. ¾ *M*, good cuisine; Ross, Löwe, Sonne, Stern, Weil, Zur Eisenbahn (the last two by the station), etc. Also **numerous** *Hôtels Garnis* and lodging-houses, the best being those above **the Anlagen.** — Restaurants of *Funk* and *Schmidt* , moderate; *Funk's Brewery*. — **Cab** (one horse) 1 *M* per ¼ hr. — Visitors' *Tax* for four days **or more, 12** *M*. — English Church (*Holy Trinity);* service in summer.

Wildbad (1426 ft.), a celebrated watering-place (3500 inhab.), situated in the narrow, pine-clad ravine of the *Enz*, possesses warm alkaline springs, used as a cure for gout and rheumatism. The greater part of the town lies on the right bank of the Enz, while the station is at the lower end of it on the left bank. In the *Curplatz*, at the end of the Haupt-Strasse, are the handsome *Curhaus* or *Bad-Hôtel*, with reading and ball rooms and a café (music in the morning and afternoon), and the large *Badgebäude*, with its admirably equipped baths. The *Springs* (90-100° Fahr.) rise in the baths themselves, and their efficacy (for gout, rheumatism, etc.) is chiefly ascribed to their being thus used in a fresh and natural condition at the fountain-head. Most of the patients (about 6500 annually) prefer the system of bathing in common, as at Leuk in Switzerland. There are three well-arranged public baths for each sex (1 ℳ), as well as a number of private baths (2 ℳ). The sumptuous *Karlsbad*, with paintings by Kolb, was opened in 1892. Between the Enz and the Bellevue Hotel stands the *Trinkhalle*, a tasteful iron structure in the Renaissance style, with a band-pavilion in the centre. Higher up in the grounds is the *Theatre*. The *Katharinenstift*, a bath for the poor, is a building in the round-arch style. In the lower part of the town is *Herrenhilf*, a sanatorium for children. There are pleasant walks and grounds on both sides of the village, on the banks of the Enz: on the S. (upper) side past the new Roman Catholic church as far as the (1 M.) *Windhof*, a café; on the N. (lower) side to the (1 M.) garden '*Zum kühlen Brunnen*', a favourite resort.

EXCURSIONS. To the *Waterfalls* in a side-valley of the Enz, 3½ M. — A road ascends the Enzthal to (7½ M.) *Enzklösterle* (Waldhorn) and (3 M.) *Gompelscheuer* (Lamm); thence to *Freudenstadt* (p. 39), 16½ M. — By the small *Wildsee*, which tradition has peopled with water-sprites, to the *Kaltenbrunn* shooting-lodge ('Inn), 16½ M.; thence to the *Hohloh-Thurm* (3625 ft.), a fine point of view, ¼ hr. — To (4½ M.) *Eyachmühl*, (2¼ M.) *Dobel*, and (3 M.) *Herrenalb* (Hydropathic Establishment and several hotels), frequented as a summer-resort; see *Baedeker's* **Rhine**.

The following is a very interesting excursion for a whole day (one-horse carr. 9, two-horse 14-15 ℳ), and is also recommended to pedestrians. Viâ *Calmbach* (see p. 18) to (2 M.) *Reichenbach* (Löwe). Thence, leaving the main road, by a by-road to the right to (6 M.) *Röthenbach* (view of Hohenzollern from the height as the village is approached; carriages should be sent on from this point to Teinach) and (2 M.) *Zavelstein* (Lamm), with a picturesque ruined castle. Descent to (1½ M.) *Teinach* (p. 16); thence down to the (1 M.) Nagold-Thal, and by *Kentheim* to (3 M.) *Calw* (p. 16; also railway from this point); then (4½ M.) *Hirsau*, and (3¾ M.) *Liebenzell* (p. 18). Back to Wildbad by *Schömberg* and *Calmbach*.

4. From Stuttgart to Hanau.

118 M. RAILWAY in 5-8¾ hrs. (fares 15 ℳ 50, 11 ℳ 30, 6 ℳ 60 pf.; express 17 ℳ 70, 12 ℳ 50 pf.). This line forms the **shortest route** from Stuttgart to Berlin (16 hrs.; comp. R. 15).

From Stuttgart to (14 M.) *Bietigheim*, see R. 2. The line follows the *Enz* for a short way, and crosses it just before its influx into the Neckar, near (18 M.) *Besigheim* (*Waldhorn; Bahnhof; Krone), an antiquated little town, probably of Roman origin, very picturesquely situated on a rock between the Enz and the Neckar, with two handsome towers of mediæval castles. On the *Michaelsberg* (1280 ft.), 6 M. to the N.W., is a very ancient chapel, said to have been once a Roman temple of Luna. The line now follows the Neckar, passes through a tunnel (700 yds.) beyond (22 M.) *Kirchheim* (to the right of which is *Liebenstein*, with an interesting church and a Renaissance château), and returns to the river at —

25 M. *Lauffen* (564 ft.), the old castle and church of which stand picturesquely on two rocks, separated by the river. Beyond (28½ M.) *Nordheim*, on a height to the left, is the *Heuchelberger Warte* (1036 ft.). Above Heilbronn rise the vine-clad *Wartberg*, on the N., and the wooded *Schweinsberg* (p. 21), on the S.E.

33 M. Heilbronn (comp. Plan, p. 13). — **Hotels.** *Eisenbahn-Hôtel* (Pl. a; B, 3), with salt-baths and good restaurant, on the Neckar, opposite the post-office, R. & B. 2½-3 ℳ; *Bahnhof-Hôtel*, opposite the railway-station, R. & B. 2½, D. 2 ℳ; Badischer Hof, Kronprinz (moderate), also at the station; Falke (Pl. b; C, 3), in the Market; Krone, Lohthor-Str. (Pl. C, 3). R., L., & A. 1½-2 ℳ, B. 60 pf., D. 1½-2 ℳ.

Cafés-Restaurants. *Faessi zur Harmonie*, in the Allee; *Deutsches Haus* (see p. 21); *Hägele zum Käthchen*, Kirchbrunnen-Str.; *Weyhing zur Sonne*, Sülmer-Str.; *Frank'sche Brauerei*, Fleimer-Str. — Wine Rooms. *Zehender*, Kram-Str.; *Albrecht*, in the Allee.

Heilbronn (518 ft.), formerly a free city of the Empire, now an important industrial town with 29,940 inhab., is charmingly situated on both banks of the Neckar. The *Allee*, a pleasant avenue on the site of the old fortifications, encircles the old town, beyond which suburbs are springing up in every direction.

On our left, as we leave the station, is the *Custom House*, with the *Wilhelms-Canal*; farther on are the *Winterhafen* and *Holzhafen*. From the Bahnhof-Str. we enter the town by a broad iron bridge. On the right bank, to our right, is the handsome new *Post Office* (Pl. B, 3). In the next side-street to the right is the *Historical Museum* (Pl. 5; B, 3), comprising prehistoric and other antiquities from the environs of Heilbronn.

Going straight on, we come to the Market-Place. On the left rises the late-Gothic *Rathhaus* (Pl. 13; B, C, 3), with its lofty flight of steps, containing a curious clock constructed by Habrecht in 1580. In the council-chamber Götz von Berlichingen, immortalised by Goethe, is said to have effectually cured 'headache, toothache, and every other human malady', with blows from his 'iron hand'. Letters from him, from Franz von Sickingen, the Reformer, from Schiller, who solicits the protection of the town in 1793, and others are shown in the *Archives*. The old-fashioned house at the S.W. corner of the Market (Pl. 6; B, 3) is pointed out as that in which 'Käthchen of Heilbronn' was born; but her history is purely traditionary.

The *Church of St. Kilian* (Pl. 9; C, 3), originally an early-Gothic edifice founded in 1013, of which the nave, with pointed arcades, is the only remnant, was rebuilt in the late-Gothic style in the 15th cent., and the tower, 217 ft. in height, was completed in 1529 in the Renaissance style. The whole building has just been thoroughly restored. The choir (1480), with richly articulated pillars and network-vaulting, contains an *Altar in carved wood, by *Tilmann Riemenschneider* (1498), and a fine ciborium. — The adjoining Clara-Strasse contains handsome new buildings.

We descend the Kirchbrunnen-Str. to the right, and enter the Deutschhof-Str. to the left, with the *Deutsches Haus* (Pl. 2; B, 4), originally an imperial palace, afterwards occupied by the Teutonic Order, and now by the courts of law. The Treaty of Heilbronn was concluded here in 1633. The oldest part of the building is the lowest story, in the Romanesque style, of the tower of the adjacent

Roman Catholic church. The court on the N. side is picturesque. Opposite is the old *Schönthaler Hof* (now Restaurant zum Deutschen Hause, see p. 20), where, as a quaint inscription on the gateway (right side) **records**, Charles V. once spent four weeks and was cured of an illness by the Heilbronn waters.

Nearly opposite the Deutsches Haus is the Allerheiligen-Str., leading to the square red *Diebsthurm* or **Götzens** *Thurm* (Pl. 3; B, 4), in which Goethe, contrary to the fact, represents Götz von Berlichingen as having died (whereas he was only imprisoned here for one night in 1519; comp. pp. 20, 22). To the E. of the tower we ascend the Rosenberger-Str. to the Allee (p. 20), in which, on the right, rises the *Synagogue* (Pl. 14; C, 4), in the Moorish-Byzantine style. Farther on is the *Harmonie-Gebäude* (Pl. C, D, 3), containing the exhibition of the Kunstverein. Near it are the large *Prison* (Pl. D, 5) and the *New Gymnasium* (Pl. D, 5).

From the N. end of the Allee the Thurm-Str. leads W. to the Sülmer-Str. Here, on the left, rises the simple Gothic *Church of St. Nicholas* (Pl. 10), where the first Protestant divine service was held in 1525. The *Schiller-Haus* opposite was occupied by the poet in 1793-94. Farther on, in the Hafenmarkt, are remains of the *Franciscan Church* (Pl. 7), destroyed by the French in 1688. The tower and the cloisters of the old monastery (now a school) are well preserved.

The pretty **Cemetery** contains several interesting **tombstones**. The *Water Works*, with steam-pump and reservoir, at the base of the Wartberg, should be seen by engineers.

On the *Wartberg* (1010 ft., or 492 ft. above the Neckar; an ascent of ³/₄ hr.) are an old watch-tower and an inn. Charming view of the Neckar-Thal. Another fine point is the (1 hr.) *Jägerhaus* (*Tavern). From the Jägerhaus we may walk past the *Köpferquelle* and through wood to the tower on the *Schweinsberg* (1205 ft.; 1¹/₂ hr. to the S.E. of Heilbronn), which affords a fine *Panorama, embracing the Alb chain to the S., the Black Forest and Vosges to the S.W., the Haardt Mts. and Donnersberg to the W., the Odenwald and Spessart to the N., and the Löwenstein Mts. to the E. The *Cäcilien-Wiese* (1¹/₂ M.) presents a lively and picturesque scene at the vintage season. Another favourite point is the *Trappensee* (*Restaurant), 1¹/₂ M. to the E. of the town.

From Heilbronn to *Bretten* and *Carlsruhe*, see p. 18; to *Schwäbisch-Hall*, see p. 23.

The train now crosses the Wilhelms-Canal and the Neckar. To the right is the line to Weinsberg (R. 5); on the hill are the tower and inn on the Wartberg (see above). Near (37 M.) *Neckarsulm*, a pleasant little town with an old château of the Teutonic Order, the train returns to the *Neckar*, and beyond (39 M.) *Kochendorf* (village and château ¹/₂ M. to the E.) it crosses the *Kocher*. — 40 M. **Jagstfeld** (*Bräuninger's Bad-Hôtel*, with terrace on the

Neckar), a saline bath at the mouth of the *Jagst*, with a sanatory institute for children *(Bethesda)*. Near the station are the salt-springs of *Friedrichshall*.

From Jagstfeld to Osterburken, 24 M., railway in 3/4-1 1/2 hr. The line runs viâ *Neudenau* and *Möckmühl*. — 24 M. *Osterburken*, on the Heidelberg and Würzburg railway, see p. 71.

From Jagstfeld to Heidelberg, 35 M. (railway in 2 hrs.). The train crosses the Neckar. 2 M. Wimpfen, *Wimpfen 'im Thal'* and above it '*Wimpfen am Berg*', both 'enclaves' of Hessen, with the salt-works and saline baths of *Ludwigshall* (*Bad-Hôtel Ritter*; *Mathildenbad*; *Sonne*; wine at *Phil. Schmidt's*). The fine Gothic abbey-church in the valley was erected in 1262-78. Wimpfen am Berg, with its picturesque old houses, towers, and walls, affords fine views of the valley of the Neckar, with the Wartberg to the S.E. The remains of the Hohenstaufen residence and chapel (now a stable) are interesting. The parish-church has a Gothic choir of the 13th cent.; the Dominican church was rebuilt at the beginning of the 18th cent. in the Baroque style.

The line now traverses a hilly and partly wooded district. 5 1/2 M. *Rappenau* (*Gasthof zur Saline*) also has salt-springs. Several unimportant stations. Then (14 M.) *Sinzheim*, where Turenne defeated the Imperial army in 1674. The line traverses the *Elsenz-Thal*. At (22 1/2 M.) Meckesheim (*Zur Eisenbahn*; *Rail. Restaurant*), on the *Elsenz*, it joins the railway to Neckarelz (p. 71). 24 1/2 M. *Mauer*; 26 M. *Bammenthal*; 28 1/2 M. *Neckargemünd*, the junction of the Würzburg line (R. 15); thence to (35 M.) *Heidelberg*, see p. 72.

The train crosses the Jagst and at (42 1/2 M.) *Offenau*, with the salt-springs of *Clemenshall*, enters the charming vine-clad Neckar-Thal, with its numerous castles. The village and château of *Heinsheim* and the ruined castle of *Ehrenberg* are passed on the left bank. — 45 M. *Gundelsheim* (Prinz Karl), a small town with walls, towers, and a picturesque château on an ivy-clad rock. Opposite, on a hill on the left bank, is the ruin of *Guttenberg*. The train then passes through the *Michelsberg* by a tunnel 950 yds. long to (46 1/2 M.) *Hassmersheim* (Anker). To the right, above (47 1/2 M.) *Neckarzimmern*, rises the picturesque castle of *Hornberg*, where Götz von Berlichingen died in 1562 (comp. p. 24). — Then through the charming valley to (left) *Hochhausen*, where we cross the *Elz* to (50 1/2 M.) **Neckarelz** (436 ft.; *Rail. Restaurant*; *Kling*; *Hirsch*), the junction of the Würzburg-Heidelberg and Meckesheim railways (p. 71).

The train follows the right bank of the pretty, wooded Neckar-Thal. Beyond (52 1/2 M.) *Binau* a tunnel 850 yds. long penetrates the *Rothenberg*. — 55 1/2 *Neckargerach* (Krone), with large quarries; on the hill is the ruined *Minneburg*, destroyed in the Thirty Years' War. 57 1/2 M. **Zwingenberg** (Schiff), with a picturesque castle, now restored, property of the Grand-Duke of Baden.

64 M. **Eberbach** (440 ft.; *Leininger Hof; *Krone), an old town with a brisk trade in timber (4940 inhab.). The *Katzenbuckel* (2053 ft.), the highest of the Odenwald Mts., commanding an extensive view, may be ascended hence in 2 hrs. — To *Heidelberg* through the *Neckar-Thal*, see p. 71.

Our train quits the Neckar-Thal and turns to the right into the grassy and wooded valley of the *Itterbach*, which it crosses several times. Beyond (67½ M.) *Gaimühle* a lofty viaduct. — 71½ M. *Kailbach;* 75 M. *Schöllenbach.* The train penetrates the *Krähenberg* by a tunnel nearly 2 M. long, descends the *Mümling-Thal* to (78 M.) *Hetzbach-Beerfelden*, and crosses the *Himbächel Viaduct*, 145 ft. high. — 83 M. **Erbach** *(*Zum Odenwald; Adler)*, a town with 2800 inhab., is the principal place on the estates of Count Erbach. The *Schloss* contains several interesting *Collections (armour, firearms, antiquities). In the chapel is shown the stone sarcophagus of Eginhard and his wife Emma (early-Gothic, and therefore not genuine), brought from the church of Seligenstadt (see below) in 1810.

84½ M. **Michelstadt** *(*Löwe; Schwan;* **Dr.** *Scharfenberg's Hydropathic)*, a prettily-situated little town, with a late-Gothic church (15th cent.) and a quaint Rathhaus. Opposite, to the left, is *Steinbach*, with Eginhard's basilica, one of the most important relics of the Carlovingian epoch and earlier than the church at Seligenstadt (see below). — We pass *Schloss Fürstenau* (left) and the stations of *Zell, König, Mümling-Grumbach*, and *Höchst-Neustadt*. Tunnel. — 97 M. *Wiebelsbach-Heubach*, junction of the Darmstadt line (see **Baedeker's Rhine**). — 99 M. *Gross-Umstadt* (*Lamm); 100½ M. **Klein-Umstadt;** 104 M. *Langstadt;* 105½ M. *Babenhausen*, the **junction** for Darmstadt and Aschaffenburg (see p. 61).

112 M. *Seligenstadt*, with 3700 inhab., is famous for the abbey founded here about 827 by Eginhard (or Einhard), the biographer of Charlemagne. — 114½ M. **Hainstadt;** 116½ M. *Klein-Auheim.* — The train then **crosses the Main** and reaches (118 M.) *Hanau* (p. 59).

5. From Heilbronn to Schwäbisch-Hall *(Nuremberg)*.

34 M. RAILWAY in 1-2 hrs. (fares 4 ℳ 40, 2 ℳ 90, 1 ℳ 90 pf.; express 5 ℳ, 3 ℳ 5 pf.); express to Nuremberg by this route in 4¼ hrs. (14 ℳ 50, 9 ℳ 60, 6 ℳ 20 pf.). This **is the shortest route between** Nuremberg and *Carlsruhe* (viâ *Bretten*, p. 14).

Heilbronn, see p. 20. The train crosses the Wilhelms-Canal and the Neckar. To the left diverges the line to Eberbach and Hanau (R. 4). Tunnel (1111 yds.).

4½ M. **Weinsberg** (600 ft.; **Traube)*, an ancient and historically memorable town. The ruined castle of *Weibertreu* ('women's faithfulness'), on the height, was the scene of the events on which Chamisso founded one of his ballads. Justinus Kerner, the poet (d. 1862), occupied a house at the foot of the hill. Near it is a monument to him. The handsome Romanesque *Church*, a basilica with pointed arcades, contains a small picture of 1659, representing the women quitting the castle. During the War of the Peasants in 1525 the most savage atrocities were committed here.

We next traverse the fertile and populous *Weinsberger-Thal*. On a hill to the right, near (8 M.) *Willsbach*, is the small town of *Löwenstein* (1260 ft.), commanded by the ruined castle of the

Löwenstein-Wertheim family. In a narrow valley at the N.W. foot of the hill lies the *Thäusser Bad*, with springs containing Epsom salts and sulphate of lime; at the E. base is *Lichtenstern*, a Protestant reformatory for children, formerly a nunnery. Beyond (10 M.) *Eschenau* the train descends into the valley of the *Brettach*, which it crosses near (13 M.) *Bretzfeld*.

16 1/2 M. Oehringen (748 ft.; *Württemberger Hof*; pop. 3700) is a pleasant **town** on the *Ohrn*, with a château of Prince Hohenlohe-Oehringen, below which are vast cellars. The Gothic *Stiftskirche*, **containing** monuments of the Hohenlohe family **and good stained glass, is interesting.** — 21 M. *Neuenstein*; 24 1/2 M. *Waldenburg*, **both with châteaux of** the Hohenlohe family. Beyond (27 M.) *Kupfer* **the train reaches the** highest point (1243 ft.) of the line, and then descends rapidly to (30 M.) *Gailenkirchen* and the valley of the *Kocher*, passing through two tunnels.

34 M. **Hall**, or **Schwäbisch-Hall** (885 ft.; **Lamm; *Adler*), on **the Kocher** (pop. 9100), once a city of the empire, has a picturesque appearance from the station. The Gothic *Church of St. Michael* (1427-1525) contains as an altar-piece an Entombment, ascribed to Lohkorn (about 1480). On the **left** bank of the Kocher is the *Church of St. Catharine* (14th **cent.**), containing a fine high-altar. **Large** salt-works with saline baths.

The salt-water is conveyed in pipes from the *Wilhelmsglück **mine** (7 M.), which is more interesting than those in the Salzkammergut. Descent by a flight of steps (680), or by **a** slide. The long galleries and spacious halls, glittering with crystals of salt, are imposing. Pure rocksalt is excavated **here.** Where the salt **is less pure, it** is obtained by filling portions **of the** mine with **water, which in a few weeks** becomes saturated **with salt, and** is then drawn off and evaporated.

The interesting church (12th cent.) of the old Benedictine abbey of Komburg, at *Steinbach* (Traube), 1 1/2 M. to the S. of Hall, now a home for invalid soldiers, possesses an embossed altar-covering (antependium) in gilded copper, of 1130, and a huge candelabrum of the same period. Immediately below it is *Klein-Komburg*, with the early-Romanesque church of St. Ægidius. In the choir are frescoes of the 12th cent., discovered in 1877, now restored. Komburg and Steinbach are 1 1/4 M. from *Hessenthal* (see below).

Beyond Hall the train passes through **two tunnels and goes on** to (38 M.) *Hessenthal*, **junction of the** following line (p. 25).

6. From Stuttgart to Nuremberg viâ Backnang.

120 M. RAILWAY in 4-7 3/4 hrs. (fares 15 *M* 40, 10 *M* 20, 6 *M* 60 pf.; express 17 *M* 60, 12 *M* 40, 8 *M* 80 pf.). This railway forms the shortest line of communication between Stuttgart and Nuremberg (comp. RR. 5, 7).

To (8 M.) *Waiblingen*, **see p. 27.** The MURRTHAL RAILWAY here diverges to the left from the Remsthal **Line** (R. 7), and crosses the deep *Remsthal* by a **viaduct** and an iron bridge. 10 1/2 M. *Neustadt*, with the favourite watering-place of *Neustädtle*. Tunnel of 390 yds. 12 M. *Schwaikheim*; 14 M. **Winnenden**, a busy little town, with **the château** of *Winnenthal*, now a lunatic asylum of high repute. In the background, to the **right**, rise the spurs of the

Welzheimer Wald (Wartturm of Bürg, Buocher Höhe). Pleasant walk viâ *Buoch* (p. 27) to the Remsthal. — 16 M. *Nellmersbach*; 17 M. *Maubach*. We now enter the *Murrthal* and reach —

19 M. **Backnang** *(Post)*, a manufacturing town (6763 inhab.) with extensive tanneries. Interesting Gothic-Romanesque church of a canonry founded here about 1116. To the right, in the background, is the Murrhardter Wald (with Schloss Ebersberg); to the left are the Löwenstein Mts. — The small watering-place of *Rietenau* (Curhaus) lies $3^1/_2$ M. to the N. of Backnang.

FROM BACKNANG TO BIETIGHEIM, 16 M. (railway in $^3/_4$–$1^1/_4$ hr.). The line follows the Murrthal, passing *Burgstall* and *Kirchberg*, to ($8^1/_2$ M.) Marbach *(Post)*, a small town on a height on the right bank of the Neckar, the birthplace of Schiller (b. 10th Nov., 1759; d. 9th May, 1805). The house in which he was born, purchased by subscription in 1859, and restored to its original condition, contains reminiscences of the illustrious poet. Close to the town is the *Schillerhöhe*, a park with a beautiful view, containing a colossal bronze *Statue of Schiller*, by Rau, erected in 1876. — The line crosses the Neckar by a viaduct 100 ft. high (fine view). — $12^1/_2$ M. *Beihingen* (junction for *Ludwigsburg*, p. 16). Then (16 M.) *Bietigheim* (p. 15).

The train crosses the *Weissach* and descends into the peaceful wooded Murrthal. 22 M. *Steinbach*; 23 M. *Oppenweiler*, with the château of Hr. von Sturmfeder, and the hoary *Reichenberg*. $25^1/_2$ M. *Sulzbach*, where the mediæval *Schloss Lautereck* is now a tannery. The train crosses the Murr.

29 M. **Murrhardt** (930 ft.; *Sonne* or *Post*; *Stern*), an ancient little town (4200 inhab.), once a Benedictine abbey. The *Walderichskirche*, on the hill, perhaps occupies the site of a Roman fort. The *Stadtkirche*, formerly the abbey-church, will repay a visit. The *Walderichs-Kapelle*, adjoining the N. tower of the Stadtkirche, is in the late-Romanesque style. The Roman castrum lay to the S.E. of the town. The Roman 'limes' (p. 27) from Welzheim to Mainhardt, crossing the Murrthal, passes about $^3/_4$ M. to the E. of Murrhardt.

32 M. *Fornsbach*.

A pleasant excursion (road) may be made to the S. to the (6 M.) Ebnisee (1555 ft.), a pretty forest-lake. About 1 M. to the S.E., by the Roman 'limes' (p. 27), is *Gausmannsweiler* (Inn Zum Ebnisee).

The train passes through the 'Schanze', or E. wall of the Murrthal, by a tunnel 578 yds. long, and reaches the *Roththal* near (35 M.) *Fichtenberg*. Another tunnel, 590 yds. long, leads to the *Kocher-Thal* and ($38^1/_2$ M.) *Gaildorf*. The Kocher is crossed by a lofty bridge. 40 M. *Ottendorf*; $43^1/_2$ M. *Wilhelmsglück*, station for the salt-mines of that name (p. 24). Then ($45^1/_2$ M.) *Hessenthal*, junction of the line to *Hall* (p. 24). The station lies at the foot of the *Einkorn* (1555 ft.; view), a favourite resort from Hall ($3^1/_2$ M.), with a ruined church and pleasure-grounds.

Next stations *Sulzdorf*, where the *Bühlerbach* is crossed, *Grossaltdorf*, *Eckartshausen*, and *Maulach*, with a chalybeate spring.

From Maulach an excursion may be made to ($2^1/_4$ M.) *Burgberg* (1755'), a gamekeeper's house (rfmts.) on a hill-top enclosed by an ancient earthen rampart; extensive view.

62 M. **Crailsheim** (*Lamm*; *Hôtel Faber*; *Deutscher Kaiser*), on

the *Jagst*, a town of 5000 inhab., with a handsome Rathhaus and an old château of the Hohenlohe family (now public offices). The Gothic *Church of St. John* (15th cent.) contains a winged altar with paintings by Wohlgemut, and a ciborium of 1498.

FROM CRAILSHEIM TO MERGENTHEIM, 36½ M. (railway in 1½-2 hrs.). Stations *Satteldorf*, *Wallhausen*, **Roth am See** (p. 130), *Blaufelden*, *Schrozberg* (p. 130). 23½ M. *Niederstetten*, an old town with walls and gates, the residence of Prince Hohenlohe-Jagstberg; 28 M. *Laudenbach*; 30 M. *Weikersheim* (*Hirsch, **Lamm**), on the Tauber, with the interesting château of Prince Hohenlohe-Langenburg. (Thence to *Creglingen* and *Rothenburg ob der Tauber*, see p. 130.) Then *Markelsheim* (a wine-growing place), *Igersheim*, and *Mergentheim* (p. 70).

FROM CRAILSHEIM TO NÖRDLINGEN, 40 M. (railway in 2-3 hrs.); TO ULM, 68 M. (by *Aalen* and *Heidenheim*, in 3½-6 hrs.). The line ascends the Jagstthal towards the S.; stations *Jagstheim*, *Stimpfach*, and *Jagstzell*, where the Jagst is crossed. Then (13 M.) **Ellwangen** (1410 ft.; *Adler*; *Post*), an old town (pop. 4700) with a castle on a hill, a small ecclesiastical principality down to 1803. The *Stiftskirche*, founded in 770, rebuilt in 1124, in the Romanesque style, with a crypt under the choir, is in admirable preservation. The interior was tastefully embellished with stucco-ornamentation in the 17th century. On the walls are two epitaphs in bronze by Peter Vischer of Nuremberg. On the *Schönenberg* (1710 ft.), to the N.E., is the handsome *Church of Loretto*, a resort of pilgrims. — Near Ellwangen (¾ M. to the S.W.) are the favourite mineral baths of *Schrezheim*. At (18½ M.) *Goldshöfe* the train reaches the Remsthal Railway (p. 28).

Beyond (67 M.) *Ellrichshausen*, with a ruined castle, the train crosses the Bavarian frontier. — 69½ M. *Schnelldorf*; 72½ M. *Zumhaus*; 76 M. *Dombühl* (Rail. Restaurant, with rooms), the junction for Dinkelsbühl and **Nördlingen** (p. 111). — 82½ M. *Büchelberg*; 85 M. **Leutershausen**. — 91½ M. Ansbach (p. 130), the junction of the Frankfort and Munich line (R. 25).

The line runs for a short distance through the *Rezat-Thal*, and then turns to the N.E. by stations *Sachsen* and *Wicklesgreuth* to (100½ M.) Heilsbronn (1345 ft.; *Post*), a small town, with remains of a famous *Cistercian Abbey*, partly in good preservation. The church, a Romanesque basilica with timber roof, begun in 1150, with a Gothic choir (1263-80 and later) and a Gothic aisle (1430-35, afterwards enlarged), and the refectory (now a Roman Catholic church), with fine vaulting and Gothic turrets, are still standing; but the cloisters and other parts of the monastery were destroyed in 1770.

The abbey-church was the burial-place of the **Franconian** line of the Hohenzollerns from 1297 to 1625 and contains the ashes of the first three Brandenburg Electors of that house, Frederick I., Frederick II., and Albert Achilles. Among the finest monuments are those of the Electress Anna of **Brandenburg** (d. 1512); of Margrave George Frederick of Ansbach (d. 1603), with eight statuettes of Counts of Zollern; and of the Margrave Joachim **Ernest** (d. 1625). Observe also three winged altar-pieces with carvings and paintings by Grünewald (altar of St. Ursula) and of Wohlgemut's school (about 1500), and a late-Gothic ciborium (1515). Both the church and its works of art have suffered from the restoration in 1856-60. The spring which gave the abbey its name rises within the church.

105½ M. *Raitersaich*; 109 M. *Rossstall*, with an old church; 114 M. *Stein*, with **Faber's** celebrated lead-pencil factory (shown by special permission only). The train then crosses the *Rednitz*, and reaches *Schweinau* and (120 M.) **Nuremberg** (p. 95).

7. From Stuttgart to Nördlingen and Nuremberg.

RAILWAY (Remsthal Line) to (71 M.) Nördlingen in 2³/₄-5 hrs. (fares 9 ℳ 40, 6 ℳ 30, 4 ℳ 10 pf.; express 10 ℳ 80, 7 ℳ 70 pf); thence to (62 M.) Nuremberg (Bavarian Railway) in 2¹/₄-4 hrs. (fares 8 ℳ, 5 ℳ 30, 3 ℳ 40 pf.; express 9 ℳ 20, 6 ℳ 50 pf.). Express from Stuttgart to Nuremberg viâ Nördlingen in 5¹/₂ hrs. (viâ Crailsheim in 4 hrs.; comp. R. 6).

The Remsthal Railway diverges to **the left** from the Stuttgart and Ulm line beyond (2¹/₂ M.) *Cannstatt* (p. 13), and winds up the hill which separates the valleys of the Neckar and the Rems. From the top a fine view of Stuttgart, **the Neckar-Thal**, and the Rothenberg **(p. 29)**. — 6 M. *Fellbach* (Traube). The **line now** descends to —

8 M. **Waiblingen** *(Post; Löwe)*, **a town of** great antiquity (4786 inhab.), whence the **imperial Salic** line and the succeeding House **of** Hohenstaufen derived **their name** of *Waiblinger*, corrupted by **the Italians into** Ghibellini, once so celebrated as the name **of a faction**. The late-Gothic *Äussere Kirche*, outside **the town**, erected **1459-88**, restored 1866, has a fine tow**er**. (To *Murrhardt*, see R. 6.)

The populous, fertile, and picturesque REMSTHAL, enclosed by the **Schurwald** on the right and the spurs **of the** *Welzheimer* Wald on the left, begins here. Beyond (11 M.) *Endersbach* is a handsome viaduct. **To the right, in a lateral** valley, are *Beutelsbach* (Löwe) and *Schnaith*, wine-growing places, **the former with a very** ancient abbey-church. **To the left** lies *Gross-Heppach* (Lamm). On the height to the left of **(14 M.)** *Grunbach* is **the village of** *Buoch*, affording **a fine view of the Swabian Alb (see p. 25)**; **to the right is the** *Schönbühl*, **with a** reformatory for boys. 17 M. *Winterbach*.

18¹/₂ M. **Schorndorf** *(Krone)*, an old town once fortified (4500 inhab.), has an interesting Gothic church, with very fine portal and choir of 1477. — Near (21 M.) *Urbach* the train crosses the Rems. 22¹/₂ M. *Plüderhausen* (Stern). Above (24¹/₂ M.) *Waldhausen*, to the N., **is the** *Elisabethenburg*, where Emp. Frederick Barbarossa is said to have been born (p. 42). The vine-culture **ceases**. — To the N.E. **of** (27 M.) Lorch *(*Harmonia; Sonne; Krone)* **rises the** Benedictine monastery of that name, founded by the Hohenstaufen in 1102, partly destroyed in the War of the Peasants, and recently restored. It **contains** several tombs and **monuments** of the Hohenstaufen, **but none of the more** distinguished **members of the** family. **In the centre of the nave is a late-Gothic cenotaph, erected** in 1475 **to Duke Frederick of Swabia (d. 1105), the** founder of the mon**astery. The unimportant mural paintings** are of the 15th century.

Lorch was the site of a Roman castrum, and there was, perhaps, **another on** the monastery-hill. Here begins the *Rhine Limes* (boundary) of **the Romans**, which took the Hohenstaufen as its objective point; while at *Pfahlbronn*, **3 M. to the N.**, is the end of the *Danube Limes*, stretching towards the E. (comp. p. 127). — From Lorch a road leads to the S. to (3 M.) *Wäschenbeuern* (Hirsch) **and** (1¹/₂ M.) *Hohenstaufen* (p. 42).

The *Wäscher Schlössle*, ³/₄ M. to the N.E. of Wäschenbeuern, was the seat of **Frederick of Büren** (11th cent.), progenitor of the Hohenstaufen.

We obtain a glimpse of the Hohenstaufen to the right as the train emerges from a short cutting just beyond Lorch, and afterwards a glimpse of the double-peaked *Rechberg* (p. 42). In the valley lies *Schierenhof*, a Roman castrum.

31½ M. **Gmünd**, or Schwäbisch-Gmünd (*Rad; Drei Mohren*), formerly a free city of the Empire (pop. 16,804), possesses three very old churches, many manufactories of jewellery, and a large industrial museum. The *Arlers* or *Parlers* were once celebrated architects here. The Gothic *Kreuzkirche* was erected by Heinrich Arler in 1351-77 (completed in 1410; towers 1492); the sculptures of the portal date from 1380, and the carved altar from the 15th century. The Romanesque *Church of St. John* contains an old picture in which the castle of Hohenstaufen is represented. Outside the town is the pilgrimage-church of *St. Salvator*, with two chapels hewn in the rock. The monastery of *Gottes-Zell* is now a prison.

Omnibus from Gmünd to *Süssen* (p. 31) twice daily in 3 hrs. (fare 1 ℳ 40 pf.). Ascent of the *Rechberg*, see p. 42.

38 M. *Unter-Böbingen*, with a Roman castrum; 40½ M. *Mögglingen*. From either of these stations an excursion may be made viâ *Heubach* to the (4½ M.) *Rosenstein* (2398 ft.), with some interesting ruins and a superb view of the Alb. — At (43½ M.) *Essingen* we cross the watershed (1719 ft.) between the Rems and Kocher, and descend into the *Kocher-Thal*.

47 M. **Aalen** (*Krone*), once a free imperial town (pop. 7150), was the birthplace of the poet *C. D. F. Schubart* (d. 1791) and contains a monument to him. The Cemetery Church is adjoined by a Roman camp.

FROM AALEN TO ULM, 45 M. (railway in 2 hrs.). 2½ M. *Unterkochen*; 5 M. *Oberkochen* (1½ M. above which is the picturesque source of the Kocher); 9 M. *Königsbronn*, with large iron-works, at the point where the Brenz takes its rise in the picturesque *Brenztopf* or *Königsbrunnen*. Then through the smiling *Brenzthal*. 12 M. *Schnaitheim*. — 14 M. **Heidenheim** (*Ochs*), a thriving industrial town with 8000 inhab., commanded by the picturesque half-ruined *Schloss Hellenstein* (view-tower). A road leads to the W. viâ *Steinheim* into the (6 M.) picturesque *Wendthal* (p. 32). — 15½ M. *Mergelstetten*; 17½ M. *Herbrechtingen* (road to *Hürben*, see below, 2½ M.); 21 M. *Giengen* (Post), once an imperial town, with mineral baths. — From (24 M.) *Hermaringen* a visit may be paid to the recently discovered *Charlotten-Höhle near *Hürben*, 3 M. to the W. The road leads viâ *Burgberg*, with the picturesquely situated château of Count Carl von Linden, and the ruin of *Kaltenburg*. The cave (715 yds. long) lies in the *Hürbethal*, a characteristic Jura valley, ½ M. to the S. of the village of Hürben. It consists of several chambers of different sizes and is specially interesting on account of the beautiful stalactites pendant from the roof (electric lights; admission-fees various). Near the mouth of the cave is a restaurant. — The train follows the Brenzthal to (28 M.) *Sontheim*, and then turns to the S.W. to *Nieder-Stotzingen*. Stations *Rammingen*; *Langenau*, a thriving little town with 3650 inhab.; *Unter-Elchingen*, the scene of the battle (14th Oct., 1805) from which Ney acquired his ducal title; and *Thalfingen*. The train then crosses the *Danube* to (45 M.) *Ulm* (p. 32).

At (48½ M.) *Wasseralfingen* (*Zum Schlegel*, opposite the foundry) are extensive iron-works, with an interesting little rack-and-pinion railway ascending to the shaft on the hillside. Above rises the *Braunenberg* (view). The train quits the Kocher-Thal and ascends rapidly to (51½ M.) **Goldshöfe** (junction for the Ellwangen and Crailsheim line, p. 26), **where it turns to the E.** On a hill to the right, between (54 M.) *Westhausen* and (57 M.) *Lauchheim*, is *Schloss Kapfenburg*. Beyond **Lauchheim** the line is carried through the watershed (1905 ft.) between the Rhine and the Danube by means **of deep** cuttings **and a** tunnel (710 yds.), and enters the narrow and **picturesque** *Eger-Thal*. About 4½ M. to the N. lies the château of *Hohen-Baldern* (2060 **ft.**), belonging to the Prince of Oettingen-Wallerstein, with a **new** and lofty tower. Above Bopfingen the *Flochberg*, with a ruined castle, is seen on the right; to the left is the bare cone of the *Ipf* (2237 ft.; view), on which prehistoric stone **implements** have been found.

64 M. **Bopfingen** (1535 ft.; *König von Württemberg*), once an imperial town. The Gothic *Church of St. Blasius* contains a winged altar-piece by F. Herlen (1477) and a ciborium by H. Böblinger (1510).

The line quits the E. part of the Alb district **and enters** the *Ries* (p. 112). 76 M. *Trochtelfingen;* 68 M. *Pflaumloch.*

71 M. **Nördlingen, p. 111.** Thence to *Nuremberg*, see R. 22.

8. From Stuttgart to Friedrichshafen.
Comp. Map, p. 42.

123 M. RAILWAY to Ulm **in** 2¼-3¾ **hrs.** (fares 7 ℳ 60, 5 ℳ, 3 ℳ 20 pf.; express 8 ℳ 20, 5 ℳ 80 **pf.**); to Friedrichshafen **in** 4¼-7 hrs (fares 15 ℳ 90, 10 ℳ 50, 6 ℳ 80 pf.; express 18 ℳ, 12 ℳ 60 pf.).

To (2½ M.) *Cannstatt*, **see p. 13.** Looking **back**, we obtain a fine view of the Royal **Villa, the** Rosenstein, and the **Wilhelma** with its gilded dome. The train ascends on the bank of the Neckar, traversing **one of the most beautiful and** fertile districts **in** Swabia.

5 M. **Unter**-*Türkheim* (Krone), a village with 3200 inhab., lies at the foot of the Rothenberg (1350 ft.; *Hôtel-Restaurant Lux*), where King William (d. 1864) erected a Greek chapel, on the **site of the old ancestral castle of the princes** of Wurtemberg, **as a** mausoleum for his consort Queen Catharine (d. 1819), a Russian princess, and himself. In the interior **the four Evangelists by Dannecker.** Service of the Greek church on Sundays.

Instead of the steep, stony, and shadeless ascent **from** Unter-Türkheim, we may choose the pleasanter but rather longer **route from** *Ober-Türkheim* **(see below),** either by *Uhlbach* or direct. A still more **extensive prospect is obtained from** the *Katharinen-Linde*, **to the S.E., ½ hr. higher.** Charming walk hence to (3 M.) *Esslingen* **(see below).**

Barely ½ M. to the S.W. **of** Unter-**Türkheim, and on the left** bank of the Neckar, lies Wangen *(Krone)*, **a favourite point for** excursions from Stuttgart. A path leads from Stuttgart **through the** woods and **over the hill direct to** Wangen in 1½ hr.; beautiful **views of the city in ascending,** and of the Neckar-Thal in descending.

6 M. *Ober-Türkheim* (*Ochse*), **another favourite resort.**

9 M. **Esslingen** (757 ft.; *Hôtel Pfähler zur Krone*, R. 1½-2, B. ¾, D. 2 ℳ; *Laich zur Post*, R. 1-1½, D. 1-1½ ℳ; *Kugel's Beer Saloon*), prettily **situated on the** Neckar, with 22,156 inhab., once a free imperial **city** and still partly surrounded by walls, which were built by Emperor Frederick II. in 1216. Sparkling Neckar-wine is

largely manufactured here. The engineering works founded here by Kessler are the largest in Wurtemberg. Other branches of industry also flourish.

In the market-place is the church of *St. Dionysius*, a basilica in the transition style, founded in the 11th cent., and partly altered in the 14th and 15th, which possesses a fine screen and ciborium of 1486. *St. Paul's Church*, also in the market, in the early-Gothic style, completed in 1268, is now used by the Roman Catholics. Opposite the present Rathhaus, which was once the palace of Count Alexander of Wurtemberg, the poet, is the *Old Rathhaus*, erected in 1430, and formerly known as the 'Steinerne Haus'. It is surmounted by the imperial eagle under a gilded canopy, and another eagle forms the vane on the turret. — Farther on in the same direction is the *Wolfsthor*, on which are still seen the lions of the Hohenstaufen, hewn in stone.

The conspicuous late-Gothic **Liebfrauenkirche*, erected in 1406-1522, was restored in 1862 and again quite recently. Admirable reliefs on the three portals, especially that of the Last Judgment on the S. Portal. The interior, with its slender pillars, contains fine stained-glass windows. Adjoining the organ-loft are the tombstones of Hans and Matthæus Böblinger, two of the architects of the church. Fine perforated tower, 247 ft. in height, completed in 1526; beautiful view from the top. — The once imperial castle of *Perfried*, above the town, commands another superb view (Restaurant). — The *Maille*, an island in the Neckar laid out as a promenade, is embellished with bronze busts of *Karl Pfaff*, the historian, and *Theodore Georgii*, the gymnastic teacher.

Quitting Esslingen, the train recrosses the Neckar. 12½ M. *Altbach*. — 14 M. *Plochingen* (*Waldhorn*) lies near the confluence of the *Fils* and Neckar. Upper Neckar Railway to *Tübingen*, see R. 9. On the hill (½ hr.) is a tower, affording an extensive panorama of the Alb.

The line now follows the Fils (comp. Map, p. 42). 17 M. *Reichenbach*; 20 M. *Ebersbach*. On a wooded height to the right, near (23 M.) *Uhingen*, rises the château of *Filseck*; on the river lies *Faurndau*, formerly a Benedictine monastery, with an old Romanesque church.

26 M. **Göppingen** (1082 ft.; **Apostel*; **Sand*), a flourishing town with 14,350 inhab., re-erected after a fire in 1782, contains several weaving mills, factories of metal-wares, machine-shops, and tanneries. Large lunatic asylum of Dr. Landerer. The government-buildings were formerly a ducal castle, erected by Duke Christopher in 1562 with the stones of the castle of Hohenstaufen. At the S.W. corner of the court an artistically-hewn spiral stone staircase ('Traubenstieg', vine-stair) ascends to the tower.

Göppingen is a favourite centre for excursions in the E. ALB. To the N. lies *Adelsberg*, a former convent, with a fine view. The conical *Hohenstaufen* (p. 42), the loftiest and most conspicuous spur of the Alb, is ascended in 20 min. from *Staufen*, which is reached from Göppingen (5 M.) by carr. and pair in 1 hr. (7 ℳ.). — To the S. we may proceed viâ (7 M.) the sulphur-baths of *Boll* to the (1½ hr.) *Bosler* or (1½ hr.) *Bertaburg-Kornberg* (2555 ft.); viâ (1½ hr.) *Eschenbach* to the (1 hr.) *Fuchseck* (1920 ft.); or viâ (1½ hr.) *Schlath* to the top of the (1 hr.) *Wasserberg* (2428 ft.).

28½ M. **Eislingen**. — 31 M. *Süssen* (pp. 28, 42), opposite which (to the N.) rises the round tower of the ruined *Staufeneck*. In the old cemetery of Gross-Süssen is a curious Mont de Calvaire by Meister Christof of Urach (ca. 1520?).

A pleasant excursion may be made to the E., viâ (1 hr.) *Donzdorf*, to the top of the *Messelstein* (2455 ft.; extensive view). — Proceeding to the S. from the rail. stat. of Süssen through the village to (1 hr.) the farm of *Grünenburg*, we may thence ascend the (1 hr.) *Burren* ('Glufenkissen'; 2273 ft.), walk along the slope (sign-posts) to the (½ hr.) *Spitzenberg*, ascend to the interesting plateau of the *Michelsberg* (2463 ft.), and traverse the (¾ hr.) village of *Ober-Böhringen*, founded in 1793, to the (20 min.) *Hausener Felsen*, which **affords a** fine view of the 'Geissen-Thal'. The return may be made viâ the reservoir (distant view of the Alps) to (1 hr.) *Ueberkingen* and (1¼ hr.) *Geislingen* (see below).

33½ M. *Gingen*. To the right appear **the long ranges of the** Alb; **to** the left, on an eminence, are the rugged **ruins of** *Scharfenberg*. Farther to the S.E. is the *Kuchalb* (see below).

From Gingen two routes lead to the (1 hr.) *Kuchalb*, a hamlet with an inn. Thence we may ascend to the (10 min.) *Mairhalde* (view) and to the (¼ hr.) °*Hohenstein* (2303 ft.), which commands a splendid view to the W. and of the **valley**. We descend either by a new path to (½ hr.) *Kuchen* (hence **to Geislingen** 1 hr.) **or** to (½ hr.) Gingen, or viâ the Kuchalb to (1½ hr.) Geislingen. **The** Kuchalb may also be reached from Gingen in 1½ hr. past *Scharfenberg* (**see** above) by a good path leading partly through wood.

Near Geislingen, **to the left, opens the** *Eybach-Thal* **with the** village **of** *Eybach* **and a château of Count Degenfeld; to** the right is the *Upper Filsthal*.

38 M. **Geislingen** (1522 ft.; **Sonne; Post*, nearest the rail. station, with a good restaurant), **a busy town (5722 inhab.) in a narrow ravine at the base of the Alb, where bone and ivory are carved and turned.** There are also **factories of metal goods and machines. The** late-Gothic *Marienkirche*, **founded in 1424,** contains choir-stalls carved by Jörg Syrlin **the** Younger (1512). On a rock above the town rises the *Oede Thurm*. Opposite, beyond the *Pavilion*, are the remains of the **château** of *Helfenstein*, destroyed in 1552.

Geislingen is a good starting-point **for the central** part of the **SWABIAN ALB** (p. 42). We ascend the *Filsthal* on **foot or by** diligence (thrice daily, in 2¾ hrs.) to (3½ M.) *Bad Ueberkingen*, (3½ M.) **Deggingen**, and (5 M.) *Wiesensteig* (Post). About ¾ M. beyond **Deggingen** we pass on the left the chalybeate baths of *Ditzenbach*. From **Wiesensteig** we ascend on foot to the (1¼ hr.) °*Reussenstein* (2500 ft.), a picturesque ruined castle **on a precipitous** rock, commanding the charming Neidlinger-Thal. We then **follow** the top of the hill to the (½ hr.) *Heimenstein*, **a** dark, rocky cavity, **a few** paces below which **we obtain a** fine view of the Reussenstein and **the** valley. Then by *Randeck* (¾ M. to the S.W. the *Randecker Maar*, with peat-diggings) **and** *Ochsenwang* (Inn, rustic) **to the** (1 hr.) °*Breitenstein* (2660 ft.), a lofty spur of the **Alb** Mts.. descending precipitously to the plain. Next by **the** *Rauberhof* **and the** ruins of the *Rauberburg* (*Diepoldsburg*) **to** the top of the (1 hr.) *Teck*, whence we descend to *Owen* (p. 43). If we omit the Breitenstein, we may proceed from the Reussenstein by *Schopfloch* to (2½ hrs.) *Gutenberg* (p. 43), and thence in 2 hrs. more to *Owen*.

Other excursions may be made from Geislingen to the N. viâ *Eybach* (p. 31) and through the romantic *Roggen-Thal* to (3 hrs.) *Weissenstein*; to the (2½ hrs.) *Messelstein* (p. 31); to the E. viâ *Söhnstetten* to the *Wendthal* (to *Bibersohl*, 3½ hrs.).

The line quits the Filsthal and ascends the *Geislinger Steige*, a wooded limestone hill, rich in fossils, to the table-land of the *Swabian Alb* (R. 11), the watershed between the Neckar and the Danube. The ascent is very considerable (350 ft. in 3 M.; 1:44); and a second engine is added to the train at Geislingen. The train crosses the *Rauhe Alb*, as this lofty plain is called (stations *Amstetten, Lonsee, Westerstetten, Beimerstetten*), and then descends to the valley of the Danube. The fortifications of Ulm soon become visible. The train passes close to the (r.) *Wilhelmsburg*, the lofty citadel of Ulm, where 30,000 Austrians under General Mack surrendered to the French after the battle of Elchingen (p. 28).

58½ M. **Ulm**. — Hotels: RUSSISCHER HOF (Pl. a; A, 2), at the station, R. & A. 2½-3, B. 1, D. 2½ *M*; HÔTEL DE L'EUROPE (Pl. b; A, 2), to the left of the station, R. 1½ *M*; BAHNHOF-HÔTEL, R. 1½ *M*. In the town: *KRONPRINZ (Pl. c; D, 3), R. from 1½, D. 2¼ *M*; *BAUMSTARK (Pl. d; B, 3), R., L., & A. 1½-2½, B. ¾, D. 2¼ *M*; *GOLDENER LÖWE (Pl. e; B, 2), moderate; OBERPOLLINGER, Hirsch-Str.; *GOLDENER HIRSCH. — Beer at the *Württemberger Hof*, Platzgasse; at the *Kronprinz, Goldner Hirsch*, and *Bahnhof-Hotel* (see above); *Rother Ochse* (with rooms); *Strauss, Oberpollinger*, Hirsch-Str.; *Beer Saloon* near the guard-house. — *Wilhelmshöhe Restaurant*, a fine point of view.

Military Bands play almost every day in summer on the **Wilhelmshöhe** and other public gardens. *Organ Concert* daily in summer, 11-12 (see below).

Ulm (1568 ft.), with 36,200 inhab., formerly an important free imperial city, as its appearance still indicates, and from 1842 to 1866 a fortress of the Germanic Confederation, has belonged to Wurtemberg since 1810. It lies on the left bank of the *Danube*, which is here joined by the *Blau*, is augmented by the *Iller* above the town, and from this point downwards is navigable. The Danube is the boundary between Wurtemberg and Bavaria, to which *Neu-Ulm* on the opposite bank belongs (7800 inhab.; garrison 5000).

The *MÜNSTER (Prot.; Pl. 4), founded in 1377, built at intervals down to the beginning of the 16th cent., and restored and completed in 1843-90, is the largest Gothic church in Germany next to the cathedral of Cologne. The massive and beautifully decorated *Tower* in the centre of the W. façade, with the magnificent triple vestibule, was designed and begun by *Ulrich Ensinger* (1392-95), the third of the cathedral architects, erected by his successors as far as the top of the square portion by the end of the 15th cent., and completed in 1877-90 by *Prof. Aug. Beyer* by the addition of the octagon and pyramid from a sketch left by *Matthäus Böblinger*, the last of the original architects. Being 528 ft. in height, it is one of the loftiest stone towers in the world (Cologne 512 ft., Strassburg 466 ft.; Washington Monument 555 ft.; Eiffel Tower, in iron, 985 ft.).

The church is open free, daily 11-12, on Sun. and holidays after divine service, incl. *Performance on the organ in summer (entrance by the 'Brautthür', on the S. side, near the choir). At other times visitors require tickets and enter through the dwelling of the sacristan, adjoining the large W. entrance: for the nave and aisles 20 pf.; choir, chapels, and sacristy, with guide, 1-4 pers. 1 ℳ; extra organ-performance 10 ℳ. The main tower may be ascended from 7 to 6 in summer, 9-3 in winter, and 8-5 in spring and autumn (to the top of the square portion 50 pf., to the octagon 1 ℳ, children half-price).

The INTERIOR originally consisted of a nave with two aisles, all of equal breadth, but in 1507 the latter were divided by slender round pillars and covered with star-vaulting, so as to form four aisles. Length 139 yds., width 55 yds.; nave 141 ft., aisles 72 ft. in height. The sculpturing on the portals is worthy of inspection. On the principal W. portal are the Creation, the Fall, Apostles, etc.; on the S.E. side-portal the Last Judgment; on the S.W. side-portal the history of Mary. The magnificent *Organ*, the largest in Germany, built in 1856 (100 stops), has lately been restored. By the second pillar of the nave is the *Pulpit*, executed by Burkhard Engelberger about 1500, the *Cover beautifully carved in wood by J. Syrlin in 1510. Farther on, to the left of the entrance to the choir, is the *Ciborium*, 93 ft. in height, beautifully sculptured in stone by the 'Master of Weingarten' (1469). Above the choir-arch is a large fresco of the Last Judgment, attributed to Herlin (1470), and till lately concealed by whitewash. The *Choir Stalls*, by Jörg Syrlin the Elder, 1469-1474, whose bust adjoins the shrine of the saint, are boldly carved in oak. The busts on the N. side below embody paganism, the relief-busts Judaism, above which is Christianity in the pointed arches. On the S. side are Sibyls below, women of the Old Testament in the middle, and women of the New Testament above. High-altar by M. Schaffner (1521). Fine old stained glass of 1480 in the choir. The S. aisle contains the octagonal *Font*, with busts of prophets, mottoes, and armorial bearings, by Syrlin the Elder (1470). On the walls and pillars are numerous escutcheons of Swabian families. The octagonal *Holy Water Basin* round the E. pillar is in the late-Gothic style, by Burkhard Engelberger (1507). The *S. (Besserer's) Chapel* contains a beautiful portrait of Eitel Besserer by Martin Schaffner (1516). The *Sacristy* contains an elegant little *Altar of 1484, attributed to M. Schön. In a side-chapel is preserved an old design for the tower on parchment (1377).

In the market rises the handsome *Rathhaus* (Pl. 11), erected at the beginning of the 16th cent. in the transition style from late-Gothic to Renaissance, with remains of old frescoes. The *Fischkasten*, a fine fountain at the S.E. corner, is by Syrlin the Elder (1482).

A little to the W. is the *Neue Bau* (Pl. 8), erected in 1591 on the site of an ancient imperial palace, now containing government-offices. The quadrangle contains a fountain with a figure of St. Elizabeth. — An old patrician dwelling in the Taubengasse contains an *Industrial Museum*, with fine wood panelling, ancient sculptures in stone and wood, works in iron, Renaissance furniture, early German and other paintings, etc. — The *Stone Bridge* at the beginning of the Hirsch-Strasse affords a picturesque survey of the *Blau*, enclosed by mediæval timber-built houses. Charming walk on the Danube from the Wilhelmshöhe (p. 32) onwards. The *Friedrichsau*, or public park, also repays a visit.

FROM ULM TO KEMPTEN, 54½ M. (railway in 3 hrs.). Stations *Neu-Ulm*, *Senden* (junction for *Weissenhorn*). To the right, on the opposite bank of the Iller, lies *Ober-Kirchberg*, with a château of Prince Fugger. The line now follows the Iller. Stat. *Voehringen*; *Bellenberg*. At (15 M.) *Illertissen* (Hirsch) is a well-preserved castle, said to be of Roman origin. Near stat. *Altenstadt* the extensive château of *Illereichen*. Stations *Kellmünz*, *Fellheim*, *Heimertingen*. Then (33 M) Memmingen (*Bairischer Hof*; *Falke*; *Adler* and *Kreuz*, plain), junction of the line to Herbertingen (p. 54), an old town with 9000 inhab., a free city of the Empire down to 1802, and still partly surrounded by walls. Hops are largely cultivated here. The principal church contains 67 *Choir-stalls, carved in the richest late-Gothic style (end of 15th cent.), probably by Jörg Syrlin the Elder. Among the mediæval houses is the *Fuggerhaus*, in which Wallenstein received the news of his dismissal in 1629. Amidst beautiful woods, 2 M. from Memmingen, lies *Dikenreis*. (Branch-line to *Buchloe*, p. 198.) — To the S.E. is the pilgrimage-shrine of Ottobeuren (diligence twice daily in 1½ hr.), once a Benedictine **Abbey** ranking as a principality, founded in 764. The church, restored in the 18th cent., contains **fine** choir-stalls, a large organ, and a rich treasury. — Next stations *Grönenbach*, *Dietmannsried*, *Heising*, *Kempten* (p. 199).

From Ulm to *Aalen*, see p. 28; to *Sigmaringen* and *Radolfzell*, see R. 13.

Our line at first ascends the left bank of the Danube, and passes the influx of the *Iller*. 63 M. *Einsingen*; 65 M. *Erbach*, with a château of Baron Ulm. The as yet insignificant Danube is now crossed, and a flat district traversed. Stations *Risstissen* (with château and park of Baron Staufenberg), *Laupheim*, *Schemmerberg*, *Langenschemmern*, *Warthausen* (with château of Herr von König).

81½ M. Biberach (*Württemberg*. *Hof*, at the station; *Post; Rad*), with 8264 inhab., once a free town of the Empire, is still partly surrounded by walls and towers. Wieland, who was born in 1733 in the neighbouring village of *Ober-Holzheim*, held a civil appointment here in 1760-69, and is said to have collected materials for his 'Abderiten' from among the townspeople. A marble bust was erected to him in 1881.

About 2 M. to the S.E. of Biberach station (diligence and omnibus several times daily) is the frequented hydropathic of **Jordanbad** (pens. 4½-6 *M*), pleasantly situated in the *Rissthal*, on the margin of the wood, with a chalybeate spring ('Kneipp Cure').

The country becomes more attractive, and woods begin to appear on both sides. 84½ M. *Ummendorf;* 86 M. *Schweinhausen;* 89 M. *Essendorf;* 93½ M. *Schussenried*, with the district lunatic asylum. At (97 M.) *Aulendorf* (*Löwe), junction of the Herbertingen and Memmingen line (p. 54), is the château of Count Königsegg, with a garden commanding a fine view of the distant Alps.

The line now follows the small river *Schussen* to Friedrichshafen. The churches in Upper Swabia are frequently roofed with zinc. The population is Roman Catholic. 101 M. *Durlesbach;* 104 M. *Mochenwangen*. To the left beyond (107 M.) *Niederbiegen* rises the old Benedictine abbey of *Weingarten*, with its three towers, founded in 1053 by the Guelphs, now used as barracks. Pilgrimages are still made to the church. Towards the S. the mountains of Appenzell come in view.

110½ M. **Ravensburg** (1456 ft.; *Post; Kronprinz*), an ancient town with 12,265 inhab., surrounded by vine-clad heights, once subject to the Guelphs, then to the Hohenstaufen, and lastly a free town of the empire, still preserves its mediæval exterior, and is surrounded by pinnacled walls and towers of every variety. The slenderest of the latter is called the *Mehlsack* ('sack of flour'). The *Protestant Church*, restored in 1862, is a good Gothic structure, with fine modern stained-glass windows. — Steam Tramway to *Weingarten* (p. 34).

The **Veitsburg** (1719 ft.; Restaurant), ¼ hr. from the town, commands an extensive view of the Lake of Constance, the Alps of Appenzell. and the Vorarlberg. A still finer point is the *Waldburg (2520 ft.), 2 hrs. to the E., the well-preserved ancestral castle of the family of that name ('Truchsess von Waldburg').

Beyond Ravensburg another glimpse of the Alps is obtained. The line traverses parts of the *Seewald*. 113½ M. *Oberzell*; 116 M. *Meckenbeuern*. *Tettnang*, with the large château of the extinct Counts of Montfort, lies to the left. The Lake of Constance at length becomes visible.

123 M. Friedrichshafen. — Hotels. *DEUTSCHES HAUS, on the lake, by the station, with garden, R. 2-3, B. ¾-1, D. 2½ ℳ; *KÖNIG VON WÜRTTEMBERG, ¼ M. from the station, recommended for a prolonged stay; *KRONE, with garden, on the lake, R. 2-2½, B. ¾-1, D. 2½ ℳ; SONNE; *DREI KÖNIGE, R. 1¼-2, D. 2 ℳ, B. 80 pf.; SEEHOF, with garden. HÔTEL & RESTAURANT MÜLLER, on the harbour, with a large terrace.

Friedrichshafen (1320 ft.) lies **on the** Bodensee or Lake of Constance. **The train goes** on from the station to the quay, whence **steamers ply** 4-5 times daily to **the chief places on the lake. The** busy little town, with 3000 inhab., and a harbour, as **its name indicates,** was founded by King Frederick **of Wurtemberg,** who connected *Buchhorn*, the smallest of 'imperial cities', **with the monastery of *Hofen*,** now the palace, and gave the place its modern name. The *Schloss* **contains a few** pictures by modern Wurtemberg masters (Gegenbaur, Pflug, etc.). A pavilion in the *Riedle Park* commands a charming prospect of the lake and the Alps. The historical, prehistorical, and natural **history collections** of the *Bodensee Verein*, **in the old Hôtel** Bellevue, deserve a visit. The lake-baths attract many **visitors in summer.** *Curhaus*, with terrace on the lake.

Lake of Constance and steamboats upon it, see pp 57, 201. — At *Langenargen*, 6 M. to the S.E. (steamer in 35 min.), is the handsome château of Montfort, belonging to Princess Louisa of Prussia (charming view).

9. From Stuttgart to Tübingen and Horb.

Comp. Map, p. 42.

64 M. RAILWAY in 3¼-4¼ hrs. (fares 8 ℳ 40, 5 ℳ 60, 3 ℳ 60 pf.). Best views to the left.

To (14 M.) *Plochingen*, see R. 8. 18½ M. *Unter-Boihingen*. To the right in the valley, near *Köngen*, the Neckar is crossed by an ancient **stone bridge, from which** Duke Ulrich is said to have leaped in 1519 in **order to** escape capture by the troops of the Swabian League. Branch-line to *Kirchheim unter Teck* (p. 43). To the left rise the Teck, Hohenneuffen, and other Alb Mts. — 22½ M. *Nürtingen* (Krone), a manufacturing town (pop. 5400) on the right bank **of the Neckar (ascent of the** *Hohenneuffen*, 2 hrs., see p. 44). 25 M. *Neckarthailfingen*. The line now quits **the** Neckar for a time. Near (28 M.) *Bempflingen*, fine views of the Alb, in which the Teck

3*

and Hohenneuffen (**pp. 43, 44**) are conspicuous, are **obtained to the left**.

From (30½ M.) *Metzingen* (1108'; *Sprandel, at the **station**; Linde) a branch-line diverges to *Dettingen* and *Urach* (½ hr.; p. 44). The *Erms* is crossed here.

Fine view from the *Floriansberg* (1598 ft.), ¾ hr. to the N.E., embracing the whole **of the Alb** Mts.; above it rises the *Jusiberg* (2175 ft.). From this point a pleasant walk may be taken along the ridge viâ the *Hörnle* (2320 ft.) **and** the *Karlslinde* to the plateau **of** *Hülben* and *Hohenneuffen* (p. 44).

33½ M. *Sondelfingen*. The line skirts the *Achalm* (p. 46).

36 M. **Reutlingen (1246 ft.;** *Ochs*, in the market-place, R. 1¼, D. 2 ₰; *Kronprinz*, at the station; *Lamm*, in the Karlsplatz, **near** the station; *Falke*, near the Marktplatz), once a free city of **the** empire, **is now an industrial town** with 18,500 inhab., **on the** *Echaz*, the water of which is conducted through the **streets**. Some of the old houses are picturesque. The ancient **ramparts and fosses** have been converted into well-built streets. **In front of the station is a** monument to *Frederick List* (d. 1846), **the political economist, who was** born in a house in the Wilhelms-Strasse (indicated by **a tablet).** In the market-place, in front of the *Spitalkirche*, rises an old Gothic fountain (1570). The Gothic (Prot.) *Church of St. Mary* was erected 1247-1343 and restored in 1844, when some very early frescoes **were** discovered **in the sacristy**. The **beautiful tower** is 240 ft. high. A thorough restoration is now in progress. The octagonal stone *Font of 1499 is admirably and richly sculptured; the **reliefs** in the niches **represent the Baptism** of Christ and the Seven Sacraments. The *Holy Sepulchre in the nave (about 1480) is also very interesting. The handsome modern **altar** was designed by Beisbarth and executed by Lauer (1878). The sacristan's house is opposite the S. side of the church. — *Lucas's Pomological Institution*, the *Weaving School*, the *School of Women's Work*, and the *Refuge of Pastor Werner* ('Bruderhaus') merit a visit. The *Cemetery* contains a tasteful modern chapel in the Gothic style. **The little** sulphurbath of *Heilbrunnen* is ¾ M. from the station.

From Reutlingen to Münsingen, 21 M., railway in 1¾ hr., viâ *Honau* and *Lichtenstein*, see p. 46.

38 M. *Betzingen* is noted for its picturesque costumes, which attract many artists in summer. At (40½ M.) *Kirchentellinsfurt* the line re-enters the Neckar-Thal. To the right *Lustnau*, with a fine church.

45 M. Tübingen. — **Hotels.** °Traube, R. 1-1½ ₰, D. 1 ₰ 20, B. 75 pf.; Lamm, in the market-place, R. 1¼-1½, B. ¾ ₰; Prinz Carl, R. 1¼-2, B. ¾, D. 2 ₰; Goldner Ochse, near the railway-station, R. 1½ ₰. — Beer at °*Kommerell's*, near the Stiftskirche; *Müller's*, by the Neckar bridge; *Museum*, Wilhelms-Str.; *Schlossbrauerei*, Markt, etc. — Wine at *Seeger's*, Herrenberger-Str.; *Riess's*, Neckar-Str.; *Trautwein's*, Kronengasse.

Tübingen (1036 ft.), a town with 13,275 inhab., finely situated **on a ridge** on the Neckar, possesses a university, founded by Count Eberhard in 1477, of which the theological and medical faculties especially enjoy a high reputation (over 1400 students). Melanchthon was a lecturer here before he was summoned to Wittenberg. Near the station, in the beautiful shady promenades of the 'Wöhrd', is a bronze *Statue of Uhland, by Kietz, erected in 1873. In the plantation at the end of the avenue of planes is a monument to the authoress *Ottilie Wildermuth* (d. 1877). The house looking down on the Neckar bridge (in the Garten-Strasse) was the residence of the poet *Uhland*, who died here in 1862. His grave in the cemetery is marked by a monument of granite.

The streets of the old town are narrow and its houses insignificant. The late-Gothic *Stiftskirche of St. George* (1470-1529) contains fine old stained glass in the *Choir; twelve monuments with recumbent stone figures, chiefly of Wurtemberg princes, including Duke Eberhard im Bart (d. 1496), founder of the university, and Duke Ulrich (d. 1550); and an old German winged picture by a master of Ulm (1520). The organ-loft is adorned with a bust of Luther by Donndorf. — Adjoining the Stiftskirche is the old *Aula*, containing the *Natural History Collections* of the University, including a fossil ichthyosaurus 24$^1/_2$ ft. long. — The *Town Hall*, a richly coloured timber-built edifice, erected in 1435, was restored in 1877. The *Stift*, a Protestant seminary with 180 pupils, founded in 1536 by Duke Ulrich, is established in an old Augustinian monastery. The Roman Catholic *Wilhelmsstift*, with about 150 students, occupies the old *Collegium Illustre*, founded in 1588 for sons of the nobility. Beyond the Wilhelmsstift is the handsome new *Roman Catholic Church*, in the early-Gothic style.

In the new E. quarter of the town, in the handsome Wilhelm-Strasse and to the W. of it, are a number of imposing buildings, such as the *University*, the *Women's* and the *Surgical Clinical Hospitals*, the *Museum*, and the *Insane Hospital*. The university possesses a picture-gallery (a *Correggio*, a *Murillo*, etc., and 125 portraits of professors) and other collections, chief among which is that of *Fossils*, in the old building next to the Stiftskirche (a fine ichthyosaurus, 24 ft. in length, etc.). At the back of the university rises an obelisk in memory of *Silcher*, the composer (d. 1860). — The *Botanical Garden* of the university contains a monument to the poet *Hölderlin* (d. 1843), presented by the sculptor Andresen in 1881.

By the Town Hall (see above) a path ascends to the left to the spacious *Schloss Hohen-Tübingen*, situated on a hill commanding the town, erected by Duke Ulrich in the Renaissance style in 1535, with a richly decorated outer portal of 1606 and an inner portal of 1538 (lately restored). It contains the admirably arranged *University Library* and the *Observatory*. The cellars, which contain an immense cask (18,700 gallons), a deep well formerly descending to the level of the Neckar, and torture-chambers, are shown to visitors. Fine *View from the *Schänzle*, at the back of the Schloss (reached from the court of the Schloss through the low passage beyond the well; then to the left), and from the *Lichtenberger Höhe*. Another good point of view is the *Oesterberg* (1436 ft.), opposite the Schloss (Café Sennhütte; Wielandhöhe). On the top of this hill, 20 min. from the town, is the *Kaiser-Wilhelms-Thurm*, erected in 1893, with portraits of Emp. William I., Emp. Frederick III., and King Charles of Wurtemberg, and a memorial stone to Prince Bismarck. The view extends from the Hohenstaufen to the Plettenberg and the Hornisgrinde. — More distant points of view are the *Waldhäuser Höhe*, *Eberhards-Höhe*, *Steinenberg* (these to the N.), *Spitzberg* or *Oedenburg*, and *Buss-Thurm* (these two to the W., beyond the Schloss).

To the N. of Tübingen, 3 M. on the old Stuttgart road, lies the well-preserved old Cistercian monastery of *Bebenhausen, founded in 1185, one of the finest Gothic structures in Swabia. The building was restored in 1873-75, and is now a royal hunting-residence. The summer-refectory with a collection of ancient arms and armour, the winter-refectory with its Gobelins, and the present dining-hall with its collection of majolica (over 300 pieces) are worthy of inspection. The fine cloisters date from 1471-1496. Adjacent are the *Hirsch* and *Waldhorn Inns*.

On a height (1558 ft.), 1¼ hr. to the N.W., rises the Wurmlinger Kapelle, commanding an extensive view. Its praises have been sung by Uhland and other poets. (The chapel may be reached by a pleasant path through the wood from the Schloss at Tübingen, following the top of the hill, viâ the Schänzle, Lichtenberg, and Buss; see above.)

From Tübingen to *Hohenzollern* and *Sigmaringen*, see R. 12.

48 M. *Kilchberg*. — 51½ M. **Rottenburg** (1115 ft.; *Bär*; *Kaiser*), an old town (7027 inhab.) picturesquely situated on the Neckar, connected by two bridges with the suburb of *Ehingen*, is an episcopal see. The late-Gothic *Church of St. Martin*, with its perforated spire, is interesting. The *Bischofshof*, formerly a Jesuit convent, contains a collection of Roman antiquities found here in the old Roman station of *Sumelocenna*. The inmates of the new *Prison* are employed in agriculture. Hops abound.

At the *Altstadt* (1394 ft.), ¼ hr. to the S.E., is a Roman camp; ½ hr. farther on, beyond the village of *Weiler*, is the *Weilerburg* (1820 ft.; belvedere). — The *Sülchenkirche*, 20 min. to the N.E. of Rottenburg, once the centre of the Sülich-Gau, is the burial-church of the Roman Catholic bishops of Wurtemberg.

The train crosses the Neckar and follows the left bank. Vineyards gradually give way to pine-forest. 53½ M. *Niedernau*. The chalybeate and sulphur baths of that name lie in a valley on the opposite bank. The line crosses the Neckar, and near (55 M.) *Bieringen* the *Starzel*. To the right, beyond a long tunnel, rises *Schloss Weitenburg*, with its fine pinnacled tower, commanding a fine view. On a pine-clad hill to the left of (59½ M.) *Eyach* is the ruin of *Frondeck*.

Prettily situated in the Eyach-Thal, 2½ M. to the S. (omnibus from the station in 20 min.) are the chalybeate baths of Imnau (*Badhaus, R. 1-2 *M*, board 2 *M* 10 pf. to 2 *M* 80 pf.), chiefly visited by ladies. Good baths (mineral, pine-cone, saline, Turkish, and vapour). Pretty walks and excursions. — In the Eyach-Thal, 4 M. to the S., lies the little Prussian town of Haigerloch, picturesquely situated in a deep valley, and commanded by an old Schloss.

62 M. *Mühlen*; **64 M. Horb.** From **Horb** to *Stuttgart* viâ *Böblingen*, and to *Schaffhausen* viâ *Immendingen*, see R. 10; to *Calw* and *Pforzheim*, see p. 16; to *Hausach*, see p. 39.

10. From Stuttgart to Böblingen and Schaffhausen.

123 M. Railway in 5-8 hrs. (fares 15 ℳ 90, 10 ℳ 60, 6 ℳ 80 pf.; express 17 ℳ 95, 12 ℳ 65 pf.). This is the direct route from Stuttgart to Central Switzerland (express from Stuttgart to Zürich in $6^3/_4$ hrs.; through-carriages) and to the Baden Oberland (see below).

From Stuttgart (Central Station) to the (5 M.) *West Station*, see p. 11. Just beyond the station the train penetrates a spur of the *Hasenberg*, and then ascends (1:100), high above the suburb of *Heslach* and the gradually contracting **valley**. Pretty views to the left. The line runs through wood on the Heslacher Wand, and is carried across three deep gorges by lofty embankments. At (9 M.) *Vaihingen* the train reaches the *Filder*, the fertile upland plain to the S. of Stuttgart. The *Schönbuchwald* is now traversed to ($15^1/_2$ M.) Böblingen (1415 ft., *Waldhorn; Bär*), an old town (4300 inhab.), with a castle, prettily situated on two large ponds. The *Waldburg*, 10 min. to the N.E. of the town, with a wooded park and extensive **view**, is a favourite resort.

19 M. *Ehningen*, where the Würm is crossed; 21 M. *Gärtringen*; 23 M. *Nufringen*. — $25^1/_2$ M. Herrenberg *(Post)*, an old town in the fertile *Gäu*; to the left the hills of the Schönbuch and the Rauhe Alb. — 28 M. *Nebringen*; 31 M. *Bondorf*; $33^1/_2$ M. *Ergenzingen*. — 35 M. *Eutingen* (1550 ft.), junction for Pforzheim (p. 17).

From Eutingen to Hausach, $42^1/_2$ M., railway in $1^3/_4$-$4^1/_4$ hrs. (from Stuttgart in $3^1/_4$-6 hrs.). The line turns to the right, and as far as ($2^1/_2$ M.) *Hochdorf* (1653 ft.) coincides with the Nagold railway (p. 17). It then ascends and enters the Black Forest. Stations: *Altheim, Bittelbronn, Schopfloch, Dornstetten*. Three lofty viaducts.

$18^1/_2$ M. Freudenstadt (2362 ft.; °*Schwarzwald-Hôtel*, at the station, with fine view; °*Waldeck*, near the wood, in the Strassburger-Str.; *Post; Linde*), a loftily-situated Wurtemberg town (6270 inhab.), was founded in 1599 by Protestant refugees from Styria, Carinthia, and Moravia, and is now a summer-resort. At the N.E. corner of the extensive Platz, with its arcaded houses, rises the *Rathhaus*, and at the S.W. corner is the curious *Protestant Church*, built in 1601-8. It consists of two naves forming an angle, one set apart for male, the other for female worshippers, while pulpit and altar are placed at the apex of the angle. Observe the carved choir-stalls and the Romanesque font brought from the monastery of Alpirsbach. Near the Roman Catholic church, $1/_2$ M. from the town, we obtain a °View of the Swabian Alb, Hohenzollern, etc. — Good roads lead from Freudenstadt to the W. over the *Kniebis* to *Oppenau*, and to the N. through the *Murgthal* to *Gernsbach* and *Wildbad* (p. 18).

The train turns to the S. and enters the smiling *Kinzig-Thal* below ($22^1/_2$ M.) *Lossburg* (2148 ft.). — 28 M. Alpirsbach (1432 ft.; °*Löwe, Schwan*), with a Romanesque church of the 11th cent., has a brisk trade in timber and straw-hats. Near it is the *Krähenbad*. — $31^1/_2$ M. *Schenkenzell*; $33^1/_2$ M. *Schiltach* (Krone), at the confluence of the *Schiltach* and the Kinzig; $39^1/_2$ M. *Wolfach*; $42^1/_2$ M. Hausach, see **Baedeker's Rhine**.

The train descends the narrow valley of Mühlen, with the ruined *Staufenberg* on the left, and crosses the Neckar. — 42 M. Horb (1262 ft.; *Zum Kaiser; Krone; Bär; Zum Bahnhof*), with 2200 inhab., has a large church in the transition style. On the hill an ancient watch-tower and a pilgrimage-chapel. — Railway by *Tübingen* and *Plochingen* to *Stuttgart*, see R. 9.

The train for a short way traverses Prussian territory. 46 M.

Neckarhausen. The Danube is crossed. To the E. above *Fischingen* rises the extensive ruin of *Wehrstein*. — 50 M. *Sulz am Neckar* (Waldhorn), a little town with a Gothic church. Then a tunnel. To the left beyond it rises the ruin of *Albeck*. Near (56 M.) *Aistaig* pleasant glimpses of the valley are enjoyed. — 58 M. *Oberndorf* (Post), a thriving village to the right. The old Augustinian monastery is now a gun-factory (director, Herr Mauser). 61 M. *Epfendorf*; 64 M. *Thalhausen*. The line is carried over four bridges, through four tunnels, with various ruins to the right and left, and lastly by a long tunnel through the hill on which Rottweil lies. The station, with the extensive railway engine-factory, is 1/2 M. from the town. To the left of the station is the site of a large Roman camp, while the *Altstadt*, 1/4 hr. to the S., covers the remains of a Roman civil colony. The saline springs and baths of *Wilhelmshall* lie 1/2 M. farther to the S.

68 M. **Rottweil** (*Wilder Mann* or *Post*, R. 1 ℳ 40, B. 70 pf., D. 1 ℳ 70, pens. 4 ℳ 50 pf.; *Lamm*; Rail. Restaurant, D. with wine 2 ℳ 80 pf.), an ancient town (6912 inhab.) with well-preserved walls and towers, was a free city of the Empire down to 1802. The *Heiligen-Kreuz-Kirche*, a fine Gothic structure (1374-1473), has been restored by Heideloff. The *Kapellenkirche*, with its handsome Gothic tower of 1364, was entirely remodelled at the beginning of last century. Some good carvings on the S. side and on the panels of the doors are the sole relics of the original structure. The interesting *Collection of Antiquities* contains chiefly Roman relics. The *Chapel of St. Lawrence* in the old cemetery contains a collection of mediæval carvings, chiefly of the Upper Swabian school. In the centre is a mosaic from a Roman bath (Orpheus). The massive *Hochthurm* (148 ft.), in the highest part of the town on the W. side, commands an extensive view.

To VILLINGEN, 17 M., railway in 1¼ hr. Stations *Deisslingen*, *Trossingen*, *Schwenningen* (the source of the Neckar is 1/2 M. to the S.). The line traverses a lofty plain, the watershed between the Rhine and Danube, and beyond stat. *Marbach* descends the *Brigach-Thal* to *Villingen* (see Baedeker's Rhine).

The line crosses the Neckar and enters the broad *Primthal*. To the left, several picturesque glimpses of the *Hohenberg*, *Lemberg*, and other spurs of the Alb. 72½ M. *Neufra*. The line ascends, and then traverses a high-lying, well-cultivated plain, forming part of the *Baar*. 75 M. *Aldingen*. To the left rises the long *Heuberg*, with the *Dreifaltigkeitskirche* on the nearest peak (3225 ft.), adjacent to which is a belvedere tower (ascended from Spaichingen in 1 hr.; splendid *Panorama*). To the right in the distance are the flattened cone of the *Hohenkarpfen* and the coffin-shaped *Lupfen*. 77½ M. *Spaichingen* (2210 ft.; *Alte Post*; **Neue Post**; Krone), a straggling village; 80½ M. *Rietheim*; 82½ M. *Wurmlingen* (Bellevue), a village; on the *Faulenbach*; 1/2 M. from the railway. The line describes a long curve, and crosses the *Danube* (to *Sigmaringen* and *Ulm*, see p. 52).

85½ M. **Tuttlingen** (2130 ft.; *Post; *Hecht; Bartenbach, at the station, well spoken of), an industrial town (10,092 inhab.), lies on the right bank of the Danube. Above it rise the ruins of the *Honburg*, destroyed during the Thirty Years' War. A monument, with a medallion-portrait and a figure of *Germania, designed by Jahn, was erected here in 1892 to *Max Schneckenburger*, author of the 'Wacht am Rhein' (b. at Thalheim near Tuttlingen 1819, d. 1849). The *Witthoh* (2887 ft.), 1¼ hr. to the S., is a good point of view.

The line traverses the broad valley of the Danube, and crosses the river near (110½ M.) *Möhringen*. 92 M. **Immendingen** *(Falke; Deutscher Kaiser)*, junction for Donaueschingen and Waldshut (see *Baedeker's Rhine*).

The train recrosses the Danube, gradually ascends its S. bank, penetrates the watershed between Danube and Rhine by deep cuttings and a tunnel, and descends beyond (95 M.) *Hattingen* (Hauser). After a long tunnel and several lofty viaducts, the line runs on a high level along the E. slope of the hills. 99 M. *Thalmühle*. We now descend the wooded *Engener-Thal* to (102 M.) *Engen* (*Post), an ancient little town, where the mountains are quitted.

The train now skirts the volcanic peaks of the *Hegau*, the highest of which, the *Hohenhöwen* (2854 ft.), rises to the W. of (103½ M.) *Welschingen;* beyond it is the *Hohenstoffeln*. 106 M. *Mühlhausen*, with the ruin of *Mägdeberg*. 107 M. *Hohenkrähen* lies at the foot of a bold rock (2116 ft.), crowned with fragments of an old castle.

110½ M. **Singen** *(*Krone*, ½ M. from the station; *Adler*, at the station, well spoken of; *Ekkehard)* lies at the base of the *Hohentwiel*.

The fortress of *Hohentwiel (2273 ft.), a small 'enclave' of Wurtemberg, rises on a lofty isolated rock ¾ M. to the N.W. of Singen (3½ M. from the station). It was successfully defended during the Thirty Years' War by the Wurtemberg commandant Widerholt, to whom a monument has been erected. In 1800 it was destroyed by the French. The imposing ruins command a superb view of the Lake of Constance and the Alps. Indicator and telescope at the top. A guide, the key, and a ticket for the tower (20 pf.) are procured at the *Inn halfway up.

114 M. *Gottmadingen;* 117½ M. *Thayingen;* 120 M. *Herblingen*.

123 M. **Schaffhausen** *(*Hôtel Müller*, R., L., & A. from 2½, B. 1¼, D. 3 ℳ; *Rheinischer Hof*, similar charges; *Riese*, R., L., & A. 2-2½, D. 2½ ℳ, these three at the station; *Post; Schwanen; Tanne*, plain; *Railway Restaurant)* is a picturesque old Swiss town (12,402 inhab.) on the right bank of the *Rhine*, formerly a free town of the Empire, and now the capital of the Canton of that name. The *Münster*, an early-Romanesque basilica of 1052-1101, has recently been restored. The massive tower of *Munot* dates from the 16th century. The *Imthurneum* contains a theatre, music-school, and music-rooms. Opposite is the *Museum* with natural history specimens, antiquities, and the town-library. The *Fäsenstaub*, a pleasant promenade, commands a fine view of the Rhine and the Alps.

The *FALLS OF THE RHINE are most conveniently visited by rail from Schaffhausen to stat. *Neuhausen*, 2½ M. distant. See *Baedeker's Switzerland*.

11. The Swabian Alb.

This district, **the central part of** Swabia, is a wooded range of limestone mountains, intersected **by picturesque** valleys, bounded on the W. by the Black Forest, on the **N. by the valley** of the Neckar, and on the S. **by the Danube.** The hills **on the** side **towards the** Neckar are picturesquely grouped, affording numerous views; **the valleys** are luxuriantly fertile and partly clothed with fine beech-forest; many **of** the towns are antiquated and interesting. Pedestrians in particular will find many attractions. **Inns** generally good and inexpensive.

Between Hohenstaufen, Ipf, and Ulm stretches the E. part of the **Alb, consisting** mainly of the Härtfeld, Brenzthal, Mts. of Aalen and Heu**bach, and** the Albuch. The central Alb lies between Hohenstaufen and **Hohenzollern on one side,** and **Ulm and** Sigmaringen on the other. The **S.W. wing of the Alb is formed of the** beautiful range of hills between Hohenzollern and Lupfen, **the plateau of the Heuberg,** and the valley of the **Danube** between Tuttlingen **and** Sigmaringen. — **The** finest **points** in the E. ALB are the neighbourhood of *Bopfingen* with the *Ipf*, *Hohenbaldern*, and *Kapfenburg* (p. 29); the neighbourhood of *Aalen*, with the *Brauneberg*, and the *Source of the Kocher* near Unterkochen (p. 28); the neighbourhood of *Heubach*, with the *Rosenstein* (p. 28), *Lauterberg*, and *Bernhardus*; the *Albuch*, with the *Wendthal* (p. 32); the *Brenzthal* from Königsbronn to Brenz-Sontheim, the finest part of which, the *Buige* near Anhausen, is also not far from the *Charlotten-Höhle* (p. 28); and finally the remarkable *Lone-Hürbe-Thal* (p. 28). — The S.W. ALB is described in RR. 10, 12, 13.

Of the CENTRAL ALB, **the district about** *Geislingen* is described at pp. 31, 32. The present route embraces the side next the Neckar, the most interesting points, which may be visited in five days, being the *Rechberg* and *Hohenstaufen*, the *Geislinger-Thal* and *Upper Filsthal*, the *Lenninger Thal* and the *Teck*, *Hohenneuffen*, the *Uracher-Thal*, *Reutlingen* with the *Achalm*, the *Honauer-Thal* and *Lichtenstein*, *Tübingen* and *Rossberg*, *Hohenzollern*.

FIRST DAY. By the first train from Stuttgart to *Gmünd* (p. 28). Thence by **a good road (on which the** omnibus to Süssen runs, see p. 28) **to the** (4 M.) upper ***Rechberg** (2316 ft.), on the broad summit of which stands a much frequented pilgrimage-chapel (refreshments **at the** parsonage, but no **quarters** for the night). **The** view embraces **a fertile** and undulating landscape, sprinkled with towns **and villages,** stretching to the N. as **far as** the Welzheimer Wald **and the Waldenburg** and Limpurg hills, **from** the old-fashioned town of Gmünd in the foreground to the distant Ellwangen. To **the W.** rise the Hohenstaufen and the Black Forest Mts.; towards **the S.W. extend** the ranges of the Swabian Alb; and in clear weather the Tyrolese and Swiss Alps may be descried towards the S.E. and S.

We next visit the ruined castle of *Hohenrechberg* (burned down in 1865), on the lower peak of the hill. Thence by a distinct path on the crest of the hill in 1½ hr. to the village of *Hohenstaufen* (Ochs, Lamm, both moderate), on the slope of the ***Hohenstaufen** (2237 ft.), to which a path ascends from the village in 20 minutes. Near this path is a small *Church*, partly restored in 1860 and recently adorned with the armorial bearings of the countries over which the Hohenstaufen once held sway.

On the N. wall is an old fresco, almost obliterated, of Frederick Barbarossa (1152-1190), with inscription, of the 16th cent., recording that the emperor, '*amor bonorum, terror malorum*', was in the habit of entering the church by this door (now walled up).

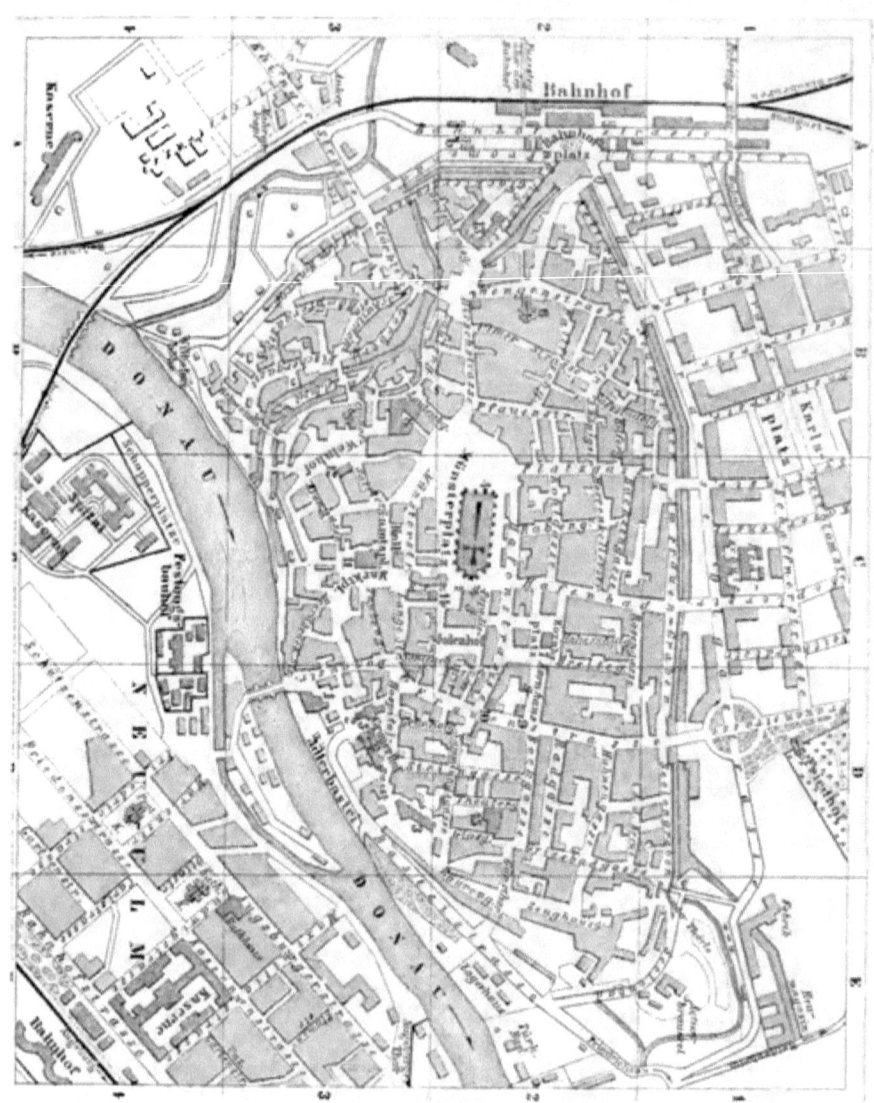

The hill commands a beautiful prospect. From 1080 until the Peasants' War in 1525 it was crowned with the ancestral castle of the illustrious family of Staufen or Hohenstaufen, which occupied the German imperial throne from 1138 to 1254 and became extinct in 1268 by the premature death of the ill-fated Conradin in Italy. A small fragment of wall on the extreme S. verge of the bare plateau is all that is now left of their abode.

A pleasant road, traversing woods for a long way, leads from the village of Hohenstaufen to (5¼ M.) *Göppingen* (rail. stat., p. 30). Thence by evening-train viâ *Plochingen* in 1½ hr. to *Unter-Boihingen* (p. 35), and in 14 min. more by *Oethlingen* to *Kirchheim unter* **Teck** (*Post; Löwe; Deutsches Haus), a small town with a handsome château, prettily situated in view of the Alb.

Or we may walk from the village of Hohenstaufen to (1¼ hr.) *Eislingen* (p. 31), take the train to (¾ hr.) *Geislingen*, and walk thence next day by *Wiesensteig* to *Owen* (comp. p. 31).

SECOND DAY. Excursion to the *Lenninger-Thal, **one of the** finest in the Alb, extending 10 M. to *Gutenberg*, a charming **drive**. From (4½ M.) the little town of *Owen* (**ow** pron. as in *cow*; Post or Krone, moderate), with a handsome restored **Gothic church**, burial-place of the Dukes of Teck, **we** ascend (in **1 hr.; following the** telegra**ph-posts and** then **turning to the** right) **to the ruined** castle of ***Teck (2542 ft.),** the ancestral seat of the Dukes of Teck (belvedere-**tower**; refreshments; **the** *Sibyllenloch* is a lofty grotto **on the** W. brink of the rock).

From the Teck we reach the *Gelbe Felsen* in 10 min. and proceed over **the** *Sattel* (2010 ft.) to the (½ hr.) ruined *Diepoldsburg* (p. 31). Thence we may either cross the plateau to the N. to (½ hr.) *Ochsenwang*, etc. (p. 31), **or** ascend the (¾ hr.) *Wielandstein* **to the** S., viâ the *Engelhof*, and descend **to** *Ober-Lenningen*.

At *Unter-Lenningen* the ruin of *Salzburg* lies to the right **and the** ruined *Diepoldsburg* or *Rauberburg* (p. 31) rises **high above us on** the left. On a steep rock at (1 hr.) *Ober-Lenningen* (Sonne, Ochs, poor) are the remains of the *Wielandstein*. At the E. **end** of the valley lies (1 hr.) *Gutenberg* (1744 ft.; Löwe, Hirsch, both well spoken of), a little to the S. of which is the ruin of *Sperberseck*, while to the N. is *Krebsstein* (see below).

Above Gutenberg, to **the** left, in the upper slope of the valley, is the (25 min.) ***Gutenberg Stalactite Grotto** ('Tropfsteinhöhle'), discovered in Dec., 1889, and well worth seeing. (Guide necessary.) We pass through the *Heppenloch*, two chambers discovered earlier, where numerous fossil bones, flint implements, etc., were found, to the 'Gothic Hall', with its splendid ice-like stalactites and stalagmites. Then through a long passage to the 'Moorish Hall' with the 'Waterfall', and past the 'Dwarf's Palace', the 'Spindles', etc., to the 'Klamm', a deep gully to which a flight of stone steps gives access. — About 5 min. **from** this cavern is the *Gussmanns-Höhle, with the 'Organ Hall' and the 'Tower' (electric light), made accessible in 1891.

A footpath **leads** to the N. from Gutenberg viâ **the** ruin of *Hohengutenberg* to (½ **hr.)** the farm of *Krebsstein*. — Another (preferable) leads to the W. viâ *Schlattstall* and the *Schröcke* to (2 hrs.) *Urach* (p. 44).

From Gutenberg we may **walk** by *Schlattstall* and *Grabenstetten* (with an ancient 'pagan' moat) to the Beuren Rock and Hohenneuffen (in 3 hrs.), without descending into the valley. Carriages drive by Owen and *Beuren* (Schlegel) to *Neuffen*.

The **Beurener Fels* ('Rock of Beuren', 2365 ft.; ascended by a good path from **Owen** or from **Beuren** in 1¼ hr.), a bold projecting rock, commands a beautiful view (Rechberg, Hohenstaufen, Black Forest, Donnersberg, Vosges). Hence across the plateau by *Erkenbrechtsweiler* and past the *Wilhelmsfelsen* in 1 hr. to the —

*Hohenneuffen (2436 ft.), a conical and conspicuous height, projecting far into the valley, and crowned by the imposing ruins of an ancient stronghold, demolished as unsafe in 1802. Fine view with charming foreground. (Refreshments when the flag is hoisted.)

From the Hohenneuffen to stat. *Nürtingen*, 1½ hr. (see p. 35). Or Urach may be reached hence in 2 hrs. by crossing the table-land and passing the *Bürrenhof* (with another old moat, comp. p. 43) and the village of *Hülben*, whence we descend into the valley. But it is pleasanter to descend by a good path through the wood to the (½ hr.) pretty little town of *Neuffen* (Ochs; Hirsch). At the lower end of the place (finger-post) we ascend to the left, take the broad track to the left where the route divides, and follow it across the *Sattelbogen*, between the view-points of *Hörnle* and *Karlslinde* (p. 36), to (1½ hr.) *Dettingen* (Löwe; Krone); thence by train to *Urach* in ¼ hr.

THIRD DAY. **Urach** (1515 ft.; **Post*, **Haus 'Zur Krone'*, both in the market-place; beer at *Heinzelmann's* and *Wenz's*; rooms at the latter), an old-fashioned little town, charmingly situated in the Ermsthal, is frequented as a summer-resort (medical boarding-houses of Dr. Camerer and Dr. Klüpfel). The *Church of St. Amandus* was built in 1472, and the *Canonry* (now a Prot. school) in 1477 by Count Eberhard im Bart, whose confessional in the church is adorned with good carving (1472). The church also contains an interesting font, executed in 1518 by Christoph of Urach; pulpit probably by the same master. In the *Schloss*, erected in 1443, partly of timber, is the 'Goldner Saal', containing reminiscences of the Counts, afterwards Dukes of Wurtemberg. Fine Gothic *Fountain* in the market-place (end of 15th cent.). Railway to *Metzingen* in ½ hr., see p. 36.

The **Uracher-Thal* from Dettingen to Seeburg, 6 M. above Urach, surpasses that of Lenningen; the slopes are richly clad with beech-forest. Several quarries of tufa. Near *Dettingen* rises the conspicuous *Rossberg* (2572 ft.); farther up, beyond the *Uracher Bleiche*, the *Runderberg*, in a side-valley on the right; then *Hohen-Urach* and the *Thiergartenberg*; on the opposite side the *Hochberg*.

Beyond Urach the road ascends by the course of the *Erms*, which drives numerous mills and a large cotton-factory, into the **Seeburger-Thal*, a picturesque, rocky, and wooded valley. Above the *Georgenau* rises the ruined *Hohenwittlingen*, under which is the fine stalactite-cavern of *Schillingsloch* (now called '*Schiller-Höhle*').

In the upper and wildest part of the valley, between lofty rocks at the mouth of the romantic *Fischburg-Thal*, lies the hamlet of *Seeburg* (Löwe, plain). On a rock high above it is the little château of *Uhenfels*. The infant Erms, though only 50 yds. from its source, most creditably drives a mill here. The excursion from Urach to Seeburg is best made in an open carriage (with one horse, there and back about 3½-5 *M*). From Seeburg to the S. through the *Seethal* to *Münsingen* (p. 47), road in about 1½ hr.

The most attractive excursion from Urach is to Hohen-Urach and to the waterfall. The hill of **Hohen-Urach** (2300 ft.; ¾ hr.; easy path; on entering the wood avoid the first path diverging to the right by the large beech) is crowned with extensive ruins and affords a good view, but is inferior in interest to the Hohenneuffen. Below the second gateway of the castle, to the left, is the chamber in which the ill-fated poet Frischlin was imprisoned; in attempting to escape he was dashed to pieces on the rocks below (1590). A path through beautiful beech-wood leads hence to (½ hr.) a sequestered grassy terrace, from which the *Waterfall of Urach takes a leap of 80 ft. (To reach it from the ruined castle, we retrace our steps for 10 min., as far as the last finger-post 'auf die Festung', turn to the right, reach another finger-post, and either go straight on to the top of the waterfall or take the path to the right leading to its foot.) The best point of view is the 'Olga-Ruhe', so named since a visit of the late Queen of Wurtemberg. The up-trains stop if desired at the entrance to this valley. Back to Urach, ½ hr.

A direct footpath (marked) leads from Urach to *Lichtenstein* in 4-5 hrs.

From Urach we may go by railway in ¾ hr. viâ *Metzingen* (to the E. of which is the *Floriansberg*, p. 36) to *Reutlingen* (p. 36); but it is far preferable to cross the hills on foot (4 hrs., guide not indispensable). On our return from the waterfall, we turn at the foot of the Runderberg into the other branch of the side-valley, to *Güterstein*; then a steep ascent by the 'Wasserweg' to a well-house beside the remains of a Carthusian monastery and past the *Vordere Fohlenhof* to *St. Johann* (Schmid's Inn, fair); or direct thither from the waterfall by the zigzag path to the right. On leaving the wood at the (½ hr.) top of the hill, the path leads straight on past a stone hut called the *Rutschenhof*. But we first follow the slope to the right as far as the boundary-stone, to obtain a charming view of the peaceful valley, with Hohen-Urach, Hohenneuffen, and Teck, one of the finest prospects in the Swabian Alb. From the Rutschenhof we either continue our route straight on, or we follow the track to the left and then, by the corner of the wood, the road to the right, to the (½ hr.) Fohlenhof above mentioned. Here a path diverges to the right (finger-post) from the path to St. Johann, and leads in 25 min. to the *Grüne Felsen* ('green rock'; 2640 ft.), a delightful point of view. We then retrace our steps and take the good road to the right leading to (20 min.) St. Johann. From

St. Johann a good road (with short-cuts) descends to (1 hr.) *Eningen* (*Bazlen), a busy market-town at the foot of the Achalm (ascent $3/4$ hr.), whence the railway runs in 6-8 min. to ($1^3/4$ M.) **Reutlingen** (p. 36).

FOURTH DAY. From Reutlingen to the summit of the ***Achalm** (2312 ft.), an isolated mountain, with vineyards **and orchards at** its base. About halfway up is a royal dairy (rfmts.). **The carriageroad to the Achalm, diverging from the Metzingen and Urach road, is much longer than the footpath, by which the summit is easily attained in** $1^1/4$ hr.: from the railway-station we ascend the Garten-Strasse and at the end of it turn to the left; in 10 min. **we reach the foot of the Achalm and the path passes under a bridge; after** 3 min. we ascend to the left towards the dairy; after 7 min. we go straight on, avoiding the path to the left, and reach the dairy in $1/4$ hr. **more; thence by a winding path to the summit in** $1/2$ **hr. On the summit is a lofty tower with** a huge vane (key at the dairy; 40 pf.). Admirable *View: Tübingen Castle, Schloss Lichtenstein, the Hohenneuffen, Rechberg, Hohenstaufen, and other peaks of the Alb; picturesque foreground; below us lies Reutlingen, to the S. Eningen.

The most attractive excursion in the neighbourhood of Reutlingen is that to SCHLOSS **LICHTENSTEIN**. Railway (p. 36) to ($6^1/2$ M.) Honau in 38 min., to (8 M.) Lichtenstein station in 56 minutes. — $1^3/4$ M. *Eningen*, $1^1/4$ M. from the village at the foot of the Achalm (see above). — 3 M. *Pfullingen* (Hirsch; Lamm), **a town of 5000 inhab., with Dr.** Flamm's lunatic asylum. **A number of pleasant** excursions may be made hence on the right bank of the Echaz (good paths with numerous guide-posts): to the *Ursulaberg* (2260 ft.) above Pfullingen; to the *Mädchenfels* (2540 ft.) and *Greifenstein* (2083 ft.) near Holzelfingen; and to the rocky ridge extending from the *Burgstein* (2400 ft.) to the *Traifelberg* (2607 ft.), above Honau. — $4^1/2$ M. *Pfullingen Paper Mill;* $5^1/2$ M. *Unterhausen Cotton Mill;* 6 M. *Unterhausen* (Adler); $6^1/2$ M. *Honau* (1722 ft.; Rössle). Hence a rack-and-pinion railway (gradient 1:10; length 2300 yds.) ascends the *Honauer Steige* to (8 M.) *Lichtenstein* (2310 **ft.).** Continuation of the railway to *Münsingen*, see p. 47.

To reach Schloss Lichtenstein from HONAU **we retrace** our steps for 60 paces, **diverge to** the left between houses, **and** ascend a meadow; after 5 min. **we enter a** beech-wood and then follow **a** new zigzag path to ($1/2$ hr.) the castle. — The direct route from UNTERHAUSEN (see above) **leads viâ (5 min.)** *Oberhausen* (Hirsch; Krone) and ascends to the right by a good road on the wooded W. slope; at the first bifurcation we keep **to the left;** after $1/2$ hr. **we leave the road at a** cutting in the rock, **ascend** a few steps to the **left**, and after 8 min. **in** a straight direction **reach the** forester's house (refreshments**), adjoining the entrance to the castle.** — FROM LICHTENSTEIN STATION (see above) the route leads past the 'Schanze' (beautiful view) and through the *Dobel Tunnel;* a footpath to the right at the upper end of the Dobel ravine then leads viâ the Old Lichtenstein to ($3/4$ hr.) the château and forester's house.

***Schloss Lichtenstein** (2985 ft.), or the '*Schlösschen*', a château **erected** in 1842 by Count Wilhelm of Wurtemberg on an isolated rock, 850 ft. above the Honau valley, is one of the most attractive points in Swabia. (Cards of admission obtained at the Duke of Urach's Palace, Neckar-Str. 68, in Stuttgart; the château is closed on Whitsunday and Whitmonday.)

The castle is approached by a draw-bridge, by which a cleft in the rock is crossed. The interior is tastefully fitted up in the mediæval style, and adorned with a number of fine old German pictures of the Swabian school, by Wohlgemut, Holbein, Schön, etc. There are also numerous antiquities, weapons, and suits of armour, but the principal attraction is the *View obtained from the lofty tower (129 ft.). In fine weather, to the S. beyond the plateau of the Alb, the Swiss and Tyrolese Alps are visible, the Glärnisch, Churfirsten, Sentis, Vorarlberg Mts., and Zugspitze; to the N., far below, the picturesque green Honauer-Thal, through which the Echaz and the railway wind; beyond it the Achalm and the extensive plain. Even the Königsstuhl at Heidelberg is said to be visible. On a projecting rock outside the château the duke has erected a monument to the novelist Hauff (d. 1827), by whose romance the old castle of Lichtenstein has been immortalised. — About 10 min. to the S. is the ruin of Old Lichtenstein.

The Nebelhöhle, a stalactite grotto, 200 yds. long and 75 ft. high, 3 M. to the W. of Lichtenstein, is frequently visited, but the brilliancy of the stalactites has been sullied by the smoke of the torches. Adm. 40 pf. each person, guide 1 *M*, each torch 40 pf., Bengal fire 50 pf.; key and guides at the Hirsch at Oberhausen (p. 46). A national festival is held here on Whitmonday, when the cavern is illuminated. The cavern is 2¼ M. from Oberhausen, and about as far from Lichtenstein. The path to the latter runs as follows: on the plateau, 5 min. from the cave, bear to the left, due S.; bear to the left again at the cross-roads after 5 min. more; 5 min. farther on, a field, where we skirt the wood to the right; 5 min. more, turn to the left, and cross the moor to a group of trees where the tower comes into view. Descent from Lichtenstein to Honau 20 minutes.

The Olgahöhle at *Honau* is smaller than the Nebelhöhle, but cleaner and more easily accessible. It is seen to advantage by electric light (40 pf. each person). — About 10 min. distant is the *Source of the Echaz*, with the figure of a nymph.

The RAILWAY TO MÜNSINGEN proceeds from (8 M.) Lichtenstein (see p. 46) across the plateau of the Alb. — 9½ M. *Klein-Engstingen* is the starting-point for a visit to the Karlshöhle, near *Erpfingen*, 3¾ M. to the S.W., another and more interesting grotto, the stalactites being still uninjured. Visitors can drive to the entrance. Some of the stalactites here bear a striking resemblance to Gothic architecture, others to human figures, etc. — 11½ M. *Kohlstetten*. Near (13½ M.) *Offenhausen*, where there is a stud-farm, is the source of the *Grosse Lauter*. The railway descends the pretty valley of the Lauter to (15 M.) *Gomadingen* and (16½ M.) *Marbach*, with another stud-farm. Pleasant walk hence through the Grosse Lauterthal to (8 hrs.) *Untermorchthal*, see p. 53. — The line now ascends to the N.E. through the *Dolderthal* and *Baumthal*, passing *Schloss Grafeneck*, to (21 M.) Münsingen (2296 ft.; *Inns*), a town with 3000 inhab., on the plateau of the Alb, 1½ hr. to the S. of *Seeburg* (p. 45). Hence to the *Schmiechthal*, see p. 53.

A pleasant walk may be taken to the W. from the Nebelhöhle viâ *Genkingen* to the (1½ hr.) top of the *Rossberg (2864 ft.; view-tower), commanding a beautiful view of the Alb, the Black Forest, and the Alps. We may descend on the N. side to *Gönningen*, at the foot of the *Stöffelberg* (2400 ft.), whence a road runs to the N. viâ *Bronnweiler* and past the *Kugelberg* (1950 ft.; view) and *Alteburghof* to (2½ hrs.) *Reutlingen*; another to the W. to (2 hrs.) *Mössingen* or **Dusslingen** (see p. 48).

Evening train from Reutlingen to Tübingen (p. 36), ½ hr.

FIFTH DAY. Visit to the *Hohenzollern*, etc., see p. 48.

12. From Tübingen to Hechingen and Sigmaringen.

51 M. RAILWAY in 3¼ hrs. (fares 7 ℳ 10, 4 ℳ 70 pf., 3 ℳ). — Comp. Map, p. 42.

Tübingen, see p. 36. The *Hohenzollern Railway* diverges to the left at the station, describes a wide curve, and enters the *Steinlach-Thal*, noted for its thriving villages. To the left are the small *Bläsibad* and the round *Bläsiberg*, with an old chapel of St. Blasius. The Steinlach is crossed near (5 M.) *Dusslingen*. The picturesque hills of the Swabian Alb on the left are now approached: the Rossberg (p. 47), the broad-backed Farrenberg, and the precipitous Dreifürstenstein; in the background the Salmendinger Chapel. Near (10 M.) *Mössingen* the Steinlach is again crossed. On a hill to the left stands the ancient *Belsener Chapel*; to the right are the sulphur-baths of *Sebastiansweiler*.

Mössingen is the starting-point for visits to the upper *Steinlach-Thal*, the *Dreifürstenstein* (2800 ft.; 1¼ hr.), the *Salmendinger Kapelle* (2 hrs.), the *Riedernberg* (2800 ft.), and the *Bolberg* (2890 ft.; 2½ hrs.).

Beyond (13 M.) *Bodelshausen* the train crosses the Prussian frontier. We then descend to —

15½ M. **Hechingen** (1640 ft.; *Linde* or *Post*, R. 1-1½ ℳ, B. 60 pf., D. 1 ℳ 70 pf., pens. 3-3½ ℳ, omn. 40 pf.; omnibus at the station; carr. and pair to Hohenzollern Castle 6 ℳ and gratuity; *Rad*; *Löwe*, nearest the station, R. 1-1¼ ℳ, B. 60 pf.; beer at the *Museum*), formerly the residence of the Princes of Hohenzollern-Hechingen, but acquired by Prussia in 1850. It is an old town with 3700 inhab., situated on the abrupt slope of the valley of the *Starzel*. The *Parish Church*, erected in 1783, contains a relief by Peter Vischer, representing Count **Eitel Friedrich** II. of Zollern (d. 1512) and his wife Magdalena of Brandenburg (d. 1495). A footpath to the left at this church leads to (1 hr.) Hohenzollern. The small *Protestant Church* on the S. side of the town (1 M. from the station) is a tasteful modern structure in the pointed style. Opposite is the *Villa Eugenia*, with gardens, the property of the Prince. About 1 M. farther on is the *Brielhof Inn* (see below).

A road passing the *Martinsthurm* leads to the W. from Hechingen to (3 M.) the little château of *Lindich*, with a park. — **Pleasant** walks to (2 hrs.) the *Zeller Horn*, *Steigberg*, and *Hangende Stein*.

The train crosses the Starzel, passes *Stetten* in the Gnaden-Thal, the ancestral burial-place of the Zollern family, and beyond several cuttings reaches (19 M.) *Zollern* (1798 ft.; *Brielhof, ½ M. from the station; one-horse carr. to the castle 5, two-horse 7 ℳ). A good road (the windings of which are avoided by short-cuts following the telegraph-posts) leads hence to the (2½ M.) magnificent castle of *Hohenzollern (2887 ft.; adm. 25 pf.), grandly situated on an isolated wooded eminence of the Alb. It was erected by Frederick William IV. in 1850-55 as a royal château, and completed in 1867. The bold and skilful construction is as remarkable as the situation.

The old castle which occupied this site was destroyed in 1423 and repeatedly restored (the last time in 1554), but at the beginning of the present century little of it remained except the chapel. An inscription over the 'Adlerthor' (Pl.1) alludes to the history of the edifice; above it is the Prussian eagle; below it an equestrian figure representing the Elector Frederick I. Passing through the Adlerthor, the visitor enters the '*Rampenthurm*', within the narrow limits of which three bold and ingeniously contrived curves and a winding tunnel lead to the gate-tower situated 75 ft. higher. The balustrade above the entrance to the tunnel is adorned with two men-at-arms in stone. The summit of the precipitous rock is enclosed, in accordance with the ancient plan of the castle, by walls 45-65 ft. in height, in the form of a heptagon, and provided with bastions and corner-turrets. Within this enclosure stands the modern castle, a winged edifice with five towers, two of which rise to a height of 120 ft. above the external walls. The two lowest of the five stories of the building are vaulted and designed for purposes of defence. The towers are adorned with the arms of the Zollern family. On the tower of St. Michael, above the balcony of the apartments of the Em-

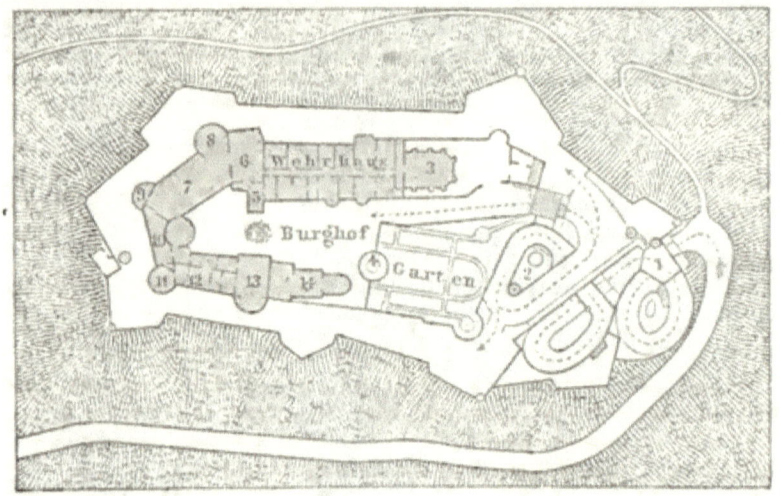

press,' is a representation of St. Michael and the Dragon in bronze. The style of the entire structure is that of the latter part of the 14th cent., which has been strictly adhered to, notwithstanding the serious difficulties encountered in constructing the approach to the castle and providing it with fortifications. The garrison consists of a company of infantry.

To the left in the upper *Burghof* is the *Burggarten*, adorned with a bronze statue of Fred. William IV. beneath a Gothic canopy (Pl. 4). Opposite, to the right, is the *Wehrhaus*, or barrack, containing a restaurant. Adjoining it is the *Protestant Chapel* (Pl. 3), in the Gothic style. To the left (S.) rises the *Michaelsthurm* with the relief-portraits and armorial bearings of the different lords of the castle. To the E. of it, in the direction of the garden, is the Roman Catholic *Chapel of St. Michael* (Pl. 14). In the centre of the quadrangle rises the noble *Königslinde*.

A lofty flight of steps (Pl. 5) by the Wehrhaus, adorned with a statue of the Count Zollern who rebuilt the castle in 1454, leads to the apartments of the interior. The *Stammbaum-Halle* (Pl. 6), containing genealogical trees, coats-of-arms, etc., is first entered. Then the sumptuous *Grafensaal* (Pl. 7), in the Gothic style, borne by eight columns of red marble, and overladen with gilding and painting. On the right of this saloon is the *Kaiserhalle* (Pl. 8), borne by a central pillar, embellished with eight painted statues of German emperors by the windows; opposite it, on the W. side of the hall, is the *Bischofshalle* (Pl. 9), with two statues and 28 medallion-portraits of prelates of the house of Zollern. Adjoining the

BAEDEKER's S. Germany. 8th Edit.

Grafensaal on the W. is the *Library* (Pl. 10), a low apartment with carved bookcases and °Frescoes by Peters illustrative of the history of the castle. From the library we proceed to the right to the *Markgrafenthurm* (Pl. 11), which contains the sitting-room and bedroom of the emperor, while to the left are the apartments of the empress (Pl. 12) in the *Michaelsthurm*. The Roman Catholic *Church of St. Michael* is the only part of the earlier structure now in existence. It contains some interesting stained glass from the monastery of Stetten.

Another attraction is the very extensive view from the balcony outside the *Bischofshalle*. It embraces the green hills of Swabia; W. the towns of Balingen and Rottweil; beyond them the Black Forest, with the Feldberg, its chief mountain; S.W. the Jura; S. and E., in the immediate vicinity, the wooded slopes of the Alb.

A little farther to the E. rises the *Zellerhörnle*, a spur of the Alb plateau, 210 ft. higher than the Hohenzollern. A pleasant path leads to the E. along the *Trauf*, as the crest of the wooded hill is called, in 2½ hrs. to *Jungingen* (°Post) or *Starzeln* (°Höfle), on the high-road to *Gamertingen* and (22 M.) *Sigmaringen*. — Another attractive route leads from the Zellerhörnle to (6 hrs.) *Laufen* on the Eyach (see below), viâ the *Zoller Steighof*, *Blasenberg*, *Stich*, *Hundsruck*, *Zillhausen*, the *Böllatfels* (3018 ft.), *Burgfelden* (with an old Romanesque church and mural paintings of the 11th cent.), and *Schalksburg* (see below).

The Zollern long remains in sight. — 21½ M. *Bisingen*; 24 M. *Engstlatt* (interesting painting of the Ulm school in the church), whence the *Hundsrück* (3054 ft.; sub-alpine flora) may be ascended. — 26 M. **Balingen** *(Schwan; Roller)*, a manufacturing town on the *Eyach*, with sulphur-baths.

An attractive excursion may be made hence to the (2 hrs.) *Lochenstein* (3153 ft.; splendid view), an ancient pagan place of sacrifice; and thence viâ the *Schafberg* (with the ruin of Wenzelstein; rock-chasms, etc.) down to the *Waldhaushof* for the (1½ hr.) ascent of the *Plettenberg* (3293 ft.).

The line now turns to the S.E. and enters the highest part of the Swabian Alb. To the right rise the *Plettenberg*, the *Schafberg*, and the bold *Lochenstein* (see above). At (29 M.) *Frommern* begins the hilly part of the railway, the gradients varying from 1:60 to 1:45. To the right of (31 M.) *Laufen an der Eyach* are the *Eyachhörnle* (3132 ft.; attractive ascent in 1¼ hr.), *Grat*, and *Gräblensberg*, to the left the rock of *Schalksburg* (with a ruined castle of the Zollern family). The train passes through a cutting in the rock, with the *Thierberg* on the right and the *Heersberg* on the left. Beyond (33½ M.) *Lautlingen* the line enters another amphitheatre of hills and soon reaches its highest point (2420 ft.), the watershed between the Rhine and the Danube. It then descends gradually to —

37 M. **Ebingen** (2395 ft.; *Schiff; Post; Adler; Stern*), an ancient industrial town, prettily situated among hills. The tower on the *Schlossfelsen* (3122 ft.; good path, ¾ hr.) commands a superb survey of the Alps from the Zugspitze to the Bernese Oberland. The train descends the winding *Schmeien-Thal* and crosses the Prussian frontier. 41 M. *Strassberg*; on a bold rock to the left is the château of that name. Below Strassberg the valley is wild and impracticable, and presented great engineering difficulties (19 bridges and countless cuttings). 43 M. *Kaiseringen*; 45 M. *Storzingen*. The train passes through several defiles (the 'Drei Burgen', 'Hexen-Küche',

'Bettel-Küche'). Beyond (48½ M.) *Oberschmeien* (1945 ft.; ¾ M. to the E. is the *Fürstenhöhe*, with fine view) the line is carried through another defile and two tunnels, and beyond the ruins of *Gebrochen-Gutenstein* enters the valley of the *Danube*.

50 M. *Inziykofen* (Kreuz; Erbprinz), with a beautiful park on the steep and wooded S. bank of the Danube, rendered accessible by flights of steps, and containing several natural grottoes. The Danube flows so slowly here as to resemble a small lake. The walk by *Laiz* (Inn) to (¾ hr.) Sigmaringen (see below) is also interesting.

Sigmaringen now comes in sight. The train runs direct towards the *Mühlberg* (p. 52), passes through a cutting, crosses the Danube, and reaches —

54 M. **Sigmaringen** (1860 ft.; *Deutsches Haus*, R. 1½ ℳ, B. 60 pf.; *Löwe*, R. 1-1½; D. 1½ ℳ, B. 60 pf.; *Kronprinz*; *Traube*, R. 1-2, B. ½, pens. 2½-3 ℳ; *Adler*, moderate), a handsome little town with 4200 inhab., the residence of **Prince Hohenzollern**, and seat of the Prussian administrative authorities, recently embellished with new streets and promenades.

The handsome SCHLOSS, on a rock rising abruptly from the Danube, contains a *Museum*, chiefly formed by Prince Karl Anton (d. 1885), and surpassing most collections of the kind both in extent and choiceness. It is admirably arranged in the *Kunsthalle*, a fine Gothic hall, with frescoes by Müller of Düsseldorf, and in two cabinets. Excellent catalogues by Hofrath Lehner. The Museum is open daily (festivals excepted) from 10 to 12 and 2 to 4; admission 40 pf.

The COLLECTION OF PICTURES (230 works) chiefly illustrates the early German school, the Swabian masters being particularly well represented. Nos. *81-86. Wings of a large altar-piece: Annunciation, Nativity, Circumcision of Christ, Adoration of the Magi, and the Procession to Calvary, by *M. Schaffner*; *132-139. Scenes from the life of the Virgin, by *Barth. Zeitblom*; 158-164. Seven scenes from the history of the Virgin, by *Hans Schülein* (three masters of Ulm, 15-16th cent.); 3. *Altdorfer*, Adoration of the Magi; *Amberger*(?), Portraits of a man and woman. The Lower Rhenish School, especially that of Cologne, is also numerously represented (*e.g.* *91. *B. Bruyn*, Crucifixion, in an appropriate landscape). The best of the early-Flemish works are: *2 and 4. Annunciation, by *Gerard David*; 5. *Herri met de Bles*, Adoration of the Magi; 29. Virgin Mary, with a background of tapestry, and *38. Virgin Mary, in a landscape, by *Rogier van der Weyden*(?); 61. *Gerritt van Haarlem*, Crucifixion; 129. *Lucas van Leyden*, Adoration of the Magi. — The other sections of the **museum contain** specimens **of mediæval and** Renaissance **carved work (statuettes,** reliefs, furniture), **metal-work**, jewelry, textile works, including Gobelins of the 14th and **15th cent.**, glasses, enamels, and a rich collection of Italian majolica, French porcelain, and Dutch, Rhenish, and Swiss pottery. — In the upper **rooms** is an extensive *Palaeontological Collection* (2000 objects).

The *Library*, **with** its valuable books, incunabula, **and** MSS., the *Armoury*, **and the** other richly furnished rooms of the palace are also worth seeing.

In front of the Schloss is a *Statue of Prince Karl Anton* (d. 1885), by Donndorf. In the Karls-Platz is the *Prinzenbau* (now the resi-

4*

dence of the Prince), in front of which is a colossal bronze bust of Prince *Karl* (d. 1853), erected in 1869.

On the *Brenzkofer Berg* (1/2 hr.), on the opposite (N.) bank of the Danube, is the *War Monument*, in memory of the Hohenzollerns who fell in the campaigns of 1866 and 1870-71. It represents Germania, on a lofty pedestal, holding an oak-wreath. The platform commands a charming view of the town and environs, with the distant Alps. At the foot of the hill, 1/2 M. to the W., is the *Zollerhof*, a favourite restaurant, with a garden; and near it stands the pretty *Villa Leibbrand* with beautiful grounds (open to visitors). — The *Mühlberg* (easy path to the summit) is another fine point of view.

From Sigmaringen to Tuttlingen, 26 1/2 M., railway viâ the picturesque winding *Valley of the Danube, which will even repay pedestrians (to Beuron 6 hrs., thence to Tuttlingen 4 hrs.). — 3 1/2 M. *Inzigkofen* (p. 51). The line crosses the *Schmeie* and the Danube, passes the ruin of *Dietfurt*, situated on a rock, and beyond a short tunnel reaches (6 M.) *Gutenstein* (Sonne), a picturesque village with a half-ruined château. Above the Danube tower the rocks of *Rabenfels* and *Heidenfels*. Traversing another tunnel (300 yds. long) the train halts at (10 1/2 M.) *Thiergarten* (Hammer), with disused iron-works; and then, beyond the ruin of *Falkenstein* (on the right) and the village of *Neidingen*, at (11 1/2 M.) *Hausen im Thal* (*Steinhaus; beer at the Adler), with a lofty ruin near it. In front rises the conspicuous old château of *Werenwag*, the property of Prince Fürstenberg, a splendid point of view (fine echo; *Inn at the top). At the foot of the castle-rock lies the hamlet of *Langenbrunn*. The railway leads through a narrow and romantic part of the valley and pierces the *Käpfle Tunnel* (200 yds.), beyond which, on the left, is seen the handsome castle of *Wildenstein* (now used as a forester's house), with interesting defensive works, partly hewn in the rock. The line follows the windings of the Danube. To the right, on the high-road, is the pretty *Chapel of St. Maurus*, erected in 1868-71; and close to it, on the left, lies the dairy-farm of *St. Maurus im Fels*.

15 1/2 M. Beuron (2050 ft.; *Pelikan*; Stern; *Sonne*), a charmingly situated village, contains an old Benedictine monastery, founded in the 11th cent., suppressed in 1876, and now a school of art. The handsome church (restored 1874-75) contains fine ceiling-paintings by Wegscheider. A footpath to the left in the neighbouring wood leads to the (20 min.) *Petershöhle*, a spacious grotto entered by wooden steps.

Beyond Beuron the railway ascends the left bank of the Danube, then diverges to the right through a tunnel (750 yds.) to (18 M.) *Fridingen*, 1 M. to the N. of the little town of that name (Sonne; Bär; Löwe). Rounding a mountain-ridge, whence the ruined pilgrimage-church of *Mariahilf* looks down, we reach (21 M.) *Mühlheim*. The town (Krone; Hirsch, etc.) is picturesquely situated on an eminence to the left, with a château of Baron Enzberg. Numerous Roman remains have been discovered near the station.

Beyond (23 M.) *Nendingen*, a considerable village with an elegant new church and the ancient chapel of St. Blasius, and the royal foundry of *Ludwigsthal*, the train passes through a deep cutting and crosses the Danube to (26 1/2 M.) *Tuttlingen* (see p. 41). Hence to (6 M.) Immendingen, see R. 10.

From Sigmaringen to *Ulm* and *Radolfzell*, see below.

13. From Ulm to Radolfzell and Constance.

Railway from Ulm to (86 M.) *Radolfzell* in 6 1/4-7 1/2 hrs. (fares 11 ℳ 30, 7 ℳ 50, 4 ℳ 90 pf.); from Radolfzell to (12 1/2 M.) *Constance* in 1/2-3/4 hr.

Ulm, see p. 32. The line diverges to the left from the Stuttgart railway (R. 12) and at (1 1/4 M.) *Söflingen* enters the smiling valley of the *Blau*. On the left, near (4 1/2 M.) *Herrlingen*, lies *Klingenstein*, with a château of Dr. Leube. From Herrlingen a pleasant excursion leads via *Schloss Ober-Herrlingen* to (1 hr.) *Lautern*. The weather-beaten rock protrudes at various points in fantastic forms from the wooded sides of the valley. On the right the ruined castle of *Hohe-Gerhausen* or *Rusenschloss*; opposite to it the rock of *Rucken*. The train crosses the Blau.

10 M. **Blaubeuren** *(*Post; Ochs)*, an old town with 2950 inhab., lying picturesquely in a basin. The **Blautopf*, a deep, pale-blue pool, just above the town, is the source of the Blau. Beside it is a monument to King Charles. The late-Gothic church of the old **Benedictine** Abbey, now a theological seminary, contains choir-stalls, carved by Jörg Syrlin the Younger (1493), a fine and richly carved high-altar, with statues by the same master, and paintings (history of John the Baptist) of the Swabian school.

At **Blaubeuren is** situated **one of** the pumping-stations of the **Alb Water Works** (*Albwasserversorgung*), constructed under the direction of the late Dr. von Ehmann since 1870, which extend over nearly the whole of the Rauhe Alb and supply drinking-water to the numerous communities situated on its arid plateau. The water is pumped up through cast-iron pipes from springs lying nearly 700 ft. below the level of the plateau, while the motive power is afforded by a few small tributary-brooks of the Neckar and the Danube, assisted only slightly by steam-power. There is another pumping-station at Eybach near Geislingen (p. 31), which may be conveniently visited by tourists.

Tourists who **desire to explore the** *Rauhe Alb* may follow the **somewhat** monotonous route **from Blaubeuren to** (22½ M.) *Urach*, viâ **Suppingen**, *Feldstätten* (*Post), **Zainingen**, and **Böhringen** (Hirsch).

The line leads through the valley of the *Aach*, passing the *Hohlefels* (on the left), a prehistoric habitation, to (14 M.) *Schelklingen*, with a ruined castle, 1 M. to the N.W. of which is the prettily situated former nunnery of *Urspring*. At (14½ M.) *Schmiechen* the line enters the *Schmiechthal*.

Pleasant **expedition in the** upper Schmiechthal viâ (¾ hr.) *Thalsteusslingen* (with the ruin of *Steusslingen* above, to the left) to (¼ hr.) *Hütten*, **at the** mouth of the wild *Bärenthal*; and thence past the ruin of *Justingen* (on the right) viâ *Gundershofen* to (¾ hr.) *Springen*, at the head of the valley. A road leads hence **in 2 hrs.** to *Münsingen* (p. 47), viâ *Mehrstetten*. Railway from Schmiechen to Münsingen proposed.

17 M. *Allmendingen*. — 20½ M. **Ehingen** *(Württemberger Hof*, at the station; *Kreuz; Kronprinz; Traube)*, an old town with 4100 inhab., near the confluence of the Schmiech and the *Danube*. The *Church of St. Blasius*, in a debased style, has an old Gothic tower. The *Kaiser-Wilhelms-Thurm* on the *Wolfert* commands a fine view.

The line traverses the broad valley of the winding Danube. 23 M. *Dettingen*; 25½ M. *Rottenacker*; 28 M. *Munderkingen*, an ancient little town encircled by the river. The new bridge over the Danube here has the largest stone-arch in Germany (164 ft.). — 30 M. *Untermarchthal*, below the romantic ravine of the *Grosse Lauter*.

Pleasant excursion in the *Grosse Lauterthal*, with its numerous ruined castles, viâ (1 hr.) *Lauterach*, (½ hr.) *Wolfsthal*, and (¼ **hr.**) *Laufenmühle*, with the ruin of *Reichenstein*, to (¾ **hr.**) *Unterwilzingen*; and thence past the ruins of *Nonsberg* and *Wartstein* (on the right), *Maisenburg* (left), and *Schülzburg* (right) to (3/4 hr.) *Anhausen*. Farther up are: 1/4 hr. *Indelhausen*, with the ruins of *Athayingen* **and the** *Gerbershöhle*; 1/4 **hr**. *Weiler*, with the *Bettelmannshöhle*; then past **the ruin** of *Derneck* (on the left) to (1/2 hr.) *Gundelfingen*, with two ruins. **1/2 hr.** *Bichishausen*; 1/2 hr. *Hundersingen* (ruins at both); 1/2 hr. *Buttenhausen* (**road hence** to the N. in 11/4 hr to *Münsingen*, p. 47); **1** hr. *Wasserstetten*; then past *Schloss Grafeneck* (on the right) to (1/2 hr.) *Marbach*, **a** station on the railway between Münsingen and Reutlingen (p. 47).

Farther on are the imposing buildings of the old monastery of *Obermarchthal*, the property of the Prince of Thurn and Taxis. 32 M. *Rechtenstein*, with the ruined castle of the Steins of Rechtenstein, is the prettiest point on the railway. The train crosses to the right bank of the Danube, and recrosses the river both before and beyond (351/2 M.) *Zwiefaltendorf*, with a fine stalactite cavern, discovered in 1891.

A road ascends the *Aachthal* hence to (1 hr.) Zwiefalten, a former convent (now a lunatic asylum), with a fine church. Thence to the *Wimsener Höhe*, 3/4 hr.; via Count Normann's château of *Ehrenfels* and the ruin of *Old Ehrenfels* to the romantic *Glasthal*, 11/2 hr.

381/2 M. *Unlingen*. The village lies to the left, **at the foot of the** *Bussen* (see below). — **40** M. *Riedlingen* (Post), **a small and ancient town on the left bank of the** Danube, 3/4 M. from **the railway.**

Pleasant excursion (2 hrs. via *Unlingen* to the E.; also carriage-road) hence to the top of the °*Bussen* (2515 ft.), an isolated hill rising from the upper Swabian plain, and commanding a view of the whole of Upper Swabia and of the Alps. On the hill is a pilgrimage-church, at its base the *Federsee*.

44 M. *Ertingen*, with a castle of the Prince of Thurn and Taxis. 47 M. *Herbertingen*. Opposite is the *Donauheuneburg*, near *Thalhof*; farther to the W. are other Huns' forts ('Heuneburgen') at *Pflummern*, *Langenenslingen*, and *Heudorf*.

FROM HERBERTINGEN TO MEMMINGEN, **62** M. (railway in 31/4-4 hrs.). Stations: 51/2 M. *Saulgau*, a little town with an interesting Gothic Church; 8 M. *Hochberg*; 12 M. *Altshausen* (to Pfullingen **and** Schwakenreute, see below); 15 M. *Steinenbach*; 171/2 *Aulendorf* (p. 34), junction of the Ulm-Friedrichshafen line; 23 M. *Waldsee*, prettily situated between two lakes, with a **Schloss** and **a 15th** cent. Gothic church; 28 M. *Rossberg*; 32 M. *Wolfegg*, with **the** Schloss of Prince Waldburg-Wolfegg; 361/2 M. *Kissleg* (Post), with two interesting old castles and a remarkable rococo church (branch-line to *Wangen* and *Hergatz*, p. 200). — 43 M. *Leutkirch*, **a** busy town with 3160 inhabitants. [Branch-line hence to (10 M.) **Isny**, capital of a Wurtemberg district of that **name**, prettily situated **on the** *Argen*. A fine carved altar in **the** Prot. church of **St. Nicholas.** The °*Schwarze Grat*, 2 hrs. to the E., commands a splendid view of **the Alps and Lake** of Constance.] Pretty scenery, but unimportant stations: *Unterzeil*, *Aichstetten*, *Marstetten-Aitrach*, *Mooshausen*, *Thannheim*; 591/2 M. **Buxheim**, once a Carthusian monastery, now a château of Count Waldbott-Bassenheim. — **62** M. *Memmingen*, see p. 33.

51 M. **Mengen** *(Siegerist; Rail. Restaurant)*, on the *Ablach*.

FROM MENGEN TO SIGMARINGEN, **6** M. (railway in 24 min.). Near (21/2 M.) *Scheer* the train passes through a short tunnel and crosses to the left bank of the Danube. 41/2 M. *Sigmaringendorf*. Then past the mouth of the *Lauchert*, and via *Stetten*, *Mariaberg*, *Gammertingen*, *Veringen*, etc., finally recrossing the river. — 6 M. *Sigmaringen* (see p. 54).

The line follows the *Ablach-Thal*. 54 M. *Zielfingen*. 561/2 M. *Krauchenwies* (°Goldner Adler), with **an** old castle, the summer-

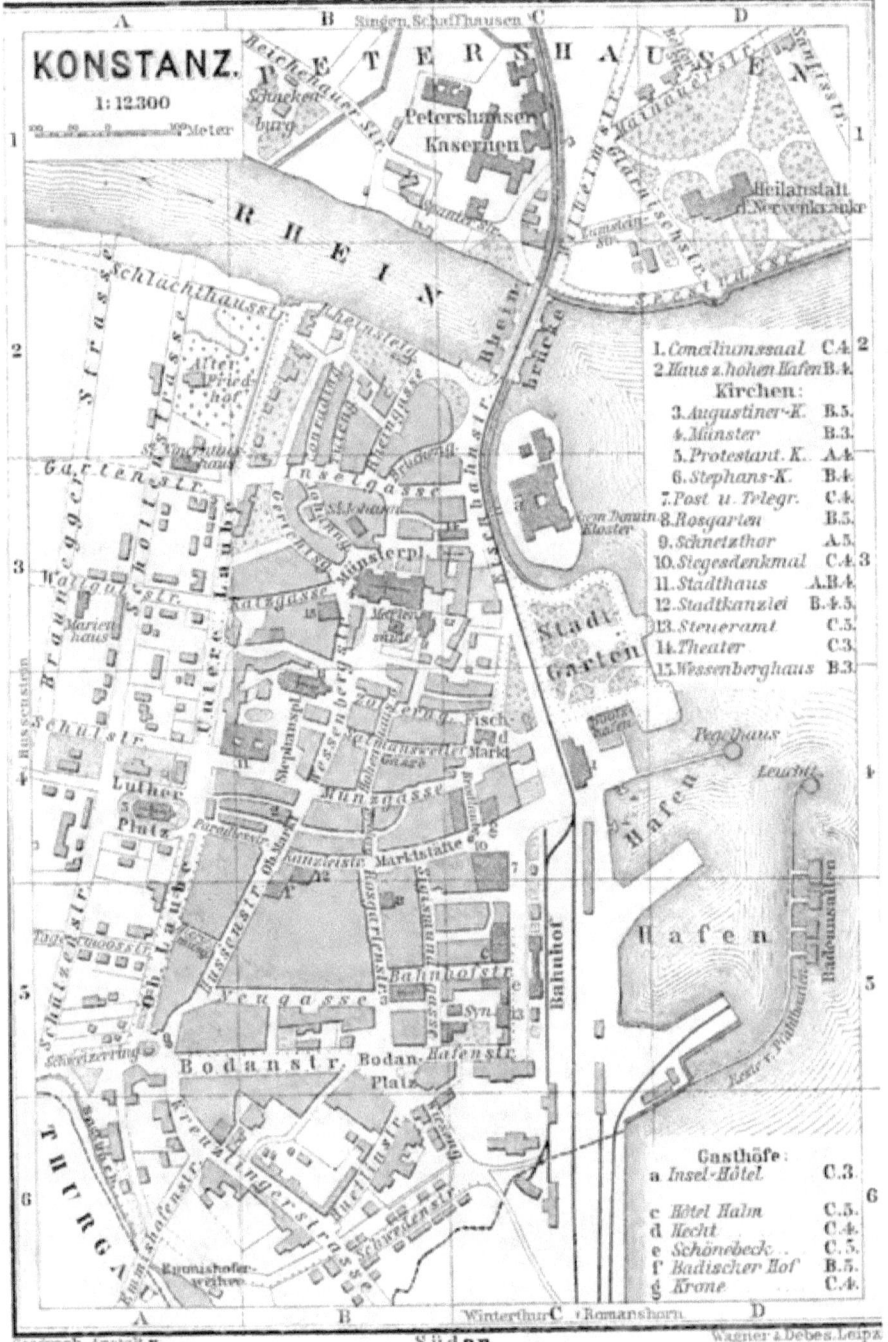

residence of the Prince of Hohenzollern; interesting erratic boulders on the *Andelsbach*, in the park. (Branch-line to *Sigmaringen* viâ *Josephslust*, 5½ M., in 24 min.) — 59 M. *Göggingen*; 61 M. *Menningen*.

63 M. **Messkirch** (**Löwe*; *Adler*; *Sonne*), a considerable little town, with a château of Prince Fürstenberg. A monument has been erected to Konradin Kreutzer, the composer, born here in 1782. The old church contains an altar-piece by H. Schäufelein (?) and monuments of the 16th cent. (epitaph of Count von Zimbern by Labenwolf). Traces of a Roman settlement have been found in the old town. — 64½ M. *Bichtlingen*; 66½ M. *Sauldorf*; 69 M. **Schwakenreute**.

FROM SCHWAKENREUTE TO AULENDORF, 30 M. (railway in 2-3 hrs.). 3 M. *Sentenhart*; 7½ M. *Aach-Linz*; 10 M. *Pfullendorf* (Schwan; Restaurant in the Rother Ochs), a very ancient town (charming excursion to *Heiligenberg*, see p. 58; 2¼ hrs.; diligence 1½, carriage 12 ℳ). Stations *Burgweiler*, *Ostrach*, *Hosskirch-Königsegg* (1½ M. to the S.E. is the partly preserved castle of *Königsegg*), *Kreenried*, and (25½ M.) *Altshausen*, junction of the Herbertingen and Aulendorf line (p. 54).

At (71 M.) *Mühlingen* we enter the wooded ravine of the *Stockach*. 73 M. *Zizenhausen*; 76 M. *Stockach* (Krone; Post), prettily situated, near which the French under Jourdan were defeated by Archduke Charles in 1799; fine view from the (½ hr.) ruin of *Nellenburg*. Then through smiling green valleys, by *Nenzingen*, *Wahlwies*, and *Stahringen*, to (86 M.) **Radolfzell** (**Schiff*; *Krone*; *Sonne*), an old town on the *Unter-See*, with a Gothic church of 1436, where the line unites with the Bâle and Constance railway. Near it, on the lake, is the *Villa Seehalde*, with a monument to its former proprietor, the poet Victor von Scheffel (d. 1886).

The railway from Radolfzell to Constance intersects the neck of land between the Unter-See and the *Ueberlinger See* (p. 57), and passes stations *Markelfingen*, *Allensbach*, and *Reichenau*. On the island of *Reichenau* in the Unter-See (visible from the train) are the buildings of a Benedictine abbey, which was suppressed in 1799 (see *Baedeker's Switzerland*). The island is joined with the mainland on the E. by a dyke. The train crosses the Rhine by an iron bridge, adorned with statues.

12½ M. **Constance**. — Hotels. °INSEL-HÔTEL (Pl. a; C, 3), in the old Dominican monastery, with garden and view of the lake, R., L. & A. 3-6, pens. 7-10 ℳ; HALM (Pl. c; C, 5), opposite the station, R. 2-3, B. 1, D. 3, pens. 7-8 ℳ; °HECHT (Pl. d; C, 4), R., L., & A. 3, B. 1, D. 3 ℳ; °SCHÖNEBECK (Pl. e; C, 5), opposite the station, R., L., & A. 2-2½, B. 1, D. 2½, pens. from 6 ℳ; °BADISCHER HOF (Pl. f; A, 5); °KRONE (Pl. g; C, 4), ANKER, SCHIFF, FALKE, BARBAROSSA, BODAN, LAMM, °SCHNETZER, second class, moderate charges. — Restaurants. °*Schönebeck*, see above, *Victoria* (beer), both opposite the station; *Engler's Biergarten*, near the public park; *Café Maximilian*, Bahnhof-Strasse.

Post Office (Pl. 7; C, 4), near the station. — *Baths* in the lake (Pl. D, 4, 5), well fitted up (bath 40 pf.; ferry 10 pf.). — *English Church Service* in summer. — The former *Constanzer Hof* (Pl. D, 1), on the lake, is now an *Institute for Nervous Patients* (Dr. G. Fischer).

Constance (1335 ft.), a free town until 1548, after the Reformation subject to Austria, and since the Peace of Pressburg in 1805 a town of Baden, has now only 17,000 inhab., though it once numbered 40,000. It is situated at the N.W. extremity of the *Lake of Constance*, or *Bodensee*, at the point where the *Rhine* emerges from it. The episcopal see, founded in 781 and held by 87 bishops in succession, was deprived of its temporalities in 1802 and suppressed in 1827.

The *Cathedral (Pl. 4; B, 3), founded in 1052, was rebuilt in its present form in 1435 and 1600. Gothic tower erected in 1850-57; the perforated spire is of light grey sandstone; on either side is a platform commanding a charming view (adm. 20 pf.).

On the *Doors* of the principal portal are °*Bas-Reliefs*, in 20 compartments, representing scenes from the life of Christ, carved in oak by Sim. Haider in 1470. The °*Choir Stalls*, with grotesque sculptures, are of the same date. The organ-loft, richly ornamented in the Renaissance style, dates from 1680. In the nave (Romanesque), the arches of which are supported by 16 monolithic pillars (28 ft. high, 3 ft. thick), sixteen paces from the principal entrance, is a large stone slab, a white spot on which always remains dry, even when the remaining portion is damp. Huss is said to have stood on this spot when the Council of 6th July, 1415, sentenced him to be burnt at the stake. In the N. chapel, adjoining the choir, is a *Death of the Virgin*, coloured stone figures life-size, 1460. Adjacent is an elegant spiral staircase. — The *Treasury* (custodian $^{1}/_{2}$-1 $\mathcal{M}$) contains a missal embellished with miniatures, 1426. On the E. side is a crypt, containing the *Chapel of the Holy Sepulchre*, with a representation of the sepulchre in stone, 20 ft. high, dating from the 13th century. On the exterior of the N. side stand two aisles of the once handsome °*Cloisters*, erected about 1480 in the Gothic style.

The Wessenberg Haus (Pl. 15; B, 3) contains books, pictures, and engravings, bequeathed to the town by the proprietor J. H. von Wessenberg (d. 1860), who for many years acted as the chief superintendent of the diocese. A number of pictures, bequeathed by the artist, Marie Ellenrieder (d. 1863), are also exhibited here.

The Church of St. Stephen (Pl. 6; B, 4), a late-Gothic building of the 15th cent., near the cathedral, with a slender tower, contains some interesting wood-carving and sculptures, but the exterior has been disfigured by modern restoration.

The Wessenberg-Strasse leads hence to the S. to the *Obere Markt*, at the corner of which stands the house 'Zum Hohen Hafen' (Pl. 2; B, 4), where Frederick VI., Burgrave of Nuremberg, was created Elector of Brandenburg by Emp. Sigismund, 18th April, 1417. Adjacent to it is an ancient building with arcades (now the Hôt. Barbarossa), styled by an inscription '*Curia Pacis*', in which Emp. Frederick I. concluded peace with the Lombard towns in 1183. — A little to the W. is the new *Protestant Church* (Pl. 5; A, 4).

The Stadt-Kanzlei, or *Town Hall* (Pl. 12; B, 4, 5), erected in the Renaissance style in 1593, was decorated in 1864 on the exterior with frescoes illustrative of the history of Constance. The apartments of the groundfloor contain the valuable *Municipal Archives*, comprising 2800 documents, the most interesting of which date from the period of the Reformation. Fine inner court. — In the Rosgarten (Pl. 8; B, 5), formerly the guild-house of the butchers, is the *Rosgarten Museum*, a rich and well-arranged collection of antiquities relating to Constance (from lake-dwellings, etc.) and of objects of natural history (adm. 40 pf.). — In the market-place is a *War Monument* (figure of Victory), by Bauer (Pl. 10).

The KAUFHAUS, or *Merchants' Hall* (Pl. 1; C, 4), by the lake, **erected in** 1388, **contains the** great *Council Chamber*, supported by massive oaken pillars, where the conclave of cardinals met at the time of the Great Council (1414-18). The hall was restored in 1866 and decorated in 1875 with frescoes illustrative of the history of the town, by *Pecht* and *Schwörer* (adm. 20 pf.). The upper floor contains a collection of Indian and Chinese curiosities (30 pf.).

The ancient *Dominican Monastery* (Pl. a; C, 3), in which Huss was confined, situated on an island in the lake, near the town, has been in part converted into a hotel (Insel-Hôtel, see p. 55). The well-preserved Romanesque cloisters, **and the** adjoining refectory **with** its graceful vaulting, repay inspection.

The house in which Huss was arrested, in the Husen-Strasse near the Schnetzthor (Pl. **A**, 5), bears a memorial tablet with his effigy, put up in 1878. Adjoining **it is an old** relief, dated 1415, with satirical verses. Some houses farther on, at the 'Obere Laube', a bronze tablet with an inscription marks the spot where Jerome of Prague was imprisoned in 1415-16. **In** the suburb of *Brühl*, $1/2$ M. to the W. of the town, is the spot where Huss and Jerome suffered martyrdom, indicated by a huge mass **of rock** with inscriptions ('Husenstein').

The *Stadt-Garten* on the lake, between the harbour and the Dominican island, affords a **pleasant** walk and a charming view of the lake **and** mountains. A **bust** of the Emp. William I. has been placed here.

The abbey of **Kreuzlingen** (*Helvetia*; **Löwe**; *Pens. Besmer*), on Swiss territory, $3/4$ **M. beyond the** S. gate, **is now a** normal school. **The** church contains **a curious piece** of wood-carving, with about 1000 small figures, executed in the 18th century.

A fine view of the lake and of the Vorarlberg **and** Appenzell Alps is obtained from the *Allmannshöhe* ($3/4$ hr.), with belvedere (Restaurant), 5 min. above the village of *Allmannsdorf*, on the road to the Mainau. — Among other pleasant objects for a walk may be mentioned the *Loretto-Kapelle* ($1/2$ **hr.**); the *Jacob*, a restaurant with **a** fine **view** ($1/2$ hr.); and the *Kleine Rigi*, above Münsterlingen (Inn; 1 hr.).

In the N.W. arm of the Lake of Constance (*Ueberlinger See*), $4 1/2$ M. **from** Constance, is situated the beautiful island of *Mainau*, formerly the **seat of a lodge of** the Teutonic Order, as **a cross** on the S. side **of the** château **(1746) indicates.** It is $1 1/2$ M. in circumference, and **is** connected with **the** mainland by a bridge 650 paces in length. Since 1853 it has been the property of the Grand-Duke of Baden, and **is** now entirely covered with pleasure-grounds, with cypresses and other semi-tropical plants. Plain restaurant near the château. Steamboat from Constance in 55 min.; rowing-boat (in 1 hr., a pleasant trip) 5 ℳ and gratuity; one-horse carr. 5-6, two-horse 8 ℳ. Pedestrians take **a shorter** route (1 hr.), partly through woods.

On **the** N. bank **of the** lake, opposite Mainau (steamboat in 40 min.), lies **Meersburg** (1463 ft.; *Seehof*, near the quay, pens. 4 ℳ, well-arranged lake-baths in the neighbourhood; *Schiff*, *Wilder Mann*, both on the lake; *Löwe*; *Pens. zum Frieden*, $1/2$ M. to the E.), a pleasant little town, with many old houses, and good and inexpensive summer-quarters. The *Old Castle*, with the Dagobert Tower (ca. 800), is said to have once been a seat of the Hohenstaufen. The old mill in the adjacent ravine is highly picturesque. The *New Castle*, long an episcopal residence, is now a deaf-and-dumb asylum. Fine views from the *Känzeli* and from the °*Edelstein*, 2 M. from the harbour. The churchyard contains the tomb of the celebrated *Mesmer* (d. 1815), the discoverer of mesmerism. The wines of Meersburg are the best on the lake.

From Meersburg the steamer plies in ³/₄ hr. more to **Ueberlingen** (°*Bad-Hôtel*, with shady garden, pension 5 ℳ; °*Löwe*; *Schiff*; *Engel*; *Krone*; *Wilder Mann*; *Adler*; *Beck*, and other restaurants; private lodgings), an ancient town with 4000 inhab., now frequented for its lake-baths and mineral spring. Pleasant grounds have been laid out on the bank of the lake. The town contains several mediæval buildings, prominent among which is the °*Town Hall*, a richly-decorated Gothic structure. The hall with its carved wood-work is an object of great interest. The 39 statuettes on the walls, representing the various elements of the German Empire (3 spiritual and 4 temporal Electors, 4 Margraves of the Empire, Landgraves, Counts, Barons, Knights, Burghers, and Peasants), are by Jacob Rues (1490). Opposite to them are portraits of the Emperors, beginning with Rudolph II. — The adjacent *Minster*, of the 14th cent., with double aisles, contains an altar with fine wood-carving of the 17th century. The *Stadt-Kanzlei*, in the Münster-Platz, has a fine doorway, of the end of the 16th century. Adjacent is an *Ethnographical and Industrial Museum*. The *Steinhaus Museum* contains a *Historical Collection* and a *Cabinet of Natural History*. Fine views of the lake from various points. The Appenzell Mts. are visible hence; also, to the S.E., the summits of the Rhætikon Mountains. About 1¹/₂ M. to the N. of Ueberlingen are the *Heidenlöcher*, mentioned in Scheffel's novel 'Ekkehard'. Excursions may also be made to the (¹/₂-³/₄ hr.) *Spezgarder Tobel* and the *Hödinger Tobel* (a picturesque ravine with waterfalls) and to *Bodmann*, on the W. shore of the lake, with an old imperial residence from which the lake (Bodensee) took its name.

A pleasant excursion may be taken from Ueberlingen or Meersburg to *Heiligenberg*. A diligence plies twice daily in 3³/₄ hrs. from Meersburg to Heiligenberg, viâ Salem; carriage and pair, there and back 18 ℳ, from Ueberlingen 12 ℳ. It is best to proceed direct from Ueberlingen to Heiligenberg, visiting Salem on the return journey. Heiligenberg (°*Adler*, pension 5 ℳ; °*Winter's Inn*, pension 4-4¹/₂ ℳ), an insignificant place, with the extensive château and park of Prince Fürstenberg, lies picturesquely on a rocky terrace 1000 ft. above the Lake of Constance. The château contains a magnificent Renaissance hall, 110 ft. long and 40 ft. broad, with a beautifully-carved wooden °Ceiling (16th cent.), probably the finest in Germany. The °Chapel (restored) is also noteworthy. The °°View from the château is strikingly beautiful: it embraces the Lake of Constance, and the entire chain of the Vorarlberg and Swiss Alps, from the Hochvogel to the Jungfrau; still better from the 'Sieben Linden' (seven lime-trees), ³/₄ M. from the village. — The same view is enjoyed from several parts of the flower-garden, on the left of the road to the castle; also from the °*Freundschafts-Höhlen*, a number of grottoes, ¹/₄ hr. to the N.W. of the inn. — From Heiligenberg to *Pfullendorf*, see p. 55.

Below Heiligenberg, to the S.W., 9¹/₂ M. from Ueberlingen, lies the suppressed Cistercian convent of Salem (*Post*), now partly occupied by the Margrave William, with large halls (the finest of which is the 'Kaiser-Saal') in the rococo style, a collection of paintings, etc. The Gothic °*Church* of the 14th cent. is lavishly adorned within with sculptures in marble (28 altars), dating from the late-Renaissance period; fine late-Gothic ciborium.

Railway from Constance to Schaffhausen and Bâle, see *Baedeker's Rhine* or *Baedeker's Switzerland*.

BAVARIA.

14. From Frankfort to Nuremberg by Würzburg.

145 M. Railway in 5¹/₄-11 hrs. (fares 18 ℳ 80, 12 ℳ 50, 8 ℳ 50; express 22 ℳ 10, 15 ℳ 60 pf.). — Trains for Hanau start from the Central Station, on the left bank of the Main, as well as from the E., or Hanau Station, outside the Allerheiligen-Thor, ³/₄ M. from the Zeil.

Frankfort, see *Baedeker's Rhine*. Soon after leaving the E. Station, we pass *Bornheim* on the left; *Offenbach* (see below) lies to the right, on the opposite bank of the *Main*. 3 M. *Mainkur;* 6 M. *Hochstadt-Dörnigheim;* 9 M. *Wilhelmsbad,* with pleasant promenades: all resorts of the Frankforters. On the Main, ¹/₂ M. to the S., is *Philippsruhe,* the seat of Landgrave Ernest of Hessen, with extensive orangeries. Near (10 M.) *Hanau* the train crosses the *Kinzig*.

From Frankfort Central Station to Hanau, 13 M. (railway in ¹/₂-³/₄ hr.). The train crosses the Main below Frankfort. 2 M. *Sachsenhausen*, a suburb of Frankfort; 3 M. *Oberrad*. 5 M. Offenbach *(Stadt Kassel)*, a manufacturing town with 35,773 inhab., founded by French refugees at the end of the 17th century. Its fancy-goods rival those of Paris, Vienna, and Berlin. There are also important engine-factories, foundries, etc. The town is commanded by a castle of Count Isenburg, built in the Renaissance style in 1564-72. — 9 M. *Mühlheim;* to the left, on the Main, is the village of *Rumpenheim*, with a château of the Landgrave of Hessen. 12¹/₂ M. *Klein-Steinheim.* The train then crosses the Main, and enters the E. station of *Hanau*.

Hanau (**Adler; *Riese; Post*, plain), a pleasant town, in the fertile *Wetterau*, with 25,000 inhab., has two railway-stations, East and West, 1¹/₄ M. apart. The modern part of the town owes its origin to Flemish and Walloon Protestants, who were banished from the Netherlands in 1597 on account of their creed. Their handicrafts, such as weaving, diamond-cutting, and the manufacture of gold and silver trinkets, still flourish. In the Parade-Platz is the house (marked by a marble tablet; now the police-office) in which the brothers Jacob (1785-1863) and *Wilhelm Grimm* (1786-1859) were born.

Near Hanau, on 30th and 31st Oct., 1813, Napoleon with 80,000 men who had retreated from Leipsic defeated Marshal Wrede with 40,000 Bavarians, Austrians, and Russians. The battle took place near the *Lamboiwald*, on the Leipsic road, beyond the Kinzig. A small stone in the wall of the Kinzig bridge bears the name of Wrede, who was wounded there.

From Hanau to *Eberbach* and *Stuttgart*, see R. 4; to *Fulda* and *Bebra* (for Leipsic and Berlin), see *Baedeker's Northern Germany*.

To the left rises the *Hahnenkamm* (p. 60). To the right *Steinheim*, a small town on the Main, with a conspicuous castle with five towers. 12¹/₂ M. *Gross-Auheim*. Just beyond it, to the right, lies *Gross-Krotzenburg*, on the site of a Roman camp, with remains of the Roman ramparts. — 15¹/₂ M. Kahl *(Krone; Lambertus)*.

From Kahl we may visit the Kahlgrund, a pretty, wooded valley, the most populous in the Spessart (p. 63). The road leads E. to (3 M.) *Alzenau*.

60 *Route 14.*   ASCHAFFENBURG.   *From Frankfort*

(410 ft.; Post; Bayr. Hof, with brewery), with a Schloss now occupied by the district court, and a ruined castle. (Diligence twice daily in 1 hr. to *Dettingen*, see below.) Ascent of the *Ludwigsthurm* on the *Hahnenkamm* (1433 ft.), a fine point of view, ³/₄ hr.— Then viâ *Kälberau* to (2¹/₂ M.) *Michelbach*, where wine is produced, *Steinbach*, and (6 M.) *Mömbris* (Karpfen; Kempf), where we cross the river *Kahl*. From (8 M.) *Schimborn* (Rosenberger), we proceed by the road coming from Aschaffenburg to the E. viâ *Erlenbach*, at the foot of the *Klosterberg* (1260 ft.; fine view), and *Kleinblankenbach* to (15¹/₂ M.) Schöllkrippen (*Fleckenstein; Steigerwald; Mähler*), whence we may visit the forester's house '*Am Engländer*' (rfmts on Sun. and Thurs.), descending to *Jakobsthal* and through the *Lohrbach-Thal* to the station of (1¹/₄ hr.) *Heigenbrücken* (p. 62). About **20 min.** to the S. of the forester's **house** is the *Steigkoppe* (1650 ft.), with a scaffolding which affords a fine view. — From Schöllkrippen to Aschaffenburg (**see** below) omnibus daily in 3 hrs.; to Gelnhausen in 4 hrs.

18¹/₂ M. **Dettingen**, where the British, Hanoverian, Austrian, and Hessian troops, commanded by George II. of England, defeated the French on 27th July, 1743: the first decisive success of Austria in the War of Succession. To Alzenau, see above. — 21¹/₂ M. *Klein-Ostheim*.

25¹/₂ M. **Aschaffenburg**. — Hotels. *PRINZ-REGENT LUITPOLD, opposite the station; *ADLER (Pl. a; C, 3), R. & B 2¹/₂-3, D. 2¹/₂ *M*; *GOLDNES FASS (Pl. b; B, 2), R. 1 *M* 60-2 *M* 50, B. 80 pf., pens. from 5 *M*; FREIHOF (Pl. c; C, 3); GEORGI, EISENBAHN-HÔTEL, both at the station. — **Weiss's Restaurant*, at the 'Riese', Herstall-Str.; beer at the *Adler* and *Kalte Loch*.

Aschaffenburg (341 ft.), with 13,609 inhab., was for centuries the summer-residence of the Electors of Mayence, but since 1814 has belonged to Bavaria. The extensive *Schloss*, with its four lofty towers (170 ft.), erected 1605-14, contains a *Library* (open Tues. and Thurs., 11-12) with valuable 'Incunabula' (*e.g.* Guttenberg's forty-two-line Bible) and books of the Gospels with admirable miniatures (the finest by Glockenton, an artist of Nuremberg, 1524); also a collection of 20,000 engravings and a **Gallery of Pictures* (346 in number). Adm. 9-12 and 2-6 (50 pf., incl. adm. to the Pompeianum. p. 61).

No. 34. *J. Pynar*, **Raising** of Lazarus; 35. *Seb. Vranck*, **Marauders**; *37. *Sal. van Ruysdael*, River-scene; °55. *A. Elsheimer*, Christ on the way to Emmaus; °58. *Rembrandt* (or *Arnold van Gelder?*), Ecce Homo (1660); 62. *Rubens*, Silenus; *A. van Everdingen*, Norwegian landscape; 85. *Eglon van der Neer*, Conversation-piece; 96. *Jan Brueghel*, 102. *H. Sachtleven*, Landscapes; 109. *G. Dou*, Dentist; 99, 112, 113. *J. Momper*, Landscapes; °125. *A. van Ostade*, Cottage interior (1639); °132. *N. Berchem*, Sunny landscape; 136, *142. *A. van der Neer*, Landscapes; 139. *J. D. de Heem*, Still-life; 143. *Ph. Wouwerman*, Horseman at a tavern (youthful work); 144. *D. Teniers*, Soldiers gambling; 148. *G. du Bois*, Edge of the wood; *149. *P. de Bloot*, Peasants in a village-street; *160. *D. Verburgh*, Large landscape; 169. *A. van de Velde*, Horsemen; 171. *Angelica Kauffmann*, Madonna; °176. *H. Sachtleven*, Large mountain landscape (1651); *L. Giordano*, 198. Esther, 199. Queen of Sheba; 206, 217, 225, 238, etc. *A. de Gelder*, Passion of Christ; 209. *Raph. Camphuisen*, River-scene; 210. *Rembrandt*, Resurrection; 211. *C. Netscher*, Portrait; °218, 221, 226, °228. *Corn. de Heem*, Fruit and flower pieces; 214, 227. *C. Huysmans*, Landscapes; °220. *A. Cuyp*, Cavaliers with landscape (finest specimen of this master in Germany); 222. *Bonaventura Peters*, Sea-piece; 233. *J. Jordaens*, St. Augustine; 234. *Manfredi* (not P. **Lastman**), Herodias; 235. *De Heem*, Still-life; °248, 251. *C. de Vos* (or *Mirevelt?*), Man and his wife; 249. *A. Keirinex*, Wood-scene; 250. *D. Seghers*,

Flowers; 255. *J. Duck*, Looting a house; 256. *J. van Goyen*. Large river-scene (1646); 258. *N. Berchem*, Landscape with gipsies; 261, 290. *H. Baldung*, Nativity, Crucifixion.

Visitors with tickets (comp. p. 60) are admitted to the garden and follow a picturesque path, with steps and arbours, to the exit opposite the Pompeianum (see below).

The Romanesque *Stiftskirche (Pl. 14; abbey-church), founded in 980, but frequently altered, has cloisters of the 12th century.

The INTERIOR has been skilfully restored since 1881. In the right aisle is a *Monument in bronze, with a gilded sarcophagus said to contain the relics of St. Margaret, dating from 1540. In the choir is the monument of Albert of Brandenburg (d. 1545), Elector of Mayence, cast in 1525 during his lifetime, by *P. Vischer*, and opposite to it a Madonna in bronze by *Joh. Vischer*. To the right of the principal entrance is a large monument in alabaster of the last Elector, Frederick Charles Joseph (d. 1802). The church also possesses three valuable paintings by *M. Grünewald*, who lived for some time at Aschaffenburg (Resurrection, Pietà, and St. Valentinian, belonging to the altar-piece in the Pinakothek at Munich).

The old abbey-buildings now contain the *Municipal Collections* (open Sun. 10-12; at other times on application to Hr. Broili, the director): Roman antiquities found at Aschaffenburg (votive tablets, altars, vases, bronzes), prehistoric relics of the stone age, minerals, reminiscences of the electoral period, etc.

The *Church of St. Agatha* (Pl. 10; B, 2), to the N.E. of the Schloss, built in the Transition style in 1115 and of late judiciously restored, contains many ancient tombstones.

To the W. of the church, on the lofty bank of the Main beyond the Schloss-Garten, stands the *Pompeianum (Pl. A, 2; adm. 8.30-12 and 2-6, 50 pf., comp. above), a villa erected by King Ludwig I. in 1824-49 in imitation of the 'House of Castor and Pollux' at Pompeii, and adorned with mural paintings. The mosaic (Juno and Jupiter) on the wall of the summer dining-room was presented by Pope Gregory XVI. View from the platform.

Pleasant walk through the *Schönthal* (Pl. D, 3) and the (¼ hr.) *Fasanerie* to the *Schmerlenbacher Wald*. — On the left bank of the Main, 2 M. to the W., where the river is crossed by a bridge constructed in 1430, is the *Schöne Busch* (comp. the Plan), a royal park with a château, orangery, and inn. — Another pleasant walk is by (4½ M.) *Johannesberg*, with its new belvedere, to the *Ludwigsthurm* on the *Hahnenkamm* (p. 60). Then down by *Alzenau* (p. 60).

FROM ASCHAFFENBURG TO MAYENCE, 46½ M. (direct railway in 1½-3½ hrs.). The through-trains from Mayence (and Cologne) to Munich and Vienna travel over this line. 9 M. *Babenhausen* is the junction for Hanau and Eberbach (p. 23). 26 M. *Darmstadt*, and (46½ M.) *Mayence*, see Baedeker's Rhine.

FROM ASCHAFFENBURG TO AMORBACH, 28 M. (railway in 1¾-2 hrs.). Soon after quitting the station the line sweeps round towards the S., passing the Fasanerie (see above) on the left, and follows the right bank of the Main, rich in vines and fruit-trees. 4 M. *Obernau*; 5½ M. *Sulzbach*, 3½ M. to the E. of which lie the picturesque baths (*Curhaus*) of *Sodenthal*, with springs containing salt and bromine; 9 M. *Kleinwallstadt*; 11 M. *Obernburg* (Kunig), opposite which, on the other side of the river, is the little town of that name, with a busy trade in timber and wine. At (15 M.) *Wörth*, a small town with an old château, the train crosses the Main. 16 M. *Klingenberg* (Hirsch; Krone); the small town, noted for its excellent red wine and its fire-proof clay, lies on the opposite bank. 18½ M. *Laudenbach*. 20½ M. *Kleinheubach* (Adler), with Schloss and park of Prince Löwenstein-Wertheim-Rosenberg (chapel with *Frescoes by E. Steinle). On the opposite bank lies *Grossheubach*, 1 M. to the S.E. of which is the Franciscan monastery of *Engelsberg*, with a pilgrimage-church (view), where Dom Miguel of Braganza (d. 1866), pretender to the throne of Portugal, is buried. In a wood near this (1½ M. from the village) are the so-called *Hain-* or *Heunen-Säulen*, twelve huge columns of sandstone, remains of an ancient quarry of the Roman period, which seems to have been suddenly abandoned.

22½ M. Miltenberg (395 ft.; *Engel; Riese*), a thriving little town of 3500 inhab., in a charming situation, stretches for a considerable distance between the river and the wooded height on its bank. Its quarries of variegated sandstone were known in the time of the Romans. The old Schloss of the Electors of Mayence, built in the 15th cent. and destroyed in 1552, contains Hr. Conrady's valuable collection of antiquities and objects of art (admission free). The *Municipal Collection of Antiquities* is in the old hospital. Several interesting timber-built houses. — Then *Weilbach* and (28 M.) Amorbach (*Badischer Hof; Post*), a small town with 2500 inhab. and mineral baths, seat of the Prince of Leiningen, whose handsome English-Gothic château of *Wald-Leiningen* lies 6 M. to the S. The old abbey-church, with two early-Romanesque towers and a nave rebuilt in the rococo style in the 18th cent., is now used for Protestant services. The abbey-mill and other Gothic edifices in the town, and the rococo library-hall in the former chapter-house should be noticed. — Hence to the Odenwald, see *Baedeker's Rhine*.

FROM MILTENBERG TO WERTHEIM, 18 M. (diligence twice daily in 3¾ hrs.). The picturesque road, which will repay even walkers, runs on the left bank of the Main through the fertile and well-wooded valley, dotted here and there with ruined castles, viâ *Bürgstadt* (near which, on the *Wannenberg*, are an ancient Germanic rampart and a deserted Roman quarry), to (5 M.) Freudenberg (*Rose*), a picturesque little place, with the ruins of a castle of the 12th cent. destroyed in the Thirty Years' War. Farther on, to the left, are the extensive quarries of *Reistenhausen;* then *Fechenbach* with the ruined *Kollenberg, Dorfprozelten,* and *Stadtprozelten* (*Post; Adler*), with a castle of the now extinct Schenks of Klingenberg, destroyed by the French in 1688. Thence by *Mondfeld* and *Grünenwörth* to *Wertheim* (see p. 63).

The line passes a monument (r.) to the Austrians who fell in 1866, and ascends by (30 M.) *Hösbach* and (32 M.) *Laufach* to the long tunnel of (36½ M.) *Heigenbrücken* (Fleckenstein's Inn, at the station). About 3½ M. to the N., above *Jakobsthal*, is the *Steigkoppe* (p. 60). The line here enters the higher regions of the *Spessart* (p. 63), winds through the wooded and grassy *Lohrbach-Thal*, and runs across numerous bridges and through many cuttings in the red sandstone to (45 M.) *Partenstein* and (49 M.) *Lohr*, on the Main. About 1 M. to the S. is Lohr (*Kessler; Hirsch; Krone; Röder*), an industrial little town, prettily situated. The Rathhaus and the Parish Church are interesting.

FROM LOHR TO WERTHEIM, 23 M. (railway in 2 hrs.). The train ascends the pleasant valley of the Main, following the right bank of the winding river. 1 M. *Stadt Lohr* (see above); 2½ M. *Rodenbach;* 5½ M. *Neustadt am Main*, with a well-restored church (Romanesque basilica), dating from a Benedictine monastery founded in the 8th century. 9½ M. *Rothenfels* (Anker, good wine), with large quarries and a château of Prince Löwenstein-Wertheim-Rosenberg. 11 M. *Hafenlohr;* 12½ M. *Marktheidenfeld* (*Post; Schöne Aussicht*), with a handsome bridge over the Main and near a large trout-breeding establishment. Nearing (16 M.) *Trennfeld*, we observe on the right *Schloss Triefenstein*, once an Augustinian provostry, now the property of Prince Löwenstein-Wertheim-Freudenberg, very handsomely fitted up (tapestry, collection of arms); beautiful park and charming view. On the left bank are *Homburg*, with an old castle, and the

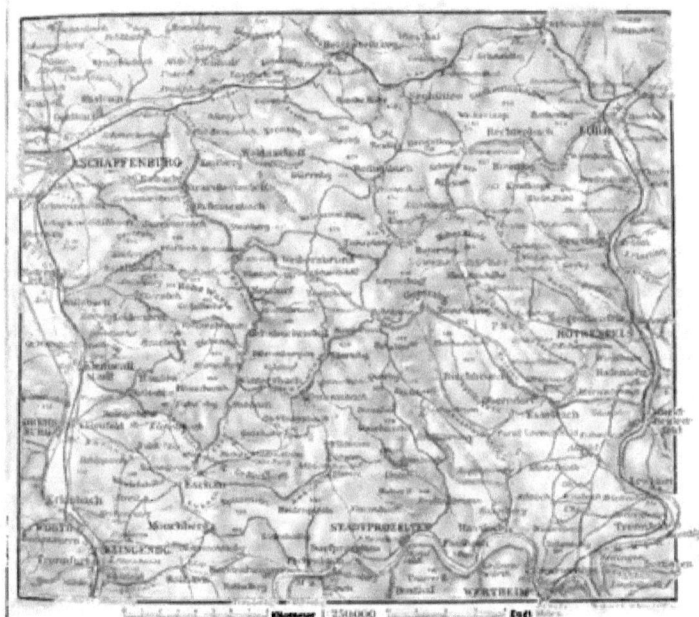

Burkardus-Höhle, the cave in which St. Burkhard, first bishop of Würzburg, died in 752. A tunnel, 550 yds. long, below the *Bettinger Berg*, brings us to (21 M.) *Kreuzwertheim*. — 23 M. **Wertheim** (*°Badischer Hof*, in the town; *°Held*, on the Main, with garden and fine view; *Löwensteiner Hof, Löwe, Ochs*, unpretending), an old town with 3540 inhab., the residence of Prince Löwenstein-Wertheim-Freudenberg, is prettily situated at the influx of the Tauber into the Main, at the foot of a wooded hill, crowned by the extensive and partially preserved ruins of a castle destroyed in the Thirty Years' War. Several quaint houses of the 16th century. The situation of the town, with the imposing red sandstone ruin above it, somewhat resembles that of Heidelberg. The church contains fine monuments of Counts Joh. and Mich. von Wertheim (15th and 16th cent.).

The S. part of the Spessart, the finest and most extensive forest-district in Germany, noted for its gigantic oaks and beeches, and its game, is washed on three sides by the Main, and is bounded on the N. by the valleys of the Aschaff and the Lohr, through which the railway from Aschaffenburg to Lohr runs. Almost in the centre of this district rises the *Geyersberg* (1920 ft.), from which long hills radiate to the W., S., and E., on the crests of which we may walk in the delicious leafy shade for hours at a time (as in the Vosges Mts.). On the W. slope of the Geyersberg, 11 M. from Stadtprozelten (p. 62) and as far from Marktheidenfeld (p. 62), Wertheim (see above), and Lohr (p. 62), lies **Rohrbrunn** (1520 ft.), a summer-resort consisting of two forester's houses and a new inn (pens. 3 1/2 ℳ), and a good centre for exploring the Spessart. Opposite is (10 min.) a hunting-lodge of Prince Luitpold, behind the forester's house of Diana, where the wild swine are fed at 5 or 6 p.m. To the S. (20 min.) is the *Annahöhe* or *Hohe Warte* (1210 ft.), a forester's house, whence we survey the vast leafy ocean of the Spessart. We may also visit a venerable oak, 1000 years old, 8-10 min. to the S.W. To the N.E. a beautiful forest-path leads past the (1 1/4 hr.) forester's house of *Jägerverein* to (1 hr.) **Lichtenau** (785 ft.; °Inn), prettily situated in the wooded valley of the *Hafenlohr* (wild swine feeding). Thence we either descend the valley to (3 1/2 hrs.) *Hafenlohr* (p. 62), or go to the N. through fine timber across the *Schwarze Rücken* to *Rechtenbach* and (3 1/2 hrs.) *Lohr* (p. 62). — A road leads from Rohrbrunn to the S.W. past the forester's house of *Diana* and through the *Dammbach-Thal* to (1 1/2 hr.) *Krausenbach* (Inn), whence we ascend to the left (guide advisable) to the (1/2 M.) *Gaishöhe* (1705 ft.), on which a view-tower has recently been built. We descend past the ruined *Wildenstein* to (1 1/4 hr.) *Eschau* (670 ft.; °*Krone*), whence a carriage-road ascends the *Elsawa-Thal* to *Hobbach* (Villa Elsawa of Dr. Websarg, pension 4-4 1/2 ℳ) and Mespelbrunn (see below), and descends to (4 1/2 M.) *Obernburg* (p. 61). — Charmingly situated, 1 3/4 hr. to the N. of Rohrbrunn (guide advisable), lies *Mespelbrunn*, the ancestral castle of the founder of Würzburg University (p. 68; refreshments in the forester's house, to the left). From this point a pleasant route (guide-posts) leads by *Neudorf* and the *Hohe Warte* (1210 ft.) to (2 hrs.) *Bad Sodenthal* and (1 1/4 hr.) *Sulzbach* (p. 61).

54 1/2 M. *Langenprozelten*. Near (58 M.) **Gemünden** *(Kreiser; Rail. Restaurant)* we cross the *Fränkische Saale*, which here falls into the Main. The little town lies picturesquely at the foot of wooded hills, commanded by the ruins of *Schorenberg*, which was destroyed in 1243.

FROM GEMÜNDEN TO ELM, 28 1/2 M. (railway in 1 1/4-2 3/4 hrs.). The line runs through the pleasant *Sinnthal*. Stations *Rineck*, *Burgsinn*, *Mittelsinn*, *Jossa* (to Brückenau, see p. 85), *Sterbfritz*, *Vollmerz* (near it, to the E., the ruins of the *Steckelburg*, once the seat of Ulrich von Hutten); then *Elm*, a station on the Bebra-Hanau Railway (see *Baedeker's Northern Germany*).

FROM GEMÜNDEN TO HAMMELBURG (17 1/2 M.), railway in 1 1/4 hr. through the pretty *Saale-Thal*. Stations: *Schönau*, with a convent on the hill to the right; *Wolfsmünster*, *Gräfendorf*, *Michelaubrück*, *Morlesau*, *Diebach*. — **Hammelburg** (°*Post*; °*Schwarzer Adler*), an ancient town, picturesquely situated on the right bank of the Saale, presented by Charlemagne to the abbey of Fulda. On the opposite bank, on a vine-clad hill, rises

Schloss Saaleck. — From Hammelburg to *Kissingen* (p. 83), 12½ M., diligence thrice daily in 3 hrs., viâ *Fuchsstadt*, *Trimberg*, with a well-preserved ruin, and *Euerdorf* (Stern). Walkers pass to the left of Fuchsstadt.

FROM GEMÜNDEN TO SCHWEINFURT (Kissingen), 31½ M., railway in 1¾ hr. — Beyond (2 M.) *Wernfeld* (see below) the line turns to the left into the fertile and smiling *Wernthal*, running now on one side of the stream, now on the other. 4 M. *Gössenheim*, 2½ M. to the N. of which is the ruined castle of *Homburg*; 7½ M. *Eussenheim*; 11 M. *Thüngen*, with a château; 15 M. *Mildesheim*; 17½ M. *Arnstein*, a small town with an old château; 21 M. *Mühlhausen*. The line quits the Wernthal, passing *Schloss Werneck* (p. 82) on the N.E., and at (25 M.) *Weigolshausen* joins the railway from Würzburg to (31½ M.) *Oberndorf-Schweinfurt* (p. 82).

59½ M. *Wernfeld* (see above). — 66 M. *Karlstadt* (530 ft.), once the fortified frontier-town of the episcopal see of Würzburg, and still surrounded with walls and towers, is said to have been founded by Charles Martel, and extended by Charlemagne. Professor Bodenstein, the instigator of the Puritanical iconoclasm, was born here, and has thence been surnamed 'Karlstadt'. On the opposite hill, on the left bank of the Main, is the ruined *Karlsburg*; and farther on, at *Laudenbach*, is a château of Prince Wertheim, destroyed during the War of the Peasants. — 71 M. *Retzbach*; 73 M. *Thüngersheim*; 77 M. *Veitshöchheim*, with a royal château and park; 78½ M. *Zell*. Opposite the vine-clad *Steinberg* lies the old monastery of *Oberzell*, now König & Bauer's printing-press factory.

81 M. Würzburg. — Hotels. °KRONPRINZ VON BAYERN (Pl. b; D, 2), Residenz-Platz, R., L., & A. 2½-3½, B. 1, D. 3 ℳ; °RUSSISCHER HOF (Pl. a; C, 2), Untere Theater-Str., near the station, R., L., & A. from 2¼. B. 1, D. 2½ ℳ; °SCHWAN (Pl. c; B, 3), Büttnersgasse, with view of the river, R. & A. 2 ℳ-2 ℳ 80, B. 90 pf., D. 2½ ℳ; °RÜGMER (Pl. d; C, 2), by the theatre; WÜRTTEMBERGER HOF (Pl. e; C, 2), in the Markt, R., L., & A. 2 ℳ 80 pf., B. 1, D. 2½ ℳ, commercial; °BAHNHOF (Pl. k; C, D, 1), °NATIONAL (Pl. 1; C, 1), with café-restaurant, ZÄNGLEIN (Pl. m; C, 1), °SCHOTT (*Zum Deutschen Kaiser*; Pl. n, C, 1), all near the station and moderate. FRÄNKISCHER HOF (Pl. f; C, 2), Eichhorn-Str.; ADLER (Pl. g; B, 2), Marktgasse; WITTELSBACHER HOF (Pl. h; B, 2), in the Markt; LANDSBERG (Pl. i; C, 2), Semmels-Str. — PENSION HEFFNER, Petersplatz 6, R. 1-2, pension 3-4 ℳ, well spoken of.

Cafés-Restaurants. °*Alhambra*, Franziskaner-Platz; *Schnitzer* (Vienna Café), Kürschnerhof; *Café National*, at the station, etc. — WINE. *Haderlein*, Dominikaner-Platz, with garden; *Ziegler*, Julius Promenade; *Stümmer*, Martinsgasse; *Bäuerlein*, Alte Brücke; wine-rooms in the *Juliusspital*, to the right of the entrance, and the *Bürgerspital* (Pl. C, 2), Semmels-Str.; *Wend*, Domerpfarrgasse, wine-room, preserved meats, etc. (the last three are closed at 8 p.m.). — BEER. *Platz'scher Garten*, outside the Rennweger Thor (Pl. D, E, 3), concerts several times weekly; *Letzter Hieb* (Pl. F, 3), a garden-restaurant about ½ M. farther on, with fine view; *Hutten'scher Garten*, outside the Sander-Thor (Pl. C, 4), at the tramway-terminus, etc.

Cabs. From the station to the town: 1-2 pers. 60, 3-4 pers. 80 pf. — By time: each ¼ hr. of the first hour, 1-2 pers. 40, 3-4 pers. 50 pf.; each additional ¼ hr. 30 or 40 pf.; from 10 p. m. to 6 a. m. double fares.

Tramway from the station viâ the Kaiser-Str., Dom-Str., and Sander-Str. to Sanderau station (10, 15, or 20 pf.).

Post & Telegraph Offices in the Parade-Platz (Pl. C, 2) and at the station.

Theatre (Pl. C, 2); performances in winter only.

River Baths. *Wellenbad*, by the quay below the old bridge; *Damenbad*, above the old bridge, etc. Warm Baths: *Dr. Wirsing*, Strohgasse; *Jäger*, at the Holzthor.

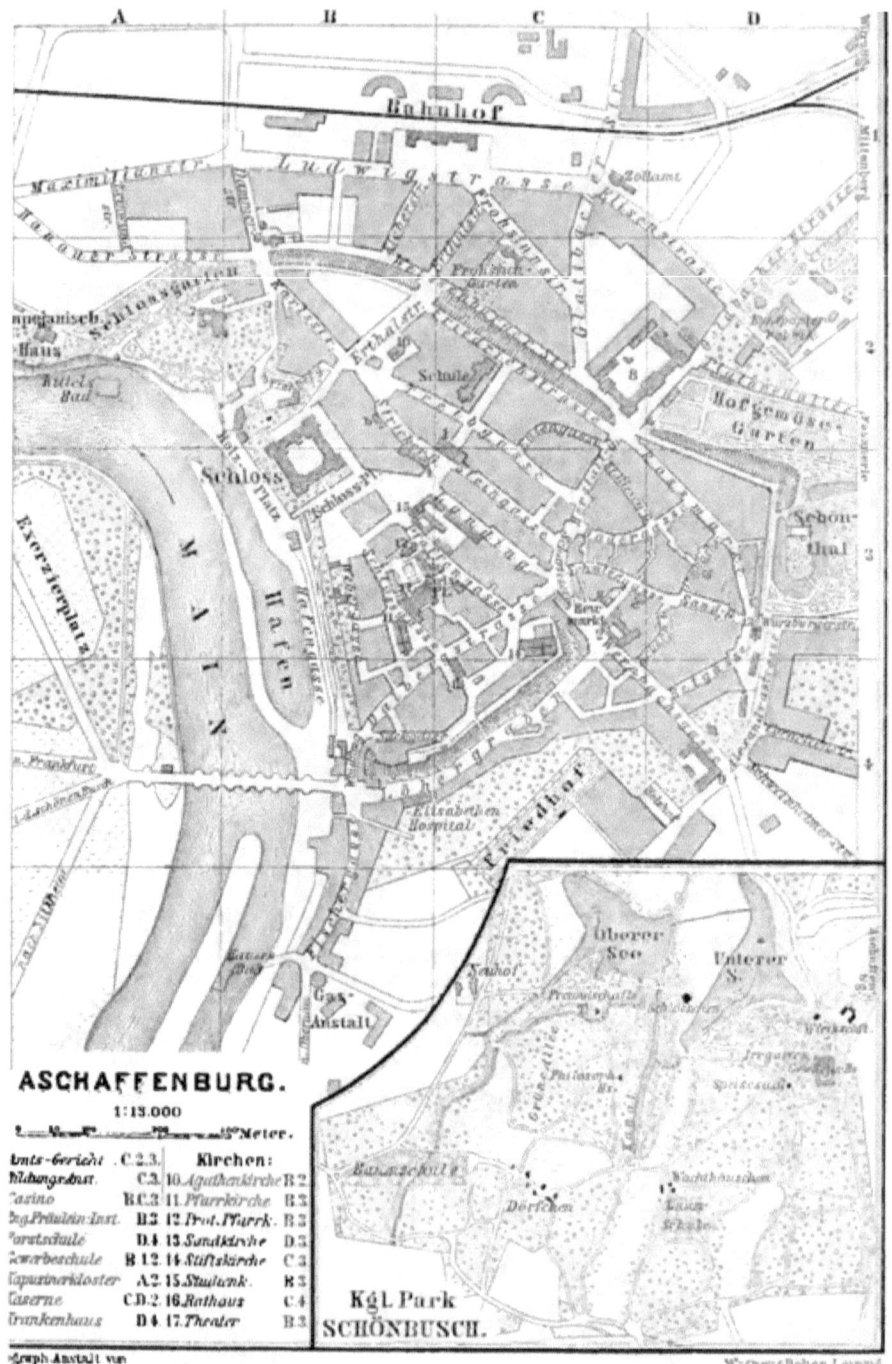

Würzburg (575 ft.; 61,032 inhab., 10,000 Prot.), **the** ancient capital of an episcopal principality, and now that of the **Bavarian province** of Unterfranken or Lower Franconia, **is charmingly situated in the vine-clad** valley of the Main. The inner and **older part of the town, of which churches** and ecclesiastical buildings form the chief feature, **is encircled** with well-kept promenades, nearly 3 M. in length, while **the modern quarters,** including the new university buildings, present a bright and handsome appearance.

Würzburg is one of the most venerable cities in Germany, having been the seat of **a bishop** since 741, when Burkardus, the first bishop, was consecrated **by** St. Boniface. The bishops soon attained to great **wealth and power, and were** created dukes of Franconia in 1120, a dignity confirmed to them by Emp. Frederick I. in 1168. Down to 1803, when Würzburg was incorporated with Bavaria, the principality was governed by an unbroken line of these bishop-princes, whose sway in the 17th and 18th cent. often included the see of Bamberg also. From 1805 to 1813 Würzburg was the capital of a grand-duchy of the Rhenish Confederation. The fortifications were removed in 1869-74.

From the **Bahnhof-Platz** (Pl. C, 1), where the *Kilian Fountain* was erected in 1895, the Kaiser-Strasse and Theater-Strasse (comp. p. 67) lead to the (10 min.) *Residenz-Platz* (Pl. D, 2, 3), in which **rises the Luitpold Fountain,** erected in 1894 on the 70th birthday **of the Prince Regent Luitpold by the** circles of Lower Franconi a and **Aschaffenburg. The fountain, designed by** *F. von Miller,* is surmounted by a figure of Franconia, with a portrait-medallion of Prince Luitpold below; still lower are lifesize figures **of** Tilmann Riemenschneider, Matthias Grünewald, and Walther von der Vogelweide.

The **extensive** royal, formerly episcopal, *Palace *(Residenz),* one of the grandest and most effective of 18th cent. edifices of the kind, was erected in **1720-44** in the rococo style from *Neumann's* **designs.** It is 550 **ft. long, 290 ft.** deep, **and 70** ft. high, and contains **7** courts, 283 **rooms, a chapel, and a theatre.**

The principal STAIRCASE, in the central structure, to the left, **is** very imposing; its lofty ceiling is adorned with a fresco by *G. B. Tiepolo* of Venice, representing Olympus and the four quarters of the globe. The ceiling-painting in the large KAISERSAAL, depicting the marriage of Emp. Frederick I. and Beatrix of Burgundy, which took place at Würzburg in 1156, is also by *Tiepolo.* The PALACE CHAPEL, which **contains two** altar-pieces by Tiepolo, is sumptuously enriched with marble **and** bronze. The former episcopal apartments are richly decorated with French tapestry (Battle of Alexander, presented by Louis XIV.), etc. Magnificent *Mirror Saloon. — The PICTURE GALLERY is particularly rich in still-life pieces by *G. B. Weenix, J. van Streeck, Elias Vonck, B. van der Meer, C. Luyks, A. van Utrecht,* etc. Among other **works** may be mentioned: **N. Berchem,* Juno and Argus (an early work); **M. Stoop,* Robbers in a cottage; *H. van Balen,* Holy Family (lifesize); **J. Livens,* Mourning for Christ; *J. Verkolje,* Party on a harbour. — The huge CELLARS, probably the largest in Germany, **contain 200 casks of** excellent Franconian wine produced by **the** royal **vineyards. — The** palace is shown daily at 10, 11, 2, and **3 o'clock** (50 pf. each; the **visit takes** 3/4 hr.). **Visitors ring for the castellan in the back-** court **of the left wing.** Adjacent is **the office of the cellarer.**

The left (N.) wing of the palace contains **the** *Collection of the Historical Society* (open on Sundays in summer, 10-12; at other times 50 pf. each pers.), and in the right **wing is the** *Picture Gal-*

lery of the Kunstverein (daily, except Sat., 10-3). — The **Hofgarten*, at the back of the palace, laid out in 1729, and afterwards frequently altered, is a favourite promenade. It contains a new *Orangery* (20 pf.), with figures from Herrenchiemsee, and a café.

In the broad Hofstrasse, leading W. from the palace to the cathedral, is the *Maxschule* (Pl. C, 2), containing the commercial and grammar schools and the collections of the polytechnic society.

The **Cathedral** (Pl. C, 2), in the Parade-Platz, a cruciform basilica in the Romanesque style, begun in 862 and consecrated in 1189, was materially altered in 1240 (to which date the two E. towers and the apse belong).

The INTERIOR, marred by 18th cent. restoration, contains numerous monuments of bishops: those of Bibra (d. 1519) and *Scherenberg (d. 1495), by the 6th and 7th pillars on the right, were executed by *Riemenschneider* (p. 77). The left aisle contains several fine brasses with low reliefs, *e.g.* that of Peter von Aufsess (d. 1522), by the 9th pillar. On the left side of the nave is a font of 1279. Altar-pieces of the 17-18th centuries. In the choir hangs a large crucifix by Riemenschneider.

Adjoining the cathedral on the N. rises the **Neumünster Church** (Pl. C, 2), of the 11th century. The red rococo façade towards the Kürschnerhof was constructed in 1711-19 by Pezani; the dome was added in 1731. The well-proportioned interior was decorated with stucco and gilding in the 18th century. On the choir of the Neumünster Church, facing the cathedral, is a tablet with a Latin and a German inscription (the latter by King Ludwig I.), erected in 1843 to the memory of *Walther von der Vogelweide* (d. about 1230), the greatest of the mediæval German poets, who was interred in the old cloisters.

A sum of money was left by the poet for purchasing food for the birds, and a vase was placed on the top of the original tomb for this purpose. The new monument is similarly provided, but the bequest has long since been diverted to the use of the canons themselves.

The Martinsgasse leads hence to the MARKT (Pl. B, C, 2), in which rises the elegant Gothic **Marienkapelle*, erected in 1377-1441, and restored in 1856, when the perforated spire was added.

The reliefs on the three portals (Annunciation, Last Judgment, Virgin enthroned) are coeval with the church. The *Statues by the S. portal (Adam and Eve) and on the buttresses (four restored) are by *Riemenschneider*. Observe in the interior the tombstone of a knight (1499) and wooden *Statues (SS. Dorothea and Margaretha) by *Riemenschneider*.

To the S.W. of the market-place lies the old *Rathhaus* (Pl. B, C, 2), the oldest part of which, the so-called Grafen-Eckartsthurm, built in 1453-56, faces the Domstrasse. In the same street is the *Vierröhren-Brunnen*, a fountain erected in 1733. The Domstrasse leads to the Old Main Bridge, see p. 68.

From the Domstrasse the Augustinergasse and the Neubaustrasse lead to the S. to the JULIUS MAXIMILIAN **UNIVERSITY**, founded in 1582 by Bishop Julius (p. 68), and attended by about 1550 students, of whom about 900 are medical. The University Buildings (Pl. C, 2), designed by Adam Kal in 1587, contain various collections: the *Zoological*, the *Mineralogical and Geological*, the *Art-*

History Museum (Wagner's collection of antiquities, including Greek monuments, vases, fragments of statues, casts from antique works, tapestry, wood-carvings by *Riemenschneider*, early **Christian** lamps, **rings**, etc.), a somewhat extensive *Picture Gallery* (open Thurs. **9-1**), the *Cabinet of Engravings* (Mon. and Wed., 9-12), etc. All the collections are closed in vacation, though strangers may obtain admission for a fee.

PICTURE GALLERY (artists' names not all authenticated). *Spinello Aretino*, **Altar**-piece; *Raphael* (?), Madonna with the carnation; *Bellini* (?), Rest on the Flight into Egypt; works by *Tiepolo*, *Tintoretto*, *Pordenone*; *Poussin*, Bacchanalian scene; *Millet*, Italian landscape; *Bourguignon*, Battle; *Greuze*, Girl's head; *Velazquez* (?), Two portraits; *Skreta*, Three portraits; *Van der Neer*, Moonlight scene; *Brueghel & Van Balen*, Landscape; *Hogarth*, **Street**-scene; *'Hell-fire' Brueghel*, Temptation of St. Antony; *Sachtleven*, River-scene; *Hondecoeter*, Poultry-yard; *Snyders* (?), Greengrocer; *Rubens* (?), Roman battle; *Van Dyck*, St. Jerome; *Peters*, Flight into Egypt; *Fr. Hals*, Portrait; *Clueisz & De Heem*, Still-life; *Elshaimer*, Destruction of Sodom; *Cranach*, **Lot and** his daughters; *Denner*, Old woman; *Schütz*, Four landscapes, etc.

The S.W. side of the quadrangle, in the Neubau-Strasse, is occupied by the *University Church* or *Neubau-Kirche*, built in 1582-91 in a curiously mixed Gothic and Renaissance style and recently well restored. The tower is used as an *Observatory* (Sat. 2-4). Adjoining the church on the E. is the *University Library*, containing over 250,000 vols., and adjacent is the *Michaelis-Kirche* or **Seminar-Kirche** (1765). — To the W. of the University is the early-Gothic *Franciscan Church*, with a monastery of the 13th cent. (Pl. C, 3).

From the Neubau-Strasse the Peter-Strasse leads to the S. to the *Peterskirche*. On the S. side of the Platz is the old *Mint* (now a school); on the E. side is the *Regierungsgebäude*, or government offices, once a Benedictine abbey, the *Church* of which, now Protestant, was tastefully decorated in the interior in the rococo style in 1782-89.

From this point the Otto-Strasse leads to the S.E., past the (left) new *Justizgebäude* (Pl. D, 3; law-courts) and the monument of *Phil. Franz* **von** *Siebold*, the naturalist and traveller (1796-1866), to the promenades by the *Sander Glacis* (p. 68).

From the Residenz-Platz (p. 65) the THEATER-STRASSE runs to the N.W. On the right we notice the *Ludwigshalle* (Pl. D, 2), formerly railway-offices, now used for exhibitions, in front of which rises a monument to **von Zürn** (d. 1884), a public-spirited burgomaster of Würzburg. To the right, farther on, at the corner of the **Semmels**-Strasse, is the *Bürgerspital* (Pl. C, 2), with its popular wine-room (p. 64). Opposite to it the Haugerpfaffengasse leads to the right to the *Hauger Church* (Pl. C, 1), with two towers and a lofty dome, built in 1670-91 by Petrini, in the rococo style. The interior is overladen with gilding.

At the end of the Theater-Strasse the Kaiser-Strasse leads to the right to the railway-station, while the JULIUS PROMENADE leads to the left to the Main. To the right in the latter is the extensive and admirably organised Julius Hospital (Pl. C, 1, 2), founded in

1576, and richly endowed, its property being now worth 9,000,000 *M*. Upwards of 600 persons, of whom 400 are patients, are daily boarded and lodged here. The clinical institutions connected with the hospital since the beginning of the 17th cent. also form a medical school. The *Statue* of the founder, *Bishop Julius Echter von Mespelbrunn* (d. 1617), in the lower Julius Promenade, is by Schwanthaler. Behind the hospital is the *Botanic Garden*.

From the W. end of the Julius Promenade, where the **Custom House** (Pl. B, 2) is situated, we follow the bank of the Main to the N., past the 'crane-quay' and the municipal *Abattoir*, to the new **Luitpold Bridge** (Pl. B, 1), which spans the river with seven arches and affords a fine view of the valley. On the opposite bank are large new barracks. In the PLEICHER RING, leading to the S.E. from the bridge to the Kaiser-Strasse and the railway-station, are the new *Zootomical Institute*, the '*Anatomie*', and the *Pathological*, *Physiological*, and *Physical Institutes*, all belonging to the university. Pleasant grounds on the left. Beyond the Kaiser-Platz (Pl. C, 1) we reach the *Hauger* and the *Rennweger Ring*, and beyond the Hofgarten (p. 65) the *Sander Ring* (Pl. B, 4), which extends to the Main.

The Dom-Strasse (p. 65) leads to the **Old Main Bridge** (Pl. B, 2, 3), 644 ft. in length, constructed in 1474-1607, and adorned with statues of saints. On the left bank, immediately to the right, is the small *Hofspital-Kirche*, containing the '14 guardian saints' carved by T. Riemenschneider. The Gothic *Deutschhaus-Kirche* (Pl. A, 2), now used for military purposes, was built in 1287-1303. — To the left, 5 min. above the bridge, rise the grey towers of **St. Burkard** (Pl. B, 2), the only church of Würzburg of intact exterior, erected in 1033-42 in the Romanesque style and restored in 1168, with late-Gothic choir of 1494-97. In the interior (now being restored) it has shared the fate of the other churches. The nave contains a late-Romanesque offertory-box in sandstone, and the S. transept a carved altar of 1590.

Through a vaulted passage below the choir of St. Burkard the Burkardergasse leads to the *Burkarder Thor* (Pl. B, 3), beyond which runs the Mergentheim road. The first road diverging to the right beyond the gate is the 'Leisten-Strasse', near which the excellent 'Leistenwein' is produced. The second road diverging to the right from the high-road (by the garden-restaurant of Leimsud) leads to a Station Path, which ascends in 10-12 min. to the octagonal MARIEN-KAPELLE ('*Käppele*'; Pl. A, 4) on the *Nicolausberg* (1178 ft.), a pilgrimage-chapel, built in 1748-92 and containing good altar-pieces. The terrace in front of it affords fine views of the town and fortress. If we ascend the steps behind the chapel, we may follow the slope to the left (beautiful view) to the (10 min.) *Schützenhof Restaurant*, and thence regain the town in 1/4 hr.

On the hill opposite Würzburg, 427 ft. above the river, rises the fortress of **Marienberg** (1016 ft.; Pl. A, 3), constructed since

1650 on the site occupied successively by a Roman fort and an episcopal castle, which was taken by Gustavus Adolphus in 1631. To reach it we cross the bridge, turn to the right, and ascend to the left by the 'Erste Schlossgasse' (12 min.). We apply to the guard above the second covered gateway and are conducted to several fine points of view (cards of admission at the 'Kommandantur'; gratis).

In 1525 the insurgent peasantry lost time and strength in a vain attempt to capture this castle, after which the episcopal troops entered the town and executed 60 of the ringleaders. Near Würzburg the Archduke Charles defeated the French General Jourdan in 1796. In 1866 the campaign of the Prussian army of the Main terminated at Würzburg with the bombardment of the fortress (27th July). An armistice was concluded next day.

Railway to *Bamberg*, R. 17; to *Munich*, R. 25; to *Heidelberg*, R. 15.

The line to Ansbach (p. 130) and Gunzenhausen diverges here. The next stations on the Nuremberg line are (86 M.) *Rottendorf* and (90 M.) *Dettelbach* (a town on the Main, 3 M. to the E.).

$95^1/_2$ M. **Kitzingen** (625 ft.; **Schwan; Rothes Ross; Stern*, on the right bank of the Main), a busy trading town, with 7541 inhab., noted for its beer, is connected by an ancient stone bridge, 886 ft. long, with the suburb of *Etwashausen* on the left bank. In 1525 Margrave Casimir of Ansbach ordered seven of the burghers to be executed in the market-place, and many others to be deprived of sight, as a punishment for their participation in the Peasants' War. On a hill near the station, $1/_2$ M. to the S.W. of the town, are the *Waterworks*, supplied from the Main by steam-power. Above the station is the *Neue Schiesshaus*, which affords a charming view of the vine-clad hills of the Main and of the Steigerwald.

The line crosses the Main by a handsome bridge, 290 yds. long, and runs to the S.E. through a hilly district, passing the *Schwanberg*. Stations *Mainbernheim*, *Iphofen* (with walls, towers, old town-gates, and a Gothic church), *Markt-Einersheim*, **Hellmitzheim**, *Markt-Bibart*, *Langenfeld*, and (120 M.) *Neustadt*, on the *Aisch*, a hop-trading place, with remains of old walls and towers (4100 inhab.).

BRANCH RAILWAY by *Dottenheim* and *Ipsheim* to ($9^1/_2$ M.) **Windsheim**, an ancient little town on the *Aisch*, once a free town of the empire, and still surrounded with walls.

Beyond (125 M.) *Emskirchen* we cross the *Aurach* by a fine viaduct, 132 ft. high. 128 M. *Hagenbüchach*; 134 M. *Siegelsdorf* (branch-line to *Langenzenn*); $136^1/_2$ M. *Burgfarrnbach*, with a château of Count Pückler. Then across the *Rednitz*. On the right the *Alte Feste* (p. 70).

140 M. **Fürth** (964 ft.; *Hôtel Kütt*, *Hôtel National*, both at the Fürth and Nuremberg Railway Station; *Schwarzes Kreuz*, *Drei Könige*, in the town, plainer; *U.S. Consul*), a busy town with 42,659 inhab., vies with Nuremberg in its staple commodities of toys and fancy-articles, and possesses very extensive manufactories of gold-leaf and of mirrors. Conspicuous among the buildings is the modern

Rathhaus with its lofty tower. The Gothic *Church of St. Michael* (14th cent.) contains a beautiful late-Gothic *Ciborium, 25 ft. high. The Rednitz, which joins the *Pegnitz* below the town to form the *Regnitz*, is crossed by a railway and a suspension-bridge.

From Fürth to Cadolzburg, 8 M., local railway in 35 min., viâ *Dambach* and (2½ M.) *Alte Veste*. At the **Alte Veste** (1184 ft.), on a hill on the Rednitz, the battle between Gustavus Adolphus and Wallenstein, which compelled the Swedish monarch to retreat, was fought on 4th Sept., 1632. The headquarters of Gustavus were at the inn 'Zum Grünen Baum', in the street now named after him. Six different attacks on the intrenched camp of Wallenstein had proved unsuccessful. Extensive view from the tower. The adjoining restaurant is a favourite resort of the Nurembergers. — The line proceeds viâ *Zirndorf, Weiherhof*, and *Egersdorf* to (8 M.) Cadolzburg, a market-village with 1237 inhab. and a well-preserved *Castle* of the Counts of Hohenzollern, with their armorial bearings on the outer gate. The oldest part of the castle dates from the 9th cent., the newer parts from 1410.

The main line between Fürth (junction for the line to Bamberg, p. 81) and (5 M.) Nuremberg is the Staatsbahn or governmentrailway; trains also run hourly (in ¼ hr.) on the *Ludwigsbahn* (station at Nuremberg outside the Spittler-Thor), the oldest line in Germany (1835); and there is also a tramway (p. 96). Our train crosses the Ludwigs-Kanal near (141 M.) *Doos*, runs for a little way parallel with it, and then turns to the E. into the (145 M.) Nuremberg station (p. 95).

15. From Würzburg to Heidelberg.

99 M. Railway in 3¾-5½ hrs. (fares 12 ℳ 80, 8 ℳ 50, 5 ℳ 50 pf.). — From Würzburg to *Stuttgart*, express in 4 hrs. viâ Osterburken and Heilbronn; Berlin to Stuttgart viâ Würzburg in 16 hrs.; comp. R. 4.

The line coincides with the Munich line as far as (4 M.) *Heidingsfeld* (p. 128), diverges to the right, and ascends through a monotonous hilly region. 6½ M. *Reichenberg;* the village, in the valley to the left, is overlooked by a handsome Schloss on the hill above. 10 M. *Geroldshausen;* beyond (14 M.) *Kirchheim* we cross the Baden frontier. The line now descends. Beyond (17 M.) **Wittighausen** several deep cuttings and a tunnel. Then through the wooded and grassy valley of the *Grünbach* to (20½ M.) *Zimmern*, where the vine-culture begins. 22½ M. *Grünsfeld*, an old town, with part of the walls still standing. The handsome church contains a good monument to a Countess von Wertheim (d. 1503) by Tilman Riemenschneider. 25½ M. *Gerlachsheim*. The train crosses the *Tauber*, and turns to the left to (27 M.) **Lauda** (*Rail. Restaurant)*, junction of the Wertheim line.

From Lauda to Wertheim (20 M.) railway in 1 hr. through the smiling Tauber-Thal. 2½ M. *Distelhausen;* 5 M. *Tauberbischofsheim* (Adler; 3400 inhab.), the scene of an engagement between the Prussian and Wurtemberg troops in July, 1866; 7½ M. *Hochhausen;* 12 M. *Gamburg*, with an old castle. Two bridges and two tunnels. 15 M. *Bronnbach;* the old Cistercian abbey, with a transition-church of the 12th cent., now belongs to Prince Löwenstein. 17 M. *Reicholzheim;* 19½ M. *Wertheim* (p. 63).

From Lauda to Mergentheim, 6 M., railway in 25 min., by *Unterbalbach* and *Edelfingen*. — **Mergentheim** (670 ft.; *Hirsch*, in the town;

Deutscher Hof, **at the** station) is an **old town on** the Tauber (pop. 4400), where the Master of the Teutonic Order resided down to 1805. The large Schloss, built in the Renaissance style in 1572, is now a barrack. The most interesting of the churches is *St. John's*, in the Gothic style (13th cent.). The *Karlsbad* (*Curhaus, closed in winter), near the town, has springs containing salt and magnesia. — From Mergentheim to *Crailsheim*, see p. 26.

$28^1/_2$ M. **Königshofen** *(Deutscher Hof)*, **a small and** ancient **town** at the confluence of the *Umpfer* and the **Tauber**, where the insurgent **peasants** were defeated in 1525.

The line quits the Tauber, and turns **to the S.W. into the** *Umpfer-Thal*. **31** M. *Unterschüpf;* **33** M. *Schweigern;* **34** M. *Boxberg-Wölchingen*. At Boxberg **a** ruined castle. **The church of Wölchingen** (to the right), in the transition-style **of the 13th cent., has** handsome **portals and** interesting **Romanesque capitals. It** contains **the** tombstones **of several** knights **of Rosenberg (14th** and 15th **cent.).** Beyond a **tunnel,** (41 M.) *Eubigheim*. Then through the *Kirnach-Thal* to *Hirschlanden, Rosenberg*, and ($48^1/_2$ M.) **Osterburken** (*Kanne*, **opposite the** station), an ancient town **on the site of a Roman** camp.

FROM OSTERBURKEN TO JAGSTFELD, $23^1/_2$ M., railway in $1^1/_4$ hour. The **line crosses** the *Kirnach*, and traverses the valley of that stream **to** *Adelsheim*, a small town on the E. spurs of the Odenwald. Then through the *Seckach-Thal* to *Sennfeld, Roigheim*, and (10 M.) *Möckmühl*, **an** old town, with walls and towers, at the influx of the Seckach into the *Jagst*, stoutly defended **by Götz von** Berlichingen against **the** Swabian League in 1519; at the N. end are the extensive ruins of the castle. — We cross the Jagst and follow the left bank to *Züttlingen, Siglingen, Neudenau, Unter-Griesheim*, and *Jagstfeld* (p. 21).

The Baden railway diverges to the right from the Wurtemberg line, passes through a tunnel, and traverses pleasant wooded and **grassy** valleys on the S.E. fringe **of the** Odenwald. 50 M. *Adelsheim;* the little town is $^3/_4$ M. distant (see above). The line now runs through the Seckach-Thal. Several tunnels. 53 M. *Seckach;* 56 M. *Eicholzheim;* 57 M. *Schefflenz;* 60 M. *Auerbach*. Near (62 M.) *Dallau* **the** *Elz* is crossed. 63 M. *Neckarburken.* 66 M. **Mosbach** (*****Prinz Karl;** *Badischer Hof; Rail.* **Restaurant),** **an old and busy** little town on the Elz, with 3500 inhabitants.

68 M. **Neckarelz** (435 ft.; *Rail. Restaurant*), **at the influx** of the **Elz** into the *Neckar*, **is the junction of the** Stuttgart and Hanau **line (p. 22).**

FROM NECKARELZ TO MECKESHEIM, 20 M., railway in $1-1^1/_2$ hour. The **train crosses** the Neckar. Beyond a short tunnel is the little château of *Neuberg* on the right. Two tunnels. Stations *Asbach*, *Aglasterhausen*, *Helmstadt, Waibstadt* (with **a** Gothic church). We **next** follow the *Schwarzbach-Thal*. $15^1/_2$ M. *Neidenstein*, with **a château;** 17 M. *Eschelbronn*. — 20 M. *Meckesheim,* junction of **the** Heilbronn and Heidelberg railway (see p. 22).

From Neckarelz to (80 M.) *Eberbach*, junction for Darmstadt and Hanau, see p. 22. Beyond the next tunnel is (85 M.) *Hirschhorn* (*****Zum Naturalisten),** picturesquely situated at the foot of the fine castle of that name. 87 M. *Neckarhausen*. — 89 M. Neckarsteinach (*****Harfe,** **with a** garden on **the** Neckar), **with four old** castles of the Steinachs, surnamed the Landschaden ('land-scourges'). The *Mittelburg*, one of these castles, has been restored in the mediæval style. Opposite, on a wooded hill, rises the ancient castle of *Dilsberg*. Beyond a tunnel the train crosses the Neckar.

93 M. **Neckargemünd** *(Pfalz; Hirsch),* where the Neckar receives the *Elsenz,* is the junction of the line to *Meckesheim* and *Neckarelz* (see p. 71). Opposite (95½ M.) *Schlierbach* is the abbey of *Neuburg*. A number of villas are passed as we near Heidelberg. The train stops first at the *Carlsthor* station (for the upper town), and then passes through a long tunnel below the castle to the (99 M.) principal station (see *Baedeker's Rhine*).

16. From Leipsic to Nuremberg by Bamberg.

220 M. RAILWAY, express in 8-9¼ hrs. (fares 29 ℳ 50, 21 ℳ 40, 15 ℳ 10 pf.), ordinary trains in 13 hrs. (fares 28 ℳ 70, 20 ℳ 20, 13 ℳ 30 pf.). — Express from Leipsic to Munich by Nuremberg in 13¼ hrs. (fares 44 ℳ 20, 31 ℳ 70 pf., 24 ℳ); to Lindau by Nördlingen and Augsburg in 18 hrs. (fares 62 ℳ 40, 44 ℳ 60, 29 ℳ 30 pf.). — The express from Berlin to Nuremberg and Munich runs viâ Halle, Weissenfels, Zeitz, Gera, Saalfeld, Probstzella, and Hochstadt (see p. 74; time 14 hrs. 25 min.; viâ Leipsic and Hof-Wiesau 12 hrs. 48 min.), and is joined at Zeitz by the train from Leipsic, starting from the Thuringian Station.

Leipsic, see *Baedeker's Northern Germany*. We start from the Bavarian Station. 5½ M. *Gaschwitz;* 9 M. *Böhlen;* 13 M. *Kieritzsch,* where a branch diverges to *Chemnitz*.

24½ M. **Altenburg** *(Hôtel de Saxe; Hôtel de Russie,* etc.), with 31,440 inhab., capital of the Duchy of Sachsen-Altenburg, is overlooked by the ducal *Schloss*. Late-Gothic church (1410), and fine park. (See *Baedeker's Northern Germany*.)

33½ M. *Gössnitz,* junction for *Glauchau* and *Chemnitz* to the E., and *Gera* to the W.; 39 M. *Crimmitzschau;* 46 M. *Werdau* (junction for *Zwickau),* all with spinning and weaving factories. To the left, on a wooded hill, *Schloss Schönfels*. 51 M. *Neumark,* junction for *Greiz*. — 56½ M. *Reichenbach (Lamm; Deutscher Kaiser;* *Rail. *Restaurant),* a manufacturing town with 21,595 inhabitants. — Carriages are changed here for Eger (see below).

The train crosses the deep *Göltzsch-Thal* by a grand viaduct with four rows of arches one above the other, 706 yds. in length and 285 ft. high. Below, to the left, lies the little town of *Mylau*. 59½ M. *Netzschkau;* 63 M. *Herlasgrün* (branch-line by *Auerbach* and *Falkenstein* to *Oelsnitz,* see below). Then another lofty viaduct across the deep, wooded *Elster-Thal*.

72 M. **Plauen** *(*Deil's Hotel; Blauer Engel; Wettiner Hof; Fürstenhalle; Stadt Dresden;* U. S. Consular Agent, *T. W. Peters),* a busy manufacturing town on the *Weisse Elster* (47,000 inhab.), is the capital of the *Voigtland,* overlooked by the old castle of *Hradschin,* anciently the seat of the Voigt or governor.

FROM PLAUEN TO WIESAU VIÂ EGER, 62½ M., railway in 3¾ hrs. The line diverges to the left from the Hof and Nuremberg line and leads through the picturesque Elster-Thal, a hilly district with numerous factories. 2 M. *Neundorf;* 6 M. *Weischlitz* (junction for the *Elsterthal Railway* to *Greiz* and *Gera);* 7½ M. *Pirk;* 12½ M. *Oelsnitz* (branch to *Auerbach* and *Zwickau);*

20½ M. *Adorf* (branch to *Chemnitz*). Then (22½ M.) **Elster** (*Hôtel de Saxe*, with the Cursaal; °*Wettiner Hof*; *Bauer*, etc.), a pleasant watering-place, with alkaline and saline springs.

The train quits the Elster and crosses the watershed between the **Elster** and the *Eger*. 31 M. *Brambach*. At (37 M.) *Voitersreuth*, the Austrian **frontier-station**, luggage is examined. 42 M. *Franzensbad*, junction for *Hof* (see below). — 46½ M. **Eger** (luggage from Munich examined here; °*Rail. Restaurant*). Description of the town, and routes hence to *Carlsbad* and *Prague*, and to *Vienna* viâ *Pilsen*, see *Baedeker's Austria*.

Beyond Eger the train quits the Austrian territory. At (53½ M.) **Waldsassen** is a Cistercian abbey, founded in 1128, suppressed in 1803; handsome church in the baroque style; fine carving in the library-hall. 56 M. *Steinmühle*; 59 M. *Mitterteich*, on the watershed between the Eger and the Nab. To the right is the *Kösseine*, p. 92. At (62½ M.) *Wiesau* (p. 134), the line unites with that viâ Hof to Munich.

79 M. *Mehltheuer*; 82½ M. *Schönberg* (branch to *Schleiz*). Beyond (87½ M.) *Reuth* the train enters Bavaria. The blue outlines of the Fichtelgebirge (see Map, p. 88) become visible on the left.

102½ M. **Hof** (1656 ft.; *Kaiserhof; *Hirsch*, *Wittelsbacher Hof*, both at the station; *Lamm; *Prinz-Regent; *Goldner Löwe, R. 1¼-2 ℳ, B. 70 pf.; *Rail. Restaurant), a considerable town on the *Saale*, with 24,548 inhab., is the junction of the Munich line viâ Wiesau and Ratisbon (R. 27). Gothic *Rathhaus* of 1563. The fine *Michaelskirche*, consecrated in 1299 and frequently altered, was thoroughly restored in 1884. On the *Theresienstein* (*Restaurant) is the pretty public park; ½ M. farther off is the *Labyrinthenberg* (1866 ft.), with a ruin and a belvedere: view of the rounded summit of the *Döbraberg* (2325 ft.) to the W., in the Franconian forest.

BRANCH RAILWAY, 14½ M., in 28 min., viâ *Naila* to *Marxgrün*, whence a diligence runs twice daily in ½ hr. to (3 M.) Steben (2130 ft.; °*Neues Cur-Hôtel*; *Cur-Hôtel & Bayrischer Hof*; *Anker*; *Pension Spörl*), a loftily situated chalybeate bath, well fitted up. The little town (800 inhab.) was almost entirely burned down in 1877 and has been handsomely rebuilt. In 1796-97 Alexander von Humboldt was mining superintendent here; the house he occupied is denoted by a tablet. Excursions to the °*Höllenthal*, to the *Langenauer-Thal*, and to *Blankenberg*, prettily situated on the Saale. — From Steben to *Kronach* (p. 74) diligence daily in 6 hrs., viâ *Geroldsgrün*, *Steinwiesen*, and *Unterrodach*.

FROM HOF TO EGER, 37½ M. (railway in 2½ hrs.). 3½ M. *Oberkotzau*; 8½ M. *Rehau* (on the right the *Grosse Kornberg*, with a view-tower); 15½ M. *Selb*. — 20 M. **Asch** (*Post*), a Bohemian manufacturing town, with 13,200 inhab., contains monuments to Luther and Joseph II. Fine view from the *Hainberg*, ½ hr. to the N., the highest point of the Elstergebirge. [A branch-line runs from the station, which is 1¼ M from the town, by *Asch-Stadt*, *Neuberg*, and *Thonbrunn*, to (8¾ M.) *Rossbach*, with considerable manufactories.] — Then stat. *Hasslau*, *Antoniushöhe-Stöckermühle*, *Franzensbad*, and (37½ M.) *Eger* (see above).

The line traverses a hilly district, running near the winding Saale. 106 M. *Oberkotzau*, junction of the line to Ratisbon and Munich (R. 27); 109 M. *Schwarzenbach*, on the Saale; 113½ M. *Seulbitz*. — 117 M. **Münchberg** (*Bayr. Hof; branch-line to *Helmbrechts*, 5½ M., in 35 min.).

The °*Waldstein* (2890 ft.) is most easily ascended hence (comp. p. 91). Pleasant footpath (or by omnibus twice daily in 50 min.) to (3 M.) *Sparneck* (Post); thence by a distinct path to the top in 50 minutes.

123½ M. *Stammbach*. On the left rise the Waldstein (see above),

Schneeberg (p. 91), and Ochsenkopf (p. 90), the highest points of the Fichtelgebirge. 127½ M. *Falls-Gefrees*; the village of *Gefrees* lies in the *Lübnitz-Thal*, 3 M. to the E. 131 M. *Markt-Schorgast* (1660 ft.) lies in the valley to the right (to Berneck, see p. 89). The engineering of the line here is interesting (gradient at first 1 : 40; descent to Neuenmarkt 575 ft.): cuttings, embankments, and dark pine-clad valleys in rapid succession. To the left in the distance is the former Cistercian abbey of *Himmelkron*, known for the legend of the Countess of Orlamünde (the 'White Lady'; d. 1382), ancestress of the Brandenburg-Kulmbach family. Gothic cloisters and the burial-vaults of the counts.

131½ M. *Neuenmarkt* (junction for *Bayreuth* and *Schnabelwaid*, etc., see p. 86 and R. 25); 1½ M. to the N. is *Wirsberg* (1470 ft.; Hôt. Werner, etc.), a summer-resort, with pretty walks. — 139 M. *Unter-Steinach*; 3 M. to the N. lies *Stadt-Steinach*. Country picturesque, especially near (142 M.) **Kulmbach** (1075 ft.; *Goldner Hirsch*, R. 1 ℳ 60-2, B. ¾, D. 1 ℳ 80 pf.; *Rail. Restaurant*), a town with 7000 inhab., famed for its beer, formerly the residence of the Margraves of Brandenburg-Kulmbach, on the *Weisse Main*, commanded by the *Plassenburg* (1390 ft.), now a prison.

Near (146½ M.) *Mainleus*, by *Schloss Stemenhausen*, the *Weisse* and *Rothe Main* unite to form the *Main*. 149½ M. *Mainroth*; 152½ M. *Burgkunstadt*, a little town with an old Rathhaus and Schloss. We cross the Main to (155½ M.) *Hochstadt-Marktzeuln*, junction of the Probstzella, Saalfeld, and Berlin line.

FROM HOCHSTADT TO SAALFELD (50 M.) railway in 2½-3½ hrs. through the pretty *Rodach-Thal*. 2½ M. *Redwitz*, at the entrance of the *Steinach-Thal*; 5 M. *Ober-Langenstadt*; 6½ M. *Küps*, a considerable village with a château of Herr von Redwitz. — 10 M. Kronach (*Goldner Wagen* or *Post; Sonne*), a small town (4000 inhab.) at the confluence of the *Hasslach* and *Rodach*, formerly fortified and bravely defended during the Thirty Years' War, was the birthplace of the painter Lucas Müller, known as Cranach (1472-1553). The Gothic church (1518-1607) stands on a lofty rock, which ascends to the imposing and well-preserved fortress of *Rosenberg* (1240 ft.; now pleasure-grounds, with restaurant and a small historical museum). Thence through the *Hasslach-Thal* by stat. *Gundelsdorf* to (15½ M.) *Stockheim*, with valuable coal-mines in the vicinity. The line now ascends by *Rothenkirchen* and *Förtschendorf* to (26 M.) *Steinbach* (1950 ft.), on the watershed between the Rhine and the Elbe, and descends into the *Loquitz-Thal* to (29 M.) *Ludwigsstadt* (branch-line in 40 min. to *Lehesten*, with extensive slate-quarries). By the hamlet of *Lauenstein* the train quits Bavaria, enters Saxe-Meiningen, and reaches (34 M.) Probstzella (*Rail. Restaurant*), where it joins the Prussian State railway. Then *Marktgölitz*, *Unterloquitz*, *Eichicht*, and (50 M.) *Saalfeld*, junction of the lines to Jena, Grossheringen, Halle, and Berlin, and to Weida, Zeitz, and Weissenfels or Leipsic: see *Baedeker's Northern Germany*.

161 M. **Lichtenfels** (866 ft.; *Anker*, R. 1-1¼ ℳ, *Hôtel Moulin*, both near the station; *Krone*, in the market) is the junction of the Werra line (see *Baedeker's N. Germany*). *Schloss Banz* on the right (1¼ hr. from Lichtenfels) and *Vierzehnheiligen* on the left (1 hr.) are conspicuous objects. Pleasure-grounds on the *Burgberg*.

Carriage to Vierzehnheiligen 4½, to Banz 6 ℳ (return included). We may visit both on foot by going from Lichtenfels to Vierzehnheiligen

(1 hr.), and thence to Banz (1½ hr.), and descending to (¾ hr.) stat. Staffelstein (see below). By the direct road Banz is 1½ hr. from Lichtenfels; we follow the direction of the railway, cross the Main at the ferry-houses, and then ascend the hill.

The once celebrated Benedictine Abbey of **Banz** (1380 ft.; *Inn*), **founded in 1096**, was dissolved in 1803. The extensive buildings on a wooded height, 400 ft. above the Main, now belong to Duke Charles Theodore of Bavaria. Delightful view from the terrace. Valuable collection of fossils found in the lias of the neighbourhood (fine saurians, colossal ammonites, etc.). The Egyptian collection is unimportant. A Descent from the Cross, a **relief in silver**, presented by Pope Pius VI. to his godson Duke Pius of Bavaria, is erroneously attributed to Benv. Cellini.

Opposite Banz is **Vierzehnheiligen** (1270 ft.; *Hirsch*), the most frequented shrine in Franconia, visited by about 50,000 pilgrims annually. The church, with its two towers, was rebuilt in the rococo style in 1743-72. An altar in the centre of the **nave** marks the spot, where, according to the legend, the 14 'Nothhelfer' ('helpers in need') appeared to a shepherd-boy in 1446, and gave rise to the foundation of the church. The two W. chapels contain numerous thank-offerings, such as figures in wax, etc. — The traveller who has visited Banz is not recommended to go to Vierzehnheiligen also, unless for the sake of extending his excursion along the top of the hill to the (3 M.) chapel (Restaurant) and the verge of the precipitous Staffelberg (see below).

Near (166 M.) *Staffelstein* the *Staffelberg* (1770 ft.) with its chapel, on the left, rises abruptly from the valley; and farther on, to the S., is the *Veitsberg* (1515 ft.), with a chapel and ruined castle. 169 M. *Ebensfeld*; 172½ M. *Zapfendorf*; 177 M. *Breiten-Güssbach* (to the left, *Schloss Giech*); 179½ M. *Hallstadt*. Near Bamberg the line from *Schweinfurt* (p. 83) joins ours on the right.

181 M. **Bamberg**. — **Hotels.** *BAMBERGER HOF (Pl. a; C, B, 2), Grüner Markt, R., L., A. 2 ℳ 50, B. 70-80 pf., D. 2½ ℳ. — **DEUTSCHES HAUS** (Pl. b; C, 2), König-Str., R. & B. from 1½ ℳ; *DREI KRONEN (Pl. d; B, 3), Lange-Str., R., L., & A. 1½-3, B. ¾, D. incl. wine 2 ℳ 70 pf.; ERLANGER HOF (Pl. c; C, 1), near the station, R., L., & A. 1½-3, B. ½ 1, D. 2½ ℳ; HÔT. & RESTAURANT LUITPOLD, Luitpold-Str., near the station.

Restaurants. *Messerschmitt*, corner of the Langen-Str. and **Promenaden-Str.** (good Franconian wine); *Rathskeller*, Kessler-Str.; *Deutsches Haus*, see **above**; *Tambosi* and *Wittelsbach*, with gardens, both on the Promenade; *Angra*, at the Sophienbrücke; *Theater-Restaurant*, Schiller-Platz; *Villa Remeis*, with view (p. 79). Beer at the *Fässlein*, König-Str. etc. Beer-Gardens on the Michaelsberg, Stephansberg, Kaulberg, and Jakobsberg, much frequented on summer-evenings, with fine views.

Cab into the town, with **one** horse 75 pf., **with two** horses 1½ ℳ; to the Jakobsberg 1 or 2 ℳ, to the Michaelsberg 1¼ or 2½ ℳ; to the Altenburg 6 ℳ (two horses). Within the town: ¼ hr. 50 pf. or 1 ℳ, ½ hr. 1 or 2 ℳ, 1 hr. 2 **or** 3 ℳ.

Post Office (Pl. C, 3), Schiller-Platz and **at the station** (Pl. D, 1). — **Telegraph Office** (Pl. 10; B, 3), at the lower **bridge**.

Swimming Baths at the *Theresienhain* (p. 80), above the town.

United States Consular Agent, *Louis Stern, Esq.*

Bamberg (785 ft.), a town with 35,248 inhab., lies in a very fertile district on both banks of the *Regnitz*, at its junction with the *Ludwigs-Canal* (connecting the Main and the Danube, little used) and 3 M. above its confluence with the Main. The town already enjoyed municipal privileges in 973, was erected into a bishopric by Emp. Henry II. in 1007, and since 1802 has belonged to Bavaria. About half of the town is built upon a chain of hills, crowned with churches. Busy industries have sprung up here of late years (cotton-spinning, weaving, brewing, etc.).

The Luitpold-Strasse leads from the station to the town. In the St. Gangolph-Platz, on the left, is the church of *St. Gangolph* (Pl. C, 1, 2), founded in 1063, originally Romanesque, with a Gothic choir, but disfigured by alterations. In the chapel in the N. transept, behind the altar, there is a crucifix with a draped and crowned figure of Christ in repose, over lifesize.

The E. branch of the Regnitz is crossed by three bridges, the *Sophienbrücke* (Pl. C, 2), the new *Peuntbrücke* (Pl. D, 3), and the *Kettenbrücke* (Pl. C, 2). The chief traffic crosses the Kettenbrücke, or chain-bridge, constructed in 1828-29, from which the Hauptwach-Strasse leads to the S. to the Maximilians-Platz and the Grüne Markt.

In the MAXIMILIANS-PLATZ (Pl. B, C, 2), on the right, is the *Priester-Seminar* (Pl. 3). In the centre rises an imposing **Fountain** (Pl. 13), executed in 1880 by *Miller* of Munich, with statues of Maximilian I. of Bavaria, Emp. Henry II., his wife Kunigunde, Bishop Otho the Saint, and Emp. Conrad III.

Farther on is the GRÜNE MARKT (Pl. B, 2, 3), where the well-stocked vegetable-market is held in the forenoon. On the right, at the corner of the Jesuiten-Strasse, is the church of **St. Martin** (Pl. 1), built by *Andr. Pozzo* in the Baroque style in 1686-1720, with a dome and massive barrel-vaulting; the tower, 180 ft. high, affords a good survey of the town. Adjoining the church is *St. Martin's Pfarrhof*, formerly a university and Jesuit college, now the *Royal Lyceum* (Pl. 4). The entrance, 2 Jesuiten-Strasse, leads into a court, in the arcades at the back of which are the entrances to the *Linder Cabinet of Natural History* (10-12; on the right) and to the *Library (Pl. 5, B, 2; on the left). The latter, formed by the union of the Jesuits' library with collections from several convents, now contains 300 000 vols. and upwards of 3000 MSS.

The library is open daily (except Sun., holidays, and Sat. afternoons), 8-12 and 2-4; during the summer-holidays visitors are admitted from 9 to 12. Some of its most interesting contents are exhibited under glass in the principal hall: fine parchments from the library bequeathed by the Emp. Henry II. to the chapter of Bamberg; several Gospels and missals of the Carlovingian period, including the so-called '*Bible of Alcuin*', probably written at Tours; prayer-books of Henry II. and his wife Kunigunde, with fine Byzantine ivory diptychs of the 11th cent.; also numerous miniatures, rare printed works, interesting drawings, water-colours, etc., including several ascribed to *Dürer* (?).

The Grüne Markt, in which rises the *Neptune Fountain* ('Gabelmann'; Pl. 14), erected in 1698, and the Obstmarkt lead to the *Obere Brücke* (Pl. B, 3), a bridge over the left arm of the Regnitz, completed in 1455, with a stone Crucifix of 1715. On an artificial island halfway across stands the Rathhaus (Pl. 7), rebuilt in 1744-56, and adorned externally with allegorical frescoes in the taste of the period. The old tower covering the entrance to the bridge is adorned with rococo balconies. — A little lower down is the *Untere*

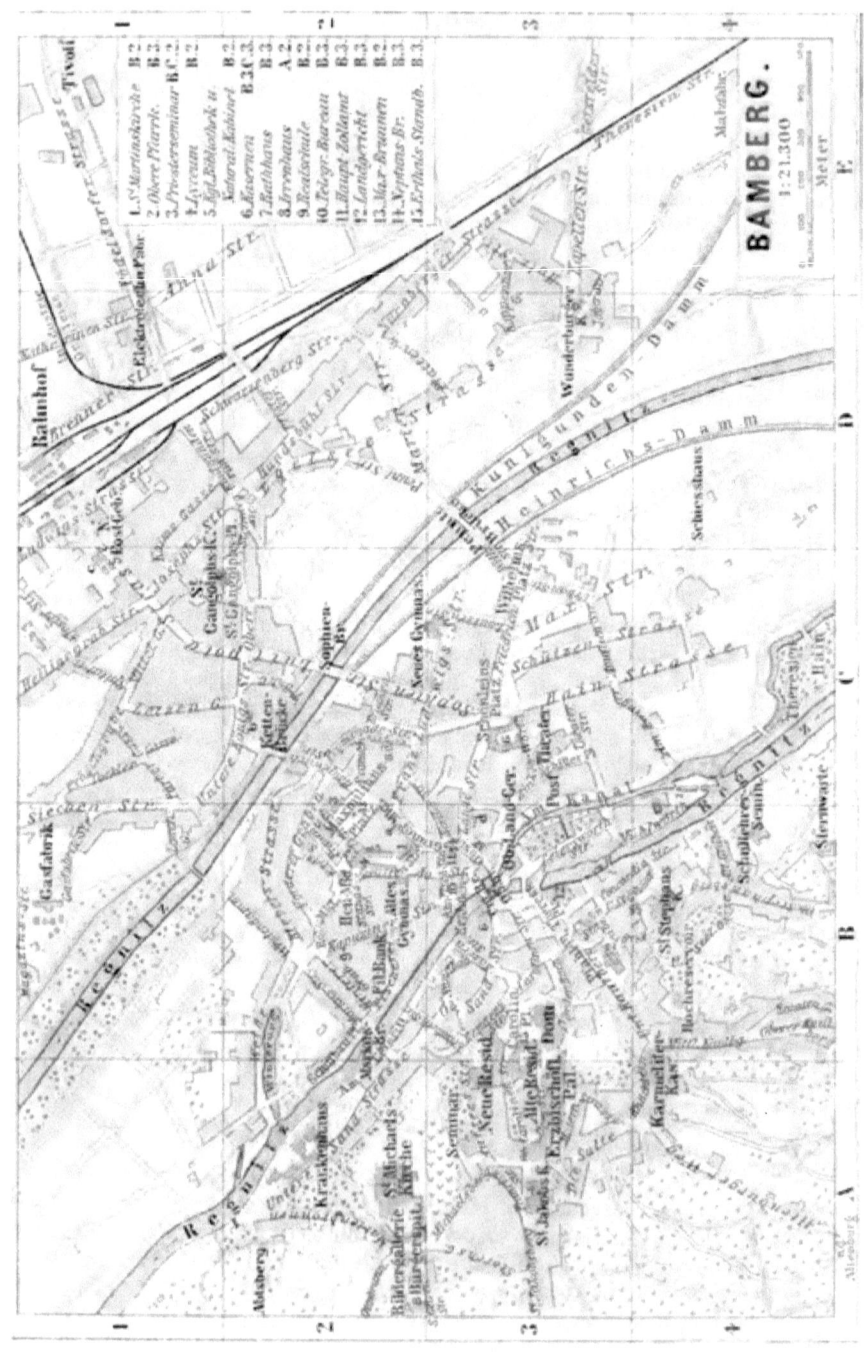

Brücke, an iron bridge constructed in 1858. Above is another iron bridge crossing from the right bank to the *Geierswörth*, an island with an old episcopal palace, now a court of justice. The two chief bridges afford fine views of the river and the picturesque houses on its banks. — From the **Upper Bridge** the Carolinen-Str. ascends to the Carolinen - Platz, a square enclosed by the cathedral, the old, and the new palace.

The *Cathedral (Pl. B, 3) with its four towers, one of the grandest Romanesque edifices in Germany (312 ft. long, 92 ft. wide, and 86 ft. high), was founded by Emp. Henry II. in 1004, but dates in its present form from the close of the 12th and the beginning of the 13th century. The W. choir, with the transept in front of it, is later, as its pointed style and moulded pillars indicate, perhaps dating from 1274, when an indulgence was granted to the promoters of the building, and the nave covered with its pointed ceiling. The four eight-storied towers are 265 ft. in height; the two at the E. end are in pure Romanesque, but the open-work turrets on the W. towers reveal the influence of the early French - Gothic style. The sculptures are among the best examples of German plastic art between the late-Romanesque and the early-Renaissance periods.

The sculptures on the recessed Principal Portal (*Fürstenthor*, N.), which resembles the **'Goldene Pforte'** of Freiberg Cathedral, represent the Last Judgment, the **Apostles** standing on the shoulders of the Prophets, and symbolical figures of Church and Synagogue (the last with its eyes bandaged). The two smaller portals to the right and left of the E. Choir, approached by a fine flight of steps, are also embellished with sculptures: on the S.E. portal (the 'marriage-door'), the usual entrance to the cathedral, are figures of Adam and Eve, SS. Peter and Stephen, and the Emp. Henry II. and his consort Kunigunde; the N.E. door (the 'Mother of God' or 'Grace' door) has fine columns with elaborate capitals; above the architrave, the Virgin worshipped by saints.

The °Interior (open 5.30-10.30 a. m.; in the afternoon only during service on Sun., Wed., & Sat.) was judiciously restored by King Lewis I. in 1828-37 and purged of disfigurements. (The sacristan, who shows the choirs and treasury, lives at the back of the W. choir; entrance in the Carolinen-Platz; fee 1/2-1 *M*.)

In the centre of the Nave is the *°Sarcophagus* of the founder Henry II. (d. 1024) and his consort Kunigunde (d. 1038), executed, in a fine-grained limestone resembling marble, by Tilmann Riemenschneider, the famous sculptor of Würzburg, in 1499-1513. On the highly ornate sarcophagus repose the emperor and empress, over lifesize, in the fantastic costumes of the 15th century. The reliefs on the sides represent scenes from their lives: 1. The Empress proves her innocence by walking over red-hot plough-shares; 2. She pays the workmen who erected the church founded by her; 3. The Emperor cured of an illness by St. Benedict; 4. He implores pardon for sin; 5. His death. — Modern *Pulpit* by Rotermundt.

To the left of the approach to the St. George's or E. Choir is an *Equestrian Figure of Emp. Conrad III.*, who died at Bamberg in 1153 and was buried in the cathedral (or perhaps of Stephen, King of Hungary, who was baptized here). — The stone screens separating the E. choir from the aisles are adorned with interesting sculptures, representing the Apostles and Prophets (in pairs) and the Annunciation, all of the early 12th cent.; between these, on the N. side, are three fine statues (Madonna, Sibyl, an angel) of the end of the 13th century. Adjacent is the monument of the last prince-bishop (d. 1808). — The E. Choir contains, on the right, the monument of the prince-bishop *George II.* (d. 1505), from Peter Vischer's studio, and the sarcophagi of *Bishop Otho II.* (d. 1196; Romanesque) and *Bishop Günther* (d. 1066; 13th century). The figure of Christ, in bronze, over the altar, was designed by Schwanthaler, as were also the 22 reliefs of saints on the altar. The choir-stalls are modern. — The CRYPT, below the E. choir, is severely Romanesque; the vaulting is borne by 14 round and octagonal columns. It contains the simple sandstone sarcophagus of Emp. Conrad III. and a well.

In the St. Peter's or W. CHOIR is the low marble sarcophagus of *Pope Clement II.* (d. 1047), once Bishop of Bamberg, with reliefs of the 13th century. On the walls are the monuments of the prince-bishops *Schaumburg* (d. 1475), *Gross-Trockau* (d. 1501), *Pommersfelden* (d. 1503), the last two being from Peter Vischer's studio, and *George III. of Limburg* (d. 1522), by Loyen Hering, one of the earliest Renaissance monuments in Germany. The choir-stalls are of the Gothic period.

In the S. TRANSEPT, to the left of the W. choir, is an ivory crucifix said to date from the 4th cent., and presented to the church by Emp. Henry II. in 1008. — The two doors in the S. transept lead to the sacristy and to the NAGEL-CAPELLE (Chapel of the Nail), added in the 15th cent., which contains 64 monumental brasses of canons (1414-1540), a carved reredos of the 15th cent., and an Entombment after Ann. Carracci. The adjacent ANTONIUS-CAPELLE contains an altar-piece by *Lucas Cranach* (1513) representing the Madonna in a garland of roses, with saints and portraits of Emp. Max I., the Pope, and other princes of that period. — The TREASURY contains, among other curiosities, a nail of the True Cross in a mounting of the 15th cent., the skulls of Emp. Henry II. and Kunigunde, the Emperor's crown, his sword, drinking-horn, and knife, combs of the Empress, a chasuble embroidered by her, and the enamelled head of St. Otho's crozier.

From the cathedral we may cross over to the *Oberpfarrkirche* in 2 min. through the 'Obere and Untere Bach'.

The W. side of the Carolinen-Platz is bounded by the picturesque *Alte Hofhaltung* or **Alte Residenz** (Pl. A, B, 2), with a lofty gable and handsome jutting window and portal, built in the second half of the 16th cent. on the site of an older palace of the Counts of Babenberg, in which the Lombard King Berengarius died in captivity in 966, and Count Palatine Otho of Wittelsbach slew Emp. Philip of Swabia in 1208. In front of this palace rises a monument (Pl. 15) to the prince-bishop *Von Erthal* (d. 1797), erected in 1865.

The N. and half of the E. side of the Carolinen-Platz are occupied by the **Neue Residenz** (adm. 10-11 and 2-4; on Sun. and holidays 10.30 to 12 and 2-3; 50 pf.), or *New Palace*, erected by Bishop von Schönborn in 1698-1704. Here, in Oct., 1806, Napoleon issued his declaration of war against Prussia. From 1806 to 1837 this palace was the residence of Duke William of Bavaria, father-in-law of the French Marshal Berthier. On 1st June, 1815, the marshal, whose mind had been unhinged by the return of Napoleon from Elba, threw himself from one of the windows on the E. side and was killed. — The S. wing contains the *Archives*.

The Obere Carolinen-Strasse, between the two palaces, leads from the Carolinen-Platz to the Jakobsberg and the St. Jakobskirche (Pl. A, 3), a flat-roofed Romanesque church of the 11th cent., with a Gothic W. choir and an E. choir which was transformed in 1771 into a rococo façade, all recently restored. At the back of the W. choir, to the left, is Schmidt's interesting *Porcelain Painting Establishment*

A little to the N. of St. Jakob's is the Michaelsberger-Str., by which we ascend to the *Michaelsberg (Pl. A, 2), with its conspicuous church and other buildings of a Benedictine abbey founded by Emp. Henry II. The court, which we enter by the W. gateway, affords a good picture of a mediæval convent on a large scale, though most of the present buildings date only from last century.

The CHURCH OF ST. MICHAEL, a Romanesque edifice of the 12th cent., with Gothic additions, tastelessly restored last century, has been entirely renovated in the interior.

The INTERIOR contains many monuments of bishops (16-18th cent.), transferred hither from the cathedral. Behind the high-altar is that of St. Otho (d. 1139), dating from the 14th cent.; at the back is a painted statue of the saint, probably a relic of an earlier monument. The altar contains his pastoral staff, mitre, and chasuble. Handsome rococo choir-stalls of the 18th century.

The S. E. wing of the abbey-building now contains the municipal GALLERY OF ART. Entrance adjoining the church-steps (adm. Sun. 10-12, free; week-days 10-12 and 2-5, in winter 10-12 and 2-3, adm. 50 pf.; catalogue 50 pf.).

ROOMS I & II. Early German Masters: 64 paintings by *M. Wohlgemut, Hans von Kulmbach, Hans Baldung Grien, M. Strigel, H. Schäufelein, Lucas Cranach*, and others. — ROOMS III & IV. contain (according to the catalogue) 61 pictures by *A. del Sarto, C. Dolci, M. Caravaggio, Sassoferrato, C. Maratta, Tiepolo*, and other Italian masters, and 11 pictures by *Spagnoletto* and other Spanish painters. — ROOMS V, VI, & VII. Dutch and Flemish Masters of the 16th and 17th cent., including *C. de Crayer, Honthorst, Jordaens, Sal. Ruysdael*, and *Jan van Goyen*. — ROOM VIII. French School. — ROOM IX. Heller Collection: 319. *Corn. Janszoon van Ceulen*, Portrait; 322. *A. Dürer*, Head of St. Paul, a study. — ROOMS X, XI, & XII. contain modern works, chiefly by artists of Bamberg and Munich; 489 Head 'al fresco' by *Cornelius*. — Also water-colours, miniatures, crayon sketches, and small works of art in ivory, alabaster, and wood. — On the first floor a large carpet of the end of the 15th cent. with scenes from the Passion.

On the N. side of the church is the old abbey, now the *Bürgerspital* or poor-house. To the left are the secular buildings, now a brewery and restaurant. Passing the terrace of the restaurant, we reach the *Monastery Garden*, laid out in the 18th cent., where an avenue of limes affords charming views of the town.

From the Michaelsberg we may go to the W., past the little church of *St. Getreu* and the *Lunatic Asylum* (Pl. 8), to the *Villa Remeis*, now the property of the town, which commands a fine panorama (restaurant, see p. 75).

To the W. of the Upper Bridge (p. 76) the Lugbank ascends to the left to the Pfahl-Platz and the *Kaulberg*. On the Untere Kaulberg, to the left, stands the Gothic *Obere Pfarrkirche zu Unserer Lieben Frauen (Pl. 2; B, 3), erected in 1320-87, disfigured in the 18th cent., but of late thoroughly restored. The Gothic choir contains 11 altars. Good wood-carving on the organ-case by *Veit Stoss* (1523). On the N. side is the *Ehethür* ('wedding-gate'), with an elegant porch borne by two slender columns and containing figures of the Wise and Foolish Virgins.

From the Pfahl-Platz (see above) we may go to the S. through the Judengasse and ascend the Stephansberg to the new *Observatory* ('Sternwarte'; Pl. B, 4), built with a bequest of the late Hr. Remeis.

Beautiful walk up the Kaulberg (see blue notice-boards), past the *Karmeliter-Kaserne* (barracks; Pl. A, 4), then down a little to the right, and lastly straight up the hill to the (40 min.) *Altenburg (1265 ft.; café at the top). The castle, probably founded in the 10th cent. and after 1251 a castle of the bishops, was destroyed in 1553 by Margrave Albert of Bayreuth, but afterwards partly restored. Fine view from the tower (162 steps; afternoon light best). The chapel, restored in 1834, contains monuments of the 16th cent. and stained glass.

The **Theresienhain** and **Luisenhain** (Pl. C, 4), with their promenades skirting the Regnitz, afford pleasant walks. They are reached from the new town in 10-15 min. by the Sophien-Brücke, the Schönleins-Platz (with a bust of the famous physician of that name; d. 1864), and the Hain-Str.; and from the old town by the Geierswörth-Str. and the Mühlendamm. Near the centre of the park is a café, and at the end of it, 2 M. from the town, is the little village of *Bug* (pron. 'book'). — On the right bank of the Regnitz, to the S. of the station, lies the suburb of *Wunderburg*, with its extensive market-gardens.

Interesting excursion to *Banz* and *Vierzehnheiligen* (p. 75). — *Franconian Switzerland*, see p. 92.

The environs of Bamberg form a vast orchard and market-garden, of which, however, little is seen from the train. Pine-plantations and hop-gardens are traversed. The railway, high-road, Regnitz, and Ludwigs-Canal run parallel. 188 M. *Hirschaid;* 192 M. *Eggolsheim*. To the left on the height near Forchheim rises the *Jägersburg* (1184 ft.), once a hunting-lodge of the bishops of Bamberg.

196 M. **Forchheim** (870 ft.; *Hirsch; Zettelmaier, Zur Eisenbahn*, both at the station), once a frontier-fortress of the bishops of Bamberg, was a place of some importance as far back as the time of Charlemagne. Pop. 6000. The Gothic *Church* contains twelve scenes from the Passion, of Wohlgemut's school and wood-carvings and reliefs by Adam Krafft and Veit Stoss. The spacious *Schloss*, of the 14th cent., is now occupied by public offices. The rapid *Wiesent* falls into the Regnitz here. — Excursion to the *Franconian Switzerland*, see p. 92.

About 11 M. to the N.W. of Forchheim is Count Schönborn's beautiful château of **Pommersfelden**, built in 1711-17 in the baroque style and sumptuously fitted up in the interior, though the best specimens of the once famous picture-gallery were sold in 1867. Large park. Visitors apply at the steward's office.

To the right, near (201 M.) *Baiersdorf*, are the ruins of *Scharfeneck*, destroyed by the Swedes in 1634. Beyond a tunnel of 374 yds. the Regnitz-Thal and Ludwigs-Canal are seen on the left.

205½ M. **Erlangen** (920 ft.; *Schwan; Wallfisch; *Blaue Glocke;* beer in the *Gute Quelle*, etc.; *Rail. Restaurant*), with 17,565 inhab.

(3800 Rom. Cath.), still partly enclosed by its ancient **walls**, owes its regular construction to a fire in 1706, which destroyed most of **the houses**, and its prosperity **mainly to** French Protestants, exiled **by the revocation of** the Edict **of Nantes** (1685), **who** transferred **their industries hither, and** also to German Protestants who took **refuge here when** the French devastated the Palatinate.

The *University* (1000 students, chiefly of medicine and theology), was founded in 1743 by Margrave **Alexander** of Brandenburg-Bayreuth. In front **of the** building, originally the palace of the margraves, **is a** *Statue* **of the** founder by Schwanthaler. In the marketplace **opposite rises the** modern *Pauli Fountain*, with Tritons, Nereids, and bronze figures **of** Erlanga and Alma Mater. The *University Library* contains **several** curiosities, including a Bible with miniatures of the 12th cent., and a **valuable** collection of drawings **by** Netherlandish **and German masters of the** 15-16th cent. **(some of** them damaged), **Dürer being** represented **by about** 20 sketches. The university also contains natural history collections and an 'aula' with numerous **portraits. The beautiful** palace-garden, **which now belongs to** the university, contains several university institutions, **chief of which is the** *Collegienhaus*, completed **in 1889, with a façade adorned with figures of the four Faculties. Near it are an unfinished statue of the Great Elector and a large fountain with 45** statuettes, said **to be portraits of the first French refugees who settled** here. The **Luitpold-Platz is adorned with a bronze** statue of *Prof. Herz*. In **the Bahnhof-Platz is a tasteful little fountain** in bronze.

Pleasant **walks** on the *Rathsberg* (belvedere and restaurant) and the *Altstädter Berg*, **a** spur of the Jura, at the foot of which a fair is held at Whitsuntide. On the W. slope is the *Canal Monument*, by Schwanthaler, erected by Ludwig I. in memory of the completion of the Ludwigs-Canal (p. 75), with figures of the Danube and Main, Navigation and Commerce.

BRANCH RAILWAY (17½ M., in 2¼ hrs.) to the E. to *Gräfenberg* (Post; Stadelmann), **a** little town with a Schloss, prettily situated at the foot of the *Eberhartsberg*, a fine point of view. (Entrance to Franconian Switzerland **by** the **charmingly** situated *Egloffstein*.)

Near **(208 M.)** *Eltersdorf* **we have** a pretty view, **to the left,** of **the** château of *Grossgründlach* (formerly the Himmelsthron Convent, burial-place of the 'White Lady', p. 74). The **line** crosses the Ludwigs-Canal to **(210 M.)** *Vach* and joins **the** Würzburg railway (see p. 69); **to the** right rises **the Alte Feste (p.** 70). The *Regnitz* is crossed; fine view of Fürth **to the left. 215 M. Fürth,** and thence by *Doos* to (220 M.) **Nuremberg, see pp. 69, 70.**

17. From Würzburg to Bamberg. Kissingen.

RAILWAY to (62 M.) **Bamberg in** 2-3⅓ hrs. (fares 8 ℳ 10, 5 ℳ 40, 3 ℳ 50 pf.; express 9 ℳ 30, **6 ℳ 60 pf.**). From Oberndorf-Schweinfurt to Kissingen, see p. 83.

Würzburg, **see p.** 64. **Beyond** (5 M.) *Rottendorf* (p. 69), junction for Nuremberg, the line turns towards the N.E. 10½ M. *Selig-*

enstadt; 14 M. *Bergtheim* (watershed, 376 ft. above Würzburg, 257 ft. above Schweinfurt); 17 M. *Essleben;* 20 M. *Weigolshausen*, where the direct line to Gemünden (p. 64) diverges (to the left *Schloss Werneck*, now a lunatic asylum); 23 M. *Bergrheinfeld*. — 26½ M. **Oberndorf-Schweinfurt** (*Rail. Restaurant; Inn*, opposite the station, plain; omnibus to the town 20 pf.), junction for the Gemünden (p. 64) and the Kissingen lines (see below).

To the S.E. of Weigolshausen, prettily situated on the Main, lies (5½ M.) Ludwigsbad Wipfeld *(Curhaus)*, with sulphur-springs and peat-baths, etc. Omnibus from Schweinfurt station in 1½ hr.; one-horse carr. from Weigolshausen or Seligenstadt 4½ ℳ.

28 M. **Schweinfurt** (**Rabe; *Deutsches Haus; *Krone; Café-Restaurant Victoria; Post)*, with 12,430 inhab., once a free town of the Empire. In the market-place is a **Statue of Rückert*, the poet (1788-1866), by Thiersch and Ruemann. The house in which Rückert was born, at the corner of the Rückert-Str., is indicated by a relief. The handsome *Rathhaus* of 1570-72 contains the municipal library (over 10,000 vols.) and the *Museum* of mediæval art and historical relics (adm. 9-12 and 2-5). The Protestant church of *St. Johann* (recently restored) dates from the 14th century. The *Gymnasium*, or grammar-school, founded in 1631 by Gustavus Adolphus, was transferred to a handsome new building to the N. of the town in 1881. Engine-works, dye-works, sugar-factories, etc., flourish here, and a large cattle-market is held every fortnight. Pleasant walk to the chief *Reservoir* of the water-works; also to the *Wehrwäldchen* (left bank). On the (¼ hr.) *Peterstirne* is a belvedere built in 1872, with a collection of weapons and fresco-paintings.

The line follows the Main. On the hill to the left is the château of *Mainberg*. 31½ M. *Schonungen;* 35 M. *Gädheim;* 39 M. *Ober-Theres*. To the left rises the old château of *Theres*, founded as a seat of the Babenberg family before 900, converted into a monastery in 1043, and dissolved in 1803. Adjacent is a modern château.

42 M. **Hassfurt** *(Post)*, a small town with walls and massive gateway, possesses a fine Gothic chapel, the **Marien-Capelle*, or *Ritter-Capelle* (middle of 15th cent.), restored by Heideloff. On the outside of the choir is a triple row of the armorial bearings of the members of an ecclesiastical brotherhood of nobles, founded in 1413, which contributed to the cost of building the chapel. Others are carved on the pillars and on the vaulting in the interior (in all 248).

BRANCH RAILWAY in 55 min. to (9½ M.) *Hofheim*, viâ (5 M.) *Königsberg*, in the Duchy of Coburg, with 1000 inhab., birthplace of the famous mathematician Johann Müller, surnamed Regiomontanus (d. 1476), to whose memory a fountain was erected here in 1871.

To the left of (46½ M.) *Zeil*, another walled town, rises the ruined fortress of *Schmachtenberg*, erected in 1438, destroyed by Albert of Brandenburg in 1552. On the left bank, opposite (50 M.) *Ebelsbach*, lies the small town of *Eltmann*, commanded by the ancient watch-tower of the castle of *Waldburg*, a thousand years old. 52 M. *Stettfeld;* 54 M. *Staffelbach;* 58 M. *Oberhaid*. To the right the towers

KISSINGEN.
1:9800

UMGEBUNG VON KISSINGEN.
1:150000

1. Actien-Badhaus	B.3.	7. Krug-Magazin	B.3.	
2. Conversationssaal & Arkadenbau	B.2.	8. Kgl. Post & Telegraphen-Amt	C.1.	
3. Kgl. Bezirksamt & Bade-Commissariat	C.1.	**Mineralquellen.**		
4. Kgl. Kurhaus	B.C.2.	9. Rakoczy	B.3.	a. Russischer Hof ... B.3.
Kirchen.		10. Pandur	B.3.	b. Hôtel Victoria ... B.3.
5. Alte Kathol. K.	C.1.	11. Maxbrunnen	B.2.	c. Central-Hôtel ... C.2.
6. Protest. K.	C.3.	12. Standbild Max II	B.2.	d. Hôtel Sanner ... B.4.
Neue Kathol. K.	D.2.	13. Theater	D.2.	e. Engl. Hof ... C.2.
				f. Wittelsbacher Hof ... C.1.

Gasthöfe.

g. Württemberger Hof ... D.1.
h. Preuss. Hof ... C.2.
i. Hôt. Holzmann ... A.1.
k. Schmitt ... A.1.
l. Zapff ... C.4.
m. Metropole ... A.1.

of St. Michael's, the Altenburg, and lastly Bamberg with the four **cathedral-towers become visible**. The Main is then crossed.

62 M. **Bamberg**, see p. 75.

From Oberndorf-Schwbinfurt to Kissingen, $14^{1}/_{2}$ M. (railway in $^{1}/_{2}$-1 hr.). $3^{1}/_{2}$ M. *Oberwerrn*; 6 M. *Poppenhausen*; $8^{1}/_{2}$ M. *Ebenhausen*, where the line to Meiningen (p. 85) diverges. We skirt wooded hills, **pass the ruin of** *Bodenlaube* (p 84), and enter the valley in which this famous 'Bad' is situated.

$14^{1}/_{2}$ M. **Kissingen.** — Hotels. °Curhaus (Pl. 4; B, C, 2), with baths, R., L., & A. from 4, B. 1 *M* 20, D. $3^{1}/_{2}$, pens. from 9 *M*; °Hôtel de Russie (Pl. a; B, 3), R. 2-10 *M*, L. & A. 90, B. 1 *M* 40, D. 3 *M* 50 pf., pens. from 7 *M*; °Hôtel Victoria (Pl. b; B, 3); °Sanner (Pl. d; B, 4), R., L., & A. 3-5, B. 1 *M* 20 pf., D. 3, pens. $7^{1}/_{2}$-10 *M*; all in the Curhaus-Strasse. — °Englischer Hof (Pl. e; C, 2), Theater-Str.; °Holzmann (Pl. i), Métropole (Pl. m), R. 3-6, B. $1^{1}/_{4}$, D. $2^{1}/_{2}$ *M*; Höt. & Villa Diana, Schmitt (Pl. k), R. from 2 *M*, L. 80 pf., D. 2 *M* 60 pf., all on the opposite bank of the Saale (Pl. A, 1); °Zapf (Pl. 1; C, 4), at the station, R. from 2 *M*, L. 30 pf., pens. 6 *M*. — Second-class: °Wittelsbacher Hof (Pl. f); Preussischer Hof (Pl. h), R. 2-4 *M*, B. 80 pf., pens. from 5 *M*; Württemberger Hof (Pl. g); °Central-Hotel (Pl. c; C, 2), all in the town, and open in winter also. — **Hôtels Garnis**: *Grand Hôtel Garni*, *Hailmann*, both by the Curgarten. On the other side of the Saale: *Dr. E. Diruf*, *Fürstenhof*, *Pilartz*, *Minerva*, *D. Vay*, *Gleissner*, *Ölmühle*, *Keyser*, *Erhard*, *Villa Franconia*, *Westend-Haus*, *Park Villa*, *Vier Jahreszeiten*, *Villa Holländer*, *Teutonia*, *Thuringia*, *Martin*, *Altenberg*, *E. Vay*, *Bavaria*, *Monbijou*. In the town: *Frau von Bolling*, with garden; *Dr. Scherpf*, *Habermann*, *Hohmann*, *Gayde*, *Dr. Stöhr*, *Göbel*, *Büdel*, *Dr. Sotier*, *Villa Bauer*, *Villa Stella*, *Villa Elsa*, *Herrnhof*. In the Curhaus-Str.: *Bergmann*, *Will*, *Dr. G. Diruf*, *Herbert*, *Fischer*, *Rieger*, *Abt*, *Villa Krampf*, *Singer*, *Bernhardt*.

Restaurants. *Casino* (p. 84); *Cursaal*; *Messerschmidt*, near the Curgarten; *Federbeck*, Hartmann-Str.; *Frühlingsgarten*, Theater-Str.; *Schweizerhaus*, on the right bank of the Saale; wine at *Halk's* (old-German wineroom), *Arnold's*, *Dauch's*, *Karch's*, all in the market.

Carriage with two horses to the salt-baths $1^{1}/_{2}$ *M*, to *Bocklet* 13, *Hammelburg* 23, *Brückenau* 30 *M*; with one horse one-third less. For short drives in the town and environs there are *fiacres* with a fixed tariff.

Reading Rooms at the *Curhaus* (gratis) and at the *Casino* by the Actien-Badhaus (adm. for non-subscribers 50 pf.); also *Weinberger's*, by the Curgarten (per week $2^{1}/_{2}$, per month 6 *M*).

Theatre (Pl. 13), performances daily **during the** season.

Tax payable by patients whose stay **exceeds** a week 30 *M* for the **head** of a family, and 10 *M* for each additional person, or 20 and 6 *M*, **or 10** and 3 *M* respectively, according to the rank of the parties. Children under fifteen and servants pay one-half less.

Baths (10-1 und 3-6) at the *Curhaus*, at the *Actien-Badhaus*, and in the *Salinen-Badeanstalt*. — *Pneumatic Institute* (Dr. Dietz), Schloss-Str. 6.

English Church (Pl. D, 1); service during the summer.

Kissingen (660 ft.), **the most frequented** watering-place **in Bavaria** (4250 inhab.), lies picturesquely in the valley of the *Fränkische Saale*, enclosed by wooded hills. **The sanatory properties of the waters were** known **as early as** the 16th cent., **and the** Prince Bishops of Würzburg took the place under their **protection**; but at the beginning of the present century it was still **a** mere village. The growing repute of the springs and increasing number of visitors have now converted the place into a handsome and well-built town, which

6*

is visited by over 14,000 patients annually, many of whom are English and Russians.

The extensive **Curgarten** between the *Curhaus* and *Cursaal*, the principal promenade, is embellished with a marble *Statue of King Lewis I., by Knoll of Munich, a Hygeia imparting to the Rakoczy and Pandur their healing influence, and a statue of King Maximilian II., both in marble, by Arnold, a native of the place. On the S. side are the chief drinking-springs, the *Rakoczy* (300,000 bottles of which are annually exported) and the *Pandur*, which is also used for baths. On the N. side is the *Maxbrunnen*, resembling Selters water. From 6 to 8 a.m., the hour for drinking the waters, the Curgarten presents a lively scene, and a band plays in fine weather. From 5 to 7 p.m. the band again plays, and the fashionable world reassembles.

Opposite the garden, on the right bank of the Saale, stands the **Actien-Badhaus** (Pl. 1), a large edifice of red sandstone, with two wings (left, baths for ladies; right, for gentlemen), and an enginehouse in the centre. Adjacent is the *Casino*, with reading-room, restaurant, etc. — A tablet on the house of Dr. Diruf, also on the right bank, commemorates the attempted assassination of Prince Bismarck in 1874 (see below).

Pretty walk, through the Von-der-Tann-Strasse and by the *Stationsberg*, or by the path (Pl. C, 4, 5) to the left, above the Hôtel Zapf, to the ruins of (25 min.) *Bodenlaube* (1128 ft.), the N. tower of which commands a fine view (Restaurant zur Linde, below the ruin). We may return by the road leading through *Unterbodenlaube*, with its interesting old lime-tree. Well-kept walks lead to the *Lindesmühle*, the *Altenberg*, the *Staffelsberg* (fine view from the *Ludwig Tower*), the *Wichtelshöhlen*, the *Kaskaden-Thal* and *Altenburger Haus*, the *Klaushof* (Hotel, in the wood), the *Klaushöhe* (omn. five times every afternoon, 1 ℳ, there and back 1½ ℳ), etc.

On 10th July, 1866, Kissingen was the scene of a sharp engagement between the Prussians and Bavarians. The latter were, however, eventually obliged to yield. Near the cemetery, ½ M. from the Curgarten, is a handsome monument in memory of the fallen.

The **Saline Springs** with the extensive evaporating-sheds, situated on the *Saale*, 1½ M. to the N., are reached by walks on both banks. A small steamboat plies on the Saale to the springs every 20 min. (fare 30, return-fare 50 pf.). A handsome bath-house (*Salinenbad*) has been erected over the *Artesian Well, which is 330 ft. in depth (containing two per cent of salt; temperature 63° Fahr.) and frequently rises to a height of 10 ft. in its covered reservoir. Near it is a *Statue of Prince Bismarck*, who has frequently visited the *Obere Saline*, ½ M. farther on.

At the village of *Hausen*, ¾ M. farther on, is the Schönbornsprudel, a shaft upwards of 2000 ft. in depth, by which it was intended to reach an extensive stratum of salt. The work has, however, been given up, as it injured the other mineral springs at Kissingen. A square tower, 100 ft. in height, built over the shaft, is open to visitors from 4 to 6 p.m.

BRÜCKENAU.   *17. Route.* **85**

Bocklet, another watering-place with powerful chalybeate springs and mud-baths (about 350 patients annually), is prettily situated on the Saale, 6 M. to the N. of Kissingen (diligence daily at 10 a.m.; fare 1 ℳ). Rooms at the *Curhaus*, in *Plank's Inn*, various villas, etc. Between the Curhaus and the *Badhaus* with its *Trinkhalle* are pleasant grounds with fine old trees.

°*Schloss Aschach*, on the Saale, 3/4 M. to the S. of Bocklet, restored in the mediæval style, the property of Count Luxburg, contains a collection of old goblets, carving, etc. (fee). — Attractive excursion through the Saalethal to (6 M.) *Neustadt* (see below).

The third of these Franconian baths (20½ M. from Kissingen; diligence daily in 4½ hrs.; fare 2 ℳ 90 pf.) is Bad Brückenau *(Cur-Hôtel* and *Curhäuser*, R. 1-4 ℳ, B. 70, D. 2 ℳ 20 pf.; *Schloss-Hôtel;* **Hot. Füglein*, R. from 1 ℳ, D. 1 ℳ 70 pf., pens. 4-5 ℳ; *Bayrischer Hof; Schwan; Villa Knell, Villa Heil, Sinnthalhof)*, in the grassy valley of the *Sinn*, enclosed by wooded hills, 2 M. to the W. of the little town of *Brückenau* (Post). Handsome Cursaal in the Italian style, built in 1827-33, with restaurant and public rooms. The *Stahl, Wernarzer*, and *Sinnberger Springs*, impregnated with carbonic acid, are beneficial in cases of poverty of blood, indigestion, kidney disease, etc. About 1400 patients annually. Visitors' tax 5 ℳ; band-subscription 2 ℳ weekly.

Beautiful walks in the environs. Shady paths with views (*Ludwigs-Platz, Washington-Platz, Amalienruhe*, etc.) lead to the N. through the *Harthwald* to (1½ hr.) *Kloster Volkersberg;* to the W. to (2 hrs.) *Schwarzenfels*, with its old castle; to the S. by the *Sinnberg* to the (2 hrs.) *Dreistelzberg* (2385 ft.), with belvedere tower. — Finest of all the excursions is the ascent of the Kreuzberg (3050 ft.), the highest of the *Rhön Mts.*, crowned with a Franciscan monastery (to the N.E., 4 hrs.). Road, following the *Sinn*, as far as (7 M.) *Wildflecken;* thence to the top (with guide) in 1½ hr. Extensive view of N. Franconia as far as the Fichtelgebirge, and W. as far as the Taunus. The hills around Würzburg and the Steigerwald close the view towards the S., and the Thuringian Forest and the hills of Fulda to the N.

From Brückenau to Jossa, 11 M., local railway in 1 hr. (fares 1 ℳ, 65 pf.). Stations: *Stadt Brückenau* (see above); 1¼ M. *Sinnthalhof* (see above); 1¾ M. *Bad Brückenau* (see above). Then along the *Sinn*, viâ *Eckarts, Zeitlofs*, and *Altengronau* to (11 M.) *Jossa* (p. 63).

From Kissingen to Meiningen, 46 M. (railway in 3 hrs.). 5½ M. *Ebenhausen* (p. 83); the line diverges here to the left from the Schweinfurt railway, and leads by *Rottershausen* to (15½ M.) Münnerstadt (°*Fränkischer Hof)*, a small town on the *Lauer*, with an interesting church in the transition style. 18½ M. *Niederlauer*. — 21 M. Neustadt (°*Goldner Mann)*, an antiquated town prettily situated on the *Saale*. Near it (3/4 M.) is the °*Salzburg*, an ancient palace probably built by Charlemagne, now one of the largest and most picturesque ruins in Germany. At the foot of the hill lies Bad *Neuhaus* (°Curhaus), with salt and carbonic acid springs.

[From Neustadt to Bischofsheim, 12 M. (railway in 1½ hr.). The line traverses the wooded *Brendthal*, passing *Brendlorenzen* (with a venerable church, said to have been erected by King Carloman in 770), *Schönau*, and *Wegfurt*. Bischofsheim 'vor der Rhön' (*Stern; Löwe)*, an ancient town with 1350 inhab., lies at the N. foot of the *Kreuzberg* (see above), which may be ascended hence viâ *Haselbach* in 1½-2 hrs.]

A little beyond Neustadt the line quits the Saalethal and turns to the left into the valley of the **Streu**. Stations: *Heustreu; Unsleben; Mellrich-*

stadt, with an old church disfigured by restoration. 36½ M. *Rentwertshausen*. The train here crosses the low watershed between the Saale and the Werra, and descends to (41 M.) *Ritschenhausen* and (46 M.) **Meiningen** (see *Baedeker's Northern Germany*).

From Kissingen to *Gemünden* viâ *Hammelburg*, see p. 63.

18. From Neuenmarkt to Weiden. The Fichtelgebirge.

49 M. RAILWAY to *Bayreuth*, 28-40 min. (fares 1 ℳ 70, 1 ℳ 20, 75 pf.); from Bayreuth to *Weiden*, 1½-2 hrs. (fares 4 ℳ 70, 3 ℳ, 1 ℳ 95 pf.). Express from Bayreuth to *Munich*, 6½ hrs.

Neuenmarkt, see p. 74. Our line turns to the S., and runs through the broad valley of the *Weisse Main* to (3 M.) *Trebgast*, then through a narrow valley, which afterwards expands. 6 M. *Harsdorf*; 10½ M. *Bindlach*. Near Bayreuth extensive meadows are traversed. Avenues of poplars on the left, and the Wagner Theatre and the large lunatic asylum on the right are conspicuous. The suburb of *St. Georgen* is passed. At the station is a large cotton-factory.

13 M. **Bayreuth**. — Hotels. °SONNE, Richard-Wagner-Str., R. from 2, D. 2½ ℳ; °ANKER, Opern-Str.; °REICHSADLER, Maximilian-Str. (Markt), R. 1½-2, D. 2 ℳ, B. 80 pf.; °BAHNHOF-HÔTEL, opposite the station; SCHWARZES ROSS, Ludwigs-Str.; TRAUBE, Richard-Wagner-Strasse.

Restaurants. Beer at *Hopfmüller's* (Reichsadler), in the market-place; *Vogel*, Prinz-Luitpold-Platz; *Baals*, *Bencker*, Maximilian-Str. (wine); °*Café Sammet*, Harmonie-Brücke, with the 'Wagner room' and garden, moderate; *Café Vogel*, etc.

Baths. *Bad Rosenau*, *Städtische Bade- und Schwimmanstalt*, both in the Bade-Strasse.

Post Office, at the railway-station. — Telegraph Office, Markt 80.

Cabs. Per drive in the town (¼ hr.), with one horse, 1-2 pers. 40, 3-4 pers. 60 pf.; with two horses 50 or 75 pf. To the Wagner Theatre 2 ℳ, with two horses 3 ℳ; to the Bürgerreuth, Rollwenzelei, Oberkonnersreuth, or Geigenreuth (a farm adjoining the Fantaisie Park) 2 or 3 ℳ; to the Eremitage 3 ℳ, with two horses 4-5 ℳ; to the Fantaisie 4-6 ℳ. Gratuities included in these fares.

Porter in the town or to the station, for 33 lbs. 15 pf., for 110 lbs. 20 pf.

All charges are raised during the Wagner festivals; the 'Wohnungs-Comité' should be applied to for accommodation.

Bayreuth (1180 ft.), with 24,556 inhab. (3300 Rom. Cath.), the capital of Upper Franconia, residence of the Margraves of Brandenburg-Culmbach from 1603 to 1769 and Bavarian since 1810, is mainly indebted for its present appearance to Margrave Christian (d. 1655), who transferred his seat from Kulmbach hither, to George William (d. 1726), and to Frederick (d. 1763), husband of Wilhelmine, the talented sister of Frederick the Great. Under the last-named prince many handsome buildings were erected.

At the end of the street ascending to the right as we quit the station, is seen the Richard Wagner Theatre (p. 88). To the left the Bahnhof-Str. leads over the Main to the Luitpold-Platz, in which (to the right) rises the *Palace of Duke Alexander of Wurtemberg*. Farther on, to the left beyond the Harmonie-Brücke, is **the** Opern-Strasse, with the *Opera House*, a sumptuous building erected by Margrave Frederick in 1747, and richly decorated in the interior in the rococo style. At the end of the Opern-Str. is the Maximilian-Platz, whence the Maximilian-Str. diverges to the W., the Ludwig-Str. to the S., the Bad-Str. and the Richard-Wagner-Str. to the E. The *House of Richard Wagner*, Richard-Wagner-Strasse 283^1/$_2$, built in 1873-74 by Wölfle, bears the inscription: 'Hier wo mein Wähnen Frieden fand, *Wahnfried* sei dieses Haus von mir benannt'. Above is a sgraffito by Krausse, representing Wotan as a wanderer. In front of the house is a bust of King Lewis II. Wagner (d. 1883) is buried in the garden.

The Ludwig-Str. (see above) leads to the Residenz-Platz, in which is the *New Palace* (Pl. 2), a long building with wings, now a royal residence, erected in 1753. The left wing now contains the picture-gallery of the Kunst-Verein (open Sun., Tues., & Thurs., 11-1). The *Palace Garden* and *Park* are used as public promenades (military band on Sun. and holidays). The large *Fountain* in front of the Palace bears an equestrian *Statue of Margrave Christian Ernest* (d. 1712), a marshal in the imperial service, erected in 1700. The four allegorical figures in sandstone at the foot of the pedestal represent the four quarters of the globe.

In front of the *Gymnasium* rises Schwanthaler's *Statue of Jean Paul Friedrich Richter* (d. 1825; Pl. 3), whose house in the Friedrich-Strasse (No. 5, to the right) bears an inscription.

From the N. end of the Friedrich-Str. the Kanzlei-Str. leads to the right to the Maximilian-Str. and the old palace. The Gothic *Stadtpfarrkirche* (Prot.; Pl. 4), built in 1439-46, contains several pictures by *Riedel*, a native of Bayreuth. Beneath the church is the *Fürstengruft*, in which most of the princes from the 17th to the 18th cent. are interred.

The *Old Palace* (Pl. 1), begun in 1454, burned down in 1758, and soon after rebuilt, is now occupied by public offices. The octagonal *Tower*, erected in 1603, with a remarkably fine double spiral staircase, affords a good survey of the environs (key at the sacristan's, Richard-Wagner-Str. 291; fee 40 pf.). In front of the Palace rises a *Statue of Maximilian II.* in bronze, by Brugger, erected on the 50th anniversary of the union of the principality with the kingdom of Bavaria.

The *Roman Catholic Church* beside the palace (formerly the palace-church) contains the tombs of Margrave Frederick and his consort Wilhelmine (p. 86). Close by is the *Harmonie*, a pretty little Renaissance building. — The Maximilian-Strasse (marketplace) is embellished with several fountains. Many of the houses possess handsome oriel windows. In the Schul-Strasse, which diverges to the right, is the handsome school, in front of which is a bronze bust of *J. B. Graser* (d. 1841), the schoolmaster, by Zumbusch. In the cemetery to the W. of the town (Erlanger Str.) are the graves of *Jean Paul Richter* (see above) and *Franz Liszt* (d. 1886), the latter in a small domed chapel.

To the N. of the town, 1 M. from the station, on the hill

below the Bürgerreuth, stands the *Wagner Theatre*, where the 'Nibelungenring' was first performed in 1876 and 'Parsifal' in 1882. The theatre, built by Brückwald of Leipsic, contains 1650 seats. Higher up is the *Bürgerreuth*, a restaurant which commands a fine view of Bayreuth and the environs. Above the Bürgerreuth to the N. towers the *Hohe Warte* (1525 ft.), on which rises the *Siegesthurm* (55 ft.) in memory of the war of 1870-71, commanding an extensive view.

St. Georgen, commonly called the '*Brandenburger*', situated on a hill to the N.E., is a suburb of Bayreuth, founded by Margr. George William (d. 1726) at the beginning of the 18th century. The road to it passes through a tunnel below the railway, beyond which, on the left, is the large *Cotton Factory* mentioned at p. 86. The road divides here. The branch to the right, a maple and chestnut avenue, flanked with handsome modern houses, leads to St. Georgen. The linden avenue to the left, planted in 1723, leads past a large spinning-mill (left), the new *District Prison* (right), and the *St. Georgen House of Correction* (left), to the *Military Hospital*, once the chapter-house of the knights of an '*Ordre de la Sincérité*', instituted in 1712 by George William and changed to the Order of the Red Eagle (Roter Adler-Orden) in 1734 by Margrave George Frederick Charles. The meetings of the order were held in the church of St. Georgen (still called '*Ordenskirche*'), built in 1705-18. The balustrade of the gallery is adorned with the arms of the knights down to 1767. — At the other end of the principal street is the *Abbey Church of Gravenreuth*.

The **Eremitage**, 3 M. to the E. of Bayreuth, a château with gardens, fountains, artificial ruins, etc., was erected by George William in 1715. It contains a number of family-portraits, including Frederick the Great, as a child, and as king, and his sister the Margravine Wilhelmine, who wrote her memoirs here; among those in the lower part of the Schloss is that of the Countess Orlamünde (the 'White Lady', p. 74). In the vicinity is the 'Grosse Bassin,' an imitation of that at Versailles, surrounded by a temple of the Sun and its two detached wings. The walls of these buildings are fantastically inlaid with coloured stones, rock-crystal, etc. The interior of the temple is sumptuously fitted up, and contains handsome columns of striped marble. Between the château itself and the offices (now a restaurant) is a pretty garden. Adjacent are the Roman theatre and the large water-tower, containing 1000 gallons of water for the fountains. The water-works play on Sundays about 5 p.m. (adm. gratis) and may be seen at other times for a fee of 2 $\mathcal{M}$.

About halfway to the Eremitage, at the point where the road turns at a right angle to the N., is a small inn, called *Rollwenzel's Haus*, with a room where *Jean Paul Richter* used to write, containing some memorials of him.

The **Fantaisie**, a château 3½ M. to the W. of Bayreuth, built in 1758 and tastefully fitted up, the seat of Duke Alex. of Wurtemberg (d. 1881) from 1828 to 1881, is charmingly situated on a richly wooded hill, near the village of *Eckersdorf*. The gardens and park, with bath-house, pheasantry, fountains, etc., are kept in excellent order. The grounds attract numerous visitors from Bayreuth (*Hôtel Fantaisie, by the park). — In the vicinity is *St. Gilgenberg*, a lunatic asylum, prettily situated.

Eckersdorf lies on the direct route to the Franconian Switzerland (diligence daily in 4 hrs. to *Waischenfeld*, p. 94). A pleasanter route

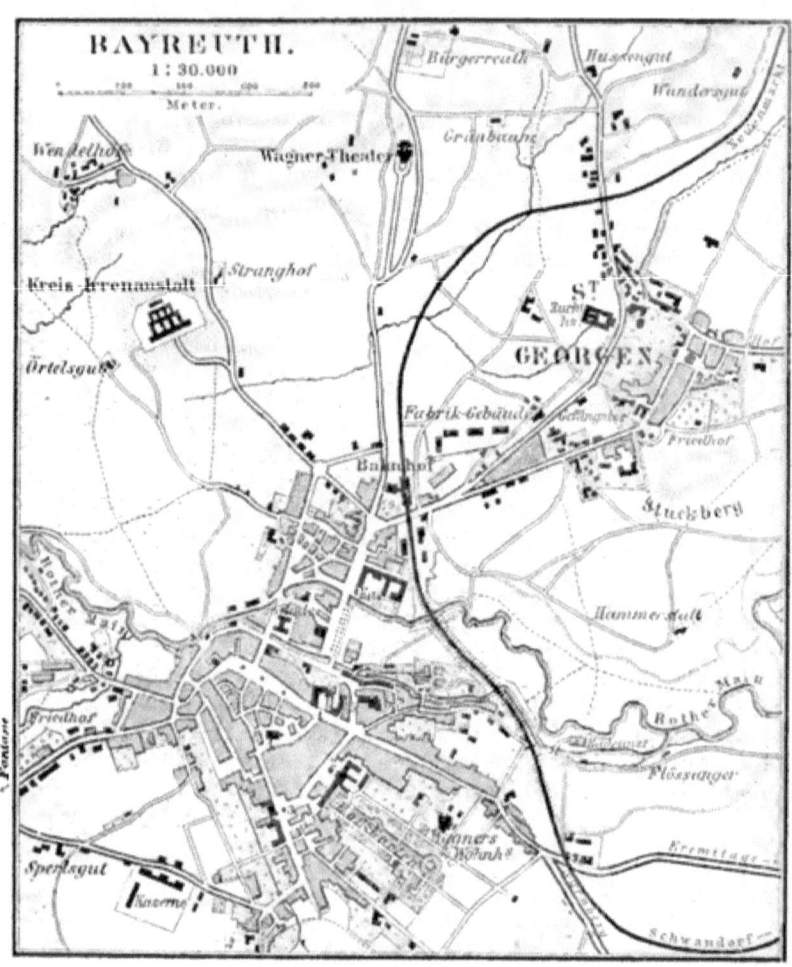

for pedestrians is by *Mistelgau*, *Glashütten*, *Volsbach*, and *Kirchahorn* to *Rabenstein* (p. 94) in 4-5 hrs.

To the left, as Bayreuth is quitted, are St. Georgen and the **Eremitage**, to the right wooded hills. 18 M. *Stockau*; 20½ M. *Seybothenreuth*; 25 M. *Kirchenlaibach* (junction for the Nuremberg and Eger Railway, p. 110). 29 M. *Kemnath-Neustadt*; on the right the *Rauhe Kulm* (2240 ft.), on the left the S. spurs of the Fichtelgebirge. We follow the valley of the **Heidenab**. 32 M. *Trabitz*; 36 M. *Pressath*; 39½ M. *Schwarzenbach*; thence through extensive **pine-forests** *(Parksteiner* and **Mantler Wald)** to (41½ M.) *Parksteinhütten* and **(49 M.)** *Weiden* (p. 134).

The Fichtelgebirge.

DILIGENCE once daily from Bayreuth to (9½ M.) *Berneck* in 2 hrs. From stat. *Markt-Schorgast* (p. 74) to (3½ M.) Berneck omnibus twice daily in 40 minutes. — From Berneck through the *Goldmühl-Thal* (valley of the Weisse Main) to *Bischofsgrün*, diligence daily in 1¾ hr. (carr. 6-8 ℳ, incl. fee). Then **on foot over** the Ochsenkopf and Schneeberg **to** *Weissenstadt* in 6 hrs. — **Walk to the top of the** *Waldstein* and back (2½ **hrs.**); drive from Weissenstadt **by** Wunsiedel to the *Alexandersbad* in 2 **hrs.**; ascend the *Luisenburg* with guide, and return to *Wunsiedel* (3 hrs.). **From** Wunsiedel by train in 10 min. to *Holenbrunn*, **on** the Fichtelgebirge Railway, p. 118. — *Carriage* and *pair* from Bayreuth to Alexandersbad by Berneck, Seehaus, Tröstau, Schönbrunn, and Wunsiedel in 8-9 hrs., 40-45 ℳ. — *Guides* (4-5 ℳ per day) **are** seldom **required, as** the German Alpine Club **and** local associations **have** made **paths** and provided finger-posts.

Bayreuth, see p. 86. The road leads through *St. Georgen* (p. 88) to (3 M.) *Bindlach* (p. 86), where it begins to ascend. Fine view as we look back on Bayreuth. Near Berneck we cross the *Weisse Main*.

9½ M. **Berneck** (1273 ft.; *Löwe*; *Hirsch*, R. 1½-2 ℳ, B. 60 pf.; *Krone* or *Post*, R. 1-1½ ℳ, D. 1 ℳ 40 pf.; *Stadt Bayreuth*; *Bube*, with **garden**-restaurant; *Schmidt's Restaurant*, **in the** market-place; *Bäreneck Restaurant*, with pretty view), picturesquely situated **in a** narrow valley watered **by** the *Oelsnitz*, is a favourite summer-resort (1500 inhab.). In the **main** street is the *Curhaus*, **with reading-room,** garden, and restaurant. **On** the Oelsnitz, at the foot of the Schlossberg, **is the** *Cur-Colonnade*, where a band plays several times a week. (Visitors' **tax for** a stay of more than five days, 4 ℳ, two pers. 6 ℳ, etc.). **On the** steep hill above **the town are the** ruins **of two** castles and **of a** chapel. A pleasant **path along the** Oelsnitz gradually ascends the wooded hill in 20 min. **to the** *Obere Burg* (1548 **ft.**), **destroyed by the** Hussites **in 1430**. Fine view hence; still finer from the *Engelsburg*, 10 min. farther on, **and the** adjacent *Kirchleite* (1935 ft.; belvedere).

Another excursion is to (¾ hr.) the ruined castle of *Stein*, romantically situated in the valley of the Oelsnitz. Thence **we may** walk through the valleys of the Oelsnitz and the *Lübnitz*, past the ruin of *Grünstein*, to (¾ hr.) *Gefrees* (p. 74). — Pearl-mussels (Unio margaritifer) are found in the Oelsnitz in considerable quantities; the shells are opened and the pearls removed every 6-7 years by a government official.

Omnibus from Berneck to *Markt-Schorgast* and *Bischofsgrün*, see above. Carriage and pair 12-15 ℳ a day, or 6-8 ℳ for half a day, incl. gratuity. — *Himmelkron*, mentioned at p. 74, lies 4 M. to the W.

The NEW ROAD from Berneck by *Goldmühl* (Heisinger; Zapf; Schwarzes Ross) to (9 M.) Bischofsgrün crosses the Oelsnitz. (On the hill-side is the arboretum *Blüchersruhe*, with its belvedere.) It then leads to the left through the *Goldmühl-Thal*, or valley of the *Weisse Main*, to the *Glasenmühle* (see below), passing a chalybeate spring 1½ M. before reaching Bischofsgrün. The shorter, but less interesting FOOTPATH, on the E. side of the valley, at first ascends rapidly; then, generally level, leads through wood, passing (¾ hr.) *Bärnreut* (1700 ft.). Thence it partly follows the road to (1¼ hr.) *Wilfersreut* (2296 ft.), descends by the *Weisse Main* to the *Glasenmühle* (1952 ft.), and lastly ascends again to (1 hr.) Bischofsgrün (2225 ft.; *Schmidt; Puchtler*), a village conspicuously situated at the N. base of the Ochsenkopf, almost entirely rebuilt since a great fire in 1887, with large manufactories of beads.

The path to the **Ochsenkopf** (3363 ft.; ascent 1 hr.; guide not indispensable: Ochsenkopf 2 ℳ, Ochsenkopf and Schneeberg 4 ℳ) leads through wood, and except at one place, the ascent is gradual. At the top it traverses blocks of granite and passes the *Schneeloch*, a hollow where snow lies till June. At the top is a slab with a very ancient carving of an ox's head (frequently restored). From the *View Tower* we gain an extensive view of the Fichtelgebirge, Franconian Switzerland, etc., including the Thuringian Forest to the N.W. About 5 min. to the S. of the tower is a spot known as the 'Aussicht' (view), commanding a picturesque glimpse of Warmensteinach.

The route by *Warmensteinach* to Bischofsgrün and the Ochsenkopf, 2 hrs. longer than the above, is preferable. The road quits the valley of the Main beyond Goldmühl, and ascends to the right in the valley of the *Zoppatenbach* to (20 min.) *Brandholz*. The antimony, lead, and silver mines once largely worked here, as numerous heaps of rubbish still testify, are now exhausted. About ½ hr. beyond Brandholz we cross a meadow and ascend the road. In a few minutes more, where the path divides, the branch to the left leads to (1¼ hr.) **Warmensteinach** (2065 ft.; *Trassel's Inn*), prettily situated. The shingle-roofed houses lie scattered along the slopes of the upper valley of the *Steinach*. Glass-making and glass-polishing are the chief industries.

A road leads hence through the *Löchle-Thal*, a romantic wooded ravine (tavern), to (1 hr.) *Grassemann* (2405 ft.), a former mining settlement, situated on an open plateau. Before the village we pass the *Ludwigs-Quelle*. Thence either to Bischofsgrün in 1½ hr. by a distinct path (short-cut to the right just beyond the finger-post), or direct to the summit of the *Ochsenkopf* (see above; path indicated by white marks; guide not necessary).

From the Ochsenkopf we descend the saddle to the E., which connects the Ochsenkopf and Schneeberg; 20 min., *Source of the Main* (*Weissmainquelle*; 2910 ft.), an excellent spring, the only one for a long distance (benches; inscription); 10 min., the *Weissmainfelsen* (2857 ft.), a group of rocks affording a fine view of the

Schneeberg and Nusshard, and towards the S. The Bischofsgrün and Fichtelberg road, in the valley which separates the Schneeberg from the Ochsenkopf, is now followed to (3/4 M.) *Karches* (2410 ft.; beer). We here enter the wood to the left, and ascend to (1 hr.) the *Nusshard* (3190 ft.), a group of huge blocks of granite rendered accessible by steps. The nine round hollows on the top of the rock are called 'the Druids' dishes'. The (1/2 hr.) Schneeberg (3454 ft.) is crowned with a group of rocks, 30 ft. high, named the *Backöfele* ('oven'), rendered accessible by a ladder. On the top is a hut built by the Fichtelgebirge Club. *Panorama uninterrupted, except towards the S.W. by the Ochsenkopf: to the S.E. is the Kösseine, to the left the Luisenburg; N.E. the Erzgebirge in the distance; N. the Rudolfstein, Weissenstadt, and the Waldstein; N.W. the Thuringian Mts. and the Gleichberge.

We now descend in 40 min. to the '*Drei Brüder*' (2736 ft.), three lofty groups of granite slabs, that in the middle resembling a wolf; 7 min., the *Rudolfstein* (2848 ft.), a huge and imposing group of granite rocks, ascended by steps, commanding a superb view. We next descend through wood, passing the Staff-Reizenstein monument, to the (1/2 hr.) plain and (1 1/2 M.) Weissenstadt. Before crossing the *Eger* we observe several rock-cellars on the left.

Weissenstadt (2070 ft.; *Adler* or *Alte Post*; *Löwe*), a small town with 2600 inhab., lies in a somewhat marshy valley, on the Eger, which rises 6 M. to the S.W. Ackermann's stone-polishing works enjoy a high reputation.

The °Grosse Waldstein (2920 ft.) may be ascended from Weissenstadt in 1 hr. (without guide). By the barns on the N. side of Weissenstadt, the path diverges from the Kirchenlamitz road to the left and leads into the wood to a (3/4 hr.) finger-post on the left, 'zum Waldstein', 1/4 hr. more. This is another group of granite rocks made accessible by paths and steps, and crowned with an iron pavilion; extensive and picturesque *Panorama, with wooded foreground. The castle of *Waldstein*, of which fragments remain, a robbers' stronghold, was destroyed by the Swabian League in 1523. Adjacent is the finely situated *Waldhaus* (2897 ft.; Rfmts.). — We may now descend to the *Source of the Saale* (2312 ft.), either direct by the *Bärenfang* (path pointed out by the forester) in 1/2 hr., or by (1/2 hr.) *Zell* (2020 ft.), and thence to the S. to the spring in 1/2 hr. more. Thence 3/4 hr. more to the Gefrees and Weissenstadt road. From Zell or from the Waldstein viâ *Sparneck* to *Münchberg* (rail. stat., p. 73), 2 hrs.

A marked path, running first to the N.W. then to the E., and crossing the road from Weissenstadt to Sparneck, leads from the Waldhaus to the (1 3/4 hr.) Epprechtstein (2600 ft.), with a ruined castle and a beautiful view; thence by *Buchhaus* (rfmts.), or direct, to (3/4 hr.) *Kirchenlamitz* (°Löwe), 1 1/2 M. from the station, p. 134.

The shadeless road from Weissenstadt to (2 3/4 hrs.) Wunsiedel is unattractive to walkers. (Carr. and pair to Alexandersbad in 1 1/2 hr., 7-8 *M*; diligence to Röslau, p. 134, twice daily in 1 1/4 hr.)

Wunsiedel (1755 ft.; *Kronprinz, R. 1 *M* 20 pf.; *Einhorn, R. 1 *M*, B. 50 pf.; *Müller's Restaurant;* one-horse carr. to Alexandersbad 3, two-horse 5 *M*), a pleasant, well-built town with 4000 inhab., on the *Rösla* or *Rösslau*, was the birthplace of *Jean Paul Fried-*

rich Richter (p. 87), whose bust by Schwanthaler has been placed in front of the house where he was born, adjoining the church.

The **Alexandersbad** (1915 ft.; **Chalybeate Baths and Hydropathic*, the property of a company, D. 2½ *M*; **Hôtel Weber*, also with pine-cone baths, D. 1½ *M*; **Roglermühle Inn*, on the Dünkelhammer, ¼ M. from the Hôt. Weber), 2 M. to the S.E. of Wunsiedel, is named after the last Margrave of Ansbach-Bayreuth. The chalybeate springs and the pine-cone and mud-baths, combined with the pleasant scenery, attract numerous visitors.

The **Luisenburg* (2266 ft.), the most striking point in the environs, so named after the visit of Queen Louisa of Prussia in 1805, formerly called *Luxburg*, with a few traces of an old castle, lies 1½ M. to the W. of the Alexandersbad and 2 M. to the S. of Wunsiedel. (Guide desirable: from Wunsiedel or from Alexandersbad to the Luisenburg 2, to the Luisenburg and Kösseine 3 *M*.) The Luisenburg is, as it were, a mountain in ruins. Huge masses of granite of fantastic form are piled together in wild confusion, the result of disintegration; they are partly overgrown with thick moss, interspersed with pines and bushes, and are rendered accessible by steps, bridges, etc. At the entrance to the labyrinth is the *Gesellschafts-Platz*, with a restaurant (2255 ft.). Numerous inscriptions on the rocks. This rocky labyrinth affords a beautiful walk, ascending in ½ hr. to the *Bundesstein* or *Kreuz* (2575 ft.). The finest point is the **Burgstein* (2858 ft.), 20 min. farther on, a group of rocks on the top of the hill, with a railing, affording a panorama towards the E., N., and W.

The **Haberstein* (2785 ft.), ¼ hr. farther on, consisting of four lofty rocks, is another good point of view. The **Kösseine* (3078 ft.), ¾ hr. from the Haberstein (1½ hr. direct from Alexandersbad) commands the finest and most extensive view in the Fichtelgebirge, embracing the greater part of the Upper Palatinate towards the S. (Temple at the top; a little below it is a simple restaurant; good water 10 min. below the summit on the E. side.) — From this point a path leads by the *Mütze* (2670 ft.) and the *Girgelstein* (2400 ft.) to the (2 hrs.) *Silberhaus* (forester's house, with two beds), whence we may ascend by the forester's house of (1 hr.) *Seehaus* to the Nusshard and the (1 hr.) Schneeberg (p. 91).

RAILWAY in 10 min. from Wunsiedel to (2¼ M.) *Holenbrunn* on the Fichtelgebirge Railway (p. 134).

19. Franconian Switzerland.

Comp. Map, p. 77.

The small hilly district dignified with this title (1600 ft. above the sea-level), with its pretty valleys watered by the *Wiesent*, its wooded heights, forming the W. spurs of the Fichtelgebirge, and lying nearly in the centre of a triangle formed by Nuremberg, Bamberg, and Bayreuth, owes its reputation chiefly to its STALACTITE CAVERNS, containing remains of antediluvian animals, specimens of which are preserved in almost every museum in Europe. The 'Jura' limestone and dolomite rock-formations are also picturesque, occasionally assuming the most grotesque shapes.

The finest points are accessible to walkers only. A guide (seldom necessary) may generally be procured for 2-3 *M* per day. — RAILWAY from *Forchheim* to *Ebermannstadt*, 9½ M., in ¾ hr. — POST OMNIBUS from Ebermannstadt viâ *Streitberg* and *Behringersmühl* to *Waischenfeld*, 17½ M., in 4¼ hrs.; from Pottenstein to *Pegnitz* (railway-station, see p. 110), twice daily in 1¾ hr.

From *Forchheim* (see p. 80) the local railway leads in a wide curve to the E. into the pleasant *Wiesent-Thal*, and passes the stations of *Pinzberg* (**Terrasse Inn*, ½ M. from the station, with beautiful view), *Gosberg, Wiesenthau, Kirchehrnbach*, and *Pretzfeld*. 9½ M. *Ebermannstadt* (957 ft.), the terminus, lies at the junction of the *Lange-Thal* (see below) and the *Wiesent-Thal*. A road (carr. at the station) leads hence, viâ *Gasseldorf*, to (¾ hr.) —

2 M. Streitberg (1046ft.; *Curanstalt*, recommended for some stay, R. 5½-14 ℳ per week, D. 2 ℳ; *Goldener Löwe*, or *Post*, with garden, R. 1 ℳ 20 - 2 ℳ, B. 50 pf., D. 1½, pens. 4 ℳ; *Adler*), a picturesquely situated village, **frequented as** a summer-resort (visitors' tax 3 ℳ, families 5 ℳ). **Pretty walk to the** (¼ hr.) *Muschelquelle*. Fine views from the (10 min.) ancient *Streitburg* and the (¾ hr.) ruin of *Neudeck*, opposite; still finer from the *Hummerstein*, ¾ hr. to the W., on which is a refuge-hut (key at the inn at Gasseldorf), and the *Guckhüll*, 1 hr. to the N.E. Pleasant excursions through the *Lange-Thal* and the '*Felsenschlucht*' to the (1 hr.) *Schönsteinhöhle*, a grotto with fine stalactites (guide for one pers. 1 ℳ, for several 40 pf. each), and through the *Leinleiter-Thal* to (1 hr.) *Unterleinleiter*, with a fine park of Baron Seckendorf.

The road goes on from Streitberg, on the right bank of the Wiesent, to (2½ M.) **Muggendorf** (1060 ft.; *Curhaus & Hotel zur Fränkischen Schweiz*, D. 1½ℳ; *Stern*, R. 1, D. 1½ ℳ; *Wolfsschlucht*, with reading-room; *Schwan*, *Sonne*, *Türkei*, less pretending; restaurants *Rosenau* and *Erholung*, with pretty views; *Kohlmann*), prettily situated, and a good centre for excursions. (Christoph Brendel is a good guide; 2 ℳ per day.) Shady promenades on the opposite bank of the Wiesent.

Below Muggendorf (½ hr.) is the *Rosenmüller's Höhle*, the entrance to which is visible to the left from the road (guide, usually at the cave, and lights for 1-6 pers., 2 ℳ). It contains fine stalactites and fossil remains of animals. The *Oswaldshöhle* (½ hr.) may be visited also, if time permit. Near it are the *Wundershöhle* and *Witzenhöhle*. The latter is said to contain a heathen altar (?). The *Kuppenburg*, near the Rosenmüller's Höhle, **the** *Hohenstein*, **and the** *Hohe Wacht*, above the Oswaldshöhle, are good points of view. The village of *Wichsenstein*, the highest point (1944 ft.) of the Franconian Switzerland, commanding an extensive panorama, **may be reach**ed from Muggendorf in 2½ hrs., viâ *Windisch-Gailenreuth*. In the *Trubach-Thal*, 3 M. to the S., is the picturesque château of *Egloffstein* (p. 81).

At Muggendorf the **road** divides. The branch to **the right leads to the** S.E. **through the** Wiesent-Thal past (3 M.) **the** picturesque little château **of** *Burggailenreuth* (p. 94; to the right, on the hill), **and the** (3 M.) *Stempfermühle* (p. 94), with the *Drei Quellen*, whence Gössweinstein, on **the** height to the right, may be reached in ¾ hr., to (¾ M.) **Behringersmühl** (*Post*, R. 1 ℳ; *Hartmann*), a village much frequented as **a summer-resort**, charmingly situated **at the junction of the** Wiesent-Thal, **the** Ailsbach-Thal, **and the** Püttlach-Thal. The *Pfaffenstein*, ½ hr. to the W., commands **a fine view**. — The road to the left crosses the hills **towards the** E. **to** (3 M.) *Doos* (p. 94). **From this** road another **leads to the** right, just beyond Muggendorf, **to** (2 M.) *Engelhardsberg* (Wunder; key of the Riesenburg, see p. 94), 10 min. from which rise the bold *Adlerstein* (1740 ft.), a splendid point of view, and the (10 min.)

Quakenschloss, a jagged grauwacke rock (whence we return by Engelhardsberg). To the N. of the village rises the (¼ hr.) **Riesenburg*, a wild group of dolomite rocks rendered accessible by paths and bridges (adm. 50 pf., 2 pers. 35 pf. each, 3-4 pers. 25 pf. each, 5 or more pers. 20 pf. each). Charming view of the **Schotter-Thal* or *Schauder-Thal*, one of the most beautiful valleys in this district. At the S. end, ¾ hr. from the Riesenburg, lies Behringersmühle (see above). We descend into this valley, turn to the left, and in ¼ hr. reach the *Doos* or *Toos Inn* (1118 ft.; unpretending), where a key of the Riesenburg is also kept.

Here begins the picturesque *Rabenecker-Thal*, watered by the Wiesent. We quit the road (which goes on to Waischenfeld, 2 M.) at a mill (1¾ M.), and beyond the Wiesent ascend to the right, on the left side of the partly preserved *Burg Rabeneck*, to a lofty plain; then take the path to the left by the wood, turning off to the right after a few yards, and passing (25 min.) *Schönhof*, reach (½ hr.) Burg Rabenstein (1456 ft.), a pinnacled castle restored in 1829, looking down upon the *Ahorn-Thal*, 160 feet below. In the latter, at the foot of the hill, lies the *Neumühle* (Restaurant).

The custodian shows the remains of antediluvian animals found in the caves, and conducts the visitor to the (¼ hr.) **Sophienhöhle** or Rabenstein Cavern, the most interesting in the district owing to the abundance of the fossil bones and the perfection of the stalactites it contains. An hour is required to explore it (fee 3-4 ℳ; full illumination 9 ℳ; magnesium wire 40 pf. extra for each of the three chambers). The *Ludwigshöhle* on the opposite side of the Ahorn-Thal hardly merits a visit.

We may now cross the hill separating the Ahorn-Thal and Wiesent-Thal to (1 hr.) **Waischenfeld** (1137 ft.; *Görl*; *Hoffmann*), pleasantly situated on the Wiesent, and environed with watch-towers and ruined castles. The *Förstershöhle* (20 min.; key at Görl's Inn; one pers. 1 ℳ, each additional visitor 50 pf.), a dome-shaped vault, contains fine stalactites. — Post-omnibus hence to *Bayreuth* (p. 86), daily in 4¼ hrs. (2 ℳ).

Walkers may go from Rabenstein across the table-land direct in 2 hrs. to Pottenstein (see below): by the Neumühle (see above) we cross the bridge and ascend to the left to *Zaupenberg*; then, leaving the villages of Ailsdorf and Kleinlesau on the right (see finger-posts), we reach, beyond *Waidmannsgesess*, the road leading from Oberailsdorf to Pottenstein. — To reach (2 hrs.) *Behringersmühl* we return for a few hundred paces on the Schönhof road, then take the Oberailsdorf footpath to the left (whence a direct path leads to Tüchersfeld, see below), and follow the path through the pretty and sequestered valley of the Ailsbach. From Behringersmühl to Tüchersfeld and Gössweinstein, see below.

The road from Muggendorf to Pottenstein crosses the Wiesent at Behringersmühl and again divides: the road to the right ascends rapidly to (½ hr.) **Gössweinstein** (1617 ft.; *Distler*, with garden; *Amschler* 'zur Fränk. Schweiz'; *Gold. Adler*; *Löwe*; *Rose*), where there is a large pilgrimage-church and a *Château*, completely restored in the Gothic style (visitors admitted). The Burg, the *Kreuz* behind the church, and the *Wagnershöhe*, all command a **View of the greater part of the Franconian Switzerland, including the valleys of the Ailsbach, Wiesent, and Püttlach, which converge at Behringersmühl. Through the grounds in the government forest we descend in ½ hr. to the Stempfermühle (p. 93), and thence reach Muggendorf in 2 hrs.

Near *Burggailenreuth* (p. 93), 1½ hr. to the W. of Gössweinstein, is the **Gailenreuther Höhle**, or Zoolith Cavern (the forester at Baron Horneck

NUREMBERG. *20. Route.* 95

von Weinheim's Schloss dispenses modest refreshments and shows the cavern; 1-3 pers. 1 ℳ each, 4-6 pers. 50 pf. each, larger parties 25 pf. each; light 10 pf. for each pers.), which has attained a European celebrity owing to the investigations of Esper, Rosenmüller, Cuvier, and Goldfuss. It consists of three or four stories, one above the other, each containing chambers filled with numerous remains of bears, lions, wolves, hyænas, etc. These wild beasts probably lived in the caves to which they brought their prey, and where they afterwards themselves died. There are several other **caverns here** of the same character, such as the *Kapps-Höhle* (difficult of access), containing beautiful stalactites. Scientific men are recommended to visit these interesting caves; the ordinary traveller will probably be satisfied with the Sophienhöhle (p. 94).

The road **leads to the E.** from Behringersmühl through the romantic *Püttlach-Thal* to (1½ M.) **Tüchersfeld** (*Seiller,* rustic), a most picturesque village, commanded by lofty pinnacles of rock. Thence to (3 M.) **Pottenstein** (1425 ft.; *Distler, Schöpff),* a beautifully situated little town, with a château. Diligence twice daily in 2 hrs. to *Pegnitz* (p. 110).

Pleasant excursion to the S. through the **romantic Schutter-Thal** or **Kühlenfelser-Thal,** past the *Schutter* and *Klumper* **mills** (by the first of which are the stalactite caverns called the *Grosse* and *Kleine Teufelsloch),* to (4½ M.) *Kühlenfels.* Back by *Kirchenbirkig* to (3½ M.) **Pottenstein.** — A road also leads from Pottenstein on the hill, past a chapel (*View), to (3½ M.) Gössweinstein (p. 94).

20. Nuremberg.

Hotels. *BAYRISCHER HOF (Pl. a; C, 2), Karl-Str. **1**, in a quiet situation, R., L., & A. from 3, B. 1, D. 3 ℳ; *STRAUSS (Pl. **c**; C, 3), Karolinen-Str. 43, R., L., & A. 3-4, B. 1 ℳ 20 pf., D. 3 ℳ, with lift, electric light, and good café-restaurant; *GOLDNER ADLER (*Hôt. Schlenk;* Pl. b, D 2), Adler-Str. 15, with lift, R. & A. 2½-3, B. 1, D. 3 ℳ; WÜRTEMBERGER HOF (Pl. d; D, 4), near the station, R. & A. from 2, B 1, D. 3 ℳ; these four of the first class. — *WITTELSBACHER HOF (Pl. f; D, 3), Pfannenschmiedsgasse 22, with **small garden** and restaurant, R. & A. 1½-3 ℳ, B. 80 pf.; *DEUTSCHER KAISER (Pl. **g**; D, 3), *MONOPOL (Pl. **h**; D, 3), both with cafés-restaurants; *KAISERHOF (Pl. k; D, 3); ROTHER HAHN (Pl. i; D, 3), all in the König-Str.; MAXIMILIAN (Pl. **e**; E, 3), Lorenzer-Str. 8. — *NÜRNBERGER HOF (Pl. **l**; D, 3), unpretending, HERZOG MAX, both in the König-Str., R. 1½-2 ℳ, B. 80 pf., D. 1½ ℳ; HIMMELSLEITER, **Karolinen-Str.** 53, R. 1½ ℳ; WOLFSSCHLUCHT, Johannesgasse 4; EINHORN, **Breitegasse** 76, near the Germanic Museum, R. 1 ℳ 20-2 ℳ, B. 60-80 pf.

Restaurants. At the *Hôtels Strauss, Wittelsbacher Hof,* and *Deutscher Kaiser,* **see** above. Also *Stadtpark,* Maxfeld (p. 109); *Rosenau* (Pl. A, B, 2, 3; p. 109). — **Wine.** *Giessing,* Rathhausgasse 8 (closed in **the** evening); *Herrenkeller (Föttinger),* Theatergasse 19; *Nassauer Keller,* in the Nassau House (p. 99); *Posthörnlein (Döring),* near the chapel of St. Maurice; cold meat, etc., at **the** last three. — **Beer.** *Strauss, Deutscher Kaiser, Monopol, Wolfsschlucht,* **see** above. Also *Wartburg,* Weinmarkt 7; *Bratwurst-Glöcklein* (p. 102), **at the** back of the Moritzcapelle, quaint; *Bratwurst-Herzle,* Herzgasse 9. — *Marienthorzwinger* (formerly *Schellmannszwinger*), at the Marienthor.

Cafés. *Monopol,* see **above**; *Krauss,* Kaiser-Str. 46; *Central,* Karolinen-Str. 23; *Merkur,* Klaragasse 7; *Noris,* Josephs-Platz 1; *Gisela,* Spittlerthorgraben 1. — **Confectioners.** *Eisenbeiss,* König-Str. 2a, at the Museum Bridge; *Merklein,* Rathhausgasse 10; *Scheuermann,* Schustergasse 3, behind the Sebaldus **church.**

Baths. *Ludwigsbad,* Breitegasse 91, at the Weisse Thurm; *Wildbad,* on the Schüttinsel, E. side of the town.

Cabs. For ¼ hr. 1-2 pers. 60 pf., 3-4 pers. 1 ℳ; ½ hr., 1 or 1½ ℳ;

³/₄ hr., 1¹/₂ or 2 ℳ; 1 hr., 2 ℳ or 2¹/₂ ℳ; small articles free, box 20 pf. — *Porter* into the town: under 33 lbs. 35 pf.; between 33 and 110 lbs. **50 pf.**

Tramways. 1. From the *Maxfeld* (Stadtpark; to the N.E. of Pl. F, 1) to the *Bahnhof-Platz* (Pl. D, E, 4), *Plärrer* (Pl. B, 3), and *Fürth* (p. 69; from the Central Station to Fürth, ³/₄ hr., 20 pf.); white lamps, etc. — 2. From the *Maxfeld* to the *Rathhaus-Platz* (Pl. D, 1, 2) and the *Schlachthof* (to the S.W. of Pl. A, 4); green lamps. — 3. From the *Lauferthor* (Pl. F, 1) to *St. Jobst* (p. 109); yellow lamps. — 4. From the *Bahnhof-Platz* to *Steinbühl* (p. 109; to the S. of Pl. C, 4). — 5. From the *Bahnhof-Platz* to the *Hauptdepôt* (New Barracks; to the N.W. of Pl. A, 3); blue lamps. — 6. From the *Plärrer* (Pl. B, 3) to the *Lorenzer-Platz* (Pl. D, 3) and *Dutzendteich* (p. 118; 20 min.; 20 pf.).

Post Offices, Bahnhof-Platz 1 (Pl. E, 4; poste restante). **Several branch-offices.** — **Telegraph Offices.** Bahnhof-Platz 7, Hauptmarkt 12 (next the Frauenkirche; Pl. D, 2), and at most of the post-offices.

Theatres. *Stadt-Theater* (Pl. D, 3), by the Lorenzkirche (closed in summer). — *Summer Theatre* at the Wittelsbacher Hof, Pfannenschmiedsgasse 22. — **Music Halls.** *Wolfsschlucht* (see p. 95), Johannesgasse 4 (closed in summer); *Reichshallen-Theater*, König-Str. 50. — Bands in the *Stadtpark* (p. 109), on Tues., Thurs., and Sun. (afternoon and evening); at the *Rosenau* (p. 95), etc.

Shops. NUREMBERG WARES: *Wahnschaffe*, Josephs-Platz 18, carved wood, etc.; *C. Quehl*, Kaiser-Str. 5, at the corner of the Fleischbrücke, etc. — IMITATIONS OF ANCIENT WORKS OF ART, in terracotta (stoves, vases, etc.), metal, papier-maché, and wood (furniture): *Fleischmann*, Hirschelgasse 28; *Eysser*, in Peller's house, Aegidien-Platz 23 (p. 105). — FANCY ARTICLES in wood, in the Renaissance style (caskets, frames, etc.): *Schmid-Daler & Co.*, Panier-Platz 9. — WOOD MOSAICS: *Adelhard*, Flaschenhof-Str. 18. — IVORY CARVING: *Behl*, Kaiser-Str. 37. — FANCY GOODS: *J. G. Kugler, L. Döhler*, König-Str. — ARTISTIC GLASS AND PORCELAIN, etc.: *Ostermayr*, Lorenzer-Platz; *C. Neumarck*, Adler-Str. 33. — STEEL GOODS: *Leykauf*, König-Str. 16. — ANTIQUITIES: *Pickert*, Dürer-Platz 10; *Helbing*, Karl-Str. 6; *Wohlbold*, Augustiner-Str. 11; *F. Neumann*, Trödelmarkt 31-33. — BOOKSELLERS AND ART-DEALERS: *J. L. Schrag, Soldan*, both in the König-Strasse. — Lebkuchen (a kind of gingerbread). *Metzger*, Josephs-Platz 6, Rathhausgasse 6, and Hauptmarkt 23; *Häberlein*, König-Str. 6, Winkler-Str. 35, and Ludwig-Str. 34; *Richter & Co.*, Josephs-Platz 2 and Bindergasse 11; Zinn, in the Frauenthor, etc. — All the shops are shut on Sundays and holidays.

English Church Service in summer at the Bayrischer Hof.

United States Consul, *William J. Black*, Esq.

Collections and Objects of Interest.

Albrecht Dürer's House (p. 102), daily 8-1 and 2-6; 50 pf.

°*Germanic Museum* (p. 106), daily 10-1 and 2-4.30 (in winter to 4), 1 ℳ, 4-5 pers. 3 ℳ, free on Sun. (and Wed. in winter).

Industrial Museum (p. 105): Industrial products, week-days 9-12 and 2-5, Sun. 10-12 (closed on Sat.); Collection of Models and Library, week-days 8-12 and 2-6, Sun. 10-12 (closed on Sat.); adm. free.

Municipal Library (p. 102), daily 9-12 and 3-6.

Natural History Museum (p. 106), Sun. 10-12, free; other times 50 pf.

Panorama, Rothenburger-Str. (Pl. A, 3), all day, 1 ℳ; Sun. and holidays 50 pf.

Permanent Exhibition of the Dürer Association (modern paintings), in the building of the Telegraph Office next the Frauenkirche (Pl. 7; D, 2), week-days 11-3, Sun. and holidays 10-2 (closed on Sat.); adm. 80 pf.

Permanent Industrial Exhibition (p. 105), week-days 9-12 and 2-5 (in winter 10-12 and 2-4), Sun. 10-12; free.

Rathhaus (p. 100), Sun. 10.30-12.30, free; at other times, fee.

School of Industrial Art (p. 105), daily; fee.

Principal Attractions: St. Lawrence (p. 99), Frauenkirche, especially the Portal (p. 99), Schöne Brunnen (p. 100), St. Sebaldus (p. 101), Burg (p. 103), Germanic Museum (p. 106).

Nuremberg, Germ. *Nürnberg* (1148 ft.), pop. 142,500, a free city of the Empire down to 1806, has since belonged to Bavaria.

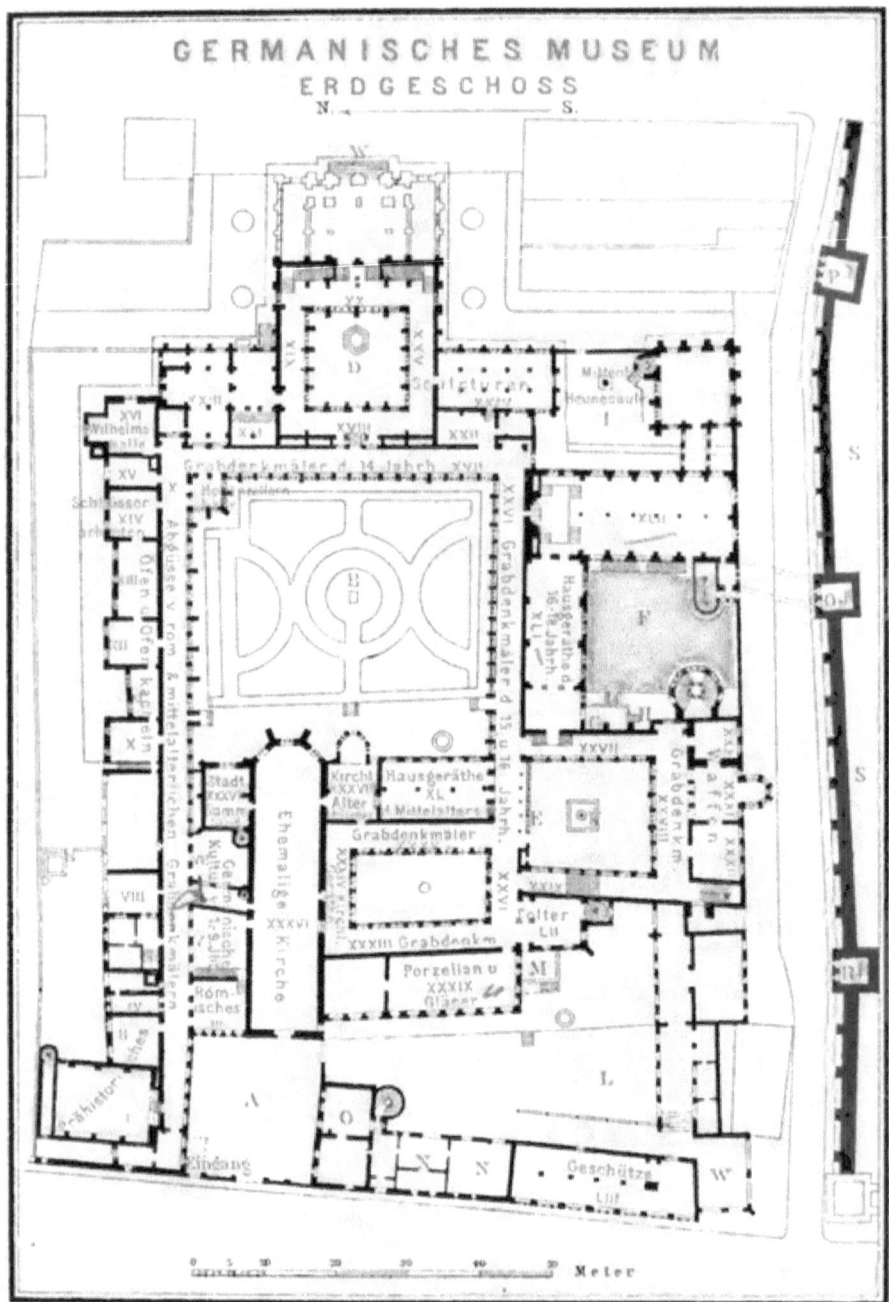

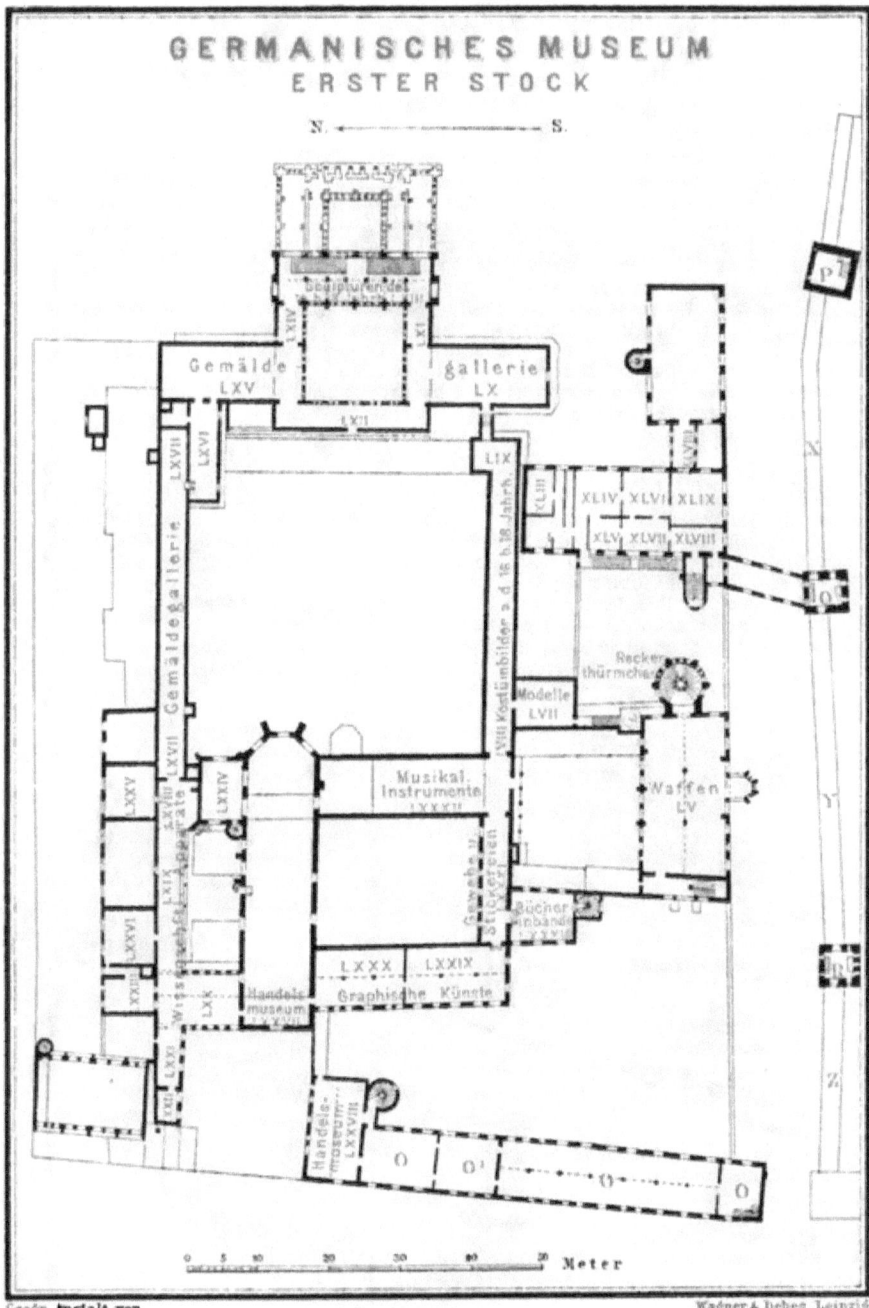

There is probably no town in Germany still so mediæval in appearance, or so suggestive of the wealth, importance, and artistic taste of a 'City of the Empire'.

Nuremberg is first mentioned in history in 1050. The establishment of a market, the miracles wrought by the relics of St. Sebaldus, and the frequent visits of the emperors rapidly attracted new inhabitants, who at first settled between the castle and the river. The city thus sprang up under the Hohenstaufen dynasty, and the castle was frequently occupied by Conrad III. and Frederick Barbarossa, two illustrious members of that family. The progress of the city was greatly promoted by the high privileges accorded to it by these and other emperors. The government was originally vested in the patrician families. These were expelled by the civic guilds in 1349, but only to return and obtain a firmer grasp of power the same year. The office of Burggrave, originally a deputy governing in the name of the emperor, was first held by Frederick I. (d. 1218) of the Zollern family under the Emp. Henry VI. These governors soon acquired independent power, and in 1363 became 'Fürsten', or princes; but after, Frederick VI. was invested by the Emp. Sigismund with the Mark of Brandenburg in 1411, they formally ceded to the town (1427) their castle, which was situated in front of the citadel. The constant dissensions and bitter feuds between the citizens and the margraves Albrecht Achilles (1449) and Frederick (1502) did not interfere with the continuous growth of the town, which at the beginning of the sixteenth century had become, like Augsburg, one of the chief depôts of the trade between Germany, Venice, and the East. At this period, too, it attained its zenith of distinction in the sphere of art as well as of politics.

To this period belongs most of the interesting old DOMESTIC ARCHITECTURE which renders Nuremberg so quaint and picturesque. The general style of the lofty houses, with their high-peaked gables, is Gothic, but the ornamentation of the façades is usually in the Renaissance style. Special care has also been bestowed upon the courts in the interior.

The zeal with which the art of SCULPTURE was cultivated is exemplified by the numerous interesting signs and figures of saints, of the 14-16th cent., with which the houses are embellished. Some of the finest are in the König-Str.; on the Glockengiesserhaus; at the corner of the Albrecht-Dürer-Platz; opposite the Moritzkapelle; in the Obstmarkt, behind the Frauenkirche; at the corner of the Weinmarkt (Rothes Ross); in the Burgstrasse; at the corner of the Bindergasse; and in the Hirschelgasse. The last-named (original now in Berlin), a statue of the Virgin, has often been ascribed to an Italian artist on account of its beauty and delicacy of form. Another similar figure of Mary at the foot of the Cross, now in the Germanic Museum (p. 95), ranks among the finest works of its time, but is also by an unknown master.

Foremost among the Nuremberg workers in stone stands *Adam Krafft* who flourished here after 1492, and died at Schwabach in 1507. His principal works are the Stations on the way to St. John's Cemetery, the tasteful tabernacle in St. Lawrence's, and the reliefs at the Frauenkirche, St. Sebalduskirche, and Aegidienkirche. Of wood-carvers the chief is *Veit Stoss* (d. 1532), who at first exercised his craft at Cracow and is therefore sometimes, though erroneously, described as a Pole. His *chef-d'œuvre* at Nuremberg is in the church of St. Lawrence (p. 99). Both of these masters are rooted in the traditions of mediæval art, and of conservative tendencies. The brass-founder *Peter Vischer* (d. 1529), on the other hand, breathes the spirit of the Renaissance, and is endowed with versatile imagination and a delicate sense of form. His sons and *Pancraz Labenwolf* (d. 1563) also produced much meritorious work. Among the specialities of Nuremberg art in the 16th cent. were the casting of medals and goldsmiths' work, the most celebrated die-cutters being *Ludwig Krug* (at the beginning of the 16th cent.), *Peter Flötner* (d. 1546), and *Hans Lobsinger*; and the most renowned goldsmiths *Wenzel Jamnitzer* (1508-85), and his son-in-law *Valentin Maler*.

PAINTING was sedulously cultivated as early as the 14th cent., as is proved by the altar-pieces in the Frauenkirche and Jakobskirche. The

Imhoff altar-piece of the Coronation of the Virgin in St. Lawrence's dates from the first half of the 15th cent., and resembles the crude productions of the Cologne school. In the latter half of the same century *Hans Pleydenwurff* and *Michael Wohlgemut* (1434-1519) was the most prominent of Nuremberg painters. In order to understand the wide-spread fame of the Nuremberg school we must keep in mind that printing had recently been invented, engendering a taste for illustrated books, engravings, and wood-cuts; for the importance of Nuremberg art lies less in the products of the paint-brush than in the humorous and thoughtful creations embodied by means of the burin and the chisel. The characteristic tendency to depth of meaning shows itself in the pictures of *Albrecht Dürer* (1473-1528), a pupil of Wohlgemut, and the greatest painter whom Nuremberg has produced. Nuremberg itself, however, now possesses few products of his fertile genius; the only certified examples of his brush in his native town are the 'Hercules' (an early work), portraits of Emp. Charlemagne and Emp. Sigismund, and a Pietà, all in the Germanic Museum. His best works are to be seen at Vienna, Munich, and Berlin. None of Dürer's pupils developed their activity to any great extent in Nuremberg itself, where, indeed, painting rapidly declined. On the other hand the artistic handicrafts, such as the engraving of medals and the manufacture of artistic cabinets, flourished here till far on in the 18th century, and are again practised with growing success at the present day.

The principles of the Reformation found favour at Nuremberg as early as 1525, and in the following year Melanchthon founded the Gymnasium. The discovery of the sea-route to India somewhat impaired the prosperity of the town; it suffered still more severely during the Thirty Years' War, and during the 18th cent. its decline was hastened by the feeble rule of the patrician families. Since 1806, however, when Nuremberg became a Bavarian city, it has prospered greatly, and it is now the most important commercial and manufacturing town in Southern Germany. Hops form one of the most important staple commodities.

The **Fortifications**, dating from the middle ages, form the most interesting feature of the town, but have unfortunately been removed at places. They consist of a rampart encircling the inner city, provided at intervals with round and square towers, and of a dry moat 35 yds. wide and 33 ft. deep. A walk round the walls will reveal the variety and beauty of their architectural effects. The most picturesque parts are between the Spittlerthor and Maxthor (early morning or late afternoon best light). The four round towers at the Neue, Spittler, Frauen, and Laufer gates received their present form from Georg Unger in 1555-68.

The *Pegnitz* divides the old town into two nearly equal parts, the Lawrence and the Sebald sides, the latter being the older and more interesting. It is crossed by several Bridges. The single-arched *Fleischbrücke* (Pl. D, 2), built in 1596-98, is an imitation of the Ponte Rialto at Venice. Two obelisks on the *Karlsbrücke* (Pl. C, 2), one with a dove and olive-branch, the other with the imperial eagle, are memorials of a visit of Emp. Charles VI., 'the peace-bringer', in 1728. The *Suspension Bridge* (Pl. C, 2) was one of the first of its kind in Germany (1824). Picturesque views are obtained from it as well as from the *Henker* (*i.e.* hangman's) *Foot-bridge* (Pl. C, 2), near which are a few relics of the earlier fortifications of the 13th century.

From the **Railway Station** (Pl. D, E, 4) we enter the town by the *Frauenthor* in a straight direction, and in 5 min. reach the church of St. Lawrence; then cross the Museums-Brücke to the Frauenkirche, and proceed to the left, past the Schöne Brunnen, to the Rathhaus, St. Sebald's, Dürer's statue, Dürer's house, and the Burg. This order is observed in the following description.

The Gothic church of *St. Lawrence (Pl. D, 3; Prot.), the finest in Nuremberg, was erected at the end of the 13th and the beginning of the 14th cent. on the site of a small Romanesque church. In 1403-45 the nave was widened, and in 1439-77 the choir was rebuilt on a larger scale by *Konrad Roritzer* of Ratisbon. The whole edifice was carefully restored in 1824 under the superintendence of *Heideloff*. Rich W. *Portal with numerous sculptures (1332); above it a superb rose window, 30 ft. in diameter. To the left of the portal is a modern Gothic fountain by *Wanderer*. The N. Tower, with its roof of gilded copper, was burned down in 1865, but has since been re-erected in its original form. The sacristan, who lives at No. 7 Lorenz-Platz, is generally in the church in summer. (Knock loudly at the N. door; fee 40 pf.; the printed description obtained in the church is inaccurate.)

INTERIOR. Seven of the beautiful stained-glass *Windows in the choir date from the 15th and 16th cent.; the finest are the 6th to the right ('Volkamer window'), representing the genealogy of Christ with the portrait of the donor, and the 9th or 'Tucher window'. The four Evangelists and Apostles (after Dürer; comp. p. 162) in the 7th window are modern, as also the 8th ('Kaiserfenster'), put up in 1881 in memory of the 84th birthday of Emp. William I. — The finest work of art in the church is the *CIBORIUM, or receptacle for the host, in the choir, beautifully and elaborately executed in stone, in the form of a tower, 65 ft. in height, and enriched with many sculptures of scenes from the life of Christ. The apex of the tower is bent like a bishop's crozier. It rests upon the three kneeling *Figures of the sculptor *Adam Krafft* and his two assistants, who were engaged in the work from 1493 to 1500. In front of the altar, suspended from the roof, is a curious *Work in carved wood with numerous figures, by *Veit Stoss*, representing the Salutation. The Gothic brass candelabrum in the choir is also noteworthy. Handsome modern pulpit and high-altar by *Heideloff* and *Rotermundt* (1839). The Krell Altar (end of the 15th century), behind the high-altar, bears the earliest known representation of the town. The various carved wooden altars and altar-pieces of the 15th cent. in the aisles repay inspection; especially the Imhoff Altar (ca. 1420) on the gallery over the N. entrance.

The *Tugendbrunnen*, a fountain on the N.W. side of the church, with numerous figures in bronze, was executed in 1589 by Benedikt Wurzelbauer (covered in winter). To the left of it, at the corner of the Karolinen-Str., is the so-called *Nassauer Haus*, erected in the Gothic style in the 14th cent. (wine-room, see p. 95). — In the adjoining Adler-Strasse rises the *Warriors' Monument*, by Wanderer and Rössner, a granite column surmounted by a figure of Victory (1876). — On the Pegnitz is the *Museum* (Pl. 4; a club; adm. only on the introduction of a member).

The Gothic *Frauenkirche or Marienkirche (Pl. D, 2; Rom. Cath. since 1816), in the market-place, was erected in 1355-61 on the site of a synagogue destroyed in 1349 during the persecutions of the Jews. The church was restored in 1878-81 by *Essenwein*. Fine façade. Over the portal of the W. *Portico, with its rich sculptur-

7*

ing, is a curious old clock, known as the 'Männleinlaufen', **constructed in 1506-9 by G. Heuss and Seb.** Lindenast, with moving figures of the seven German electors (best seen at noon). The N. aisle (open 7-10 a.m.; sacristan, Vordere Spitalhof 9) contains an *Epitaphium of the Pergenstorfer family of 1498, by *A. Krafft*, with a relief of the Madonna as Mother of Mercy. Adjacent is the Tuchersche Altar, with a winged picture on a gold ground, one of the finest works of the Nuremberg school in the first half of the 15th century. Old stained glass in the choir, with the armorial bearings of many Nuremberg families.

In the Gänsemarkt, behind the Frauenkirche, is a quaint fountain-figure in bronze, by Pancraz Labenwolf, called the *Gänsemännchen* ('little goose-man'; Pl. 2), a peasant carrying a goose under each arm.

The *Schöne Brunnen (Pl. D, 2), opposite the Frauenkirche, erected in 1385-96, by *Meister Heinrich*, the '*Balier*', and restored in 1821-24, is a Gothic pyramid 63 ft. in height, adorned with numerous figures (originally painted). The *Statues below represent seven electors and the nine worthies (*viz.* Charlemagne, Godfrey de Bouillon, Clovis, the Christian worthies; Judas Maccabæus, Joshua, David, the Jewish worthies; Cæsar, Alexander, Hector, the pagan worthies); those above, Moses and the seven prophets. In the iron railing of the fountain, on the N.W. side, is a small movable iron ring, ingeniously wrought, which the travelling apprentices regard as the cognisance of the city. — No. 19, Hauptmarkt (Pl. D, 2; tablet), opposite the Schöne Brunnen, was the residence of the celebrated humanist *Pirkheimer* (born at Eichstätt in 1470; died at Nuremberg in 1530). No. 15, adjacent, adorned with frescoes designed by Wanderer (1886), is the house in which *Martin Behaim*, the cosmographer (1459-1507), was born. Until the introduction of the Reformation the crown-jewels were exhibited annually in front of this house (comp. p. 107).

The **Rathhaus** (Pl. D, 1, 2; adm., see p. 96; entrance opposite the guard-house; bell for the custodian on the first floor to the right), 290 ft. in length, was erected by *Jakob Wolf* in 1616-22 in the Italian Renaissance style, incorporating an earlier building of the 14-15th centuries. The late-Gothic part of the building at the back, with a fine façade towards the Theresien-Str. and an interesting court, was added by *Essenwein* in 1885-89.

The great hall, with its timber roof, belongs to the older part of the building, erected in 1340, and is adorned with badly-preserved frescoes designed by *Dürer*, representing the triumphal procession of the Emp. Maximilian, Town Musicians, and Calumny (after Apelles); it also contains stained glass by *Veit Hirschvogel*, etc. On the central buttress is a mural painting, executed in 1613 (restored in 1824), representing an execution by the guillotine, proving that this instrument is not a modern invention. — On the wall of the staircase to the second floor is a large painting by *Paul Ritter* (1883): The representatives of Nuremberg entering the town in triumphal procession with the imperial regalia in 1424. — The ceiling of the long corridor in the second floor is adorned with a relief in stucco representing a tournament held at Nuremberg in 1446, executed by **Hans** and *Heinrich Kuhn* in 1621 (restored in 1891). On the **3rd** floor is the MUNICIPAL PICTURE GALLERY (chiefly modern paintings). Room **I.** *Jäger*, Emp. Maximilian I. visiting A. Dürer in 1518; *Schuch*, Funeral of Gustavus Adolphus; *Ans. Feuerbach*, Battle of Amazons; *Bauer*, Body of Emp. Otho III. being brought across the **Alps**. — R. II. *Joachim von Sandrart*, Banquet in the Rathhaus in 1619; **Maar. The** Schöne Brunnen, 1424; *Mayer*, Interior of St. Sebald's. — R. **III.** *Kreling*, Magdeburgers besieged by Tilly receiving the Sacrament; also portraits of distinguished Nurembergers.

The tasteful *Fountain* in the old **court is by** Pancraz Labenwolf, 1557. **The gallery in the S.E.** corner **of the court,** resting upon curious carved **brackets,** and with **Gothic balustrades, is by** Hans **Behaim (1425).** Under the Rathhaus are subterranean passages, partly fallen in, **leading from the old dungeons to** the deep well at the Burg (p. 103) **and in other** directions; these **may** be inspected by the curious.

The church of *St. Sebaldus (Pl. D, 2; Prot.), originally **a** Romanesque structure of the 11th cent., restored in the Transition style at **the** beginning of the 13th cent., was converted **into a Gothic church** in 1361-77. The W. choir with the Löffelholz **Chapel, the lower** part of the towers (completed in the 15th cent.), **and the nave,** date from the 13th cent., while **the** present E. choir in the pure Gothic style **was** added during the later alterations. The church **is** now undergoing restoration under **the direction of** *Hauberrisser*. The sacristan (Burg-Str. 6) is generally **in the church;** visitors knock at the **N.** side-door; **donations go to the building fund. The printed** description obtained **at the church is worthless.**

Exterior. The visitor should **inspect the** N. Portal, or *'Bride's Door'*; the reliefs on the buttresses of the **E. choir,** representing the Passion; the 'Schreyer Monument' (opposite the Rathhaus), with numerous lifesize figures **in stone,** representing the Bearing **of the** Cross, the Entombment, and the **Resurrection,** executed in 1492 by *Adam Krafft*, and the richest and most important **of his works;** the Last Judgment over the S. entrance.

Interior. In the E. ambulatory, to the right, three reliefs by *Veit Stoss* (1449): Last Supper, Christ on the Mt. of Olives, and the Kiss of Judas. Above these, the 'Markgrafenfenster', a fine stained-glass window executed by *Veit Hirschvogel* in 1515, representing the Margrave Frederick **of** Ansbach and Bayreuth, with his wife and eight children; **to the** left, a triple fresco (Christ washing the Disciples' feet, Last **Supper,** Christ on the Mt. of Olives), and a winged picture on the Tucher'sche altar, painted in 1513 by *Hans* **von** *Kulmbach*, from drawings by *Dürer*, probably **the** master's finest work. °Crucifix and wooden figures **of the Virgin and St. John,** over **the high-altar, the** latest work of *Veit Stoss.* High-altar **in** wood (1821) by *Rotermundt* and *Heideloff*. — °°*St. Sebald's Monument* **(eight tons in weight, for which** the trustees of **the** church paid 3145 florins), **the masterpiece of** *Peter Vischer*, the celebrated artist in bronze, was completed by him with **the aid of** his five sons in 1519, after thirteen years' labour. **The twelve Apostles in** niches around the sarcophagus containing **the relics of the saint are admirable;** above **are** twelve smaller figures **of church-**fathers and **prophets; below,** about seventy allegorical figures of genii, mermaids, **animals,** etc. The miracles performed by the **saint are** pourtrayed **in four beautiful reliefs** below the sarcophagus. In **the** niche at the **W. end is St. Sebaldus, and in** the E. niche is the artist himself with apron **and chisel, a beautiful statuette.** Near the fine **modern** wooden pulpit (by *Rotermundt;* 1859) **is** a copy of the Pietà by Dürer now in the Germanic Museum. The *Löffelholz Chapel*, W. choir, contains a Gothic font in bronze, of the beginning, and an altar of the middle, of the 15th century

The *Parsonage of St. Sebald*, on the N. side, with its fine Gothic *Oriel-window ('Chörlein'), dating from 1318, was once occupied by Melchior Pfinzing (d. 1535), provost of St. Sebald, and author of the 'Teuerdank', an allegorical narrative of the wooing of Mary of Burgundy by Emp. Maximilian I.

Opposite St. Sebald's, on the N., is the Gothic *Chapel of St. Moritz* (Pl. D, 1), transferred hither from the Hauptmarkt in 1313, and restored in 1829. Adjoining is the *Bratwurst-Glöcklein* (p. 95), mentioned as early as 1519. At No. 6 Halbwachsengasse, behind, is the *Rotermundt Collection* of antiquities, casts of ancient Nuremberg sculptures, etc.

To the S.W. of St. Sebald's, Winkler-Str. 29, is *Palm's House* (Pl. 5; C, D, 2), with the inscription: 'Here dwelt John Palm, bookseller, who fell a victim to the tyranny of Napoleon in 1806'. The patriotic Palm had published a pamphlet on the 'Degradation of Germany', written in a tone derogatory to France, for which the Emperor caused him to be condemned by a court-martial and shot (p. 234). — At the corner of the adjacent Augustiner-Strasse, on the site of an Augustinian monastery, stand the Courts of Law (Pl. 3; C, D, 2), erected by *Solger* in 1877. In the hall are marble busts of the jurists Anselm von **Feuerbach** and Rud. von Holzschuher; the court of the Chamber of Commerce contains a large painting by **A. Feuerbach**: Emp. Lewis the Bavarian conferring privileges on the merchants of Nuremberg.

Opposite Palm's house, over the gateway of the *Stadtwage*, is a good relief by *Krafft* (1497). Near this (Winkler-Strasse 20) is the house in which Dürer was born, with inscription.

*Dürer's Statue (Pl. D, 1), erected in 1840 on the Albrecht-Dürer-Platz, was designed by the eminent *Rauch*, after Dürer's portrait of himself at Vienna. Some hundred paces to the N.W., No. 39 Albrecht-Dürer-Strasse, near the **Thiergärtner-Thor**, is *Dürer's House* (Pl. 1; C, 1), the property of the city, and marked by a medallion. It contains a collection of antique furniture and utensils, and also copies of Dürer's paintings. Adm., see p. 96.

We return to the Rathhaus (p. 100). Opposite, on the right side of the Burgstrasse, is the old Dominican monastery, containing the *Municipal Archives* on the groundfloor. The upper floor contains the **Town Library** (Pl. D, 1; adm., see p. 96), of 70,000 vols. and 2000 MSS., including a missal with fine miniatures by the brothers Glockendon, miniature-painters of Nuremberg; also early specimens of typography, *e.g.* the Rationale of Durandus (1459), one of the first books printed by Gutenberg; autographs of Luther, Melanchthon, Ulrich von Hutten, Hans Sachs, etc.; and various curiosities.

The Burg-Strasse ascends the **Burg Hill** (1164 ft.; Pl. C, D, 1) to the N., a sandstone rock on the N.W. side of the town. At the top the route forks; the left branch leads by the 'Himmelsweg' direct to the Kaiserburg (p. 103); that to the right leads past a *Mt. of*

Olives (1499) to the *N. Freiung* and the *Pentagonal Tower* ('Alt-Nürnberg'), the oldest building in the town.

This tower and the *Walpurgis* or *St. Ottmar's Chapel* (restored in 1892), situated opposite, are relics of the old *Burg* of the Hohenzollern burggraves, destroyed in the war of 1420. The tower (adm. **20 pf.**) contains a torture-chamber with the 'Iron Virgin', a hollow figure with iron spikes in the interior, into which the victim was thrust, and a collection of antiquities. — Next this tower, on the right, is the old *Granary* (now a barrack), built by Hans Behaim the Elder in 1494-95 and named '*Kaiserstallung*' ('imperial stables'). To the E. of this lies the *Luginsland*, with turrets at its four corners said to have been built by the townsfolk in **1367** in order to watch the Hohenzollern-Burg. — We return to the *N. Freiung* or *Landfreiung*, commanding a view of the wide moat and the N. suburbs. On the parapet are shown two hoof-shaped impressions, which are said to have been left by the horse of a captive robber-knight (Eppelein von Gailingen) in the 16th cent., who escaped by leaping over the moat. This incident gave rise to a sarcastic proverb: 'The Nurembergers hang no man, unless they have caught him'. — We then pass through a gate to the S.W. to the *S. Stadtfreiung*, with a view of the city and of the 'Nuremberg Switzerland'. Another gateway brings us to the *Vestnerthor-Thurm* (view from the top; 10 pf.), and farther on is the *Deep Well*, the depth of which is shown by lowering candles into it, or by reflecting the daylight upon the surface of the water by means of a mirror (10 pf.). — Straight on is the —

*Kaiserburg, founded in the 11th cent. and enlarged by Frederick Barbarossa in the 12th. It was restored in the Gothic style and fitted up as a royal residence in 1854-56, and since 1866 has belonged in common to the Bavarian and Prussian royal families (ring at the gate; fee $1/2$-1 $\mathcal{M}$).

The venerable *Lime Tree* in the court, said to have been planted by the Empress Kunigunde, wife of Emp. Henry II. (1002-24), died in **1893**. A niche in the wall contains a statue of the Saxon ambassador *Glansdorf*, who died at Nuremberg during the Thirty Years' War. The *Heidenthurm*, by the castle-gate, contains two Romanesque chapels of the 12th cent., one above the other: the lower, *St. Margaret's Chapel*, is built over the burial-vault of the Burggraves; the upper, the *Kaiser-Capelle*, with groined vaulting resting on slender marble columns with Romanesque capitals, and pictures by Wohlgemut, Krafft, and Holbein the Elder, was used for divine service. In the Audience Chamber, next the Kaiser-Capelle, are several pictures, chiefly copies of later Italian **works**. Handsome old stoves and panelled ceilings in this and other rooms. Most of the rooms and particularly the new balcony on the W. side of the castle afford splendid **views of the** city and environs. — The castle-enclosure (**now a royal garden**), on the S.W. side of the castle hill, is **open to the public.**

On the **S.W. side** of the castle is the *Thiergärtner Thor* (Pl. C, 1), **with its** square tower, beyond which, in the Burgschmiet-Str., is the **Bronze** *Foundry of Prof. Lenz*, with a collection of models (formerly *Burgschmiet*; Pl. C, 1). The road leads **on past** the *Stations*, consisting of seven sandstone pillars with **reliefs** of the Passion, and the *Kalvarienberg*, all by *Krafft* (now **mostly replaced** by copies; originals **in the** Germanic Museum).

The *Holzschuher Chapel* in **St. John's Cemetery** (Pl. A, 1) contains a good Entombment with fifteen lifesize figures by *A. Krafft* (1507) and an altar by *Veit Stoss*. The Gothic *Church of St. John* (14th cent.) has an altar-piece by *Altdorfer*. — The graves in the old part of the cemetery are nearly all adorned with good brass-plates. In the 8th row to the S. of the conspicuous Müntzer tomb (1560; 23 ft. in height) is the grave of *Al-*

brecht *Dürer* (d. 1528; No. 649), close to which is that of *Wenzel Jamnitzer* (d. 1585; No. 665), with a fine epitaph by Jost Amman. Farther to the W. lie *Veit Stoss* (d. 1533; No. 268) and the poet *Grübel* (p. 105; No. 200). A few rows farther on, near St. John's church, is the grave of *Paumgärtner* (d. 1679) and a few rows still farther, that of *Sandrart* the painter (d. 1688). Pirkheimer's tomb (No. 1414) is nearer the entrance, in the 6th row to the right of the Holzschuher chapel. The wife of the chief sexton (house to the right of St. John's) affords all information (50 pf.).

The new **Central** *Cemetery*, also in the Johannis Suburb, to the N.W., has a fine portal by Hase (1879).

On the way back to the town a visit may be paid to the Gothic *Heiligkreuz Capelle* (Pl. B, 1; entrance Johannis-Str. 24; fee 30 pf.), built in 1390, which contains a fine altar in carved wood, with an architectural top and double wings painted by *Wohlgemut*.

We now proceed past the *Neuthor* and *Hallerthor* to the *Spittlerthor* (Pl. B, 3; comp. p. 98). In this neighbourhood is the Ludwig Station (Pl. A, B, 3; for *Fürth*, see p. 70), in front of which, on the **Plärrer**, a *Monumental Fountain* was erected in 1890 in memory of the opening of this, the first railway in Germany (p. 70). — In the Rothenburger-Str., which diverges to the S.W. from the Plärrer, are the *Panorama* (p. 96), and the *Cemetery of St. Rochus* (Pl. A, 3), with **the grave of the celebrated** *Peter Vischer* (d. 1529; No. 90, ninth stone on the right). The Imhof Chapel (1519) contains an interesting altar and stained-glass windows by *Hirschvogel*. At the end of the street is the *Harbour* of the Ludwigs-Canal (p. 76), 370 yds. long.

The broad **Ludwigs-Str.** leads from the Spittler Thor to the **St. Jakobskirche** (Pl. B, C, 3), founded in 1209, restored in the **14-15th** cent., rebuilt in 1692, and restored by Heideloff in 1824.

It contains a Gothic high-altar with winged paintings (14th cent.) and four figures of Apostles (six others of the series being now in the Germanic Museum). On the N. and E. sides of the choir and in the windows are the armorial bearings of **Teutonic** Knights. Many fine sculptures in wood and stone. At the E. end of the N. aisle is a triptych by *Veit Stoss*, restored by *Burgschmiet*. Stained-glass **windows** with the arms of Nuremberg families. Escutcheons of Teutonic **Knights**. The Dillherr Chapel contains a Lamentation for Christ by *Veit Stoss*.

Opposite are the old *Deutsche Haus*, or **Teutonic Lodge**, now an infantry-barrack, and the Roman Catholic **Church** *of St. Elizabeth*, built in **1785** as the Deutschhaus-Kirche, in the Italian baroque style, with a massive dome. — The Jakob-Str. leads to the E. from the Jakobs-Platz to the Germanic Museum (p. 106). To the N.E. we may pass through the *Weisse Thurm* ('white tower'), a relic of the 13th cent. fortifications, and thence cross the Häfner-Platz and follow the Karolinen-Str. to the church of St. Lawrence (p. 99).

From St. Lawrence's the Lorenz-Strasse leads to the **E.** to the Marienthor and the Marien suburb. To **the** right is the *Stadt-Theater* (Pl. D, 3). In the **Peter-Vischer-Gasse**, nearly opposite, are *Peter Vischer's House* (Pl. 10; No. 23) and the Gothic *Church of St. Catharine* (Pl. E, 2), long used by the Meistersingers as their school.

In the *Nonnengarten*, the garden of the former **Convent of St. Catharine**, rises the —

Bavarian Industrial Museum (Pl. E, 2, 3), a handsome building erected in 1893-95 for the collections hitherto exhibited at König-Str. 3 (adm., see p. 96). The museum, founded in 1872, is to be transferred to its new quarters in 1896. — Adjoining, at No. 8 Marienthorgraben, is the *Permanent Industrial and Commercial Exhibition* (Pl. E, 2; adm., see p. 96).

To the N.W., **beyond** the island of *Schütt*, is the Spital-Platz (Pl. D, 2), in the centre of which is a bronze *Statue of Hans Sachs*, by Krauser (1874). *Sachs's House*, in which the poet was born in 1494, is in the adjacent Hans-Sachs-Gasse (Pl. 9; No. 17; tablet). — On the E. side of the square **is the** new *Synagogue* (Pl. D, 2), built in 1869-74 in the Moorish style, **by** Wolf. The *Heiligegeist-Spital* (Pl. D, 2), on the S. side, was founded by Conrad Gross in 1331; in the court are the old *Heinzel Fountain* and a small chapel built in 1459 on the model of the Holy Sepulchre. The Gothic *Spital-Kirche* or *Heiligegeist-Kirche*, built in 1331-41 and modernized in the 17th cent., was from 1424 to 1796 the depository of the imperial regalia (now **in Vienna**; **casket** in the Germanic Museum, p. 107).

Not far off, at the corner of the Tucher-Str. and the Neue Gasse (Pl. E, 2), is a tasteful fountain with a bronze figure (by Wanderer) of *Konrad Grübel* (1736-1809), a popular poet of **Nuremberg**; the charming bronze reliefs on the pedestal refer to Grübel's poems. — The Rothschmiedsgasse and Judengasse lead hence to the N.W. to **the** Theresien-Platz (Pl. D, 1, 2), with a monument to the navigator *Martin Behaim* (p. 100), by Rössner (1890). — The Bindergasse (fine Madonna by *Adam* **Krafft** on **No. 1**, **to the** right) **and** the Theresien-Strasse run to the **W. to the** Rathhaus (p. 100). In the Theresien-Strasse are *Paumgärtner's House* (No. 23), with a relief of St. George and the dragon above the door, by *Krafft*; then, at the corner of the Tetzelgasse, the *Post and Telegraph Office* (1894) **of** the Sebaldus quarter; and *Krafft's House* (No. 7; on the right), with a fine court.

To the N.E., above the Theresien-Platz, is the *Ægidien-Platz* (Pl. D, E, 1), on the N. side of which rises *Peller's*, now *Eysser's*, **House** (No. 23; Pl. 6), with its rich Renaissance façade (1605) and fine court in the interior. It contains a magnificent old timber ceiling, and has **been** handsomely and tastefully fitted **up** and furnished by the owner, a furniture-manufacturer of Bayreuth (fee). To **the** right, in front of the *Gymnasium*, is a statue of *Melanchthon* by Burgschmiet. No. 13 Ägidien-Platz (tablet) **was the** house of the famous printer *Anton Koberger* (1470-1513).

St. Ægidius (Pl. E, 1; key at the gymnasium), originally a Romanesque basilica, erected in 1140, and burned down in 1696, was rebuilt in 1711-18 in the degraded style of that period. It contains a Pietà by *Van Dyck*, and at the back of the **altar two** reliefs in bronze by the sons of *P. Vischer*. Adjacent is the Romanesque *Eucharius Chapel* (end of the 12th cent.), with two altars by *Veit Stoss*. In the Gothic *Tetzel-Kapelle* (1345) a Coronation of the Virgin in stone, by *A. Krafft*.

To the E., in the old *Landauer Kloster*, is the *Royal School of Industrial Art* (Pl. E, 1; adm., see p. 96), which, however, is to be transferred in 1896 to a new building in the Reindel-Strasse (Pl. F, 3). The fine vaulting of the *Chapel* is borne by two spiral columns (1507). For this chapel, in 1511, Dürer painted his celebrated All Saints altar-piece, now at Vienna.

We next cross the Weber-Platz with the Sieben Zeilen, *i.e.* seven rows of weavers' houses, to the Hirschelgasse (Pl. E, 1), where the *Tucher'sche Landhaus* (No. 11; 1533-44) and *Rupprecht's* **House** (1534) are worth seeing. The latter contains a beautiful early-Ital. Renaissance hall (called 'Hirschvogelsaal' after its builder), of 1534, recently well restored. The figure of the Virgin on the outside is a cast of the original, now in Berlin (comp. p. 97).

Retracing our steps, we cross the Weber-Platz to the Max-Thor, whence the Lange Gasse to the right leads to the Laufer Thor. — To the left is the Paniers-Platz, on the N.W. side of which is *Topler's*, now *Petersen's*, *House* (Pl. 8; D, 1), built in 1590.

Near this, in the house 'Zur Blume', Schildgasse 12, is the **Natural History Museum**, containing zoological, botanical, ethnographical, and anthropological collections (adm., see p. 96). At No. 23, opposite, the *House with the Golden Shield*, decorated with mural paintings in 1888, the first twenty-three articles of Charles IV.'s Golden Bull were composed in 1356, providing amongst other points, that every German emperor should hold his first diet in Nuremberg.

The *Germanic National Museum (Pl. C, D, 3; entrance, Karthäusergasse 7), an institution for the illustration of German historical research, founded in 1852, is established in a suppressed *Carthusian Monastery*, a Gothic building of the 14th cent., with a fine church and extensive cloisters. The museum was enlarged in 1873-75 by the addition of the Augustine monastery (founded about 1450), formerly occupying the site of the Law Courts (p. 102), but removed thence and re-erected here. Since 1866, owing to the energy of the late director *Dr. von Essenwein* (d. 1892) and the munificence of private donors, the museum has become one of the finest in Germany. The objects of general interest are exhibited in 83 rooms (some badly lighted), while others are reserved for the use of artists and students. Admission, see p. 96. Catalogue at the entrance, 50 pf.; the numbers correspond with the red numbers on the exhibits. (See plans, pp. 96, 97.) Simple refreshments in R. XLII, on the groundfloor.

The long *Cloister Wing IX*, which we enter first, contains casts of Roman tombstones of the 1-4th cent. and of mediæval monuments down to the 14th century.

To the left. *Room I.* Prehistoric antiquities, objects from lake-dwellings, stone articles, funereal urns. — *R. II.* Prehistoric bronze antiquities, iron weapons and tools, etc. — *III, IV.* Roman antiquities; beams from the Roman bridge at Mainz. — *V-VII.* Germanic antiquities **of the** 4-9th centuries: ornaments, weapons, coffins, etc.; No. 264 **(in R. V), Greek** epitaph of a Germanic Christian of Constantinople (3rd **or 4th** cent.); No. 258 (in R. VII), Copy of the 'Treasure of Athanarich', **King of the** Visigoths (d. 381), found at Petreosa in Roumania (original at **Bucharest).** — *VIII.* Recent acquisitions. — *X-XIII.* Stoves and stove-tiles. — *XIV, XV.* Locksmith's work. — *XVI* (corner-room), called the '*Wilhelmshalle*', from a window presented by Emp. William I. (when King of Prussia) in 1861, representing the foundation of the Carthusian monastery in 1381 by Burggrave Frederick of Nuremberg, executed at Berlin from designs by Kreling. Original model of Luther's monument at Worms, by Rietschel. — Opposite, at the angle of the cloisters, is the '*Hohenzollernhalle*' (Pl. C), with four Gothic windows bearing the arms of the provinces of Prussia, presented by Princes Charles and Albert **of** Prussia, and Charles Anthony and Leopold of Hohenzollern.

Cloister Wing XVII (Ludwigsgang). Casts of tombstones of the 14th century. — *Cloisters XVIII-XX* and *XXV, Courts XXI* and *XXII,* and *Rooms XXIII* **and** *XXIV (Victoria* and *Friedrich Wilhelm Building):* Casts of sculptures **of** the 10-16th centuries. — The above-mentioned cloisters enclose the *Reichshof* (Pl. D), containing **a copy in stucco** of the Roland Column at Bremen.

Cloisters XXVI and *XXVII-XXIX* (adjoining on the left): Tombstones **of** the 15-16th centuries. Fine old and modern stained glass (Pl. E, five windows presented by the Austrian imperial house). — *Rooms XXX-XXXII* contain **armour and** weapons, from the 10th to **the** beginning of the 16th century.

Cloisters XXXIII-XXXV. Casts of tombstones **from the 16-18th cent.;** casts of ecclesiastical implements; book-bindings. — **We then pass through** the CHAPEL *(XXXVIII)* and enter (to the left) —

XXXVI, formerly the CHURCH, which contains **a** collection of °Sculpture, chiefly of the 15-16th centuries. On the N. wall: 775. *Veit Stoss,* Kneeling Madonna; °785. *Tilmann Riemenschneider,* St. Elisabeth; 792, 793. *School of Michael Pacher,* SS. Leonard and Stephen; 770. Top of an altar. On the S. wall: 771, 772. *Swabian School* (early 16th cent.), SS. Gereon and Catharine. In the centre: 745. *Veit Stoss,* Madonna and Child. Also, 852. Silvermounted casket in which the imperial jewels of the Holy Roman Empire were formerly kept (from the Spital-Kirche, p. 105). Small carvings in ivory, alabaster, mother-of-pearl, etc.; ecclesiastical vessels and vestments. On the S. side is a 'Mural Painting by *W. von Kaulbach* representing Emp. Otho III. visiting the tomb of Charlemagne in 1000, symbolical of the object of the institution to bring to light the treasures of the past.

The CHAPEL *(XXXVII)* contains (on the left) the NUREMBERG ART COLLECTION: 741. Model of *Labenwolf's* Gänsemännchen (p. 100); 738. Statue of St. Wenzel, the model of *P. Vischer's* bronze statue in the cathedral of Prague; °732. Frame of the All Saints' picture from the Landauer Brüderkapelle, executed in 1512 from a design by Dürer, who here shows his genuine Renaissance tendency. On the window-wall: 736. Reliquary of St. Sebastian (15th cent.); 733, 734. Two 'Palmesel' (asses used on Palm Sunday). Back-wall: 740. Weeping Virgin, an admirable statue in wood from a group of the Crucifixion (about 1500), spoiled by a coat of grey paint and badly placed; *Veit Stoss,* 742. The rosary, a circular wood-carving, 743. Justice, 744. Coronation of the Virgin, in high relief. — In the centre: °739. Bronze archer (Apollo), by *P. Vischer the Younger* (1532).

The COLLECTION OF DOMESTIC ANTIQUITIES occupies RR. XXXIX-LI. — *Room XXXIX.* German and Venetian glass, porcelain, majolicas, pottery, **etc.** — *XL-XLI.* Domestic life of 16-18th cent., illustrated by furniture **and** utensils. In R. XL: 1034. Richly carved wardrobe (ca. 1500); 1040. Large Gothic bedstead of the Fürer family (ca. 1500). In R. XLI: 1142. **Bedstead in ebony** with alabaster ornamentation (early 17th cent.); in the centre, ornamental vessels, goblets, ewers; also 1344. Silver travelling-service, adorned with agate (Augsburg; 17-18th cent.). — *XLII.* Antique portal from the monastery of Heilsbrunn (13th cent.). — Above this are *Rooms XLIII-LI*, containing Tyrolese, Swiss, and Nuremberg wainscoting of the 16th and 17th cent.; also a mediæval kitchen. Returning to the ground-floor, we turn to the left at the end of Cloister XXVI, and enter —

Hall LII. Instruments of torture. — *Hall LIII*, in the S.W. part of the building, contains a collection of cannon. — We next ascend the open spiral staircase (Pl. H), passing the Dantsic 'Beischlag' or balcony (Pl. G), to the —

SECOND FLOOR. *Room LIV*, fitted up by the German 'imperial' towns, contains a collection of costumes. — The staircase on the W. side descends to *R. LV*, fitted up by the German 'Standesherren', or nobles of the highest rank, which is occupied by a very complete historical collection of fire-arms and other weapons (16-19th cent.), including some magnificent specimens acquired with the Sulkowski Collection in 1889. — We now descend on the S. side by the 'Reckenthürmchen' (*LVI*) to the —

FIRST FLOOR. *LVII.* Ordnance of 17-19th cent., tents, military apparatus, etc. — Through *Gallery LVIII* and *Cabinet LIX*, containing pictures of costumes (16-18th cent.), we reach the *Galleries and Rooms LX-LXVII*, containing casts of sculptures of the 16-18th cent. (*R. LXIII*), coins (*LXV*), and the *PICTURE GALLERY (Catalogue 1½ *M*), unsurpassed for its works of the upper and lower German Schools of the 15th and 16th centuries. *R. LXII* (to the right): 7. (black numeral) *In the style of Meister Wilhelm of Cologne*, Madonna with the pea-blossom; 2078. *Stephan Lochner*, Crucifixion, with six saints; 2080. *Early Flemish School* (15th cent.), Coronation of Emp. Frederick III.; to the left, 2079. *Master of the Lyversberg Passion*, Annunciation; 2086. *Victor & Hein. Dünwegge*, Pietà; *2083. *Hugo van der Goes*, Cardinal Bourbon; to the right, 2090. *Master of the Imhof Altar-piece*. Pietà; to the left, 2095. *A. Dürer* (?), Portrait; 2091. *Hans Pleydenwurff*, Crucifixion. — *LXVI.* 2107, 2108. *Hans Baldung Grien*, Two nude allegorical female figures; *Alb. Dürer*, 2099. Emp. Maximilian I., no number, Hercules (1500); 2103. *H. L. Schäufelein*, Crucifixion with John the Baptist and King David; 2100. Copy of *Dürer's* All Saints picture (p. 106); 2115. *Hans Burgkmair*, Madonna; 2110, 2111. *Hans Holbein the Elder*, Madonna enthroned; 2105. *A. Altdorfer*, Crucifixion; 2119. *L. Cranach the Elder*, Luther. — LXV. 2109. *B. Zeitblom*, Pietà; 2093. *A Dürer*, Emperors Charlemagne and Sigismund (freely retouched); 2092-2094. *M. Wohlgemut*, Four wings from the Peringsdörfer altar-piece, with the legend of St. Vitus and saints (from the Augustine church; ca. 1490); *2097. *A Dürer*, Pietà; 2101, 2102. *Hans von Kulmbach*, SS. Cosmas and Damian; 2112. *Burgkmair*, St. Sebastian and Emp. Maximilian. — *LX* contains chiefly Netherlandish works of the 17th century. Exit-wall: 2123. *P. Hooch*, Party; *Rembrandt*, 2121. Portrait of himself (ca. 1629), 2125. St. Paul; 2122. *Corn. Begas*, Tavern-scene. In the middle of this room are various small sculptures in bronze (2155. Figure of a boy, 2157. Dog, 2158. Genius, all ascribed to *Peter Vischer*), lead (goldsmiths' models; 16-18th cent.), and ivory. At the window to the left: 2150. A number of exquisite wood-carvings attributed to *P. Flötner*, but really by various hands.

LXVIII-LXX. Scientific apparatus, calendars, and maps. — *LXXI-LXXIII.* Pharmaceutical Collection (*LXXII.* Apothecary's shop). — *Chapel LXXIV.* Ecclesiastical Art of the 16-18th centuries. — *Room LXXV.* Antiquities of guilds. — *LXXVI.* Models. — *Church Gallery LXXVII* and *R. LXXVIII.* Commercial Museum, interesting models of ships and waggons; weights and measures. — *LXXIX, LXXX.* Collection of documents illustrative of the arts of writing and printing; MSS., incunabula, woodcuts, engravings. — *LXXXI (Gallery).* Weaving and embroidery. — *Hall LXXXII* (fitted up by the nobility of Mecklenburg). Musical Instruments. — *LXXXIII.* Book-bindings.

The extensive *Manufactories* of Nuremberg chiefly lie outside the old town. The *Nuremberg Machine Co's* (formerly *Cramer-Klett's*;

Pl. F, 2) works are outside the Wöhrder Thor. On the S. side, beyond the Färber-Thor, near the railway, are the *United Ultramarine Factories* (formerly Leverkus, Zeltner, & Co.; Pl. B, C, 4); and in the suburb of Steinbühl are *Schuckert & Co.'s* dynamo-electric machine works. *Faber's* lead-pencil factory is at *Stein* (p. 26), 6 M. from Nuremberg. The largest breweries are *Henninger's* in the Maxfeld (now in the hands of a company), *Tucher's* in the Waizen-Strasse (Pl. C, 2), and *Kurz's* (J. G. Reif), Lorenz-Str. 6.

The most popular pleasure-grounds at Nuremberg are the *Stadt-Park* or *Maxfeld*, on the N. side (*Restaurant; music frequently; tramway, see p. 96), and the *Rosenau* (Pl. A, B, 2, 3; restaurant; music frequently). — Pleasant excursion to *Dutzendteich* (p. 118; tramway); thence a beautiful walk through wood, by *Falznerweiher* (restaurant) and *Schmaussenbuck* (rustic inn), with its view-tower (20 pf.), to *Mögeldorf* (station; see p. 234). — Viâ Fürth to the Alte Veste (old fortress) and *Cadolzburg*, see p. 70. To the *Nuremberg Switzerland*, see below.

21. From Nuremberg to Eger by Schnabelwaid.

94 M. RAILWAY in 5¼-6½ hrs. (fares 12 ℳ 20, 8 ℳ 10, 5 ℳ 20 pf.).

Nuremberg, see p. 95. Soon after leaving the station the train diverges to the left from the lines to Ratisbon and Amberg, and crosses the *Pegnitz-Thal* by means of a long embankment and several bridges to (2½ M.) *St. Jobst*. It then skirts the hills on the N. side of the Pegnitz-Thal, running parallel with the Amberg railway (p. 234) on the S. side. On the left, *Schloss Platnersberg*, restored by Heideloff. 6 M. *Behringersdorf;* 8 M. *Rückersdorf* (3 M. to the N. is the *Ludwigshöhe*, a summer-resort with view-tower); 10½ M. *Lauf* (Rail. Restaurant), with a château, on the Pegnitz (½ M. to the S. is the station of the Amberg line, p. 234); 12½ M. *Schnaittach*, which lies 3 M. to the N. of the station, with the ruin of *Rothenburg* rising above it (a fine point of view); 15 M. *Reichenschwand*, at the base of the *Hansgörgl-Berg* (see below), with a château and park.

17 M. Hersbruck (1100 ft.; *Post;* *Traube*, in the market-place; *Rother Hahn*), a prosperous little town (3800 inhab.) on the right bank of the Pegnitz, at the foot of the *Michelsberg*, surrounded by hop-gardens. The station on the right bank of the Pegnitz (*Heissmann's Restaurant*) lies on the N. side of the town, 1½ M. from the station on the left bank of the Pegnitz (p. 234).

The **Michelsberg** (1428 ft.), ascended from the right bank station in ¼ hr., affords an admirable survey of the town and district. A still finer point of view is the *Hansgörgl-Berg* (1979 ft.), 1 hr. from *Reichenschwand*, or 1½ hr. from Hersbruck viâ the *Galgenberg* and the *Hagenmühle*. On the top is a pavilion.

At (20½ M.) *Hohenstadt* the line turns to the N. and enters the narrow and tortuous Upper Pegnitz-Thal; to the right, prettily situated at the mouth of the *Hirschbach-Thal*, lies the summer-resort of *Eschenbach*, with a Schloss and a Curhaus. We cross the Pegnitz twice, and pass *Alfalter* and *Düsselbach* on the left. 25 M. **Vorra** (*Krone). Then five bridges and two short tunnels. 27 M. **Rupprechtstegen** (1184 ft.; *Inn 'Zur Fränkischen Schweiz'*, with a huge lime-tree), the centre of the 'Nuremberg Switzerland'. The *Cur-Hôtel*, pleasantly situated on the slope to the left, is a favourite resort in summer.

The *Ankathal*, with its beautiful woods and picturesque groups of rocks, affords a pleasant walk. The path then crosses a lofty plain to (2 hrs.) the ruin of *Hohenstein* (2080 ft.), rising above the village of that name (Inn zur Felsburg; beer at Maier's); fine view from the wooden belvedere (key at the village). — Walk on the left bank of the Pegnitz to the (1 hr.) castle of *Hartenstein*, mentioned in the 'Parzival' of Wolfram von Eschenbach.

Ten bridges and five tunnels (90 to 350 yds. in length) in rapid succession. The walk through the Pegnitz-Thal to Velden is interesting. 29 M. *Velden*, a picturesquely-situated town (Krone), with an ancient gate, lies 1/3 M. to the N.W. of the station. The valley now expands. 31½ M. *Neuhaus* (Rossbach's Inn, at the station; Wilder Mann), commanded by the watch-tower of the old castle of *Veldenstein*.

Near the village of *Krottensee* (Zur Grotte), 1½ M. to the E., is the *Maximilianshöhle, or *Windloch*, a large stalactite grotto, made accessible in 1878 (adm. 1 pers. 75 pf., 2 pers. 1 *M*, etc.; guide necessary; magnesium wire 75 pf. extra).

We cross and recross the Pegnitz several times. 33½ M. *Ranna*; 37 M. *Michelfeld*; 41½ M. *Pegnitz* (Lamm; Ross), a district-town on the Pegnitz, which rises at **Lindenhart**, 9 M. to the N. (diligence daily in 2¾ hrs. by *Pottenstein* to *Gössweinstein*, p. 95). The train now ascends to (46½ M.) **Schnabelwaid**.

BRANCH RAILWAY TO BAYREUTH (11 M., in 40 min.) by (4 M.) *Creussen*, an old town in the valley of the *Rothe Main*, noted for its earthenware, and (7 M.) *Neuenreuth*. 11 M. *Bayreuth* (see p. 86).

The train turns to the E., and near (50 M.) *Engelmannsreuth* passes through the watershed between the **Pegnitz** and the *Nab* by a cutting 880 yds. long. Beyond (53½ M.) *Vorbach* the *Hard* is penetrated by a tunnel of 490 yds.

58 M. **Kirchenlaibach**, junction for the Neuenmarkt and Weiden line (p. 89). The train pursues a N.E. direction. Near (63½ M.) *Immenreuth* it crosses the *Heidenab*, and at *Oberwappenöst* it passes under the watershed between the Heidenab and the *Fichtelnab* by a tunnel of 935 yds. The valley of the latter stream is crossed near *Riglasreuth* by a lofty iron viaduct. 70 M. *Neusorg* (1827 ft.); branch hence to (9½ M.) *Fichtelberg*. Near *Langentheilen* the watershed between the Nab and the *Röslau* is pierced by another long tunnel. 75 M. *Waldershof* (1805 ft.); **2 hrs. to the W.** is the *Kösseine* (p. 92). — 77 M. **Markt-Redwitz** (1742 ft.; *Anker*, at the station; *Weisses Ross* and others, poor), a busy little town on the *Kössein*, with a Protestant church in the transition style;

junction of the line from Hof to Wiesau (p. 134). The line now turns to the N.E. and follows the Röslau, which it crosses twice. 81½ M. *Seussen*; 83½ M. *Arzberg*; 86 M. *Schirnding*. Before reaching (88½ M.) *Mühlbach* we enter Austrian territory. The train now follows the *Eger*, intersects the plateau to the S. of Eger at a depth of 56 ft., and, curving to the N., enters the station of (94 M.) Eger (see *Baedeker's Austria*).

22. From Nuremberg to Augsburg.

105 M. RAILWAY, express in 3½-4 hrs. (fares 16½, 11 *M*), ordinary train in 6 hrs. (13 *M* 60, 9 *M*, 5 *M* 80 pf.).

The train crosses the *Ludwigs-Canal* immediately after quitting Nuremberg, and beyond (5 M.) *Reichelsdorf* the *Rednitz*.

9 M. **Schwabach** (*Engel; Rose; Stern*, unpretending), an old town with 8190 inhabitants. The late-Gothic church of *St. John*, erected in 1469-95, contains a grand *Altar-piece with carving by *Veit Stoss* and paintings by *Wohlgemut* (1506) and *Dürer* (? Entombment); in the Rosenburg chapel are other paintings by *Wohlgemut*, *Martin Schön* (Virgin in a garland of roses), *Grünewald*, etc., and a Gothic ciborium, 42 ft. high, by *A. Krafft* (1505), to whom **a monument** was erected in the church in 1889. (The sacristan **lives in the** Kirch-Platz, in a small house to the left of the bookseller's.) The *Schöne Brunnen* in the market-place, erected in 1716, was restored in 1856. 'Schwabach type' is an old German text now revived. The 'Articles of Schwabach' form the Protestant creed adopted in 1528-29.

Near (15½ M.) *Roth* is the old château of *Ratibor* (1535). A little farther on, the *Swabian* and *Franconian Rezat* unite to form **the Rednitz**. From (21 M.) *Georgensgmünd* a branch-line leads in 25 min. to *Spalt*, a small town prettily situated on the Swabian Rezat, the birthplace of G. Spalatin (d. 1545), the friend of Luther and Melanchthon. On a wooded eminence to the left rises *Schloss Sandsee*, the property of Prince Wrede. 27 M. *Pleinfeld*, on the Rezat, junction of the Nuremberg and Munich railway (viâ *Treuchtlingen*, p. 130). 33 M. *Langlau*.

37 M. **Gunzenhausen**, on the *Altmühl*, junction of the Würzburg and Munich line (see p. 130). Beyond (42 M.) *Kronheim* the line reaches the *Wörnitz*. To the right of (46 M.) *Wassertrüdingen* **rises** the long *Hesselberg*. 48½ M. *Auhausen*. 54 M. *Oettingen*, a small town with 3200 inhab., on the Wörnitz, residence of the Prince of Oettingen-Spielberg. Beyond (57 M.) *Dürrenzimmern*, the *Ipf* (p. 29) becomes conspicuous on the W. The village on the right near Nördlingen is *Wallerstein* (p. 112), with **a ruined** castle.

62 M. **Nördlingen** (1410 ft.; *Hôt. Kiehneyer*, at the station; *Krone; Deutsches Haus; Weisses Ross;* Beer at the *Sonne*), formerly an imperial town, is still surrounded with walls and towers. **Pop.** 8000. In the gardens outside the station is a bronze bust of the

poet *Melchior Meyr* (d 1871), author of 'Erzählungen aus dem Ries'. The Gothic *St. George's Church*, erected 1428-1505, contains a fine late-Gothic ciborium (1511-25), a good stone pulpit of the same period, a curious winding staircase to the organ-loft, paintings by *Schäufelein* (Mourning for Christ, in the Baptistery) and *Herlen*, and good stained glass. Fine prospect from the tower (290 ft. in height), extending over the Ries with its numerous villages, of which 99 are said to be visible. The late-Gothic *Rathhaus* contains a large mural painting by *Schäufelein* (1515), of the history of Judith and Holofernes; on the upper floor a collection of old German pictures (chiefly by *Schäufelein* and *Herlen*), autographs, coins, local antiquities, etc. (Apply to custodian on first floor.)

During the Thirty Years' War the Imperial Generals Ferdinand of Hungary and the Cardinal Infanta Don Fernando gained a signal victory here over the Swedes under Bernhard of Weimar and Horn, 27th Aug., 1634.

A diligence plies daily from Nordlingen viâ *Fessenheim* to (12 M.) Wemding (*Kreuz; Sonne*), on the *Dosbach*, near which is the small bath of *Wemding*, with a sulphurous spring.

Remsthat Railway from Nördlingen to Stuttgart, see R. 7.

FROM NÖRDLINGEN TO DOMBÜHL, $33^{1}/_{2}$ M. (railway in $2^{1}/_{2}$-$3^{1}/_{4}$ hrs.). $2^{1}/_{2}$ M. *Wallerstein*, with a picturesque ruined castle. *Marktoffingen*, 1 M. to the E. of which lies *Maihingen*, formerly a convent, with the valuable library, armoury, and other collections of Prince Oettingen-Wallerstein. Then *Fremdingen*, *Wilburgstetten*. — $18^{1}/_{2}$ M. Dinkelsbühl (*Goldne Rose*), an old imperial town on the *Wörnitz*, still surrounded with walls and towers (4484 inhab.), was the birthplace of *Chr. von Schmid* (d. 1854), a popular writer for the young, to whom a statue has been erected in the marketplace. The late-Gothic *Church of St. George* (built in 1441-99), with its handsome ciborium and carved altars, and the *Deutsche Haus* (15th cent.) are interesting. — $22^{1}/_{2}$ M. *Schopfloch*; 27 M. *Feuchtwangen* (Post), an old town with a Gothic abbey-church; 30 M. *Dorfgüttingen*. $33^{1}/_{2}$ M. *Dombühl*, see p. 26.

$67^{1}/_{2}$ M. *Möttingen*; to the left, the *Lierheimer Schloss*. Beyond (70 M.) *Hoppingen* we enter the *Ries*, a remarkably fertile tract, probably once the bed of a lake. 72 M. *Harburg*, a little town belonging to Prince Wallerstein, with a well-preserved castle, picturesquely perched on a rock. $75^{1}/_{2}$ M. *Wörnitzstein*. The train follows the fertile valley of the winding *Wörnitz*.

$79^{1}/_{2}$ M. **Donauwörth** (1365 ft.; *Krebs*, unpretending, R., L. & A. 1 ℳ 20 pf., B. 60 pf.; *Becher*), an old town on the *Danube*, with 3733 inhabitants. The buildings of the suppressed Benedictine Abbey of the *Holy Cross* are now the property of Prince Wallerstein. A chapel adjoining the abbey-church contains the sarcophagus of the ill-fated Mary of Brabant, consort of Duke Lewis of Bavaria, by whose order she was beheaded in 1256 on a groundless suspicion of infidelity. The fortress of *Mangoldstein*, where the execution took place, to the right near the station, was destroyed by Emp. Albert I. in 1308, and the ruins were removed in 1818. A tablet in the rock, bearing the words '*Castrum Woerth*', now marks the site of the castle, and a cross above indicates the scene of the execution. The *Schellenberg*, above the station, was stormed with severe loss by Lewis of Baden in 1704. Its capture formed a prelude to the disastrous battle of Höchstädt (see next page).

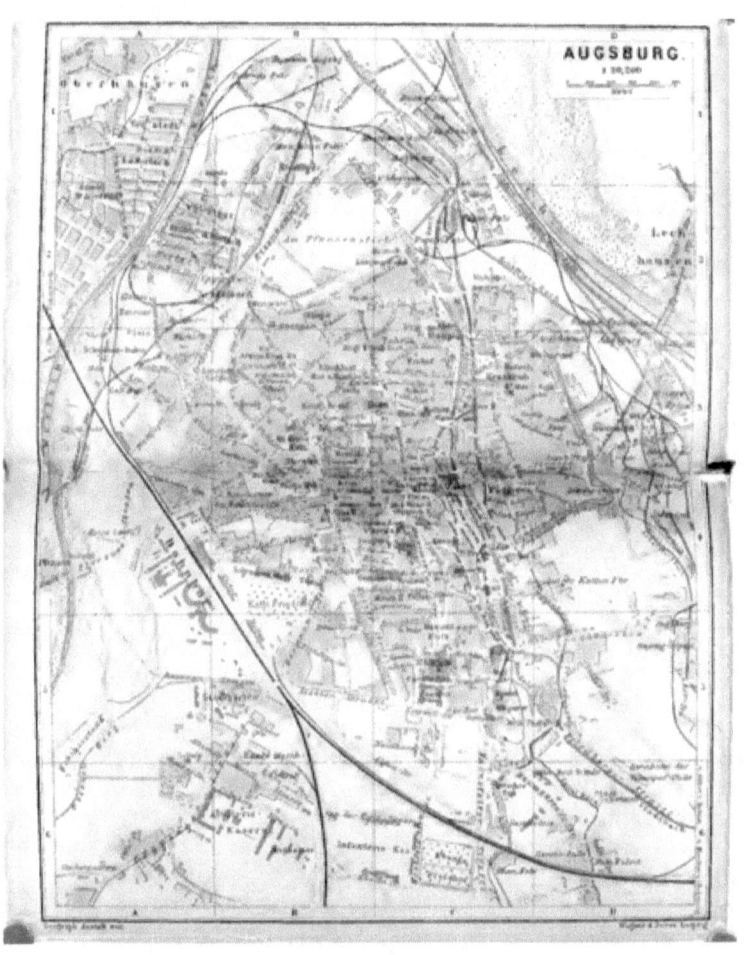

From Donauwörth to Neu-Offingen, 27½ M., railway in 1½ hr. (to Ulm in 3 hrs.). The line skirts the N. side of the town, turns to the S.W., and traverses the valley of the tortuous *Danube*. 5 M. *Tapfheim*; 9 M. *Blenheim*, or *Blindheim*; 12 M. *Höchstädt*. Each of the last two names recalls more than one fiercely contested battle. Here in 1083 Guelph I. of Bavaria was defeated and deprived of his duchy by Emp. Henry IV. In 1703 Elector Max Emanuel of Bavaria and Marshal Villars gained a victory at Höchstädt **over the** Imperial troops under Count Styrum; but the Elector and Marshal Tallard were signally defeated, at Blenheim, by **Prince Eugene** and the **Duke of Marlborough**, 13th Aug., 1704. Nearly a century later, on 19th June, 1800, the Austrians under Kray engaged the French under Moreau at Höchstädt. — 11½ M. *Steinheim*. — 17 M. Dillingen (°*Bayrischer Hof*; *Stern; °*Deutscher Kaiser*, unpretending), a thriving town of 5770 inhab., which has belonged to Bavaria since 1802, was formerly the seat of a university, suppressed in 1804. The old château once belonged to the bishops of Augsburg. — 19 M. Lauingen, a busy town of 3845 inhab., the residence during the middle ages of the Bavarian **dukes** of Pfalz-Neuburg, whose burial-vault is below the Roman Catholic church. The isolated *Hof-Thurm*, 180 ft. high, in sixteen stories, was erected in 1478. A bronze statue of the celebrated scholar *Albertus Magnus* (1193-1280), a native of Lauingen, was erected in the market-place in 1881. — 22½ M. *Gundelfingen*, a small town on the *Brenz*, with the ruins of the castle of *Hohen-Gundelfingen*, destroyed during the Thirty Years' War. The line turns towards the S., crosses the Danube, **and** joins the Ulm and Augsburg line (p. 133) at (27½ M.) *Neu-Offingen*.

From Donauwörth to *Ingolstadt* and *Ratisbon*, see R. 24.

The train crosses the **Danube, and then the** *Schmutter*. Stations *Bäumenheim*, *Mertingen*, *Nordendorf* **(right, the château** of Count Fischler-Treuberg), *Meitingen* (right, **on the height, the** castle of *Markt*, once a Roman fort, the property of **Prince Fugger**), *Langweid*, *Gersthofen*, and *Oberhausen* (to *Ulm*, see **p. 133**). We cross the *Wertach*, near its union with the Lech.

105 M. **Augsburg. — Hotels.** °Drei Mohren (Pl. a; C, 4), Maximilian-Str., R., L., & A. from 3, B. 1, D. 3 ℳ, omn. 70 pf., one of the oldest hostelries in Germany, but lately rebuilt. °Kaiserhof (Pl. i; B, 4), Halder-Str., with frequented restaurant; °Goldne Traube (Pl. b; C, 4), Maximilian-**Str., R.** 1½ ℳ, D. 2 ℳ 20 pf., B. 70 pf.; °Bayrischer Hof (Pl. d; **B,** 4), Drei Kronen (Pl. e; B, 4), with garden, both in the Bahnhof-Str.; Weisses Lamm (Pl. c; B, 3), Ludwig-Str., R. 2-3 ℳ, B. 70 pf., good cuisine; Mohrenkopf (Pl. f; C, 4), Predigerberg; Eisenhut (Pl. g; C, 3), Obstmarkt, R. 1-1½ ℳ. — **Restaurants and Cafés.** °*Railway Restaurant;* °*Kaiserhof*, see above; *Kernstock, Steingasse, D. 1 ℳ 20 pf.; °*Restaurant* in the *Stadt-Garten; Augusta* and *Stötter*, in the Fugger-Str.; *Mussbeck*, *Bavaria*, in the Maximilian-Str. — Wine. °*Metzler-Hofmann* (*Grünes Haus*), in the St-Anna-Str.; *Lamberger zur Weiberschule*, **Bei** der Metzg (C, 182); *Eisenhut*, see above; *Rathskeller*, Eisenberg (C, 323). — Beer. *Hering*, at the Schmidtberg; *Kohleis* (Reichskrone), Burgergässchen.

Baths. *Ott'sche Badeanstalt*, Baumgartner-Str., **outside** the Rothe Thor (Pl. C, 6; cold, warm, and vapour baths); *Augustusbad*, Kreuz-Str.; *Grünwald*, at the Katzenstadel (F, 152). *Municipal Swimming Bath* (Pl. D, 6); *Swimming* **School (Pl.** A, 3).

Post & **Telegraph Office** (Pl. B, 3, 4), Grottenau, at the corner of the Ludwig-Str.

Cabs. Drive (¼ hr.), 1-2 pers. 50 pf., 3 pers. 60 pf.; **from the** station **20 pf. more. At night (10 to 6)** double fares. Each box of 56lbs. 20 pf.

Tramways (comp. **Plan**): from **the** Ludwigs-Platz (Perlach; Pl. C, 4) to Oberhausen 10 pf., to **the** Ulrichs-Platz 10 pf., the railway-station 10 pf., Pfersee 15 pf., Göggingen (p. 118) 20 pf.; from the Metz-Platz to Lechhausen 10 pf.

114 *Route 22.* AUGSBURG. *Cathedral.*

Augsburg (1340 ft.), with 75,523 inhab. ($1/3$ Prot.), the Roman *Augusta Vindelicorum*, situated at the confluence of the *Wertach* and the *Lech*, is one of the most important towns in S. Germany. Its abundant water-power, utilised by canals traversing the town, has given rise to various industries (weaving, cotton-spinning, etc., chiefly outside the town).

In the middle ages (from 1268) Augsburg was a free imperial city, and the great centre of the traffic between N. Europe, Italy, and the Levant. It reached the height of its prosperity in the 15th and 16th centuries, and several of its citizens enjoyed princely wealth and power. Three daughters of Augsburgers were married to princes: Clara von Detten to Elector Frederick the Victorious of the Palatinate; Agnes Bernauer, the beautiful daughter of a barber, to Duke Albert III. of Bavaria (p. 236); and Philippina Welser to Archduke Ferdinand of Austria. Bartholomew Welser, another citizen, fitted ont a squadron to take possession of Venezuela, which had been assigned to him as a pledge by Emp. Charles V. The Fugger family raised themselves within a century from the condition of poor weavers to that of the wealthiest merchants at Angsburg, or perhaps in Europe. They were the Rothschilds of their age and like them ennobled; and they frequently replenished the exhausted coffers of the emperors Maximilian I. and Charles V. A separate quarter of Augsburg, founded by Joh. Jacob Fugger 'the Rich' in 1519, is still called the *Fuggerei* (p. 115), closed by its own gates, and consisting of fifty-three small houses, tenanted at a merely nominal rent by indigent Roman Catholic citizens. — At Augsburg Charles V. held his famous diets; that of 1530, at which the Protestant princes presented to the Emperor and the estates the '*Augsburg Confession*', a reformed creed framed by Melanchthon; that of 1548, at which the 'Interim' was issued; and that of 1555, by which a religious peace was concluded. The delivery of the Confession took place in a hall of the episcopal palace, which is now a royal residence.

The present appearance of Augsburg still recalls its ancient importance. Most of the houses are in the Renaissance style of the 16th and 17th cent., and several are still adorned with well-preserved frescoes. Those of greatest historical interest are indicated by tablets. The old fortifications have been removed, and handsome new streets erected on their site (comp. p. 118).

The principal street is the handsome, broad *Maximilians-Strasse* (Pl. C, 4; between the Maximilians-Platz and the Ludwigs-Platz), with its continuation, the busy *Karolinen-Strasse* (Pl. C, 3). At the N. end of the latter rises the **Cathedral** (Pl. B, C, 3), an irregular Gothic pile, originally a Romanesque basilica, begun in 995, consecrated in 1006, and altered 1321-1431. It now consists of a nave with low vaulting, borne by square pillars, and double aisles separated by slender round columns with foliage-capitals. The N. and S. portals of the E. choir, with sculptures of the 14th cent., are particularly fine.

The W. choir contains a very ancient episcopal throne and an ancient Gothic altar in bronze. In the nave hangs a fine bronze candelabrum of the 14th century. The richly carved Gothic pulpit and the high-altar in the E. choir are modern. The bronze doors of the S. aisle, dating from about 1050, contain representations of Adam and Eve, the Serpent, Centaurs, etc., in thirty-five sections. Fine stained glass, ancient and modern; the S. Romanesque windows of the nave (11th cent.) are among the oldest in existence. The altar-pieces of the first four side-altars are by *Holbein the Elder* (1493); the other altar-pieces in the ambulatory of the choir are by *Zeitblom, Amberger, Wohlgemut, Burgkmair*, and others. On the back wall of the N. aisle are portraits of all the bishops from 596 to the present day. The choir-chapels, containing the tombs of many bishops, are separated from the choir by tasteful iron screens. The fine cloisters on the N. side (late-Gothic, 1474-1510) contain tombstones, some of them very old.

To the W. of the cathedral, in the Frohnhof, with its handsome *War Monument* by *Zumbusch*, is the *Royal Palace* (Pl. B, 3), now government-offices; to the E., in the Karolinen-Platz, the *Episcopal Palace* (Pl. C, 3).

On the right, in the Karolinen-Str., is the *Riedinger House*, the handsome court of which is fitted up as a winter garden. At the S. end of the street is the *Ludwigs-Platz* (Pl. C, 4; usually called 'Eiermarkt' or 'Perlach'), the busiest part of the town, in the centre of which rises the *Fountain of Augustus*, the founder of the city, whose statue was cast by the Dutch master Gerhardt in 1594. On the right is the *Exchange*; on the left the *Perlach-Thurm*, a clock-tower, erected in 1063 as a watch-tower, heightened in 1615, with a fine view from the top. — The *Barfüsserkirche* (Pl. C, 4; Prot.), to the E. of the Perlach-Thurm, contains pictures of the 17th and 18th cent. and an excellent organ. — The *Jacober-Strasse*, the E. continuation of the Barfüssergasse, is still one of the most mediæval streets in existence. Near it is the *Fuggerei* (p. 114). — In the 'Vordere Lech' is the house, in which Holbein the Elder (p. 117) lived and Holbein the Younger was born.

The *Rathhaus (Pl. A, 4; bell in the vestibule to the right, in the middle; in summer the keeper is usually in the hall upstairs), a handsome Renaissance edifice, was erected in 1615-20 by *Elias Holl*. On the gable in front is a large pine-cone in bronze, the heraldic emblem of the city. The lower vestibule contains an eagle, with gilded beak and claws (1606), and busts of Roman emperors from Cæsar to Otho; on the back-wall is a bust of Emp. Frederick III., who commanded the Bavarian troops in the war of 1870-71. An antechamber on the first floor, borne by eight columns of red marble, has a fine wooden ceiling and a statue of Chr. von Schmid (d. 1854; see p. 112), the educational writer. On the second floor is the *'*Golden Hall*', 118 by 62 ft., and 54 ft. in height, one of the finest halls in Germany, with rococo decorations in the Italian style. The adjoining *Fürstenzimmer* also have fine wooden ceilings, wall-panelling, artistic stoves, and a few pictures, casts, flags, etc.

To the S.W., in the Ludwigs-Platz, opens the Philippine-Welser-Strasse, in which a *Statue of Joh. Jac. Fugger* (1516-1575) was erected in 1858. To the E. of the monument is the handsome house in which Philippina Welser lived from 1530 to 1550. To the W. is the **Maximilians-Museum** (Pl. B, C, 4), a Renaissance edifice of the 16th cent., containing the collections of the *Historical* and *Natural History Society* (daily, except Sat. afternoon, 10-1 and 2-5; Oct.-March, 10-12 and 2-4; tickets, 50 pf. each). On the ground-floor are Roman antiquities from the neighbourhood of Augsburg; on the first floor the mediæval collections, including sculptures,

8*

wood-carvings, seals, coins, drawings, etc. The pictures include portraits by *Amberger*, and an Adoration of the Magi by *Gumpolt Giltlinger*, a rare contemporary of Holbein. The natural history department embraces valuable collections of zoological botany, mineralogy, palæontology, ethnography, etc.

In the neighbouring St. Anna-Strasse is the church of St. Anna (Pl. B, 4; Prot.), built in 1472-1510 in the late-Gothic style, with a central part altered to the Renaissance style.

In the interior are an altar-piece (Jesus receiving little children) and portraits of Luther and Elector John Frederick of Saxony, by *Cranach*; the Wise and Foolish Virgins, by *Amberger*; Feeding of the four thousand, by *Rottenhammer*; Portrait of the Patrician von Oestreicher, by *Van Dyck* (?); Christ in Hell, by *Burgkmair*, etc. To the left of the altar is a fine relief in stone of the Raising of Lazarus (16th cent.). The paintings on the wings of the large organ are by *Burgkmair*, those on the small altar are attributed to *Holbein the Younger*. At the W. end is the rich Italian Renaissance burial-chapel of the Fugger family, built by Jacob Fugger the Rich (p. 114). Numerous tombstones in the cloisters.

We return hence to the Maximilians-Strasse, where there are two fountains, the *Mercury* and the *Hercules*, by **Adr. de Vries**, erected in 1599 and 1602. — On the right is the long Fuggerhaus (Pl. C, 4), the property of Prince Fugger-Babenhausen, adorned with modern frescoes by *F. Wagner*, illustrating the history of the town and the Fugger family.

Subjects of these scenes (from left to right): 1. Emp. Rudolph of Hapsburg confirms the municipal privileges of Augsburg (1273); 2. Emp. Lewis the Bavarian takes Augsburg under his protection (1315); 3. Jacob Fugger founds the Fuggerei (1519); 4. Emp. Maximilian I. holding his court at Augsburg (1500); 5. Anthony Fugger interceding for the town with Charles V. (1547). Friezes with allegorical groups of children form a kind of frame to these paintings. Between the windows of the first floor are the armorial bearings of distinguished families of Augsburg. Over the principal portal is a Madonna.

The office of the Fugger estates ('Domänenkanzlei', at the back of the Fuggerhaus, in the Zeugplatz, entered from the Apothekergässchen) contains the so-called *Fugger Bath Rooms*, two sumptuous apartments in the Italian style (1570-72), now used for the meetings and exhibitions of the Augsburg Art Union (open Sun., Mon., Tues., 10-4; at other times on application to the keeper). Opposite is the *Arsenal* (Pl. C, 4), an imposing edifice with a façade by Elias Holl (p. 115; 1602). Above the portal, which bears the inscription '*pacis firmamento, belli instrumento*', is a bronze group, by Reichel, of St. Michael smiting Satan (1607).

At the S. end of the Maximilians-Strasse are the two churches of **St. Ulrich** (Pl. C, 5), one Protestant, the other, the *Church of St. Ulrich and St. Afra*, Roman Catholic. The lofty nave of the latter was erected in 1467-99, and in 1500 the foundation of the choir was laid by Emp. Maximilian I. The tasteful pentagonal porch of the N. portal was added in 1881. The tower (305 ft.), completed in 1594, commands a fine view (adm. 20 pf.).

Interior (always open). The nave and aisles are shut off by a highly elaborate iron *Screen, of the 16th cent., which when seen from the choir produces a striking effect of perspective. The *Fugger Chapel*, between the 2nd and 3rd pillar on the left, with its fine iron railing of 1568, contains the *Tomb of Hans Fugger (1589), a marble sarcophagus with recumbent figure by A. Colins of Malines; also an altar with fine early-German carvings (14th cent.), recently erected. In the chapel of St. Bartholomew (left aisle) is a Roman sarcophagus, said to be that of St. Afra. The three handsome *Renaissance altars date from 1604. Below that to the right is a vault with the marble sarcophagus of Bishop Ulrich (10th cent.), patron of the see of Augsburg. Finely carved confessionals of the beginning of the 17th century. In the nave is a Crucifixion in bronze by Reichel and Neidhardt, cast at the beginning of the 17th century. The 16th cent. paintings above the choir-stalls represent the foundation of the choir and the procession of the emperor and estates.

To the W. of the Hercules Fountain opens the Katharinen-Strasse, in which is situated the *Picture Gallery, in the old monastery of St. Catharine (Pl. C, 4; open daily from 9 to 1, and for strangers at other times; fee 1/2-1 ℳ; catalogue 1 1/2 ℳ, out of date). The collection, founded in 1836, consists of over 700 paintings from the suppressed churches and convents of Augsburg, the convents of Kaisheim and Schönfeld, the Boisserée and Wallerstein cabinets, and the old galleries of Düsseldorf, Mannheim, and Zweibrücken. It is chiefly interesting for its early German masters, in particular the works of *Hans Holbein the Elder* and *H. Burgkmair*, whose names mark the zenith of art in Augsburg (beginning of 16th cent.). Good photographs sold by the attendant. Director, *Herr von Huber*.

VESTIBULE. Four paintings representing the legend of St. Nicholas of Cusa and SS. Jerome and Ambrose, by a *Tyrolese Master of about 1480 (Michael Hans Pacher?)*. — ROOM I. In the centre, marble bust of the younger Holbein after his portrait of himself at Bâle, executed by *Lossow*. 16-27. Cycle of paintings belonging to the old convent of St. Catharine, relating to an indulgence granted to its inmates; the seven principal churches of Rome are represented; above, Scenes from the Passion. 16-18. *Holbein the Elder*, Basilica of S. Maria Maggiore (1499); *Burgkmair*, 19. Basilica of St. Peter (1501), 20-22. S. Giovanni in Laterano (1502); 23. *L. F.* (?), SS. Lorenzo and Sebastian (1502); 24. *Burgkmair*, S. Croce (1504); 25-27. *Holbein the Elder*, S. Paolo fuori (ca. 1504); 42, 43. *Wohlgemut*, Ascension and Crucifixion; *Ulrich Apt*, 47-49. Christ on the Cross and the two malefactors, 50, 51. (grisaille) Annunciation; 52, 53. *Burgkmair*, Emperor Henry II. and St. George (1519); 59. *Gittlinger* (comp. p. 116), Adoration of the Magi; *79-82. *Zeitblom*, Legend of St. Valentine; 84-86. *Holbein the Elder*, Triptych, Transfiguration, Feeding of the four thousand, Healing of the demoniac (1502); 87. The Same, Passion. — ROOM II. Netherlands schools. 99. *Aart de Gelder*, Garland; 109. *Schellincks*, Sea-piece; 113. *M. Sweerts*, Concert; 103. *G Schalcken*, Mocking of Christ; 118. *Van Dyck* (?), Portrait of a marine painter; 97. *Snyders*, Bear-hunt; 121. *Cuyp*, Pastoral scene; 143. *Pieter Lastman* (teacher of Rembrandt), Ulysses and Nausicaa (1619); 205, 206. *Van Dyck*, Sketches (grisaille) for engravings; 169. *Kneller* (after Van Dyck), Queen Henrietta Maria; 164. *Rubens*, Arabs fighting with crocodiles (studiopiece). — ROOM III., chiefly Italian artists. 426. *Rosalba Carriera*, Head of a child; 424. *S. Bourdon*, Idyl; 372. *Ribera*, St. Sebastian; 266. *Millet*, Classical landscape. Second division: 265. *Tintoretto*, Christ at the house of Mary and Martha; 293. *Fr. Zurbaran*, St. Francis. Third division: 382. *Jacopo de' Barbari*, Still-life (1504); *388. *Parmigianino*, Madonna and Child, with a monk; 883. *Imitator of Leonardo da Vinci*, Head of a girl; 287. *Gian Pietrino*, Mary Magdalen. Fourth division: 304. *J. A. Koch*, St. George and the dragon, in a heroic landscape. Last wall: 271. *Fr. Torbido*, Transfiguration. — In the five CABINETS are many excellent small pictures. I. 538. *Adr. van Ostade*, Portrait of himself; 631. *Jan van Os*, Flowers. —

II. 548. *I. van Ostade*, Peasant's hut; *120. *Jan Steen*, Merry party; 635. *B. Cuyp*, Circumcision of Christ. — III. 601. *Hobbema*, Sylvan path; 623. *Philip Wouwerman*, Hawking; 100, 569, 584, *586. *Van Goyen*, Landscapes; 565. *Pynacker*, A wanderer; 628. *Poelenburg*, Waterfall. — IV. 13. *Cranach the Elder*, Pharaoh and his host overwhelmed in the Red Sea; *44-46. *Burgkmair*, Christ on the Cross and the two malefactors (1519); no number, *B. Strigel*, Isaiah and Zachariah; ʻ2. *Altdorfer*, Angel-choirs in a church, with the Holy Family in front. — V. *Holbein the Elder*, 674. Legend of St. Ulrich; 676. Beheading of St. Catharine (1512); 683-685, Crucifixion, Descent from the Cross, Entombment; 6-8. *Burgkmair*, Christ and Mary enthroned, with saints (1507); 673, 675. *Holbein the Elder*, Madonna, St. Anna, and the Infant Christ, Crucifixion of St. Peter; *Dürer*, 668, Virgin with the pink (1516), 669. The Virgin as mediatrix (1497); ʻ696. *Barthel Beham*, Portrait (1535); 672. *North German Master of about 1520*, Portrait of a woman.

The new W. quarters near the railway-station (comp. p. 114) contain several handsome buildings: in the Fugger-Strasse the *Courts of Law* (Pl. B, 4; built 1871-75) and the *Theatre* (Pl. B, 3; built 1876-77); in the Schäzler-Strasse the *Municipal Library* (Pl. B, 3, 4; built 1893), with upwards of 150,000 vols.; and in the Halder-Strasse the *Gymnastic Hall* and the *Corn Market* (Pl. B, 4).

On the E. side of the town extends the public *Park*, at the upper end of which are the large water-works in the Lech called the 'Ablass', for conveying water to the town (*Restaurant). Adjacent are the *Water Works* for supplying the town with drinking-water. — In the Wertach-Thal, 2½ M. to the S.W. (tramway, see p. 113), is *Göggingen* (Dr. Hessing's Curanstalt), with a palm-house, summer-theatre, concerts, etc.

From Augsburg to *Munich*, see R. 26.

23. From Nuremberg to Ratisbon.

62 M. Railway in 2¼-5¾ hrs. (fares 9 ℳ 30, 6 ℳ 60, or 8 ℳ 10, 5 ℳ 40, 3 ℳ 50 pf.). — From Nuremberg to Ratisbon by *Schwandorf*, see R. 41 and p. 134; from Ratisbon to Linz, see R. 42.

Nuremberg, see p. 95. The line at first runs through wood. 2 M. *Dutzendteich* (*Restaurant Dutzendteich; *Waldlust), a favourite resort of the Nurembergers (tramway to Nuremberg, see p. 96). At (7½ M.) *Feucht* branch-lines diverge E. to *Altdorf*, and W. to *Wendelstein*. From (10 M.) *Ochenbruck*, a pleasant walk into the romantic *Schwarzach-Thal*, 1½ M. to the W., by *Schwarzenbruck*. 16½ M. *Postbauer*. The line crosses the Ludwigs-Canal.

22½ M. **Neumarkt** *in der Oberpfalz* (1385 ft.; *Gans*; *Egner*, near the station), a prettily-situated town of 5080 inhab., on the *Sulz*, with chalybeate and sulphureous springs. Observe the Gothic *Church* and the 15th cent. *Rathhaus*. The *Schloss* contains the law-courts. Fine views from the (1 M.) *Mariahilfsberg* (1918 ft.) and the (3 M.) ruins of *Wolfstein* (1905 ft.). — Branch-lines to *Freystadt* and *Beilngries*.

The line traverses the broad *Sulzthal* and enters a wooded and hilly region. Beyond (29 M.) *Deining* it crosses the *Laber* near its source. 35 M. *Seubersdorf*; 39½ M. *Parsberg*, picturesquely

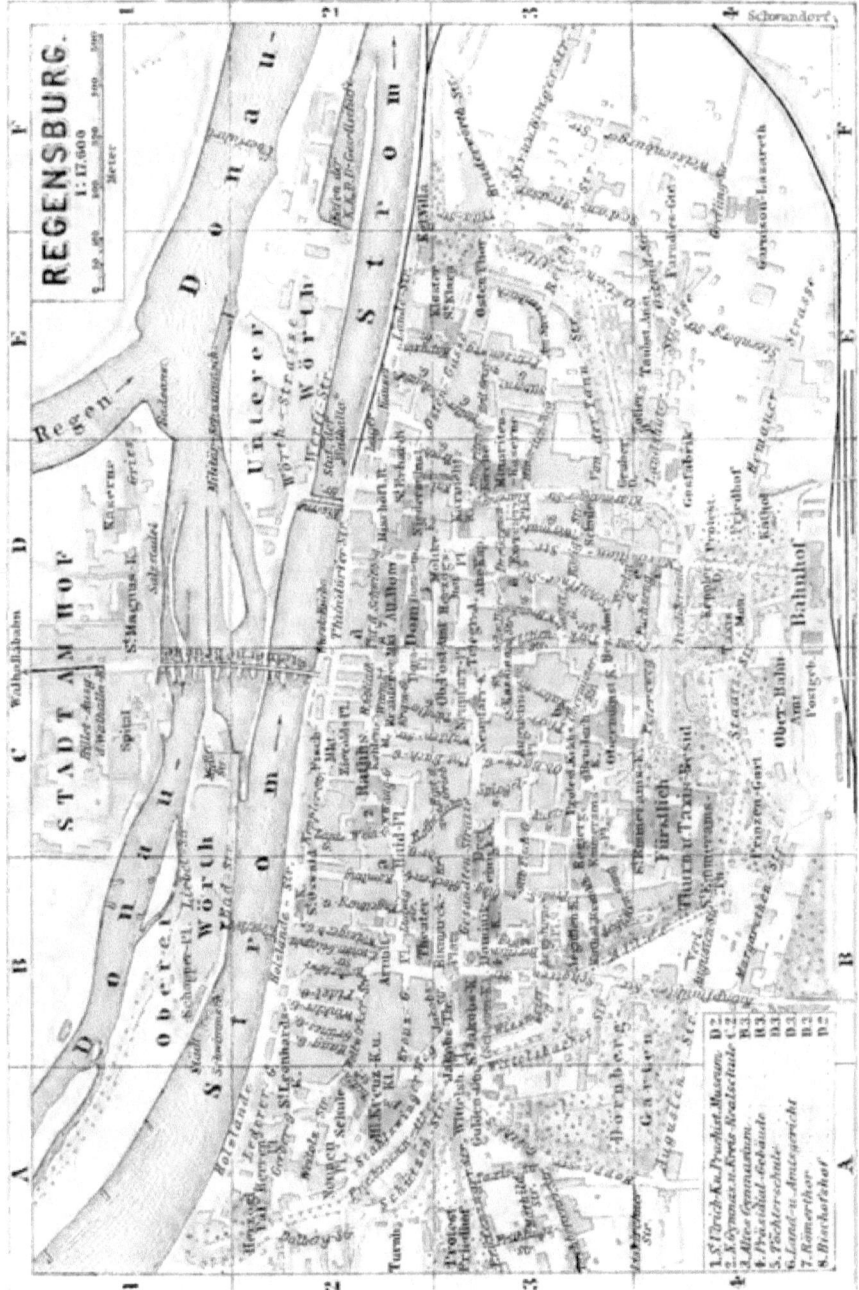

situated on the slope of a hill, which is crowned by an old château, now the district tribunal. The church contains a late-Gothic font of the 15th century. 43 M. *Mausheim.*

Near (46 M.) *Beratzhausen* the train enters the valley of the *Schwarze Laber*, wild and romantic at places, passes *Laber, Deuerling*, and *Eichhofen*, describes a wide circuit towards the E., and enters the pleasant *Nabthal*. Near (56 M.) *Etterzhausen*, much visited from Ratisbon, is the '*Robbers' Cave*', a lofty dome-shaped cavern in the rock.

The line follows the slope on the right bank of the Nab, crosses the *Danube* near (60 M.) *Prüfening*, above the influx of the Nab, and reaches —

62 M. **Ratisbon.** — Hotels. GOLDENES KREUZ (Pl. a; B, 2), Haidplatz, R., L., & A. 2-3, B. 1, D. 3 *M*; *GRÜNER KRANZ (Pl. d; C, 3), Obermünster-Str., R., L., & A. 1½-2½, D. 2½ *M*; *MAXIMILIAN (Pl. c; D, 4), near the station, with restaurant and garden; *NATIONAL (Pl. e; D, 4), *WEIDEN-HOF (R. 1 *M* 20 pf. - 2 *M*), ACHNER, *KARMELITENBRÄU, all in the Maximilian-Str.; WEISSER HAHN (Pl. d; D, 2), near the bridge.

Restaurants. *Rail. Restaurant*; *Maximilian*, **near** the station, with concert-garden; *Neues Haus*, Bismarck-Platz; *Café-Restaurant Central*, Pfauengasse; *Weisse Lilie*, near the **station**; *Guldengarten*, outside the Jakobsthor; *Wurstküche*, quaint, below the bridge (open 6-11 a.m.). — Schillfisch and Scheidfisch, or *Waller*, are good kinds of fish.

Wine. *Diem*, Ludwig-Str.; *Monn*, Plauengasse, beside the **cathedral**. — Beer. At the *Bischofshof*, Domplatz; *Obermünsterbrauerei*, **Obermünster-Str.**; *Weisses Bräuhaus*, Schwarze Bären-Str.; *Jesuitenbräu*, Obermünster-gasse; *Karmelitenbräu* and *Hochsteller*, Maximilian-Str.; *Pfalter*, Ludwigs-Str.; at the *Katharinenspital*, in Stadt-am-Hof, to the left of the bridge.

Post Office at the station and in the Dom-Platz. — **Telegraph Office**, Neupfarr-Platz.

Cabs. To or from the station, one-horse cab (1-2 pers.) 60, two-horse 80 pf. (3-4 pers. 1 *M*); in the town, one-horse cab, ¼ hr. 50 pf., ½ hr. 1 *M*, two-horse 1 *M* or 2 *M*. To the Walhalla, one-horse, 1-2 pers. 5 *M*, 3 pers. 5½ *M*, two-horse, 1-2 pers. 5½ *M*, 3-4 pers. 6½, 5 pers. 7 *M*. (The hirer should insist on being driven up to the Walhalla, as the drivers are apt to stop at the foot of the hill.)

Steam Tramway from Stadt am Hof (p. 124) to *Donaustauf*, 5½ *M*, in 35 min.; fare 75 or 45 pf., return 1 *M* 10 pf. or 75 pf.; it starts close to the bridge on the left bank, 10 min. from the railway-station.

Steamboat to *Donaustauf (Walhalla)* from the Untere Wöhrd by the lower bridge (Pl. D, 2), in July and Aug. thrice; in June, Sept., and Oct. twice daily in ½ hr. (back in 1-1¼ hr.); return-fare 1st cl. 1 *M* 20 pf., 2nd cl. 80 pf.

Baths. *Otto-Bad*, Keppler-Str. and Fischmarkt. — River-baths (20 pf.) at the Obere and the Untere Wöhrd.

Ratisbon, Germ. *Regensburg* (1115 ft.), situated at the confluence of the Danube and *Regen*, with 37,936 inhab. (6000 Prot.), the *Castra Regina* of the Romans, the Celtic *Ratisbona*, and since the 8th cent. the seat of an episcopal see founded by St. Boniface, was from the 11th to the 15th cent. one of the most flourishing and populous cities of S. Germany. At an early period it was a free town of the Empire, and from 1663 to 1806 the permanent seat of the Imperial Diet. By the Peace of Luneville it was adjudged to the Primate Dalberg; and in 1810 it became Bavarian, after the disastrous defeat of the Austrians beneath its walls the preceding year, when part of the town had been reduced to ashes.

Some of the numerous mediæval houses still retain the armorial bearings of their ancient owners, and several still possess their **towers of** defence, a reminiscence of early German civic life now preserved at Ratisbon alone. Of these the *Goldene Thurm* in the Wahlen-Strasse **is the** most conspicuous, near which, in the Watmarkt, is a tower with a relief said to be a portrait of Emp. Henry I. Observe also the *Goliath*, the ancestral seat of the powerful Thundorffer family, opposite the bridge, restored in 1883; the so-called *Römerthurm*, adjoining the ancient 'Herzogsburg' in the Kornmarkt; and the **tower of the** 'Golden Cross' hotel. Ratisbon is one **of the** earliest **homes of art in** Germany, and **so far back as the late** Carlovingian **period** possessed many interesting buildings.

Of *Roman Buildings* there are still a few relics. Thus the remains of the *Porta Praetoria* in the street 'Unter den Schwibbögen', opposite No. F, 112, on the N. side of the Bischofshof (Pl. D, 2). Parts of the old Roman walls were found during building operations, but have been covered in again. The foundations of a Roman building to the S. of the railwaystation were excavated in 1885. During the construction of the railwaystation in 1870-74 a large Roman and Merovingian burial-ground was discovered; the objects found there are now in the Roman **museum in** St. Ulrich's (p. 121).

The *****Cathedral** (Pl. D, 2) of *St. Peter* was begun by Bishop **Leo** Thundorffer on the site of an earlier edifice in 1275, and completed during the following centuries (down to 1534), with the exception of the towers. The symmetrical proportions of the interior recall Strassburg Cathedral. Peculiarities of construction are that the transept does not project beyond the sides of the aisles, and that the choir is destitute of the ambulatory and chapels usual in Gothic churches. The W. façade, with the chief portal and a curious triangular *Porch, is of the 15th century. A gallery, with open stone balustrade, is carried round the roof, and affords a good survey **of** the town. On the N. side of the transept rises the *Eselsthurm*, or Asses' Tower, containing a winding inclined plane. The elegant open *Towers were completed in 1859-69 by *Denzinger*; and a slender wooden spire, coated with zinc, has been raised above the centre of the transept. Length of interior 306 ft., breadth 125 ft.; nave 132 ft. high. (Admission 5-10 a.m.; the sacristan's house is Domgarten, F, 125, at the back of the choir; enter by the gate on the S. side.)

Interior. The nave **contains a monument** in bronze **erected in 1598 to** Bishop Philip William, **Duke of Bavaria.** In a niche **in the N. aisle**, partly concealed from view, is **the monument** of the Primate Prince Dalberg (d. 1817), designed by Canova, and executed in white marble. On the N. side of the choir the °Monument **of** Margaretha Tucher in bronze, by *P. Vischer* (1521), representing Christ **with** the sisters of Lazarus. On the opposite wall of the choir is a marble relief **in** memory of Bishop Herberstein (d. 1663), representing Christ feeding the five thousand. Adjacent, the altar-tomb of Bishop Wittmann (d. 1833). **The** high-altar, presented in 1785 **by** the Prince-Bishop Count Fugger, is entirely of silver; **adjoining it is the elegant** °Ciborium, 56 ft. in height, with numerous **statuettes,** partly executed by Roritzer in 1493. On the S. side of the choir **are two** other modern monuments to bishops, by Eberhard; near them a **well 66 ft. in** depth, with an elegant covering sculptured in stone, executed in 1501 by the cathedral-architect Wolfgang Roritzer, who was beheaded in 1514, for 'rebellion against the imperial authority'. The aisles contain five altars with handsome Gothic canopies and modern pictures. The finest of these is in the N. aisle, with statues of Emp. Frederick II. and the Empress Cunigunde. Late-Gothic pulpit of 1482. An elegant open gallery runs round the interior of the church below the windows. The treasury contains old and costly crucifixes, reliquaries, and other valuables.

The *Cloisters on the N. side of the cathedral are shown by the sacristan. The central hall contains beautifully-sculptured windows of the 16th cent.; the pavement is formed by the tombstones of canons and patricians of Ratisbon. Adjoining this hall on the E. is the Romanesque *All Saints' Chapel*, erected in 1164, with the remains of early frescoes and an interesting antique altar. On the N. side of the cloisters is the *Old Cathedral* (*St. Stephen's*), a very early building in the circular style, with four recesses in the sides. The altar in the apse, a block of stone partly hollowed out, with elegant little round-arched windows, in which relics are said once to have been kept, is evidently of great antiquity.

Just beyond the cathedral is **St. Ulrich**, or the *Alte Pfarre*, a curious but elegant church in the transition-style of the first half of the 13th century. It now contains the older collections of the *Historical Society* (see below), prehistoric and Roman, including several sarcophagi and over thirty inscriptions. The gallery contains the bronzes and other smaller antiquities (adm. daily 8-6, 50 pf., Sun. 9-12, 20 pf.; catalogue 30 pf.). — To the N.E., beyond the cathedral-garden, lies the church of *Niedermünster*, of early foundation but entirely rebuilt in the baroque style. Adjoining is the *Bishops' Palace*, occupying part of the old convent of St. Erhard. The interesting little *Crypt of St. Erhard*, in the Niedermünstergasse, behind the church, dates from the 11th century. In the Kallmünzergasse is the handsome new Roman Catholic *Vereinshaus* **St. Erhard**, with a fine Gothic hall ('Dollinger-Saal'). On the upper floor are the archives, library, coins, drawings, seals, weapons, pictures, etc., belonging to the *Historical Society* (adm. on application to the custodian in St. Ulrich's church).

In the OLD KORNMARKT (now the Moltke-Platz; Pl. D, 3), to the S.E. of the cathedral, are the *Herzogshof* (now the Forestry bureau) and the *Römerthurm* or *Heidenthurm* (p. 118). On the S. side is the *Alte Kapelle*, originally a Romanesque church with a Gothic choir, restored in the 18th cent. in the baroque style. Opposite, to the E., is the little *Karmelitenkirche* (1641-60), in the Ital. baroque style. On the Minoriten-Platz rises the Gothic *Minoritenkirche*, built early in the 14th cent., with a fine lofty choir. Part of it is now a military gymnasium, and the adjacent monastery is now a barrack.

From the cathedral we pass through the Kramgasse to the W. to the **Rathhaus** (Pl. C, 2), a gloomy, irregular pile, partly erected in the 14th cent. and partly after 1660. The Imperial Diet met here from 1663 to 1806. Observe the façade towards the Rathhaus-Platz, with an elegant bow-window and a fine portal. Cards of admission at the police guard-room (50 pf. each).

The great *Imperial Hall* contains what is groundlessly called the imperial throne, covered with leather and studded with brass nails. The walls are hung with **tapestry**. The stained-glass windows exhibit the armorial bearings of **Emperors** Charles V. and Matthias. In the *Fürstenkollegium* is preserved **tapestry** of the 14-15th cent.: Æneas and Dido, Coronation of Esther, **Contest of the virtues and the vices**; also embroidery of the same period ('**the heart's joys and sorrows**'); tapestry of the 15-17th cent. (mythological **and hunting scenes**). The *Nebenzimmer* (entrance under the gallery of the **Imperial Hall**) contains old flags, portraits, views of Ratisbon (1725) and **Nuremberg (1637)**, etc. In the *Model Room* are eighty-eight models of buildings in Ratisbon, antiquities, etc. Subterranean dungeons and a torture-chamber are also shown.

Farther to the W. is the HAIDPLATZ (Pl. C, 2), in which is the hotel '*Zum Goldnen Kreuz*' (Pl. a). The massive tower on the E. side of the hotel bears a medallion-portrait of Don John of Austria (modern).

This celebrated general, a natural son of the Emp. Charles V. and the beautiful Barbara Blumberger, was born at Ratisbon on 25th Feb., 1547. The Emperor lodged, during the Diet of 1546, at the 'Golden Cross', then the house of Bernard Kraft auf der Haid, but that Don John was born here is a fiction.

Going hence through the Ludwig-Str. to the Arnulf-Platz, and turning to the left, past the *Neue Haus* with the *Theatre* (Pl. B, 2), we reach the church of the old *Benedictine Abbey of St. Jakob*, usually called the **Schottenkirche** (Pl. B, 3), the abbey having originally belonged to Scottish or Irish monks. The famous Romanesque portal is adorned with curious sculptured figures of men and animals, perhaps symbolical of the victory of Christianity over paganism. The church, a Romanesque basilica of the latter half of the 12th cent., containing columns with interesting old capitals, has lately been restored. The old monastery is now a seminary for priests. — In the vicinity, outside the Jakobsthor, is a Gothic *Column* of 1459 with scriptural scenes and statues of saints, restored in 1855.

To the E. of the Jakobskirche is the BISMARCK-PLATZ (Pl. B, 3), with pleasure-grounds, on the S.E. side of which rises the large Gothic *Dominikanerkirche*. The Gesandten-Str. (Pl. B, C, 3), with its handsome houses, leads straight on to the E. to the Neupfarr-Platz, passing the Prot. *Dreieinigkeitskirche*. In the adjoining court a number of interesting tombstones are built into the wall. Farther on the house of Herr Schwarz (C, 93) contains the *Collections of the Natural History Society* (adm. on the 1st and 3rd Sun. of each month, 10-12).

The Bereiterweg leads to the S. from the Bismarck-Platz, passing the *Präsidialgebäude* (Pl. 4), on the right, and the *Old Gymnasium* (Pl. 3), on the left, to the ÆGIDIEN-PLATZ (Pl. B, 3), where are situated the Rom. Cath. **Krankenhaus** and the Gothic **Aegidienkirche** (13th cent.), recently restored. The Marschall-Str. to the left leads thence past the *Regierungsgebäude* to the EMMERAMS-PLATZ (Pl. C, 3), embellished with a statue of *Bishop Joh. Mich. Sailer* (d. 1832), in bronze, by Widnmann, **erected by** Ludwig I. in 1868.

The old *Benedictine Abbey* of **St. Emmeram** (Pl. C, 3, 4), one **of** the oldest in Germany, was founded in the 7th cent., and suppressed in 1803. The Romanesque church, with two choirs and a crypt, dates from the 11th cent., and was restored **early** in last century in

Obermünster.   RATISBON.   *23. Route.* **123**

a degraded style. (**The** sacristan's house is to the **right of** the church, C, 152.)

The entrance is from the Emmerams-Platz, through a **double** door, above which are faded **frescoes**. Between the doors is a **relief of** Christ bearing the Cross (1511). On the wall to the right are blind arches resting upon columns; to **the left in the garden** is the isolated church-tower, adorned with statues (16th cent.). The porch adjoining the church-door contains an ancient **stone seat**, known as the *Heinrichs Stuhl*, because the Emp. Henry II. is supposed to have sat upon it. On the wall to the right is the tombstone of the historian Aventin (d. 1534). The principal altarpiece is a painting by Sandrart (1666), the **martyrdom** of St. Emmeram; in the pavement in front of the altar a **slab** bearing the imperial crown denotes the **tombs of** Emp. Arnulph (d. **899) and** Emp. Lewis the Child (d. 911). The aisles contain some interesting ancient sculptures; in the left aisle: monuments **of** Empress Uta, wife of Arnulph (13th cent.); **Count Warmund von** Wasserburg (d. 1010); **Dukes Arn**ulph (d. **937) and Henry** (d. 995) **of Bavaria; and** St. Aurelia (d. 1027), daughter of Hugh Capet, erected in 1335. This aisle also contains the altar of the **martyred** Maximianus, with his relics; and a cabinet (opened **by the sacristan) with** relics of SS. Emmeram and Wolfgang, reliquaries, ecclesiastical antiquities, etc. In the right aisle: monuments of St. **Wolfgang** (d. 994); beneath an iron grating, Bishop Tuto, chancellor under Arnulph, and St. Emmeram; also the altar of St. Calcedonius with his relics. In the vaulted treasury are a handsome sarcophagus, hewn at Ratisbon in 1423 and containing the relics of St. Emmeram, and other **curiosities**. Below the W. choir is a crypt of the **year** 1052, restored in 1878.

The fine old *Cloisters* on the S. side of the church (13th and 14th cent.) are enclosed by the extensive abbey-buildings, which have been the residence of the Princes of Thurn and Taxis since 1812. The way to the cloisters (open daily, 11-12) is to the right of the church, past the *Reitbahn*, or riding-school (with sculptures by Schwanthaler); then through a portal to the left into the large court with the old *Kaiserbrunnen* (with figure said to represent Emp. Arnulph); and again to the left to a door with a glass roof, where we find the porter (fee). In the centre of the cloisters is the modern *Chapel*, adorned with stained'glass; in the choir is a statue of Christ by Dannecker (p. 11); the crypt contains the family burial-vault. At the end of the E. wing of the cloisters is a fine iron gate, said to date from the 11th century.

The adjacent abbey-church of **Obermünster** (Pl. C, 3), an 11th cent. basilica resembling St. Emmeram's, contains some old frescoes and tombs. The convent is now an episcopal school for boys. — We may return hence to the cathedral viâ the Neupfarr-Platz, to the N., in which is the Prot. *Neupfarrkirche*.

Outside the Petersthor (Pl. D, 4; now pulled down), in the **Anlagen**, or pleasure-grounds, laid out on the site of the old ramparts, is the *Prediger-Säule*, or 'preacher's column', with reliefs of the 13th or 14th cent. (restored in 1858). In the vicinity is a small circular temple, erected in 1808, with a bust of *Kepler*, the astronomer, who died here in 1630 whilst on a journey. The Anlagen contain several other monuments. The *Royal Villa* in the Gothic style, on an old **bastion at the** lower end of the town, **near the** Ostenthor (Pl. E, 2), **commands** an extensive view.

A stone bridge over the Danube, 380 yds. in length, built in the 12th cent., **connects** Ratisbon with **Stadt am Hof, a** suburb on the opposite bank, which was almost entirely burned down by the Austrians in 1809. Below Stadt am Hof the *Regen* empties its turbid water into the Danube.

Pleasant walk through Stadt am Hof to the *Dreifaltigkeitsberg* and the (³/₄ hr.) *Seidenplantage* (Restaurant; fine view, best by **evening** light).

To the Walhalla, a most attractive **excursion; there and** back in about 3 hrs. (steam-tramway, steamboat, or carriage, see **p. 119**). The Walhalla-Bahn traverses Stadt am Hof, crosses the *Regen*, and **intersects the** railway (p. 134; passenger-station) at the station of *Walhalla-Strasse*. Thence it crosses the plain of the **Danube,** via *Schwabelweis* and *Tegernheim*, to (6³/₄ M.) **Donaustauf or** *Stauf* (1068 ft.; *Restaurant zur Walhalla*, at the upper end). On a limestone rock above the long village rise the ruins of the castle of *Stauf* (1385 ft.), destroyed by the Swedes in 1634, with pleasure-grounds (view finer than from the Walhalla).

Two routes ascend from the upper end of Donaustauf to the (20-25 min.) Walhalla; one immediately to the left (at first a carriage-road, then ascending steps and by a footpath to the right, past the house of the custodian), approaching the Walhalla from the back, and preferable for the view suddenly disclosed. The other, a footpath, ascends direct to the grand flight of 250 steps by which the edifice is approached from the Danube. The sculptures in the S. tympanum are only seen to advantage from the upper part of the flight. The best general view is obtained from the opposite bank of the Danube. — Travellers arriving by steamer do not enter the village, but follow the first road to the right, and then either ascend to the left through the grounds to the route first described, or go on at the foot of the hill to the flight of steps.

The *Walhalla (*i.e.* 'Hall of the Chosen', the Paradise of the ancient Germanic tribes), a German 'Temple of Fame', stands very conspicuously on a hill planted with oaks and laid out with walks, 280 ft. above the Danube (1348 ft. above the sea-level). This magnificent edifice, **founded** by King Lewis I. in 1830, and designed by *Klenze*, was completed in 1842. Admission daily from April 1st to Sept. 1st, 8-12 and 1-7; in March and Sept. **8-12** and 1-6, in Oct. **8-12** and **1-5**; other months 9-12 and 1-4 (free).

The Exterior (246 ft. long, 115 ft. broad), surrounded by fifty-two **fluted** columns, a fine example of the purest **Doric** order, closely resembling the Parthenon at Athens, is massively constructed of unpolished grey marble (most of it quarried at the Untersberg; some of the blocks about fifteen tons in weight). The Pediments both in front and at the **back contain** groups in marble: S., **towards** the Danube, Germania, regaining her liberty **after** the battle of Leipsic; N. the 'Hermannschlacht', or Battle of Arminius, both by *Schwanthaler* (d. 1848). The roof is of iron, covered with **plates** of copper.

The Interior, of the Ionic order, consists of a superb hall 180 ft. long, 50 ft. broad, and 56 ft. high, with richly decorated and gilded ceiling, and lighted from above. The pavement is of marble-mosaic. The lateral walls are divided into six sections by means of projecting buttresses, two on each side, and are lined with marble. The beams of the ceiling are supported by 14 painted Walkyries (warrior-virgins of the ancient German Paradise), by *Schwanthaler*. Around the entire hall runs a frieze, executed by *Wagner*, representing in 8 sections the history and life of the Germanic race down to the introduction of Christianity. Above the cornice are 64 marble tablets bearing the names of famous Germans of whom no portrait could be obtained. The busts are arranged chronologically (beginning on the left side by the entrance) in groups, separated by six admirable °°VICTORIES by *Rauch* (the finest of which is that in the middle of the left side). At the farther extremity is the 'opisthodomos', separated from the principal hall by two Ionic columns; in front of it is a seated marble statue of **King** Lewis I., by F. **von** Miller (1890). The general effect of the interior **is grand** and impressive, although the association of classical Greek arch**itecture** with an ancient barbarian Paradise and modern German celeb**rities** may appear somewhat incongruous. — The °BUSTS, 101 in number, **represent** celebrated Germans **who were deemed worthy by** the illustrious **founder** to grace his temple **of fame. Among** them are **the** emperors Henry the Fowler, Fred. Barbarossa, and **Rudolph** of Hapsburg; also Gutenberg, Dürer, Luther, Wallenstein, Fred. **the Great,** Blücher, Schwarzenberg, and Radetzky; Lessing, Mozart, **Beethoven, Kant,** Schiller, Goethe, etc.

*View of the dark slopes of **the Bavarian** Forest; below **flows the** Danube; beyond it **the** fertile plain of Straubing; right, **Donaustauf** and Ratisbon; left, in clear weather, the snow-capped Alps.

From Ratisbon to the °*Befreiungshalle*, at Kelheim, see below.

24. From Ratisbon to Donauwörth *(and Augsburg)*.

RAILWAY to (18½ M.) *Kelheim*, 1-1½ hr. (fares 2 ℳ 30, 1 ℳ 70, 1 ℳ 5 pf.); to (46 M.) *Ingolstadt*, 2½-3 hrs. (fares 6 ℳ, 4 ℳ, 2 ℳ 60 pf.); to (78½ M.) *Donauwörth*, 4-6 hrs. (fares 10 ℳ 30, 6 ℳ 90, 4 ℳ 50 pf.); to (87½ M.) *Augsburg*, 5 hrs. (fares 11 ℳ 30, 7 ℳ 50, 4 ℳ 80 pf.).

The line passes under the Nuremberg and Ratisbon railway at (2 M.) *Prüfening* (p. 119) and crosses the *Danube*, which is here flanked by the spurs of the *Franconian Jura*. 4 M. *Sinzing*, at the **mouth of the** *Schwarze Laber* (branch-line to *Alling*, with large **paper-mills**). Then on the left bank of the Danube; pretty scenery. **Opposite** (9 M.) *Gundelshausen* lies *Oberndorf*, where Count **Palatine Otho** of Wittelsbach, the murderer of the German Emperor **Philip (p. 78)**, was overtaken and slain **in** 1208. Farther on is *Abbach* (***Curhaus), the** birthplace of Emp. Henry the Saint (972), **with sulphur-baths, a new** church, and a ruined **castle.** We then **cross the Danube to (12 M.)** *Abbach;* the station is 2 M. **from the village.** The **train skirts the** *Teufelsfelsen***, where many** Roman **coins were** found **during the** construction **of the** railway **in** 1873. **The** Befreiungshalle **is** visible **to the left. On the** *Ringberg* are well-defined traces **of** an extensive Roman **camp.** — 15½ M. *Saal*.

To KELHEIM (3 M.), branch-railway in 14 minutes. **The** terminus lies on **the** right bank of the Danube, which is **crossed by a fine** new bridge. On **the** left bank are the government-offices, **in an old Schloss of** the Dukes **of Bavaria;** in the garden **are** the remains **of a** Roman watch-tower.

Kelheim (1150 ft.; °*Ehrenthaller*, **at the** Donauthor; *Richl's Inn, Haberl, Lang,* restaurants with gardens and **view; carr.** with one horse to the Befreiungshalle and back to the station, 1½ hr., 3 ℳ) is a busy little town (3400 inhab.) with partly preserved walls and gates, at the influx of the *Altmühl*, and through it of the *Ludwigs-Canal* (p. 75) into the Danube. The market is adorned with statues of Lewis I. and Maximilian II. by *Halbig.* The late-Gothic *Church* (1468), lately restored and adorned with polychrome painting, contains altars of white Kelheim limestone. The fine group (Coronation of the Virgin) on the high-altar is by Obermeyer; **on** the altar to the left is a Pietà by Veit Stoss, on that to the right a St. Anna by Knabl. The choir-frescoes are from drawings by Prof. Klein of Vienna.

The *Befreiungshalle ('Hall of Liberation'; 1480 ft.), on the *Michaelsberg*, to the W. of the town, a magnificent classical edifice, designed by Gärtner and Klenze, was founded by Lewis I. in 1842, and inaugurated on 18th Oct., 1863, the 50th anniversary of the Battle of Leipsic. A rotunda, 191 ft. in height, is borne by a substruction 23 ft. high, and is reached by a flight of 84 steps. On the exterior are 18 colossal female figures, emblematical of different German provinces; in front of, and below these, 18 candelabra; on the coping above the external arcade, 18 trophies. The interior, which is entirely lined with coloured marble, contains *34 Victories in Carrara marble by Schwanthaler; between these are 17 bronze shields made of the metal of captured French guns, bearing names of victories. Above the arcades are the names of 16 German generals on white marble tablets; higher up, the names of 18 captured fortresses. Below these is a gallery borne by 72 granite columns, 20 ft. in height, with bases and capitals of white marble. The richly-fretted dome, 70 ft. in height and 105 ft. in width, is lighted by a cupola 19 ft. in diameter. Opposite the portal is a staircase (opened by the custodian; fee) ascending to the inner gallery, which affords a good survey of the interior (fine echo). A narrow staircase leads thence to the outer gallery, where a view of the valleys of the Danube and Altmühl is enjoyed. — Admission daily 8-10 and 2-6 o'clock (in winter 10-12 and 2-4). The custodian lives in a house a short distance to the left.

Pleasant excursion from Kelheim up the Altmühl-Thal to (10 ^{1}/$_2$ M.) *Riedenburg* (carr., in 1 ^{3}/$_4$ hr., 6 *M*, with two horses 9 *M*). The road follows the left bank of the Altmühl, skirting a bare slope, with *Neu-Kelheim* and the extensive Kelheim Quarries, and passes *Gronsdorf* and (2 ^{1}/$_2$ M.) *Oberau*. To the right, halfway up the hill, is the *Schullerloch*, a large cavern affording a fine view of the valleys of the Altmühl and the Danube (Restaurant). [Pedestrians should follow the road to the Befreiungshalle on the right bank of the Altmühl, as far as the first kilomètre-stone, and take the path to the right, skirting the wood, to the *Schottenhof*, above which, at the *Hesselberger* in the *Au*, is a ferry to the Schullerloch. Or they may follow the right bank to *Schellneck*, Alt-Essing and Neu-Essing.] 4 ^{1}/$_2$ M. *Neu-Essing* (Graf's Brewery), commanded by the ruin of *Randeck*. 7 ^{1}/$_2$ M. *Nusshausen* (Brewery); to the right, on a precipitous and isolated rock, the château of *Prunn*. To the left diverges a footpath to the *Klamm*, a mass of rock towering amid the woods on the hillside to the right, and affording a good survey of the Altmühl-Thal (direct and shady footpath hence to Riedenburg). — 10 ^{1}/$_2$ M. Riedenburg *(Post; Riemhofer)* possesses three castles *(Rosenburg, Rabenstein,* and *Tachenstein)*, situated on rocky spurs, which appear to close up the valley. To the left opens the pretty *Schambach-Thal*.

The Valley of the **Danube** between Kelheim and (3 M.) *Weltenburg* is very picturesque. The barren and rugged rocks, the gorges and summits of which are wooded, rise abruptly from the river to a height of 300-400 ft. Each of the more conspicuous rocks is named from some fanciful resemblance or from some legend, such as the *Three Brothers*, *Maiden*, *Peter and Paul*, *Pulpit*, *Napoleon*, etc. The Benedictine Abbey of Weltenburg, founded by Duke Thassilo of Bavaria in 775 and rebuilt in the 18th cent., lies at the foot of a strongly-fortified Roman station. The present church is a neat rococo structure. The best plan is to take the train to stat. *Thaldorf*, walk thence to the (3 M.) village and (^{1}/$_2$ M.) abbey of Weltenburg (*Restaurant), or direct to the latter (3 M.); then descend the river in a small boat (1-6 pers. to Traunthal 2, to Kelheim 3 *M*) to the monastery ('*Klösterl*') of *Traunthal*, romantically situated on the left bank (pleasant garden-restaurant), whence a walk of 20 min. through wood brings us to the Befreiungshalle. A good forest-path (red marks) leads in 1 hr. from the Befreiungshalle to the bank of the Danube opposite Weltenburg (ferry). Three so-called 'Roman Walls', probably of pre-Roman origin, cross the ridge between the valleys of the Danube and the Altmühl; one of them is upwards of 2 M. long.

The line quits the Danube and runs to the S.W. through a wooded and hilly district to the valley of the *Hopfenbach*. 20 M.

Thaldorf. Then through the N. part of the *Holledau*, a hop-growing district. — 25 M. Abensberg (1213 ft.; *Kuchelbauer*), a small town on the *Abensfluss*, with an old castle (now containing the local court of justice) and an interesting Carmelite church in the Gothic style, was the birthplace of the Bavarian historian Johann Thurmayer, surnamed Aventinus, to whom a monument has been erected in front of the Schloss. Napoleon defeated Archduke Charles here in 1809. To the S. are the pilgrimage-church of *Allersdorf* and the Romanesque abbey-church of *Biburg* (1125-50).

From Abensberg a road leads to the N.W. to (4½ M.) *Eining*, on the Danube, near which are the interesting remains of the Roman frontier-station of Abusina, the chief Roman military post in Bavaria. [Eining is 6 M. from Neustadt (see below), from which it may be reached by a foot-path viâ *Gögging*, a village with a strong sulphur-spring and an old Romanesque church-portal.] The Romans recognised the importance of this spot as the junction of the military roads connecting the Danube territories with the Rhine and with Gaul, and as soon as they had conquered the district (B. C. 15) they established a station here, which they maintained, with three interruptions, down to the end of their sway (5th cent.). The remains, excavated since 1879, include a great part of the S. castrum, a bath, with a hypocaust in still usable condition under the floor, and the bath-keeper's house. A guide may be obtained at the parsonage, where some of the objects found here are preserved; but most of them are in the collection of the Historical Society at Landshut.

From Eining (Inn; better, Stipberger's Brewery, in *Hienheim*, opposite) we may ascend the Danube by boat to (5 M.) Weltenburg (1-6 pers. 5 *M*, each addit. pers. 60 pf.) and Kelheim. *Haderfleck* ('Locus Hadriani'), on the left bank, marks the end of the *Limes Romanus* (*Teufelsmauer*, *Pfahlrain*), a frontier-rampart with towers, constructed about 100 A.D. to protect the Roman Empire against the incursions of the Germans, and extending from the Danube, past Weissenburg am Sand (p. 131), to Wiesbaden, on the Rhine (comp. p. 27). — Pleasant walk from Hienheim across the Teufelsmauer, through the *Hienheimer Forest*, with its huge oaks, and past *Schloss* to the *Klamm* and (3½ hrs.) *Riedenburg* or (3 hrs.) *Neu-Essing* in the Altmühl-Thal (p. 126).

About 8½ M. to the S.E. of Abensberg (diligence daily in 1¾ hr.) lies Rohr *(Inn)*, with an interesting abbey-church in an elaborate baroque style.

Beyond (28½ M.) *Neustadt an der Donau* (1165 ft.) the country becomes flatter. The train skirts the extensive forest of *Dürnbuch*. 33½ M. *Münchsmünster*, on the *Ilm*, formerly a Benedictine abbey. 37½ M. *Vohburg* (village on the Danube, 3 M. to the N.E.); 41 M. Manching. — 46 M. Ingolstadt (p. 132).

From Ingolstadt to Augsburg, 41 M., railway in 2 hrs. The scenery is monotonous, the line running at first along the E. margin of the *Donaumoos* (see below). 3½ M. *Zuchering*; 15½ M. *Schrobenhausen*, a town on the *Paar*, with a late-Gothic brick church of the 15th cent.; 22 M. *Radersdorf*. Near (25½ M.) *Aichach*, to the N.E., is the ruined castle of *Wittelsbach*, the ancestral seat of the reigning house of Bavaria, destroyed in 1209, with an obelisk erected in 1832. 32 M. *Dasing;* 37 M. *Friedberg*, an ancient little town on the *Ach*, with a modern church, decorated with frescoes by F. Wagner; 38½ M. *Hochzoll* (p. 133). The train then crosses the *Lech* and reaches *Augsburg* (p. 113).

The railway to Donauwörth traverses the *Donaumoos*, an extensive marshy district, partly drained and rendered cultivable during the last century. 52 M. *Weichering;* 55 M. *Rohrenfeld*, with a royal stud.

58 M. **Neuburg** (1410 ft.; *Post*), a pleasant town with 7500 inhab., on the slope of a hill rising from the Danube. The older part of the large *Schloss* of the Dukes of Pfalz-Neuburg is now a barrack. The W. wing, in the Renaissance style, added by Elector **Otho Henry** in 1538, contains the district archives. Fine vaulted gateway and two rooms with rich timber **ceilings**. The *Historical Society* possesses four large pieces of tapestry of the 16th century. The *Hofkirche*, adjoining the château, contains a valuable collection of ecclesiastical vestments. Herr Grasegger has a collection of antiquities found in the duchy of Neuburg. The town-library and the old throne-room in the town-hall are also interesting.

The line now traverses a uninteresting district, running 1-3 M. from the right bank of the Danube. From (62 M.) *Unterhausen* Count Arco-Stepperg's château of **Stepperg** is seen in the distance to the right, on the wooded left bank of the river. Farther on is *Bertholdsheim*, the large Schloss of Count Dumoulin. 66 M. *Burgheim*; 71 M. *Rain*, where Tilly, at the age of 73, was mortally wounded in 1632 while defending the passage of the Lech against Gustaphus Adolphus. The line crosses the *Lech* to stat. *Genderkingen*, joins the Augsburg Railway, and crosses the Danube to —

78½ M. **Donauwörth** (p. 112).

25. From Frankfort to Munich by Ansbach and Ingolstadt.

253 M. Railway in 10-13½ hrs.; fares 31 ℳ, 21 ℳ 80 pf., 14 ℳ, express 38 ℳ, 26 ℳ 80, 18 ℳ 90 pf.

As far as *Würzburg*, see R. 14. The Ansbach line here turns to the S.; to the right the Marienberg. 83 M. *Sanderau*, on the S.E. side of the town. Near (85 M.) *Heidingsfeld*, once a fortified town, of which the church-tower alone is visible (interesting relief in the church by *T. Riemenschneider:* Mourning for Christ), we cross the *Main*. (The Heidelberg line diverges to the right, see p. 70.) — 89 M. *Winterhausen*; 91 M. *Gossmannsdorf*. — 94 M. *Ochsenfurt* (545 ft.; *Schnecke), with a Gothic church surmounted by a Romanesque tower; opposite, the late-Gothic chapel of St. Michael (1440), with a fine portal. The old fortifications, with their numerous towers, are well preserved. — At (97 M.) *Marktbreit*, with its old watch-towers, we quit the Main and approach the W. slopes of the *Steiger Wald*. 104 M. *Herrnbergtheim*; 108½ M. *Uffenheim*; 112 M. *Ermetzhofen*. — 116½ M. *Steinach* (*Goldenes Kreuz*, unpretending).

Branch Railway from Steinach viâ *Hartershofen* in 40 min. to (7 M.) **Rothenburg on the Tauber** (1550 ft.; °*Hirsch*, Schmiedgasse, R. 2, D. 2 ℳ, B. 60 pf., charming view from the windows overlooking the Taubergrund; *Bär*, R. 1 ℳ; *Lamm*; beer at *Dickhaut's*, *Hachtel's*, and *Beck's*; wine at the *Eisenhut*), a charming mediæval town (7000 inhab.), with red-tiled, gabled houses and well-preserved fortifications. As in Nuremberg the churches are Gothic, the secular buildings Renaissance. Rothenburg is already spoken of as a town in a document of 942, and from 1274 to 1803 it was a free city of the Empire. In the 14th and 15th cent. it was an energetic member of the Franconian League, in 1525 it joined the insurgent peasantry, and in 1543 embraced the Reformation. During the Thirty Years' War the town was repeatedly besieged and taken.

A visit of 4-5 hrs. suffices for a visit to the chief points of interest. From the railway-station we walk to (5 min.) the Röder-*Thor*, the E. entrance of the town, and thence to (5 min.) the MARKET. In front of us is the broad Herrengasse; to the left diverges the Obere Schmiedgasse, containing the so-called *Haus des Baumeisters* (No. 343), of 1596, with its handsome façade adorned with Caryatides and its interesting court. At the beginning of the Herrengasse (see below), to the left, is the *Fountain of St. George*, erected in 1606, beyond which is the *Gewerbehalle*, with a small collection of antiquities (ring). To the right rises the handsome *Rathhaus, the older part of which is in the Gothic style, with a tower 230 ft. high, while the later is a beautiful Renaissance structure of 1578, with a projecting rustica portico and balcony (of 1681), an oriel, and an elaborate spiral staircase. The staircase in the interior of the older building ascends to a vestibule with a fine timber-roof supported by Ionic columns. Beyond this is the spacious Court Room (now 'Kaisersaal'), in which an annual festival commemorates the capture of the town by Tilly in 1631. (A picture by Schuch in the Council Room, on the upper floor of the new Rathhaus, refers to the same event.) In the cellars are torture-chambers and dungeons, where, among others, the burgomaster Toppler, accused of treason, perished in 1408. The court contains an antique Renaissance portal. The tower (193 steps) commands a splendid view of the town and the Tauber-Thal.

The neighbouring church of **St. James (Jakobskirche)*, with its two towers and a choir at each end, built in 1373-1471, is remarkable for its fine proportions and the purity of its style (restored in 1851). It contains three fine carved wooden altars: the *Altar of the Holy Blood, dating from 1478 (an early work of *T. Riemenschneider*); the Virgin's Altar, of 1495; and the *High Altar of 'the twelve messengers', with wings painted by *Fritz Herlen* (1466). The beautiful stained-glass windows of the choir date from the end of the 14th cent. and were restored in 1856. The sacristan lives opposite the E. choir (fee 50 pf.). The *Toppler Chapel*, to the S. of the church, contains the tomb of the above-mentioned burgomaster. Adjoining the W. choir is a handsome Renaissance house with an oriel, now the parsonage. In the street passing below the W. choir is the entrance to the *Chapel of the Holy Blood*, with old sculptures and paintings by Herlen, Wohlgemut, and others. The *Gymnasium*, in the Kirchplatz, was built in 1589-91.

From the passage under the W. choir of the Jakobskirche we proceed straight towards the N. to the *Klingen-Thor* and the small Gothic Church of *St. Wolfgang*, of 1473-83, the N. side of which forms part of the town-wall. — A pleasant promenade outside the wall leads to the left to (6-8 min.) the gate of the grounds laid out on a hill once occupied by a *Castle* of the Hohenstaufen (fine view of the town and of the deep Tauber-Thal). Below it is the *Topplerschlösschen*, which once belonged to the unfortunate Burgomaster Toppler (see above). We now return through the Burgthor to the Herren-Strasse, which leads to the market (see above), and contains the early-Gothic *Franciscan Church* (keys kept by the sacristan) and several houses of patricians of Rothenburg, including the *Staudt'sche Haus* (No. 16, on the left), with a curious old court. The house No. 48 also has a fine court.

The Schmiedgasse (see above) and its prolongation the Spitalgasse lead past the Leper Hospital (now a pawnbroker's), the Gothic *Church of St. John* (R. C.), with the *Johanniterhof* (now district offices), and the *Spital* (1570-76), with its quaint court, to the *Spitalthor*, a fortified gateway with a circular bastion (1542). — The following walk (ca. 1 hr.) affords charming views of the town. Turning to the right outside the gate, and after 200 paces following the narrow path which leads straight from the tower by the edge of the fields, we reach the *Essigkrug*, a hill commanding a good view of the town from the S. side. We then descend into the Tauber-Thal, where we reach in succession the *Wildbad* (Hotel; garden-restaurant), with a cold sulphur-spring, the late-Gothic *Cobolzeller Kirche* (R. C.; shut), and the old bridge over the Tauber (1330), with its double row of arches (beyond the bridge two forest-inns). We continue to follow the **Tauber-Thal** to the *Topplerschlösschen* (see above) and the old village of *Dettwang* (Inn, wine), with a very fine carved °Altar, and return to the Klingenthor by a bridge across the Tauber.

DILIGENCE daily in 2½ hrs. from **Rothenburg** to (11 M.) *Creglingen* ('Lamm). The adjacent *Hergottskapelle* (¼ hr.) contains a celebrated carved °Altar (uncoloured) by Tilman Riemenschneider. (The *old* road to Creglingen commands, near *Schwarzenbronn*, a charming survey of Rothenburg.) From Creglingen diligence thrice daily in 2½ hrs. to (11 M.) *Weikersheim* (p. 26). — A diligence also runs from Rothenburg daily in 3 hrs. to (13 M.) *Roth am See* (p. 26), and in 3 hrs. via *Schillingsfürst* (Bremer) to (12½ M.) *Dombühl* (p. 26). — Carriage from Rothenburg to (10 M.) *Schrozberg* (p. 26) in 2 hrs.

118¼ M. *Burgbernheim*; 1½ M. to the S.W. lies *Wildbad* (an unpretending little watering-place). At (124 M.) *Oberdachstetten* we enter the valley of the *Franconian Rezat*. The *Petersberg* (1660 ft.), visible to the left, may be ascended hence in 1-1¼ hr. (view). — 128 M. *Rosenbach*; 131 M. *Lehrberg*.

136 M. Ansbach (1325 ft.; *Stern*, with restaurant and garden; *Zirkel*, unpretending; *Joh. Wedel*; *Krone*; *Benkher's*, *S. Wedel's*, and *König's Wine Rooms*), with 14,267 inhab. (2000 Rom. Cath.), on the *Rezat*, is the capital of Central Franconia. It is surrounded by park-like woods. The *Schloss*, built in the Italian Renaissance style in 1713-32 and once the seat of the Margraves of Brandenburg-Ansbach, is a veritable treasure-house of baroque and rococo art, both of which are seen at their best in the elegant equipment of the 22 state apartments. The picture-gallery is also interesting, especially that section of it which illustrates the history of the Hohenzollerns. In front of the Schloss stands Halbig's bronze statue of the poet *Aug. von Platen* (d. 1835). The house in which he was born, in the Platen-Strasse, is indicated by a tablet with an inscription, above which is an old coat-of-arms (1696), an eagle gazing at the sun, with the motto, '*Phoebo auspice surgit*'. The *Hofgarten* near the Palace, a well-kept park with a double avenue of lime-trees, contains a pavilion with modern frescoes, an orangery (Restaurant, plain), a monument to the poet *Uz* (d. 1796), and another marking the spot where *Caspar Hauser* was assassinated, with the inscription: '*Hic occultus occulto occisus 14. Dec. 1833*'. Caspar Hauser's tombstone in the churchyard is inscribed, '*Hic jacet Casparus Hauser aenigma sui temporis, ignota nativitas, occulta mors 1833.*' It is believed that this ill-fated youth was a victim, throughout his life and in his death, to the unscrupulous ambition of some noble family to whose dignities he was the lawful heir.

The finest church is the Protestant °*Gumbertuskirche*, with three Gothic W. towers (1483-93 and 1597) and a late-Gothic choir (1523).

The choir, known as the '*Schwanritterkapelle*', contains stone monuments of knights of the Order of the Swan, transferred in 1825 from a now partly walled-up chapel of St. George, which the Elector Albert Achilles meant to make the central point of the order in S. Germany. The chief of these is the *High Altar*, erected by Albert Achilles in 1485 and restored at the instance of Emp. Frederick III., with carvings and paintings of the school of Wohlgemut. On the walls are scutcheons of Knights of the Swan and the old banners used at the funerals of the Margraves. The stained glass dates from the 15-16th centuries.

On the N. side of the church is the *Hofkanzlei*, now law-courts, a handsome gabled edifice of 1563. — In the Obere Markt is the Protestant *St. Johanniskirche*, a Gothic structure of the 15th cent., with two towers of unequal height. Below the choir is the burial-vault of the Margraves, originally constructed in 1660. — Between the two churches is the old *Landhaus* (now a druggist's), a Renaissance edifice of 1531. Adjacent is a fountain with a statue of Margrave George the Pious (d. 1543), who introduced the Reformation into Franconia. — The collections of the *Historical Society* (in a wing of the château), the new *Municipal Museum*, and the china and glass collections of *Herr Hirsch* (on the Promenade) are all interesting. Near the station are the *Slaughter House* and a large factory of preserved food for the army. — Favourite resorts are *Drechsel's Garten* (reached in 20 min. from the Schloss by crossing the Schlossbrücke and ascending the Schlossgasse), with a fine view of the town and environs (café-restaurant), and the *Tivoli Restaurant*, with a garden. Near the Rezat is a large *Bathing Establishment*.

From **Ansbach** to *Heilsbronn* and *Nuremberg*, see p. 26; to *Craitsheim* and *Stuttgart*, see p. 26; to *Rothenburg* (viâ *Steinach*), see p. 128.

142 M. *Winterschneidbach*. — 146 M. **Triesdorf**, a former château of the Margraves, with a fine park. About 3 M. to the N.E. is *Eschenbach*, birthplace of the poet Wolfram von Eschenbach (d. 1228), with a monument to him. — 149½ M. *Altenmuhr*, on the *Altmühl*. — 152½ M. **Gunzenhausen**, junction for Augsburg and Nuremberg (R. 22). The line crosses the Altmühl and follows its valley to Eichstätt. — 158 M. *Windsfeld*; 162½ M. *Berolzheim*; 165 M. *Wettelsheim*. — 167½ M. **Treuchtlingen**, junction of the line from Munich to Nuremberg, which runs hence viâ *Grönhard*, *Weissenburg am Sand*, and *Ellingen* to *Pleinfeld*, and there joins the Augsburg and Nuremberg line (p. 111).

The Altmühl is crossed twice. — 171 M. **Pappenheim** (1330 ft.; *Eisenbahn-Hôtel*; *Deutsches Haus*; *Krone*), charmingly situated, is commanded by the extensive ruins of a castle of the ancient counts of that name. The massive Roman Tower, 100 ft. in height, commands a beautiful view. The town contains two châteaux of Count Pappenheim, one of them a fine modern building by Klenze (1820).

Beyond a tunnel the line crosses and recrosses the Altmühl. To the S. of (175 M.) *Solnhofen* are extensive slate-quarries, once worked by the Romans, where upwards of 3000 workmen are employed. The slate, used for lithographing purposes, table-slabs, etc., is largely exported. Numerous fossils.

A long tunnel. Then (179 M.) *Dollnstein*, a small and old town, still surrounded by walls. Below it, on the left bank of the Altmühl, rises the conspicuous, serrated *Burgstein*. Farther on is the pretty

9*

village of *Ober-Eichstätt*. The line quits the valley of the Altmühl and reaches the (185½ M.) station of *Eichstätt*, situated in a cutting, whence a narrow-gauge branch-line runs in 25 min. to (4 M.) —

Eichstätt (1270 ft.; *Schwarzer **Adler**; Schwarzer Bär*), an old town with 7475 inhab., seat of an ancient episcopal see founded in 740 by St. Willibald, a companion of St. Boniface. In the Residenz-Platz are a '*Mariensäule*' of 1777, 60 ft. high, with a gilded figure of the Virgin, and the handsome *Law Courts*, formerly the residence of the archbishops. The *Cathedral*, begun in 1042, with Romanesque towers and the choir of St. Willibald in the transition-style, Gothic nave and E. choir of 1365-96, has recently been tastefully painted. It contains the monument of St. Willibald with his statue, and tombstones of bishops. Good relief (1396) on the N. Portal (Death of Mary), and fine stained glass in the choir. Beautiful cloisters with Romanesque columns. The fountain in the market-place is adorned with an admirable bronze statue of St. Willibald (1695). The *Walpurgiskirche*, containing the tomb of St. Walpurgis, from which a 'miraculous oil' exudes, is visited by numerous pilgrims on 1st May (St. Walpurgis' Day). The barrel-vaulting of the *Jesuits' Church* (1640) is fine. — Above the town rises the dilapidated *Willibaldsburg*, the residence of the bishops down to 1730; the tower commands a striking view, best in the evening (apply to the castellan). The well is 295 ft. deep. On the *Blumenberg*, to the N.W., numerous rare fossils (pterodactyl, archæopterix) have been found.

The line traverses a hilly and wooded tract by means of deep cuttings. 188½ M. *Adelschlag*; 1½ hr. thence is *Pfünz*, above the Altmühl, with extensive remains of the Roman fort of Vetonianis, recently excavated. 193 M. *Tauberfeld*; 198 M. *Gaimersheim*.

200 M. *Local Station* of Ingolstadt (**Wittelsbacher Hof*, R. 1¼-2 ℳ, B. 70 pf.; *Adler*; *Bär. moderate), with 17,600 inhab., a strongly fortified town on the Danube, once the seat of a famous university, founded in 1472 by Duke Lewis the Rich, and transferred to Landshut in 1800 and to Munich in 1826 (p. 151). At the end of the 16th cent. it was attended by 4000 students. The *Jesuits' College*, founded in 1555, was the first established in Germany. The town was besieged by Gustavus Adolphus in 1632, while his antagonist Tilly lay mortally wounded within its walls (see p. 128). The French General Moreau took the place in 1800 after a siege of three months, and dismantled the fortifications, but they have been reconstructed since 1827. On the right bank of the Danube are strong têtes-de-pont with round towers of solid masonry and the Redoubt Tilly. — The Gothic *Frauenkirche* of 1439, with two massive towers in front, contains the tomb of Dr. Eck (d. 1543), the opponent of Luther, and monuments to Tilly, who was buried at Alt-Oetting (p. 233), and the Bavarian General Mercy, who fell at Allersheim in 1645.

The line skirts the glacis, crosses the Danube (to the right is the tête-de-pont), and reaches the (202 1/2 M.) *Central Station of Ingolstadt* (*Dintler's Inn, plain), 2 M. from the town, with which it is connected by tramway (20 pf.).

Railway to *Donauwörth, Augsburg,* and *Ratisbon*, see R. 24.

Stations *Oberstimm, Reichertshofen, Wolnzach*, and (221 M.) *Pfaffenhofen* (a busy place with 3000 inhab., on the *Ilm*). The line follows the Ilm as far as (225 M.) *Reichertshausen*, beyond which it reaches the *Glon*, an affluent of the Amper. 230 M. *Petershausen*; 235 1/2 M. *Röhrmoos*. Then down the *Amper-Thal*, crossing the river, to (241 1/2 M.) *Dachau* (1328 ft.; *Zieglerbräu*), a small town with 4000 inhab., commanding a splendid view of the plain and the Alps. The railway intersects the extensive *Dachauer Moos*, crosses the *Würm* at (246 M.) *Allach*, skirts the extensive Park of *Nymphenburg*, and reaches —

253 M. Munich (p. 137).

26. From Stuttgart to Munich.

149 M. RAILWAY in 5-9 hrs. (fares 19 ℳ 30, 13 ℳ 30, 8 ℳ 60 pf.; express 22 ℳ 10, 15 ℳ 70, 8 ℳ 30 pf.).

From Stuttgart to (58 1/2 M.) *Ulm*, see R. 8. The line here crosses the Danube, and enters the Bavarian dominions, to which *Neu-Ulm* belongs. 64 1/2 *Burlafingen*. Near (67 M.) **Nersingen** the town and abbey of *Elchingen* are seen on the opposite bank, the heights of which were occupied by the Austrians under Laudon, 14th Oct., 1805, but were stormed by the French under Ney. From this victory the marshal derived his title of Duc d'Elchingen (comp. p. 28). 69 1/2 M. *Leipheim*.

74 M. Günzburg *(Bär)*, the Rom. *Guntia*, a town with numerous towers, lies picturesquely on a hill, at the confluence of the *Günz* and Danube. Pop. 4100. The Schloss was erected by Margrave Charles, son of Archduke Ferdinand of Tyrol and Philippina Welser (p. 114). We next notice a range of wooded hills to the right, crowned by the castles of *Reisenburg* and *Landestrost* (the latter almost entirely removed). 79 M. *Neu-Offingen* is the junction for Donauwörth (p. 113) and Ratisbon (p. 128).

The train quits the Danube. Near *Offingen* it crosses the *Mindel*. 83 M. *Burgau*, with 2200 inhab. and an old château. 85 M. *Jettingen*; 89 M. *Gabelbach*. The country becomes flatter. On a hill to the left is the small château of **Zusameck**. Stations *Dinkelscherben* (where we cross the *Zusam*), *Mödishofen* (beyond it across the *Schmutter*), *Gessertshausen, Diedorf, Westheim*. 109 M. *Oberhausen* is the junction of the Nuremberg line (p. 113). The train then crosses the *Wertach* and reaches (110 1/2 M.) Augsburg (p. 113).

Beyond Augsburg (to the right, the Protestant Cemetery) the line crosses the *Lech* and traverses a sterile plain. 113 1/2 M. *Hochzoll*, junction for Ingolstadt (p. 127). To the left lies the small town of **Friedberg** (p. 127). The Lech is now quitted. Stations *Mering, Alt-*

Hegnenberg (with château), *Haspelmoor, Nannhofen, Maisach, Olching* (where the *Amper*, the discharge of the Ammersee, is crossed), *Lochhausen*. The *Dachauer Moos* is then traversed. At (144½ M.) *Pasing* the train crosses the **Würm**, by which the Lake of Starnberg is drained. Near Munich the park and palace of *Nymphenburg* (p. 194) are seen on the left; then the *Marsfeld*, or military drilling-ground.

149 M. **Munich**, see R. 28.

27. From Leipsic to Munich viâ Hof and Ratisbon.

296 M. Railway in 9¾-16½ hrs. (express fares 44 ℳ 20, 31 ℳ 70 pf., 24 ℳ). This route is quicker than that by Eger (comp. Baedeker's *Northern Germany*).

From Leipsic to (103 M.) **Hof**, see R. 16. Beyond Hof the line traverses a hilly district, running near the winding Saale. 108 M. *Oberkotzau*, junction for Eger (p. 73) to the left, and Nuremberg (p. 73) to the right. 110½ M. *Martinlamitz*; 115 M. *Kirchenlamitz* (1834 ft.; 1¼ hr. to the W. rises the *Epprechtstein*, p. 91). 118 M. *Marktleuthen*, where the train crosses the *Eger*. 122½ M. *Röslau* (1916 ft.; diligence twice daily in 1¼ hr. to *Weissenstadt*, p. 91). At (125 M.) *Holenbrunn* (1846 ft.) a branch-line diverges to (2½ M.) *Wunsiedel* (p. 91). At *Untertholau* we cross the valley of the *Röslau* by a viaduct 115 ft. high. — 130 M. *Markt-Redwitz* (Rail. Restaurant), a busy little town on the *Kössein*, junction of the Nuremberg-Eger line (p. 111). 136 M. *Groschlattengrün*.

139 M. **Wiesau** (1736 ft.; *Rail. Restaurant*), with a chalybeate spring *(König Otto-Bad)*, junction for Eger (p. 73). — 146 M. *Reuth*. Then through the valley of the *Fichtelnab* to (150½ M.) *Windisch-Eschenbach* and (156½ M.) *Neustadt an der Waldnab* (branch-line to *Waldthurn* and *Vohenstrauss*).

160 M. **Weiden** (1300 ft.; **Post*), a pleasant little town (5820 inhab.), junction for *Bayreuth* (p. 89) and *Neukirchen* (p. 235). — 163 M. *Rothenstadt*. At (165 M.) *Luhe* (1270 ft.) the *Heidenab* and *Waldnab* unite to form the **Nab**. 171 M. *Wernberg* (to the left the village, with an old castle); 175 M. *Pfreimd*; 178½ M. *Nabburg*; 185 M. *Irrenlohe* (junction for Nuremberg, see p. 235). The train now crosses the Nab to (188 M.) **Schwandorf** (1204 ft.; *Bär; Kloster; Pfälzerhof*), a prettily situated little town (4840 inhab.), the junction for Furth and Prague (R. **41**).

192 M. *Klardorf*. From (197 M.) *Haidhof* a branch-line runs to the rail-factory of *Maximilianshütte*, 1¼ M. to the W.; 2½ M. to the W. is *Burglengenfeld*, with a picturesque ruined castle. — To the right beyond (198½ M.) *Ponholz* rises *Schloss Birkensee*. Near (204 M.) *Regenstauf* the *Regen* is crossed. 209 M. *Wutzlhofen*. On the right Ratisbon with its cathedral, and on the left the Walhalla come in sight. Beyond (211 M.) *Walhallastrasse* (p. 124) the train crosses the *Danube* by an iron bridge, **700 yds. long**.

213 M. **Ratisbon**, see p. 119.

The Munich line traverses an uninteresting district. Stations *Obertraubling* (to Passau, see R. 42), *Köfering*, *Hagelstadt*, and *Eggmühl*, where the French under Davoust (Prince d'Eckmühl) defeated the Austrians, 22nd April, 1809. The *Grosse Laber* is now crossed. Stations *Steinrain*, (238 M.) *Neufahrn*, on the *Kleine Laber* (branch by *Geiselhöring* to *Straubing*, see p. 236), *Ergoldsbach*, and *Mirskofen*.

252 M. **Landshut** (1290 ft.; *Kronprinz*, R., L., & A. 1¼-2 ℳ, B. 70 pf., D. 2 ℳ; *Dräxlmeier*, R. 1-1½, B. 30-50 pf.; *Bernlochner*; *Drei Mohren*; *Rail. Restaurant*; omn. from the station to the town, 1½ M., 20 pf.), with 18,870 inhab., a pleasant town with wide streets and gabled houses, lies picturesquely on the *Isar*, which forms an island within the town. The quarter on this island is called *Zwischen den Brücken*. The chief attractions are in the broad main street, named the 'Altstadt'. The three principal churches, *St. Martin's* (about 1392-1495), *St. Jodocus* (1338-68), and the *Holy Ghost* or *Hospital Church* (1407-61) are fine structures in brick, adorned with sculpturing in stone. The lofty tower of St. Martin's is 462 ft. in height. Among the numerous tombstones on the outer walls of this church is (on the S. side, protected by a railing) that of *Stetthammer* (Hans der Steinmetz, d. 1432), the builder of this church and the Hospital Church, with his bust and a half-length figure of the Saviour. The late-Gothic pulpit, of limestone, dates from 1422. Beautiful late-Gothic high-altar (1424), the back of which is also interesting. The lofty choir-windows contain modern stained glass. — The *Post Office* (formerly *House of the Estates*) is decorated with old frescoes of the sovereigns of Bavaria from Otho I. to Maximilian I. — The *New Palace* (1536-43), begun by German, and completed by Italian architects, exhibits features both of the German and Italian Renaissance. Its columned court and fine upper rooms, with beautiful friezes, are among the best Renaissance works in Germany. (Custodian in the portal, to the right.) Some of the rooms contain an instructive collection of industrial models, established by Dr. Gehring (Sun., 10-1; at other times a fee). — The *Rathhaus*, originally erected in 1446, has been entirely restored. New façade, 1860-61. The late-Gothic *Council Chamber (apply at the Registry Office on the first floor), with its fine timber ceiling and chimney-pieces, is adorned with a huge mural painting in tempera, by Seitz, Spiess, and other artists, of the marriage of George the Rich. In front of the Rathhaus stands a bronze *Statue of Maximilian II.*, by Bernhard (1868). The university of Ingolstadt was transferred to Landshut in 1800, and thence to Munich in 1826. A statue of the founder, *Duke Lewis the Rich* (d. 1479), has been erected in front of the government-buildings. — In the suburb of the *St. Nicola*, to the N.W., is a War Monument for 1870-71.

*Burg Landshut or Trausnitz (1530 ft.), an old castle rising above the town, formerly the residence of the Dukes of Lower Bavaria, begun by Duke Ludwig of Kelheim in 1204, was frequently altered, and has suffered greatly from the ravages of time. The pleasantest approach to it is through the *Hofgarten* with its pretty promenades. The *Chapel* (1304-31), which lately underwent thorough renovation, is the only part remaining of the original structure. The balustrades, decorated with stone figures, the large relief of the Annunciation, the mural paintings of the altar-recess, and the ciborium (1471) are worthy of notice. Some of the apartments are finely painted in the Renaissance style (1576-80), and others contain handsome wooden ceilings and panelling. The mural paintings on the '*Fools' Staircase*', representing **scenes from Italian comedies**, deserve inspection. The upper **floor has been** sumptuously fitted up for the reception of the King of Ba**varia (adm. on** application to the Archivist, Dr. Jörg, in the castle). In **the court is a** well, surmounted by a fine wrought-iron framework; the pails in bronze (executed, according to the inscription, in 1558) are now kept inside the castle. Conradin, the last of the Hohenstaufen, was born at the neighbouring castle of *Wolfstein* (now a ruin) in 1252 and spent a **great part of his** childhood at the Trausnitz. The best descent is afforded **by the flight** of steps leading to the Heiglkeller (upper town). — Beyond **the Trausnitz** lies the village of *Berg*, separated from (1¼ M.) Landshut by **the Hofgarten.** — From the garden-restaurant on the (1¼ M.) *Klausenberg*, **a fine view is obtained of** the town, **the** castle, and the valley.

From Landshut to Landau, 28 M., railway in 2 hrs., the shortest route from Munich to Eisenstein, Pilsen, and Prague. The train follows the left bank of the *Isar*. Stations *Altheim*, *Ahrein*, *Wörth*, *Loiching*, (18 M.) *Dingolfing*, an old town on the right bank of the Isar. Then across a tract of moorland to *Gottfrieding*, *Schwaigen*, *Pilsting*, and *Landau* (p. 244).

A railway also runs from Landshut, viâ (8 M.) *Geisenhausen*, (14 M.) *Vilsbiburg*, and (20½ M.) *Egglkofen*, to (24½ M.) *Neumarkt an der Rott* (p. 244).

The railway ascends the valley of the *Isar*. 257½ M. *Gündlkofen*; to the left, *Schloss* **Kronwinkel**. 259 M. *Bruckberg*, with a small château to the **right of the line**; then on the right *Schloss Isareck*. The *Amper* is crossed. **264 M. *Moosburg*, a very ancient town on** the Isar; **the Romanesque church contains a** fine old **carved altar. In clear weather the** Alps **soon become visible.** 268 M. *Langenbach*.

274½ M. **Freising** (**Ettenhofer; Zur Eisenbahn*, unpretending; omn. into the town 20 pf.), a town with 9485 inhab., on the Isar, and partly on a hill (Domberg), has been the seat of an episcopal see (now Munich-Freising) from the 8th cent. to the present day. Otho von Freising, the historian, grandson of Emp. Henry IV., was bishop here from 1137 to 1158 (statue in the Domhof). The Romanesque *Cathedral* (1161-1205), with its two towers and double aisles, was marred by internal alterations in the 17th century. Observe the late-Romanesque portal (partly disfigured) and the curious quadruple crypt, the vaulting of which rests on short round and polygonal columns, with rich capitals. In the raised vestibule, to the left on entering, are statuettes of **Frederick Barbarossa** and his wife **Beatrix** (?), of 1161. Gothic choir-stalls. The cloisters contain some fine tombstones. The *Church of St.* **Benedict**, connected with the cathedral by cloisters, **contains a** fine **old and** two modern stained-glass windows. The *Clerical Seminary*, opposite the cathedral, **contains early German** paintings, sculptures, etc. — To the W. lies (20 min.) the loftily-situated **Weihenstephan**, formerly an abbey, **now an agricultural** college **and** brewery.

Next stations *Neufahrn*, *Lohhof*, (288 M.) *Schleissheim* (p. 194), *Feldmoching*, (293½ M.) *Schwimmschule*, and (296 M.) **Munich**.

28. Munich.

Railway Stations. 1. *Central Railway Station* (Pl. C, 4; °Restaurant), a large building erected in 1876-84, forming a terminus for most of the lines. The omnibuses of the larger hotels meet the trains here (3/4-1 ℳ). — 2. *Starnberg Station* (Pl. B, 4), to the N. of the Central Station, for the trains to Starnberg, Murnau-Partenkirchen, and Penzberg. — 3, 4. *Southern Station* (Pl. B, 9) and *Eastern Station* (Pl. I, 7, 8), supplementary stations of the Rosenheim and Simbach lines, without importance for the ordinary tourist. — 5. *Isarthal Railway Station* (Pl. B, 10, 11), for the local line to Wolfratshausen (p. 191). — Porter from the station to a cab, 20 pf. up to 110 lbs., 40 pf. up to 220 lbs.; into the town, small articles 20 pf., trunk under 110 lbs. 40 pf., under 220 lbs. 80 pf. — Cab from the station to the town with one horse, 1-2 pers. 50, 3 pers. 60 pf.; with 2 horses, 1-4 pers., 1 ℳ; from 10 p.m. to 6 a.m. double fare and 20 pf. extra for waiting. Small articles of luggage free, trunks under 55 lbs. 20 pf., above 55 lbs. 40 pf.

Hotels (often full in the season). °VIER JAHRESZEITEN (*Four Seasons*; Pl. a; F, 4, 5), Maximilian-Strasse 4, R., L., & A. 4-7 ℳ, B. 1 ℳ 20, D. at 1 p.m. 4, at 5 p.m. 4½, omn. 1 ℳ; °GRAND HÔTEL CONTINENTAL (Pl. e; D, 3, 4), Otto-Str. 6; °BAYRISCHER HOF (*Bavarian Hotel*; Pl. b, E 4), Promenade-Platz 19, R., L., & A. 5-6 ℳ, B. 1 ℳ. 30 pf., D. at 1 p.m. 3½, at 5 p.m. 4½ ℳ; °HÔTEL BELLEVUE (Pl. c; C, 4), Karls-Platz 25, R., L., & A. from 5, D. 4, B. 1 ℳ; °RHEINISCHER HOF (Pl. d; C, 4, 5), Bayer-Str., near the Central Station, R., L., & A. from 4 ℳ, B. 1 ℳ 20 pf.; °DOM-HÔTEL (*Hôt. Detzer*; Pl. e, E 5), Kaufinger-Str. 23, R., L., & A. 3½, B. 1, D. 3, pens. 5-7 ℳ, omn. 70 pf.; ENGLISCHER HOF (Pl. f; E, 5), Diener-Str. 11, R., L., & A. from 4 ℳ, B. 1 ℳ 20 pf., D. 3½ ℳ; HÔTEL LEINFELDER (Pl. g; D, 4), Karls-Platz 1, R., L., & A. 2½-3 ℳ, B. 80 pf., D. 3 ℳ; °MARIENBAD (Pl. h; D, 3), Barer-Str. 11 and 20, with a large garden and baths, R., L., & A. 3½-5, B. 1½, D. 3-4, pens. in winter 7 ℳ. — Second-class: °HÔTEL MAXIMILIAN (Pl. i; F, 5), Maximilian-Str. 44, R. & L. 3-3½, B. 1 ℳ; °MAX EMANUEL (Pl. k; E, 4), Promenade-Platz, R. & L. 2-3 ℳ, B. 80 pf.; °KAISERHOF (Pl. p; C, 4), Schützen-Str. 12, R., L., & A. 1½-3, D. 2½ ℳ, B. 80 pf.; DEUTSCHER KAISER (Pl. r; C, 4), °HÔT. NATIONAL (Simmen; Pl. a, B 4), °BAHNHOF-HÔT. STECHER, all three in the Arnulf-Str., near the Central Station (N. exit, to the left), R. from 1½ ℳ; °HÔT. DE L'EUROPE (Pl. 1; C, 4, 5), °HÔT. NEUSIGL (Pl. q; C, 5), FRÄNKISCHER HOF, all three in the Senefelder-Str., near the Central Station (S. exit, to the right); °GRAND HÔT. GRÜNWALD (Pl. w; C, 4), Dachauer-Str. 3, near the Central Station, R. from 1½ ℳ; HÔT. HÖRL (Pl. v; C, 4), moderate, Bahnhofs-Platz; HÔT. STACHUS (Pl. m; C, 5), Karls-Platz 24, R., L., & A. from 2 ℳ, B. 80 pf.; OBERPOLLINGER (Pl. n, D 5; p. 138), Neuhauser-Str. 41, commercial; BAMBERGER HOF (Pl. o, D 5; p. 141), Neuhauser-Str. 26; HÔT. ACHATZ (Pl. u, D 4; p. 141), with garden, HÔT. SCHNÖLL (formerly *Abenthum*; Pl. t, D 4), both in the Maximilians-Platz; TREFLER'S HOTEL, Sonnen-Str. 21; ÖSTERREICHISCHER HOF (Pl. d; B, 5), WITTELSBACHER HOF, POST, all in the Bayer-Str.; SCHWEIZER HOF (Pl. x; C, 4), Louisen-Str. 1½; HÔT. KRONPRINZ (Pl. z; C, 5), Zweig-Str. 10, R. 2-2½ ℳ, B. 70 pf., all near the Central Station. — Hôtels Garnis. °WOLFF (Pl. b; C, 4), Arnulf-Str. 3, at the Central Station (N. side); GASSNER (Pl. c; C, 5), Bayer-Str. 37, at the station (S. side); °HÔTEL (Pl. s; F, 5), Neuthurm-Str. 5, R. & L. 2½ ℳ; ROYAL, Karls-Platz 21. — Pensions. *Fuchs*, *Bellevue*, both at Brienner-Str. 8 (6-8 ℳ per day); *Finckh*, Brienner-Str. 46; *Waltenberg*, Brienner-Str. 47; *Glocker*, Maximilian-Str. 5; *Seiler*, Karl-Str. 10; *Frau Rath Stremel*, Jäger-Str. 15; *Fontana*, Maximilians-Platz 2; *Kreitmayr*, Maximilians-Platz 12; *Reindel-Belleville*, Fürsten-Str. 9; *Vincenti*, Kaulbach-Str. 40; *Cortin-Gehr*, Kaulbach-Str. 47; *Dümler-Haus*, Leopold-Str. 21; *Fortuna*, Kanal-Str. 46a; *Bluhm-Piquet*, Max-Joseph-Str. 1; *Hoffmann*, Luisen-Str. 38; *Bürger*, Luisen-Str. 42f; *Scheidemann*, Adalbert-Str. 48; *Frau Geret*, Blüthen-Str. 8; *Pens. North*, Schnorr-Str. 9; *Frau Dr. M. Fischer*, Wittelsbacher-Platz 2; *Quisisana*, *Washeim*, Theresien-Str. 30 and 34; *Bauer*, Theresien-Str. 100; *Neumann*, Schelling-Str. 87; *Hursach*, Schelling-Str. 62; *Quistorp*, Schelling-Str. 78; *Spangenberg*, Schelling-Str. 85 (Fürstenhaus); *Mme. Borel*, Schönfeld-Str. 11.

138 *Route 28.* MUNICH. *Cafés.*

Restaurants at the *Kaiserhof, Deutscher Kaiser*, **Grünwald**, *Oberpollinger, Bamberger* **Hof, Achatz,** *Schnöll, Trefler, Roth*, and other hotels (see p. 137); at most of the wine and beer houses (see below); at the cafés *Luitpold, Maximilian, de l'Opéra, Victoria, Heck, Gisela*, and *Gasteig* (see below). Also: *Hof-Theater*, Max-Josephs-Platz; *Eberlbräu* (handsome rooms), Karlsthor; *Isarlust* (p. 141), on the Isar island, pleasant on warm evenings; *Englisches Café*, Otto-Str. 16; *Paul*, Gärtner-Platz. The usual hour for dinner is 12-1, for supper 6-8.

Wine Saloons (also restaurants): *Schleich*, Brienner-Str. 6, D. 12-3 p.m. 2 ℳ; *Restaurant Français*, Brienner-Str. 8, D. from 3 ℳ; *Rathskeller* (p. 189); *Eberspacher*, in the Kunstgewerbehaus (p. 188), Pfandhaus-Str. 7, and Kaufinger-Str. 15; *Grodemange*, Maximilian-Str. 23; *Junemann (Eckel)*, Burg-Str. 17; *Kurtz*, Augustiner-Str. 1; *Gillitzer*, Prielmayer-Str. 18; *Elsässer Weinstube*, in the Hôt. Schnöll (see above); *Rüdesheimer Weinstube*, Karmeliter-Str.; *Dürkheimer*, Frauen-Platz (Palatinate wines); *D'Orville*, Marien-Platz 21; *Neuner*, Herzogspital-Str. 20; *Michel*, Rosen-Str. 11, Hungarian wines; *Veltliner Weinhalle*, Luitpold-Str. 5; *Stadt Patras* (Greek wines), Maximilians-Platz 14; *Continental Bodega* (Spanish wines; cold dishes), Neuhauser-Str. 12; *Italienische Weinstube*, Kapellen-Str. 5.

Beer. The *Hofbräuhaus*, in the Platzl (Pl. F, 5), famous among Bavarian beer-houses, and one of the sights of Munich, is always crowded by persons of all classes. In the vicinity (with Hofbräu beer): *Platzl*, *Regensburger Wurstküche*, *Nürnberger Wurstküche*, all in the Münz-Str.; *Orlando di Lasso*, Platzl 4; *Zur Scholastica*, Lederergasse 25; *Franziskaner*, Residenz-Str. 9; *Bürgerbräu*, Kaufinger-Str. 6; *Pschorr*, *Spatenbräu*, and *Augustiner*, in the Neuhauser-Str.; *Deutsches Haus*, Sophien-Str. 1a; *Nürnberger Bratwurstglöckl*, Frauen-Platz 9; *Lohengrin*, Türken-Str. 50; *Sternecker*, *Metzgerbräu*, in the Thal; *Hackerbräu*, *Eberlbräu*, Sendlinger-Str.; *Café Bock*, outside the Isarthor, etc., etc. — The large 'Bierkeller' outside the gates also attract numerous visitors in summer; they generally possess gardens and fair restaurants. *Hofbräukeller* (Pl. H, 6), Wiener-Str., near the Maximilianeum; *Löwenbräukeller* (Pl. B, 2; p. 141), Stiglmayer-Platz, with a terraced garden and a large concert-room, often crowded; *Franziskanerkeller* (Pl. G, H), Hoch-Str. 7, with view-terrace; *Münchner Kindlkeller* (Pl. G, 7; p. 141), Rosenheimer-Str. 15, with large concert-room; *Bürgerliches Bräuhaus* (Pl. G, H, 7; p. 141), Rosenheimer-Str. 29; *Steneckerkeller* (Pl. G, 6, 7), these on the right bank of the Isar (p. 192); *Augustinerkeller* (Pl. A, B, 3), Arnulf-Str.; *Spatenbräukeller* (Pl. A, 5), Bayer-Str. 109; *Hackerkeller* (Pl. A, 4), Bayer-Str. 34; *Bavariakeller* (Pl A, 5), Theresienhöhe. — In the cellars and breweries the beer is served only in large earthenware mugs holding a litre ('Mass'), but in the restaurants the glasses or mugs contain ½ litre only ('eine Quart' = ¼ litre). The following kinds of beer are drunk in spring only: *Salvator* (strong), at the *Zacherl-Keller*, Au suburb (p. 192), for about a week from the Sun. before 19th March; *Bock* (first introduced from Eimbeck in the 16th cent.), usually in May, and at the festival of Corpus Christi in June, at the *Hofbräuhaus*, etc.

Cafés (most, with the exception of those already mentioned among the restaurants, closed in the evening). *Luitpold*, Brienner-Str. 8, with English and other newspapers; *Maximilian, de l'Opéra, Victoria* (with garden), all in the Maximilian-Str.; *Prinz-Regent*, Prinz-Regenten-Str.; *Putscher, Lutz, Heck (Arkaden-Café)*, in the arcades of the Hof-Garten, seats outside in summer; *Gisela*, Fürsten-Str. 2; *Central*, Brienner-Str.; *Börsen-Café*, Maffei-Str.; *Wittelsbach, Danner, Probst*, and *Karlsthor*, near the Karlsthor; *Royal*, **Karls-Platz** 21; *Impérial*, Schützen-Str. 1a, outside the Karls-Thor; *Union*, Herzogspital-Str. 12; *Schelling*, Schelling-Str. 56, near the New Pinakothek; *Mikado*, Müller-Str. 3a; *Türkisch-Arabisches Café*, Rumford-Str. 2; *Neptun*, Steinsdorfer-Str. 31, near the Ludwigs-Brücke (p. 192); *Gasteig*, Innere Wiener-Str. 31, etc.

Confectioners. *Rottenhöfer*, Residenz-Str. **26**; *Brienner Bäckerei*, Odeons-Platz 1; *Eyerich*, Theatiner-Str.; **Hof, Promenaden-Platz 6**; *Bernhardt*, Theresien-Str. 25.

Key to the Plan of Munich.

Academy of Art. . F, 1
   „ of Science D, 5
Alte Hof . . . . . . E, 5
Anatomie . . . . . . C, 6
Archiepis. Palace . E, 4
Art Union . . . . . F, 3
Bank, Bav. . . . . E, 4
Bavaria . . . . A, 7
Blind Asylum . . . F, 2
Botan. Garden . . C, 3, 4
Bronze Foundry . . B, 1
Cadets, Corps of . . A, 2
Cemetery,
   Southern . C, D, 7, 8
—, new . . . . C, 8
—, Northern . . . . D, 1
Chem. Laboratory C, 3, 4

Churches.
Allerheiligen
  (Court-) Chapel F, 4
St. Anna . . . . . G, 4
Auer (Maria-
  hilf) Kirche . . **F, 8**
Basilica . . . . . . C, 3
Carmelites . . . . D, 4
Frauenkirche . . . E, 5
Heiliggeist . . . . E, 5
St. John . . . . . D, 6
Ludwigskirche . F, 2
St. Luke's (Prot.) G, 5, 6
St. Mark's (Prot.) E, 3
St. Matthew's
  (Prot.) . . . . C, 5
St. Michael's . . . **D, 5**
St. Peter's . . . . **E, 5**
Theatine Ch. . . **E, 4**
Civic Arsenal . . . **E, 6**
Clinical Inst. D, 5, C, 6
Colosseum . . . . . D, 7
Commandant's
  Residence . . . F, 3
Corn Hall . . . D, **E, 6**
Crystal Palace . . **C, 4**
Deaconess Institute D, 1
Exchange . . . . . E, 4
Exhibition Building C, 3
Feldherrnhalle . . **E, 4**
General Hospital . **C, 6**
Georgianum . . . . F, 1
Glyptothek . **C, D, 2, 3**
Government
  Buildings . . . . G, 5
Herzog Max Burg . D, 4
Hofbräuhaus . . . . **F, 5**
Hospital of St.
  Elizabeth . . . . C, 6
Hygienic **Institute** . B, 6
Industrial **Art**
  School . . . . . C, 2

Industrial Exhibition D, 4
Isarthor . . . . F, 6
Karlsthor . . . . D, 4, 5
Law Courts . . . C, D, 4
Library . . . . F, 2
Lotzbeck Collection D, 3
Lunatic Asylum . . H, 8
Mary Column . . . E, 5
Maximilianeum . . H, 5
Max-Joseph Inst. . F, 1
Military Hospital . A, 1
  „ School . . A, 2
Ministry of Finances F, 3
  „ of For-
    eign Affairs E, 4
  „ of the In-
    terior . . . E, 4
Mint . . . . . . F, 4, 5

Monuments.
Deroy, Schel-
  ling, Rumford,
  Fraunhofer . F, G, 5
Elector Maximi-
  lian I. . . . . . . E, 3
— Max Emanuel E, 3
Gabelsberger . . D, 4
Gaertner, Klenze E, 6, 7
Goethe . . . . . . D, 4
King Lewis I. . . E, 3
  „ Max I. . . . E, 4
  „ Max II. . . G, 5
Liebig . . . . . . D, 4
Nussbaum . . . . C, 6
Schiller . . . . . . E, 3
Senefelder . . . . D, 6
Westenrieder,
  Gluck, Kreit-
  mayr, Orlando E, 4
National **Museum** F, G, 5
Obelisk . . . . D, 3
Odeon . . . . E, 3

Palaces.
Duke Max . . . . **E, 3**
— Ludwig . . G, H, 6
Prince Luitpold . **E, 3**
Prince Ludwig
  Ferdinand . . . **E, 3**
Wittelsbach . . . E, 3
Panoramas . **A, 5, D, 1**
Pathological **Inst.** . **C, 6**
Pharmacological
  Inst. . . . . . . C, 6
Physiological **Inst.** C, 6
Pinakothek, **Old** . D, 2
—, New . . . . . D, 2
Police Office . . . . E, 5
Polytechnic School D, 2
Post Office . . . . E, 4, 5
Priests' **Seminary** . F, 2

Propylæa . . . . . . C, 3
Railway Station,
  Central . . . . C, 4
Rathaus, Old . . . E, 5
—, New . . . . . . E, 5
Reichsbank . . . . **F, 3**
Riding School . . . **F, 4**
Royal Palace . E, **F, 4**
— Stables . . . . **F, 4**
Schack's Picture
  Gallery . . . . C, 3
Schwanthaler
  Museum . . . . C, 5
Schüssel, Passage . **E, 5**
Siegesthor . . . . . **F, 1**
Slaughter House . . B, 8
Ständehaus . . . . . E, 4
Synagogue . . . . . D, 4
Telegraph **Office** . C, 4

Theatres.
Hof-Theater . . . **F, 4**
Residenz-Theat. . **F, 4**
Gärtner-Platz-
  Theater . . . . E, 7
Volks-Theater **C**, D, 5
Turnhalle . . . . . B, 1
University . . . . . F, 1
Veterinary School F, G, 1
War Office . . . F, 2, 3

Hotels.
a Four Seasons **F**, 4, 5
b Bavaria . . . . . E, 4
c Bellevue . . . . . C, 4
d Rheinischer Hof C, 4, 5
e Continental . D, 3, 4
f Englischer Hof . E, 5
g Leinfelder . . . . D, 4
h Marienbad . . . D, 3
i Maximilian . . . F, 5
k Max-Emanuel . E, 4
l Hôt. de l'Europe C, 4, 5
m Stachus . . . . . C, 5
n Oberpollinger . . D, 5
o Bamberger Hof D, 5
p Kaiserhof . . . . C, 4
q Neusigl . . . . . C, 5
r Deutscher Kaiser C, 4
s Roth . . . . F, 5
t Schnöll . . . . . D, 4
u Achatz . . . . . . D, 4
v Hörl . . . . C, 4
w Grünwald . . . . C, 4
x Schweizer Hof . C, 4
y Dom-Hôtel . D, E, 5
z Kronprinz . . . . C, 5
a National . . . . B, 4
b Wolff . . . . . . C, 4
c Gassner . . . . . C, 5
d Oester. Hof . . . B, 5

Baths. *Maximiliansbad* (Pl. F, 5), Kanal-Str. 19, with **swimming-bath**; *Kaiser-Wilhelm-Bad*, Lindwurm-Str. 70, with garden and **restaurant**; *Bavariabad*, Türken-Str. 68b; *Centralbad* (Pl. C, 4), Lämmer-Str. 3; *Marienbad* (see p. 137); *Giselabad*, Müller-Str. 29, 30; *Wöstermayr*, Müller-Str. 45, with swimming-baths. — Baths in the *Würm*, at Schwabing (p. 152), to the N.E. of the terminus of the tramway-line mentioned below: *Ungerer*, with garden, etc.; *Germania-Bad*. Also at *Gern*, at the terminus of the Nymphenburg steam-tramway.

Cabs. (*Droschke*, a one-horse vehicle, for 2-3 pers. only; *Fiaker*, with two horses.) One-horse: 1/4 hr., 1-2 pers. 50, 3 pers. 60 pf.; 1/2 hr. 1 ℳ or 1 ℳ 20 pf.; 3/4 hr. 1 ℳ 50 or 1 ℳ 80 pf.; 1 hr. 2 ℳ or 2 ℳ 40 pf.; 1 1/4 hr. 2 1/2 or 3 ℳ; 1 1/2 hr. 3 ℳ or 3 ℳ 60 pf.; 2 hrs. 4 ℳ or 4 ℳ 80 pf.; 3 hrs. 5 ℳ 60 or 6 ℳ 80 pf.; each additional 1/4 hr. 40 or 50 pf. — Two-horse: 1/4 hr., 1-4 pers. 1 ℳ, 5-6 pers. 1 ℳ 10 pf.; 1/2 hr. 2 ℳ or 2 ℳ 20 pf.; 3/4 hr. 2 ℳ 50 or 2 ℳ 80 pf.; 1 hr. 3 ℳ or 3 ℳ 40 pf.; 1 1/4 hr. 3 ℳ 70 or 4 ℳ 20 pf.; 1 1/2 hr. 4 ℳ 40 pf. or 5 ℳ; 2 hrs. 5 ℳ 80 or 6 ℳ 80 pf.; 3 hrs. 8 ℳ 60 or 9 ℳ 80 pf.; each 1/4 hr. additional 70 or 80 pf. — Tariff for drives to the following places, for a *Droschke* with 1-2 pers., and a *Fiaker* with 1-4 pers. respectively: the Bavaria 1 ℳ or 1 ℳ 80 pf.; Chinese Tower 70 pf. or 1 1/2 ℳ; Brunnthal 80 pf. or 1 ℳ 80; Bogenhausen 1 or 2 ℳ; Kleinhesselohe 1 ℳ or 2 ℳ 20 pf.; Nymphenburg 2 ℳ or 3 ℳ 60 pf. If the carriage is used in returning, the return-drive is paid for by time. — The fare for the first 1/4 hr. must be paid in full, however short the drive; for less than 5 min. of an additional 1/4 hr., 10 or 20 pf. only is paid. From dusk till 10 p.m., 10 pf. per 1/4 hr. is charged for the lamps. From 10 p.m. to 6 a.m. double fares, also from the stations after 9 p.m. double fares and 20 pf. extra as waiting-money. Luggage up to 55 lbs., 20 pf., above 55 lbs., 40 pf.; small articles free.

Steam Tramway from the Arnulf-Str. (N side of the Central Railway Station; Pl. B, 4), viâ *Neuhausen* and the villas of *Neu-Wittelsbach*, to *Nymphenburg* (p. 194), every **hour** in the morning, every 1/2 **hr.** in the afternoon (on Sun. every 10 min.), in 25 min. (fare 20 pf.).

Tramways (with system of correspondence-tickets; 1 or 2 sections 10 pf., each addit. section 5 pf.). The first cars start at 7 a.m., the last at 10 and 11.30 p.m. — 1. Ring Line: From the *Central Station* (Pl. C, 4) by the **Sendlingerthor-Platz** (Pl. D, 6), Isarthor-Platz (Pl. F, 6), Maximilian Monument (Pl. G, 5), Gallerie-Str. (Pl. F, 3), Ludwig-Str., Theresien-Str., and **Augusten-Str.** (Pl. C, 1-3), back to the *Central Station* (red lamps, etc.). — 2. From *Schwabing* (p. 152) by the Ludwigs-Str., Maximilians-Platz (**Pl. E, D, 4**), Bayer-Str., and Theresienhöhe, to the *Landsberger-Strasse* (Pl. A, 4, 5; green). — 3. From *Neuhausen* (to the **N.W.** of Pl. A, 1, 2) by the **Nymphenburger-Str.**, Dachauer-Str., Central Station, Bayer-Str., Promenaden-Platz (Pl. **F, 4**), and Barer-**Str.** (Old and New Pinakothek) to the *Hermann-Strasse* (to the N.E. of Pl. E, 1; white; yellow board on cars going towards the Pinakothek). — 4. From the *Hof-Theater* (Pl. F, 4) by the Maximilians-Str., Johannes-Platz (Pl. H, I, 6), the East Railway Station (Pl. I, 7, 8), Orleans-Str., and Rosenheimer-Str., to the *Ludwigs-Brücke* (Pl. G, 6, 7; white). — 5. From the *Arnulf-Strasse* (Pl. B, 4) by the **Bayer-Str.**, Karlsthor, Marien-Platz (**Pl. E, 5**), and Ludwigs-Brücke to the *Wiener-Strasse* (Pl. H, 6; **yellow**). — 6. From the *Karls-Platz* (Pl. C, 5) by the Sendlingerthor-Platz (**Pl. D, 6**) and the Lindwurm-Str. to the *Sendlingerberg* (to the S.W. of Pl. A, 8; blue). — 7. From the *Frauen-Strasse* (Pl. E, 6) by the Reichenbad-Brücke (Pl. E, 8) to the *Freibad-Strasse* (Pl. E, 10; green). — 8. From the *Bahnhof-Platz* (Pl. C, 4) by the Goethe-Str., Kapuziner-Str. (Pl. C, 8), and Wittelsbacher-Brücke to *Giesing* (Pl. E, 10). — 9. Electric tramway from the *Färbergraben* (Pl. E, 5) by the Sendlinger-Strasse, the Thalkirchner-Str. (S. cemeteries), and South Railway Station to the *Isarthal Railway Station* (Pl. B, 10, 11).

Post Office in the Max-Joseph-Platz (Pl. E, 4, 5; poste restante); also at the Central Railway Station. Branch-offices at Thekla-Str. 3, Zweibrücken-Str. 37, Theresien-Str. 31 and 43, Neuhauser-Str. 51 (Old Academy), Adalbert-Str. 9, Leopold-Str. 62 (Schwabing), etc. Offices open from 8 a.m. to 8 p.m.; on Sun. and holidays, 8-9, 11-12, & 5-7. — **Telegraph Office**

(Pl. C, 4) at Bahnhof-Platz 1; also at the General Post Office, and at the three first-mentioned branch post-offices. — **Telephone Offices** at the telegraph office, at the Central Station, and at the post-offices.

Tourist Agents. *Schenker & Co.* (agent for *H. Gaze & Son*), Promenade-Platz 5. — *Private Intelligence Office*, Kaulbachstr. 47.

Porters. For an errand of ½ M. within the city with 33 lbs. of luggage 20 pf., each addit. ½ M. 10 pf.; for a message without luggage 10 pf. per 5 minutes. The porter should give a counter-check.

Theatres. *°Hof- und National-Theater* (Pl. F, 4; p. 148), performances almost daily (closed in July). Ordinary charges for operas: dress-circle (*balkon*) 4-6 ℳ, parquet (*i.e.* reserved seats in the parterre or pit) 4-5 ℳ, parquet standing-place 3-4 ℳ, pit 1 ℳ 40 pf. - 1 ℳ 60 pf. (charges much higher at the Wagner Performances in Aug. and Sept.: dress-circle 15-25 ℳ, Erster Rang or gallery above the dress-circle 10-15, Zweiter Rang 6-10 ℳ, etc.). Charges for plays: parquet 2-3½ ℳ; dress-circle 3½-4 ℳ; pit 2 ℳ. Performances usually begin at 7 p.m. (long operas at 6 p.m.). Performances at reduced prices are given occasionally. Box-office open 9-1 and 5-5.30 o'clock; entrance in the Maximilians-Str.; booking-fee for next day 30 pf.; tickets also sold at the Kiosque in the Maximilians-Platz, adjoining the Herzog-Max-Burg (Pl. D, 4; open 8-6; fee 10 pf.). — *°Residenz-Theater* (Pl. F, 4; p. 148), where plays are performed on Sundays, Tuesdays, and Saturdays: parquet and pit-boxes 3½-4 ℳ (prices raised in Aug. & Sept.). Tickets at the box-office of the Hof-Theater and at the Kiosque (see above). Performances begin at 7 p.m. — *Gärtner-Platz Theatre* (Pl. E, 7; p. 192), for comedies, operettas, and ballet: front-row of first gallery 3½, parquet 2 ℳ. Tickets at the box-office (see above), at the Kiosque, and at Haber's music-shop, Marien-Platz 3. Performances begin at 7.30 p.m. — *Volks-Theater* (Pl. C, D, 5; p. 191), Sonnen-Str. 5 (entr. in the Josephspital-Str.), for farces, popular pieces, and operettas; reserved seat 1 ℳ. Performances at 8 p.m. — *Marionette Theatre*, Mars-Str. 13, on Sun. afternoons in winter. — **Variety** Theatres (with restaurants): *°Kil's Colosseum* (Pl. D, 7), **Colosseum-Str. 2**; *°Blumensäle* (Pl. D, 7), Blumen-Str. 29; *Monachia*, Herzog-**Wilhelm-Str., near** the Karlsthor.

Concerts. *Löwenbräukeller* (**p. 138**; military band almost every evening in summer); *Isarlust* (p. 156); *Münchener Kindl-Keller* (p. 138); *Bürgerliches Bräuhaus* (p. 138); *Achatz* (p. 137); *Oberpollinger*, *Bamberger Hof* (p. 137; popular songs; for men only); *Volksgarten* at *Nymphenburg* (p. 194). — High-class concerts in winter at the *Odeon* (Pl. E, 3; p. 150) and in the *Museum*, Promenade-Str. (Pl. E, 4).

Military Band daily at 12 at the guard-house, Marien-Platz (Pl. E, 5; p. 189), and on Tues., Thurs., Sat., and Sun. in front of the Feldherrnhalle (Pl. E, 4; p. 131) at the same hour. In summer also every Wed. evening, 5-6, in the Hofgarten, and on Sat. evenings near the Chinese tower in the English Garden at the same hour (p. 193).

Church Festivals. Music at the *Court Church of St. Michael* (p. 190) on Sun. **at high mass, 9 a.m.; on** the Sundays of Advent and Lent, and during Passion Week, **vocal** only; on Holy Thursday and Good Friday at 7 p.m. a grand Miserere (by Allegri, etc.), when the church is illuminated by a cross composed of 800 flames; military mass with military music in the same church at 11 (only **when** the court is present). — Church-music in the *Frauenkirche* (p. 189) at **9, in** the *Allerheiligenkirche* (p. 148; only when **the court is present**) at **11** a.m. — On *Corpus Christi Day* (2nd Thurs. after Pentecost) a great procession, shared in by **the** court and the chief officials, wends from the Frauenkirche through the chief streets of the city — On the days of *All Saints* and *All Souls* (Nov. 1st & 2nd) the *Cemeteries* **are** decorated with flowers, etc., and the *Royal Vaults* **in** the Hofkirche, Frauenkirche, and Theatinerkirche are open to **the public.**

Popular Festivals. During the *Carnival* large **public masked** balls ('Redouten') are held in Kil's Colosseum (see above), **the** Blumensäle, the Centralsäle, Neuturm-Str., the Münchener Kindl-Keller, the Löwenbräukeller (p. 138), and other resorts. On the first Sun. of May and the third Sun. of Oct. a *Dult*, or fair, is held at the suburb of Haidhausen (p. 157). **On** Whitsunday there is a *Church-Fair* ('Kirchweih') at Grosshesselohe

(p. 193). The so-called *Magdalen Festival* takes place at Nymphenburg (p. 194) from July 22nd to July 29th. On the Sun. after July 25th (Day of St. James) there is a *Dult* at Au (p. 192). The *October Festival*, founded by King Lewis I. **in 1810 and** celebrated on the Theresienwiese (p. 191) from the end of **Sept. to the** middle of Oct., attracts large crowds of peasants from Upper Bavaria; it includes an agricultural show, horse-races, etc. The so-called *Metzgersprung* ('Butchers' Festival') takes place in the Marien-Platz **(p. 189)** on Carnival Monday every third year. The *Schäfflertanz* ('Coopers' Dance') is celebrated every seven years. —

Collections, etc. (adm. free unless the contrary is stated): —

Academy of Science **(p. 190)**, palæontological, **mineralogical**, and zoological collections, **Sun. 10-12**, Wed. and Sat. **2-4 (in winter** Sun. & Sat. only); **at** other times for a fee.

Anatomical and Pathological Collections (p. 191), on **week-days, 12-2** (adm. by ticket, 50 pf., obtained in the Academy, **Neuhauser-Str.**, between 10 & 12).

Antiquarium **(in** the New **Pinakothek, p. 179), Tues. and Sat., 8-12; in** winter, **Tues.** only, 10-12.

Arco-Zinneberg Collection of Antlers (p. **157**), **daily on** application (fee).

Arsenal and Military Museum (p. 187), in **summer**, Tues. and Frid. 9-12 and 3-5, and Sun. 9-12, free; on Mon. **and Thurs.** 9-12 and 3-5, 1 *M.*

Art Exhibition of the Münchener **Künstlergenossenschaft** at the Exhibition Building (p. 184) daily 9-5, Nov. **to Feb. 9-4**, adm. 50 pf. — *°Annual **Exhibition** of the same society in the **Crystal Palace** (p. 187), from **1st June** to 31st Oct., daily 9-6, 1 *M.* — *°International Exhibition of the Verein Bildender Künstler* (the so-called '*Secession*'), at the Exhibition building in the **Prinz-Regen**ten-Str. (Pl. F, 3; p. 149), daily from 1st June to 31st Oct., 9-6; 1 *M.* — Other **exhibitions**: *Wimmer & Co.*, Brienner-Str. 3; *Neumann*, Maximilians-**Str. 33**; *Fleischmann*, Maximilians-Str. 2, etc.

Art Union or *Kunstverein* (p. 149) daily (except Sat.), 10-6. Strangers are admitted gratis once, on application to the secretary **(first** floor), or when introduced **by a** member; ticket for four weeks 2 *M.*

°Bavaria and **Ruhmeshalle (p.** 191), 9-12 **and** 2-7, in winter **10-12 and** 2-4; adm. 40 pf.

Botanical Garden (p. 187), **week-days, 8-6;** palm-house on Mon. & Thurs., 2-5, with guide; closed **on** Saturdays and Sundays.

Bronze Foundry **(p.** 186), week-days 1-6, Sun. 12-2, adm. 40 pf.

Cabinet of Coins **(at** the Academy, p. 190), by special permission.

Cabinet of Drawings (Old Pinakothek, p. 172), Tues., Frid., 9-1.

Cabinet of Engravings (Old Pinakothek, p. 172), in summer, Mon. & Thurs. 9-12, Tues. & Frid. 9-1; in winter, Tues. & Frid. 9-1.

Cabinet of Natural History (p. 190), see *Academy of* **Science.**

Cabinet of Vases (p. 173), in the Old Pinakothek, **9-1, daily** except Wed. & Sat. (in winter, Sun., Tues., and Thurs.).

Collection of Fossils (p. 190), see **Academy** *of* **Science.**

°Festsaalbau, see *Palace.*

Frauen-Kirche, N. tower (p. 189), daily, tickets from the sacristan 40 pf.

Glass-Painting, Brienner-Str. 33; show-room daily, 9-12 & 3-5.

°Glyptothek (p. 180), free on Mon. and Frid. **8-12** and 2-4, Wed. 8-12 (in winter Mon. and Frid. 9-2, Wed. 9-1). **On other days at** the same hours 1 *M.* Closed during the 'October Festival' **(see above).**

Hof-Theater (p. 148), **arrangements of the interior, Mon., Wed.**, Sat. at 2 p.m. precisely; **50 pf.**

Hofwagenburg (*Royal* **Coach** *Houses*; **p.** 148), **week-days 9-12 and** 2-4, Sun. and holidays 9-12 (50 pf.); Wed., 2-4, free.

Kaulbach Museum (p. 150), daily, 2-4.

Kunstgewerbehaus (p. 188), Pfandhaus-Str. 7, exhibition and sale of art-industrial objects, week-days 8-7, Sun. and holidays 11-1, free.

Kunstverein, see Art Union.

°Library (p. 150), for readers on week-days, 9-1 (Sat. 8-12); for visitors ('Cimelien'), in summer, daily, 9-12; fee ½-1 *M.*

Lotzbeck's Collection (p. 158), Tues. and Frid. 9-3; fee 50 pf.

Maillinger Collection (p. 192), Sun., Tues., & Frid., 9-1.
Maximilianeum (collection of modern historical paintings, **p.** 156), in summer, Wed. and Sat. 10-12.
Mayer's Collection of Ecclesiastical Ornaments, Stiglmayer-Platz, **daily**.
Minerals, Collection of, see *Academy of Science*.
°*Museum, Bavarian National* (p. 153), daily, May to Sept. 9-3, **Oct. to April 10-2**; closed on Mon.; gratis **on** Sun. and Thurs.; on other days 1 *M*.
Museum of the City of Munich, Historical (p. 192), Sun., Mon., & Thurs., **9-1**.
Museum, Ethnographical **(p.** 149), Wed. and Sun., 9-12; in winter, **Sun.** only, 10-12.
Museum of Plaster Casts **(p. 149), Mon., Wed., Thurs., and Sat., 3-5,** in winter 2-4.
*Nibelungen Rooms (p. **147), in the** Palace, **see below.**
Observatory (p. 193), Tues. **&** Frid., 8-11 & 2-5.
Palace (p. 145): *Kaiserzimmer* (p. 146), *Trierzimmer* (p. 146), *Papstzimmer* (p. 146), °*Festsaalbau* (p. 147), and °*Nibelungen Saloons* (p. 147) daily at 11 a.m. precisely, except Sun.; tickets 1 *M* (obtained at the approach to the broad flight of steps, to the left in the passage, by Herzog Christofs-Stein, a little before 11 a.m.). The *Odyssey Saloons* are at present closed. The *Treasury (p. 146; June to Sept., Tues. and Frid., 9-11 a.m.) and the °*Reiche Capelle* (p. 146; Mon. & Thurs., 9-11 a.m.) are shown by tickets, which are issued between 9 and 10.30 a.m. at the Grottenhof, adjoining the Gensdarmes' Guard-room **(2** *M*).
Panoramas. In the Theresien-Str. (Pl. **D, 1;** p. 180): Emp. Constantine entering Rome in 312, by Bühlmann and Wagner; daily from 9 till dusk, 1 *M*. — On the Theresienhöhe (Pl. A, 5): The Battle of Orleans, by Diemer and Nisle (adm. 1 *M*).
St. Peter's Church, tower (p. 189), daily, tickets from attendant, 40 pf.
°°*Pinakothek, Old* (p. 158), Sun., Tues., Wed., and Frid. 9-3 (in winter 9-2); Mon. and Thurs. 9-5 (in winter 9-4); closed on Saturday.
**Pinakothek, New* (p. 173), Sun., Tues., Thurs., Sat., 8-12 and 2-4 (in winter 10-2); porcelain-paintings, same days and hours.
°*Porcelain Paintings* (New Pinakothek, p. 174), see above.
Rathhaus, New (p. 189): admission to the council-rooms 2-3 **(Sun.** 10-12), on application to the custodian (fee).
°*Reiche Capelle* (p. 146), in the Palace (see above).
°*Schack Picture Gallery* (p. 184), daily 2-5, in winter 2-4.
Schwanthaler Museum (p. 191), Mon., Wed., Frid., 9-2; at other times, adm. 35 pf.
Slaughter Houses and *Cattle Market* (p. 191), week-days **8-5,** Sun. 10-2; tickets at the restaurant (20 pf.).
Synagogue (p. 190), daily, except Sat., 9-12 and 2-4 (40 pf.).
Treasury (p. 146), in the Festsaalbau, see Palace.
Churches. The *Frauenkirche* (p. 189) is open all day (best seen 12-4), the *Theatinerkirche* (p. 149) and *Auerkirche* all day except 11-1, the *Basilica* (p. 187) except 12-1, and the *Ludwigskirche* (p. 151) except 12-2. The *Court Church of St. Michael* (p. 190) is closed after 11 a.m. The *Allerheiligen-Hofkirche* (p. 148; entr. usually from the Brunnenhof) is shown by tickets (20 pf.) obtained in the Sacristy **after midday** (in July, **Aug., &** Sept. after 10.30 a.m.).

Diary (summer). DAILY: Botanical Garden 8-6, closed on Sun.; Kunstgewerbehaus 8-7, Sun. and holidays 11-1; Old Pinakothek 9-3 (Mon., Thurs., 9-5), exc. Sat.; Library 9-12, exc. Sun.; Pictures of the Kunstverein 10-6, exc. Sat.; Bronze Foundry 1-6, Sun. 12-2; Palace at 11, exc. Sun.; National Museum 9-2, exc. Mon.; New Rathhaus 2-3, Sun. 10-12; Schack's Gallery 2-5; Anatomical collections 12-2; Panoramas, from 9 a.m.; Exhibition of Art in the Kunstausstellungs-Gebäude 9-5 (Sun. & holidays 9-1), in the Crystal Palace 9-6, in the Prinz-**Regenten**-Str. ('Secession') 9-6; Bavaria and Ruhmeshalle 9-12 and 2-7; **Kaulbach** Museum 2-4, **exc.** Sun.; Hofwagenburg 9-12 and 2-4, Sun. 9-12.

SUNDAYS: Military and Church Music, see p. 141. New Pinakothek and porcelain-paintings 8-12, 2-4. Cabinet of Vases 9-1. Ethnographical Museum 9-1. Maillinger Collection 9-1. City of Munich Museum 9-1.

144 *Route 28.*   MUNICH.   *History.*

Military Museum 9-12. Mineralogical and Palæontological Collections 10-12.
— MONDAYS: Glyptothek 8-12 and 2-4. Reiche Capelle 9-11. Cabinet of
Engravings 9-12. Military Museum 9-12 and 3-5. Cabinet of Vases 9-1.
Munich Museum 9-1. Schwanthaler Museum 9-2 (see p. 191). Hof-Theater
(interior) 2. Plaster Casts 3-5. — TUESDAYS: New Pinakothek and porcelain-
paintings 8-12, 2-4. Observatory 8-11 and 2-5. Treasury 9-11. Military
Museum 9-12 and 3-5. Cabinets of Drawings and Engravings 9-1. Cabinet
of Vases 9-1. Antiquarium 8-12. Maillinger Collection 9-1. Lotzbeck
Collection 9-3. — WEDNESDAYS: Glyptothek 8-12. Maximilianeum 10-12.
Museum of Casts 3-5. Mineralog. and Palæont. Collections 2-4. Hof-
Theater (interior) 2. Schwanthaler Museum 9-2. Ethnograph. Museum 9-1.
Military music in the Hofgarten 5-6. — THURSDAYS: New Pinakothek and
porcelain-paintings 8-12, 2-4. Cabinet of Engravings 9-1. Reiche Capelle
9-11. Military Museum 9-12 and 3-5. Cab. of Vases 9-1. Munich Museum
9-1. Plaster Casts 3-5. — FRIDAYS: Treasury 9-11. Glyptothek 8-12, 2-4.
Drawings and Engravings 9-1. Schwanthaler Museum 9-2. Maillinger Col-
lection 9-1. Observatory 8-11 and 2-5. Military Museum 9-12 and 3-5.
Lotzbeck Collection 9-3. — SATURDAYS: Old Pinakothek closed. New
Pinakothek and porcelain-paintings 8-12, 2-4. Maximilianeum 10-12. Museum
of Casts 3-5. Mineralog. and Palæont. Collections 2-4. Antiquarium 8-12.
Hof-Theater (interior) 2. Military music, at the Chinese Tower in the
Engl. Garden 5-6. — A *Drive (fiacres see p. 140) in the English Garden
(p. 198) or in the Gasteig Grounds (p. 157), is recommended after a morning
of sight-seeing; also excursions by the Isarthal railway (p. 194) or on the
Starnberger See (p. 195).

GREATEST ATTRACTIONS: Old Pinakothek (p. 153), New Pinakothek
(p. 173), National Museum (p. 153), Basilica (p. 187), Palace (p. 145), Glyptothek (p. 180). Schack Gallery (p. 184).

English Church Service in the Odeon (p. 150) at 11 a.m. and 3.30 p.m.
(in winter 3 p.m.).

British Minister Resident: *V. A. W. Drummond, Esq.*, Barer-Str. 15,
11-2; Consul, *John S. Smith, Esq.*, Barer-Str. 14, 11-1. — American
Consul: *Ralph Steiner, Esq.*

Munich (1703 ft.), the capital of Bavaria, with 350,600 inhab.
(incl. **6100 Jews** and a garrison of **9300 men**), lies on the S. side
of a sterile plain, 50 sq. M. in area, chiefly on the left bank of the
Isar, which emerges from a narrow gorge (10 M. long) about 4½ M.
above the city. The lofty situation of the city and its proximity to
the Alps render it liable to sudden changes of temperature, against
which visitors should guard, especially towards evening. The high
mountains, about 25 M. to the S. of the city, become very distinct
after a thunder-storm or on the approach of bad weather.

History. Munich was founded by Henry the Lion, who constructed a
bridge over the Isar, a custom-house, a mint, and a salt-depôt on the site of
the present city in 1158. The land is said to have belonged to the monks
of Schäftlarn or Tegernsee, whence the name of *Forum ad Monachos, Muniha*,
or Munich. Under the Wittelsbach princes the town prospered. Otho the
Illustrious (d. 1253) transferred his residence to Munich, and his son Lewis the
Severe built the Alte Hof (p. 184). Emp. Lewis the Bavarian almost entirely
re-erected the city, which was loyally attached to him, after a fire in 1327 (his
tomb in the Frauenkirche, see p. 163). Duke Albert V (1550-73) founded the
Library and the Kunstkammer, to which the Antiquarium, cabinet of coins,
and part of the National Museum owe their origin. Elector Maximilian I.
(1597-1651) erected the Arsenal, the Old Palace, and the Mariensäule (p. 162).
In 1631 Gustavus Adolphus paid a lengthened visit to the city. Elector Maximilian III. Joseph founded the Academy (p. 190) in 1757, and his successor
Charles Theodore of the Palatinate removed the old fortifications. King
Maximilian I. Joseph (d. 1825) contributed materially to the improvement
of the city by the dissolution of the religious houses and the erection of

new buildings, but for its modern magnificence Munich is chiefly indebted to his son LEWIS I. (d. 1868). That monarch, who even before his accession had purchased several valuable works of art (*e.g.* the Ægina Marbles, the so-called Ilioneus) and attracted Cornelius and other artists to Munich, raised the city during his reign of 23 years (ending in 1848) to the foremost rank as a school of German art. *Klenze* (d. 1864) was chiefly instrumental in carrying out the architectural plans of the monarch, and he was ably seconded by *Gärtner*, *Ohlmüller*, and *Ziebland*. The indefatigable *Schwanthaler* (d. 1848) provided the plastic embellishment, and *Cornelius* (d. 1867) and his pupils enlivened the walls with paintings of a monumental character. The harmony of this period, however, was soon disturbed by a difference between Cornelius and Klenze, and when the king showed that his sympathies were with the latter, Cornelius removed to Berlin. As *Kaulbach* (d. 1874) also for the last ten years of his life worked chiefly at Berlin, and *Schwind* (d. 1871) at the Wartburg, the glory of Munich as an art-centre began to pale. The decline, however, was transient; for while Munich has lately produced nothing of the first rank in architecture or sculpture, it has maintained its position as a leading school of painting, though under completely altered conditions. The elder Munich artists were distinguished for their accuracy of drawing and composition, and prided themselves on having revived the romantic style of art; the latest generation, under the lead of *Karl Piloty* (1826-1886), on the contrary, has fixed its attention chiefly on the study of colouring, and bestows the utmost care upon technical perfection of finish.

The MAX-JOSEPH-PLATZ (Pl. E, 4), the centre of the city and its traffic, situated between the old quarters and the new, is adorned with the *Monument of King Max Joseph (d. 1825), erected by the city on the 25th anniversary of that monarch's accession, modelled by *Rauch* of Berlin, and cast in bronze by *Stiglmayer*. The colossal statue in a sitting posture rests on a pedestal adorned with reliefs emblematical of Agriculture, Art, Constitution, and Religious Toleration.

The N. side of the Max-Joseph-Platz is bounded by the royal Palace (Pl. E, F, 4), which consists of three parts: on the S. side towards the Platz the *Königsbau*, N. towards the Hofgarten the *Festsaalbau*, and between these the *Alte Residenz*, or old palace, facing the Residenz-Str.

The **Alte Residenz**, built by *Hans Reifenstuel* in 1596-1619, under Elector Maximilian I., comprises four courts, Kaiserhof, Küchenhof, Brunnenhof, and Kapellenhof (*i. e.* courts of the emperor, kitchen, fountain, and chapel). The simple façade is embellished with two handsome bronze doors and a bronze statue of the Virgin by *Hans Krumper*. By the door to the right we enter the *Kapellenhof*. The passage thence to the Brunnenhof contains 'Duke Christopher's Stone' (an inscription on the wall). A staircase to the left ascends to the *Hercules Saloon*, where visitors to the palace assemble at 11 o'clock sharp (comp. p. 143). To the right of the Kapellenhof is the *Grottenhof*, with a small garden and a fantastic shell-grotto; in the centre a bronze Perseus, after B. Cellini. From the S.E. corner a passage leads to a larger court, with fountain-figures of Neptune, etc., from which the Nibelungen Saloons in the Königsbau are entered (p. 147). The *Brunnenhof*, to the E. of the Kapellenhof, is embellished with a statue of Otho of Wittelsbach and other figures in bronze by *P. Candid*. The Allerheiligenkirche

(p. 148) adjoins this court on the E.; to the S. a passage leads to the Hof-Theater (p. 148).

The apartments of the Alte Residenz are sumptuously fitted up in 17th cent. style. Visitors are first conducted to the KAISERZIMMER or REICHEN ZIMMER, which include the *Ante-Room*, with a portrait of King Lewis II. by Piloty; the *Audience Chamber*, with twelve Roman emperors by an unknown Venetian painter; the *Throne Room*, occupied in 1809 by Napoleon I.; the *Green Gallery*, containing Italian and Dutch pictures of little value; the *Bed Chamber*,

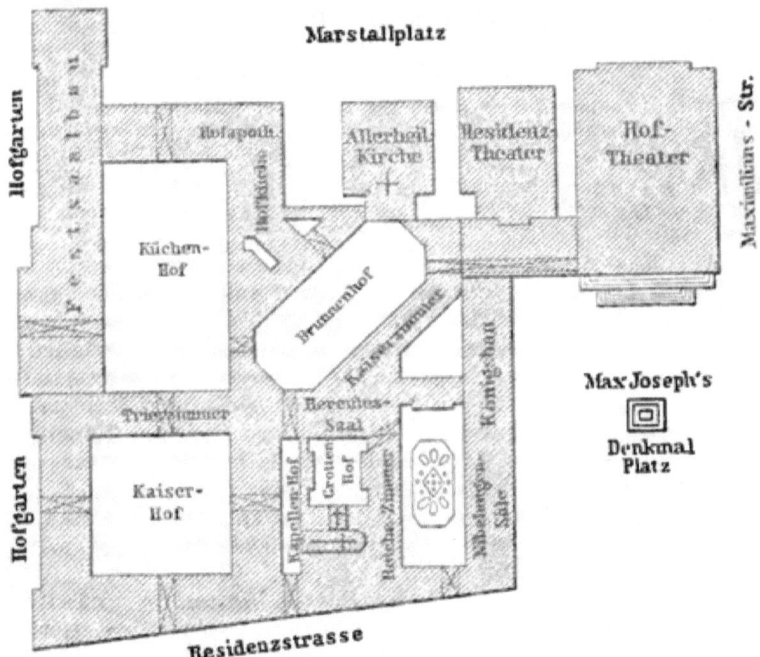

with a richly-gilded bed; the *Mirror Cabinet*, with valuable crystal; the *Miniature Cabinet*, with miniatures. — The TRIERZIMMER (for royal guests) and the PAPSTZIMMER, occupied in 1782 by Pope Pius VI., with furniture, tapestry, etc., of the 17th and 18th cent., are now usually shown after the visit to the Festsaalbau (p. 147).

The *Treasury (admission, see p. 143) contains jewels and precious trinkets, including the Bavarian 'Hausdiamant', a magnificent blue diamond, and the 'pearl of the Palatinate', half black; goblets, orders, regalia, including the Bohemian crown of Frederick V. of the Palatinate, captured at Prague in 1620, and the crowns of Emp. Henry II. ('the Saint') and his wife Cunigunde, of the year 1010; group of St. George and the Dragon, with the knight in chased gold, the dragon of jasper, and the whole adorned with diamonds, rubies, emeralds, and pearls; model of Trajan's Column, executed by the goldsmith Valadier (1763-83); violin of tortoise-shell.

The *Reiche Capelle (adm., see p. 143) contains costly objects in gold and silver, many of them of high artistic worth; two miniature altars by

Benv. Cellini (?), the enamelled pocket-altar of Mary Queen of Scots, about 6 in. in length, and a Descent from the Cross in wax by Michael Angelo (?).

The *Festsaalbau (façade towards the Hofgarten, 256 yds. long), a 'building of festive halls', erected in 1832-42 by *Klenze* in the later Italian Renaissance style, possesses a handsome porch of 10 Ionic columns, surmounted by two lions, between which are 8 **allegorical figures in** marble-limestone by *Schwanthaler*, representing **the different provinces of the kingdom. The** unsightly structure on **the roof was the winter-garden of King Lewis II**. The six saloons **of the groundfloor are decorated with** encaustic MURAL PAINTINGS **FROM THE ODYSSEY, by** *Hiltensperger*, **from designs** by *Schwanthaler* (closed at present).

A broad marble staircase ascends to the first floor from **the passage on** the E. side of the Küchenhof. Visitors, however, **are usually** conducted from the Hercules Saloon to the ante-chambers **by a long** corridor.

STAIRCASE, with six handsome columns of marble **from the Untersberg.** ANTE-CHAMBER, **with reliefs** by *Schwanthaler*; 2nd ante-chamber decorated **in** the Pompeian style **by** *Hiltensperger*. — Magnificent BALL ROOM, tribunes supported by marble columns and bearing Caryatides of papier-maché, coloured reliefs (dancing genii) by *Schwanthaler*. Two CARD ROOMS with thirty-six *Portraits of Beautiful Women* by *Stieler*. — BATTLE SALOON: Fourteen large pictures representing scenes from the wars in 1805-15. — *HALL OF CHARLEMAGNE, with six encaustic paintings (mural paintings **on** wax ground) designed by *Schnorr*. Charlemagne anointed by Pope Stephen II. as Defender of the Church; Charlemagne entering after his victory over the Lombard king Desiderius; victory over the Saxons, felling of the sacred oak, and erection of the cross; synod at Frankfurt; coronation; **also twelve** smaller scenes from the emperor's life. Between the windows Alcuin, Arno, and Eginhard. — *BARBAROSSA HALL, with six mural paintings by the same masters: election as emperor, entry into Milan, reconciliation with Pope Alexander III. at Venice, imperial festival at Mayence, battle **at** Iconium, death. Reliefs above by *Schwanthaler*. — *HAPSBURG SALOON, with four paintings, mainly by *Schnorr*: Rudolph's meeting with the priest; his acceptance of the imperial sceptre; victory over Ottocar of Bohemia on the Marchfeld; Rhenish robber-knights summoned before his tribunal. Frieze by *Schwind*, **representing** the Triumph of the Arts, etc. — *THRONE SALOON. Twelve magnificent gilded bronze statues, **over life-**size, by *Schwanthaler*, of the ancestors of the House of Wittelsbach, **from** Otho the Illustrious **to** Charles XII. of Sweden.

The **Königsbau** (façade towards the Max-Joseph-Platz, **136** yds. long), erected in **1826-33** by *Klenze* in imitation of the Pitti Palace at Florence, **but** of inferior effect owing to necessary deviations from the original plan, is adorned in the interior with sculptures, frescoes, and other works of art (not accessible).

The S.W. apartments on the groundfloor (entered from the Grottenhof, p. 145) are adorned with the magnificent *NIBELUNGEN FRESCOES **by *Schnorr*, begun** in 1861. Five saloons with large paintings; in the lunettes, numerous smaller paintings.

ENTRANCE HALL: the principal persons of the poem, right, Siegfried and Chriemhild; then Hagen, Volker, Dankwart; above, the dwarf Alberich, keeper of the Nibelungen treasure, and Eckewart, Chriemhild's messenger; left, Gunther and Brunhild; Queen Ute (Gunther's mother) with her sons Gernot and Giselher; Siegmund and Siegelinde, Siegfried's parents; next, King Attila and Rudiger, Dietrich **of Bern** and Meister Hildebrand. MARRIAGE

Hall: Siegfried's return from the war against the Saxons; Brunhild's arrival at Worms; Siegfried and Chriemhild's nuptials; opposite, by the window, the delivery of the girdle. Hall of Treachery: (by the window) quarrel of the queens Chriemhild and Brunhild in front of the cathedral at Worms. Siegfried murdered by Hagen at the well; Chriemhild finds Siegfried's corpse at the door of the cathedral: Hagen proved to be the murderer by the corpse beginning to bleed afresh. Over the door: Hagen throwing the Nibelungen treasure into the Rhine. Hall of Revenge: Fall of the heroes (by the window); Chriemhild expostulates with Volker and Hagen; combat on the staircase of the burning palace; Dietrich conquers Hagen; Chriemhild's death. Over the doors: the last combat of the heroes; Hagen brought before Chriemhild by Dietrich; Attila's lament. Hall of Mourning: Burial of the fallen heroes; the sad tidings conveyed to Burgundy; Bishop Pilgram of Passau causes mass to be sung for the repose of the dead (by Schnorr's pupils).

The **Hof- und National-Theater** (Pl. F, 4; performances, see p. 141), on the E. side of the Max-Joseph-Platz, one of the largest in Germany, accommodating 2200 spectators, was erected by *Fischer* (d. 1822) in 1818, but was burned down in 1823 and re-erected in its original form by *Klenze* within eleven months. Handsome portico of eight Corinthian columns. The pedimental frescoes designed by *Schwanthaler* (Pegasus and the Horæ, Apollo and the Muses) were replaced in 1894 by glass mosaics. The building is 145 ft. high, 188 ft. broad, and 332 ft. deep; the stage measures 95 ft. in breadth by 115 ft. in depth. The interior deserves a visit (which takes an hour; adm., see p. 142); fine view of the Alps from the roof. — Between the Hof-Theater and the Allerheiligenkirche is the **Residenz-Theater**, built in 1752-60 and restored in 1857, richly decorated in the rococo style (room for 800 spectators).

The *****Allerheiligen-Hofkirche** (All Saints' Church), or *Court Chapel* (adm., see p. 143; music, see p. 141), on the E. side of the palace, erected in 1837 by *Klenze* in the Byzantine-Romanesque style, is sumptuously fitted up. The arches rest on columns of variegated marble, the walls are covered with different coloured marbles; and the vaulting, window-arches, and choir are adorned with frescoes on a gold ground by *Hess*, *Schraudolph*, and *Koch*. The concealment of the windows causes the light to enter in a very effective manner.

At the back of the Alte Residenz, in the Marstall-Platz, are the **Royal Coach Houses and Harness Rooms** (*Hofwagenburg*; adm., see p. 142), containing an extensive collection of vehicles belonging to the rulers of Bavaria in the 17-19th centuries. Among the most noteworthy objects are the *State Coaches and **Sleighs of** Elector Max Emmanuel (1679), the Carriage of Elector Charles **Albert** (1726), and the *State Sledges and Carriages of King **Lewis II.**

Adjoining the Festsaalbau on the N. is the Hofgarten (Pl. E, F, 3, 4), or palace-garden, laid out in 1614. Originally a pleasant park, with fountains and a pond, it is now simply a square planted with trees, and bounded on two sides by open **Arcades**, which are adorned with faded frescoes of landscapes and historical subjects, painted in 1827-34.

By the entrances next to the Palace are three frescoes by *Kaulbach*, representing Bavaria and the rivers Danube, Rhine, Isar, and Main. The historical frescoes on the W. side, of events from the history of Bavaria, were executed by **pupils of** Cornelius (most of them restored); beyond them are masterly **landscapes** from Italy and Sicily by *Karl Rottmann* (d. 1850). Each scene **has its name** annexed. The distichs above the pictures are by King Lewis I. On the N. side, at the top, are thirty-nine small encaustic paintings **from the Greek War of** Independence, from sketches by *P. Hess* (p. 177). — In the seven niches at the N.E. end are the labours of Hercules in colossal **wooden groups**, executed by *R. Boos* (1796-1810) and restored in 1852. — In the **middle** of the Hofgarten is a fountain-temple with a good bronze **figure of Bavaria** (16th cent.).

The groundfloor of the N. wing contains the **Museum of Plaster Casts** of classic sculptures (adm., see p. 143), affording a good survey of the development of the plastic art from the 6th cent. before Christ down to the present day. Director, Prof. Furtwängler. Catalogue 30 pf. — The extensive **Ethnographical Museum** occupies seven rooms on the upper floor (adm., see p. 143; Conservator, **Dr.** Buchner; **Catalogue** 50 pf.). — Opposite, **to the** right of the exit, **is the Art Union**, or *Kunstverein* (Pl. F, 3; entrance in the Arcades; adm., see p. 142), containing paintings and sculptures by living **artists**, some of them the property of the society, others for sale. — The *Barracks* on the E. side of the Hofgarten are to be torn down.

From the just-mentioned exit a few **steps bring us to** the PRINZ-REGENTEN-STRASSE (Pl. F, G, H, **3, 4**), which is now undergoing a thorough reconstruction. **It begins** opposite the *Palace of Prince Charles* (now the Austrian **Embassy**), skirts the left (S.) side of **the** *English Garden* **(p.** 193), **passes** (right) the *Exhibition Building of the 'Secession'* (p. 142), and leads straight to the Isar, which it crosses by the *Luitpold-Brücke*. On the farther bank, below the *Luitpold Terrace* (p. 157), to which two roads ascend, are pleasure-grounds and a large fountain.

Most of the buildings in the handsome LUDWIG-STRASSE (Pl. F, E, 4-1; tramway-line 2, p. 140), originated by King Lewis I., 40 yds. in width, and $^3/_4$ M. in length, are in various Renaissance **forms**, constructed of brick **and stone** skilfully combined.

The **Feldherrnhalle** (Pl. E, 4), or *Hall of the Generals*, at the S. end, a copy of Orcagna's Loggia dei Lanzi at Florence, erected in 1844 by *Gärtner*, contains the *Bavarian Military Monument*, by F. von Miller (unveiled in 1892), and statues of the Bavarian generals Tilly and Wrede, by *Schwanthaler*.

The **Church of the Theatines** (Pl. E, 4), erected by *Barelli* in 1662-75 in the debased Italian style, overladen with decoration, contains the Royal Vaults. Façade of 1767. Pictures in the interior (restored in 1856) by *Tintoretto, Zanchi, Karl Loth, Cignani*, and others. To the right is the mortuary chapel of King Maximilian II. (d. 1864) and Queen Marie (d. 1889). In the sacristy, on the left, an Entombment by *H. Hess*.

In the Odeons-Platz rises the equestrian **Statue of Lewis I.**

(d. 1868), by *Widnmann*, erected in 1862. — To the left is the **Odeon** (Pl. E, 3), erected in 1828 by *Klenze*, and destined for concerts and balls; one of the apartments is fitted up as an *English Chapel* (see p. 144). The ceiling of the concert-room is decorated with frescoes by *W. von Kaulbach* and others, the orchestra with busts of celebrated composers (partly concealed by the organ). — On the N. side of the square, on the left, stands the **Palace of Prince Regent** Luitpold, formerly that of the *Duke of Leuchtenberg* (Pl. E, 3), erected by *Klenze* (unoccupied). Opposite (Fürsten-Str. 1) is the *Palace of Prince Ludwig Ferdinand*.

Then, farther to the N., in the Ludwig-Strasse (left), the **Palace of Duke Max** (Pl. E, 3), by *Klenze*, with frescoes by *Langer*, *Kaulbach*, and *Zimmermann*, and a marble frieze representing the myth of Bacchus, by *Schwanthaler*. On the right, the **War Office** (Pl. F, 2, 3), also by *Klenze*. — In the vicinity, Kaulbach-Str. 12, is the **Kaulbach Museum**, an interesting selection of the pictures and sketches left by the eminent painter *W. von Kaulbach* (d. 1874). Adm., see p. 142.

The *Royal Library (Pl. F, 2; adm., see p. 142), an imposing edifice, was built in 1832-42 by *Gärtner* in the Florentine style. The steps are adorned with colossal seated figures of Aristotle, Hippocrates, Homer, and Thucydides. *Staircase with broad marble flight of steps; above, on each side, is a gallery, borne by 16 marble columns; on the walls are medallion-portraits of celebrated poets and scholars. At the entrance to the library are statues of Albert V., the founder, and Lewis I., the builder of the library, both by *Schwanthaler*. The library (Director, Dr. Laubmann), one of the most extensive in Europe, comprises upwards of 1,800,000 vols. and 30,000 MSS., and is especially valuable for its theological and biblical literature and German MSS. The most interesting rarities ('Cimelien', from the Greek χειμήλιον, a treasure) are exhibited in the *Fürsten-Saal*.

FIRST SECTION: Specimens of substances used to write on; bronze and wax tablets, papyrus, parchment, cotton and linen paper, palm-leaves, bark, woven materials. Also brazen *tabulae honestae missionis*, or certificates of honourable discharge of Roman soldiers; wax tablets with inscriptions; the *Codex Purpureus*, a Latin Book of the Gospels of the 9th cent., written on purple vellum with gold and silver letters. — SECOND SECTION: Precious manuscripts in different old and modern languages. The most numerous are the Latin MSS., of which, for showing the development of writing, specimens of every century from the 6th to the 16th are exhibited. One of the oldest is the *Breviarium Alarici*, an extract from the Code of Theodosius the Great, made in Spain by order of Alaric, King of the Visigoths, 484-506. Earliest German MSS.: The *Wessobrunner Gebet*, a fragment of an alliterative epic with a prayer in prose, written before 814, from the monastery of Wessobrunn in Upper Bavaria; *Heliand*, a harmony of the Gospels in early Low German (the Gospels in alliterative verse), written about 830 by a Saxon ecclesiastic; *Otfried of Weissenburg's* Gospel in verse, composed between 863 and 871 and copied at Freising about 900; oldest (13th cent.) MS. of the *Nibelungen Lied*, from the monastery of Hohenembs near Bregenz; *Tristan and Isolde*, poem by Godfrey of Strassburg, MS. of 1240, with paintings; *Parcival and Titurel*, by Wolfram von Eschenbach, **with** paintings. Among the Oriental MSS. several Arabic **specimens** are remarkable for their splendour and beautiful writing; among **the** modern MSS. a copy of *Petrarch* with graceful marginal drawings **and a** manuscript of *Calderon* with a final note **from** the author's **own hand may** be mentioned. Then follow several **musical** compositions with old notes, among them also ancient Greek hymns of Dionysius and Mesomedes. — THIRD SECTION: Sumptuous old bindings. °*Codex Aureus*, written **in** gold uncial letters in 870 by order of **Emp.** Charles the Bald; **the** cover consists of **a plate of** embossed **gold, with** jewels **and pearls.** °**Four Books of Gospels and a Missal** of Emp. Henry **II.** (1024). presented **to the** cathedral **of Bamberg, with a** similar cover. Then a collection **of bindings** from the **11th to the 17th** cent. and a series of **ivory covers, showing the** development of ivory carving from the Roman **period to the end of the 16th** century. — FOURTH SECTION: Illuminated MS. °**Prayer-book of Emp. Maximilian I.**, with marginal drawings by Albert **Dürer and Cranach.** Latin prayer-book with miniatures by Memling (?). The Jewels **of Anne** of Austria, consort of Duke Albert V. of Bavaria, miniature-paintings by Hans Miclich. Prayer-book of Duke Albert V. of Bavaria, by Giulio Clovio (1574). Calendarium of the 16th cent. by Brueghel (?). °*Livre de Jehan Bocace des cas des nobles hommes et femmes*, translation made in 1458 for Maître Etienne Chevalier, **with** admirable miniatures by Foucquet and his pupils. Latin prayer-book with illustrations by Sinibaldi of Florence (1485), richly bound like the preceding. **Several** books **of arms** and weapons, among them the tournament book of **Duke William IV. of** Bavaria, painted in 1541-44. — FIFTH SECTION: Typographical specimens in illustration of the history of printing. Block-books (*i.e.* books printed from carved blocks of wood) of the 15th century. Then the earliest printed books, including the Mazarin Bible, printed **by** Gutenberg and Fust (Mayence, 1455); stereotype plate of 1553. Dürer's **Passion of** 1511, **the** first edition of Holbein's Dance **of Death,** Sandro Botticelli's engravings (Florence, 1481), the first **editions of** Columbus' and **Amerigo** Vespucci's letters on the New World; **broadsides** and title-pages, etc. — SIXTH, SEVENTH, AND EIGHTH SECTIONS: Interesting early maps; autograph writings of celebrated men; book-plates ('Exlibris') from the 16th cent. to the present day.

The *National Archives* of Bavaria, in the vaults of the groundfloor, **contain** about 500,000 documents and include an interesting collection of medals and of impressions of the seals of German emperors, princes, and noblemen (shown on application). Archivist, Hofrath von Rockinger (office-hours 9-2).

The *Ludwigskirche (Pl. **F, 2**; adm., see p. 143), erected in **1829-44** in **the** Italian Romanesque style by *Gärtner*, is a handsome cruciform structure. Façade flanked with two towers 210 **ft. in** height. Mosaic **roof** of coloured tiles. Above the portal, Christ and the four Evangelists, by *Schwanthaler*.

INTERIOR (dark; best light in the afternoon). The entire wall at the back **of** the high-altar is covered with the °Last Judgment, the largest of the frescoes of *Cornelius* (1836-40), 60 ft. high, 36 ft. broad. The other **frescoes,** designed by Cornelius, were executed by his pupils (God the **Father, the** Nativity and Crucifixion, Patriarchs, Prophets, Martyrs). — In **the adjacent** grounds **are** frescoes by *Forstner* at fourteen different shrines.

Opposite is the **Blind** Asylum (Pl. F, 2), erected by *Gärtner* in **1834-38 in** the **Florentine style.** The portals are embellished with **statues of** the four patron-saints of the blind, by Eberhard.

The **University** (Pl. F, **1**) on the left, the *Priests' Seminary*, or *Georgianum*, opposite, **and** the *Max-Joseph School* form a large square, intersected by the Ludwig-Strasse, and adorned with two *Fountains* copied from those by Bernini in the piazza of St. Peter **at Rome. The university (about** 3500 students), founded in 1472 at

Ingolstadt (p. 132), was transferred to Landshut (p. 135) in 1800, and thence to Munich in 1826. The *University Library*, on the second floor, contains upwards of 300,000 vols. (open daily, 9-12).

The *Siegesthor (Pl. F, 1), or *Gate of Victory*, erected by Lewis I. 'to the Bavarian army', begun by *Gärtner* in 1843 and completed by *Metzger* in 1850, is an imitation of the triumphal arch of Constantine at Rome. It is crowned with 'Bavaria' in a quadriga drawn by lions, in bronze, designed by *Wagner* (comp. p. 174). Over the Corinthian columns at the sides are figures of Victory; on the walls reliefs, representing warlike exploits (below) and the different provinces of the kingdom (above). This fine arch forms an appropriate termination to the Ludwig-Strasse.

Beyond the Siegesthor, to the left, is the imposing *Academy of Art, in the Italian Renaissance style, designed by *Neureuther* (1874-85). The central portion is 610 ft. long, while the wings at the ends project 105 ft. On the flight of steps in front of the main entrance are mounted figures of Castor and Pollux, cast in bronze by *F. von Miller* from the designs of *Widnmann*.

From the Siegesthor the LEOPOLD-STRASSE leads past the *Palace of Prince Leopold* and several villas to the suburb of Schwabing (*Salvator Brewery; Grosser Wirt*), which, with its large bath-establishments (p. 140), was incorporated with Munich in 1861.

On the S. side of the Max-Joseph-Platz is the **Post Office** (Pl. E, 4, 5). The façade towards the Platz was constructed by *Klenze* in 1836. The open arcade contains six paintings of horse-tamers on a red ground in the Pompeian style, by *Hiltensperger*. The original façade towards the Residenz-Str. is in the Italian palatial style (1740). — To the right a short street leads to the *Alte Hof*, the oldest palace of the Dukes of Bavaria, erected in 1253-56, and now occupied by public offices. A passage to the left in front of it leads to the *Hofbräuhaus*, or 'Court Brewery' (Pl. F, 5; p. 138).

The *MAXIMILIAN-STRASSE (Pl. F, G, H, 5; tramway-line 4, p. 140), 1 M. in length and 25 yds. in breadth, was constructed by desire of King Max II. in a novel style of domestic architecture. First, on the right, is the *Mint* (Pl. F, 5), a building of the 16th cent., remodelled by Gärtner in 1809, with arcades embellished with statues. The old court is in the Renaissance style. Farther on, the street expands into a square, relieved with pleasure-grounds; on the left the *Government Buildings* (Pl. G, 5; 1858-64), on the right the *National Museum* (p. 153). In the centre rise four monuments: to the left a *Statue of General Deroy* (Pl. 19; killed at Poloczk in 1812), by *Halbig* (1856); adjoining it, that of *Count Rumford* (d. 1814), founder of the English Garden, by Zumbusch (1868). Opposite are the statues of *Schelling*, the philosopher (d. 1854), designed by Brugger (1861), and *Fraunhofer*, the optician (d. 1826), by Halbig (1861).

The *Bavarian National Museum (Pl. F, G, 5; adm., see p. 143), founded by King Max II. in 1855 and originally exhibited in the Herzog-Max-Burg (p. 188), contains a rich collection of objects illustrating the progress of civilisation and art. The building was erected in 1858-66 by *Riedel*. On the central portion, 95 ft. in height, is enthroned a 'Bavaria' with the lion, in zinc. The façade is richly adorned with caryatides, statues, reliefs, and other enrichments. Director, *Prof. Dr. W. N. von Riehl*.

The Bavarian National Museum contains works of art of every kind, dating from the prehistoric Roman periods down to the present day, and representing every civilised country, but with special reference to Bavaria. The plans hung up at the entrance afford a general outline of the arrangement. The collections are divided into two principal sections: 1. *General Collection* ('Allgemeine Sammlung') of the products of human industry, from hoar antiquity to the present day; 2. *Special Collections* ('Fachsammlungen') illustrating special branches of art or industry, and too extensive to be embraced in the General Collection. The *General Collection* begins in the arcades and in the two prehistoric rooms on the E. side of the ground-floor, is continued throughout the whole of the rooms on the W. side, and ends with the modern rooms (16-19th cent.) on the second floor. The *Special Collections* begin in the third room on the E. side of the ground-floor and are continued in the thirty rooms on the first floor. These last are embellished with large *Mural Paintings* of the history of Bavaria. At the back of the building is a GARDEN, which contains monuments and gravestones extending from the Roman period to the 18th cent. (including the tomb of Orlando di Lasso, the composer; see p. 188); also a colossal *Group of Mars and Venus in bronze, by Hubert Gerbard (ca. 1590), and the so-called 'Miltenberg Column'. — The Museum further includes an extensive *Library of Technical Works* and a copying-room, the use of which is granted to artists and students on application. The larger groups and other objects of importance in the various sections are labelled. The briefest visit to the whole museum takes two hours. Those who are pressed for time should confine themselves to the second floor. Printed guide 50 pf.; also several special catalogues.

GROUND FLOOR. In the *Vestibule* are cannon, a relief of St. George, and in the centre the stone monument of a Count of Haag (d. 1566), with a recumbent figure. In the Arcades to the *left* are Roman relics. — *Room I (left).* Cases 3-7. Prehistoric antiquities, chiefly from tumuli in different parts of Franconia. Works of the bronze period (ca. 1400-900 B.C.?), the early iron period (ca. 900-450 B.C.?), and the later iron period (from ca. 450 B.C. to the Roman period; Celtic antiquities). In Case 2 is the Golden Hat (shield-boss) of Schifferstadt (ca. 400 B.C.). Cases 8, 11-14. Roman antiquities, including (Case 13) fine glass vessels and fragments of early-Christian glass from the Catacombs. Cases 1, 2, 9, 10. Germanic antiquities of the Merovingian period (5-8th cent. A.D.), objects from tombs at Wittislingen, Nordendorf, etc. The walls are hung with handsome Brussels carpets (continuation of this collection on second floor). — *Room II.* Roman antiquities; mosaic from Westerhofen, near Ingolstadt; an altar from Rheinzabern; and stone monuments. — *Rooms 3-9* contain the following SPECIAL COLLECTIONS: 3-5. Iron-work, from the 15th cent. onwards (fine iron screen of ca. 1735 from the Dominican church at Ratisbon, at the entrance of R. 3; painted Gothic screen from Küfstein); 6. Utensils in bronze, copper, brass, and tin; modern work in metal; 7-9. Plaster casts from famous originals. — To the left, at the foot of the staircase to the first floor, is a *Torture Chamber*.

We return to the entrance. To the *right* is the department of 'Mediæval Art, ranging from the early Christian epoch to the beginning of the 16th century. The *Arcades* contain architectural fragments of the Romanesque and early-Gothic periods. — *Room I* (Romanesque period). Romanesque architectural members. In the glass-cases are smaller works of art, chiefly ecclesiastical, such as ciboria, aquamaniles, crucifixes, monstrances, reliquaries, censers, and candelabra. Special attention is deserved by the ivory carvings (reliefs of the Resurrection and Ascension, 6th cent.; jewel-casket of St. Cunigunde from Bamberg Cathedral) and the enamel-work **on metal** (11-14th cent.). On the walls are large wooden crucifixes; stone sculptures from Wessobrunn (ca. 1250); mural paintings from the monastery of Rebdorf (13th cent.); stained glass from Seligenthal (ca. 1300). On the entrance-wall are early-Russian and modern Greek paintings and small objects **in metal and wood.** — *Room II* (Gothic, 14th cent.). The **cases** contain **miniatures** from mass-books and **antiphonies** (12-15th cent.); crucifixes, **aquamaniles**, osculatories; small sculptures, originals and casts. On the **walls are larger** sculptures, chiefly tombstones with reliefs; altar-piece from **Rosenheim, with** the oldest panel-paintings of Bavaria (beginning of the 14th cent.); **small** reliquary-altar, with paintings in tempera in the Lower Rhenish style (ca. 1350). — *Room III*. Panel-paintings and sculptures of the 14-15th **cent.**, including a *Winged Altar from Pähl near Weilheim (No. 9) and a **rich** Gothic domestic altar from Nuremberg (**No. 15**), both of the first half of the 15th century. — *Room IV*. Large triple **altar** from **the old** Franciscan **church** at Bamberg (perhaps by Meister Berthold of Nuremberg; 1429); **stained** glass from the Franciscan church of **Ratisbon**. — *Room V*. Ceiling and panelling **from the** old Weavers' Hall **at Angsburg** (1457); bridal coffers, **cabinets; figures of** the twelve Apostles **in wood** from Lübeck (15th cent.). — *Room VI*. The glass-cases contain **incunabula** (1440-1500); mediæval **coins and dies**; original documents, etc. On the partition-wall, wooden figure of St. Willibald; large piece of Flemish tapestry, representing **the Nativity and** Adoration **of the Magi** (ca. 1500). — *Room VII*. Rich Gothic **ceiling in** lime-wood **from the** castle of Oberhaus near Passau. The cases **contain sculptures in wood**, fine miniatures (Flemish prayer-books of the 16th **cent.**, etc.), two **small oil-paintings** by Memling, late-Gothic goldsmith's **work. By the walls, handsome** carved **cabinets;** bedsteads; **panel-**paintings **of different Upper German schools.** — *Room VIII*. Staircase **and** gallery **from Neu-Ötting (15th cent.); altar of the Virgin** from **Weissenburg (15th cent.); wooden figure of St. George (14th cent.);** so-called 'Palmesel' (comp. p. 107; **16th cent.**). — *Room IX* ('Kirchensaal', in seven sections). Altar **from Geroldshofen** **(ca. 1515), figures of the Virgin** and the Magdalen, bust of St. Afra, wooden statu**ettes of the** Apostles, and o**ther works by** Tilmann Riemenschneider; Death of the Virgin, a group carved in wood, from Ingolstadt (1490-1500); two procession-poles of the Fishermen's Guild of Ingolstadt (1509); winged altar with gilded carving and paintings, of the school of Michael Pacher (ca. 1500); armorial shield of Milan; high-altar from the former Franciscan church at Munich (1492). The cases of the 6th and **7th sections** contain church-vessels **in metal**. Good stained glass in the **windows**. — *Room X*. Winged altar carved in oak, from Calcar **(ca. 1520); fine** late-Gothic goldsmith's **work; large** Flemish tapestry worked **in gold thread** with allegorical scenes **(16th** cent.).

We now ascend the staircase, adorned with weapons and reliefs, to the FIRST FLOOR, **which** contains the HISTORICAL FRESCOES and the continuation of the SPECIAL COLLECTIONS (see **above**). To the right, Rooms I-XII. Weapons, **armour**, uniforms, costumes, **ornaments**, etc., from the 12th cent. to the **present day.** — *Room I* (12-16th cent.). Helmets, chain-mail, shields, targes, etc. — *Room II* (1400-1520). **Pikes**, halberds, etc.; two-handed swords. — *Room III* (1500-1570). Caron**nades**, cross-bows, stone projectiles; swords of knights and 'Landsknechte', ornamented swords and daggers; fine wheel-lock muskets. — *Room IV* (1570-1620). Pikes, halberds, swords, battle-axes; 15. Gilded **armour of** Bishop Dieter von Raitenau, **of Salzburg** (1587-1612), by **the armourer** Piccinino of Milan. — *Room V* (1540-1650). Light armour; **armour for** man and horse (ca. 1540); ornamented **weapons**; 9. Wedding cloak **of Duke** William V. (1568); 11. Women's dress **and** ornaments of the 16-17th cent.; 13, 14. Jewels and clothes, chiefly **from** the graves of the Counts-Palatine of Neuburg, at Lauingen; breech-loading 'cannons. — *Room VI* (1600-1660). Light armour, chiefly of the period **of** the Thirty Years' War; 3. Tilly's coat; 4. Official robes of a

Nuremberg councillor; collection of shoes from the Roman period to the present day. — *Room VII*. South-German costumes of the first half of the 19th century. — *Room VIII* (1620-1780). Collection of models of the cannon used in the Thirty Years' War; Oriental saddles and weapons, captured at Belgrade by Max Emanuel (1688); 8. Handsome rococo sword; 9. Memorials of Frederick the Great. — *Room IX* (1640-1800). Ladies' costumes of the beginning of the 18th cent.; 9. Headdresses and coiffures of patrician ladies of Nuremberg and Augsburg; 15. Napoleon's sword. — *Rooms X-XII* (1740-1871). Robes and garments of the Bavarian sovereigns Max Joseph I., Lewis I. and his consort Theresa, and Max II., of Otho, King of Greece and his wife, of Fieldmarshal Wrede, and of General von der Tann; uniforms, weapons, and trophies. — *Room XIII*. Musical instruments from the 15th to the 19th century. — *Room XIV*. Objects **used** in the Jewish divine service; examples of Nuremberg bismuth-painting and brazier's work; toys; playing-cards; book-covers. — *Room XV*. Collection of seals from Charlemagne to the present day.

The *Central Saloon* (XVI) contains a collection **of old** ship-models, including that of the vessel of Charles V. in his attack on Algiers in 1541; also models of Bavarian and other towns, churches, castles, and fortresses; compasses and sun-dials of the 15-19th cent.; Schiller's writing-table. — To the *left* of the entrance, in *Rooms XVII-XXIV*, is the *Textile Collection*, consisting of lace, embroidery, and materials for dress, and including Egyptian and late-Roman costumes (R. XVII), ecclesiastical vestments (R. XVIII), Oriental carpets (R. XIX), and the *Bed of Lewis II., from Linderhof (R. XXIII). Next, in *Rooms XXV-XXVIII*, is the *Ceramic Collection*, from Roman times to the present, including specimens of the chief manufactories of the world, among the finest of which are the Italian majolicas of the 16-17th cent. (R. XXVII), the Japanese and Chinese porcelain of the 15-18th cent., and the Meissen and Nymphenburg china of the 18th century. In *Room XXIX* is the *Glass Collection*, from the Roman period down to our own. *Room XXX*. Ornaments **in** wood

The SECOND FLOOR contains works of art of the *Renaissance and Modern Times*. The staircase has a fine wooden ceiling from the château at Dachau, and three pieces of Brussels *Tapestry, representing the battles of Hannibal, after Giulio Romano. The various rooms are hung with **tapestry** after different masters (from Flanders, Germany, France), and contain ceilings from Dachau, Neuburg, Donauwörth, Nuremberg, and the Frauenkirche and the Royal Palace at Munich. The first five rooms are devoted to the 16th century. Among the choicest contents are: *Room I*. MSS., miniatures, and rare prints; finely ornamented drinking-cups and utensils, chiefly from Nuremberg and Augsburg; reliefs in wood representing the ten commandments (1524); draughtsmen with portrait-medallions, partly by Hagenauer. — *Room II*. Cast of the monument of St. Sebald by *Peter Vischer* at Nuremberg, and (No. 4) two bronze statues by *Vischer*. Bridal casket of Duchess Jacobæa of Bavaria (No. 7), with beautiful Italian intarsia. — *Room III*. Vessels in Limoges enamel, including eight by P. Reymond. *Silver-gilt hammer, designed for the use of Pope Julius III. at the opening of the great Jubilee Festival in 1550; 5. Winged altar of the Nuremberg school from Artelshofen (1514). — *Room IV*, Gold goblet of the Augsburg butchers' guild; 3. Domestic altar, with carvings by G. Bockschütz (1561); 5. Two tables, of Spanish workmanship; bed of Countess Palatine Susanna. — *Room V*. In the centre the complete boudoir of a Countess Fugger from the château at Donauwörth (1546). — *Room VI* (1500-1650). Table utensils in ivory and enamel; 3. Ivory caskets with portraits of Elector Maximilian I. and his sister. — *Room VII*. (This and the next four rooms illustrate the period of Elector Maximilian I., 1597-1651.) Table of Kelheim stone, elaborately engraved with portraits, arms, perpetual calendar, etc.; two tables in scagliola-work (imitation of mosaic); carved furniture. — *Room VIII*. Nos. 1,2. Cabinets inlaid with tortoise-shell and mother-of pearl; 5. Cabinet in Florentine mosaic; 13, 17. Cabinets of ivory, silver, enamel, and lapis lazuli, by Chr. Angermaier of Weilheim; vessels of rock crystal set in gold and enamel. — *Rooms IX-XI*. Works in amber and silver filigree, the latter chiefly from Augsburg; fine groups in bronze, etc. — *Rooms XII-XIII* (time of Elector Ferdinand Maria, 1651-79). Gilded ceiling from the palace at Munich; large silver watches from Augsburg; Buhl furniture; cabinet with paintings by W. van Bemmel; portrait of Electress Adelheid (d. 1676), ascribed to Kneller. — *Room XIV* (time of Max Emmanuel, 1679-1726). Miniatures and medallions of Bavarian and other royal personages. — *Room XV*. 'Ivory carvings, several by Elhafen (ca. 1720) and Simon Troger (d. 1769). 'Cabinet for coins by Angermaier of Weilheim (1624). — *Rooms XVI-XVIII*. Tapestry from the Munich manufactory; wood-carvings in the rococo style; miniatures and medals; fans. — *Room XIX* (modern period). First attempts at reviving the art of staining glass. Memorials of Max I. Joseph, Lewis I., and Max II.

At the end of the Platz rises the *Monument of King Maximilian II. (d. 1864), erected by his 'faithful people' in 1875. The colossal figure of the king in his coronation robes, $16^{1}/_{2}$ ft. high, stands upon a lofty granite pedestal. In his right hand he holds the roll of the constitution; his left rests on a sword. At the base of the pedestal sit allegorical figures of Peace, Enlightenment, Strength, and Justice; at the upper angles are four figures of children bearing the Bavarian coat-of-arms and laurel-wreaths. All the figures are in bronze, cast by *Miller* from models by *Zumbusch*.

The Thiersch-Str. and the Pfarr-Str. lead hence to the N. to the St. Anna-Platz, with the St. Annakirche (Pl. G, 4), a Romanesque edifice built in 1892-94 from the designs of *Gabriel Seidl*.

Just beyond the monument the Maximilians-Str. reaches the Isar. The handsome *Steinsdorfer-Strasse* (Pl. G, 5,6), a wide, new quay, ascends hence to the S.W., along the left bank, to the new Protestant *Lukaskirche*, in the transition style, and on to the Ludwigs-Brücke (p. 192). Opposite, in the river, are two islands united by the '*Muffatwehr*'; the lower or *Prater-Insel* is prettily laid out and contains the Isarlust Restaurant (p. 138).

The Maximilian-Str. crosses the river and the Prater-Insel by the *Maximilians-Brücke*, 540ft. long, which was constructed by Zenetti in 1859-64 and has recently been embellished with a monument to *Burgomaster von Ehrhardt* (d. 1888). In the grounds below the bridge is a monument to *M. von Schwind*, the painter, with figures of Legend and Fantasy by Hähnel. On the right bank the street ascends the *Gasteighöhe* in two branches. On the slope, forming a suitable termination to the grand street, rises the —

Maximilianeum (Pl. H, 5), founded by King Max II. for the higher instruction of students who have shown special aptitude for the civil service. The architect was *Bürklein*. Admission, see p. 143.

A broad circular approach ascends to the façade, which rises in two series of arches on a lofty terrace. The slightly curved central part of the structure is adjoined by open arcades on each side, flanked with corner-towers. Beautiful view of the river, the city, and the mountains.

At the top of the handsome staircase are the sketches in oil for the paintings by *K. von Piloty* on the façade (now destroyed): in the middle, Emp. Lewis the Bavarian founding the monastery of Ettal (1330); to the right, Wolfram of Eschenbach at the 'Sängerkrieg' in the Wartburg; to the left, Duke Lewis the Rich founding the University of Ingolstadt. — Three rooms on the upper floor contain thirty large oil-paintings, illustrative of momentous events in the world's history; adjoining these on the right and left are two saloons adorned with frescoes.

ENTRANCE HALL: left, 1. *Cabanel*, Fall of man; right, 2. *A. Müller*, Mahomet's entry into Mecca. — Room to the left. Wall of the entrance: *3. *G. Richter*, Construction of the Pyramids. To the right: 4. *Otto*, Belshazzar's banquet at Susa; *5. *Kaulbach*, Battle of Salamis; 6. *Foltz*, Age of Pericles; 7. *Hiltensperger*, Olympian Games; 8. *A. Müller*, **Wedding of Alexander the Great** at Susa; 9. *Conräder*, Fall of Carthage; 10. *Joh. Schraudolph*, Nativity; 11. *Gunkel*, Battle of Arminius; 12. *Hiltensperger*, Age of Augustus; 13. **Hauschild**, Crucifixion; 14. **Deger**, Resurrection. — Room to the right. Entrance-wall: 15. *Köckert*, Haroun al-Raschid. On the left: 16. *F. Kaulbach*, Coronation of Charlemagne; 17. *Echter*, Battle on the Lechfeld; 18. *Schwoiser*, Henry IV. at Canossa; 19. *Piloty*, Godfrey de Bouillon; 20. *Foltz*, Frederick Barbarossa and Henry the Lion; 21. *Ramberg*, Emp. Frederick II. at Palermo; 22. *Kreling*, Coronation of Lewis the Bavarian; 23. *Schnorr*, Luther at Worms; 24. *Piloty*, Queen Elizabeth of England; 25. *Piloty*, Elector Maximilian I. founding the Catholic League; 26. *Kotzebue*, Peter the Great founding St. Petersburg; 27. *A. Adam*, Battle of Zorndorf; 28. *Pauwels*, Louis XIV. receiving a Genovese embassy; 29. *E. Hess*, Washington; 30. *P. Hess*, Battle of Leipsic.

The 'loggie' and side-rooms contain busts and portraits of great men.

On both sides of the Maximilianeum lie the ***Gasteig Promenades**, laid out under King Max II. from the designs of *Effner*, and commanding beautiful views. They extend up the Isar (*'Am Gasteig'*) to the Ludwigs-**Brücke** (p. 192), and down (*'Maximilians-Anlagen'*) to Brunnthal and **Bogenhausen** (p. 193). In the Maximilians-Anlagen, opposite the Prinz-Regenten-Str. (p. 149), is the *Luitpold Terrace* (Pl. H, 4), constructed in **1894 and** affording a fine view of the city. — To the E. of the Maximilianeum is the suburb of *Haidhausen*, with the Gothic **Church of St. John** (Pl. H, 6), erected in 1852-74; central tower, 286 ft. high. The interior, without aisles, has groined vaulting, marble altars, and stained-glass windows in the choir.

———

The handsome *Brienner-Strasse*, 3/4 M. long, leads **to the W. from the Odeons-Platz** to the Propylæa and the Glyptothek. The Wittelsbacher-Platz, on the right, is adorned with the equestrian ***Statue of Elector Maximilian I.** (Pl. E, 3; d. 1651), founder and chief of the Roman Catholic League, and victor at the Weisse Berg near Prague, designed by *Thorwaldsen* in 1839, and cast by *Stiglmayer* with the metal of captured Turkish cannon. — Count Arco-Zinneberg's Palace, Wittelsbacher-Platz 1, contains a rare and interesting **Collection of Antlers* (adm., see p. 142).

At the E. end of the Maximilians-Platz (p. 164) is a *Statue of Schiller* by Widnmann (1863). To the right, farther on, is the red **Wittelsbach Palace** (Pl. E, 3), in the mediæval English pointed style, built in 1843-50 from plans by *Gärtner*, the residence of Lewis I. **in 1848-68**, now that of Prince Ludwig, the present heir to the throne, and **Prince** Arnulf. Part of it is shown on application to the castellan (to the right in the court). Fine court and staircase.

In the Gabelsberger-Str., a little to the N.E., is the Protestant *Church of St. Mark* (Pl. E, 3), erected by Gottgetreu in the Gothic style in 1873-77.

In the *Carolinen-Platz* (Pl. D, 3) rises an **Obelisk**, 105 ft. in height, cast almost entirely of the metal of captured guns, 31 tons in weight, and erected by Lewis I. in 1833 to the memory of 30,000 Bavarians who had perished in the Russian war.

At No. 3, Carolinen-Platz, in the garden-building, to the right, is the **Lotzbeck Collection of Sculptures and Paintings**, transferred in 1890 from the Château of Weyhern to Munich (adm., see p. 143; catalogue 30 pf.).

CENTRAL SALOON. Sculptures: 1. *Halbig*, King Lewis I.; °2. *Thorwaldsen*, Venus; 3. *Hoyer*, Psyche; *Troschel*, 7. Adonis, 8. Zethus and Amphion, 9. Perseus and Andromeda, 10. Bellerophon and Pegasus (four reliefs). Paintings: °11. *Riedel*, Sakuntala; *Consoni*, 14. The Muses, 15. Dante and Virgil in the Inferno; *Ary Scheffer*, 16. Faust and Gretchen, 17. Walpurgisnacht; *B.* and *F. Adam*, 20. Stable, 21. Hunt; 24. *Schiavoni*, Melancholy; 25. *Gail*, Storming of a Spanish cloister; 26. *Catel*, Burial of a Crusader. — LEFT WING. Sculptures: 28. *Troschel*, Sleeping maiden; 29. *Holbeck*, Rape of Proserpine (relief). Modern pictures: 30. *Manuel*, Baron C. L. von Lotzbeck; *Rottmann*, 37. Untersberg, 38. Perugia; 39. *Kirner*, Raphael visiting Michael Angelo; 40. *Simonsen*, Fight with pirates; *Bürkel*, 41. Village-smithy, 49. Mountain-pasture; 45-48. *Kunz*, Cattle; 51. *Marko*, Death of Adonis. Old pictures: 97. *Antonello da Messina*, Portrait of a man; 102. *Italian School* (ca. 1630), Portrait of a woman; 98. *Lor. Lotto* (?), Rest on the Flight into Egypt; 99. *Ang. Bronzino* (?), Same subject; 100. *Torbido*, Portrait of a man; 101. *Jac. Bassano*, Portrait of a woman. — RIGHT WING. Sculptures: 55. *Tenerani*, Flora. Modern pictures: °60. *Riedel*, Medea; 61. *Morgenstern*, Rorschach; 64. *A. Adam*, Arabian horses; 65. *Bayer*, Hora; *Catel*, 66. Illumination, 67. In a gondola; °68. *Dias*, Girl in a landscape; 71, 72. *Carl Werner*, Venetian scene; 76. *Maes-Canini*, Italian peasant family; 77. *Bayer*, Erwin Column in Strassburg Cathedral; *P. Hess*, 78. Engagement between French and Cossacks, 79. Scene on the Loire; 83. *Pollack*, Girl reading. Old pictures: 89. *Cologne School* (ca. 1530), Portrait of a man; 94. *Livens*, Portrait of a boy; 95. *Teniers the Younger*, Peasant with a hare; 91. *Upper German School*, Princess Elizabeth, daughter of Emp. Ferdinand I. (1534); 96. *School of Giotto* (ca. 1360), St. Peter.

The Barer-Strasse on the right leads to the —

****Old Pinakothek** ('Repository of Pictures', from the Greek; Pl. D, 2; adm., see p. 143; reached by tramway-lines 1 & 3, p. 140), erected in 1826-36 by *Klenze* in the Renaissance style. The building is 500 ft. long, 90 ft. wide, and 90 ft. high. On the S. side, on the **attic story above**, are twenty-four statues of celebrated painters from sketches by *Schwanthaler*. It contains upwards of 1400 pictures, arranged in periods and schools, in twelve saloons and twenty-three cabinets. Each picture is labelled. Catalogue 1½ *M*, or with 120 photographs 15 *M* (comp. Hirth and Muther's '*Cicerone*', with 188 illustrations, and the section in Morelli's '*Italian Painters*', devoted to the galleries of Munich and Dresden). The cabinets should be visited immediately after the rooms to which they belong, in order to preserve the historical sequence. Director, *Prof. Dr. von Reber.*

ORIGIN OF THE COLLECTION. This fine picture gallery has been formed by the union of three different collections. As early as the 16th and 17th centuries the Bavarian princes were noted for their love of art. Elector Maximilian I. in particular was an enthusiastic admirer of Dürer, and secured at Nuremberg several of that master's finest works. In 1805 this collection was enriched by the removal to Munich of the celebrated Düsseldorf Gallery, founded by the Electors of the Palatinate. This was done to save the collection from being carried off to Paris, and it was afterwards regarded as part of the inheritance of the Palatinate which fell to Bavaria. The numerous examples of Netherlandish masters of the 17th cent., including the fine Rubens collection, formed part of the Düsseldorf Gallery. The third constituent part of the Pinakothek is the *Boisserée Collection*, being works of the Lower Rhenish School rescued by the brothers Sulpice and Melchior Boisserée and their friend Bertram from churches and monasteries suppressed at Cologne in 1805-1810. The addition of this valuable collection to the Pinakothek in 1827 placed it in the foremost **rank as a** gallery for the study of northern art. Under King **Lewis I. the gallery was** further extended by the addition of the Wallerstein collection **in 1828, and** of several valuable works purchased at different times **in Italy**.

The pre-Raphaelite Italian schools **are scantily** represented in **the** Munich Gallery; probably the most important examples are the **Madonna** by *Francesco Francia* (Room VIII, No. 1039) and *Perugino's* **Vision of** St. Bernard (R. **VIII,** No. 1034). The finest of the works by *Raphael* **is** undoubtedly the Madonna of the Tempi family (Cab. XIX, 1050), **painted in his Florentine** period; **the contemporary** Madonna of the **Canigiani family (R.** VIII, 1049) **has suffered greatly from** cleaning, the angels at **the top** having entirely vanished. There exist **several** replicas **of the Madonna della** Tenda (Cab. XIX, 1051; Roman period) at Turin and elsewhere, but the Munich example is **considered the best.** The portrait of Bindo Altoviti (R. VIII, 1052), freely retouched, was formerly regarded as **a** portrait of Raphael himself. Not **one of** the **five** works **ascribed to** *Correggio* is indisputably authenticated. **The best** example **of the** Venetian school is **the** Christ crowned with thorns, by *Titian* (R. IX, 1114). *Murillo's* Beggar Boys (R. XI), perhaps **the** most popular **work** in the gallery, is sure of attention. Early Flemish painting is seen to the greatest advantage in *Rogier* **van der Weyden's** Triptych **(R. II, 101-103) and** St. Luke (R. **II, 100),** *Memling's* **Seven Joys of Mary (Cab.** III, 116), the winged altar-pieces and the triptych **by** *Dierick Bouts* (Cab. III, **107-111),** and the **Adoration of the Magi** ascribed **to Gerard** David **(R. II, 1**18). The Cologne works **of the 15th** and 16th centuries **will chiefly** attract the professional **eye, while** several works **of the Swabian and Franconian schools are of** general interest **and high artistic importance. Promin**ent among these German masters **stands** *Holbein the Elder*, to whom the altar-piece with St. Sebastian (R. III, 209-211) is now rightly ascribed. *Dürer's* **Four** Apostles, or **the** 'Four Temperaments' (R. III, 247, 248), **deserve the** closest study, especially the magnificent St. Paul **in the famous** white robe, unrivalled **in** its plastic modelling. **The** Battle of Arbela (Cab. IV, 290) by *Albrecht Altdorfer* (ca. 1480-1538), remarkable for its almost fantastic excess of realism, the Finding of the Cross (R. III, 267) by the **rare master** *Barthel Beham* **(d.** 1540), and the Portrait (Cab. V, 286) by *Hans Baldung* **Grien are also** worthy of notice. Of the altarpiece formerly attributed to *Grünewald* (R. III, 281 et seq.) **No. 281** alone is by this artist, while the wings are in the style of **Cranach.**

Next to Antwerp and Vienna, Munich best shows the versatility of *Rubens*. Among the eighty-nine pictures formerly catalogued here under **his name are many school-pieces** and mediocre works, but they also include several of his finest creations. The vast range of his genius may be estimated by glancing from the stupendous Last Judgment to the Lion Hunt, from the Battle of the Amazons to the Children with garlands of fruit, from the sketches for the Medici pictures in the Louvre to the Bacchanalian scenes. Rubens's best pupil, *Van Dyck*, is also well represented by several portraits (R. VII, 844, 845). The Descent from the Cross (Cab. VIII, 326) is the finest of the numerous examples of *Rembrandt*. The canvases of *Adrian Brouwer* (Cab. XVI, 879, 883, 885, 893), notable partly for their rarity, the genre-pieces of *Terburg* and *Metsu*, and the humorous subjects of *Jan Steen* also deserve attention. The works of the Italian painters of the 17th cent. generally meet with

```
+----------+---------------------------------------------------------+----------+
| XII.     |                    North.                               | II.Lower |
| French   |                                                         | Rhenish  |
| School.  |                                                         | School.  |
+----------+---------------------------------------------------------+----------+
|          |23|22|21|20|19|18|17|16|15|14|13|12|11|10|9|8|7|6|5|4|3|2|1| I.     |
|          |IX.     |VIII.   |VII.    |VI.     |V.    |IV.   |III.   |Cologne  |
|  X.      |Venet.  |Italian |Flemish |Rubens  |Flem. |Dutch |Upper  |School.  |
| Italian  |School. |School. |School. |Saloon. |Schl. |Schl. |Germ.  |Hall of  |
| School.  |        |        |        |        |      |      |School.|the Foun-|
|          |        |        |        |        |      |      |       | ders.   |
+----------+---------------------------------------------------------+----------+
|          |                   Loggie.                               | Vesti-   |
+----------+---------------------------------------------------------+ bule.    |
| XI.      |                   South.                                |          |
| Neap. &  |                                                         |          |
| Sp. Sch. |                                                         |          |
+----------+---------------------------------------------------------+----------+
```

scant notice, but the Ascensions of *Guido Reni* and *Cignani*, at least, do not merit this fate. The Mourning over the body of Christ, by *N. Poussin* (R. XII, 1321), is a work of great beauty.

Vestibule. Portraits of the founders and enrichers of the gallery from Elector John William (d. 1719) to King Lewis I. (d. 1868). — We pass to the right into Room I.

Lower Rhenish and Early Netherlandish Schools (Rooms I, II; Cab. I-III). — I. Room. To the left: *1. *Meister Wilhelm of Cologne* (?), St. Veronica with the napkin; 3, 4. *In the style of Stephan Lochner*, Saints; 31-33. *Master of the Lyversberg Passion or of the Life of Mary*, The Twelve Apostles; 9-18. *School of Stephan Lochner*, Wings of a shrine from Heisterbach, with scenes from the Annunciation to the Gift of Tongues and Death of the Virgin, and figures of saints.

II. Room. To the right (S. wall): *55, 56, 57. *Master of the Death of the Virgin*, Triptych, in the centre Death of the Virgin, on the wings the donors with their patron-saints. — E. wall: *118. *Gerard David* (?), Adoration of the Magi; 97, 98. *Coxie*, The Virgin Mary, John the Baptist (copies of figures in the Ghent altar-piece by Hubert van Eyck); *134. *Quentin Matsys* (?), Pietà. — N. wall

169, 170. *J. van Hemessen*, Call of Matthew, Isaac blessing Jacob. — W. wall: *101, 102, 103. *Rogier van der Weyden the Elder*, Triptych, in the centre Adoration of the Magi, on the wings Annunciation and Presentation.

'No picture of the master is more imbued with religious feeling; none is more happily arranged and carried out.' — '*The Early Flemish Painters*' by *Crowe and Cavalcaselle*.

Above, 162, 163, 164. *Flemish Master* (ca. 1530), Adoration of the Magi; *100. *Rogier van der Weyden*, St. Luke painting a portrait of the Virgin; above, 139. *Marinus van Roymerswale*, Room of a lawyer (1542). — S. wall: *48, 49, 50. The so-called *Master of the Boisserée St. Bartholomew* or of the *Altar of the Holy Cross* (in the Cologne Museum), Triptych: in the centre SS. Bartholomew, Agnes, and Cecilia; on the wings SS. Christina, James, John, and Margaret.

CABINET I. To the right (W.): 5. *School of Stephan Lochner*, Madonna in a bower of pinks; *Master of the Lyversberg Passion*, 28. Assumption, 27. Visitation. — S. wall: 29. *Cologne Master*, Coronation of the Virgin; *Master of the Lyversberg Passion*, 23. Nativity of the Virgin, 22. Meeting of Joachim and Anna, 34. Crucifixion. — E. wall: *Master of the Lyversberg Passion*, 24. Purification in the Temple, 26. Annunciation, 25. Marriage of the Virgin; 2. *School of Meister Wilhelm*, Virgin enthroned.

CABINET II. To the left (E.): *Flemish School* (ca. 1510), 126. St. George, 125. Madonna; 89, 80-83, 88. *Barth. Bruyn*, Saints; 140. *Patinir*, Crucifixion; 161. *Flemish Master* (ca. 1530), Nativity. — S. wall: 143. *Patinir*(?), St. Rochus; 122. *Netherlands School* (about 1500), Madonna. — W. wall: Portraits, chiefly by unknown masters; 68-72. *B. Bruyn*, Altar-piece; 133. *Quentin Matsys*, Portrait of Jehan Carandolet.

CABINET III. To the left (E.): 110, 111. *Dierick Bouts*, Two wings belonging to the Last Supper in the church of St. Peter at Louvain: Abraham and Melchisedech, and Gathering manna; *107-109. *Dierick Bouts*, Triptych, in the centre Adoration of the Magi, at the sides SS. John the Baptist and Christopher; *115. *Memling*, John the Baptist; 155. *Gossaert*, surnamed *Mabuse*, Madonna and Child. — S. wall: 151. *J. Mostaert* (?), Repose on the Flight into Egypt; 146, 147. *Herri met de Bles*, Adoration of the Magi; *Lucas van Leyden*, *148. Virgin with Mary Magdalen and St. John, 149. Annunciation. — W. wall: 117. *Gerard David*, Marriage of St. Catharine; 114. *Hugo van der Goes* (?), Annunciation. — *116. *Memling*, The seven Joys of Mary (1480).

'We feel at once, in looking at this picture, the absence of linear perspective and atmosphere; yet the episodes are so complete in themselves, and so cleverly arranged and executed, that they produce a deep impression; and the colours are so bright, so clear, and so admirably contrasted, that we necessarily yield to a grateful sense of rest'. — *C. & C.*

145. *Herri met de Bles*, Annunciation; 138. *M. van Roymerswale* (after *Matsys*), Money-changer and his wife (1538).

UPPER GERMAN SCHOOLS (R. III; Cab. IV, V). — III. ROOM.

To the left (E.): *240, *241, *242. *Dürer*, The Paumgartner altarpiece, a triptych, in the centre the Nativity, on each side the donors in armour; above, 278. *Lucas Cranach the Elder*, The Woman taken in adultery (half of it a later enlargement); 197, 198, 199, 200. *Holbein the Elder*, Crown of Thorns, Ecce Homo, Bearing of the Cross, Resurrection. — S. wall: *M. Schaffner*, 214. Annunciation, 215. Presentation in the Temple; 231. *M. Wohlgemut*, Crucifixion; 258. *Style of Hans von Kulmbach*, Adoration of the Magi and Descent of the Holy Ghost; *M. Schaffner*, 216. Pouring out of the Holy Ghost, 217. Death of the Virgin; 229. *M. Wohlgemut*, Resurrection; above, 259. *Style of H. von Kulmbach*, Resurrection of Christ and Coronation of the Virgin. — W. wall: 209, *210, *211. *H. Holbein the Elder*, Triptych: centre, Martyrdom of St. Sebastian; at the sides, SS. Barbara and Elizabeth.

This work may be styled the artist's master-piece, and far transcends any of his previous efforts. Without excessive or violent motion, the picture is full of dramatic power. The head of the saint is well individualised and expressive of a high degree of patient suffering, while the nude body shows careful observation of nature. See '*Holbein und seine Zeit*', by Professor *Alfred Woltmann*.

175, 176. *Zeitblom*, SS. Margaret and Ursula; 225. *H. Burgkmair*, Esther before Ahasuerus; *Holbein the Elder*, 201. Purification in the Temple, 204. Nativity, 202. Annunciation, 203. Visitation; 254-257. *H. von Kulmbach*, Saints; 238. *Dürer*, Pietà (1500); above, 267. *Barthel Beham*, Invention of the Cross; 205, 206, 207, 208. Works by *Holbein the Elder*. — N. wall: *Dürer*, **247. SS. Peter and John, **248. SS. Paul and Mark (completed in 1526).

The four Apostles are at the same time prototypes of the four 'Complexions', St. John representing the melancholic, St. Peter the phlegmatic, St. Paul the choleric, and St. Mark the sanguine temperament. The panel with SS. Paul and Mark is the finer of the two. St. Paul is one of the most majestic figures ever conceived by the master, and appears as if just on the point of battling for his faith with word or blow. A great deal more labour in the details has been bestowed upon St. Paul than upon the other figures, and it is also the best-preserved. The white mantle is a marvel of plastic painting, and is admirably shaded. — '*Dürer*', by *Prof. Moriz Thausing*.

233. *Hans Pleydenwurff*, Crucifixion; 297a, 297b. *Tyrolese Master of about 1480 (M. Pacher?)*, SS. Gregory and Augustine; 188, 189. *B. Strigel*, Portraits of the Rehlingen family, patricians of Augsburg; *281. *Matthias Grünewald*, Conversion of St. Mauritius; 282-285. Four altar-wings belonging to the last, with SS. Mary Magdalen, Lazarus, Chrysostom, and Martha, by an unknown master; *Hans Pleydenwurff*, 234. Marriage of St. Catharine, 234a. Adoration of the Holy Child. — E. wall: 271. *L. Cranach the Elder*, Death of Lucretia; 244. *Dürer*, Same subject (1518); 222. *Burgkmair*, St. John in Patmos; above, 193-196. Works by *Holbein the Elder*.

CABINET IV. To the left (E.): 295. *M. Feselen*, Siege of Alesia (Burgundy) by Julius Cæsar; 292. *Ulrich Apt*, Pietà; 221. *H. Burgkmair*, SS. Liborius and Eustace. — 270. *Cranach*, Madonna; *A. Dürer*, 250. Mater dolorosa (1515), *249. Jacob Fugger the Rich;

177. Zeitblom, St. Bridget. — W. wall: 228. *Jörg Breu*, Scipio's victory at Zama; **183**. *B. Strigel*, David with the head of Goliath; *A. Altdorfer*, *289. The chaste Susanna, 290. Alexander's victory at Arbela.

CABINET V. To the left (E.): 245. *A. Dürer*, SS. Joachim and Joseph (from the so-called Jabach altar-piece); *213. *H. Holbein the Younger*, Portrait of Sir Bryan Tuke, treasurer of King Henry VIII.; *A. Dürer*, **239. Portrait of himself (dated 1500, but shown by the style of execution to be of later date), *236. Portrait of Oswolt Krell (1499); 191. *B. Strigel*, Emp. Maximilian I.; **246**. *A. Dürer*, SS. Simeon and Lazarus (from the Jabach altar-piece). — S. wall: 286. *H. Baldung Grien*, Pfalzgrave Philip the Warlike. 292a. *Ulrich Apt*, Triptych: in the centre, SS. Narcissus and Matthew in a landscape; at the sides, Virgin and Child and St. John. 220. *M. Schongauer*, Portrait of himself (1483; a later copy by *H. Burgkmair*); 287. *H. Baldung Grien*, Margrave Bernhard III. of Baden. — W. wall: 223, 224. *School of Ratisbon*, William IV., Duke of Bavaria, and his consort Maria Jacoba (1526); 293. *A. Altdorfer*, Mountain-landscape; *L. Cranach the Elder*, 275. Moses with Aaron and two Prophets, 272. Madonna; *243. *A. Dürer*, Portrait of his teacher Wohlgemut (1516); 291. *A. Altdorfer*, Virgin and Child, with angels playing on musical instruments; 294. *M. Feselen*, Siege of Rome by Porsenna; *212. *H. Holbein the Younger*, Half-length of Derich Born (1530); *237. *A. Dürer*, Portrait of a young man (Hans Dürer?); 174. *In the style of M. Schongauer*, Nativity; 288. *A. Altdorfer*, St. George fighting the dragon.

DUTCH SCHOOL (R. IV; Cab. VI-XI). — IV. ROOM. To the left (E.): 640, 641. *Weenix*, Still-life; 317. *Nic. Eliasz Pickenoy*, Admiral Tromp. — S. wall: 315, 316. *B. van der Helst*, Portraits; *579. *Jan Wynants*, Landscape by morning-light, accessories by *A. van de Velde*; *359. *Frans Hals* (more likely of the *Flemish School?*), Family-portraits; 645. *Weenix*, Poultry; 313. *M. J. Mierevelt*, Portrait; 319, 320. *J. van Ravesteyn*, Portraits; *580. *Wynants*, Landscape by evening-light, accessories by *A. van de Velde*; 307. *Bloemaert*, Raising of Lazarus; 322. *De Vries*, Portrait. — W. wall: 338, 339. *F. Bol*, So-called portrait of Govert Flinck and his wife; 554. *J. van der Meer of Haarlem* (?), Forest-scene; 343. *G. Flinck*, Soldiers gaming; *Honthorst*, 312. Cimon and Pera, 310. St. Peter liberated from prison; 646. *Weenix*, Boar-hunt; *Rembrandt*, *333 (?). Portrait of himself, 325. Portrait of a man in Turkish costume (1633); 335, 336. *Lievens*, Portraits of old men; 487. *A. van de Velde*, Landscape with cattle by evening-light; 350. *G. van den Eeckhout*, Isaac blessing Jacob. — N. wall: 647. *M. de Hondecoeter*, Cock-fight; 451. *A. van der Werff*, Mary Magdalen; 332. *Rembrandt*, Abraham's sacrifice (studio-copy); 594. *N. Berchem*, Landscape with ruins; *324. *Rembrandt*, Holy Family (1631); 644. *Weenix*, Game; 588. *J. Both*, Autumnal scene in Italy; 648. *Hondecoeter*, Cock-fight; 609. *Beerstraten*, Storm at sea. — E. wall: 566.

A. van Everdingen, Norwegian landscape with waterfall; **592.** *N. Berchem*, Laban and Jacob.

Cabinet VI. To the left (E.): *A. Cuyp*, **475.** Landscape, **474.** Officer with a grey horse; 530. *Es. van de Velde*, Skaters. — S. wall: **491.** *A. van de Velde*, Cattle; **471.** *P. Potter*, Cows and goats; **490.** *A. van de Velde*, Shepherd at a well. — W. wall: *472. *Paul Potter*, Cattle; 541, 540. *S. van Ruysdael*, Landscapes; *Isaac van Ostade*, *378. Winter-scene, 381. Village-fair; **321.** *J. van Ravesteyn*, Portrait; 314. *M. J. Mierevelt*, Portrait of himself; *J. van Goyen*, 535. Landscape, 537. View of Leyden.

Cabinet VII. To the left (E.): 551. *Jac. van Ruysdael*, **Group of oaks and a torrent**; *424. *Gabr. Metsu*, Twelfth Night; *542. *Sal. van Ruysdael*, River-scene; 624. *J. de Heem*, Flowers; 629. *A. van Beyeren*, Still-life. — S. wall: 597. *N. Berchem*, 587. *J. Both*, Landscapes. — W. wall: *548. *Jac. van Ruysdael*, Marshy forest; ***478.** *K. du Jardin*, The sick goat; *544. *Jac. van Ruysdael*, **The sandy road (1667)**; 610. *L. Bakhuysen*, Antwerp harbour; 351, 352. *J. Backer*, Portraits.

Cabinet VIII. To the left (E.): *Rembrandt*, *331. Adoration of the Shepherds (1646), *326. Descent from the Cross, *327. Crucifixion (1633); 348. *G. van den Eeckhout*, Jesus teaching in the Temple. — S. wall: *583, 584. *J. Both*, Landscapes with Mercury and Juno; *623. *J. de Heem*, Fruit; 401. *G. Dou*, Old woman cutting bread; *369. *A. van Ostade*, Peasants drinking and **smoking**. — W. wall: *Rembrandt*, ***328.** Ascension (1636), *329. **Resurrection**, *330. Entombment (1639).

This remarkable series of scenes from the history of Christ (Nos. 326-331) was executed in 1633-39 for Prince Frederick Henry, Stadtholder of the Netherlands. The finest of the series is the Entombment, which is painted with a broad and vigorous touch, and is of ample, dry, and granulated impasto. The colouring in general is sombre, and in the background and the figures in the foreground there are shades of **brown** which recall the Spanish colourists. A powerful effect is produced by the group on which the high light falls, where the colours have been laid on with great freedom. — '*Rembrandt; sa Vie et ses Œuvres*', by *C. Vosmaer*.

Cabinet IX. To the left (E.): 372. *A. van Ostade*, Merry peasants; *545. *Jac. van Ruysdael*, Forest-scene; 577. *J. Wynants*, Landscape; *409. *F. van Mieris the Elder*, Oyster-breakfast; 371. *A. van Ostade*, Boors brawling; 392. *J. Steen*, Physician feeling the pulse of a patient; *G. Dou*, 403. Old woman eating, 396. Girl with a light at a window, 402. Old woman at a window; 370. *A. van Ostade*, Merry peasants; 546. *J. van Ruysdael*, Forest-scene; 373. *A. van Ostade*, Peasants drinking. — S. wall: *Isaac van Ostade*, 377. Scene on the ice, 376. Interior of a cottage; 353. *S. de Koninck*, Jesus in the Temple; 510. *Ph. Wouwerman*, Grey horse. — W. wall: 419. *F. van Mieris*, Trumpeter; 477. *K. du Jardin*, Sheep and goats; 425. *G. Metsu*, Cook in the larder; *388. *G. Terburg*, Trumpeter bringing a lover-letter; 539. *J. van Ruysdael*, Landscape;

G. Dou, 398. Woman selling herrings; *397. Portrait of himself; *389. *G. Terburg*, Boy with a dog.

CABINET X. To the left (E.): *423. *F. van Mieris*, Lady at her mirror; 407. *G. Dou*, Lady at her toilet; 391. *J. Steen*, Card-players quarrelling; *F. van Mieris*, *415. Lady playing the lute, *417. Lady in a swoon, *414. Lady with a parrot; 614. *J. van der Heyden*, Street-scene; *G. Dou*, 393. Old painter at an easel, 399. Hermit. — S. wall: *G. Dou*, 395. Old market-woman, 408, 400. Hermits; *550. *J. van Ruysdael*, Waterfall; *361. *Th. de Keyser*, Man and wife; *628. *A. van Beyeren*, Still-life; 374. *A. van Ostade*, Man drinking. — W. wall: 404. *G. Dou*, Old **woman combing** a boy's hair; 553. *J. van der Meer van Haarlem*, Margin of a forest; 427. *Slingeland*, Cradle; *G. Dou*, *394. Quack, *405. Girl emptying a can; 627, 622. *J. de Heem*, Flowers and fruit; *F. van Mieris*, *420. Officer asleep, 422. Boor cutting tobacco; 549. *J. van Ruysdael*, Thaw in the village.

CABINET XI. To the left (E.): *Ph. Wouwerman*, 503. Watering horses, 501. Stable; 488. *A. van de Velde*, Ferry; 652, 653. *J. van Huysum*, Fruit and flowers; *582. *J. Wynants*, Landscape; *Ph. Wouwerman*, *496. Deer-hunt, 499. Leaving the stable; 513. Draught of fishes. — S. wall: 506. *Ph. Wouwerman*, Battle of Nördlingen; 613 **Willem van de Velde the** *Younger*, **Calm sea**; 436. *Eglon van der Neer*, **Lady in a faint**; 567. *A. van Everdingen*, Storm at sea; 507. *Ph. Wouwerman*, **Plundering of a village**. — W. wall: 468. *W. van Mieris the Younger*, Fishmonger; 505. *Ph. Wouwerman*, Scene on the ice; *651. *J. van Huysum*, Fruit; *426. *Pieter de Hooch*, **Interior** with woman reading; *Ph. Wouwerman*, 500. Waggoners at a ferry, 508. **Sportsmen** resting, 502. Watering horses; 625. *J. de Heem*, **Fruit**; 406. *Dou*, Woman baking cakes.

FLEMISH SCHOOL (RR. V-VII.; Cab. XII-XVI). — V. ROOM. To the left (E.): 786. *Rubens*, Portrait of a young **man** (after *Joost van Cleve*); *813. *J. Jordaens*, The satyr and the peasant; 871. *G. de Crayer*, **Portrait**. — S. wall: *663. *Neufchatel*, Neudorfer, the mathematician, and his son; 934. *K. E. Biset*, Picture-gallery **(the pictures on** the walls by various Antwerp artists); 869. *G. de Crayer*, **Madonna** enthroned with saints; 664, 665. *Neufchatel*, **Portraits**; **944.** *F. Millet*, **Landscape**; 961. *P. de Vos*, Bear-hunt. — W. wall: *Frans Snyders*, 957. Two young lions pursuing a roe-deer, 956. **Lioness killing a wild** boar; 969. *P. Boel*, **Still-life**. — N. wall: 812. *C. de Vos*, **Family** von Hutten; *814. *J. Jordaens*, **As the old cock crows, the young one** learns; **925.** *D. Teniers the Younger*, Fair at Florence (after Callot); *955. *Snyders*, Kitchen-piece. — E. wall: *729. *Rubens* and *J. Brueghel*, Madonna **in a** garland of flowers; 954. *Snyders*, Poultry-dealer.

VI. ROOM, with the adjoining Cabinet XII. (see p. 166), contains exclusively works **by** *Rubens* or from his studio. To the left (E.): **734. Lion-hunt. — S. wall: **737. Perdition of lost souls;

724. Seneca; *752. Meleager and Atalanta; **782. Portraits of **Rubens and his first wife**, Isabella Brant; 726. Martyrdom of St. Lawrence; *735. The Last **Judgment** (the large picture); *794. Portrait of his second wife, Helena Fourment; 750. SS. Peter and Paul; **757. Massacre of **the Innocents**; *784. Earl and Countess of Arundel; *728. Seven **children with festoons of fruit**; *754. Drunken **Silenus**. — W. wall: 787. **Philip IV. of Spain**; *798. **Rubens and Helena Fourment in a garden**; *799. **Portrait of a scholar**; 749. **The Trinity**; *800. **Portrait of Dr. van Thulden**; *744. **Samson betrayed by Delilah**; 788. **Elizabeth of Bourbon, first wife of Philip IV. of Spain**. — N. wall: *797. **Helena Fourment and her son**; 731. **Diana**; *795. **Portrait of Helena Fourment**; 730. **Nymphs surprised by satyrs**; 739. **The woman of the Apocalypse**; *746. **Christ and the penitents**; **759. **Pastoral scene**; *791. **Franciscan**; *748. **Crucifixion**; 790. **Cardinal Don Ferdinand of Spain**; 736. **Fall of the Angels**; **727. **Rape of the daughters of Leucippus by Castor and Pollux**; 725. **Drunkenness** and Wantonness **overcome by Virtue and** Temperance. — E. wall: 755. War and Peace; 753. **Reconciliation of** the Romans and the Sabines.

Cabinet XII. Contains exclusively pictures by, or attributed to, *Rubens* (comp. R. VI, p. 165). To the left (E.): 762. St. Christopher. — 838. The Last Judgment (the small picture).

'Very happily and with a proper feeling of his own powers, Rubens has here given only a corner in the background to the Blessed, whose heavenly calm and ethereal existence he was incapable of expressing; and he has devoted the whole of the remaining space to the fall of the Damned, his true sphere.... The whole produces an admirable effect by the broad manner in which the light is managed. The colouring is powerful, but not extravagant; the treatment particularly **easy and** clever'. — '*Life of Rubens*', by *Prof. Waagen*.

758. Pietà. — S. wall: 743. Satyrs; *745. **The chaste Susanna**; 733. Conversion of Paul; *761. Landscape, with rainbow; 760. Browsing cattle; 732. Destruction of Sennacherib's army. — W. wall: *793. Portrait **of a girl**. — **742. Battle of the **Amazons**.

'The admirable effect of the whole is increased by a decided and masterly arrangement of the light; the colouring is forcible without being overcharged, and the execution of the principal parts **must be called** *careful* for Rubens. In the whole range of **modern** art there exists no other historical battle-piece worthy of being compared with Raphael's Battle of Constantine; and in fact it has **the** advantage over the latter in the well-planned concentration **of interest**, and in the contrast afforded by **the male and** female figures, which **is** admirably employed.' — *Waagen*.

792. Old woman; *780. Mourning for Decius (sketch for a picture in the Liechtenstein Gallery, Vienna); *764-779. Sketches of events in the life of Maria de' Medici, for the pictures painted in 1621-26 for the Luxembourg in Paris, now in the Louvre.

VII. Room. To the left (E.): *A. van Dyck*, 848. The organist Liberti of Antwerp, 827. Rest on the Flight into Egypt, 836. Portrait of Marchese Spinola (unfinished); 939. *J. van Arthois*, Landscape. — S. wall: *Van Dyck*, 828. SS. Mary and John with the body of Christ, 834. Petel, the sculptor, 823. Martyrdom of St. Sebastian; 781.

Snyders, Boar-hunt, the figures by *Rubens*; 832. *A. van Dyck* and *P. Snayers*, Henry IV. of France defeating the Catholic League; *A. van Dyck*, *822. Susanna at the ba**th**, *833. Portrait of himself, 866. Portrait of Queen Henrietta Maria of England (studio-piece). — W. wall: 868. *G. Kneller* (after **Van Dyck**), Queen Henrietta **Maria** of England; *A. van Dyck*, *846. T**he** painter Jan de Wael and his wife, 849. **Portrait** of Mary Ruthven, Van Dyck's wife; 964. *J. Fyt*, Bear-hunt. *Van Dyck*, 847. Malery the engraver, *830. **Pietà, 835. Portrait of Marchese** Mirabella; 965. *J. Fyt*, Boar-hunt. — N. wall: *A. van Dyck*, 842. **Duchess of Croy**, *843. Portrait, *841. **Duke of Croy,** *824. St. Sebastian; 968. *P. Boel*, Dog watching dead game; *Van Dyck*, *839, 840. So-called Burgomaster of **Antwerp and his wife,** *837. Duke Wolfgang Wilhelm of the Palatinate; *J. Fyt*, **963. Roe** pursued by dogs, *966. Still-life. — E. wall: *A. van Dyck*, *844, *845. The sculptor Colyn de Nole and his wife, *826. **Holy** Family; 940. *Arthois*, Landscape.

Cabinet XIII. To the left (E.): *Van **Dyck*** (sketches), **856.** General Tilly, 851. Maria de' Medici, 859. Palame**desz**, the painter, 860. **V**an Uden, **the** painter, 857. John, Count of **Nassau**; 708, 709. *H. van Balen* and *J. Brueghel*, **Spring**, Summer. — S. wall: 921. *D. Teniers the* **Younger**, Apes carousing; 831. *Van Dyck*, Pietà, 719. *Vinkboons*, **Bearing of the Cross;** 922. *Teniers*, **Monkeys.** — W. wall: *A. van Dyck*, **854. Gustavus** Adolphus; **844. Wallen**stein, 853. Margaret **of Lorraine, 852.** Prince Thomas of Carignan, **858.** Cæsar Alexander **Scaglia**; **710,** 711. *Van Balen* and *Brueghel*, **Autumn,** Winter.

Cabinet XIV. To the left (E.): 697, 682, 689. *J. Brueghel the* **Elder**, Landscapes; *909. *Teniers the Younger*, Violin-player; 850. **Van Dyck,** Snayers, the painter; 675. *Bril*, Landscape; 919. *Teniers*, **Witchcraft.** — S. wall: 713, 712. *Balen* and *Brueghel*, Nymphs **fishing, Nymphs** and game; 705. *Brueghel* and *Rubens*, Flora. — W. wall: *Teniers*, 917. **Lot and his** daughters, 912. Village-concert; *J. Brueghel*, 704. **Madonna with a** garland of flowers, 683. Landscape; 715. *Van Balen* and *Brueghel*, Feast of the Gods.

Cabinet XV. To the left (E.): *Teniers*, 902, 903. Tavernscenes, 926-929. Old picture-gallery at **Brussels**; 894. *A. Brouwer*, Peasants singing. — W. wall: 916. **Teniers**, Municipal guardroom; *880. *Brouwer*, Village-surgeon; **Teniers**, 911. Peasant couple, 905. Peasant wedding.

Cabinet XVI. To the **left** (E.): *879. *Brouwer*, Card-players quarrelling; *907. **Teniers**, Boors drinking; 887, 889, 890, 895, 896. *Brouwer*, Tavern-**scenes**; 945. *Millet*, Italian coast-scene. — S. wall: *Brouwer*, 882, 883, 884, 891, 892. Scenes of peasantlife, *885. Village-surgeon. — W. wall: 904. *Teniers*, Villagetavern; 888. *Brouwer*, **Card**-players; 825. *A. van Dyck*, Crucifixion; *910. *Teniers*, Cottage-interior; 946. *Millet*, Italian landscape; *893. *Brouwer*, Soldiers gaming.

ITALIAN SCHOOL (RR. **VIII-X**; Cab. XVII-XX). — **VIII.** ROOM. To the left (E.): 984a, b. *Agnolo Gaddi*, SS. Nicholas and Julian; *1033. *Cima da Conegliano*, **Madonna with Mary Magdalen and St. Jerome**; **1044.** *School of Leonardo da Vinci*, Madonna; 1016a. *Lorenzo di Credi*, **Virgin and Child**, with an angel, an early work; *1083. *Lor. Lotto*, **Marriage of St. Catharine**; 1008. *Filippino Lippi*, Christ appearing to the Virgin. — S. wall: *1011, 1012, 1013. *Dom. Ghirlandajo*, **Madonna with SS. Catharine and Lawrence**; 1057. *Mariotto Albertinelli*, Annunciation; **1010.** *Sandro Botticelli*, **Pietà**; *1080. *Garofalo*, Pietà; **1026.** *Marco Palmezzano*, **Madonna and Saints**. — W. wall: no number, *Luca Signorelli*, Madonna (studio-piece); 1022a. *Liberale da Verona*, Pietà; 1017. *Lorenzo di Credi*, **Holy Family**; 1085. *Rocco Marconi*, St. Nicholas with John the Baptist and St. Philip; 1066. *A. del Sarto*, **Holy Family** (injured); **1095.** *Correggio*, Madonna with SS. Ildefons and Jerome (retouched). — N. wall: **1034. *Perugino*, **The Virgin** appearing to St. Bernard; **1035.** *Perugino*, **Virgin adoring the Holy Child**; *1052. *Raphael*, **Portrait of Bindo Altoviti**, probably painted in Rome about 1512 (injured); 1045. *Bern. Luini*, St. Catharine; *1049. *Raphael*, **Holy Family**, of the Canigiani family; 1087. *Seb. del Piombo* (?), Portrait of a priest; 1073. *Sodoma*, Madonna; 1060. *Innocenzo da Imola*, Virgin and saints. — *1039. *Franc. Francia*, Madonna **in a bower** of roses.

This panel 'affords a rare example of dignity in Francia's works; it is also distinguished by a more tender blending and harmony of silvery tone than any we have hitherto met with'. — '*History of Painting in North Italy*', by *Crowe and Cavalcaselle.*

1009. *Filippino Lippi* (?), Pietà. — E. wall: 1086. *Bissolo* (?), The relatives of Christ; **1006.** *Fra Filippo Lippi*, Madonna; **1040.** *F. Francia*, **Madonna and Child** with two angels; 1005. *Fra Filippo Lippi*, Annunciation; *1031. *M. Basaiti*, Madonna with SS. Sebastian and Jerome; 987, 988. *Spinello Aretino*, **Two altar-pieces** with five saints in each.

IX. ROOM. To the left (E.): 1127. *Jac. Tintoretto* (?), **Vesalius, the anatomist**; *1112. *Titian*, Charles V. (1548); 1147. *Jac. Bassano*, **Entombment**. — S. wall: *Paolo Veronese* (?), **1134.** Cupid with two tiger-hounds, **1135.** Portrait of a lady in brown silk; 1117. *Franc. Vecellio*, Madonna and saints; 1116. *Titian*, Venus initiating a girl in the service of Bacchus (studio-piece); 1128. *Jac. Tintoretto* (?), **Nobleman introducing his son to the Doge.** — W. wall: 1152. *Leandro Bassano*, Christ with Mary and Martha; 1113. *Titian*, Madonna (injured); 1149. *Jac. Bassano*, **Moses smiting the rock.** — *1109. *Titian*, **Madonna with Jesus** and John the Baptist.

'The head and foot of St. John, and the head of the Virgin are damaged by abrasion and retouching; yet the picture is still a lovely one of Titian, and the landscape to the right, with blue mountains and nearer ranges dotted with church and campanile, is beautifully painted'. — '*Titian*', by *Crowe and Cavalcaselle.*

1124. *Moroni*, Portrait; **1115.** *Titian* (?), Venetian noble. — **1108.** *Palma Vecchio*, **Holy** Family.

'The flesh tints are flayed, and there is some retouching in this little picture, but the figures and action are still attractive by their grace; and the colours almost equal those of Titian in richness and power'. *C. & C.*

N. wall: *1123. *Moretto* (more likely *Moroni*?), **Priest**; 1275, 1274. *Rotari*, Genre-scenes; *School of Jac. Tintoretto*, **1132**. Portrait of Grimani, Venetian admiral, 1129. Annunciation; *1110. *Titian*, Vanity of earthly things (an early work, damaged); 1239. *B. Strozzi*, The Tribute Money; **1111.** *Titian*, Portrait of a man; 1156. *Palma Giovane*, Adoration of the Shepherds. — *1114. **Titian**, Christ crowned with thorns (of his latest period).

'It is impossible to conceive better arrangement, greater harmony of lines, or more boldness of movement. Truth in the reproduction of nature in momentary action is combined with fine contrasts of light and shade, and an inimitable richness of tone, in pigment kneaded, grained, and varied in surface beyond anything that we know of this time'. *C. & C.*

1136. *P. Veronese*, The Centurion of Capernaum; 1121. *Paris Bordone* (?), Man offering jewels to a woman; 1155. *Palma Giovane*, Entombment. — E. wall: 1120. *P. Bordone*(?), Portrait. — *1107. *Palma Vecchio* (more likely *Cariani*?), Portrait of a man.

'A noble portrait by Palma Vecchio', probably of the painter himself. 'Whoever he may be, the man is of strong and energetic mould; the glance of his eye is so rapid, open, and expressive as to convey the best impression of nature's instant action; there is a breadth of modelling and a variety of toning beyond measure telling and truthful; and the play of the features is admirable'. *C. & C.*

P. Veronese, 1137. Holy Family (copy ?), 1140. Cleopatra (studio-piece); 1271. *Giov. Batt. Tiepolo*, Adoration of the Magi (1753).

X. ROOM. To the left (E.): 1174. *Guido Reni*, St. Jerome; 1176. *Domenichino*, Susanna at the bath; 1182. *Guercino*, Dido on the funeral pyre; *1211. **Camillo** *Procaccini*, Holy Family; 1215. *Cavaliere d'Arpino*, Madonna. — S. wall: 1194. *Cantassi*, Mary Magdalen borne to Heaven by angels; 1171. *G. Reni*, Apollo flaying Marsyas. — W. wall: 1259. *Cignani*, Assumption. — N. wall: 1054. *After Raphael*, St. Cecilia (original at Bologna); 1105. *Fed. Baroccio*, Mary Magdalen receiving the Eucharist; 1197. *A. Turchi*, Hercules and Omphale; *1170. *G. Reni*, Assumption; 1165. *Lod. Carracci*, Angel appearing to the sleeping St. Francis. — E. wall: 1164. *Lod. Carracci*, Entombment; 1185. *Tiarini*, Rinaldo in the enchanted forest (from Tasso); 1104. *Baroccio*, Christ appearing to Mary Magdalen.

CABINET XVII. To the left (E.): 1023. *Ferrarese School* (about 1480), Madonna enthroned; *989-991. *Fra Angelico*, Legend of SS. Cosmas and Damianus; 992. *Fra Angelico*, The dead Christ; **1040a.** **Leonardo da Vinci** (more likely *School of Verrocchio*?), Madonna and Child; 1000. *Florentine School* (about 1400), St. Jerome; 983. *Giotto*, Last Supper. — S. wall: 1022. *Francesco di Giorgio*, St. Anthony of Padua; *Florentine School*, 1001. The Magi. 999. St. Francis; 1007. *Fra* **Filippo** *Lippi*, Annunciation; 993, 994. *School of Fra Angelico*, Annunciation. — W. wall: *Giotto*, 982. Christ in Hades, 981. Crucifixion; 986. *Lippo Memmi* (?), Assumption; 996, 997. *Florentine School*, Portraits; 1030. *School of Gentile Bellini*, Portrait.

CABINET XVIII. To the left (E.): **995**. *School of Fra Angelico*, Head of a monk (in fresco); 1053. *Raphael*(?), Head **of St. John** on a tile. — S. wall: **1081.** *Garofalo*, Madonna with St. **Michael** and John the Baptist. — W. wall: 1032. *M. Basaiti*, **Descent from** the Cross.

CABINET XIX. To the left (E.): **1078**. *Umbro-Bolognese School* (about 1510), Portrait of a young man (forged **inscription**); 1242. *Salvator Rosa*, Soldiers drinking; 1059. *Girol. del Pacchia*, St. Bernardino. — ****1050**. *Raphael*, Madonna **Tempi (so named from the Casa** Tempi at Florence, where it was purchased by Lewis I. in 1829; much damaged).

Both in tone and execution this beautiful **work is** closely allied **to** the celebrated Madonna of the **House** of Orleans. **The** colours are laid **on** thinly, with a somewhat fuller impasto **in** the whitish light. It is a true touch of nature which makes **the mother** accompany the close embrace with a look of tender affection, **while the child** receives the caress more mechanically **and** gazes **straight out of the picture.** — 'Raffael und Michelangelo', by *Prof. Anton Springer.*

1223. *Sassoferrato*, **Madonna**; **1058**. *Pacchia*, Madonna and angels; 1186. *Franc. Albani*, **Venus** and Adonis. — S. wall: 1038, **1037**. *Raphael* (more probably *Perugino?*), Baptism and Resurrection of Christ; *1094. *Correggio*, Faun playing the flute, **early** work; 1074. *Sodoma*(?), Archangel Michael. — W. wall: **1184**. *B. Gennari*, Salvator Mundi; *1051. *Raphael*, Madonna della **Tenda** (so named from the green curtain; purchased in England by Lewis I. in 1814); 1227. *C. Dolci*, **Mary Magdalen.** — N. **wall:** 1224. *C. Dolci*, Madonna.

CABINET XX. To the left (E.): *Bern. Belotto (Canaletto)*, 1268. The Piazzetta, 1270. Vegetable-market at Venice; *1133. *Paolo Veronese*(?), Jupiter and Antiope; 1145. *Paolo Veronese*, Adoration of the Magi (studio-piece). — S. wall: 1168. *Ann. Carracci*, **Pietà**; 1192. *Lanfranco*, Christ on the Mt. of Olives; 1200. *Cigoli*, St. Francis. — W. wall: 1267. *Belotto (Canaletto)*, Canal Grande at Venice; 1233. *Carlo Maratta* (?), Portrait of a cardinal.

SPANISH MASTERS (chiefly). — XI. ROOM. To the left (N.): **1291**. *Zurbaran*, St. Francis of Assisi; **1254**. *L. Giordano*, The father of the artist; ***1308**. *Murillo*, **Old woman** cleansing a boy's head; 1253. *L. Giordano*, Portrait of himself. — E. wall: 1309. *Clodio Coello*, St. Peter of Alcantara walking **on the sea**; 1280. *Ribera*, Body of St. Andrew removed from **the** cross; 1298. *Ant. Pereda*, **Portrait**; 1281. *Ribera*, Death of Seneca. — S. wall: 1310. *José Antolinez*, The Conception; *Murillo*, *1306. Beggar-boys gambling, 1303. St. Thomas of Villanuova healing a paralytic, *1307. Girls selling fruit; 1279. *Franc.* **Ribalta**, The Virgin and St. John returning from the Sepulchre. — W. wall: *Ribera*, 1285. St. Onuphrius praying, 1282. Egg-dealer; 1300. *Pedro de Moya*, Conversation-piece; *1305. *Murillo*, Two beggar-boys with a puppy;

1284. *Ribera*, St. Bartholomew; 1293. *Velazquez*, Portrait; 1299. *P. de Moya*, Fortune-teller; 1302. *Careño*, Donna Maria **Anna de Austria**. — N. wall: 1292. *Velazquez*(?), Portrait of himself (injured); 1283. *Ribera*, Peter's repentance; **1304. *Murillo*, Two beggar-boys **eating grapes** and melons; 1301. *Alonso Cano*, Vision of St. Anthony of Padua.

XII. ROOM. FRENCH and LATER GERMAN MASTERS. To the left (N.): *1326, 1327. *Claude Lorrain*, Landscapes. — W. wall: 1322. *N. Poussin*, Midas and Bacchus; 1374. *J. Vernet*, Storm at sea; 1340. *Ph. de Champaigne*, Turenne; *1324, *1325. *Claude Lorrain*, Landscapes; *1321. *N. Poussin*, Entombment. — S. wall: 1330. *Le Sueur*, Christ in the house of Lazarus. — E. wall: 1433. *Ant. Graff*, Portrait of himself; 1425. *J. Kupetzky*(?), Portrait of a woman; *Chr. Schwarz*, 1380-82. Madonna in clouds, at the sides SS. Jerome and Catharine, 1379. Family of the artist; 1431. *R. Mengs*, Portrait of himself; 1432. *Ang. Kauffmann*, Portrait of herself.

CABINET XXI. To the left (E.): 1316. *A. Crabeth* (?), Portrait of a young lady; 1331. *Le Sueur*, Mass of St. Louis; 1368. *C. J. Vernet*, Morning by the sea; 1366. *Ant. Pesne*, Girl with straw-hat; 1376. *Chardin*, Cook paring turnips; 1369. *Vernet*, Evening near Rome. — W. wall: 1377. *Greuze*, Head of a girl; 1314. *J. Clouet*, Portrait of a young man; 1315. *François Clouet*, Claude, daughter of Henry II. of France. — N. wall: 1320. *S. Vouet*, Madonna.

CABINET XXII. GERMAN MASTERS, chiefly 17th century. — To the left (E.): *Casp. Netscher*, 1398. Musical entertainment, 1399. Lady with parrot; *Rottenhammer*, 1383. Judgment of Paris, 1384. Last Judgment, 1385. Diana and Actæon; 1426, 1427. *Denner*, Old man and old woman; 1416. *J. H. Roos*, Before the battle; *Netscher*, 1400. Bathsheba at the bath, 1402. Pastoral scene. — S. wall: *1391. *Elsheimer*, Moon-light scene, with the Flight to Egypt as accessory; 1401. *Netscher*, Boy playing the flute; 1404, 1405. *Mignon*, Fruit and flowers; *Rottenhammer*, 1386. Madonna in a landscape, 1387. Boys dancing. — W. wall: 1388. *Rottenhammer*, Marriage at Cana; 1403. *Lingelbach*, Hay-harvest; 1415. *Roos*, Landscape with cattle; 1390. *Elsheimer*, Destruction of Troy.

CABINET XXIII contains a series of religious pictures painted for Elector Palatine Johann Wilhelm by *Adrian van der Werff*, and a few other works by the same hand (440-61, 464, 438, 446).

On the S. side are the *Loggie (entrance from the Platz, to the left), an arcade in twenty-five sections, with frescoes designed by *Cornelius*, illustrating the history of painting in the middle ages, the first thirteen relating to Italian art, the remaining twelve to art in Germany, the Netherlands, and France.

E. SERIES: 1. Dome: *Religion in union with the Arts.* Arabesques; King David (lyric poetry), **Solomon** (architecture), St. Luke (painting), St. Cecilia (music). King Lewis conducted by his genius into the grove of poets and artists; the three heads to the right on the outer arch are Klenze, Cornelius, and Zimmermann. — 2. *The Crusades awaken Art.*

Bernard of Clairvaux preaches the Crusade. Battle of Iconium. Giov. Pisano shows the magistrates of Pisa his design for the Campo Santo. — 3. *Cimabue* (d. 1300). He is taught by Byzantine painters; his **Madonna** brought into the church. — 4. *Giotto* (d. 1337), when a shepherd-boy, becomes Cimabue's pupil; shows his pictures to Pope Benedict XI.; King Robert of Naples visits Giotto; the painter accompanies Pope Clement V. to Avignon. — 5. **Fra** *Angelico da Fiesole* (d. 1455). **Ordination as** Dominican; he paints in the cells of the **monastery; receives the blessing of** Pope Martin V. **after** having painted **a chapel in the Vatican;** shows Duke Cosimo de' **Medici at** Florence the plan **of** the monastery **of St.** Mark; he declines an archiepiscopal see. — 6. *Masaccio* (d. 1443) shows his designs to a cardinal; paints in the church del Carmine at Florence. — 7. *Perugino* (d. 1524), Raphael's teacher. — 8. *Predecessors and Contemporaries of Raphael*. Signorelli's Vision of the Last Judgment. — 9. *Leon. da Vinci*'s birth (d. 1519); Leonardo **as a teacher** and a portrait-painter; his death in the **presence** of Francis I. **of France.** — 10. *Correggio* (d. 1534) among his pupils; allegories. — 11. **Venetian School.** Dürer visits Bellini; Bellini at Constantinople paints the **Sultan and his mistress**; Titian paints Emp. Charles V.; the heads of the **School visit Titian.** — 12. *Michael Angelo* (d. 1563). Allegory in allusion **to his threefold capacity as** painter, sculptor, **and** architect; he paints **the ceiling of the Sistine** Chapel; works as a **sculptor at** night; designs the dome **of St. Peter's.** — 13. *Raphael* (d. 1520) **when a boy** in his father's studio; **enters the school** of Perugino; is **introduced to** Pope Julius II.; paints **in the Stanze of the** Vatican.

W. **Series** (beginning at the end): **1. Allegories** similar to those **in the first loggia on the** E. — 2. Charles Martel's victory over the Saracens **at Tours (732). Boniface** preaches Christianity. Charlemagne surrounded by scholars, **bards, and** poets. — 3. Emp. Henry, the 'founder **of** cities'. The architect Meister Gerhardt delivers **the** model of Cologne cathedral to Bishop Conrad; relics of the Magi; **death of St. Gereon and** St. Ursula. — 4. *Meister Wilhelm of Cologne* (d. 1380). **Vision of the** Virgin; **his** death. Influence on the pictures **of** Holbein **and** other masters. — 5. *John* (d. 1442) and *Hubert* (d. 1426) *van Eyck*: the latter **invents** oil-painting; teaches **his brother** and sister; shows Philip the Good of Burgundy his pictures; instructs Antonello of Messina in the art of oil-painting. Allusions to their celebrated 'Immaculate Lamb'. — *John Memling* (d. 1499) paints in St. John's Hospital at Bruges; his death; vision of the Last Judgment. — 7. *Lucas van Leyden* (d. 1533): drawing on his death-bed. — 8. *Hans Holbein* (d. 1543): the Virgin appears to him (allusions to his Dresden Madonna); he receives **letters** of introduction **from** Erasmus for England; paints Sir Thomas More and his family; introduction to Henry VIII.; he draws the Dance of Death. — 9. *Albert Dürer* (d. 1528), pupil of Wohlgemut; his friend Pirkheimer reads to **him**; Emp. Maximilian holds the ladder for him; his flattering reception among the painters of Antwerp. — 10. *Rembrandt* (d. 1669); on the dome *Claude Lorrain* (d. 1682). — 11. *Le Sueur* (d. 1655) working at night, **among** the Carmelites; *Nic. Poussin and his School* at Rome; protection from envy. — 12. *Rubens* (d. 1640) at his easel, sprinkled with flowers by the goddess of fortune; at his feet Cupid and Bacchantes; allusions to the tendency of his pictures; **the** master in the presence of Marie de' Medici; ambassador in England.

Ground Floor of the Pinakothek. On **the N.** side are **the Cabinet of Engravings** (adm., see p. 142), upwards of 300,000 in number (Dutch and German well represented), and the **Cabinet** of Drawings (adm., see p. 142), containing 22,000 by old and modern **masters** (four by *Raphael*, ten by *Fra Bartolommeo*, **seal of the academy of Florence by** *Benvenuto Cellini*, with explanation **in his own** handwriting, sketches by *Rembrandt* and *Dürer*, portraits by *Holbein*, etc.).

Good reproductions (photographs, photo-lithographs, etc.) **of** rare engravings, etchings, and drawings are sold by the attendants in the Cabinet of Engravings. Prices 25 pf. to 3 ℳ.

Old Pinakothek. MUNICH. *28. Route.* 173

The **Cabinet of Vases** (adm., see p. 142; catalogue 1 *M*), occupying five **rooms** in the W. wing of the groundfloor of the Old Pinakothek, **comprises** about 1500 specimens, obtained by King Lewis I. **from the** Candelori (from **Vulci**), Canino (Etruscan), Dodwell **(Greek),** Panitteri and Politi **(Sicilian),** and Lipona (Lower **Italian)** collections.

I. ROOM. Centre-table: 2. Woman playing the lyre; 3. Hercules wrestling with Antæus; 7. Theseus carrying off Antiope; 10-41. Drinking cups, mostly inscribed with toasts. Table to the left: **54.** The Gorgon pursuing Perseus (archaic); 58, 60. Hercules stealing the Delphic tripod; 65. Achilles killing Troilus at the altar (on the battlements of Troy are Priam, Hecuba, and other figures); 89. Achilles lying in wait for Polyxena and Troilus behind a fountain; 114. Hercules and Antæus; 120, 122. Women with pitchers on their heads at a fountain; 123. Zeus, Hermes, Hera, and **Aphrodite** caricatured; 124. Achilles attacked by Hector, **Æneas,** and **Deiphobus** after the death of Troilus (very early); 125. **Atalanta and Peleus** struggling; 134. Hercules vanquishing **the** Triton; 170. **Fight between** Theseus and the Minotaur.

II. ROOM. Near the door, **fragments of old mural** paintings. Table to the right (behind a grating): *211. **Dodwell Vase**, found at Corinth (on the lid, boar-hunt with names **inscribed;** on the vase, figures of animals). Table to the left: 299. Triptolemus **in the winged chariot. On the small** table near, 329. **Theseus and Ariadne.**

III. **ROOM (r.).** First table to the right: **331.** Peleus overcoming Thetis; 334. **Cups with** pleasing **inscriptions in** dialogue; *336. Triptolemus in the winged chariot (patera); **337.** Youth on horseback (Castor?); 342. Combat between Hercules and Busiris; 343. Medea with **the ram** practising magic; 345. Gæa delivering Erichthonius to Athena. Second table: *370. Large cup with raised and gilded ornamentation, Achilles slaying Penthesilea; **376. Boreas carrying** off **Orithyia; 378. Hector** arming **himself;** 383. Orpheus pursued by a Thracian woman. — Third table. 404. **Seated** youth with a wreath; 418. Chariot-races.

IV. ROOM (left from II. Room). The nine tables round the walls bear **nothing of** importance. Near the pillars stand Athenian prize amphoræ, **the pattern** of which was imported into Italy in oil-jars, *e.g.* 449, 498, **544, with** representations of Athena and warlike sports. On the windows **wire-cages** with specimens of small **vessels**, some **of them** of very handsome shape. **On the table** (No. 10) nearest the entrance: *745. The contest **between** Idas **and Apollo** for Marpessa; 748. Boreas pursuing Orithyia; ***753.** (flower-pot or wine-cooler?), Alcæus and Sappho. Eleventh table (towards the window) 776. Hephæstus intoxicated, surrounded by Bacchantes; 781. Large cooler or mixing-cup, **with** five sailing-ships on the brim, inside. Twelfth table (in **a** line with **No.** 10): *805. Scenes from the Argonautic expedition; 807. Peleus pursuing Thetis; *810. Large coloured **amphora from** Canosa in Apulia: Vengeance of Medea, death of Creusa in **the poisoned garment,** Medea slays her children and departs in the chariot **drawn by dragons.** — Thirteenth table: *849. **Large** amphora, Orpheus in **Hades,** companion vase to the beautiful No. **810** and like it found at Canosa; **853.** Lycurgus and Dionysus, beautifully ornamented, Apulian, from the same tomb as Nos. 810 and 849. Then, **drinking** utensils representing heads of a woman, griffin, sheep, ram, horse, and deer.

V. ROOM. On Table I, left: **Old Etrurian utensils** in black clay with **stamped figures;** on Table II some very ancient yellow ones with animals. **Table IV, right: Plain Cyprian vessels.** On Table III: 1035. Large vase with **combats between war-chariots. On the floor** a large antique ***Mosaic, Gæa, goddess of the earth, surrounded by the** seasons, also Helius in the zodiac, **found in the Romagna on the property of** the Duke of **Leuchtenberg.**

The ***New Pinakothek** (Pl. D, 2; tramway-lines 1 & 3, p. 140; adm., see **p.** 143; catalogue, incl. the porcelain collection, 80 pf.), erected by *Voit* in 1846-53, contains exclusively *Modern* **Pictures**, mainly by Munich masters (650 works, in eleven rooms and fourteen cabinets). The frescoes on the exterior, which have suffered from exposure on the W. and S. sides, were executed by *Nilson* from Kaulbach's designs (see 5th small saloon, p. 176). In the entrance-hall is the model of Wagner's Quadriga on the Siegesthor (p. 152). Near it, to the left, is the **entrance to two rooms** containing **Paintings** *on Porcelain* (adm., see p. 143; catalogue, see above), copies of the best pictures in the Old Pinakothek, and of the gallery of beauties in the Palace. The groundfloor also now contains the *Antiquarium* (p. 179), in five rooms.

Ground Plan of the Upper Floor.
North.

	14	13	12	11	10	9	8	7	6	5	4	3	2	1	
VI	V		IV		III			II			I				Staircase.
	I		II		III			IV			V				

South.

I. Room: **W. von Kaulbach*, Portrait of King Lewis I.; (r.) *Kaulbach*, Portrait of King Maximilian II.; (l.) *Holmberg*, Prince Regent Luitpold. Malachite vase presented by Emp. Nicholas; porphyry vases from King Charles John of Sweden. Tables of green granite (erbetto antico) and Egyptian granite; vases of serpentine, porphyry-breccia, and antique alabaster.

II. Room. *1. *C. von Piloty*, Seni before the corpse of Wallenstein; 24. *Jacobs*, Wreck; *2. *C. von Piloty*, Thusnelda in the triumphal procession of Germanicus; *230. *Andr.* **Achenbach**, Storm at sea; *3. *Anselm Feuerbach*, Medea; 7. *Piglhein*, Christ bearing the Cross; 8. *Füger*, Mary Magdalen; 9. *Albert Becker*, Raising of the daughter of Jairus; 10. *Winkler*, Mountain-scene by moonlight; 11. *Stange*, Venice burying its doge; 15. *Schorn*, Deluge (unfinished); 17. *J. A. Koch*, 20. *Chr. Reinhart*, Historical landscapes. This and the following three rooms also contain (above) cartoons for windows in the cathedral of Cologne and the Auer-Kirche at Munich, by *J. A. Fischer*.

III. Room. *Wenglein*, *27. Collecting lime in the bed of the Isar at Tölz, 28. Moorland in Upper Bavaria; 524. *Ed. Schleich*, Moonlight; *32. *Heffner*, Isola Sacra near Rome; 33. *A. Zimmermann*, Mountain-scene; *36, 37. *Makart*, Gifts of the water and the earth (Abundantia); 38. *Coroënne*, The Dauphin taking leave of his mother Marie Antoinette in 1793; *40. *W. von Kaulbach*, Destruction of

Jerusalem (which suggested the cycle of frescoes in the New Museum at Berlin); 39. *Flüggen*, Ante-chamber of a prince.

IV. Room 618. W. *Räuber*, The conversion of St. Hubert; 636. **Fr.** *Roubaud*, In the Caucasus; 588. L. *Herterich*, St. George; 609. W. *Lindenschmit the Younger*, Venus and Adonis; 55. **H.** *von Hess*, Last Supper (unfinished); 607. *William Stott*, Bathing-place; 623. W. B. *Tholen*, Sand-pits among the Dunes; 34. A. *Zimmermann*, Historical landscape; 504. *Luigi Nono* (Venice), Vegetable-seller; *Zwengauer*, 77. Moor, 78. The Benediktenwand (evening-scenes); 139. P. *Höcker*, Dutch girl; 589. G. *Kühl*, Sunday afternoon in Holland; 615. P. *Paul Müller*, By the pond; 587. *Herm. Baisch*, Dutch pasture; 590. A. *Laupheimer*, Cardinal; 79, 80. *Millner*, Kampenwand; 605. O. *Strützel*, Environs of Munich; *516. Ed. *Schleich*, Scene on the Isar; 54. *Fr. Navez*, Women of Fondi spinning; 606. *Anderson-Lundby*, Winter-day; *123. A. *Böcklin*, Among the waves; 83. *Joh. Schraudolph*, Christ healing the sick; 591. *Fr. Skarbina*, Farm-house in Picardy; **597. P.** *J. Clays*, Open sea; 53. *Heimlein*, Waterfall near Salzburg.

V. Room. 119. *Fr. August von Kaulbach*, Entombment; 58. *H. von Hess*, Apollo and the Muses; 109. *Fischer*, Entombment; 85. *Joh. Schraudolph*, The Virgin, Mary Magdalen, and St. John on Mt. Calvary; 108. L. *Brüls*, The Saviour; *Schraudolph*, 84. Miraculous draught of fishes, 81. Mary with Jesus and John the Baptist, 88a. Ascension; 116. *Fr. Overbeck*, Italy and Germany; 82. *Schraudolph*, St. Agnes; 62, 63. P. *von Hess*, King Otho entering Nauplia in 1833 and Athens in 1835; 107. W. *von Schadow*, Holy Family; 97. *Angelica Kauffmann*, Christ and the Samaritan Woman; 613. *Ed. Gebhardt*, Crucifixion; 91. *Wichmann*, Venetian woman distributing fruit; 57. *H. von Hess*, Virgin enthroned; *115. *Overbeck*, Mary and Elizabeth, Jesus and John **the Baptist** (1825).

VI. Room. *Rottmann*, Twenty-three Greek landscapes (1845-50), encaustic paintings admirably lighted from above.

Smaller Rooms (beginning from the large Room V).

I. On the right: 633. L. K. *Müller*, Study of a head (Coptic girl); 156. H. *Lang*, Storming of Fröschweiler; 602. *Raffet*, Soldiers of the First Republic; 157. H. *Lang*, Bavarians crossing the Marne at Corbeil; A. *Adam*, 159. Battle of Custozza (1848), 160. Battle of Novara (1849); *140. *Putz*, Bavarian riflemen at Bazeilles; 5. *Ans. Feuerbach*, Portrait of himself; 141. *Fr. Bodenmüller*, Battle **of Wörth**; *122. *Fr.* **von** *Lenbach*, Portrait **of** Dr. Döllinger; 593. *R.* **Hirth** *du Frênes*, The artist Schuch; 142. *Bodenmüller*, Incident in the Battle of Sedan; 158. A. *Adam*, Storming the lines of Düppel (1849); 642. H. W. *Jansen*, Dutch harbour; 652. V. *Müller*, Romeo and Juliet; *578. *Cr. Bisschop* (The Hague), Sunshine in house and heart; 124. A. *Böcklin*, Pan among the reeds; 563. *Jan Blommers*, Fresh fish; *121. *Lenbach*, Prince Bismarck; 126. *F. Adam*, Battle of Orléans; 581 *Frenzel*, **The** favourite; *120 *Lenbach*, Pope Leo XIII.

II. To the right: 631. *George Innes*, Sunrise; 572. *V. Geza*, Ducks; 570. *A. von Pettenkofen*, Hut in Slavonia; 565. *Fr. von Uhde*, A painful walk; 61. *P. von Hess*, Battle of Austerlitz; 622. *F. Brütt*, The decisive moment; *643. *Franz Stuck*, Sin; 127. *F. Adam*, Attack at Mars-la-Tour; *584. *A. Kampf*, Emp. William I. lying in state; 640. *O. Jernberg*, In the fields; 51. *W. von Kobell*, Battle of Hanau (1813); 594. *A. Langhammer*, Supper; 625. *H. Herkomer*, Cares (water-colour); 604. *Ad. Menzel*, The levy (gouache), 568. *John Lavery*, Tennis-court; 567. *A. Kunz*, Still-life; 562. *Fr. Courtens*, A field of hyacinths; 638. *G. Hackl*, The first quarters; 616. *Nic. Gysis*, Carnival in Greece; 47. *B. Adam*, Cattle; no number, *Munkacsy, Visit to a sick woman; 174. *Steffan*, Mountain-scene; no number, *J. Benlliure* (Valencia), St. Francis; 182. *Ad. Echtler*, Fallen; 169. *Chr. Morgenstern*, Landscape in Alsace; 149. *Van der Meer*, Winter-scene in the Netherlands; 626. *L. Brunin*, The sculptor; 644. *Aless. Milesi*, Twilight; 577. *H. Bartels*, At full steam.

III. To the right: 186. *G. von Canal*, Old palace-garden; 184. *Diday*, The Wetterhorn; 187. *E. Zimmermann*, Adoration of the Shepherds; 191. *Willroider*, The Deluge; 192. *H. Kaulbach*, At a friend's grave; *193. *A. Gabl*, Vaccination in Tyrol; 194. *M. Zimmermann*, Oak-forest; 519. *Ed. Schleich*, Coming storm; 198. *Joh. Fischbach*, Convent-park; 201. *L. von Hagn*, Concert in a garden; *202. *Kurzbauer*, Festival in the country; 203. *Stademann*, Winter-scene; 189. *Loefftz*, Body of Christ; 185. *G. von Maffei*, Turn-spits (Dachshunde); 183. *Winterhalter*, Portrait.

IV. To the right: *215. *Wilkie*, Opening the will; 216. *J. Vermeersch*, Harbour-scene; 229. *Chr. Mali*, Mountain-pasture; 165. *W. Lichtenheld*, Moonlight-scene; 242. *Jos. von Brandt*, Cossack horses in a snow-storm; 236. *B. Fries*, Scene on the Tiber, near Rome; 210. *A. Riedel*, Girl of Albano; 635. *Fr. Roubaud*, Wounded; *243. *J. von Brandt*, Defence; 235. *Voltz*, Herd returning home; 231. *Andr. Achenbach*, Autumn morning in the Pontine Marshes; 239. *L. Gallait*, Monk feeding the poor; 178. *R. Zimmermann*, Mountain-scene in winter; 241. *Verboeckhoven*, Sheep-pen; 537. *Grützner*, Convent-scene; 561. *Le Mayeur*, High-tide; 228. *Mali*, Scene in Verona; *227. *Wopfner*, Fishing in the Chiemsee; 224. *Schindler*, March; 206. *A. Riedel*, Judith; 223. *Ad. Lier*, The Theresienwiese at Munich; 221. *Ramberg*, After dinner; 205. *A. Riedel*, Neapolitan fisher-family.

V. Above: *W. von Kaulbach*, Sketches for the frescoes outside the building (p. 174), representing the artistic activity of King Lewis I. at Rome and Munich, with numerous portraits. To the right: 244. *Marcó*, Landscape with the Flight into Egypt; 250. *A. von Bayer*, Franciscan Church in Salzburg; 254. *J. Lange*, The Gosau-See by morning light; *257. *J. Geyer*, Concilium medicum; 271. *Jos. Stieler*, Portrait of Goethe (1828); *260. *Defregger*, Storming the Red Tower at Munich in 1705; 258. *J. Geyer*, Return from the masked ball; 59. *H. von Hess*, Portrait of Thorwaldsen; 255. *J.*

Lange, The Gosau-See by evening-light; 261-269, **274**-279. *Stieler, Schrotzberg*, etc., Portraits of the Bavarian royal family; *Ainmüller*, 246, 247. Interior and Choir of Westminster Abbey; 249. *Steinle*, The Parzival cycle (water-colours).

We now pass through Room I to the CABINETS (chronologically arranged).

1. Cabinet. To the right, 281. *Graff*, Portrait of Chodowiecky; 98. *Angelica Kauffmann*, King Lewis I. when crown-prince; 18. *Jos. A. Koch*, Italian vintage-festival; **opposite**, 298. *Catel*, Crown-prince Lewis in the Spanish artists' **tavern** on the Ripa Grande at Rome; 19. *J. A. Koch*, Schmadri Fall in Switzerland.

2. Cabinet. To the right, 307. *A. Schelfhout*, By the shore; *Rottmann*, *319. Monte Pellegrino near Palermo, 320. Acropolis of Sicyon; *Fr. Catel*, 302. Near Castel Gandolfo, 303. Bay of Palermo; 321. *Rottmann*, Island of Ischia; opposite, 316. **Fr. Granet**, Savonarola; 317. *Koekkoek*, Sea-piece; 337. *Regemorter*, Dutch room; 44. *W. von Kaulbach*, King Lewis I.; back-wall, *Quaglio*, 341. St. Sebald's at Nuremberg, 342. Cathedral of Orvieto; 355. *Dillis*, Tegernsee; 358. *Neher*, Trausnitz Chapel, near **Landshut**; 372. *Heydeck*, Lion-gate at Mycenæ.

3. Cabinet. To the right, 309. *J.* **W. Preyer**, Still-life; *P. von Hess*, 64. Italian tavern, 67. Greek peasants on the **shore**, **66. Marino**, in the Alban Mountains; *B. Stange*, 12. Shipping in the Lagoons of Venice, 13. Italian villa; 374. *K. W. von Heydeck*, Bridge of Cuenca in Spain; 324. *Rottmann*, Eibsee; opposite, 297. *Jos. Rebell*, Near Capri; 68. *P. von Hess*, Capturing horses in Wallachia; *Rottmann*, 325. The Hohe Göll, 326a. Corfu; 313. *J. Schnorr*, Scenes from the Nibelungen; rear-wall, 305. *Catel*, Garden of the Capuchins at Syracuse.

4. Cabinet. To the right, no number, *P. von Hess*, Departure of King Otho for Greece; 162, 163. *A. Adam*, Horses; 308. *Schelfhout*, Winter-scene; 272, 273. *Jos. Stieler*, Emp. Francis I. of Austria and his wife; 377. *Heydeck*, Approach to the Acropolis; opposite, *Rottmann*, *322. Taormina with Mt. Etna, 323. Tomb of Archimedes at Syracuse; 384. *Schendel*, Market-place at Antwerp; 385. *Monten*, **Napoleon** I.; rear-wall, 128. *F. Adam*, French cuirassiers at the burning of Moscow; 340. *Ferd. Braekeleer*, Street-musician; 70-74. *P. von Hess*, Sketches for the scenes from the Greek War of Independence in the Arcades (p. 149).

5. Cabinet. To the right, 392, 393. *H. Adam*, Views of Munich; ***394**. *M. von Schwind*, A symphony; opposite, 344. *D. Quaglio*, Villa Malta, at Rome; 166. *W. Lichtenheld*, Castle-yard with treasure-diggers by moonli**ght**; **25.** *J. Jacobs*, Harbour of Constantinople; 402. *L. van Kuyck*, Stable; rear-wall, 412. *J. Kirner*, Fortune-teller; 415. *Aiwasowsky*, Near St. Petersburg; 172. *Gerhardt*, Interior of St. Mark's at Venice; 414. *W. Schön*, Girl listening.

6. Cabinet. To the right, *420. *L. Robert*, Woman of Procida; 421.

N. de Keyser, Monk at an alms-box; 200. *Fischbach*, The Tennengebirge; 424. *J. H. van de Laar*, Genre-scene; 14. *B. Stange*, The tower-window; opposite, 386. *W. Lindenschmit the Elder*, Death of Duke **Luitpold** at the battle of Pressburg (sketch); 429. *H. Bürkel*, Winter-scene; 406. *Enhuber*, Grandfather and grandson; 433. *Lepoittevin*, **Adrian Brouwer** painting a sign in a tavern; *Hasenclever*, *438. Jobs undergoing examination, 439. Sulking couple; rear-wall, 419. *A. Löffler*, Twenty-two sketches from the East.

7. *Cabinet*. To the right, 222. *Ramberg*, The morning-prayer; 443. *L. Faustner*, Frauenkirche at Munich; 251. *Bayer*, Conventhall; 448. *Frey*, Memnon columns at Thebes; opposite, 430. *H. Bürkel*, Aqueduct in the Roman Campagna; 413. *Kirner*, Baden freelances in **1849**; rear-wall, 345-348. *D. Quaglio*, Views of Munich; 460. *Foltz*, The singer's curse.

8. *Cabinet*. To the right, 462. *Scholz*, Officer's widow in church; 464. *Spitzweg*, The poor poet; 213. *Riedel*, Karl Rottmann; 434. *Camphausen*, Scene from Cromwell's time; 467. *R. Eberle*, Shepherd; opposite, *431. *H. Bürkel*, Rain in a mountain-village; 248. *M. Ainmüller*, Rheims Cathedral; 86. 87. *J. Schraudolph*, Angels; 56. *H. von Hess*, Portrait; 359. *M. Neher*, St. Martin's at Brunswick; 432. *Bürkel*, Roman Campagna; rear-wall, 349-352. *Quaglio*, Views of Munich; 219. *Vermeersch*, Canal Grande at Venice.

9. *Cabinet*. To the right, 232. *And. Achenbach*, On the North Sea; 481. *Bamberger*, Gorge at Cuenca in Spain; 505. *A. Fink*, Winter morning among the mountains; *Spitzweg*, 465. In the attic, 466. Hermits; 252. *Bayer*, Convent-yard; 233. *A. Achenbach*, Sea-piece; 49. *B. Adam*, Stable; 482. *Bamberger*, San Geronimo in Castile; 485. *Hendrik Schmidt*, Dutch school-room; 486. *Bosboom*, Interior of a church at Amsterdam; 35. *A. Zimmermann*, Mountain-torrent.

10. *Cabinet*. To the right, 224a. *E. J. Schindler*, Saw-mill in Upper Austria; 510. *Bischof*, The first snow; 600. *W. Trübner*, Herreninsel, in the Chiemsee; 512. *K. Hoff*, At the palace of Würzburg; 648. *Willroider*, Near Fürstenfeld-Bruck; 558a. *Rob. Schleich*, Hay-harvest in Upper Bavaria; *H. Rhomberg*, 436. The first cigars, 437. Sledge-carver; *Neher*, 365. Prague Cathedral, 367. Lichtenthal, near Baden-Baden; 649. *E. Meissonier*, The bravoes.

11. *Cabinet*. To the right, 574. *Weishaupt*, Cattle; 26. *J. Jacobs*, Sunrise in the Archipelago; *583. *Rob. Haug*, Parting; 585. *Fröhlicher*, Landscape; opposite, **534**. *A. Holmberg*, Scholar; *564. *Ed. Dantan* (of St. Cloud), **Potter's** work-room; 150. *G. Schönleber*, Dutch village.

12. *Cabinet*. To the right, 540. *Gebler*, Reynard's end; 497. *Gabriel Max*, Ape-critics; 571. *J. R. Reid*, Unwelcome news; 608. *José Villegas*, Doge **Foscari** after his deposition (water-colour); 566. *J. H. de Haas*, Cattle at pasture; opposite, 536. *Grützner*, The devil and the Silesian roysterer; 538. *Fr. Amerling*, Study of a head; 637. *Favretto*, Venetian art-dealer; *569. *W. Leibl*, Peasant interior;

543. *A. Seitz*, Vagabonds; rear-wall, 88. *J. Schraudolph*, Madonna; 592. *Hans Thoma*, Scene in the Taunus.

13. Cabinet. To the right, 494, 495. *Olga Wiesinger-Florian*, Flower-pieces; *496. *Gab. Max*, Catharine Emmerich in a state of ecstasy; opposite, 542. *A. D. Bouveret* (Paris), Madonna; 610. *O. Sinding*, Boys bathing; 516-528. *Ed. Schleich*, Landscapes.

14. Cabinet. To the right, 550. *Al. Gierymski*, Wittelsbacher-Platz at Munich; *547. *Benlliure*, Month of Mary at Valencia; 552. *Max Liebermann*, Old woman with goats; 498. *Bauernfeind*, Ruined temple at Baalbek; opposite, 503. *Nono* (Venice), Garden-scene; 500. *Mauve*, Cows pasturing; *551. *Squindo*, The **royal** family brought back to Paris in 1789; 560. *A. Newhuys*, Spring.

The **Antiquarium**, on the groundfloor of the New Pinakothek, contains the smaller Greek and Roman and a few Egyptian antiquities, **including some** fine terracottas and bronzes **(adm.**, see p. 142; good catalogue, 60 pf.).

I. ROOM. Cork models **of the Pantheon and** the so-called temples **of** Vesta at Rome and Tivoli. **Ancient terracottas of** Italian and Greek origin, some of them reproductions **of celebrated works** in **bronze or** marble. *4th Cabinet*, *258. Winged **Victory**, **a Roman work** after **the Nike** of Paionios at Olympia. *Case to **the left of the entrance:*** *653. Satyr carrying off a girl, from Tanagra; °659. **Greek funeral feast**; **662**. Diomede; 667. Europa and the bull; 671. Nereid. *Over the Case by the E. wall:* 894. Dancing mime with a wreath; above, **926-929**. Reliefs of vintage-scenes and winemaking. *Case to the right of the entrance:* 761. Winged sphinx; 762. Nike, with traces of painting; 770. Eros; 774. Flask; 775. Painted beaker in the form of a barbarian's head; *777. Perforated glass goblet, from a Roman sarcophagus at Cologne; 790. Votive tablet with Aphrodite and Hermes, from Rosarno in Calabria; 791. Young Bacchant with ivy-wreath; 803. Fortuna and Cupid; 805. Sphinx; 806. Victory, gilded terracotta from Attica. *Case by the W. wall:* *846. Draped female figures from an Attic grave with well-preserved painting; 848. Triton and Eros; 849. Head of the so-called 'Dying Alexander'; 908. Leda. By the *Window-Wall:* 923. Marble fragment with three old men; 923. Arimaspe and **a** griffin. — II. ROOM. Models in cork of the Arch of Constantine, the Temple of Neptune at Pæstum, etc. The *Wall-Cases* contain small antiquities of the most diverse nature. — III. ROOM. Cork and plaster models (Colosseum, **House of** Sallust at Pompeii, etc.). The *Round Case in the centre* contains gold **and silver** ornaments and works in ivory (shelves 1, 2, & 6, Trinkets from Etruria; shelf 3, °Gold wreath from a Greek tomb at Armento, S.Italy; shelf 4, Gold ornaments from Greece and Cyprus; shelf 8, Egyptian gold ornaments **from** the great Pyramid of Meroë). In the *Wall-Cases* are Roman lamps, bronze ornaments and utensils, etc. — IV. ROOM. *5th Wall-Case*, Ancient weapons and armour, including a handsome suit **of bronze armour from the** tomb of a Greek warrior in S. Italy. Among the **small** bronze figures in the *Case to the left of the entrance* are: 349, 350. Mercury; 352. Jupiter Pluvius; 357. Youthful Mars; °361. Venus loosening her sandal; °363. Discobolus, after Myron; 369. Pallas Athena; 372. Hercules, probably after Lysippus; **373. Zeus**. *Case to **the** right of the entrance:* **647**. Silver goblet **with** representations of the destruction of Troy, by **a Greek** master, 652. Onehandled silver pitcher with reliefs of Lapithæ and Centaurs; 666. Marble disk with representations of Hercules; 671. Early-Greek standing mirror from Hermione, in Argolis (5th cent. **B.C.**). The early-Etruscan bronze reliefs by the *E. Wall* belong to the same series as Nos. 32-38 in the Glyptothek. By the middle window of the *N. Wall:* 920. Cist from Præneste. — EGYPTIAN ROOM (to the left of Room I). Egyptian collection: sarcophagi, mummies, cippi, etc.

At No. 78 Theresien-Strasse, behind the New Pinakothek, is

12*

a *Panorama representing the Emp. Constantine entering Rome in 312, by *Bühlmann* and *Wagner* (adm., see p. 143).

In the Schelling-Strasse (Nos. 83-93), near the New Pinakothek, are the so-called *Fürstenhäuser*, a row of private residences elaborately adorned with frescoes by Ferd. Wagner; in the court of No. 87 is the kiosque from the old winter-garden of Lewis II. A little to the N., in the Arcis-Str., lies the new *Northern Cemetery* (Pl. D, 1; p. 193). Opposite the W. side of the Old Pinakothek rises the **Polytechnic School** (Pl. D, 2), a handsome brick edifice in the Italian Renaissance style, with ornamentation in granite and sandstone, by *Neureuther* (d. 1887). The cornice is adorned with seventy-two medallion-portraits of celebrated architects, mathematicians, and naturalists. *Staircase worthy of inspection. The valuable technical collections are shown during the vacations only, and occasionally on Sundays (apply to the custodian, groundfloor). — In the neighbouring Luisen-Strasse is the *Art-Industrial School*.

The *Glyptothek (Pl. C, D, 2, 3; adm., see p 142), or 'Repository of Sculptures', in the Königs-Platz, contains ancient sculptures collected chiefly by Lewis I. when crown-prince, in 1805-16. The building, erected by *Klenze* in 1816-30, is externally in the Ionic style, with a porch of eight columns; the interior is vaulted, and tends to the Roman style. The group in the tympanum, designed by *Wagner*, and executed by *Schwanthaler* and others in marble, represents Minerva as protectress of the plastic art. The thirteen halls are lighted from the quadrangle in the centre. The niches in front and on the sides contain marble statues of famous sculptors. Excellent catalogue by *Prof. Dr. Brunn* (d. 1894), 2 *M*.

I. *Assyrian Hall*. At the entrance, two colossal lions with human heads, casts of the originals from the **palace** of Sardanapalus III. at Kalah (Larissa; 884-859 B.C.), now in the Louvre. In the hall, seven reliefs in alabaster, originally coloured, with winged genii, etc., and cuneiform inscriptions.

II. *Egyptian Hall*. 5, 6. Statues of priests in black marble, of the time of Hadrian; 7, 8. Recumbent sphinxes, in basalt, of Roman workmanship; *13. Statue of Ra, the god of the sun, with the head of a hawk, in black granite, early Egyptian; 14. Portrait-statue of a man (not Egyptian); 15. **Antinous** as Osiris, in rosso antico, of Hadrian's time; 16. and 24. Groups of husband and wife in a sitting posture, in sandstone, the former with traces of painting; 17. Isis, and 23. Horus, of a late period; 25. Quadruple head of Brahma; 29. Head of Buddha (specimens of Indian art from Java); *30. Sitting statue of a high priest, in limestone, early Egyptian, the most valuable object in this part of the collection; 31. (in the centre) Obelisk in syenite, of Roman origin.

III. *Hall of the Incunabula* (Greek and Etruscan art, 'in cunabulis', *i.e.* 'in its cradle', and copies). *41. So-called Apollo of Tenea, probably a portrait-figure, archaic (middle of the 6th cent.

B.C.; found at the foot of the Acro-Corinth); 43. Roman lady as Fortuna, in imitation of the archaic style, of Hadrian's time; 46. Spes, Roman, a similar work; 44. Triangular base of a candelabrum from Perugia, a very ancient Etruscan **work, embossed** and riveted; 47, 48. Etruscan cinerary urns; *49. **Head of** a youth, a copy in marble of a bronze original (?); 50. Bearded Bacchus, archaistic; 32-38. Early-Etruscan reliefs in bronze found at Perugia, some of them probably from a chariot.

IV. **Æginetan Hall*. Sculptures in marble from a Temple of Minerva in the island of Ægina, found in 1811, purchased by Crown-Prince Lewis in **1812**, and restored with the aid of Thorwaldsen. They are **of great importance in the history** of art. They consist of two pediment groups **from** the temple erected by the Æginetans **after the** Persian wars, **and commemorate the exploits of their heroes,** (1) Telamon and (2) Ajax and **Teucer**, his sons, in the war against the Trojans. The first group (E. pediment) consists now **of five figures only; the** other (W. pediment) **has ten.** The figures are somewhat thickset, with mask-like **heads and** open mouths. A

			North.		
VII. Hall of Niobe.	VIII. Hall of Gods.	Small Vestibule.	IX. Trojan Hall.	X. Hall of Heroes.
VI. Hall of Bacchus				
V. Hall of Apollo.		COURT.		XI. Roman Hall.
IV. Æginet. Hall.		I. Assyr. Hall.		
III. Hall of Incunab.	II. Egyptian Hall	Vestibule.	XIII. Modern Works.	XII. Colored Sculptures.
		South.		

small model of the temple on the wall above affords a convenient survey of the left group. Group on **the right: Telamon and** Hercules fighting over the body of Oicles against Laomedon, the perjured king of Troy. 54. Hercules, 55. Dying Trojan, **56.** Champion of the Trojans, 57. Fallen warrior, 58. Youth stooping forwards. Group on the left: Greeks fighting against the Trojans around the body of Achilles. **59. Minerva,** 60. Achilles, 61. Ajax Telamonius, 62. Teucer, 63. **Greek combatant** (son of Ajax Oïleus?), 64. Wounded Greek, **65. Æneas,** 66. Paris, 67. Trojan **kneeling,** 68. Wounded **Trojan.** By the walls are smaller fragments.

V. *Hall of Apollo.* **79.** Ceres; 80. Bearded Bacchus; 81. Jupiter Ammon; **82. Rhodian vase;** 83. **Head of an** athlete, a Roman copy of Lysippus; 85a. **Relief of a** family sacrificing to Æsculapius and Hygieia, from Corinth; 87. Draped female statue (Roman portrait-figure; **head** ancient, but not belonging to this statue); 88. Attic cinerary urn, with relief; *89. Girl's head (Muse?), an admirable original of the **Attic** School (ca. 400 B.C.); 90. Colossal **statue of** Apollo Citharœdus; 91. Head of Mars; *92. Pallas, Roman copy of a bronze original; 93. Statue of Diana, Roman.

VI. *Hall of Bacchus*. In the centre: **95. Sleeping satyr, the 'Barberini Faun', a Greek original (ca. 300 B.C.; partly restored); *96. **Eirene and Plutus**, a copy of the bronze original by Cephisodotus the Elder, father of Praxiteles (**beginning of the** 4th cent. B.C.); 97. Apollo; 98. **Silenus**, copy from a Greek original in bronze; *99. Head of a laughing **satyr**, after a bronze original; 100. Bacchanalian **sarcophagus**; upon it, 101. Sitting satyr, Roman copy of a Greek work in marble; *102. **Young Pan with** horns, known as 'Winckelmann's Faun'; 103. **Bacchus anointing** himself; *105, 106. Satyrs, probably after Praxiteles; 108. **Bacchus**, late-Roman; 109. Satyr with a wine-skin, Roman copy of a Hellenistic bronze; 112. Ariadne; *113. Diana, restored by Thorwaldsen as Ceres; *114. Silenus with the young Bacchus, freely **restored**. By the wall to the left, 115. **Nuptials of Neptune and Amphitrite**, a Greek relief from the **workshop of Scopas (4th cent. B.C.)**.

VII. *Hall of the Children of Niobe*. 123. Hermes, **resembling the** Hermes of Praxiteles; 124, 129. Busts of Roma and Minerva with bronze helmet (modern); 125. Female figure in relief (Roman); 127. Rustic scene, a **Hellenistic** relief; *128. Head of Medusa ('Medusa Rondanini'), alto-relief; 130. Venus; *131. Venus of Cnidos, after Praxiteles; 136. Decoration **of a** herma, relief; 135. Head of Paris; 138. Draped figure, restored **by** Thorwaldsen as Clio. In the centre, 140. Boy struggling with a goose, a Roman copy of the bronze original of Boëthus; 141. Dying child of Niobe; *142. Torso of a youth, an admirable Greek original of the 4th cent. B.C., formerly mistaken for Ilioneus (son of Niobe).

VIII. *Hall of the Gods*. This and **the next** two **rooms are adorned with beautiful *Frescoes** by **Cornelius, executed in 1820-30. The principal scenes are: 1.** The infernal regions, Orpheus entreating **Pluto and** Proserpine to restore him his wife Eurydice; 2. Marriage **of Neptune and** Amphitrite; Arion; Thetis; 3. Olympus; Jupiter **and Juno;** Hercules receives the cup of nectar from Hebe; Ganymede and the eagle. On the vaults are the four Elements, the Seasons, **and the** Quarters of the Day. **Over the** doors reliefs by Schwanthaler. — *Small* **Vestibule.** Minerva imparts a soul to the man formed by **Prometheus;** Prometheus released by **Hercules; Pandora opens** her casket. In the niches are Roman busts; to the left, *147. Marcus Aurelius, in peperino.

IX. *Hall of the Trojans*. Frescoes: 1. Quarrel of Achilles and Agamemnon over the abduction of Briseïs; 2. **Contest for the body of Patroclus;** 3. Destruction of Troy, with Priam, **Hecuba, Cassandra,** Æneas, and **Anchises. The nine** smaller paintings on the ceiling represent **episodes** before and during the Trojan war.

X. *Hall of the Heroes.* On the left: 152. Æsculapius; 153. Alexander the Great (much restored, arm wrongly); 155. Hippocrates (?); 156. Hunter; 157. Pericles; 158. Domitian; 159. Themistocles (?); 160. **Statue of a** Greek king, after an early-Attic original; 162. Diomedes carrying off the Palladium, after a Greek original in bronze (the Victory not part of the original); 163. Philosopher (Zeno?); *165. Athlete, probably a copy of an early-Attic original in the style of Myron; 166. Socrates; 149. Demosthenes; *151. (in the centre), Mercury, after a bronze original of the school of Lysippus (head not belonging to the statue).

XI. *Hall of the Romans* (in three sections), with a valuable collection of busts, chiefly of the Roman Empire. Section 1: to the left, *172. Unknown; 236. Tiberius; VIII B. Messalina; *219, 183. Augustus; *216. Cicero (?); 181, 202. Nero; 261. Corbulo (?); 211. Mæcenas (?); 187. Unknown; to the right, 272. Seneca (?); 271. Otho; 238. Vitellius (? modern). — Sec. 2: to the left, 211. **Julia**, daughter of Titus; 186. Vespasian; *268, 196. Trajan; *198. Antoninus Pius; 199. Titus; 217. Hadrian (?); 180. Lucius Verus; 242. Marciana, sister of Trajan; 276. Plotina, wife of Trajan; 193. Marcus Aurelius; **to the right,** 237. Sabina (?), wife of Hadrian; 195. Ælius Cæsar (?); **256.** Antinous. — Sec. 3: **to the** left, 245. Pertinax; 220. Plautilla, wife of Caracalla; 194. Tranquillina, wife of Gordianus Pius; **240.** Otacilia Severa, **wife** of Philippus Arabs; 200. Septimius Severus; 255. Commodus; EHB. Junius Brutus (?); **to** the right, 201. Geta (?); 182. Unknown; 231. Lucius Verus. — By the doors: 167-170. Four Caryatides, Roman. By the left wall: 175. Statue of Agrippina the Elder, wife of Germanicus; 188. Sarcophagus with the Muses, Athena, and Apollo; 192. Statue of Septimius Severus; 205. **Sarcophagus with** the children of Niobe; 206. **Reliefs** from a **frieze, Victories** sacrificing; **209.** Augustus, 226. Livia Drusilla, wife of Augustus, statues. Wall to the right: 280. Statue of Lucilla (?), wife of Lucius Verus; 264. Statue of a member of the Claudian family; 246, 262, 277. Pulvinaria (seats of the gods), with appropriate attributes; 233. Statuette of Matidia, niece of Trajan, as Ceres. In the centre: 285. Boy with a goose, on a stand; 286, 287. Candelabra; 288. Ornamental vase, with head of Medusa; **no** number, Intoxicated Roman woman.

XII. *Hall of the Coloured Sculptures.* In the centre, 293. Antique mosaic; upon it, 294. Tripod, bearing (295.) a modern (?) statuette of Silenus in bronze. (1.) 298. Ceres (?), in black and white marble, freely restored; *299. Head of a satyr, in bronze; 300. River-god, in black marble; 302. Head of an athlete, a fine bronze; 304. Girl loosening her robe, statuette in black and white marble, **a good Roman work;** 306. Alexander the Great (?), bronze; 309. Young satyr, in marble; 313. Claudius (?), bust; 314. Draped female statue, in bronze, a good Roman portrait-figure.

XIII. *Hall of Modern Masters.* To the left, *318. Paris, by

Canova; 319. Sandal-binder, *R. Schadow;* 320. Napoleon, bust by *Spalla* (1808); 321. Lewis I. when crown-prince (1821), bust by *Thorwaldsen;* 322. Paris, *Canova;* 323. Cupid and Muse, *Eberhard;* 324. The Russian Marshal Münnich, *Eberhard;* 325. Infant Christ kneeling, *Algardi;* *326. Admiral Tromp, bust by *Rauch;* 327. Barbarossa, bust by *Tieck;* 328. Bust of a young man (not Raphael), a good Florentine (?) terracotta of the close of the 16th cent.; 329. Iffland, **bust by** *G. Schadow;* *336. Statue **of Adonis**, *Thorwaldsen;* 330. Elector Palatine Frederick the Victorious, bust by *Dannecker;* 331. **General von Heydeck, bust** by *Wolf;* 332. Count Stolberg, **bust** by *Freund;* 333. Vittoria Caldoni, 'the beauty of Albano', bust **by** *R. Schadow;* 334. Catharine II. of Russia, bust by *Busch;* no number, Abel, bronze figure by *Carles;* 335. Vesta, marble statue by *Tenerani*. In the centre: Ludovica, Duchess of Bavaria, monumental figure by *Rümann;* Motherhood, marble group by *Flossmann.*

The **Exhibition Building** (Pl. C, 3), opposite the Glyptothek, in the Corinthian style, was completed by *Ziebland* in 1845. In the tympanum is Bavaria, bestowing wreaths on artists, by Schwanthaler. It contains a permanent exhibition of works by Munich artists (p. 142), most of which are for sale.

The handsome **Königs-Platz** is appropriately terminated **by the** ***Propylæa (Pl. C, 3)**, a magnificent gateway, with Doric columns **outside, and Ionic inside**, designed by *Klenze*, and completed in 1862. The reliefs by *Schefzky* **(after** *Hiltensperger*) represent scenes from the Greek War of Independence and the régime of King Otho. On the inner walls are inscribed the names of the heroes of the war and of famous philhellenists. — On the day after its inauguration (30th Oct., 1862) the ex-monarch of Greece (d. 1867) returned to his native city. — From the Propylæa to the *Basilica* and to the *Crystal Palace*, see p. 187.

The ***Schack Picture Gallery**, Aeussere Brienner-Str. 19 (Pl. C, 3; adm., see p. 143; catalogue 50 pf., bound 1 ℳ), bequeathed by **Count** *Adolf von Schack* (d. 1894), the poet, to the German **Emperor**, consists of choice modern works of German masters, such **as Genelli**, Schwind, Feuerbach, and Böcklin, and of copies (often admirable) of the great Italian and Spanish masters by Lenbach and others. It forms a valuable complement to the New Pinakothek.

GROUND FLOOR. Opposite the entrance: *Seeboeck*, Bust **of Count** Schack. — ROOM I. To the left: *Böcklin*, 12. Ideal landscape; 25. Autumn-landscape, with Death on horseback; 26. Italian villa in spring; *17. **The** shepherd's complaint; *18. Murderer pursued by **the Furies;** 23. Sacred grove; 14. Pan frightening **a shepherd;** ***15, 16**. Villa on the sea; 21. Ideal landscape in spring. *71. *Lenbach*, Shepherd-boy; 60. *L. von Hagn*, Italian garden-scene; *1. *Bamberger*, Gibraltar; 95. *Neubert*, Olevano, in the Sabine Mountains; 112. *Ross*, Grotto of Egeria; 93. *Feuerbach*, Laura at mass at Avignon, **watched by** Petrarch; *3. *Bamberger*, The bridge of St. Miguel, near Toledo; 164. *Spitzweg*, Hypochondriac; 6. *Bamberger*, Scene near Granada; 172. *Steinle*, The watchman; 122. *Schleich*, Night scene at Venice; 77. *Lenbach*, Portrait of a Franciscan; 7. *Bamberger*, **Lake** of Albufera near Valencia; 118, 119. *Rottmann*, Roman scenes; *31. *Dreber*, Sappho. — End-wall: *Preller*, 104. Ulysses and Leucothea, 105. Calypso bidding farewell to Ulysses; *Morgenstern*, 91. **Coast** of Capri, 90. Tasso's house at Sorrento. Above the door: *78. *Lenbach*, Portrait of Count Schack. — Right wall: 42. *Feuerbach*, Idyl from Tivoli; 72. *Lenbach*, Portrait of a lady; 38. *Feuerbach*, Madonna and Child with angels; 28. *Böheim*, Two satyrs pursuing a hare; 177. *Rottmann*, Greek coast with rising storm; 186. *Zimmermann*, Lake of Como; *40. *Feuerbach*, Hafiz at the fountain; 68. *Köbel*, Egeria's grotto, near Rome; 121. *Schleich*, The Lake of Starnberg; *61. *Henneberg*, The Wild Huntsman; 87. *Millner*, The Obersee, near Berchtesgaden; 35. *Feuerbach*, Francesca da Rimini and Paolo, **37.** **Children bathing**, *34. Pietà, 33. Roman woman, 32. The garden of Ariosto, 36. Nymph listening to children performing music; *Böcklin*, 19. The dragon's cave, 24. Old Roman tavern in spring, *22. Ideal landscape **with the journey** to Emmaus, 27. Nereid and Triton, 13. The anchorite, 20. Shepherdess with her flock; 41. *Feuerbach*, Mother and children at a well. — ROOM II. Copies of Giov. **Bellini**, Titian, **Palma Vecchio, Veronese**, etc., by *A. Wolf*.

FIRST FLOOR. ROOM I. *M. von Schwind* (to the left), 137. The **Erl-king**; 143. Forest-chapel; 146. Morning-prayer; (to the right) 158. The captive's dream; 135. Nymphs watering a stag; *139. The wedding-trip; 151. Number Nip. — **To the** right, ROOM II. (right), *M. von Schwind*, 147. Duel by night; 160. Hero and Leander; *129. Count Gleichen returning from the Crusades; 153. Father Rhine; 154. The Danube. 174. *Steinle*, Lorelei (first sketch of No. 175, **see below**); 48. *Genelli*, Ezekiel's **vision**. — To the left, ROOM III. *M. von Schwind*, 130-133. Morning, Noon, Evening, Night; 150. Wieland the Smith; 161. Hermit in a rock grotto. — ROOM IV. *Copies from Titian, Giorgione, Murillo, Velazquez, Rubens*, etc., by *Lenbach*; to the left of the door, 73. *Lenbach*, Portrait of himself. — ROOM V. **175.** *Steinle*, Lorelei; 123. *Schleich*, Alp in the Zillerthal; 76. *Lenbach*, The Tocador de la Reina at the Alhambra; 106. *Rahl*, Portrait of Willers, the landscape-painter; 173. *Steinle*, Tartini playing the **violin** on a tower of Padua; 84. *H. von Marées*, Watering horses; 109. **Rahl**, **Portrait of a** woman; 185. *Zimmermann*, Brocken Scene from Goethe's Faust; 64. *Kirchner*, Verona; *Genelli*, *49. Rape of Europa, *52. Lycurgus fighting **with** Bacchus and Bacchantes; **179. Willers**, Athens; *103. *K. von Piloty*, Columbus discovering the New World; 107. **Rahl**, **Portrait of an old** man; 59. *Hagn*, Garden of the Villa Colonna, at Rome; 55. *Bamberger*, The Generalifeh, near Granada; 182. *A. Wolf*, Lovers in a garden at Venice; 115. *Rottmann*, Greek landscape; 85. *Marshall*, Tartini's dream; 171. *Stange*, Piazza at Venice in moonlight. — End-wall: *62. *Hess*, Thorwaldsen; 163.

Spitzweg, Serenade; **51.** *Genelli*, Abraham receiving the news of Isaac's birth; 88. *B. Morgenstern*, Heligoland; 187. *R. Zimmermann*, Winter-scene **by night**; 5. *Bamberger*, Evening-glow in the Sierra Nevada; *50. *Genelli*, Hercules and Omphale; 2. *Bamberger*, Toledo; 74. *Lenbach*, View of the Vega, from the Torre de las Infantas at Granada; 29. *Catel*, The theatre **of Taormina**; 113. *Rottmann*, **The** Kochelsee; *81. *W. Lindenschmit*, The fisherman (Goethe); 53. *Genelli*, Bacchus and the Muses; 176. *Steinle*, Adam and Eve; 75. *Lenbach*, The Alhambra; ***53a.** *Genelli*, Composition for the **curtain** of a theatre; 69. *A. Kraus*, The Troubadour; 167. *Spitzweg*, Hermit; 114. *Rottmann*, **The** Hintersee, near Berchtesgaden; 54. *Gerhard*, Lion Court at the Alhambra by moonlight; 166. *Spitzweg*, Turkish coffee-house; 116. *Rottmann*, The spring of Calirrhoë, near Athens; 128. *Schweinfurth*, Landscape from the environs of Cervetri, near Rome; 92. *Muhr*, Gipsies; 66. *L. von Klenze*, Interior of a Saracenic château near Amalfi; 126. *Schnorr von Karolsfeld*, **The Erl-**king; *168. *Spitzweg*, Herd-girls on an alp; 79. *Lenbach*, Portrait of Count Schack; *30. *P. von Cornelius*, Flight into Egypt (of his early Roman period; the landscape in the background is painted by J. A. Koch); 67 *J. A. Koch*, Lime-kiln near Olevano. — ROOM VI (lighted from above). Copies of Bellini, Titian, Michael Angelo, Velazquez, etc., by *Linhart, Marées, Schwarzer, Wolf*, and others.

We **now return to** Room IV and descend the stairs to the right. ROOM I. **(to the** left) 94. *Naue*, Return of Kallias and Arete from the battle of Salamis (after Count Schack's poem 'The Pleiades'); **Neureuther, 97. The nun** (from Uhland), 99. Madonna, 101. Dream of Rezia **(from** Wieland's Oberon); 46. *Führich*, Introduction of Christianity into ancient Germany; 180. *Wislicenus*, Fancy borne by the Dreams; **11.** *Bode*, Legend of Charlemagne's birth; 47. *Führich*, Death of St. John Nepomuk; Copies of Titian, P. Veronese, Correggio, and Seb. del Piombo, by *Wolf*. — ROOM II. (to the left), 184. *A. Zimmermann*, Golgotha at the time of the Crucifixion; 170. *Stange*, The evening-bell; 162. *Sidorowicz*, Evening-scene; *Neureuther*, *98. Reminiscences of the Villa Mills at Rome, 96. Festival in honour of **Cornelius**, 102. Reminiscence of Villa Malta at Rome; 181. *Wolf*, Venetian banquet; 8. *M. von Beckerath*, Burial of Alaric, King of **the Goths**, in the river Busento; **198.** *Zwengauer*, The Kochelsee; 93. *Naue*, The Swan Maiden; 169. *Stademann*, Winter-scene. Copies from Venetian masters, by *Wolf* and others.

The **Bronze Foundry** (Pl. B, 1; adm., see p. 142; tramway-line 3, p. 140), in the Erzgiesserei-Str., enjoys a high reputation. Founded in 1825 by **Stiglmayer** (d. 1844), it was afterwards managed by his nephew *Ferd. von Miller*, and now belongs to the sons of the latter. The *Museum* contains **the original models of most of the statues cast here,** including **the head of the** Germania **on** the Niederwald Monument. — **A few** paces to the N.W., in the Ferdinand-Miller-Platz (**Pl. B,** 1), is the new *Church of St. Benno*, in the Romanesque style.

Farther to the N.W., on the road to Dachau, 1/2 M. beyond the **terminus of** tramway-line 3 in the Stiglmayer-Platz, is the *Zeughaus* or **Royal Arsenal**, with the *Military Museum* (arms, banners, uniforms, etc.; 15-19th cent.; adm., see p. 142; catalogue 80 pf.).

In front of the building are 22 cannons and 4 mortars, several of them with elaborate ornamentation. In the court are French field-pieces, naval guns, and mitrailleuses. — Room I. Head-pieces, helmets, and other objects from the time of Charles Theodore to the present day. The glass-cases contain early implements for artillery and models. In the middle, Bavarian, Franconian, and Swabian banners. — Room II. Flags, weapons, and armour of the 16-17th centuries. Rich collection of pikes, halberds, pole-axes, etc. — Room III. Objects of the end of the 17th and the 18th century. Trophies of the Turkish wars, including the tent of Grand-Vizier Suleyman, captured in 1687 at Mohacs by the Elector Max Emmanuel. Bavarian military types of the 18th century. — Room IV (19th cent.). Trophies of the Napoleonic wars and of 1870-71. Models of muskets, rifles, and cannon, collection of gun-locks and pistols; orders, medals, presentation swords, uniforms of Bavarian rulers and generals. — Room V. Collection of the modern weapons of different countries, either in use or projected; collection of munitions of war, bullets, cartridges, and cannon-balls. Portfolios and albums with over 3000 portraits of distinguished military men, pictures of uniforms, etc. — On the staircase and throughout the different rooms are the original plaster models of statues of Bavarian rulers, executed in the reign of King Maximilian II.

Beyond the Arsenal lie the *Military Hospital*, the *Maximilian Barracks*, and the *Artillery Work-Shops*. — **Other** large military **structures have** recently been **erected** in the Marsfeld (Pl. A, 2, 3), to the **W. of the** Stiglmayer-Platz (see above). Among these are the buildings of the *Corps of Cadets* (façade 735 ft. long), in the Mars-Platz; the *Military School*, in the Blutenburger-Str.; and the *Military Academy*, in the Pappenheimer-Str., the last with a collection of weapons and models on the first **floor**.

The *Basilica of St. Boniface* (Pl. C, 3; adm., see p. 143), an admirable imitation of an early-Christian Italian basilica of the 5th or 6th cent., designed by *Ziebland*, was completed in 1850. **Nave** 75 ft., four aisles 41 ft. in height. **The** sixty-six **columns are** monoliths of grey Tyrolese marble with **bases and capitals of white** marble. Open timber roof, richly gilded.

On the right of the entrance is a sarcophagus of gray marble, the burial-place of Lewis I. (d. 1868) and his queen Theresa (d. 1854). The choir, the side-altars, the spaces between the windows, and the walls of the nave are decorated with fine frescoes by *H. von Hess* and his pupils *Schraudolph* and *Koch*: scenes from the life of St. Boniface and Bavarian saints, Madonna enthroned, Stoning of St. Stephen, etc. Above the columns in the nave, between the arches, are thirty-four medallion-portraits of the popes from Julius III. to Gregory XVI. — Adjoining the choir of the church is a Benedictine monastery, with a fresco of the *Holy Eucharist*, by *H. von Hess*, in the refectory.

The Botanic Garden (Pl. C, 3, 4; adm., see p. 142), opposite the Basilica, **contains a large** fresh-water aquarium (Victoria Regia, etc.), a palm-house, **botanical museum**, etc. — In the Sophien-Str. is the **Crystal Palace** (Pl. C, 4; 256 yds. long; central part 75 ft. high), erected in 1854, **used for exhibitions** and festivities. (*Annual Exhibition of Art*, see p. 142.) — **A** little to the S. are the Courts of Law and the Karls-Platz (p. 190). To the E., at the corner of the Arco-Str. and the Barer-Str., is the bronze *Monument of F. X. Gabelsberger (d. 1849), inventor of a well-known system of stenography, by Eberle (1890). From this point we proceed to the E. to the —

MAXIMILIANS-PLATZ (Pl. D, 4), the pleasure-grounds of which were laid out by K. von Effner. In the middle stands the *Liebig Monument, by Wagmüller and Rümann, erected in 1883. The seated marble figure of the great chemist (1805-73) rests upon a pedestal of grey granite with laurel-wreaths and marble reliefs. Adjacent are a marble bench with a Bust of Effner (1886) and the Herma of a Satyr by Gasteiger (1894).

At the S.W. end of the grounds rises the handsome *Wittelsbach Fountain by Hildebrandt (1895), with groups emblematical of the destructive and fertilizing powers of water and masks symbolizing its different 'temperaments'. — To the W., opposite the fountain, is the Bernheimer Haus, a fine baroque edifice by Thiersch (1890). To the S., at the corner of the Pfandhaus-Str., is the Herzog-Max-Burg, built about 1580, now occupied by the military authorities and the commission for extinguishing the national debt.

To the E. of the Liebig Monument (Pranner-Str. 20) is the Landtagsgebäude (Pl. E, 4), or house of the Diet, remodelled in 1885 in the German Renaissance style. — In the Pfandhaus-Str. (see above; No. 7) is the **Kunstgewerbehaus** (Pl. D, 4; adm., see p. 142), built in 1877 in the Renaissance style, with a façade by Knab and Voit and a fine exhibition-hall. The handsome banquet-hall, designed by B. Gedon, is adorned with paintings by F. A. Kaulbach.

The Pfandhaus-Strasse ends at the **Promenade-Platz** (Pl. D, E, 4), in which are five bronze statues. In the middle is Elector Max Emmanuel (1679-1726), conqueror of Belgrade, by Brugger (1861). To the right are Westenrieder (1748-1829), the historian, by Widnmann (1854), and Gluck (1714-87), the composer, by Brugger; to the left are Kreittmayr (1705-90), the statesman, by Schwanthaler (1845), and Orlando di Lasso (1520-94), the composer (properly Roland de Lattres, of the Netherlands), by Widnmann. — The Hartmann-Strasse leads to the S. from the Promenade-Platz to the Frauenkirche (p. 190). The Maffei-Str. leads to the E. to the busy Theatiner-Str., whence we may follow either the Perusa-Str. to the N.E. to the Max-Joseph-Platz (p. 145), or the Wein-Str. to the S. to the Marien-Platz.

The **Marien-Platz** (Pl. E, 5), the centre of old Munich, is adorned with a Column of the Madonna, erected in 1638 by Elector Maximilian I. from a design by Peter Candid, to commemorate the victory on the Weisse Berg near Prague. Enthroned on the column is the Virgin, the tutelary saint of Bavaria; four genii at the corners contend against a viper, a basilisk, a lion, and a dragon (plague, war, famine, and heresy).

The **Old Rathhaus** (Pl. E, 5), on the E. side of the Platz, dates from the 14th cent. and was restored in 1865. The **tower**, under which **runs the** road to the Thal (p. 165), is adorned with stereochromatic paintings by Seitz. The gables in front bear zinc statues of Henry the Lion and Lewis **the** Bavarian. The great hall, recently restored, contains old **standards and** ensigns of the Munich guilds. — On the N. side of the **Platz is the *New Rathhaus** (Pl. 85), a Gothic edifice by *Hauberrisser* (1867-74). The façade towards the Marien-Platz is 156 ft., that towards the Diener-Strasse 230 ft. long. The central part of the former, in sandstone, 57 ft. wide, has a balcony in three sections on the second story, terminating in a lofty gable, and **embellished with** statues of the four Civic Virtues by *A. Hess.*

Below the portal, to the left, are two tablets, with handsome bronze trophies, in memory of citizens who fell in the war of 1870-71. On the second floor are the *Council Chambers*, on the left that of the town-council, on the right that of the magistrates (adm., see p. 143). In the former, filling the whole wall, is a large allegorical painting of 'Munichia' by *K. von Piloty*, illustrating the history of Munich (explanation of the portraits on the table); also portraits of Lewis II. by *F. Piloty* and Prince Regent **Luitpold** by *Kaulbach*. The *Magistrates' Room* is adorned with a mural painting by *W. Lindenschmit* (progress of Munich under Lewis I.) and admirable stained-glass windows by *R. Seitz* (nine departments of civic administration). Portraits of Prince Regent Luitpold by *Holmberg* and Lewis II. by *Lenbach*. Bust of Burgomaster von Ehrhardt (d. 1888), by *F. von Miller*. Splendid carved timber ceiling; fine mantel-piece and chandelier.

To the left of the portal is the Hauptwache or guard-house. In the sunk-floor (entrance in the Diener-Str.) is the *Rathskeller* (p. 138).

In front of the Rathhaus rises the **Fischbrunnen*, in bronze, by Knoll (1865). The figures allude to an old Munich custom called the 'Metzgersprung' (p. 142).

A few yards to the S.E. **of the** Marien-Platz is the **Church of St. Peter** (Pl. E, 5), of 1170, **the oldest** in Munich, but repeatedly restored and modernized. To **the** original building belongs the Romanesque tower (p. 126; fine view from the gallery). Altar-pieces by *Sandrart, Loth*, etc.; fine organ by Abt Vogler.

The Thal leads from the Marien-Platz to the **S.E.** to the Ludwigs-Brücke and the suburbs of Haidhausen and **Au** (pp. 157, 192), **while the** Kaufinger-Str. and Neuhauser-Str. **lead to** the N.W. to the Karlsthor and the Central Railway Station (**tramway-line 5, p. 140**). To the right is the *Frauen-Platz*, with the —

*Frauenkirche (Pl. E, 5), or Church **of Our Lady**, cathedral of the **Arch**bishopric of Munich and Freising, **a brick** edifice (320 ft. **long, 117 ft.** broad; vaulting 108 ft. high) in **the** late-Gothic **style**, **erected by** *Jörg Gangkofer* in 1468-88 and restored in 1858-68. The **two uncompleted** towers, **318 ft.** high, were covered at **the** beginning **of the 16th cent.** with clumsy helmet-shaped roofs (ascent, see p. 142). **On the outside** walls of the church are many ancient tombstones.

INTERIOR (adm., see p. 113; music, see p. 143). The nave and aisles **are** of equal height, borne by twenty-two slender octagonal pillars; rich groined vaulting. The windows, each 65 ft. high, are filled with fine **stained glass**, including the remains (sometimes wrongly arranged) of the old glazing of the 15-16th centuries. The high-altar-piece shows the Coronation of Mary, in carved **wood**, by *Knobl*, and paintings on the wings by *Schwind*. The archiepiscopal **throne** and pulpit, a modern continuation of the ancient **choir-stalls**, are by *Knabl*. Most of the modern side-altars are by *Sickinger*, the statues by *L. Foltz*. Above the choir-stalls are carved wooden figures of the 15th cent. (Apostles and Prophets). — The large Turkish flag on a pillar of the nave (l.) was captured by Elector Max Emmanuel at Belgrade in 1688. — At the W. end of the nave, under the organ-loft, is the °**Monument of Emp. Lewis the Bavarian** (d. 1347), erected in 1622 by Elector Maximilian I. (designed by *P. Candid*, cast by *H. Krumper*), a catafalque in dark marble, with figures and decorations in bronze; four knights at the corners guard the tomb; at the side are statues of the Wittelsbach princes Albert V. and William V.; an admirable brass of the 15th cent. is inserted in the pedestal, which is open at the sides. Behind this monument, opposite a relief-monument of Bishop Gebsattel (d. 1846) by Schwanthaler, is a spot from which none of the thirty windows of the church are visible except the great window behind the altar.

At the corner of the Neuhauser-Str. and the Ett-Str. rises the **Church of St. Michael** (*Hofkirche;* Pl. D, 5; adm., see p. 143), formerly a church of the Jesuits, erected in 1583-97 in the Roman baroque style, with grand barrel-vaulting. The front is adorned with a St. Michael in bronze, by *Hub. Gerhard*. The transept contains the *Monument of Eugène Beauharnais (d. 1824), Duke of Leuchtenberg, and once vice-king of Italy, by Thorwaldsen. In the royal burial-vault under the choir reposes Lewis II. (d. 1886). Church-music, see p. 141.

The old Jesuits' College, adjoining St. Michael's, contains the **Academy of Science** (Pl. D, 5), with its valuable collections (adm., see p. 142).

The °*Palaeontological Collection*, under the direction of Prof. Dr. Zittel, is probably the most complete in Europe (nine rooms); the specimens from the animal kingdom are arranged zoologically, those of plants geologically. The *Prehistoric Collection* contains many objects of the stone period and interesting relics of lake-dwellings from the Starnberger-See and Robenhausen. The °*Collection of Minerals* also deserves inspection. The *Zoological-Zootomical Collection* includes animals both stuffed and preserved in spirits. The *Collection of Physical and Optical Instruments* is interesting, especially to the scientific visitor. Of ancient Greek coins alone the *Cabinet of Coins* contains 20,000.

The Academy also contains an *Exhibition of Bavarian Exports* (free).

The narrow Herzog-Max-Strasse, at the end of the Neuhauser-Strasse, leads to the right to the **Synagogue** (Pl. D, 4; adm., see p. 143), built in the Romanesque style by *Alb. Schmidt*, in 1884-87. — The Neuhauser-Str. ends in the **Karlsthor** (Pl. D, 5). Outside the gate is the *Karls-Platz*, on the right side of which is the *Hôtel Bellevue* (p. 137), embellished with frescoes by C. Schraudolph. Adjacent, to the N., at the corner of the Prielmaier-Str. and the Elisen-Str., are the new **Courts of Justice** (Pl. C, D, 4), by *Thiersch*. Nearly opposite, at the corner of the Maximilians-Platz, is a *Statue of Goethe*, by Widnmann (1869). — *Botanic Garden*, see p. 187.

From the Karls-Platz the broad *Sonnen-Strasse*, planted with trees, runs to the S. to the Sendlinger-Thor-Platz. At the beginning of it is the Protestant **Church of St. Matthew** (Pl. C, 5), an unattractive circular building (1827-32), open only on Sundays during service (at **8**, 10, and 3). The ceiling is adorned with an Ascension by *Hermann* of Dresden. — To the E., Herzogspital-Str. 18, is the *University Ophthalmic Institute*.

The **Schwanthaler Museum** (Pl. C, 5; adm., see p. 143), Schwanthaler-Str. 90, contains models of almost all the works of the talented and prolific sculptor *Ludwig von Schwanthaler* (d. 1848), bequeathed by him to the Academy of Art. Catalogue 30 pf.

In the Sonnen-Strasse are the new *Volks-Theater* (Pl. C, D, 5; p. 141; No. 5, to the left), the *Reisingerianum* (University Clinical Institute; No. 17, to the right), and the *Frauenklinik* or *Gynaecological Institute* (Pl. C, 6; No. 16).

In the SENDLINGER-THOR-PLATZ (Pl. C, 6) are the old *Sendlinger Thor* (14th cent.) and a colossal bust of *Alois Senefelder* (d. 1834), the inventor of lithography, by Zumbusch (1877). — The busy Sendlinger-Strasse leads hence to the N., passing the *St. Johanniskirche* (Pl. D, 6; 1733-46), to the Marien-Platz (p. 188), while the Thalkirchner-Strasse (electric tramway, **p. 140**) runs to the S. to the *Southern* **Cemetery** (**p. 192**) and to the large municipal *Slaughter House* and **Cattle Market** (Pl. B, C, 8; adm., p. 143), erected by Zenetti in 1876-78. Beyond these are the *South Railway Station* (Pl. B, 9) and the *Isar Railway Station* (Pl. B, **10, 11**; p. 194).

To the S.W. of the Sendlinger-Thor-Platz are the large *General Hospital* (1813) and the *Institute of Clinical Medicine*. In the grounds in front is a **marble bust of T. N. von Nussbaum**, the surgeon (1829-90). — Adjacent, in the Nussbaum-Str., are the new *Clinical Institute of Surgery* (Pl. C, 6) and the *Pathological* and *Pharmacological Institutes*. — To the N. (Schiller-Str. 25) is the *Anatomical Institute*, with important anatomical and pathological collections (adm., see p. 142). In the Findling-Str. (Nos. 12 & 34) are the *Physiological* and *Hygienic Institutes*.

The Findling-Str. ends at the THERESIENWIESE (Pl. A, 6, 7), the scene of the October Festival (p. 142), which has recently been much diminished by the construction of new streets. On the N.E. side are the new *Church of St. Paul* (Pl. A, B, 5) and a *Panorama* (Pl. A, 5; p. 143).

The *****Bavaria** and **Hall of Fame** (*Ruhmeshalle*; Pl. A, 7) lie on the W. side of the Theresienwiese, 1¼ M. to the S.W. of the Karlsthor (tramway-line 2, p. **140**; adm., see p. 142). The colossal statue of *Bavaria*, in bronze, designed by Schwanthaler, measures 62 ft. to the top of the wreath which the figure holds aloft. The ascent, by an iron spiral staircase of sixty steps, is most comfortably made early in the morning, before the metal has been heated by the sun. *View in clear weather through apertures in the head (room for 5 persons). — The *Hall of Fame*, a Doric colonnade with projecting wings, designed by Klenze, and completed in 1853, contains **busts of** eighty Bavarian notabilities, among them Francis von Sickingen, Jean Paul Richter, Schwanthaler, the philosopher Schelling, Klenze, Cornelius, etc. (custodian's fee for **the statue and** the hall, 40 pf.). Adjoining the Ruhmeshalle is a public *Park*.

Towards the E. from the Marien-Platz (p. 188) we pass through an archway under the **tower** of the Old Rathhaus (p. 189), and enter the broad street called the *Thal*. On the right, at the beginning of it, rises the *Church of the Holy Ghost*, **rebuilt in 1885-87**, beyond which lies the *Provision Market* (Pl. E, 5, 6). Beyond the latter is the spacious **Corn Hall** (*Schranne*; Pl. D, E, 6), built in 1853. In the St-Jakobs-Platz (Pl. D, E, 6), between the Corn Hall and the **Sendlinger-Str.**, is the *Landwehr Arsenal*, containing the *Municipal Historical Museum* and the *Maillinger Art-Historical Collection*, illustrative of the history of Munich (adm., see p. 143).

At the E. end of the Thal is the ***Isarthor** (Pl. F, 6), erected at **the beginning of the 14th cent. and restored** by Lewis I. **in 1835. The pediment is adorned** with a **fresco** by Neher, representing the **Entry of Emp. Lewis** the Bavarian after the Battle of Ampfing (1831; spoiled **in 1881 by an attempt at** restoration). In the Zweibrücken-Str., beyond the gate, on the right, are the *Heavy Cavalry Barracks*, on the bank of the Isar. Opposite is the new Steinsdorf-Strasse (see **p. 156**). The *Ludwigs-Brücke* (Pl. G, 6, 7), farther on, affords a **good survey of the** Maximilians-Brücke and the Maximilianeum. The bridge was remodelled in 1891-94 and **furnished** with allegorical **figures of industry and trade (by Eberle),** fishing (by Hahn), **and art (by Kaufmann).**

In the suburb of *Au* (Pl. F, G, 7, 8) are numerous beer-gardens (comp. p. 138). The ***Mariahilfkirche** (Pl. F, 8), or *Auer-Kirche*, was erected in 1830-39 by *Ohlmüller* and *Ziebland* in the earliest Gothic style. Tower 260 ft. high. *Stained glass designed by *Schraudolph*, *Fischer*, **and** others. — Farther to the S., in the suburb of Giesing, is the *Giesinger Kirche, a Gothic building erected by Dollmann in 1866-84, with a tower 315 ft. high and an elaborately decorated interior. A little to the E. is the new *Eastern* or *Central Cemetery*.

From the Auer Kirche we return into the town by the *Reichenbach Bridge* (Pl. E, 8; tramway-line 7, p. 140). In the Gärtner-Platz (Pl. E, 6, 7), with statues of *Gärtner* (d. 1847) and **Klenze** (d. 1864), the chief architects **of** modern Munich (see **p. 145), is** the *Gärtner-Platz Theatre* (p. 141). — With a visit to Giesing may be combined an excursion to **the** *Isarauen* (p. 193), or we may drive hence to the *Southern Cemetery* (p. 192; tramway-line 8, p. 140).

The *Southern Cemetery (Pl. C, D, 7, 8) of Munich, outside the Sendlinger-Thor (p. 191), contains the finest and most artistic **tombstones** in Germany.

Among the illustrious dead may be mentioned *Fraunhofer*, the astronomer (d. 1826; arcade, W. side), *Senefelder*, inventor of lithography (d. 1834; E. side, by the wall), *Neumann*, the historian (d. 1870; central walk), and *P. von Hess*, the painter (d. 1871; central walk).

On the S. side, from the arcades, we enter the New Cemetery (Pl. C, 8), inclosed with arcades in red brick. The first graves on the right and left are those of *Ludwig von Schwanthaler* (d. 1848) and *Fr. von Gärtner* (d. 1847), the two greatest contributors to the splendour of modern Munich. Many other eminent men are also interred here. The centre *Crucifix is by *Halbig*.

The Northern Cemetery, in the Arcis-Strasse (p. 180; Pl. D, 1), not far from the New Pinakothek, laid out by Zenetti in 1866-69, contains a monument erected by the city to the German soldiers who died of their wounds at Munich in 1870-71, and also a monument to French prisoners buried here during the same period. In the centre is another marble *Crucifix by *Halbig*.

ENVIRONS. The *English Garden (Pl. F, G, H, 1, 2, 3), a park of 600 acres, originally laid out by Count Rumford, with fine old trees, and watered by two arms of the Isar, affords delightful walks in summer. At the entrance between the Hofgarten and the Prinz-Regenten-Str. (p. 149) is a marble statue known as the 'Harmlos', from the first word of the inscription, by Xaver Schwanthaler (renewed in 1890). Farther on, by the Brunnhaus, is an artificial cascade. Then, on the right, the *Dianabad*. To the left, on a height, rises the *Monopteros*, a small temple designed by Klenze; then the *Chinese Tower* (café; music, see p. 125) and the little lake of *Kleinhesselohe* (restaurant), used for boating. The *Milchhäusl* and the *Tivoli*, farther on, are both cafés. At the N. end is the *Aumeister*, a forester's house with a restaurant.

To the E. of the park is the *Max-Joseph-Brücke*, leading across the Isar Canal and the Isar to *Bogenhausen* (Pl. I, 2; Inn), on the right bank of the Isar, near which is the *Observatory* (adm., see p. 143). From the *Brunnthal*, a health institute with a shady coffee-garden, to the right of the bridge, the charming *Gasteig-Anlagen* extend to the Ludwigs-Brücke (p. 192).

On the left bank of the Isar, above the Reichenbach bridge (Pl. E, 8; p. 192), begin the °*Isarauen*, through which a road leads, crossing the *Überfälle* or weirs, to the right bank of the Isar (fine view of *Thalkirchen*, see below). Then, to the right, we enter the *Marienklause*, ascend the steps, and follow the bank through fine wood to the (1½ hr.) *Menterschwaige* and to *Grosshesselohe*.

Grosshesselohe, 7 M. from Munich, is reached by railway in 12-20 min.; it is also a station of the Isarthal Railway (see p. 194). From the Main Railway Station (p. 137) we cross the handsome bridge over the Isar to (1 M.) the *Menterschwaige* (Restaurant). The bridge affords a good view of Munich, with the deep and broad valley of the Isar below. — Pleasant walk to the *Grosshesselohe Restaurant*, ascending from the station by a path to the left on the left bank (10 min.); thence through wood to the (¼ hr.) little château of *Schwanegg*, erected by Schwanthaler (private property, not accessible); ¼ hr. farther on is *Pullach* (p. 194). We now descend to (½ hr.) *Höllriegelskreut* (Inn), on the Isar, and return by the romantic lower path

along the river (not advisable in wet weather), traversing fine beech-woods and ascending to **the station** near the Grosshesselohe bridge. Or from Höllriegelskreut we may **cross** the river by a wire-rope ferry to the **old** ducal hunting-lodge of *Grünwald* (Inn, with **view**), and follow the **right** bank to (1 hr.) the bridge.

Nymphenburg, founded in 1663, **and once a** favourite château of Max Joseph I., 3 M. to the W. of Munich **(cab, see p.** 140; steam-tramway, see p. 140), has well-kept grounds, two **fountains** 100 ft. high, **and** fine hothouses (numerous Brazilian plants). **In the central** part **of the château tickets are** issued (9-11 and 1-5) for the **Nymphenburg** itself (uninteresting), and for **the** Pagodenburg, Amalienburg, **and Badenburg** (50 pf.; park free). **In the nearer part of** the park are the *Magdalen Chapel*, **built** to imitate a ruin, **and** the *Pagodenburg*, farther to the W., on a small pond. In the **farther part of the park are** the *Amalienburg*, a pretty Renaissance structure by Cuvillier (1737), **the** *Badenburg* (1718), on a large pond, and a circular Corinthian temple. — At the terminus of the tramway is the *Volksgarten*, with a restaurant, a small zoological garden, concerts, etc. **Near the château, on the** left, is the Restaurant zum Controlor. On the **N.E. side of the château is a** *Porcelain Manufactory*, formerly belonging to **the king, now in private hands. In** the (1/2 M.) *Deer Park* (Restaurant) are **kept tame stags and white deer.**

The **château of Schleissheim** (*Schlosswirth*; *Blauer Karpfen*; *Traveller's Home*; *Restaurant zum Bergl*, 1½ M. from the Schloss), a station on the Ratisbon railway **(p. 136, reached in** 20-30 min.), erected by Elector Max Emmanuel at the **end of the 17th cent.**, possesses a pleasant garden, a picture-gallery, etc. (in the lower **rooms**, early German and Italian masters, open 11-12.30; in the upper, Dutch, etc., open 3-5).

From Munich to Wolfratshausen, 17 M., Isarthal Railway in 1 hr. 7 min. (best views to **the** left). The trains start from the Isarthal Station (Pl. B, 10, 11; p. 137), reached from the Färbergraben in 1/4 hr. by electric tramway (p. 140; 10 pf.). — The train passes *Thalkirchen* (Deutsche Eiche), with **a** hydropathic, and **beyond** *St.-Maria-Einsiedel* ascends through wood to the top **of** the plateau, crossing the **state-railway** near the Grosshesselohe station (p. 137). — 4½ M. *Grosshesselohe* (p. 193); footpath to the state-railway-station and to the **Isar** bridge, 8-10 min.; past the brewery to the **restaurant in** the wood, 1/4 hr. — Farther on we traverse wood and pass **the château of** *Schwanegg* (see above). — 5½ M. *Pullach* (1910 ft.; *Rabenwirt*, **with view-terrace**; Hydropathic, on the Isar), charmingly situated on **the** high left bank **of the Isar.** The church contains two early-Bavarian altar-pieces (1489) and a figure of the Salvator Mundi of the beginning **of** the 15th century. — 7 M. *Höllriegelskreut-Grünwald* (1955 ft.; Restaurant zum Forsthaus, near the rail. station). About 1/2 M. to the E. (left) is the *Höllriegelskreut Inn*, whence a ferry crosses **to** *Grünwald* (see **above**). — 9½ M. *Baierbrunn*; 11½ M. *Hohenschäftlarn* (2150 ft.; Häfele's **Rail. Restaurant; Kapuziner), a high-lying village with a fine view. — From (12½ M) *Ebenhausen* (Post) **we may** descend **to** (1/2 M.) the convent of *Schäftlarn*, **with an** interesting **church** (1733-64) **and** a frequented brewery. **Fine view from the** *Röschenauer Höhe* (2130 ft.; Inn), 1/2 M. to the N.W. **of the** rail. station. From Ebenhausen a marked path leads, viâ *Irschenhausen*, *Merlbach*, and *Aufkirchen*. to (2 hrs.) *Leoni*, **on** the *Lake of Starnberg* (p. 196). — **Farther** on we enjoy **a** fine view **of** the Isar valley and **the** mountains. **Beyond** (14½ M.) *Icking* **the line** descends through deep cuttings and **along** the hillside (gradient 1:33), affording a good survey of the wide valley of the Isar, with its grey sandy and gravelly islets, and the confluence of the *Loisach* and the Isar. We then cross the Loisach and reach —

17 M. **Wolfratshausen** (*Restaurant*), the station for which is 1/2 M. from the prettily-situated **town** (1890 ft. ; 1750 inhab.; *Hôt.-Pens. Kronmühle*, with garden; *Haderbräu*; *Humplbräu*; *Botengarten*). Above, on the *Calvarienberg*, are shady walks affording delightful views. The Lake of Starnberg may be reached hence by pleasant routes viâ *Münsing* (Inn) to (2 hrs.) *Ammerland* (p. 196), viâ *Dorfen*, *Höhenhain*, *Aufhausen*, and *Aufkirchen* to (2 hrs.) *Leoni*, or direct from the Calvarienberg to (1¾ hr.) *Rottmanns-*

hohe (p. 196). A road (diligence in 2 hrs.) leads to the S. from Wolfratshausen through the valley of the Loisach to (5¼ M.) *Eurasburg* and (3¼ M.) *Beuerberg*; another leads to the S.E. through the Isar valley to (9 M.) *Königsdorf* (2053 ft.; Post) and thence viâ *Unterbuchen* to (10 M.) *Tölz* (p. 215).

Pasing, the first station on the Starnberg, Lindau, and Augsburg lines (see below and pp. 198, 134; 5 M., in about ¼ hr.), is the starting-point for a visit to the churches of Pipping and Blutenburg, which possess considerable artistic interest. The church of **Pipping**, ½ M. to the N. of Pasing, was built in 1478-79. The interior has remained unchanged, and, with its old stained glass, altars, choir-stalls, and frescoes, affords a charming picture of a late-Gothic country-church of the 15th century. — A few hundred yards to the N. of this lies Blutenburg, now a school of English nuns. The church (fee 50 pf.), built in 1490, contains a high-altar and two side-altars of 1491, with paintings of the Munich school; fine wooden figures of the Apostles, the Virgin, and the Risen Christ, of the same period; and stained-glass windows of 1497.

Excursion to *Dachau*, see p. 133.

29. The Starnberger See and Ammersee. The Hohe Peissenberg.

RAILWAY from Munich (*Starnberg Station*, p. 137) to Starnberg (17½ M.) in 34-65 **min.**; to Peissenberg (38½ M.) in 2-2¼ hrs. — STEAMBOAT from Starnberg to Seeshaupt and back (round the whole lake, 2 ℳ 80, 1 ℳ 80 pf.), 10 times daily in summer (oftener on Sundays) in 3 hrs. Steamboat-tickets may be purchased at the railway-station in Munich as well as on board the steamers. A circular ticket entitles the holder to break the journey twice, but a fee of 60 pf. must be paid for each additional halt.

The train quits the Lindau line (p. 198) at (4½ M.) *Pasing*. 9 M. *Planegg*; 12 M. *Gauting*, with a sulphur-spring. Near (14½ M.) *Mühlthal* we have a glimpse of the pretty, wooded *Würmthal* to the left.

7½ M. **Starnberg** (*Bayrischer Hof; *Bellevue; **Zum Deutschen Kaiser*, all on the lake; *Zur Eisenbahn; *Pellet; *Tutzinger Hof*), a considerable place at the N. end of the lake, is generally crowded in summer. **Swimming** and other baths next the steamboat-quay. Rowing boat 80 **pf.** per hour.

The *Lake of Starnberg, or **Würmsee** (1920 ft.), 12½ M. long and 2-3 M. in width, is enclosed by banks of moderate height, which are covered with villas and parks, especially at the N. end. The principal charm of the scenery is the view of the distant mountains in clear weather. The following are the conspicuous peaks, from E. to W.: Wendelstein, Brecherspitze, Kirchstein, Benediktenwand, Karwendel-Gebirge, Jochberg, Herzogstand, Heimgarten, **Krottenkopf**, Wetterstein range with the Zugspitze, and Ettaler Mandl.

STEAMBOAT JOURNEY. On the **hill** to the right, immediately beyond Starnberg, rises the château of Count Almeida. On the bank, farther on, are a number of other villas. Stat. *Niederpöcking*. **Possenhofen** *(Inn)* lies about ½ M. from the railway-station of that name (p. 196). Duke Carl Theodor of Bavaria has a château here. The garden, enclosed by a high wall, is not shown; but the park, about 2 M. in length, is open to the public. Pleasant walk through wood, ascending to the right (way-posts), to (1 M.) *Feldafing* (see below). In the lake below lies the *Roseninsel* (shown by order obtained at the 'Oberst-Hofmarschallamt' at Munich, or from the 'Rentamt' at Starnberg).

The first station on the E. bank is **Schloss Berg** (*Wiesmayer's Inn*, 1/4 M. from the lake, with garden).

About 1/4 M. from the pier is Schloss Berg (adm. 50 pf.), a royal château with a large park, where King Lewis II. of Bavaria perished in the lake on June 13th, 1886. The château is plainly fitted up, and contains paintings and statuettes, for the most part of scenes and characters from Wagner's operas. — A road leads through the park to (1 M.) *Leoni* (see below), passing the spot where the bodies of King Lewis II. and Dr. von Gudden were found (indicated by a stone column with a cross).

Farther on, opposite Possenhofen (boat in 1/4 hr., 1 ℳ), lies the neat little village of Leoni (**Hôtel Leoni*, pens. 5 ℳ). On the hill above it rises the church of *Aufkirchen*.

*Rottmannshöhe (2195 ft.; 20 min.). The path ascends opposite the landing-place, and at the top of the hill turns to the right to the *Hotel*, the roof of which commands a beautiful survey of the lake and Alps (fee 10 pf.). On a platform in front of the hotel-veranda stands a simple monument erected by the artists of Munich to Karl Rottmann (d. 1850), the famous landscape-painter.

On the W. bank a number of parks and gardens extend from Possenhofen to (2 1/4 M.) *Garatshausen*, with a château of Prince Thurn and Taxis. Next stat. **Tutzing** (**Hôtel am See*, with a garden; **Simson's Bahnhôtel*, at the rail. station, 1/2 M. from the lake, with *View from the terrace; *Bierkeller*, a restaurant with groups of fine trees, 1/4 M. to the S. of the station), with Hr. von Hallberger's château, the pleasant grounds of which are open from 12 to 3 p.m. Below the landing-stage are a bathing-place and swimming-baths. — The *Johannesberg*, 3/4 M. to the S. of the railway-station, commands a charming view (still finer from the **Ilkahöhe*, near *Oberzeismering*, 1 hr.). The lake, which forms a bay here towards the W., called the *Karpfenwinkel*, has now attained its greatest width (3 M.).

Stat. **Bernried** *(Altwirth; Neuwirth)*, with a château of Hr. von Wendland and a fine park, open to the public (good beer at the brewery). The banks become flatter, and the mountains more conspicuous. Stat. Seeshaupt *(Post)* lies at the S. end of the lake. The steamer now steers along the wooded E. bank, passing *Ambach*, *Ammerland*, with a château of Count Pocci, and *Allmannshausen*, to Leoni and Starnberg.

RAILWAY JOURNEY. — 17 1/2 M. *Starnberg*, see p. 195. 20 1/2 M. Possenhofen (p. 195; *Hôt.-Restaurant Pöcking*, 1/4 M. to the right of the station; *Bellevue*, in the village of Pöcking, 1/4 M. farther on, both with fine views). — 22 M. Feldafing (2160 ft.; **Strauch's Hotel*, 1/2 M. from the station, with terrace; **Hôt.-Pens. Neuschwanstein*; fine view from both), 1 M. from the lake (see above). At (25 M.) *Tutzing* passengers for *Penzberg* (p. 213) change carriages. The Weilheim line turns towards the W. (view of the Zugspitze, etc., to the left).

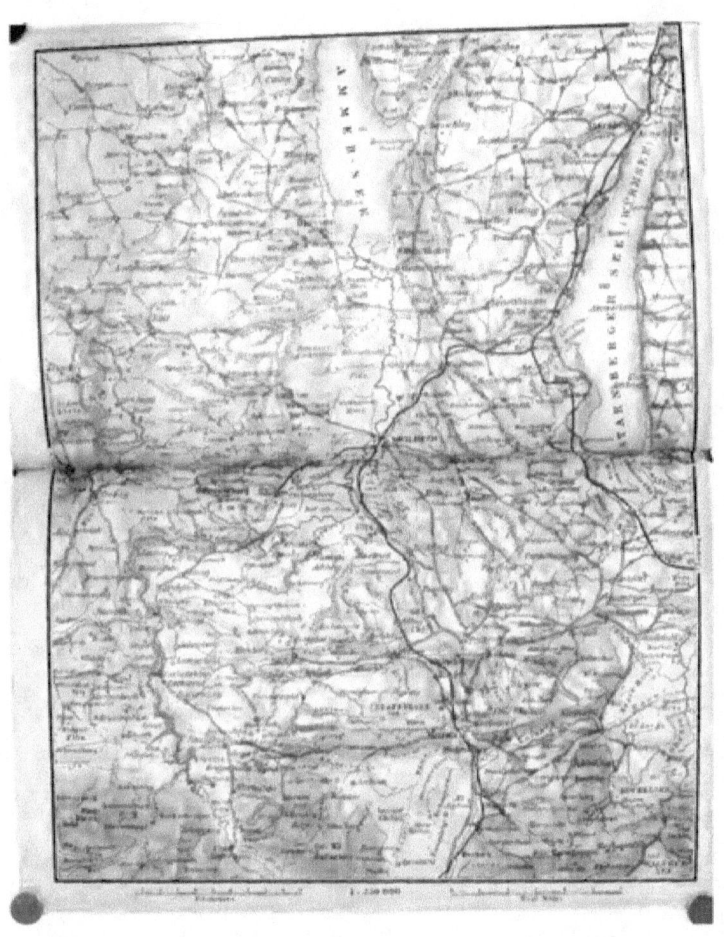

27½ M. *Diemendorf;* 30½ M. **Wilzhofen** (to the Ammersee, see below). — At (33½ M.) Weilheim (1845 ft.; **Post; *Traube; *Bräuwastl,* with garden), a small town on the *Ammer,* we change carriages for Peissenberg. (Route to Murnau and Partenkirchen, see p. 207.) Passing *Unter-Peissenberg* (Post), the train stops at (38½ M.) *Peissenberg* (1930 ft.), where the railway ends. About ¼ M. from the station is **Bad Sulz** (2020 ft.; **Hotel,* pens. 4 ℳ), with mineral springs and shady walks.

The best ROUTE TO THE HOHE PEISSENBERG (mountain-railway projected), indicated by red and white marks, leads viâ Bad Sulz, the *Sulzbach Waterfall,* the *Quellenhaus,* and the *Schöne Aussicht* (to the top 1¼ hr.; donkeys at Bad Sulz). The descent (blue marks) may be made to the S.E., across the ridge (fine views) to the *Weinbauer* (Inn, good wine), and thence in windings to (1 hr.) the railway-station of Peissenberg.

The ***Hohe Peissenberg** (3190 ft.), the Rigi of Bavaria, affords a remarkably extensive panorama owing to its isolated position opposite the centre of the Bavarian Alps. On the summit are a pilgrimage-church, a school (with an observatory on the roof; adm. 20 pf.), and an *Inn* (35 beds).

VIEW. The principal mountains visible are, from E. to W., the Wendelstein, Benediktenwand, Jochberg (beyond which in the extreme distance peeps the snowy Venediger), Herzogstand, Heimgarten (in front of which lies the Staffelsee), Karwendelgebirge, Kistenkopf, Krottenkopf, Dreithorspitze, Wetterstein range (with the Zugspitze), Daniel, Hochplatte, Hohe Bleiche, Gabelschroffen, Säuling, Grünten, and Stuiben. To the N. an extensive survey of the plain, embracing the Ammersee, Starnberger See, and innumerable towns and villages as far as Munich and Augsburg.

FROM PEISSENBERG TO OBER-AMMERGAU. A carriage-road (diligence daily to Bayersoyen) leads round the E. flank of the Hohe Peissenberg to *Böbing* (Hydropathic) and (9 M.) *Rottenbuch* (*Post), with its ancient convent, picturesquely situated on the left bank of the deep *Ammerthal.* Thence past (4½ M.) *Bayersoyen* (Inn), near the little *Soyen Lake,* and (3 M.) *Saulgrub* (p. 212), to (4½ M.) *Unter-Ammergau* and (3 M.) *Ober-Ammergau* (p. 211).

The **Ammersee** (1750 ft.), 10 M. long and 3¾ M. broad, is inferior to the Starnberger See in landscape beauty. The banks are flat and wooded. It commands a view of the distant Alps to the S., while the Hohe Peissenberg rises in the foreground. A small steamboat plies on the lake (3-4 times a day between Diessen and Stegen in 1½ hr.; fares 1½ or 1 ℳ).

From stat. *Wilzhofen* (see above) a diligence runs thrice daily in 2 hrs. viâ *Pähl,* a pleasant village commanded by the Gothic **Hochschloss* (fine view from the adjoining *Sonnenhügel*), and *Fischen* to (7½ M.) **Diessen,** or *Bayerdiessen* (**Post; *Gattinger;* Pens. *Seerichterhaus),* a straggling market-town and summer-resort at the S.W. end of the lake, with the extensive buildings of an old monastery (now a château of Count Pestalozza). Baths in the lake at the N. end of the town (20 pf.), and at *St. Alban,* ½ M. farther on.

The STEAMBOAT crosses the lake to *Fischen* (see above), and then skirts the E. bank to *Mühlfeld* and *Hersching* (*Post, moderate), the station for (3 M.) **Andechs** (2335 ft.), once the seat of the powerful counts of that name, and now a Benedictine monastery, with a favourite pilgrimage-church. The next stations are *Ried* on the E. bank, with a fine château and park (Inn), *Utting* (Inn) on the W. bank, and *Breitenbrunn* (*Belle), on the E. bank. Then, **on the** W. bank. *Schondorf* (Inn), above which, to the left, are the **village and** château of *Greifenberg* (1920 ft.; Post); at the foot of the hill **are the** chalybeate baths of that name. The *Amper* emerges from the **lake near** stat. *Stegen* (Inn), at the N. end. A small steamboat plies **on the Amper** (1/2 hr.; fares, 90, 60 pf.) to *Grafrath* (inn), 1 M. from the **railway**-station of the same name (see below; omnibus from the landing-place **to the** station, or vice versâ, 25 pf.).

30. From Munich to Lindau.

137 M. RAILWAY *(Bayrische Staatsbahn)* in 5¼-8 hrs. (fares 17 ℳ 70, 11 ℳ 80, 7 ℳ 60 pf.). Views to the left.

Munich, see p. 137. Soon **after** leaving the station **we see** on the right **the park** and château of *Nymphenburg* (p. 194). 4½ M. *Pasing* is the junction for Augsburg (R. 26) and Starnberg (R. 29). After crossing the *Würm* and passing **(7 M.)** *Aubing*, the train enters the boggy *Dachauer Moos*. — 14½ M. Bruck *(Marthabräu; Post; Ludwigshöhe)*, or *Fürstenfeldbruck*, pleasantly **situated** on the *Amper*, is visited **for its river**-baths. Near **it** is the old Cistercian **abbey of** *Fürstenfeld*, now a barrack, with an interesting church of 1673-1732. — Then across the Amper to (20 M.) *Grafrath*, **station for the** Ammersee, which is visible to the left (see above). 24½ M. *Türkenfeld*; 28½ M. *Schwabhausen*; 31½ M. *Epfenhausen*. The train crosses the *Lech* to (35 M.) *Kaufering* (1939 ft.).

BRANCH RAILWAY TO SCHONGAU (21 M., in 1¾ hr.). — 3 M. **Landsberg** (*Goggl*; *Zederbräu*), **a quaint** old town on the Lech (5300 inhab.), **with the late-Gothic** *Liebfrauenkirche*, founded in 1498. The *Rathhaus*, recently restored, contains frescoes **by** Piloty **and** Schwoiser and an excellent painting, by Hubert Herkomer, **of a** *Sitting **of the** Landsberg Magistrates*. Herkomer, who is a native of Waal, 6 M. from Landsberg, has built the so-called *'Mutterthurm'*, **in the** English castellated style, adjoining the house at Landsberg in which **his** mother died (fine views of the town and valley). On **the hill** is the *Bayerthor*, a picturesque Gothic gate-tower, with carvings in wood. Several small stations. — 21 M. **Schongau** (*Post; Stern*), an interesting and ancient little town, lies picturesquely on a hill on the Lech. The *Johannisbad* here is well fitted up.

FROM KAUFERING TO BOBINGEN, 14 M., branch-railway **in 1 hr.**, crossing the *Lechfeld*. 14 M. *Bobingen*, see below.

Near (38 M.) *Igling* is the château **of** that name on the left. — 42½ M. Buchloe (*Rail. Restaurant; Hôtel Ensslin*, near the station), **the junction of** the lines to Augsburg and Memmingen.

FROM AUGSBURG TO BUCHLOE, 25 M., railway in 50-70 min. (from Augsburg to Lindau in 5-8 hrs.). The line traverses the *Lechfeld*, the plain **between the** Wertach and Lech, where Otho I. defeated the Hungarians **in 955.** Near stat. *Inningen*, to the right, beyond the Wertach, rises the *Wellenburg*, **a** château of Prince Fugger. Stations *Bobingen* (branch-line to Kaufering, **see above**), *Grossaitingen, Schwabmünchen* (a manufacturing place), *Westereringen*. The line then crosses the *Gennach*, and reaches *Buchloe*.

FROM BUCHLOE TO MEMMINGEN (29 M., railway in 1½ hr.). Beyond (2½ M.) **Wiedergeltingen** the train crosses the Wertach. **5 M.** *Türkheim*. 12 M. *Mindelheim*, an old **town** with 3400 inhab.; in the **church is the tomb of** Georg von Frundsberg (d. 1528), a distinguished general. **Stations** *Stetten*, *Sontheim, Ungerhausen, Memmingen*, see **p. 33**.

The train enters the broad valley of the Wertach. 46½ M. *Beckstetten*; 50 M. *Pforzen*. Beyond the river is the monastery of *Irrsee*, now a lunatic asylum. The background of the landscape is here formed by **the** Zugspitze (9761 ft.), **the** Hochplatte (9837 ft.), **the** Säuling (6683 ft.), and other imposing mountains.

Near the **old town** of (54½ M.) Kaufbeuren (2241 ft.; *Sonne; Hirsch*) the line crosses the Wertach, and then winds between densely wooded hills. 58 M. *Biessenhofen* (Post; branch-line to *Füssen*, see p. 202); 61 M. *Ruderatshofen;* 69½ M. *Aitrang.* A deep cutting penetrates the watershed between the Wertach and the Iller. 69½ M. *Günzach,* with an old monastery, now a brewery, is the highest point (2628 ft.) of the line; fine view of the Günzthal; to the right *Obergünzburg.* The *Mittelberg,* ¼ hr. to the S.W., is a fine point of view.

The line descends, at first among wooded hills, and then through a broad grassy valley with large beds of peat. 76 M. *Wildpoldsried;* 77½ M. *Betzigau.* The *Iller* is crossed.

81½ M. **Kempten** (2287 ft.; *Algäuer Hof, Kronprinz, at the station; *Krone, Post, in the new town; Deutscher Kaiser, *Hanse, in the old town; Frommlet's old-German wine-room, near the station; Rail. Restaurant), the capital of the *Algäu*, with 15,700 inhab., picturesquely situated on the Iller, which here becomes navigable for rafts, was a free town of the empire down to 1803. It consists of two parts, the *Neustadt,* on the high ground near the station, and the *Altstadt* on the Iller. In the Residenz-Platz in the Neustadt stands the old *Palace* of the once powerful Prince-Abbots of Kempten, built in the 18th cent.; adjacent is the handsome *Abbey Church,* with a dome in the Italian style (1652). In the Altstadt are the *Rathhaus,* lately restored, and the *Protestant Church* in the St-Mang-Platz. In front of the Real-Schule is a *War Monument* of 1870-71.

To the S. of the town, 10 min. from the station, rises the *Burghalde, a hill with new promenades and remains of old walls and towers. Splendid view of the Algäu Alps. Still finer from the *Marienberg (3035 ft.), 1 hr. to the W., best reached by *Feilberg* and *Eggen.*

From Kempten to Ulm, railway viâ *Memmingen* in 4 hrs., the direct route from Stuttgart to the Algäu, Hohenschwangau, etc., see p. 33. — From Kempten to *Füssen* and *Reutte,* see p. 202.

Beyond Kempten, from which the train backs out, the line follows the left bank of the Iller. Finest views to the left. Beyond (85 M.) *Waltenhofen* (2362 ft.) the *Niedersonthofer See* (2240 ft.) is seen on the right, at the foot of the *Stoffelsberg* (3900 ft.). 88 M. *Oberdorf.* The line approaches the Iller. To the left is the green and sharp-edged *Grünten* (p. 200).

95 M. **Immenstadt** (2395 ft.; *Kreuz or *Post;* **Hirsch; Engel; Traube,* with beer-garden), a busy town of 3000 inhab., lies picturesquely on both banks of the *Steigbach,* near the confluence of the *Konstanzer Ach* and the Iller, at the foot of the *Immenstadter Horn* (5050 ft.) and the *Mittag* (4688 ft.).

Fine views from the *Calvarienberg* (¼ hr. to the N.) and from the *Rothenfels* (½ hr. to the NW., near the E. extremity of the Alpsee, see below). — The ascent of the *Stuiben (5790 ft.; 3-3½ hrs., guide unnecessary) is recommended. Cart-road up the Steigbach valley to the (1¼ hr.) *Almagmach Inn* (3385 ft.), and footpath thence to the (1½ hr.) *Stuiben-*

Hütte (Inn in summer), about 20 min. below the summit, which **commands a splendid view**.

From Immenstadt to Oberstdorf, 13 M., railway in 1¹/₄ hr. — 3 M. *Blaichach*; 5¹/₂ M. *Sonthofen* (Deutsches Haus, at the rail. station; Engel), whence the *Grünten (5710 ft.), another excellent point of view, may be easily ascended viâ (2¹/₂ M.) *Burgberg* in 2¹/₂-3 hrs. (Inn near the top). — 9 M. *Fischen*. — 14 M. Oberstdorf (2685 ft.; *Mohr; Hirsch; Sonne*, etc.), a favourite summer-resort, beautifully situated in the midst of the Algäu Alps, near the confluence of the *Trettach, Stillach*, and *Breitach*, the valleys of which with their ramifications afford **a great variety of excursions**: To the *Fatterbach Waterfall*, 25 minutes. — *Hofmannsruhe* (2885 ft.), ¹/₂ hr., viâ *St. Loretto* (fine view from the hill; on the S. side is the Alpenrose Inn). — °*Wasach*, 1 hr. We follow the Fischen road and beyond the Breitach bridge ascend to the left by a shady path to the Inn, where we enjoy a beautiful view of the Algäu Alps (best by evening-light). We may return viâ *Tiefenbach* (1¹/₂ hr.). — *Freiberg-See* (3085 ft.; 1¹/₄ hr.); beyond (¹/₄ hr.) *St. Loretto* (see above) a footpath diverges to the right from the Birgsau road, crosses the Stillach, and ascends through wood to the charming, dark-green lake (Restaurant and bathing-house). — °*Spielmannsau* (Trettach-Thal), 2 hrs., carriage-road viâ St. Loretto (see above) and the *Burgstall*, skirting the N. foot of the *Himmelschroffen*, to the hamlet of *Spielmannsau* (3510 ft.; °Inn), amid grand scenery. — *Hölltobel*, 1¹/₂ hr., attractive. Beyond the Burgstall (see above) we diverge to the left from the Spielmannsau road, cross the Trettach, and ascend (right) to the picturesque ravine in which the *Dietersbach* forms three beautiful waterfalls. — *Oythal* (to the *Stuiben Fall* 3 hrs.), repaying; carriage-road half the way. — *Zwingsteg* and *Walser Schänzle*, 1¹/₂ hr. A carriage-road crosses the Stillach to the W. of Oberstdorf and ascends along the hillside to the *Walser Schänzle* (Inn, good wine), just beyond the Austrian frontier, in the valley of the Breitach or Kleine Walser-Thal. About 8 min. before it is reached, a path descends to the right to the *Zwingsteg*, a bridge over the deep and narrow gorge of the Breitach. Crossing the bridge, we may descend along the left bank and return to (1 hr.) Tiefenbach, or (1¹/₄ hr.) Oberstdorf. — *Birgsau* (Stillach-Thal), by road 6 M.; footpath thence to the left along the wild gorge of the Stillach to (¹/₂ hr.) *Einödsbach* (3745 ft.; Schraudolph's Inn), grandly situated at the mouth of the huge *Bacher Tobel*, near the foot of the Mädelegabel. — For details, mountain-ascents (*Nebelhorn, Mädelegabel, Hohe Licht*, etc.) and the passes to Hinterstein, the Lech Valley, and the Bregenzer-Wald, see Baedeker's *Eastern Alps*.

The train now turns to the W. into the valley of the Ach, reaches the village of *Bühl*, on the *Alpsee* (2355 ft.; 2 M. long), and runs through the pleasant *Konstanzer-Thal*, flanked with green hills, to (102 M.) *Thalkirchdorf*. It then ascends to (105¹/₂ M.) **Oberstaufen** (2598 ft.; *Büttner*), the watershed between the Danube and the Rhine. At the end of a short tunnel, just before Oberstaufen is reached, and at several points beyond it, we obtain striking views of the deep Weissach-Thal, the wooded mountains of Bregenz, and the snow-clad peaks of Appenzell beyond. From Oberstaufen to the Lake of Constance the line descends 1280 ft.

Beyond (110 M.) *Harbatzhofen* the valley is crossed by the *Rentershofener Damm*, an embankment 577 yds. in length and 174 ft. in height. 114 M. *Röthenbach* (2319 ft.). Farther on we obtain another view of the Appenzell mountains. 123 M. *Hergatz* (1815 ft.; branch-line viâ *Wangen* to *Kisslegg*, p. 54); 128 M. *Schlachters*; 132 M. *Oberreitnau*. The line skirts the *Hoierberg* (p. 201) and then turns to the S.E. Beautiful view of the Lake of Constance; on the left Bregenz, in the foreground Lindau, and beyond it the mountains of St. Gallen and Appenzell. An embankment 605 yds. long crosses an arm of the lake to the station of —

137 M. **Lindau.** — *Bayrischer Hof, on the lake, near the station, R., L., & A. 3-4, D. 3 *M*; °Krone, *Hôtel Reutemann, °Lindauer Hof, R. 1½-2½, D. 2½ *M*, Helvetia, R. 1½-1½ *M*, all on the lake; Sonne, in the Reichsplatz; Pension Gärtchen auf der Mauer, on the mainland. — Beer at the *Krone*, and in the *Seegarten*, next the Bayrischer Hof; *Schützengarten*, with view; adjacent, *Rüpflin's* wine-saloon; *Rail. Restaurant.* — *Lake Baths* on the N.W. side of the town (30 pf.). — **English** *Church Service* in summer.

Lindau (1306 ft.; pop. 5400), formerly a free imperial town and fortress, and in the middle ages a busy trading place, lies on an island in the *Lake of Constance*, 240 yds. from the mainland, with which it is connected by the railway-embankment and a wooden bridge. It is now a favourite summer-resort and bathing-place. The Romans under Tiberius defeated the Celtic Vindelici in a naval battle on the lake, and founded on the island a fort, of which the ancient tower by the bridge (the so-called *Heidenmauer*) is a relic. On the quay is a *Statue of King Max II.* (d. 1864) in bronze, erected in 1856. At the end of the S. pier is a large lion in marble, and on the opposite pier a lighthouse. The harbour is adjoined to the S. by the *Alte Schanz*, which commands a *View of the Alps from the Scesaplana to the Sentis (mountain indicator). In the neighbouring Reichs-Platz is the *Reichsbrunnen*, erected in 1884 from a design by Thiersch and Rümann, with a bronze statue of 'Lindauia' and other allegorical figures. The handsome *Rathhaus* in the Renaissance style, erected in 1422-36, restored and adorned with frescoes in 1885-87, contains an interesting collection of antiquities (open 11-12, Sun. 2-5). Pleasant grounds by the Landthor, with a monument for 1870-71.

Excursions. Pleasant walk on the W. bank of the lake (crossing the railway-embankment, and turning to the left), to the (2 M.) charmingly situated Schachenbad (*Restaurant & Pension Freihof*, 22-30 *M* per week), with mineral and lake-baths. Near it (¼ M.) is the Lindenhof, or Villa Gruber, with a beautiful park, hot-houses, etc. (adm. Frid. free, on other days 1 *M*; closed on Sundays). Thence along the bank of the lake, by *Tegelstein* (to the right the finely situated *Schloss Alwind*) and *Mitten*, to (2 M.) Wasserburg (°*Hôt.-Pens. Springer*, with terrace), with a château and church, situated on a peninsula. Back by steamer. — Beautiful view from the (¾ hr.) °Hoierberg (1496 ft.), reached either by the path parallel with the railway, or by the road from the Landthor through *Aeschach* (Schlatter) to the hamlet of **Hoiren** at the foot of the vine-clad hill. Two **inns** and **a** belvedere at the top. Return viâ *Enzisweiler* (°Schmid's Restaurant) and *Schachen* (Schlössle).

To *Bregenz* (the *Gebhardsberg*, *Pfänder*, etc.), see Baedeker's Eastern Alps.

The **Lake of Constance** (1300 ft.) is about 40 M. in length, 7½ M. in width, and at the deepest place (between Friedrichshafen and Utweil) 837 ft. in depth. Its principal feeder is the Rhine, the deposits of which have formed a broad delta at its influx between Bregenz and Rorschach. The river emerges from the lake at Constance. This vast sheet of water, with its picturesque and well-peopled banks, its green and wooded hills on the S. side, and the view it commands of the distant snow-mountains, presents a very striking scene to the traveller approaching the Alps for the first time.

The principal places on the lake are *Friedrichshafen*, *Lindau*, *Bregenz*, *Rorschach*, *Romanshorn*, *Constance*, *Meersburg*, *Ueberlingen*, and *Ludwigshafen*, between which steamboats ply at least once a day. On the more important routes, Lindau-Rorschach (1¼ hr.), Lindau-Romanshorn (1½ hr.), Friedrichshafen-Rorschach (1¼ hr.), Friedrichshafen-Romanshorn (1 hr.), Friedrichshafen-Constance (1½ hr.), there are 3-4 trips daily. The **lake being** neutral, passengers' luggage is liable to examination at the **custom-house** wherever they land; but those proceeding from one German **port** to another **obtain exemption by** procuring a ticket for their luggage **on** starting. **The banks of the lake** belong to five different states: Bavaria, Wurtemberg, **Baden, Switzerland**, and Austria. (See *Baedeker's Switzerland*, and comp. **p. 57.**)

31. From Munich to Füssen (Hohenschwangau) and Reutte.

90½ M. RAILWAY to Biessenhofen, 58 M., in 1¾-3¼ hrs. (fares 7 *M* 60, 5 *M*, 3 *M* 20 pf.): from Biessenhofen to Füssen, 23 M., local railway in 1¾ hr. (4 *M*, 2 *M* 90, 1 *M* 80 pf.). — DILIGENCE from Füssen to Reutte (9½ M.) twice daily in 2 hrs. (fare 1 *M* 50 pf.). — CARRIAGE from Füssen to Hohenschwangau with **one horse 3**, with **two horses 5** *M*; to Neu-Schwanstein 7 or 10 *M*; to Reutte 6 or 10 *M*; to Linderhof 18 or 30 *M*; to Oberau 36 or 50 *M*. Return-journey in each case one-half more; but an arrangement must be **made as to** the length of the halt. Driver's fee 10 per cent **of the** fare.

FROM KEMPTEN (p. 199) TO FÜSSEN (25 M.), carriage-road (railway to Pfronten under construction); carr. to Hohenschwangau, with one horse 20, with two horses 36 *M*. We cross the railway-bridge (fine view) and in 12 min. reach the road to (3 M.) *Durach* (3 M. to the S. of which, near *Sulzberg*, lie the small but well-equipped iodine **baths** of *Sulzbrunn*). Thence we ascend through wood, pass *Zollhaus*, and reach (7½ M.) *Oy*, a lofty village with a fine view, beyond which we descend to **cross the** *Wertach*, remounting again to (3¾ M.) Nesselwang (2845 ft.; *°Post; °Krone; °Bär*), with 1200 inhab., 7½ M. from stat. *Weizern-Hopferau* (diligence twice daily in 2 hrs., viâ Weissbach; see below). The ascent of the **Edelsberg** (5330 ft.), which commands a splendid view extending to the Sentis and the Lake of Constance, may be made hence by an easy marked path in 2 hrs. (10 min. from the top is the open *Edelsberg Pavilion*; at the top an 'orientation' table). Descent to Pfronten (see below). — The road now leads through *Kappel* and (3¾ M.) *Weissbach* (°Haf) and past the *Weissensee* to (7½ M.) *Füssen*. — To REUTTE, a direct road diverges to the right at *Weissbach* (see above), which with the following villages of *Kirchdorf* and *Steinach* belongs to the parish of **Pfronten** (*Frons Raetiae*), consisting of thirteen villages. From *Pfronten-Halden* (1½ M. from Weissbach) we may ascend the *Edelsberg* (see above) in 3 hrs. *Pfronten-Steinach*, 2¼ M. from Weissbach, is a good starting-point for the attractive ascent of the *Aggenstein* (6505 ft.; 4 hrs., with guide). From *Pfronten-Meillingen*, 1½ M. from Weissbach, a road, constructed by King Lewis II. along with an aqueduct 450 yds. long, ascends the °*Falkenstein* (4190 ft.), at the top of which, commanding a splendid view, is a ruined castle (restaurant). The descent may be made to (1 hr.) *Schönbichl* (see below). — A pleasant path leads on the right bank of the Ach from *Pfronten-Dorf* to the (1 hr.) *Fallmühle* (3260 ft.; Inn, with pretty grounds), whence we may go on to the *Kothbach Fall*. — Beyond (2 M.) *Steinach* the road follows the broad valley of the *Vils*, crosses the **Austrian** frontier to the (2 M.) °*Schönbichl Tavern*, and leads viâ (3 M.) the small town of *Vils* (2735 ft.; Huter) to the (1½ M.) *Ulrichs-Brücke* (p. 206).

From Munich to (58 M.) *Biessenhofen*, see p. 199. The BRANCH RAILWAY to FÜSSEN diverges here to the left. — 1½ M. *Ebenhofen*; 4 M. **Oberdorf** (2395 ft.; *Alte Post; Neue Post*), a market-town with a loftily situated church and an old château. — 7 M. *Leuterschach*; 9 M. *Balteratsried*; 11 M. *Lengenwang*; 14¼ M. *Seeg*, a well-built

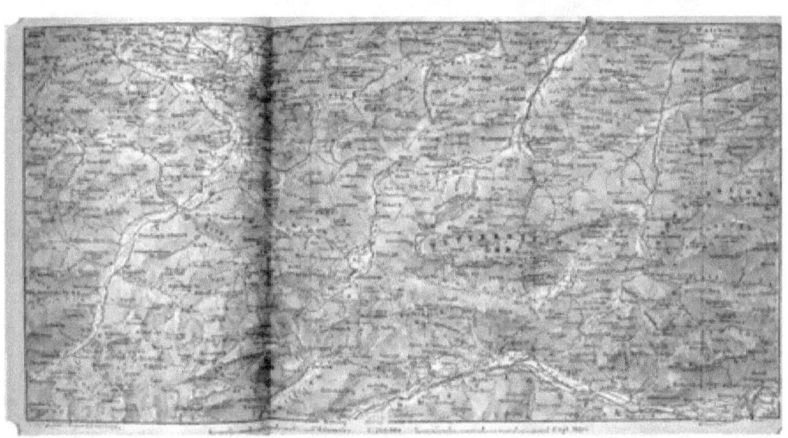

village on the hill to the right. Beyond (16 M.) *Enzenstetten* the ruin of *Falkenstein* (p. 202) appears to the right. 17½ M. *Weizern-Hopferau*; in the distance, to the left, the château of Neu-Schwanstein is visible. 20 M. *Reinertshof*, on the E. bank of the *Hopfensee*.

23 M. Füssen. — The *Railway Station* (omn. of the Hohenschwangau Inns, see below; carr., p. 202) lies a short distance from the town, at the entrance to which we follow the main street, reaching the bridge over the Lech in 6-8 minutes. — *Hotels*. Post, Mohren, both in the main street, R. 1½ *M*; Neue Post; Krone; Löwe; Sonne, etc.

Füssen (2615 ft.), a small town (3000 inhab.) on the *Lech*, with a castle erected by the bishops of Augsburg in 1322, restored by King Max II., and the remains of its old walls, presents an attractive picture of a mediæval fortified town. Below the castle are the suppressed Benedictine abbey of *St. Mang*, founded in 629 (present building, 18th cent.), and the Church *of St. Magnus*, erected in 1701 on older foundations. The gate in the town-wall between the castle and the church commands a fine view. — About ½ M. to the W. is the small sulphur bath of *Faulenbach*.

On the right bank of the Lech, a few hundred paces above the bridge, a path (guide-post) with pilgrimage-stations ascends from the church to the Calvarienberg (¾ hr.), surmounted by three crosses, and commanding a beautiful view: N. the valley of the Lech and Füssen, S.W. the Schwansee, Hohen-Schwangau, and Neu-Schwanstein. A footpath leads hence, skirting the *Schwansee*, direct to (1 hr.) Hohenschwangau.

The Road from Füssen to Hohenschwangau (3 M.) crosses the Lech, turns to the left, and ascends the right bank of the Lech, passing the Alterschroffen Inn. It then turns to the right, skirts the Schlossberg, and leads through the park to Hohenschwangau. — Pedestrians follow the road to Reutte (p. 206), to the right beyond the bridge, for 5 min., then ascend the path to the left on the slope of the Calvarienberg, which leads past the (7 min.) view-point known as the 'Kanzel', crosses a cart-track, and passes through wood to (25 min.) the saddle between the Calvarienberg and the Schwarzenberg. Here we reach the so-called *Königliche Reitweg*, which begins at the Schwarzbrücke (p. 206). We descend this path, with a view of Neu-Schwanstein and (farther on) of Hohenschwangau (to the right), and before reaching the *Schwansee* take the footpath to the right across the ridge, where the 'Alpenrosen-Weg' (see below) joins our route, to (1 hr.) the village of Hohenschwangau. — A longer route (2 hrs.) is offered by the *Alpenrosen-Weg*, which begins at the Weisshaus (p. 206) and winds along the slope of the *Schwarzenberg*, commanding beautiful views. This route may be joined from the Schwarzbrücke or from the saddle between the Calvarienberg and the Schwarzenberg (see above).

Hohenschwangau. — Hotels. Schwegerle zur Alpenrose, beautifully situated on the Alpsee, R. from 3, B. 1 *M* 20, pens. from 6 *M*; °Schwansee, ¼ M. from the Alpsee, quieter, R., L., & B. 1½-3, D. 3, pens. 6-8 *M* (in May and June 5 *M*); °Liesl Inn, plainer. — All these have omnibuses at the station of Füssen (1 *M*).

The castles of Hohenschwangau and Neu-Schwanstein are open from

May 1st to Oct. 15th, week-days 9-12 and 2-5, Sun. 10-12 and 2-5; closed on June 13th, the anniversary of King Lewis II.'s death.

Hohenschwangau (2735 ft.), a small village at the foot of a hill crowned by the castle of the same name, is a pleasant summer-resort with numerous attractive walks in the vicinity. It lies near the beautiful blue *Alpsee*, which is girdled with fine woods, while the steep crags of the Pilgerschroffen rise above its S. end. Opposite the Alpenrose Hotel begins the 'Fürsten-Strasse' (open to pedestrians only), from which (3 min.) a road to the right to Schloss Hohenschwangau and (8 min.) the above-mentioned footpath to Füssen diverge. About 40 paces farther on a footpath leads to the left to the 'Pindar-Platz', a rocky projection with a fine view of the lake (p. 206). Well-made paths make the entire circuit of the lake (1¼ hr.). — The footpath to the old Schloss ascends opposite the Liesl Inn. Tickets (50 pf.) to the right of the vestibule.

*Schloss Hohenschwangau (2930 ft.), formerly called *Schwanstein*, originally belonged to the house of Guelph, but in 1191 came into the possession of the Hohenstaufen dukes of Swabia and in 1567 passed to the dukes of Bavaria. In the 17th and 18th cent. it was several times besieged and captured. It was destroyed by the Tyrolese in 1809, sold for a trifling sum in 1820, and in 1832 purchased by King Max II. of Bavaria (d. 1864), then crown-prince, who caused the ruin to be entirely re-constructed by *Quaglio, Ohlmüller*, and *Ziebland*, and decorated with frescoes from German legend and history by *Schwind, Lindenschmit, Ruben, Monten*, and other Munich artists. The castle commands charming views of the plain, the Alpsee, and Neu-Schwanstein. It was the favourite residence of King Max II. and Lewis II., the latter of whom spent his later years almost exclusively here. The little garden, to the left of the entrance to the castle, contains a *Marble Bath*, cut out of the rock, with two nymphs, by Schwanthaler, and an imitation of the Lion Fountain of the Alhambra, by the same artist.

Opposite the ascent to Hohenschwangau, near the Liesl Inn, begins the road to (35 min.) Neu-Schwanstein, from which (5 min.) the road to the Blöckenau (p. 205) diverges to the right; 6 min. farther on (opposite the footpath from the Hôtel Schwansee) a steep footpath ascends on the right to the Jugend; and 12 min. farther on a bridle-path diverges to the right, near a workmen's barrack on the left side of the road, to the Marienbrücke and the Jugend. The road next passes a restaurant (open in summer only) and in 8 min. reaches the castle of —

*Neu-Schwanstein (3300 ft.), begun by King Lewis II. in 1869 on the site of the old castle of *Vorder-Hohenschwangau*, and beautifully situated on a precipitous rock above the profound ravine of the *Pöllat*. The castle, built in the Romanesque style by *Von Dollmann, Riedel*, and *Hofmann*, is planned somewhat after the style and arrangement of the Wartburg, but on a much larger scale.

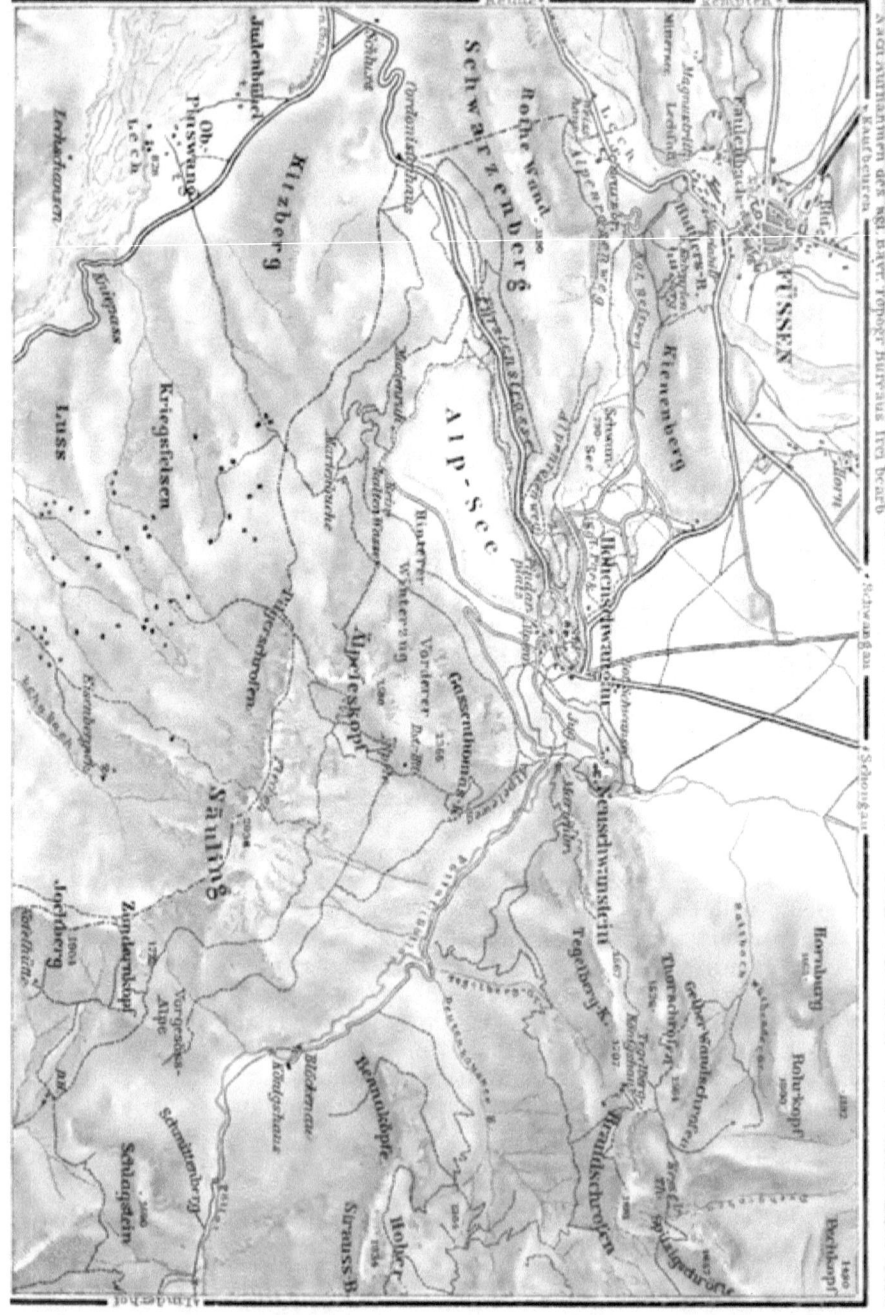

Through the *Thorbau* or *Gatehouse* on the N.E. (where tickets are obtained; 3 ℳ; adm., see p. 204) we enter the first court, in which to the right (N.W.) is the *Palas* or **main building**, to the left (S.E.) the *Kemenate* or women's apartments, and in the middle the *Ritterbau*. The visit takes 3/4-1 hr. The castle is splendidly fitted up, and its windows command beautiful views, especially of Hohenschwangau and the Alpsee to the S., and of the profound gorge of the Pöllat and its waterfall, spanned by the Marienbrücke, to the E.

The imposing PALAS has four stories: the groundfloor contains the offices, the first floor is occupied by the attendants, the second is unfinished, and the royal apartments are on the third. Visitors ascend to the third floor by a staircase of 96 steps in the massive N. tower, 195 ft. high. The landing at the top of the staircase is adorned with frescoes by Hauschild, illustrating the legend of Sigurd. To the left we pass through the *Adjutant's Room* to the *King's Study*, with scenes from the story of Tannhäuser by **Aigner**; and thence through the *Stalactite Grotto* to the former *Winter Garden*, a balcony commanding a fine view of the plain. Next follow the *Sitting Room*, with pictures from the Lohengrin legend by Hauschild; the *Dressing Room*, with scenes from the lives of Walter von der Vogelweide and Hans Sachs by Ille; the Gothic *Bedchamber*, with illustrations of the story of Tristan and Isolde by Spiess; the *Oratory*, with scenes from the life of Lewis IX. by Hauschild (fine view of the valley of the Pöllat from the balcony). The *Dining Hall* is embellished with scenes from the Wartburg under the Landgrave Hermann, by F. Piloty. The ante-chamber leads back to the landing, whence we enter the (unfinished) *Throne Room*, fitted up in the Byzantine taste, with pictures by Hauschild, representing the relations of monarchy to religion. It has a mosaic floor and an open loggia. — Aigner has also adorned the landing at the top of the staircase on the fourth floor with a series of 12 pictures from the story of Gudrun. On this floor is the *Festsaal* or *Sängersaal* (Minstrels' Hall), 90 ft. long, with pictures from Wolfram von Eschenbach's 'Parzival' by Spiess, Munsch, and Piloty.

A footpath, leaving the road at the N. angle of the castle and running under the N.W. façade, brings us to the S.W. side, near which the above-mentioned bridle-path ascends. [Before the latter is reached, a poor footpath descends to the left to the *Gorge of the Pöllat*, where we have a view of the castle and of the Pöllat Waterfall from below.] We ascend by the bridle-path and in 5 min. reach a point whence two footpaths diverge: one, to the right, leading down to the *Jugend*, a clearing in the wood commanding a view of Hohenschwangau and the Alpsee, like that from Neu-Schwanstein (the path descends still farther to the road, see below); the other, to the left, ascends to the *Marienbrücke*, a handsome iron bridge 138 ft. long, which boldly spans the rocky gorge of the Pöllat at a height of 295 ft. above the waterfall and affords the best view of the castle of Neu-Schwanstein. — Returning from the bridge, we take the path to the left, which brings us in 4 min. to the Blöckenau road, at which also the bridle-path ends (to Hohenschwangau by this road 1/2 hr.).

From Neu-Schwanstein a direct footpath leads to Linderhof (p. 212) in 6 hrs. (to the Ammerwald Inn, 3 1/2 hrs.), through the *Blöckenau* and across the Schützensteig or *Jägersteig* (4660 ft.; guide unnecessary).

To the Tegelberg Alp, 3 hrs., a pleasant excursion. We ascend the road to (3 M.) the *Blöckenau* (see above), diverging to the left at the 'Verbotener Weg' placard (permission obtained from the forester) and ascending in windings to the (2 hrs.) royal hunting-lodge on the *Tegelberg Alp*, which commands a beautiful view of mountain and plain. Hence to the top of the *Tegelberg (Brandschrofen*, 5925 ft.), marked by a cross, in 20-30 min. more (guide convenient for the inexperienced).

Other excursions (*Säuling, Schlicke*, etc.), see **Baedeker's** *Eastern Alps*.

PEDESTRIANS proceeding from Hohenschwangau to Reutte (8 M.) need not return to Füssen, but may either follow the 'Fürsten-Strasse' (p. 204) high on the W. bank of the Alpsee, or the good path past the 'Pindar-Platz' (p. 204), to the end of the lake, and then return to the road. We pass the (1³/₄ M.) **Austrian** frontier-station and descend in windings, turning to the left at the (¹/₄ hr.) *Schluxenwirth* (good wine) and following the Pinswang road to (3 M.) *Pflach* (see below).

The ROAD from Füssen to (9¹/₄ M.) Reutte leads up the right **bank of the** Lech to (7 min.) **a narrow ravine (on the left bank a bust** of King Max II.; on the **right** bank a war-monument). We then **cross** the (5 min.) *Schwarzbrücke* (p. 203) and reach the Austrian **frontier** at the (10 min.) *Weisshaus* (good wine). The main road then crosses the Lech by the (1³/₄ M.) *Ulrichs-Brücke*, passes *Musau* and the *Rossschlüg Pass*, **and** at *Unterlötzen*, **shortly** before reaching (5 M.) *Pflach* (2745 ft.; Schwan), **recrosses to the right** bank. Pedestrians will find it shorter and pleasanter **to diverge to the** left before reaching the Ulrichs-Brücke, and proceed **by** *Pinswang* and the *Kniepass* (3030 ft.), a rocky barrier narrowly confining **the Lech**, to (4¹/₂ M.) Pflach. Beyond **Pflach** the *Arch-Bach*, issuing **from the** Plansee, **is crossed (see below).** Then (2¹/₄ M.) —

32¹/₂ M. **Reutte** (2795 ft.; *Post*, R. 70 kr.-1 fl. 20 kr., D. 1 fl.; *Hirsch*; *Krone*; *Adler, plain; *Glocke*; *Mohren*, well spoken of), **a small town in the bed of an ancient lake,** intersected **by the Lech, and surrounded by lofty mountains: N. the** *Säuling* and *Dürreberg*, **E. the** *Zwieselberg* and *Tauern*, S. the *Axljoch*, *Thaneller*, **and** *Schlossberg*, S.W. the *Schwarzhanskarkopf*, **W.** the *Gachtspitz*, *Gernspitz*, and *Gimpel*.

At **the church of Breitenwang,** ¹/₂ M. to **the** E. of Reutte, **is a** monument **to the** Emp. Lothaire, who died here **in** 1137, on his return from Italy. The mortuary chapel **contains** a Dance of Death in relief. About ³/₄ M. farther on, **at the** foot **of the** Tauern, is *Bad Krekelmoos*, with mineral springs.

To the *Stuiben **Falls, a** pleasant **walk of** 2-2¹/₂ hrs., there and back. We follow the field-path, crossing the Arch above *Mühl* and recrossing to the left bank at the (¹/₂ hr.) paper-factory, **and** then follow the 'Hermannsteig' along the river (numerous rhododendrons) to the (¹/₂ hr.) **Lower Stuiben Fall*, a cascade 100 ft. in height, finely framed with trees. A footpath (finger-post) ascends hence to the right **to the road to** Reutte, which is 3 M. distant. Those who are bound for the Plansee ascend the left bank of the Arch to the (¹/₄ hr.) smaller *Upper Fall*, and turning to the right regain the (4 min.) road near a small chapel (p. 213), 10 min. from the *Little Plansee*.

From Reutte **to** *Linderhof* **and** *Partenkirchen*, see R. 33. *Upper Lechthal*, *Pass Gacht*, **and** viâ *Tannheim* to *Immenstadt*, see *Baedeker's Eastern Alps*.

FROM REUTTE TO IMST (35 M.), diligence twice daily in 10 hrs. The road passes the (2 M.) *Ehrenberger Klause*, a defile formerly defended by a castle (now **in ruins), and** leads viâ (3 M.) *Heiterwang* and (3 M.) *Bichelbach* to (5¹/₂ M.) **Lermoos (3245 ft.;** *Drei Mohren; *Post), **a** village situated **in** a wide green valley, **from** which on the E. rise the barren rocky walls of the imposing *Wetterstein Chain*, culminating in the *Zugspitze* (9725 ft.) **to the** N. (To Partenkirchen viâ *Griesen*, see p. 210.) The road to Nassereit, the finest mountain-pass between Bavaria and Tyrol, should be traversed on foot (**4 hrs.**) or in an open carriage (from **Lermoos** to **Nassereit** 4½, with two horses 7½ fl.). Beyond (1½ M.) *Biberwier* it ascends, passing the *Weissensee* (left) and the beautiful *Blindsee* (right), to the (5 M.) **Fern Pass** (3970 ft.; poor Inn), and descends in **wide curves, which pedestrians may avoid by** short-cuts. In the bottom **of the valley we pass the picturesque castle of** *Fernstein*, on the right; **at its base is the *Fernstein Inn*,** containing **two** rococo rooms fitted up **by King Lewis II.** (adm. 1 *M.*). **To the** left, the **ruins** of **the** *Sigmundsburg* rise **from the** small, wood-girt *Fernstein Lake*, the outlet of which we cross by a stone bridge. At (5¼ M.) **Nassereit** (2765 ft.; °*Post*) the road divides, the right branch leading **through the** *Gurgler-Thal* to (9½ M.) *Imst*, while the left branch (preferable) crosses **the** saddle of *Obsteig* to the **E. and** leads via *Ober-Mieming* (2840 ft.; °Post) **to** (13¾ M.) *Telfs*. For details, **see** *Baedeker's Eastern Alps*.

32. From Munich to Partenkirchen and Mittenwald.

Comp. Maps, pp. 194, 202, 208.

72 M. From Munich to *Partenkirchen*, **62** M., RAILWAY in 3-4 hrs. (fares 6 *M*, 3 *M* 85 pf.); from Partenkirchen to *Mittenwald*, **10** M., DILIGENCE twice daily in 2½ hrs.; carriage with one horse 10, with two horses **14** *M*.

Beyond (33½ M.) *Weilheim* (p. 197) the **train diverges to the left from the** Peissenberg line, **and traverses the wide valley of the Ammer.** 36 M. *Polling*; 39 M. *Huglfing*; 43½ M. *Uffing*. The line runs at some distance from the E. bank of the *Staffelsee* (2160 ft.), with its islands, passing the villages of *Rieden* and *Seehausen*, to —

47 M. **Murnau** (2265 ft.; *Restaurant*), at the S.E. end of the Staffelsee, and 105 ft. above it. (**Curhaus Staffelsee*, with chalybeate springs, on the lake, ½ M. from the railway-station; *Fuchs, moderate; good baths in the lake.) About ¾ M. from the station and the lake is the prettily-situated village of Murnau (*Post; *Pantlbräu; *Griesbräu; *Zacherlbräu*; *Angerbräu*). The *Vier Linden* (limetrees), to the W., and the *Asamshöhe* (with tower 60 ft. high), command a ***View of the mountains** (left the Heimgarten, Kistenkopf, and Krottenkopf; **right the** Ammergau Mts.; in the background of the Loisach-Thal the Wetterstein range).

To the W. of Murnau a road (diligence daily) **crosses the hills** between the Staffelsee and the Murnauer Moos to (9 M.) Kohlgrub (2690 ft.; *Adler*); ½ M. to the S.W. is the chalybeate bath and health-resort of the same name (2850 ft; °*Curhaus*, pens. 4-4½ *M*; °*Hôt.-Pens. Lindenschlösschen*, with shady grounds; *°Hôt.-Pens. Hinterlinderhof*), at the N. base of the *Hörnle* (5135 ft.). **The road goes on** via *Saulgrub* to (15 M.) *Ober-Ammergau* (p. 212). Walkers **to Ammergau save** ½ hr. **by following from the baths the direct** path, **which strikes the Ammergau road at** *Wurmesau*.

The railway **descends in a wide curve to** (49½ M.) *Hechendorf* (2040 ft.), crosses **the** *Ramsau* **and the** *Loisach* **and** proceeds on the **E. side of the broad and** marshy **Loisach valley to** (52 M.) *Ohlstadt*, **situated at the foot of** the *Heimgarten* **(5870 ft.).** The Loisach is **crossed before (54 M.)** *Eschenlohe* (Altwirth), where the valley contracts; **to the left rise the roof-shaped** Kistenkopf **and the Hochriesskopf; in the background the imposing** Wetterstein range with the Zugspitze; **on the right the Ettaler Mandl.** — 57 M. *Oberau* (2180 ft.; ***Post**) **is the station** for *Ober-Ammergau*, *Linderhof*, the *Plansee*. etc. (comp. R. 33).

Beyond (60 M.) *Farchant* the broad basin of Partenkirchen **opens** to the S. On the left is the *Kuhflucht*, a gorge with waterfalls, descending from the *Hohe Fricken*. Fine view of the Wetterstein range from the Dreithorspitze to the Zugspitze. The train again crosses the Loisach. 62 M. **Garmisch-Partenkirchen** (2295 ft.), 1/2 M. from the villages of those names (*Bayerischer Hof; Hôt. & Café Bauer, with baths; Zum Werdenfelser Michl, second-class, all at the station).

Partenkirchen. — Hotels. Post, R. 2-4 M, B. 70, omn. 50 pf.; Stern, R. from 2, B. 1, pens. 6 M; Bellevue, in an open situation above the village, R. 2, B. 1, D. 2, pens. 6 M; *Kainzenbad, see p. 210; Baumgartner, moderate; Zum Rassen; Melber, well spoken of; Werdenfelser Hof, Pischl, unpretending. — Pensions. *Schweizerhaus*, 5-6 M; *Panorama*, above St. Anton, with café and attractive view, etc. — *Private Apartments* numerous; apply at Th. Riedl's book-shop. — *Engl. Church Service* in summer.

Partenkirchen (2350 ft.), a favourite summer-resort, is beautifully situated at the base of the *Eckenberg*, a spur of the Krottenkopf. Handsome modern Gothic church (1865-71); new Protestant church, near the station. A visit may be paid to the school of carving and design, on the way to Garmisch. Good photographs sold by *Johannes*.

Garmisch. — Hotels. °Westermeier zum Husaren, R. 1 1/2-3, pens. 6-8 M; Post; °Lamm, pens. 4 M; °Reiser zur Zugspitze; °Drei Mohren; Colosseum, with theatre and concert room, R. 1-1 1/2, pens. from 3 1/2 M; Kainzenfranz. — °Hôt. Riesserbauer (see below). — Pensions. *Villa Sophia; Malerheim; Hohenleitner*, etc.

Garmisch (2290 ft.), a thriving village 1 M. to the W. of Partenkirchen, with picturesque old houses, the seat of the district-court, is another favourite resort. On the E. side of the village is the *Wittelsbach Park*, with a bust of Prince-Regent Luitpold.

Carriages are to be obtained at both Garmisch and Partenkirchen and at the railway-station. One-horse carr. to the Badersee 6, two-horse 10 M, two-horse carr. to Walchensee (3 3/4 hrs.) 20, Ober-Ammergau 20, Lermoos 20, Reutte 30, Imst viâ Lermoos 55 M. (The driver expects a fee of 10 pf. for each mark of the fare.)

Excursions (for details, see *Baedeker's Eastern Alps*). **Finest** °View from the pilgrimage-church of St. Anton (2400 ft.), to which a shady path ascends in 10 min. from Partenkirchen. The peaks, from left to right, are the Wetterwand, Dreithorspitze, Alpspitze, Waxenstein (behind it the Zugspitze), the pointed Upsberg (in the distance, beyond the Eibsee-Thörlen); to the right the Kramer, in the foreground Garmisch.

Faukenschlucht. Beyond Partenkirchen a path ascends to the E. to the ravine, and then leads on its right side to the (20 min.) waterfall of the *Faukenbach*. Through the Faukenschlucht to the (3/4 hr.) *Lukas Terrasse* (fine view of the villages and mountains) and thence back in 1/2 hr. viâ the *Schalmei-Schlucht*.

The °**Riesserbauer** (2565 ft.) is a good point of view, 1/2 hr. from Garmisch. From the post-office we cross the meadows towards the S.W., in the direction of the *Riesserkopf* (3690 ft.), a wooded height immediately below the Alpspitze. The charming little °*Riesser-See* (boating; baths) lies in a hollow behind the *Inn (also Pension), in the direction of the mountain.

°**Partnachklamm** and °**Vorder-Graseck** (1 1/4 hr.; guide unnecessary). After following the Kainzenbad road (p. 210) to the S. of Partenkirchen (see below) for about 60 paces, we turn to the right at a finger-post, and in 1/2 hr. reach the first bridge, at the mouth of the *Partnach Valley*. (From the station of Garmisch-Partenkirchen a good, and in part shady footpath, turning to the left at the Hôtel Bauer, leads along the bank of the Partnach, joining the route from Partenkirchen about 10 min. before the

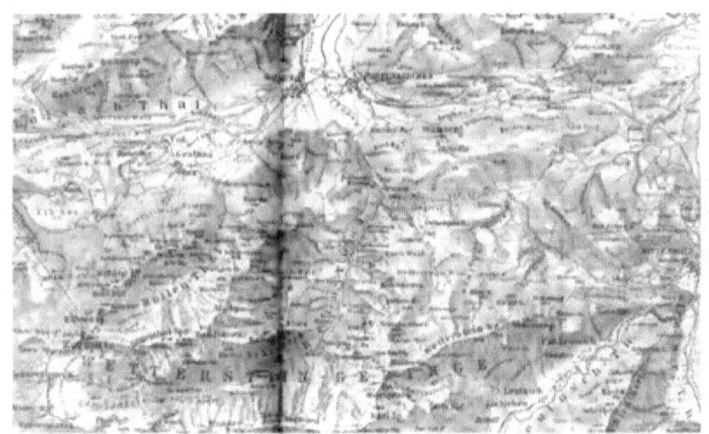

above-mentioned bridge is reached.) **Beyond** the bridge **a finger-post indicates our path to the left ('nach Graseck');** after 1/4 hr. **we** cross the stream by **a second** bridge, beyond which **the road to Graseck** ascends abruptly **to the left,** while the path **to the 'Klamm', or gorge, leads** to the right; 6 min., **third** bridge. The **(10 min.) fourth (iron) bridge** (*Klammbrücke*), **50 ft. long and 220 ft.** above **the Partnach, is the finest point. Beyond** the bridge **the path** ascends **in 10 min. to the forester's** house of *Vorder-Graseck* (2920 ft.; °Restaurant), **where a fine view is enjoyed.** — A **narrow** path (*Triftweg*), constructed for **the use of the 'lumberers' and** diverging to the left before the third bridge, **leads along the bottom of** the gorge, **close to** the water, **revealing the grandeur of the ravine to great advantage.** It is provided **at places with wire-ropes and is quite safe for** those reasonably **free from giddiness. The best plan to see the** ravine **is to follow** the **upper path to Graseck, descend thence into the** Partnach valley, **and return by the path at the bottom of the gorge (in all 3 hrs. from Partenkirchen). — From** Graseck **to** Mittenwald viâ Elmau, 3 1/2-5 hrs., **a much better route for** pedestrians **than the high-road** (p. 210). From **the forester's house we ascend the pastures for a short** distance, **and then turn** to the right. **After 20 min. we go straight on (not to the right to** *Mittel-Graseck*) to **(10 min.)** *Hinter-Graseck*; 3/4 hr., **bridge over the** Ferchenbach; **then for** 1/4 hr. **straight on through the wood, and down to (7 min.)** *Elmau* (3345 ft.; Inn). From **this point a road ascends slowly, at** first **through wood but afterwards shadeless, to** (1 1/2 M.) **the** *Ferchen-See*, **and then descends, past the** *Lauter-See*, **to (3 M.)** *Mittenwald* (p. 210). — **From Elmau to the** *Schachen* (3 1/2 hrs.), see p. 210.

The °**Eckbauer** (4062 **ft.). We may either follow a steep marked path** from the **Kainzenbad in** 1 1/2-2 hrs., **or take another steep path (also marked, usually shady in the afternoon) from Graseck (see above), which turns to** the left **at a (**1/4 hr.) **finger-post, ascends the grassy slopes in windings, passes through wood, and reaches the Eckbauer in** 3/4 hr. (*Inn*, **with 6 rooms**). The top of the hill, **2 min. beyond the house, commands an admirable panorama of the mountains: Karwendelgebirge, Wettersteinwand, Dreithorspitze with the Schachenalp and Frauenalpe, Alpspitze, Zugspitze, Kramer, and Krottenkopf; below lies the deep, wooded valley of the Ferchenbach.**

Schlattan and **Gschwandner Bauer** (2 1/4 hrs.). From Partenkirchen we ascend to the right through the *Bremstall-Wald* (finger-post) to (1 3/4 hr.) the *Schlattan Restaurant*, and thence viâ *Höfte* to the (1/2 hr.) *Gschwandner Bauer* (3345 ft.; °**Inn,** rustic). which affords **a fine view of the Wetterstein and Karwendel ranges.** We **may return** by the Mittenwald road (shady in the evening).

°**Badersee** (2720 ft.; 4 1/2 M. from Garmisch; **omnibus twice daily from Partenkirchen in** 1 1/2 hr., **starting at 7.30 a.m. and 2 p.m., returning at** noon and 6 p.m.; fare 1 *M*, return 1 *M* 80 pf.). **The road diverges to the** left from that to Lermoos, a few hundred yards beyond **the (**2 1/2 M.) *Schmelz* (Inn), **and leads viâ** *Unter-Grainau* (°Inn) **to** the small, **emerald-green lake,** 1 M. round **and 60 ft.** deep. The °*Hôtel-Pension Schäfter* (pens. 6 1/2 *M*), **on** its bank, is pleasant for a prolonged **stay. — Road hence to the (3 M.) Eibsee (see below).**

The °**Eibsee** (3145 ft.), 7 M. from Garmisch, is reached by **the** road viâ *Unter-Grainau* (omnibus from **the Post at** Partenkirchen twice daily in 2 1/2 hrs., **returning in** 2 hrs.; fare each way 1 1/2 *M*); or, from Garmisch, by **the path to the left** at the **W. end of the** village. which leads across meadows to (1 1/4 hr.) *Ober-Grainau* (2480 ft.; Wackerl's Inn), and thence to (1 1/4 hr.) the lake. The Eibsee, **3 M. long,** 2 M. wide, and 90 ft. deep. has seven small **islands and is enclosed** by dark, wooded hills, above which **tower** the enormous **rocky walls of** the Zugspitze (°*Terne's Inn*, with veranda, boats, and baths, R. 1 1/2-2, pens. 5-6 *M*). Travellers are rowed (50 pf. each) to the *Ludwigs-Insel* in the middle of the lake, where the echoes are awakened by **a shot (50 pf.). The huge Zugspitze is seen to great advantage from the lake, but on** summer afternoons **is usually shrouded in clouds.**

The °**Krottenkopf** (6880 ft.; **5** hrs.; guide 4 1/2, if a night is spent. 7 *M*).

A marked bridle-path leads from Partenkirchen viâ St. Anton, passing the parsonage, to the (2 hrs.) *Esterberg-See* (generally dry in summer) and the (10 min.) *Esterberg-Bauer* (1335 ft.; poor inn). Bridle-path thence, steep and stony at places, through the hollow between the Bischof and the Krottenkopf to the (2¼ hrs.) *Krottenkopf Club-Hut* (6450 ft.; Inn in summer), on the saddle between the Krottenkopf and the Oberrisskopf, and to (25 min.) the top (pavilion; fine *View).

*Königshaus am Schachen (6125 ft.; 5½-6 hrs.; guide, 4½ *M*, unnecessary). We follow the Triftweg (p. 209) through the Partnachklamm in 1¼ hr. to the bridge over the *Ferchenbach*, the left bank of which we skirt to (¾ hr.) the *Steilenfälle* (sometimes dry). The path then ascends rapidly to the right through the Wettersteinwald to a small shrine, turns to the left, and crosses a clearing after a few minutes, from which a broad path through the wood leads past the *Wetterstein-Alp* (4820 ft.; rfmts.), to the (3 hrs.) *Schachen-Alp*, with the small *Schachen-See*, and (¾ hr.) the *Königshaus*, built by King Lewis II. and containing a sumptuous room in the Oriental style (adm. 1 *M*; Restaurant, with 14 beds). The *Belvedere*, a few hundred paces to the W., on the brink of the abyss, commands a magnificent *View of the Reinthal below us, with the Plattach-Ferner, Schneefernerkopf, and Wetterspitzen, the Hochblassen to the right, and (to the S.) the Dreithorspitze and Wetterstein. To the N. stretches the vast Bavarian plain. — From *Elmau* (p. 209) a good bridle-path (driving practicable, but not agreeable; carr. and pair for 2 pers. 15, for 3 pers. 18 *M*) ascends to the Schachen-Alp in 3½ hrs.

Longer Excursions (*Höllenthal-Klamm*, *Rainthal* and *Blaue Gumpen*, *Alpspitze*, *Zugspitze*, etc.), see Baedeker's *Eastern Alps*.

To Lermoos (p. 206), 18 M., by a good road through the wooded Loisach-Thal (omn. daily in 3¾ hrs.; carr. 10-12 *M*). At (10 M.) the frontier-inn at *Griesen* (p. 212) we turn to the left (to the right the road to the Plansee, p. 212), cross the Austrian frontier, and proceed via the (3½ M.) old *Ehrwalder Schanze* (2950 ft.; Neuner's Inn) to (4¼ M.) *Lermoos* (p. 206). — A shorter, but unattractive path leads from the Eibsee over the *Thörlen* (5230 ft.) to *Ehrwald* and (3½ hrs.) *Lermoos*.

The road to Mittenwald (diligences, etc., see p. 207) begins to ascend at once. To the right in the valley, 1 M. from Partenkirchen, lies the *Kainzen-Bad* (*Inn, pens. 6 *M*), with a spring containing iodine, natron, and sulphur, used as a remedy for gout and cutaneous diseases. On the top of the hill, the road traverses undulating pastures; on the right rises the Wetterstein, and in front are the bold peaks of the Karwendel range. 3½ M. *Kaltenbrunn*; 2 M. *Gerold* (on the left the small *Wagenbrech-See*); 1½ M. *Klais*.

To the left, a road diverges here to the (1½ M.) Barmsee (3070 ft.), a pretty little lake embosomed in wood (fine view from the *Inn). The lake affords boating and bathing, and there are pleasant walks on its banks. Remains of lake-dwellings have been discovered here.

The road passes the small and marshy *Schmalsee*, and winds down into the *Isar-Thal*, where it unites with the road from Benediktbeuern and Walchensee (p. 214). Then (4 M.) —

10 M. Mittenwald (3020 ft.; *Post*, with clever animal-paintings by Paul Meyerheim in the veranda; *Zum Karwendel*; *Zum Wetterstein*. plain; *Pension Villa Neuner*), the last Bavarian village (1750 inhab.), overshadowed by the precipitous *Karwendel-Gebirge* (7825 ft.). The manufacture of violins and guitars, which are chiefly exported to England and America, forms the main occupation of the inhabitants. A bronze statue of *Michael Klotz* (d. 1743), who introduced the violin-industry, has been erected in front of the church.

EXCURSIONS. To the *Lauter-See (3365 ft.), ³/₁ hr., **and the** *Ferchen-See* (3400 ft.), ½ hr. farther up (see p. 209); to the *Hohe **Kranzberg** (1525 ft.), 1½ hr. (splendid view); to the *Leutasch-Klamm*, near **the** Scharnitz road (see below; 1½ hr. there and back); *Barmsee* (p. 210), 1½ **hr.**; *Leutasch Valley*, **Vereins-Alpe**, *Karwendel-Spitze*, etc., see *Baedeker's Eastern Alps*.

FROM MITTENWALD TO ZIRL, **16 M.**, diligence daily in 3½ hrs. (carriage with one horse 17, with two horses 22 *M*). The road **crosses the Isar (before** the bridge, **to the right, the** path to the Leutasch-Klamm, see **above) and traverses the level bottom** of the valley as far as the (5 M.) *Defile of Scharnitz*, **the** boundary between Bavaria and Tyrol, formerly **protected by a** strong fortress which was completely destroyed by the **French in 1805.** Beyond the adjacent village of *Scharnitz* (3160 ft.; Adler) **the road quits** the Isar and ascends to the left **to** (9½ M.) **Seefeld** (3860 ft.; *Post*)**, a** summer-resort beautifully situated on the watershed between **the Isar** and Inn. It then leads past the small *Wildsee* to (12½ M.) *Reith*, **beyond** which it **descends** viâ *Leiten* in wide curves, affording magnificent views of the Inn valley and the Tyrolese Alps, to (16 M.) *Zirl* (see *Baedeker's Eastern **Alps**).

33. From Munich to Ober-Ammergau and viâ Linderhof to Reutte-Hohenschwangau.

Comp. Map, p. 202.

RAILWAY to (57 M.) *Oberau* in 3-3½ hrs.; from Oberau to *Ober-Ammergau*, 6½ M. (on foot 2-2½ hrs.), to *Linderhof* direct 8½ M., viâ Ober-Ammergau 13½ M. (on foot 4 hrs.). — OMNIBUS from Oberau viâ *Linderhof* to *Hohenschwangau* **daily in** 12½ hrs., **starting at 7.30 a.m.**; returning from Hohenschwangau at 1 p.m. (night **spent at Linderhof**) and reaching Oberau at 2.30 p.m.; fare 7 *M*. — CARRIAGE from **Oberau to Ober-**Ammergau with one horse 10, **with two horses** 15 *M*; to **Linderhof 18 and** 30, to Reutte 30 and 40, to Füssen-Hohenschwangau 36 and **50 *M*.** — RAILWAY CIRCULAR TICKETS **may be** obtained **from** Munich to Oberau **and from Füssen** back to Munich **viâ Oberdorf (2nd cl.** 12 *M*, 3rd cl. 7 *M* 50 pf.).

From Munich to (57 M.) *Oberau*, see p. 207. The road to Ober-Ammergau leads to the W., passing the *Untermberg Inn* (½ M. from **the station), crosses the** *Giessenbach*, and ascends, at first in a wide sweep to the right, along the N. side **of a** wooded **gorge. At the bottom** of the valley **runs the steep old road**, which is shorter for **walkers.** The upper end of the gorge is closed by the *Ettaler Berg*, **which the new** road skirts, while the old road **climbs over it. 3 M. Ettal (2880 ft.;** *Landes*, moderate)**, a** convent **founded by** Emp. **Lewis** the Bavarian in 1330, **dissolved in** 1803, rebuilt after a fire in 1844, **and now** the property of Count Pappenheim. The church, **with a massive dome, was** built in **the Gothic style by Emp. Lewis, but was** remodelled in the baroque style in the 18th cent.; it contains **frescoes** by Knoller **and a famous organ. On the N. side is** a brewery **of local repute.** The village **lies at the base of the** *Ettaler Mandl* **(5385 ft.), a rocky peak,** the ascent of **which is difficult (2½-3 hrs.,** with guide).

About ³/₄ **M. farther on the road** forks, the left branch leading direct to (4½ M.) **Linderhof, the** right to (2¼ M.) **Ober-Ammergau (2760 ft.;** *Alte Post or *Schwabenwirth*; *Wittelsbacher Hof*; *Stern*, and **others), celebrated for** the passion plays performed here every ten **years (1890, 1900, etc.). Wood and ivory carving is the chief occu-**

14*

pation of the inhabitants. — About 1/4 hr. to the W., on the *Osterbühl*, at the base of the *Kofel* (3545 ft.), stands the *Crucifixion, a colossal group in Kelheim sandstone, executed by Halbig, and presented by King Lewis II. in 1875.

From Ober-Ammergau a road runs to the N., through the monotonous and at places marshy *Ammer-Thal*, viâ (3 M.) *Unter-Ammergau* (2655 ft.; Schuhwirth; Rabe) and *Wurmesau*, to (4 1/2 M.) *Saulgrub*. Thence either to the N. viâ *Rottenbuch* to (15 M.) *Peissenberg* (p. 197), or to the E. viâ *Kohlgrub* (p. 207) to (10 M.) *Murnau* (p. 207).

The ROAD FROM OBER-AMMERGAU TO (9 M.) LINDERHOF diverges to the right at the S. end of the village from the road to Ettal (p. 211), and unites 2 1/4 M. farther on with the direct Oberau and Ettal road (p. 211). 2 1/4 M. *Graswang* (2885 ft.: Inn), a village with the Bavarian custom-house, beyond which we ascend through the pleasant *Graswang-Thal*, or upper valley of the Ammer; to the left opens the wide *Elmauer Gries*, above which peeps the Zugspitze. Just beyond the (3 3/4 M.) forester's house of *Linder* (rfmts. and beds) we cross the Ammer to the right to (1/2 M.) the royal *Schloss Linderhof (3080 ft.), erected and splendidly decorated in the rococo style by King Lewis II. in 1870-78 (adm. from May 1st to Oct. 15th daily, 9-5; fee 3 ℳ, including grotto and kiosque; closed on June 13th). To the left of the entrance are the office and the *Schloss Restaurant, with 50 beds (2-3 ℳ).

The *Vestibule* of the château (adm. in parties of at least 12 pers.) contains an equestrian statue of Louis XIV., after Bosio. On the *First Floor* is a series of finely fitted up rooms with paintings of French celebrities and events in the time of Louis XIV. and Louis XV. — The extensive *Gardens* are embellished with fountains, statuary, etc., and contain the *Monopteros*, a small temple with a figure of Venus (good view), and the *Blue Grotto*, with a subterranean lake, which can be illuminated with electric light. Near the grotto is the *Moorish Kiosque*, richly gilded and decorated, with stalactite vaulting, enamelled peacocks, etc. Behind the palace are the *Cascades*, where the fountains play at noon and at 6 p.m. — A visit to the palace and gardens, including the grotto and the kiosque, takes about 2 hrs.

We continue to ascend the finely-wooded Ammerthal to the (4 1/2 M.) *Grenz-Brücke*, or frontier bridge, about 1/2 M. to the left of which (guide-post) is the *Hunding-Hütte* (3600 ft.), a blockhouse in the old German style (comp. Wagner's opera of the 'Walkyrie'; adm. daily 9-12 and 2-6, 50 pf.; rfmts.; adjacent a hermit's hut). We then skirt the N. base of the *Geyerkopf* (7095 ft.), traversing the thickly wooded *Ammerwald-Thal*, and reach (3 M.) the *Ammerwald Inn* (3575 ft.; rustic), whence the 'Schützensteig' leads to the right to (4 hrs.) Hohenschwangau (p. 205). About 3 M. farther on the road emerges from the wood and reaches the Great Plansee (3190 ft.), a fine sheet of water, 2 3/4 M. long by 1/4-1/2 M. broad and 250 ft. deep, enclosed by wooded mountains. On its bank is the *Austrian Custom-House*, near which is a monument to King Max II. of Bavaria (*Forelle*, boats for hire, lake-baths; *Alpenrose*).

FROM THE PLANSEE TO PARTENKIRCHEN (15 M.) a narrow road descends the wooded *Naiderach-Thal* to the (5 1/2 M.) Austrian and Bavarian custom-house of *Griesen* (Inn), where it joins the road from Lermoos to Partenkirchen through the *Loisach-Thal* (p. 210).

The road to Reutte, shadeless in the morning, skirts the N. bank of the Plansee, passing the *Kaiserbrunnen*. At the ($3^1/_2$ M.) W. end of the lake, in the *Gschwänd*, is the *Seespitz Inn (R. from 60 kr.). Farther on we pass the *Little Plansee*, cross the *Arch*, which flows out of it, and reach (1 M.) a chapel, near a good spring.

A footpath descends hence to the right, through wood, to the *Upper* and (20 min.) **Lower Stuiben Fall*, whence we may either ascend to the left to (40 min.) the road, or follow the Hermannsteig along the Arch to *Mühl* and (1 hr.) *Reutte* (comp. p. 206).

The road crosses the *Rossrücken*, affording a fine view of the Lechthal, with the Glimmspitze and Hochvogel in the background. We then descend the slope of the *Tauern* (6044 ft.), where the path from the lower Stuiben Fall (see above) joins the road at a stone with an inscription. The road afterwards proceeds past the small bath of *Krekelmoos* and viâ *Breitenwang* to ($4^1/_2$ M.) *Reutte* (see p. 206). From Reutte to *Füssen* and *Hohenschwangau*, see R. 31.

34. From Munich to Mittenwald viâ Benediktbeuern.
Kochelsee and Walchensee.

Comp. Maps, pp. 196, 214, 202.

$66^1/_2$ M. Railway to *Penzberg* ($38^1/_2$ M.) in $2^3/_4$ hrs. Post Omnibus twice daily from Penzberg to (5 M.) *Benediktbeuern* in $1^1/_4$ hr. (90 pf.); thence to (11 M.) *Walchensee* in 3 hrs. (1 *M* 80 pf.); and thence to (12 M.) *Mittenwald* in 3 hrs. (1 *M* 80 pf.). — Carriage and pair from Benediktbeuern to *Walchensee*, 20 *M*.

From Munich to (25 M.) *Tutzing*, see p. 196. — $28^1/_2$ M. *Bernried*; $31^1/_2$ M. *Seeshaupt* (p. 196), both $^3/_4$ M. from the railway. Farther on, the country is uninteresting. On the right lies the little *Ostersee*. — $35^1/_2$ M. *Staltach*. — $38^1/_2$ M. Penzberg (1980 ft.; *Bernrieder Hof; Zur Eisenbahn*), the terminus of the railway.

The road to Kochel crosses the *Loisach* and traverses a flat district to ($4^1/_2$ M.) *Bichl* (*Löwe; Grüner Hut), where it joins the road from *Heilbrunn* (p. 216). Then ($^3/_4$ M.) —

$43^1/_2$ M. **Benediktbeuern** (2025 ft.; *Post*; **Zur Benediktenwand*), with a once wealthy and celebrated monastery, founded in 740, and consecrated by St. Boniface, now containing a home for veteran soldiers and a stud. To the E. rises the *Benediktenwand* (5910 ft.; fatiguing ascent of $4^1/_2$-5 hrs., with guide), to the S. the Jochberg, Herzogstand, and Heimgarten.

Beyond Benediktbeuern the road skirts the E. side of an extensive marsh, and leads viâ *Ried* and *Besenbach* along the *Rohrsee* (N. end of the Kochelsee) to (48 M.) *Kochel* (Abenthum, moderate), which is separated by a hill from ($^3/_4$ M.) the lake (*Bad Kochel, with a chalybeate spring and grounds on the lake, R. $1^1/_2$ *M*; *Pens. Natalie*, also on the lake). The Kochelsee (1970 ft.), $3^3/_4$ M. long and $2^1/_2$ M. broad, is fed by the Loisach, and is bounded on the S. by the Jochberg, Herzogstand, and Heimgarten. The pavilion near Bad Kochel affords a good view.

On the opposite bank of the lake lies Schlehdorf (*Inn zum Herzogenstand*), 3½ hrs. from stat. Murnau (p. 207) and 3 hrs. from stat. Penzberg (omnibuses from both stations). The *Herzogstand* (see below) may be ascended hence in 4 hrs. by an attractive route. We follow the marked path along the lake for ¼ hr., then ascend (guide-post) viâ the *Jochplatte* to the (1 hr.) *Unterauer Alp* (about 2850 ft.), whence the *Pionier-Weg*, constructed in 1892 by the 1st Battalion of Pioneers, gradually ascends through wood, crossing several streams, and commanding beautiful views of the Kochelsee and the plain. At (1¼ hr.) the *Schlehdorfer Alpl* we join the bridle-path ascending from Urfeld; thence to the top, see below. — From Schlehdorf ferry in ½ hr., passing the *Nase*, which rises perpendicularly from the lake, to the *Müller am Joch* (Inn), at the foot of the Kesselberg. Footpath thence to the (20 min.) *Kesselberg Inn*.

About 1 M. beyond Kochel, at the *Kneipp-Bad Kochelsee*, the new road approaches the lake, and skirts it, passing the *Inn zum Grauen Bären*, to the (20 min.) *Kesselberg Inn* (ferry to Bad Kochel 80 pf.; good echo on the lake). It then ascends in easy windings to the pass of the **Kesselberg** (2825 ft.). To the right of the road are the pretty falls of the *Kesselbach*, along which a path cutting off an angle of the road ascends. From the culminating point, where the bridle-path to the Herzogstand diverges to the right (see below), we obtain a view of the Karwendel and Wetterstein ranges in the distance, and, below us, of the beautiful, deep-blue *Walchensee (2635 ft.), 4¼ M. long and 3 M. broad, surrounded by forests and mountains. At the N. end are the houses of (1½ hr.) *Urfeld* (Zum Jäger am See, R. 1½ ℳ; Inn at the fisherman's).

The *Herzogstand (5695 ft.), a remarkably fine point of view, is ascended hence in 2½-3 hrs. (guide unnecessary). A bridle-path (see above) diverges to the left (W.) from the road coming from the Kesselberg, about 8 min. from Urfeld (or a steep path leading from Urfeld direct to this bridle-track in ¼ hr. may be taken). On the saddle, ½ hr. below the top, are the *Herzogstand-Häuser* (5100 ft.), belonging to the German Alpine Club (Inn with 50 beds at 2½ ℳ). On the summit is a closed pavilion, and a little lower is an open hut. Admirable view of the mountains as far as the Oezthal glaciers, and of the plain with its numerous lakes. — A narrow arête, protected by a wire-rope, but advisable for experts only, connects the Herzogstand with the (1 hr.) *Heimgarten* (5870 ft.), to the W. — From the Herzogstand-Häuser a narrow path to the right, affording at first a fine view of the Walchensee, and then leading through wood, descends to the hamlet of Walchensee in 1½ hr.

From Urfeld to *Jachenau* and *Tölz*, see p. 216. — Boat across the lake: to Walchensee (for 1, 2, 3, or 4 pers.) 1 ℳ 20, 1 ℳ 80, 2 ℳ 10, 2 ℳ 40 pf.; to Altlach 2, 3, 4, 4½ ℳ; Obernach 2½ ℳ, 3½ ℳ, 4 ℳ 80, 5 ℳ 30 pf. — Carriage from Walchensee to Wallgau 5, with two horses 8 ℳ; to Kochel, Krün, and Jachenau 6 and 9, to Barmsee 7 and 11, to Benediktbeuern and Mittenwald 10 and 15, to Vorder-Riss 12 and 18, to Partenkirchen 14 and 21, to Lenggries and Penzberg 17 and 22, to Murnau 15 and 23, to Tölz 19 and 31, to Tegernsee 30 and 50, to Achensee 33 and 50 ℳ.

From Urfeld the road skirts the W. bank of the lake to (2 M.) —

54½ M. **Walchensee** *(Post)*, a hamlet charmingly situated on a bay of the lake, and surrounded with beautiful woods. On the opposite bank are the church and parsonage of *Klösterl*.

It is preferable to proceed from Urfeld to Walchensee by boat in ¾ hr. From the middle of the lake (the 'Weitsee') a fine view is enjoyed. On the S. bank are the houses of *Altlach*, whence a good bridle-path ascends the *Hochkopf* (4010 ft.; 1½ hr.; descent to Vorder-Riss, see p. 216). Near

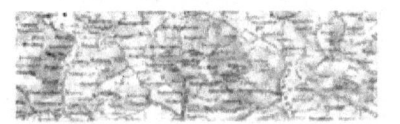

the S. bank lies the wooded islet of *Sassau* (private; no adm.). Travellers bound for Mittenwald row from Urfeld (without going to Walchensee) in 1½ hr. to the mouth of the *Obernach* (see below).

Beyond the hamlet of Walchensee the road is carried over the steep *Katzenkopf* (2775 ft.) to the (¾ hr.) forester's house of *Obernach*, at the S. end of the lake. We now gradually ascend a lonely pine-clad valley. At (1¼ hr.) *Wallgau* (Altwirth), the broad valley of the *Isar* is reached (road to Vorder-Riss and Tölz, see p. 216). — From (1½ M.) *Krün* (2895 ft.; Inn) a road leads to the right, past the picturesquely situated *Barmsee* (p. 210), to (3 M.) *Klais*, on the high-road from Mittenwald to Partenkirchen. On the S. the precipitous Karwendel-Gebirge is conspicuous; to the W. rises the Wetterstein-Gebirge. — 6 M. —

66½ M. **Mittenwald** (p. 210).

35. From Munich to Tölz and Mittenwald.

74 M. RAILWAY to (36 M.) *Tölz* in 1½-2¼ hrs. DILIGENCE from Tölz to (6½ M.) *Lenggries* twice daily, in 1¾ hr.; to (10 M.) *Benediktbeuern* via *Heilbrunn* and *Bichl* daily, in 2¼ hrs. DILIGENCE from Lenggries to *Vorder-Riss* thrice weekly (Tues., Thurs., & Sat.) in 4 hrs. One-horse carriage from Tölz to the Walchensee 10 *M*, to Mittenwald 20 *M*.

The train soon turns towards the S.; to the left are seen the Bavaria and Ruhmeshalle, to the right the distant Alps. **The line to Simbach** (R. 40) and the direct **line to Rosenheim diverge to the left** (R. 38). — 3½ M. *Mittersendling*. At (6½ M.) *Grosshesselohe* the Isar is crossed; to the left we obtain a view of the deep and gravelly bed of the river, with Munich in the distance. Then through wood. To the left, near (11 M.) *Deisenhofen*, is the large reservoir of the Munich water-works, with a capacity of 8,250,000 gallons. 16 M. *Sauerlach*. The *Teufelsgraben* ('devil's dyke'), a deep, dry hollow, is crossed, and the train reaches (23 M.) Holzkirchen (2245 ft.; Post; *Oberbräu*; Rail. Restaurant), the junction of the lines to Rosenheim (p. 222) and Schliersee (p. 220).

The line skirts the E. side of the town, and diverges to the right from the line to Schliersee. 26 M. *Ober-Warngau*; 30 M. **Schaftlach** (2480 ft.; Rail. Restaurant; to Tegernsee, see p. 217). The mountains become grander; on the left rises the Benediktenwand. 32 M. *Reichersbeuern*, with a handsome château. The (36 M.) *Tölz* station (2255 ft.; Rail. Restaurant; *Bellevue*, with fine view, adjacent) lies to the N. of the town, ½ M. from the Isar bridge (omnibus 20 pf.).

Tölz (2160 ft.; Post; *Bürgerbräu*, *Bruckbräu*, both with gardens; *Kolberbräu*; **Lechner**, etc.), a small town (4092 inhab.), with breweries and a trade in timber, is prettily situated on a hill on the Isar. Many of the houses are frescoed with Biblical subjects. The garden of the Bürgerbräu and the *Calvarienberg* (2320 ft.; ¼ hr.) command a fine survey of the Isarthal, stretching far into the distance; in the background, to the S.W., the long Benediktenwand

(p. 213) and the cone of the Kirchstein. On the left bank of the Isar, $^1/_2$ hr. from the station, are the baths of **Krankenheil** (*Cur-Hôtel*, with baths; *Sedlmair*, with baths, R. 2, D. $2^1/_4$ *M*; *Artmann*, D. $2^1/_2$ *M*; *Actienbad*; *Pension Spenger*, 5-7 *M*; *Pens. Emilia*, 5 *M*; *Pens. Villa Meister*; furnished rooms at the *Villa Bellevue*, *Daxenterger*, etc.), with a *Conversations-Saal*, *Trinkhalle*, and *Bath House* (bath 2 *M*). The water is conducted in leaden pipes from the springs, $^1/_4$ M. distant, and contains natron and iodine. About $1^1/_2$ M. to the W. is the *Zollhaus* (*Inn, with baths), on a hill near which is the *Alpenhaus* Kogel (Restaurant, D. $1^1/_2$ *M*). The left bank of the Isar, close to the town, is laid out with extensive woods and promenades.

FROM TÖLZ TO THE WALCHENSEE there are two **roads**: by *Kochel* (21 M.), or through the *Jachenau* (25 M.). The KOCHEL ROAD (one-horse carr. 12, two-horse 18 *M*) leads to the W., past the *Zollhaus* (see above), *Stallau*, and (6 M.) the **baths** of *Heilbrunn* (2235 ft.), with the *Adelheidsquelle*, containing bromine and iodine. We then pass *Enzenau* and *Steinbach*, and reach (3 M.) *Bichl* (p. 213).

The LENGGRIES AND JACHENAU ROAD (one-horse carr. to Urfeld 18, two-horse 23 *M*) crosses the Isar beyond ($6^1/_2$ M.) *Lenggries* (see below; on the opposite bank is the château of *Hohenburg*, **see** below), and reaches ($2^1/_2$ M.) *Wegscheid* (Zum Pfaffenstefll, rustic). The road now quits the valley of the Isar, skirts the wooded flanks of the *Langenberg*, and enters the Jachenau, a secluded valley watered by the *Jachen*, 10 M. in length. 8 M. *Zum Bäck Inn*. About 2 M. farther on is the village of *Jachenau* (2590 ft.; Neuwirth; Pfund). The road to Urfeld continues to ascend over the *Fieberberg* and then descends through wood to (4 M.) *Sachenbach*, at the E. end of the *Walchensee*, whence it follows the N. bank to (2 M.) *Urfeld* (p. 214).

FROM TÖLZ TO MITTENWALD (38 M.; carr. to Vorder-Riss 18, with two horses 30 *M*). The road follows the right bank of the Isar to ($6^1/_2$ M.) Lenggries (2230 ft.; *Altwirth; Post*), beyond which, on the left, is the Grand-Duke of Luxembourg's château of *Hohenburg* (with brewery and inn), and leads via *Anger* to (3 M.) *Fleck* (2275 ft.; *Inn), with large saw-mills. Beyond (1 M.) *Winkel* the valley contracts and turns to the S.W. — The road crosses the *Walchen* or *Achen*, on the right bank of which a narrow road leads to (9 M.) *Achenwald* on the Kreuth post-road (p. 219), and reaches (6 M.) *Fall* (2435 ft.; *Inn).

The valley expands. 6 M. **Vorder-Riss** (2645 ft.; *Weiss*, by the saw-mill), a royal shooting-lodge in a pine-clad dale, at the confluence of the *Rissbach* with the Isar.

THROUGH THE RISS TO THE ACHENSEE by road (30 M.). The road ascends the wooded valley past ($3^1/_2$ M.) the *Oswald-Hütte*, and crosses the Tyrolese frontier to (5 M.) **Hinter-Riss** (3055 ft.), a shooting-lodge of the Duke of Coburg, in finely-wooded environs. At the foot of the small Gothic château are the low buildings of a Franciscan monastery (*Inn*, adjoining the monastery; *Alpenhof*, 20 min. farther on). — From Hinter-Riss the road ascends gently to the (2 hrs.) *Hagel-Hütte* (3575 ft.), where the *Rissthal* turns towards the S. We then ascend in windings through wood to the ($2^1/_2$ hrs.) *Plumser Joch* (5410 ft.), which commands a limited but fine view, and descend through the wooded *Gernthal* to (2 hrs.) *Pertisau* (p. 219).

The road to Mittenwald crosses the Isar, and follows the left side of the secluded valley to (8 M.) *Wallgau* (p. 215), on the high-road from the Walchensee to ($7^1/_2$ M.) *Mittenwald* (p. 210).

36. From Munich to Tegernsee, Wildbad Kreuth, and the Achensee.
Comp. Maps, pp. 214, 218.

94 M. RAILWAY to (34 M.) *Gmund* in 2½ hrs. DILIGENCE from Gmund thrice daily to (3 M.) Tegernsee (½ br.) and (11 M.) Kreuth (2½ hrs.; fare 1 ℳ 80 pf.). POST-OMNIBUS from Tegernsee (Guggemos) to Wildbad Kreuth twice daily in 1¾ hr., and from Kreuth to the Achensee (Scholastika) daily in 3½ hrs. — CARRIAGE from *Gmund* to Tegernsee with one horse 4 ℳ, with two horses 7 ℳ; from *Tegernsee* to Kreuth one-horse 9, two-horse 12 ℳ, to the Scholastika 16 or 24, to Jenbach 26 or 42 ℳ; from the *Scholastika* to Kreuth 6 or 10½, to Tegernsee 9 or 15, to Gmund 11 or 18 fl. — STEAMBOAT on the Achensee from the Scholastika to the Seespitz (and back) eight times daily in summer in 50 min. (90, 60 kr.). — RAILWAY from the *Seespitz* to *Jenbach* (6 trains daily in ¾ hr.) in connection with the steamboat (see p. 219).

Railway to (30 M.) *Schaftlach* (change carriages), see p. 215. The branch-line to Tegernsee diverges to the left from the line to Tölz (on the right, the Benediktenwand) and reaches the *Tegernsee* (3¾ M. long, 1¼ M. broad) at (34 M.) *Gmund* (2430 ft.; Herzog Max; Bellevue; *Obermayer's Restaurant, at the station, with view), where the *Mangfall* emerges from the lake.

Kaltenbrunn (Inn), a farm of Duke Charles Theodore, at the N.W. end of the lake, 1 M. from Gmund and 4½ M. from Tegernsee by land, or reached by boat in 1 hr. (1 ℳ 40 pf.), commands the best survey of the lake.

From Gmund a road leads along the E. bank, viâ *St. Quirin*, to —

37 M. Tegernsee. — Hotels (omn. from Gmund station, 60 pf.). *POST, R. 2-3 ℳ, B. 80 pf.; *GUGGEMOS, R. 2, D. 2 ℳ; TEGERNSEER HOF; *STEINMETZ, R., L., & A. 3 ℳ, B. 80 pf., pens. 5-8 ℳ; SCHANDL, unpretending; PENSION VILLA HELENE, on the Lehberg. Lodgings may also be procured. — At *Rottach*: SCHEURER, R. from 1½ ℳ. — At *Egern*, at the S.E. end of the lake, on the road to Kreuth: BACHMAIR, moderate; GASTHOF ZUR UEBERFAHRT; *VILLA KORN. — Beer at the *Bräustübl*, in the brewery of the ducal château; *Sommerkeller*, with veranda, a little to the N. of the château (open on Sun., Wed., Frid., & Sat. afternoons). *Café am See*, with view-terrace; *Maier*, on the Albach, café and confectioner. — Boat, with rower, for 1-2 pers. 1 ℳ per hr., 3-4 pers. 1 ℳ 20, 5-6 pers. 1 ℳ 40 pf.

Tegernsee (2400 ft.), a large and charmingly situated village, attracts numerous visitors in summer. Beautiful walks in the environs. The imposing *Schloss*, formerly a Benedictine abbey, said to have been founded in 719, and suppressed in 1804, now belongs to Duke Charles Theodore of Bavaria; the N. wing contains a brewery (see above). Above the portal of the *Church* is an ancient relief in marble representing the princely founders of the abbey. Beautiful grounds.

*ENVIRONS (numerous guide-posts). A favourite point is the Grosse Parapluie, an open 'rondel', 20 min. to the S.E. The path ascends the right bank of the Albach, and in 3 minutes crosses a bridge (to the right) at the edge of the wood. Or the steps ascending to the left, about ½ M. to the S. of the S.E. angle of the Schloss, passing a memorial to the poet Carl Stieler (d. 1888), may be followed to the rondel (2680 ft.), which affords an admirable view of the lake and the encircling mountains. A path leads hence to the *Lehberger* (*Restaurant); fine view of the head of the lake. — The *Pflieglhof* (2755 ft.; rfmts.), 10 min. to the E. of the Parapluie, and the *Westerhof* (2920 ft.; rfmts.), 35 min. above Tegernsee on the N.E., also command fine views.

The **Falls** of the Rottach are situated in a picturesque ravine, 5½ M. from Tegernsee. The road leads from the *Schwaighof* (see below) on the left bank of the Rottach (or footpath on the right bank viâ the Duften-Mühle), passing *Elmau*, to (1½ hr.) *Enter-Rottach* (2565 ft. ; Inn); ½ M. farther on (finger-post) the path to the falls descends to the right and rejoins the road higher up. The road ascends hence to the **Wechsel-Alp** (3390 ft.), and descends through the picturesque wooded valley of the *Weisse Falepp* to (3 hrs.) the forester's house of *Falepp* (p. 220). Thence by the *Spitzing-See* to *Schliersee* 12 M., and from Schliersee to Tegernsee 10 M. The whole round forms a pleasant drive of 10 hrs. (carriage 20 *M*, with two horses 30 *M*.)

The *Neureut (4115 ft. ; shelter-hut at the top), to the N.E., is ascended from Tegernsee in 2 hrs. by a marked path. Splendid view (to the S. the Venediger). We may then keep along the ridge to the E. to the (1 hr.) *Gindelalmschneid* (4350 ft.), with fine views of the Schliersee, the Kaisergebirge, etc., and descend by the (10 min.) *Gindel-Alp* to (2 hrs.) *Schliersee* (see p. 220).

The *Hirschberg (5480 ft. ; 4½ hrs.) is an admirable and easily reached point of view. The ascent is best made from *Scharling*, on the Kreuth road, 3 M. from the ferry at Egern (see below). Here, or ½ M. before, on the other side of the *Lohbach Fall*, we diverge to the right from the road, pass a marble-quarry, and follow a marked path through wood viâ the *Holzpoint-Alp* (3705 ft.) to the (2 hrs.) *Ringberg-Sattel* and the (¾ hr.) *Hirschberg-Haus* (4950 ft. ; *Inn), 25 min. below the summit. Splendid view at the top (panorama by Waltenberger, 50 pf.).

Other excursions (*Riederstein*, *Risserkogl*, *Walmberg*, etc.), see Baedeker's *Eastern Alps*.

The high-road from Tegernsee to Kreuth passes the baths of *Schwaighof* (sulphur-spring), crosses the Rottach, and leads through (1¾ M.) *Rottach* (Scheurer), with its pretty country-houses. About 1 M. farther on (to the right is Egern, p. 217) it crosses the **Weissach** (*Bachmair's Inn).

Pedestrians save 1 M. by taking the ferry (5 pf.) across the S.E. arm of the lake from the (¼ M.) *Kleine Parapluie* to *Egern* (5 min.; Gasthof zur Ueberfahrt, with lake-baths); the road on the other side reaches the high-road at (¾ M.) the Weissach bridge.

The road follows the pretty valley of the Weissach viâ (1½ M.) *Scharling* (*Hoegg; ascent of the *Hirschberg*, see above). The valley contracts near the village of (1½ M.) *Kreuth* (Obermayer), to the right of which rises the conical *Leonhardstein* (4760 ft.). On the left is (¾ M.) the prettily-situated *Inn zur Rainer Alpe*, about ¾ M. beyond which a road to the left diverges to the (½ M.) —

44½ M. **Wildbad Kreuth** (2720 ft.), a large bath-house and hotel (R. 2½-3 *M* per day, 6-36 *M* per week, D. 3 *M*), the property of Duke Charles Theodore of Bavaria, situated in a broad green basin. The springs, containing salt and sulphur, have been known since 1500. Good bathing arrangements; whey-cure, etc. Shady walks in the grounds of the Curhaus.

Excursions (*Gaisalpe*, *Königs-Alpe*, *Hochalpe*, *Schildenstein*, *Schinder*, etc.), see Baedeker's *Eastern Alps*.

The road from Bad Kreuth to the W. crosses the Weissach and joins the main road. The latter gradually ascends the wooded Weissach-Thal, passing the (2 hrs.) hamlet of *Glashütte* (2930 ft.; *Inn), with the Bavarian custom-house of *Stuben*. Beyond the *Stuben-Alp* (3090 ft.), about 1 M. farther on, the road descends rapidly through

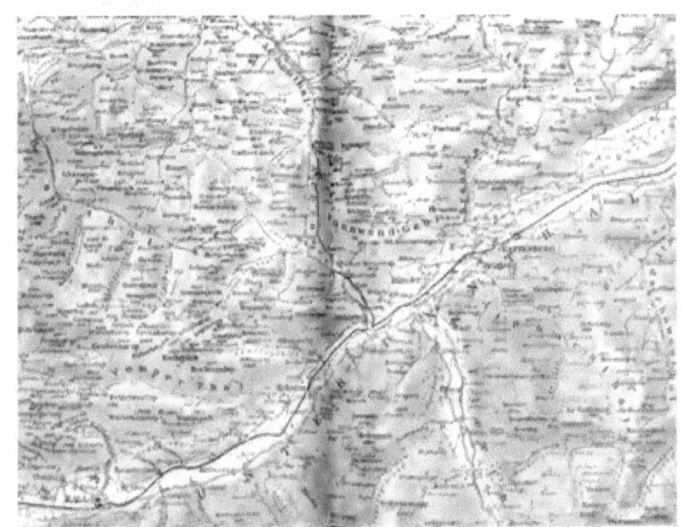

profound ravines, and at the *Kaiserwacht*, in the once strongly fortified defile of *Achen* (2860 ft.), crosses the Tyrolese frontier. The Austrian custom-house is near the village of (1¼ hr.) *Achenwald* (2695 ft.; *Inn 'Zum Hageninwald'). The road then gradually ascends along the *Achen*, or *Walchen*, the outlet of the Achensee, which rushes noisily in its deep bed. At (1 hr.) *Leiten* (Hinterer's Inn) the *Ampelsbach-Thal* opens on the left; in the background rise the grotesque rocky horn of the *Guffert* and the long ridge of the *Unnütz*.

59 M. Achenkirch (3085 ft.; *Kern; *Post, with baths, ¾ M. farther on; *Adler, good wine), a village 2½ M. long, the scattered houses of which extend almost to the Achensee. At the N. end of the lake is *Maier's Inn, a little beyond which is the *Hôtel Scholastika (R. 80 kr., D. 1 fl. 10 kr.), with a veranda, a bath-house, and the church. About ¾ M. farther on, on a green promontory, is the *Hôtel Seehof (R., L., & A. 1 fl. 20, D. 1 fl. 30 kr.), with a café on the lake.

The *Unnütz (6815 ft.; 3 hrs.; guide, unnecessary except for novices, 3 fl.) affords an easy and attractive expedition. Good paths (marked with red) ascend from the inns on the lake to the (1¼ hr.) *Kögel-Alp* (4695 ft.; rfmts.), whence the summit (*Vorder-Unnütz*) is reached in 1¾ hr. Extensive and magnificent View.

The *Achensee (3050 ft.), 5½ M. long, about ½ M. broad, and 430 ft. deep, a dark-blue lake, the finest in N. Tyrol, lies 1300 ft. above the valley of the Inn. The road, hewn in the rock at some places, leads on the E. bank to (6 M.) *Buchau* (*Pranti), at the S.E. end of the lake (a drive of 1 hr.). Preferable is the STEAMER, which plies eight times daily from Scholastika to Seespitz (and back) in 50 min., calling at Seehof, Pertisau, and Buchau (circular tour 1 fl. 30 kr.). Rowing-boat from the Scholastika to Pertisau in 1½ hr. (1 pers. 70, 2 pers. 80 kr.); to the Seespitz in 2 hrs. (1 fl. and 1 fl. 20 kr.). On the S.W. bank of the lake is the Pertisau, a green pasture enclosed by precipitous mountains and frequented as a summer-resort (*Fürstenhaus, on the lake, the property of the Benedictine abbey of Viecht. R. 90, D. 1 fl. 10, S. 45 kr.; *Hôtel Stephanie, D. 1 fl. 20 kr., pens. 3 fl.; rooms at the *Villa Wörndle*; *Pfändler* and Karl, in the village, ½ M. from the lake, unpretending; Lake Baths). Charming view of the lake; to the S. the mountains of the Innthal and of the lower Zillerthal. A road leads from Pertisau along the W. bank to the (1½ M.) Seespitz (Brunner's Inn), at the S. end of the lake.

FROM THE ACHENSEE TO THE INN VALLEY we may from the Seespitz either follow the rapidly descending road through the *Kasbach-Thal* (3½ M.) or proceed by railway (p. 217) via (1 M.) *Maurach* and *Eben* in ⅜ hr. to (4 M., 71 M. from Munich) *Jenbach*, on the railway to (94 M.) *Innsbruck* (see Baedeker's Eastern Alps or Baedeker's Austria).

37. From Munich to Kufstein viâ Schliersee and Bairisch-Zell.

Comp. Map, p. 217.

68 M. RAILWAY to (38 M.) Schliersee in 2½ hrs. From Schliersee to (10 M.) Bairisch-Zell POST-OMNIBUS twice daily in 2 hrs.; thence to (20 M.) Kufstein carriage-road, but no public conveyance. Carriage and pair from Schliersee to Kufstein in 6-7 hrs., 45 ℳ.

Railway to (23 M.) *Holzkirchen* (change carriages), see p. 215. The line diverges to the left from the Tölz line, and at (27 M.) *Darching* it enters the picturesque *Mangfall-Thal*. Opposite is *Weyarn*, formerly a monastery, now a school. — 30½ M. *Thalham* (2005 ft.); on the right rises the *Taubenberg* (3015 ft.), a fine point of view (1¼ hr.; Inn, 10 min. from the top). The train crosses the Mangfall, and traverses the wooded *Schlierach-Thal*. — 33½ M. **Miesbach** (2245 ft.; *Waizinger; *Post; *Kreiterer; Alpenrose; Wendelstein*), a thriving village and summer-resort, prettily situated. In the vicinity are several coal-mines. The train crosses the Schlierach twice, passes *Agatharied* and *Hausham* (with coal-mines), and reaches —

38 M. **Schliersee** (2575 ft.; *Seehaus; Post; Seerose*, at the station; *Wagner; Messner*, plain), prettily situated on the *Schliersee*, and much frequented in summer. Peasants' theatre on Sun. and holidays in summer at 7 p.m. The (5 min.) **Weinberg-Kapelle** affords the best view of the environs (from E. to W., the Schliersberg, Rohnberg, Eipelspitz, Jägerkamp, Brecherspitze, Baumgartenberg, and Kreuzberg). Baths at *Seebad Spitz* (*Restaurant, with rooms), ½ M. from the station, to the S.

The road skirts the E. side of the lake. 2 M. *Fischhausen* (Kellerer) lies at the S. end of the lake; high up to the left the ruin of *Hohenwaldeck*. At (¾ M.) *Neuhaus* (2655 ft.; *Eham*), a summer-resort, the road divides, the right branch leading to Falepp, the left to Bairisch-Zell. To the E. rises the finely-shaped Wendelstein; to the S. the Brecherspitze and Jägerkamp.

The ROAD TO FALEPP leads through the *Josephs-Thal*, past (½ hr.) a paper-mill (Inn), and ascends in numerous windings, which the pedestrian may cut off, between the *Brecherspitze*, on the right, and the *Jägerkamp*, on the left. Beyond the (¾ hr.) pass (3740 ft.), the road descends to the (¼ hr.) lonely Spitzing-See (3495 ft.), and follows the *Rothe Falepp*, past the (2 M.) *Waizinger Alp* (beer), to (2 M.) the forester's house of **Falepp** (2840 ft.; *Inn* at the forester's), prettily situated in the midst of wood, below the union of the Rothe and Weisse Falepp. In the vicinity is the disused *Kaiserklause*. A marked path leads from Falepp by the *Erzherzog-Johann-Klause* and through the *Brandenberger-Thal* to (9-10 hrs.) *Brixlegg* in the Inn valley. For details, and other excursions from Schliersee and Neuhaus (*Brecherspitze, Bodenschneid, Rothwand*, etc.), see Baedeker's *Eastern Alps*.

The road to Bairisch-Zell next passes (2 M.) *Aurach*, enters the wide *Leitzach-Thal* beyond (2¼ M.) *Geitau*, and leads viâ (1¼ M.) *Osterhofen* to (2 M.) **Bairisch-Zell** (2630 ft.; *Wendelstein or Neuwirth; Post* or *Altwirth*), a village prettily situated in a basin enclosed by the Wendelstein, Seeberg, and Traithen.

*Wendelstein (6035 ft.; 3 hrs.; guide unnecessary; horse to the Wendelstein-Haus 8 M, if kept overnight 12 M), a much frequented and very fine point of view. We ascend through meadows by a path (marked with white and red) past the *Tanner-Mühle* and several alps to the (2 hrs.) *Upper Wendelstein Alp* (5215 ft.) and the (3/4 hr.) *Wendelstein-Haus* (5655 ft.; *Inn, with 90 beds), whence a safe path protected by railings leads to the (20 min.) summit, a plateau 6-12 yds. broad and about 25 yds. in length, on which stand a new chapel and a cross. The *View (panorama to be obtained in the house) embraces (left to right) the Untersberg, Watzmann, Kaisergebirge, Tauern Mts. (with the Venediger and Gross-Glockner), and the Karwendel and Wetterstein ranges (with the Zugspitze); to the N. the extensive Bavarian plain with the Chiemsee, Simmsee, and Starnberger See.

From Bairisch-Zell to Oberaudorf, 4 1/2-5 hrs. A rather rough road leads by the *Tanner-Alp* and the *Grafenherberg-Alp* to the *Auer-Brücke*, and through the *Auerbach-Thal* to the (2 1/2-3 hrs.) Tatzelwurm (2510 ft.; *Inn*), near a fine fall of the Auerbach (best viewed from the lower bridge). Then by the deep Auerbach-Thal past *Rechenau* to (2 hrs.) *Oberaudorf* (see Baedeker's Eastern Alps).

The road to Kufstein (rough at places) follows the finely-wooded *Ursprung-Thal* and crosses the Austrian frontier at the (2 M.) *Bäcker-Alp* (2770 ft.). 1/2 M. farther on is the *Inn Zur Ursprung* (good wine), 2 1/2 M. Landl (2195 ft.; *Inn*), a pleasant village in the *Thiersee-Thal*. The road forks here. The branch to the left leads through the valley of the *Thierseer Ache (Kieferthal)* to (4 1/2 M.) the *Thiersee* or *Schrecksee* (2040 ft.; *Seewirth*). Thence it crosses the *Marblinger Höhe* (fine view of the Kaisergebirge), and descends through wood, passing the dark *Längsee* and the *Ed*, to (5 M.) *Kufstein*. — The more attractive road to the right from Landl ascends viâ (2 1/4 M.) *Inner-Thiersee* (Grasshammer) and (2 1/4 M.) *Vorder-Thiersee* (2200 ft.; Kirchenjackl), where the peasants perform passion-plays every tenth year, to the (3/4 M.) *Thiersee*. — *Kufstein*, and thence to *Innsbruck*, see *Baedeker's Eastern Alps*.

38. From Munich to Salzburg and Reichenhall.
Comp. Maps, pp. 214, 222, 224.

To *Salzburg*, 95 M., express in 3-3 1/2 hrs.; ordinary trains in 5 1/2 hrs. (fares 14 M 10, 9 M 90, or 12 M 40, 8 M 20, 5 M 30 pf.); to *Reichenhall*, 103 1/2 M., express in 3 3/4, ordinary trains in 5 3/4 hrs. (fares 14 M 60, 10 M 30, or 13 M, 8 M 40, 5 M 30 pf.). Travellers from Salzburg to Reichenhall or Munich should be provided with German money.

Munich, see p. 137. The railway skirts the town. Beyond the (3 M.) *Munich S. Station (Thalkirchen)* the train crosses the Isar. At (6 M.) *Munich E. Station (Haidhausen)* the Simbach-Braunau line diverges to the left (see p. 233). Stations *Trudering, Haar, Zorneding, Kirchseeon*. — 23 1/2 M. **Grafing** *(Railway Inn; Kaspersbräu)*, a considerable place, 1 1/2 M. from the railway.

From Grafing to Glonn, railway in 36 min. through the smiling *Glonnthal*, viâ *Taglaching, Moosach*, and *Adling*. From Glonn (*Inns*) pleasant excursions may be made to the (1/2 hr.) château of *Zinneberg* (fine view), to the *Glonnquelle*, to the *Steinsee*, etc.

Between *Assling* and *Oster-München* the broad dale of the *Attel* is traversed. To the right, opposite the traveller, rises the Wendelstein, to the left the Kaisergebirge, in the background the Gross-Venediger. — 36 1/2 M. *Gross-Carolinenfeld*.

40 M. **Rosenheim** (1470 ft.; *Bayrischer Hof; *König Otto; Alte Post; *Deutsches Haus, R. 1½-2 M; Zum Wendelstein, Thaller, both near the station and moderate; Rail. Restaurant), the junction of the Innsbruck, Holzkirchen, and Mühldorf lines, a town of 10,000 inhab., with salt-works, lies at the influx of the Mangfall into the Inn. The salt-water is conveyed hither from Reichenhall, upwards of 50 M. distant. About ¾ M. from the station are the *Kaiserbad, with a large park, the *Marienbad, and the Dianabad, all with salt and other baths. Pretty view of the Innthal and the Alps from the (½ hr.) Schlossberg (Restaurant), on the right bank of the Inn.

FROM MUNICH TO ROSENHEIM VIÂ HOLZKIRCHEN, 46 M., in 3 hrs. To (23 M.) Holzkirchen, see p. 215. We here diverge from the line to Schliersee and enter the Teufelsgraben (p. 215), which ends at the valley of the Mangfall. Stations Westerham, Bruckmühl, Heufeld, and (40 M.) Aibling (1575 ft.; *Ludwigsbad; *Hôtel Duschl; *Schuhbräu; *Wittelsbach, with garden and park; *Johannisbad), a small town on the Glonn, with salt and mud baths. The Kaisergebirge, and beyond (43½ M.) Kolbermoor, with a large cotton-factory, the Gross-Venediger, become visible on the right. — 46 M. Rosenheim, see above.

The train **crosses the Inn**, passes (44 M.) Stephanskirchen, the Simmsee (3¾ M. long), and (50 M.) Endorf (Post; Wieser), and runs to the S. through a hilly district to (56 M.) **Prien** (1745 ft.; *Zur Kampenwand, near the station and also a halting-place on the Chiemsee line, with view, R. 2 M; Hôtel Chiemsee, at the station; Kronprinz; Bayrischer Hof; Railway Restaurant), a favourite summer-resort, in the smiling Prienthal.

From Prien a STEAM TRAMWAY runs in 8 min. to (1 M.) Stock (Hôtel Dampfschiff, with lake-baths), the landing-place of the steamer on the Chiemsee, which plies nine times daily in ¼ hr. to the Herreninsel and six times daily in ½ hr. to the Fraueninsel (return-ticket to the Herreninsel, 2nd class in the steam-tramway, 1st class on the steamer, 1 M 80 pf.; to the Fraueninsel 2 M 60 pf.; rowing-boat there and back 1 M, with a stay of some time 1½ M). — The Chiemsee (1700 ft.), 8½ M. long and 6½ M. broad, contains three islands: the large Herreninsel, with a monastery (now the old castle) and the new palace; the Fraueninsel, with a nunnery (now a girls' school) and an interesting church; and the Krautinsel ('vegetable island'), formerly a kitchen-garden for the monks and nuns. The Fraueninsel (20 acres in area) is also the site of a fishing-village and an *Inn, a favourite resort of artists, as an album kept in the house will testify. On the extensive Herreninsel (9 M. in circumference) rises the large *Schloss Herrenchiemsee, **built in the style of** Louis XIV. by King Lewis II. after the model of Versailles, **but not** completed (adm. daily from 1st May to 15th Oct., 9-5; fee 3 M, Sun. and holidays 1½ M; closed on 13th June). A few min. walk from the pier, where tickets for the palace are obtained (to the right), is the Hôtel-Restaurant Artmann, with a veranda and garden. Thence we proceed through the **grounds** of the Old Castle and **then through** wood to (10 min.) the New Palace, built on three sides of a square (open on the E.), adjoined on the N. by a wing (unfinished) 480 ft. long. In front of the W. façade are ornamental Water-Works (without water at present), with the basins of Fortune, **Fame, Latona**, etc. The **pillared** Vestibule, adorned with an enamelled group of peacocks, opens on a Court, paved with black and white **marble**, on the right side of which is the magnificent *Staircase, richly adorned with imitation marble and painting. On the first floor, turning to the right, we enter successively the Salle des Gardes du Roi (blue and gold), the Première Antichambre (lilac), the Salon de l'Oeil de Boeuf (green; with an equestrian statue of Louis XIV., by Perron), and the magnificent *Chambre de Parade. This last apartment,

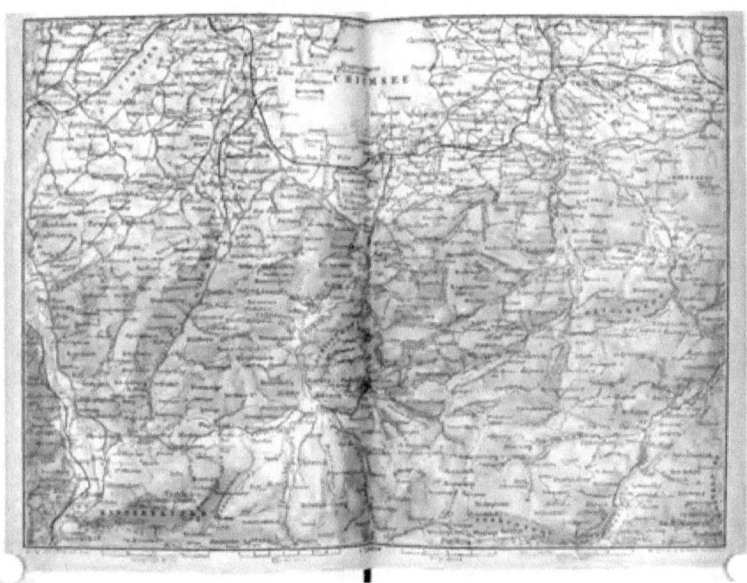

an imitation of Louis XIV.'s **Bed** Chamber at Versailles, adorned in purple and gold, with a lavishly gilded bed, is said to have cost alone over 125,000*l*. Of the remaining rooms the chief are the °*Galerie des Glaces* or *Spiegelgallerie*, 245 ft. long and illuminated with 35 lustres and 2500 candles, the *Salon de la Guerre* **and** the *Salon de la Paix*, opening on the right and left of the Galerie, the royal *Bed Chamber* and *Study*, **the** *Dining Room* (with the table descending and ascending through the floor), the *Small Gallery*, the *Oval Saloon*, and the *Bath Room*. In all the **rooms are** costly furniture, clocks, etc. — The woods clothing the S. part of **the** island afford pleasant promenades. The long chain of the Bavarian **and** Salzburg Alps forms the S. background of the landscape.

From *Seebruck* (Inn), at the S. end **of** the lake (steamer from Stock to Seebruck and Chieming in summer twice daily, except Frid.), a road leads to (3 M.) **Seeon**, an old monastery on an island in the small *Seeoner See*. About 4½ M. to the E. is the railway-station of *Stein an der Traun* (p. 224).

A BRANCH RAILWAY runs from *Prien* to the S. through the richly-wooded *Prienthal*, in 32 min., past the station of *Umratshausen*, to the charmingly-situated village of (6 M.) Niederaschau (2020 ft.; *Rest* and other inns), another summer-resort. About 1 M. to the S., in the **middle** of the valley, is the château of *Hohenaschau*, picturesquely situated on a rock, 100 ft. in height (at the foot a brewery and the *Inn zur Burg*, R. 3 *M*). Pleasant excursions to the *Hofalpe* (3350 ft.; 1½ hr.), the *Hochriss* (5115 ft.; 3½ hrs.), the *Kampenwand* (5136 ft.; 3½ hrs.), **etc.**; see *Baedeker's Eastern Alps*.

The line skirts the S. bank of **the Chiemsee.** 59½ M. *Bernau*. From (64 M.) **Uebersee** (Heindl) a branch-railway runs to *Marquartstein*. The **train crosses the** *Grosse Ache*. — 69 M. *Bergen*; **the village** (*Huber*) **is** prettily situated 1½ M. to the S.

Carriage-road from **the** railway-station (diligence twice daily in ½ hr.) via *Bernhaupten* to the baths of **Adelholzen** (2065 ft.), charmingly situated 1½ M. to the S.E., well fitted up, and possessing three different springs (saltpetre, sulphur, and alum). The hilly neighbourhood affords many pleasant walks. About 2 M. to the S.W. are the foundries and blast-furnaces **of** the *Maximilians-Hütte* (2000 ft.; °*Zum Eisenhammer*; Hütten-Schenke). — The easy and attractive ascent of **the** °Hochfelln (5480 ft.) **may** be made from the Maximilians-Hütte in 3 hrs. (guide unnecessary; horse 10, there and back 16, overnight 20 *M*), via the *Brünnling-Alpe* (3800 ft.; Inn). About 65 ft. below the summit is the *Hochfelln-Haus* (*Inn; post and telegraph office and telephone to Bergen). On the S. summit is the *Tabor-Kapelle*. The splendid °View commands the entire chain of the Salzburg, Bavarian, and Tyrolese Alps, the Chiemsee with four other lakes, and to the N. the plain as far as the Bavarian Forest.

73 M. **Traunstein** (1935 ft.; *Traunsteiner Hof*; *Krone, at the station; *Wispauer; *Post; Scheicher; Sailer; Weisses Bräuhaus, etc.; *Bad Traunstein*, with mineral, saline, and mud baths, a hydropathic establishment, and large garden, pens. 3½–7 *M*), a thriving place with 5400 inhab., on a slope of the *Traun*, is much frequented as a summer-resort. The extensive salt-works are situated in the suburb of *Au*, on the Traun; the brine evaporated here is conducted in pipes from Reichenhall (p. 224), a distance of 22½ M.

FROM TRAUNSTEIN TO REICHENHALL via *Inzell*, 22½ M. (post-omnibus to Inzell, 11 M., daily in 3 hrs.; carr. and pair to Reichenhall 22 *M*). The road, which beyond Inzell will also repay the pedestrian, leads via (4½ M.) *Ober-Siegsdorf* through the valley of the *Rothe Traun* to (4 M.) Inzell (2275 ft.; *Post*), a village in the bed of an ancient lake. It then passes between the *Falkenstein* on the left and the *Kienberg* on the right, and traverses the deep *Weissbach-Thal* to the village of *Weissbach* (1995 ft.). Farther on, the road ('Neuweg') is carried along the rocky slope on the left, adjoining the salt-water conduit, to the (6 M.) °*Mauthäusl* (p. 225). Thence to (8 M.) *Reichenhall*, see p. 225.

224   *Route 38.*   REICHENHALL..

From Traunstein to Trostberg, 13 M., local railway in 1¹/₃ hr., **through** the pretty Traunthal, viâ *Bad Empfing, Stein an der Traun* (Inn), **and (11 M.)** *Altenmarkt*. **The two** last-named are both 1¹/₂ hr. from *Seeon* (p. 223).

The Salzburg train crosses the Traun by a bridge 75 ft. in height. To the S., above the lower heights, towers the Stauffen, and farther on, **the Untersberg**. 77 M. *Lauter;* 83 M. *Teisendorf*, with the ruined castle of *Raschenberg;* 89¹/₂ M. **Freilassing** (1380 ft.; *Föckerer; *Maffei*, ¹/₄ M. **from the station**), the junction **of** the lines **to the** S. to Reichenhall **(see below)** and on the N. to *Tittmoning* (23 M. in 2 hrs.).   **The train crosses the** *Saalach* (the Austrian frontier); to the right is *Schloss Klesheim;* to the left, the church of *Maria-Plain*. The *Salzach* is then crossed; **to the** right a **view** of Hohen-Salzburg **is suddenly** disclosed.

95 M. **Salzburg**, see *Baedeker's* **Eastern Alps** or *Baedeker's Austria*.

The **Reichenhall Line** diverges to the **left at** *Freilassing* (see above) and ascends **the left bank of** the *Saalach*. **On** the right **is** the wooded *Högelberg;* **on the left** the Gaisberg **and** Untersberg. 93 M. *Hammerau*. **On the right**, near (95 M.) *Piding*, **at the** base of the abrupt Hochstauffen (p. 225), **stands the ruin** of *Stauffeneck*. The train then crosses the Saalach to —

103¹/₂ M. **Reichenhall**. — Hotels: °Curhaus Achselmannstein, **with** garden, R. & L. 4 (before the season 3), D. 3 *M;* °Cur-Hôtel Burkert, adjoining the Cur-Park, R. & A. from 3, B. 1, D. 3 *M;* °Deutscher Kaiser, with garden-restaurant, R. 1¹/₂-4, pens. 7-10 *M;* °Louisenbad; °Maximiliansbad; °Marienbad (*Dr. Hess*); °Bad Kirchberg (p. 225), all suitable for a prolonged stay. Apartments with pension: Villa Hessing, Schader, Mann, Wittelsbach, etc. — °Hôtel Bavaria, at the Reichenhall-Kirchberg station, R. 2-3, D. 2¹/₂, pens. from 6 *M;* Villa Thalfried (hôt. garni), with café-restaurant; °Russischer Hof, R. 1¹/₂-2¹/₂, D. 2¹/₂ *M;* °Post (or Krone), R. 2 *M;* °Münchner Hof; Hôtel Bahnhof, with garden-restaurant; Goldner Hirsch, R. 1-3, B. ¹/₂ *M*, unpretending.

Cafés, etc.: *Café Mayr*, also a restaurant and lodging-house (R. & A. 1¹/₂ *M*), with garden; *Staimer*, by the Cur-Garten; °*Niedermaier's Café-Meierei*, prettily situated ³/₄ M. to the N. of the Cur-Park, in the direction of the Saalach; *Fischerbräukeller*, with garden; *Railway Restaurant*. — *Schiffmann*, confectioner.

Visitors' **Tax** (for a stay of more than a week) 15 *M* (less **in** proportion for members of a family).

Baths at the *Dianabad* (with inhalation and pneumatic cabinets), at the Curhaus Achselmannstein, Louisenbad, Bad Kirchberg, etc.

Post and Telegraph Office in the market-place and at the station (poste restante).

English Church Service in summer.

Reichenhall (1555 ft.), a favourite watering-place on **the Saale** or *Saalach* (3800 inhab.), **is** picturesquely bounded on three sides by an amphitheatre **of** mountains, the *Untersberg* (6480 ft.), *Lattengebirge* (5700 ft.), *Reitalpgebirge* (6460 ft.), *Müllnerhorn* (4500 ft.), *Ristfeichtkogl* (5315 ft.), *Sonntagshorn* (6430 ft.), and *Hochstauffen* (5815 ft.). This **is the central** point of **union of the** four principal Bavarian **salt-works**, which are connected **by conduits** of an aggregate length of **50 M**. The large *Salinengebäude*, or salt-work buildings, in the market-place, contain the offices on the right, and four *Sudhäuser*

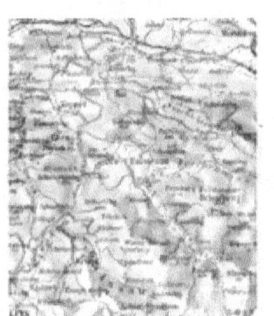

('boiling-houses', from 'sieden'; comp. Engl. seethe, suds) on the left, opposite which is the handsome *Hauptbrunnhaus*, or pump-house. In the latter (second door to the left) tickets of admission (1 ℳ) to the springs and the salt-pans are obtained.

The sources of the saline springs of Reichenhall, fifteen in number, are about 50 ft. below the surface of the soil, and are reached by a flight of 72 steps. Five of them are so strongly impregnated (Edelquelle, $25^{1}/_{2}$ per cent) that they are at once conducted to the Gradirhaus (see below), and also supply the fountain in the Gradir-Park. The fresh-water springs are conveyed to the Saalach by means of a shaft $1^{1}/_{2}$ M. in length and 8 ft. in height. The pump-house contains the two huge wheels by which the pumps are worked. On the second floor is a chapel in the Byzantine style, with stained-glass windows. In the court are two fresh-water fountains adorned with statues of SS. Virgilius and Rupert.

The *Church*, in the Romanesque style, is adorned with small frescoes by *Schwind*. A new *Protestant Church* adjoins the Cur-Garten. Above the town rises the old castle of *Gruttenstein* (1680 ft.).

Reichenhall is resorted to by patients suffering from general debility, chronic rheumatism, pulmonary affections, asthma, etc., who find relief in the mild and highly ozonized air, as well as from the salt-baths, saline and pine-needle inhalation, etc. The chief rallying-point of visitors is the *Cur-Garten*, beside the *Gradirhaus* (behind the Hôtel Burkert), with a covered promenade, a café, etc., where a band plays from 6.30 to 8 a.m. and from 5 to 7 p.m. (on Tues. and Frid. afternoons at Bad Kirchberg, see below). The Cur-Anlagen contain the *Soolsprudel*, a salt-water fountain 20 ft. in height. The *Gradirwerk* (evaporating-house), 180 yds. long, is exclusively devoted to the purposes of the inhalation cure.

Near the station of Reichenhall-Kirchberg (p. 227), a handsome new bridge crosses the Saalach to the *Kirchberg Bath-House*, with salt and mineral baths and whey-cure (board 5 ℳ per day; R. 10-36 ℳ per week, L. & A. extra).

Environs. One of the chief attractions of Reichenhall for invalids consists in the numerous shady woodland walks in the immediate neighbourhood of the town, some level and some gently ascending, e.g. in the *Nonner Wald*, *Forstplantage*, *Kirchholz*, etc. These are all marked by guide-boards and distance-posts. — On the Salzburg road, $^{1}/_{2}$ M. to the N.E. of the Curhaus, lies St. Zeno (*Hofwirth*; *Schwabenbräu*), once an Augustine monastery, of very ancient origin, but suppressed in 1803, and fitted up in 1853 as a nunnery and school. — The Königsweg, a winding path among the fine pines of the *Kirchholz*, begins behind the monastery and ascends gradually to ($^{1}/_{2}$ hr.) the *Klosterhof* (1770 ft.; Café). Hence across the hill to Gross-Gmain, 20 minutes.

To Gross-Gmain, a pleasant walk of 40 minutes The route (footpath past Staimer's café, or road past the Villas Hessing and Langenfeld) crosses the hill, turns to the left by an old lime-tree, and descends gradually Fine view of the Untersberg and Lattengebirge all the way. The pleasant little village (1710 ft.; *Untersberg*; *Kaiser Karl*) lies on the right bank of the *Weissbach*, just beyond the Austrian frontier. The picturesque ruined castle of *Plain* (popularly called *Salzbüchsel*; with belvedere) lies $1^{1}/_{2}$ M. to the E., at the base of the Untersberg.

To the W. of the Gradir-Park, beyond the ($^{1}/_{2}$ M.) *Nonner Steg* (bridge across the Saalach), extends the *Nonner Wald*, which is intersected by numerous paths. The most frequented leads straight on (where it forks,

BAEDEKER's S. Germany. 8th Edit. 15

we pass through the fence to the right) to (3/4 M.) Non (1590 ft.; *Fuchsbauer's Restaurant*), a village at the foot of the Hochstauffen, with an old church containing a Gothic °Altar of the 15th century. — The °*Padinger Alpe* (2170 ft.; café) may be reached from Non in 50 min.; splendid view of the Reichenhall valley. — Other pleasant promenades: to the *Molkenbauer* (20 min.), *Alpgarten* (1/2 hr.), *Listsee* (1 hr.), etc.; see Baedeker's *Eastern Alps*.

Among the nearer mountain-excursions, the ascent of the °*Zwiesel* (5850 ft.), the W. and highest peak of the *Stauffengebirge*, is particularly recommended (4 hrs.; guide unnecessary). Road to the (3 M.) farm of *Langacker* (rfmts.), at the foot of the mountain; bridle-path thence, for the most part through beautiful beech and pine woods, to the (2 hrs.) *Zwiesel-Alp* (4790 ft.; Inn) and the (1 hr.) summit, which commands a magnificent mountain-panorama. — The ascent of the *Hochstauffen* (5815 ft.), the E. peak of the Stauffengebirge, is laborious (2 1/2 hrs. from the Zwiesel-Alp; the ascent from *Piding*, on the N. side, is preferable, see p. 224).

°To the Mauthhäusl, 2 1/2 hrs., a very attractive excursion (carr. with one horse 6, carr. and pair 10 1/2 *M*; omnibus daily in summer at 2.30 p.m. from the Hôtel Achselmannstein, returning at 6 p.m., return-fare 1 1/2 *M*). The road leads to the W., passing *Bad Kirchberg* (p. 225), and ascends a wooded ravine. About 2 1/2 M. from Reichenhall, on two rocky eminences, are the *Chapel of St. Pancras* (1800 ft.) and the ruin of *Karlstein*, two good points of view. About 3/4 M. farther on we reach the pretty *Thumsee* (1730 ft.), 1/2 M. long and 1/4 M. broad (Restaurant on the opposite bank). The road ascends from the W. end of the lake through the picturesque *Nesselgraben* to the (1 1/2 M.) pump-house of *Obernesselgraben*, at the summit of the pass (2120 ft.), and 1/4 M. farther on divides. The left branch descends to *Schnaizlreut* and *Lofer* (see below); while the right branch, known as the *Neuweg*, maintains its high level above the valley of the *Weissbach* (opposite rises the huge *Ristfeichtkogel*, 5315 ft.; to the S.E. the Watzmann), and reaches the (1/2 hr.) °Mauthhäusl (2075 ft.; *Inn*), in a most picturesque situation above the profound gorge of the Weissbach. A path leads down to the *Gorges of the Weissbach* and the *Schrainbach Fall* in the ravine beneath. — Beyond the Mauthhäusl the road goes on, past *Weissbach* and *Inzell*, to *Traunstein* (p. 223).

From Reichenhall to Lofer, 17 1/2 M., diligence twice daily in 4 1/2 hrs.; carr. with one horse 17, with two horses 27 *M*. From (5 M.) *Obernesselgraben* (see above) the road descends abruptly to (2 M.) *Schnaizlreut* (1670 ft.; Inn), a hamlet in the Saalach valley, beyond which it crosses the *Bodenbühl* to (2 1/4 M.) Unken (1810 ft.; °*Post; Lamm*), a favourite health-resort. About 2 M. to the S. are the small baths of *Oberrain* (°Inn). A visit should be paid to the imposing gorge of the °*Schwarzberg-Klamm*, 2 1/2 hrs. to the W., and to the *Staubfall* (3 hrs.). The °*Sonntagshorn* (6436 ft.), easily ascended in 4 1/2 hrs. (guide not indispensable), commands a magnificent view. — From Unken the road traverses the *Kniepass* to (6 M.) Lofer (2096 ft.; °*Post;* °*Bräu;* °*Schweizer*), a straggling village, much visited as a summer-resort, and beautifully situated between the *Loferer Steinberge* to the W. and the *Reitalp-Gebirge* to the E. Pleasant excursions to the *Loferer Hochthal*, the *Loferer Alpe*, etc. About 6 M. to the S., on the Oberweissbach road, is the interesting °*Vorderkaser-Klamm*. For details, see Baedeker's *Eastern Alps*.

39. From Reichenhall to Berchtesgaden. Königs-See.

Comp. Map, p. 224.

12 M. Railway in 1 1/4 hr. (2nd class 1 *M* 60 pf., 3rd class 1 *M*). The tickets are sold by the conductor on the train. The view-carriages, for which 2nd class passengers have to take an additional 3rd class ticket, are scarcely recommended. — Carriage from Reichenhall viâ Hallthurm to Berchtesgaden (preferable in fine weather) in 3 hrs., with one horse 11 *M* 20 pf., with two horses 17 *M* (fee included); viâ Hintersee and Ramsau (much better than viâ Hallthurm), 15 or 27 *M*; see p. 282. —

OMNIBUS (1 *M.*) and CARRIAGES for the Königs-See (tariff, see p. 228) meet the trains at Berchtesgaden.

FROM SALZBURG TO BERCHTESGADEN: **Steam** Tramway to (8 M.) *St. Leonhard-Drachenloch* in 53 min.; omnibus **thence to** *Berchtesgaden* seven times daily in 1¼ hr., and to *Königs-See* **four times** daily in 2 hrs. Through-ticket from Salzburg to Berchtesgaden, cl. 1 fl. 20 kr., 3rd cl. 1 fl.; to Königs-See 1 fl. 70, 1 fl. 50 kr., return-ticket 2 fl. 60, 2 fl. 10 kr. Circular ticket from Salzburg to Berchtesgaden and back viâ Reichenhall, 2 fl. 90, 2 fl. 10 kr. — CARRIAGE from Salzburg to Berchtesgaden 5 or 8 fl., there and back 6 or 10 fl.; to the Königs-See and back 8 or 12 fl. (visit to the salt-mines included **in each case**; the drive from Salzburg and back, with a visit to the salt-works, **occupies** 8 **hrs.**).

Reichenhall (1555 ft.), see p. 224. The train skirts the W. side of the town to (1 M.) *Reichenhall-Kirchberg* (*Hôtel Bavaria, at the station; *Bad Kirchberg*, **to** the right, **beyond the** Saalach, p. 225) and then **ascends** to the left through **the valley** of the *Waldbach* (4 : 100). **To** the left is the château **of** *Gruttenstein* (p. 225). At (2 M.) *Gmain* (1765 ft.; Restaurant) we obtain a view of the Untersberg (left) **and the** Lattengebirge (right). **To the left** lie the village of Gross-Gmain and the ruin of Plain (**p.** 225). **The train then steadily ascends along the base of the** Lattengebirge, crosses **the Weissbach and the** old moraine of the *Fuchsenstein*, and **proceeds** through **fine wood** to (4½ M.) **Hallthurm** (2270 ft.; *Pension Hallthurm), picturesquely situated on the saddle between the Untersberg and the Lattengebirge, with an **old tower. We then descend** (2 : 100) through a wide green valley (in front, to the **right, the** Hochkalter, with the **Blaueis glacier, to** the left the Watzmann) **and skirt** the *Bischofswieser Ache*, **which** descends from the right. In front rises the Hohe Göll, to **the right the** Hagengebirge. Below (8½ **M.**) *Bischofswiesen* (2015 ft.; Brennerbascht **Inn**, Neuwirth, **p.** 229) **the** train crosses to the **left bank of the Ache. The** next part of the line lies through the wild *Tristram* **Ravine** (short tunnel) to (10½ M.) *Gmundbrücke* (1805 ft.), at **the confluence of the** Bischofswieser Ache with the *Ramsauer Ache*. **The** train runs along the bank **of the latter to** (**12 M.**) *Berchtesgaden* (1770 ft.; Hôtel Bahnhof); **the station** lies to **the** S. of the town, near the **salt-works (omnibuses for the** principal **hotels and the Königs-See in waiting**).

Berchtesgaden. — Hotels. *BELLEVUE, **with** baths, R., L., & A. 2-4, **B. 1**, D. 3, pension 7-8 *M*, omn. **60** pf.; *LEUTHAUS or POST, **R.** 2-3 *M*, **B. 80** pf., pension 6-7, omn. ½ *M*; VIER JAHRESZEITEN, at the upper end of **the village, with garden and view, R.** 2½, D. 3, B. 1, pens. 6-8 *M*; HÔTEL-PENSION & RESTAURANT DEUTSCHES HAUS, R. 1½-3. pens. 5-7 *M*; *HÔT.-RESTAURANT BAHNHOF, at the station, pens. 5½ *M*; WATZMANN, R. 2 *M*; KRONE; SALZBURGER HOF, pens. 5 *M*; NEUHAUS; NONNTHALER WIRTHSHAUS; BÄR; LÖWE; TRIEMBACHER, R. 1 *M*; ZUR KÖNIGS-ALLEE, on the Salzburg road. — Pensions: GEIGER, 5-7 *M* per day; GISELA-BAD; BERGHOF; VILLA MINERVA, **with park and** view; LUITPOLD; VILLA HOLZNER (*Café* Waldluft), **in a** cool situation; WAHLHEIM; SCHWABENWIRTH; GÖHLSTEIN; FÜRSTENSTEIN; WENIG; ZECHMEISTER. — PENS. GREGORY, with café-garden, 6-8 *M*; MALTERLEHEN, HOFREIT, VILLA KÖPPELECK, etc., in Schönau (**p.** 229); *MORITZ, STEINER, and REGINA, on the Upper Salzberg (p. 229; 1¼-1½ hr.).

Cafés. *Forstner, near the Post, with rooms; *Deutsches Haus* (see above), beer; *Café-Restaurant Göhlstein*, near the Malerhügel. — Reading Room in the Rathhaus (1st floor), adm. free.

Baths. Fresh and salt water baths at the Bellevue, the Leuthaus, and most of the pensions; *Huber*, Bahnhof-Str.; *Wilhelmsbad*, Maximilian-Str. *River Baths* in the *Gernbach*, 3/4 M. from the town, to the left of the Salzburg road, and at the *Aschauer Weiher*, 2 M. to the W. of the town (p. 229).

Carved Wares in wood, bone, and ivory, for which Berchtesgaden has been famous for centuries, are kept in great variety by *S.* and *P. Zechmeister*, *Kaserer*, *Walch*, *Wenig*, *Huber*, *Grassl*, and others.

Carriages. To the *Königs-See* and back, with stay of 3 hrs., one-horse carriage 8 *M*, two-horse 11 *M* 70 pf. (for each additional hour 1 *M* more); to *Ramsau* 8 *M* 10 or 11 *M* 70, there and back (1/2 a day) 11 *M* 10 or 15 *M* 70 pf.; *Hintersee* 11 *M* 40 pf. or 17 *M*, there and back 13 *M* 40 or 20 *M* 40 pf.; to the *Almbach-Klamm* 8 *M* 10 and 11 *M* 70 pf.; to *Vordereck* (Pens. Moritz), with two horses 11 *M* 70 pf.; to *Ilsank* 5 *M* 70 pf.; to *Reichenhall* viâ Schwarzbachwacht, returning viâ Hallthurm, 17 *M* 50 or 26 *M* 50 pf. Fees included, but tolls extra. — Omnibus from the station to *Königs-See* in connection with the trains (1 *M*); to the Wimbach-Klamm Hotel (Ramsau), twice daily in summer from the station (2 1/2 *M*); to the *Hintersee* once daily in July and August (3 1/2 *M*).

English Church Service in summer.

Berchtesgaden (1885 ft.), a small Bavarian town with 2300 inhab., **was down** to 1803 the seat of an independent provostry, or ecclesiastical **principality, the** dominions of which **were so** mountainous and **so limited in extent** (165 sq. M.), that it was jestingly said to be **as high** as **it was broad** (interesting relief-map in the above-mentioned reading-room). **One-sixth** part only was cultivated, the **remainder** consisting **of rock,** forest, and water. The handsome old **abbey is now a royal château.** The *Abbey Church* possesses Romanesque **cloisters, carved stalls,** marble tombs of the Abbots of Berchtesgaden, and an interesting crypt. The *Luitpold Park*, in front of the royal villa to **the S. of the town**, was embellished in 1893 with a bronze *Statue *of Prince Luitpold*, regent of Bavaria, by F. von Miller. This point commands a fine view: to the left the Schwarzort, Hohe **Göll, and** Hochbrett, in the background the Stuhlgebirge and Schönfeldspitze, **to the right the Kleine and Grosse** Watzmann. In the valley, on the Ache, are situated extensive *Salt Works* and the Station of the Reichenhall Railway (p. 227). Berchtesgaden is a very favourite summer-resort, and the **environs afford an almost inexhaustible variety of** beautiful **walks and excursions.**

Walks (comp. **the** guide-book **issued by** the local Alpine Club). About 3/4 M. to the E., on the Salzburg **road, is** the Salt Mine, a visit to **which** requires about **1** hr. Ticket for the regular trips at 11 a.m. and 5 p.m., 1 1/2 *M* each; at other hours, from **6 a.m.** to 7 p.m., admission for **one person** 3 1/2 *M*, **for** each additional **person** 1 1/2 *M*. Visitors of each **sex are** provided **with** appropriate miners' costumes and with lanterns. **The mine is entered** on foot, numerous flights of steps ascended, and an **occasional** descent accomplished by means of wooden slides inclined at **an angle** of 45° **or more.** The 'Salz-See', illuminated somewhat feebly by **miners'** lamps, **is traversed** in a boat. The party then passes through **several** other **chambers and** galleries, the **most** interesting of which is the **huge Kaiser-Franz chamber,** now deserted, **and reaches** the tramway **by which the mine is** quitted.

The **Lockstein* (2235 ft.; 1/2 hr.) commands an admirable view of the valley of Berchtesgaden, particularly by evening-light. We turn to the **right by the** abbey-church and ascend **the** *Doctorberg* **by the old Reichen-**

hall road; at the hospital we turn to the right, again keeping to the right where the path divides, and proceeding through the wood to the restaurant. — A few hundred paces before the hospital, a charming path to the left skirts the precipitous *Kälberstein* (see below) by the 'Soolenleitung', or salt-water conduit, to the (1/4 hr.) *Calvarienberg* (fine view), and proceeds thence, passing **above the** royal villa, to the new Reichenhall road. — Another pleasant excursion may be made by following the old Reichenhall road past the hospital (see above) as far as the (1/2 hr.) *Rosthäusl* (2185 ft.), and then proceeding to the right through the *Rostwald* to (1/4 hr.) the **Aschauer Weiher** (2135 ft.), with swimming and other baths (1/4 M. to the N.E. the °*Restaurant Dietfeldkaser*, picturesquely situated). — A pleasant return-route from the Rosthäusl to Berchtesgaden is offered by the **Königsweg**, extending for 1 1/2 M. along the wooded slopes of the Kälberstein, and joining the old Reichenhall road at the hospital (see above). — A **very** pleasant walk **may** be taken to Bischofswiesen (p. 227) by following **the** old Reichenhall road to the (3 M.) *Neuwirth* (3/4 M. farther on, near the station, the *Brennerbascht Inn*), returning by the new Reichenhall road. A fine return-route is also afforded by the beautiful **Maximilians-Reitweg**, which is reached through meadows (marked path) in about 10 min. from the railway-station of Bischofswiesen. This bridle-path traverses the *Rostwald*, on the slope of the Untersberg, and ends at the Dietfeldkaser near the Aschauer Weiher (see above). — **Another** excursion leads to **the** (1 hr.) **Böckl Weiher** in the *Strub* (1985 ft.; Restaurant; baths), viâ **the** new Reichenhall road as far as *Reitofen*, then **to** the left viâ *Urbanlehen* to the Bischofswieser Ache, the right bank **of which** we ascend (from the pond to the Neuwirth, 25 min.).

The **Schlössibichl** (1/2 **hr.**; 2075 ft.), **an** inn with a pretty view, at the mouth of the *Gerner-Thal*, **is** reached **from** Nonnthal by the *Hilgerberg*; in the vicinity are the *Etzerschlössl*, **a villa** belonging to Prince Urusoff, and the *Etzer-Mühle*, with a waterfall. **A** new road leads hence to (20 min.) the village of **Gern** (2390 ft.; *Inn*), with the pilgrimage-church of *Maria-Gern* (good ceiling-paintings and old votive tablets). A new path (red marks) ascends to the right between the school and the inn to the (23 min.) °**Marxen-Höhe** (2566 ft.), affording a splendid view.

Schönau is a scattered village on the plateau between the *Königsseer* **Ache and** the *Ramsauer Ache* (pensions, see p. 227). A picturesque walk leads from the station past the château of *Lustheim*, to the (1 hr.) *Vienna* **Café-Garden** at the Pens. Gregory and (1/4 M.) the *Kohlhiesl* (Café), returning by the Unterstein road (1 1/4 hr.) passing the *Sulzberglehen*, or viâ *Ilsank* (p. 231; 2 **hrs.**). Charming views of the Hohe Göll, Brett, Kahlersberg, etc.

The Upper **Salzberg** (**to Vordereck** or Pens. Moritz, 1 1/2 hr ; omn. from the station to Pens. Moritz daily at 3.30 p.m., 3 *M*, carr. and pair 11 *M* 70 pf.) may be reached by crossing the Ache at the rifle-range, and proceeding by a road, shaded the greater part of the way, past (1 1/4 hr.) the *Pension Steiner*. Beyond this point the road divides, the left branch leading to (1/4 hr.) the forester's lodge at *Vordereck* (3180 ft.; **Café**; adjoining the °*Pension Villa Regina*), the right to (1/4 hr.) the °*Pension & Restaurant Moritz* (3135 ft.), in a sheltered situation (pens. 8 *M*). The pensions on the Upper Salzberg (besides those already mentioned: *Bergler*; *Hötel*; *Kurz*, etc.) are steadily growing in reputation as health-resorts.

The °**Almbach-Klamm**, a picturesque gorge through which the *Almbach* descends in cascades from the Untersberg, **is** an interesting object for an excursion (1 1/2 hr.; carr. to the hotel **in** 3/4 hr.). We follow the Salzburg road to (3 1/4 M.) the °*Almbach-Klamm Hotel*, turn to the left to (5 min.) a bridge over the Ache, descend the **left** bank for 5 min., and near the *Almbach-Mühle* ascend on the left side **of** the gorge, which has recently been made **accessible by a** well-constructed path ('Pionierweg') as far as the (3/4 hr.) **Theresienklause** (2338 **ft.**). The finest point is the *Gumpe*, a rocky basin with a cascade 33 ft. high falling into a dark-green pool, about 8 min. from the entrance of the gorge.

°**Vorderbrand** (1 1/2-2 hrs.; carr. and pair there and back 13 *M* 70 pf.; donkey with attendant 10 *M*). **At the** (1/4 hr.) *Wemholz*, on the old Königs-

230 *Route 39.*   KÖNIGS-SEE.

See road, we diverge to the left to (1½ hr.) *Vorderbrand* (3485 ft.; 'Inn). Thence in 20 min. to the *Vordere* and *Hintere Brandkopf* (3795 ft.), which afford magnificent views.

*Scharitzkehl-Alp (3360 ft.; 1½-2 hrs.; guide, unnecessary, 3, donkey and attendant 10 M). From the rifle-range we ascend the *Herzogberg* to the right, passing the *Kalte Keller* (a deep rocky cleft), or diverge to the left from the Königs-See road opposite the station, and pass the *Waldhäusl*. Both routes unite near the *Schiedlehen*. The Alp (rfmts.) lies in an extensive meadow, surrounded by trees, between the Göhlstein and the Dürreckkopf. About ¾ hr. farther up is the *Endsthal*, a desolate valley at the W. base of the Hohe Göll, containing rocky debris and patches of snow. From the Scharitzkehl-Alp to *Vorderbrand* ¾ hr., to *Vordereck* 1½ hr. (p. 229).

Mountain ascents (*Knäufelspitze*, *Todte Mann*, *Jenner*, *Brett*, *Göhlstein*, *Hohe Göll*, etc.), see *Baedeker's Eastern Alps*.

The gem of this district is the clear, dark-green **Königs-See (1975 ft.), or *Lake of St. Bartholomew*, 6 M. long and 1¼ M. broad, the most beautiful lake in Germany, vying in grandeur with those of Switzerland and Italy. Some of the surrounding mountains, which rise almost perpendicularly from the water, are 6500 ft. in height above the lake. The new road, opened in 1894, crosses the Ache near the station by an iron bridge, and gradually ascends along the right bank of the stream to (1¼ hr.) the village of *Königssee* (Zum Königssee, Schiffmeister, both on the lake), on the bank of the lake, with a small bath-house.

The 'Schiffmeister' Moderegger presides over the rowing-boats and their crews, and regulates their trips. The fares are paid to him on returning; the rowers usually receive a small gratuity. The latter are sometimes stalwart peasant-girls, the sinews of whose arms might well be coveted by heroes of the Isis or the Cam. From the middle of June to 1st Oct. there are four regular trips daily round the lake, starting at 8.30 a.m., 11.30 a.m., 1.30 p.m., and 2.30 p.m., and occupying about 4¾ hrs., including ¾ hr. at the Sallet-Alp and 1 hr. at St. Bartholomä (fare for each pers. 1½ M). Small boat (2 pers.), with one rower, to St. Bartholomä 3 M; with two rowers (1-4 pers.) to St. Bartholomä 4½, to the Sallet-Alp 6½ M; with three rowers (7 pers.) 7½ and 11 M; for parties of 10 or upwards 1 M and 1½ M each. The best plan is to row direct to the Sallet-Alp (1½ hr.), and call at St. Bartholomä in returning. The most favourable light is in the early morning or late in the afternoon.

LAKE VOYAGE. To the left, on a promontory, is the *Villa Beust*; in the lake lies the islet of *Christlieger*, with a statue of St. John Nepomuk. The boat passes the *Falkenstein*, a rock with a cross commemorating the wreck of a boat with a party of pilgrims about 150 years ago. The lake now becomes visible in its entire extent; in the background rise the *Sagereckwand*, the *Grünsee-Tauern*, and the *Funtensee-Tauern*, and adjoining them on the right the *Schönfeldspitze* (8700 ft.). On the E. bank the *Königsbach* falls over a red cliff (about 2525 ft.) into the lake. A little farther on, at the deepest part of the lake (616 ft.), a long, reverberating echo is awakened by a pistol fired in the direction of the W. cliffs (*Brentenwand*). In the vicinity, on the E. bank, not far from the Kessel Fall, is a cavern on a level with the water, called the *Kuchler Loch*, from which a streamlet enters the lake. The boat touches at the Kessel, a wooded promontory on the E. bank, whence a good path, leading through the **Kesselgraben**, ascends to the (10 min.) pretty waterfall of the *Kesselbach* (bridle-path to the *Gotzen-Alp*, see below).

The boat now proceeds to the S.W. to St. Bartholomä, a green promontory, **with a chapel and a former royal** hunting château. At the **restaurant kept by the forester good salmon-trout** *(Salmo salvelinus*, Ger. *Saibling)* **may be obtained (dear).** In the cellar is **a large tank** for keeping the fish.

On the S.W. bank **of the lake the** *Schrainbach* **is precipitated into it from** a rocky gorge. The *Sallet-Alp*, a poor pasture $1/_2$ M. in breadth and strewn with moss-grown rocks, with **a villa of the Duke** of Meiningen, separates the Königs-See **from the beautiful *Obersee** (2000 ft.), a lake 1 M. long, enclosed on **three sides by lofty precipices of limestone.** To the left rises the sheer *Kaunerwand;* beyond it **tower the** *Teufelshörner* (7855 ft.), from which a brook **descends** over the *Röthswand* in several arms from **a height of 1**800 ft. **On the E. bank is the** *Fischunkel-Alp*, to **which a narrow path (not recommended) leads on** the S. bank in $1/_2$ hr.

From the Kessel (p. 230) a good path in long windings ascends **to the** ($3^1/_2$-4 hrs.; guide, unnecessary, 5 *M*) *Gotzen-Alp (5530 ft.), opposite St. Bartholomä (rustic **quarters, with 5** beds, in the *Springel-Kaser*). Magnificent view of the **Uebergossene** Alm, Steinerne Meer, Watzmann, Hohe Göll, Untersberg, etc. **The** view towards the N. is imperfect until we reach the ($1/_4$ hr.) **Feuerpalfen** (5640 ft.) on **the** N.W. margin of the Alp. **Somewhat** beyond that **point**, from the brink of the rock lower down, the **lake and** St. Bartholomä are visible 3300 ft. below **us. Descent** to the **(2 hrs.)** *Kessel*, where **a** boat (previously ordered) **should be in** waiting.

To the Ramsau a road leads direct from the Königs-See vià *Schönau* (p. 229) to ($1^1/_2$ M.) *Ilsank* (see below).

From Berchtesgaden to Reichenhall (12 M.), railway vià *Hallthurm* in $1^1/_4$ hr.; see p. 227. A far preferable route, however, **is the Road by** the Ramsau and the Schwarzbachwacht (20 M.; omn. daily to **the** Hintersee, see p. 228). The road passes the **Luitpold Park** and beyond the Theresien-Allée joins the new Reichenhall road. After $3/_4$ M. (direction-post) it descends to the **left**, crossing the ($1/_3$ M.) *Gmundbrücke* over the *Bischofswieser Ache*. At ($2^1/_4$ M.) Ilsank (1910 ft.; *Inn*, pens. 4-5 *M*) a brook descending about 400 ft. works a **pump by which the** salt-water from the mines is forced up to the *Söldenköpfl*, 1200 ft. higher, and over the Schwarzbachwacht to Reichenhall, a distance of 20 M.

A flight of steps ascends thence **to the** *Söldenköpfl* (3110 ft.; simple refreshments in the pump-house) whence a good path with fine views leads along the brine conduit to the ($1^1/_4$ hr.) *Zipfelhäusl* (rfmts.) and the ($1^3/_4$ hr.) Schwarzbach**wacht (p. 232).**

The fine new road **now runs** along the **left** bank of the **foaming** Ache; to the left **a grand view** of the Watzmann; before us **rises the** broad Steinberg. The *Ramsau is remarkably picturesque owing to **the contrast of the luxuriant vegetation of the valley with the** imposing **and** picturesquely-shaped grey mountains. — On the left ($1^1/_2$ M.) a finger-post indicates the path to the 'Jagdschloss Wimbach'.

A path crossing the bridge (2050 ft.; *Restaurant*) to the left, and ascending to the right by the 'Trinkhalle', leads to the ($1/_4$ hr.) *Wimbach-

Klamm. The clear blue water of the brook here forms beautiful falls in its rocky ravine, into which the sun shines about noon.

The ascent of the *Watzmann (6-7 hrs.; guide 10 *M*, **to the** middle peak 12 *M*; to the Watzmann-Haus, 6 *M*), is not difficult **for** experts. We ascend from (1¼ hr.) Ilsank by *Schappach* (rfmts.) to the (2¼ hrs.) *Mitterkaser-Alpe* (4570 ft.) and the (1½ hr.) *Watzmann-Haus* on the *Falzköpfl* (6830 ft.; *Inn in summer). Thence we ascend the arête to the E. of the *Watzmann-Grube* and over the *Watzmann-Anger* to the (2-2½ hrs.) *Watzmann-Hocheck* (8700 ft.), on which are a trigonometrical bench-mark and two crosses. The °View embraces the Gross-Glockner, Gross-Venediger, Krimmler Tauern, the vast Bavarian plain, the entire Salzkammergut and district of Berchtesgaden, with the Wimbach-Thal below, and the Königs-See and Obersee to the S.

On the road, ½ M. above **the** finger-post (see p. 231), is the *Inn zur Wimbachklamm* (pens. 4-5 *M*), and a little beyond it the *Inn zum Hochkalter.* Then (¾ M.) Ramsau (2190 ft.; *Oberwirth*, well spoken of). About ¾ M. farther on **the road** divides, the branch **to the Hintersee** and the Hirschbichel (see below) leading **to the left.** The ROAD TO REICHENHALL ascends **straight on** (right), past **the** small *Taubensee* (2845 ft.) and through beautiful pine-woods, **to the** (2¼ M.) Schwarzbachwacht (2910 ft.), a pump-house on the summit of the pass, beyond which the *Brine Conduit* (p. 231) runs parallel with the road (¼ M. farther on is the small *Inn zur Schwarzbachwacht*). The road then descends into the deep wooded valley between the **Reiter-Alpe** on the left and the *Lattengebirge* on the right, and (3 M.) crosses the *Schwarzbach.* At the (1 M.) *Jettenberg* pump-house (1795 ft.; rfmts.), at the end of the valley, another bridge crosses the Schwarzbach, which forms a fine cascade *(Staubfall)* here and falls into the Saalach immediately below. The road skirts the right bank of the Saalach, passing opposite *Fronau*, to (4½ M.) *Reichenhall* (p. 224).

The OBER-WEISSBACH ROAD crosses the Ache **and again forks.** The new road leads to the left, partly through wood, **with fine views** of the Reiter-Alpe, etc., and skirting the S.E. bank of the **Hinter**see, to the (1 hr.) Auzinger Inn (see below), where **it rejoins the** old road. The latter, to the right at the fork, recrosses the Ache, and ascends to the (1½ M.) **Hintersee** (2580 ft.), the W. bank of which it follows. Not far from the N.W. **end** of the lake, near the small *St. Antoni Chapel*, is the *Wartstein Inn* (pens. 4-5 *M*), affording a picturesque view of the Hochkalter with the Blaueis, the Hohe Göll, etc. About ¾ M. farther on, ¼ M. from the upper end of the lake, **are the** forester's house of *Hintersee* (2605 ft.) and the Bavarian custom-house. **Opposite** is *Auzinger's Inn.*

EXCURSIONS **from** the Hintersee (*Blaueis, Edelweisslahnerkopf, Stadelhorn, Hochkalter*, etc.), see *Baedeker's Eastern Alps.*

Those who desire to proceed to Reichenhall from the Hintersee take the road to the left at the N. end of the lake, skirting the W. side of the *Wartstein* (ascended in 25 min.; pretty view), turn to the left again 10 min. farther **on, and in** ½ hr. reach the Reichenhall road below **the** Taubensee (see above).

The beautiful valley between the *Hochkalter* (left) and the *Reiter-Alpe* (Grundübelhörner, Mühlsturzhorn; right) is now ascended to the (6 M.) **Hirschbichel** (3780 ft.; *Inn*), with the Austrian custom-house of *Mooswacht*.

The *Kammerlinghorn* (8045 ft.), ascended from the Hirschbichel in 3½-4 hrs. (somewhat fatiguing; guide, desirable, 5 *M*, from Ramsau 11 *M*), **is an** admirable point of view (Steinerne Meer, Tauern, etc.).

The road ascends **a few** hundred **paces** farther **to** its highest point (3870 ft.), **and then** descends **into** the Saalach-Thal (the marked footpath saves ¼ hr.). **Before us rise the** imposing *Leogang Steinberge*. About 2¼ M. **from the** Hirschbichel, near a saw-mill, a finger-post indicates **the way to the *Seisenberg-**Klamm, **a profound** and very picturesque gorge, hollowed **out by the action of the** *Weissbach*, which dashes over huge blocks of rock **below**. At the (25 min.) *Binder-Mühle*, at **the lower** end of the ravine, we reach the Saalach-Thal; a road leads hence to (½ M.) Ober-Weissbach (2150 ft.; **Auvogl*, near the church), where we rejoin the road from the Hirschbichel (to the left). The **Inn zur Frohnwies* lies ½ M. **to the** S.

The road to Saalfelden (one-horse **carr.** from Frohnwies 4, two-horse 6-7 fl.; omnibus twice daily **in** summer, **1** fl.) traverses a **defile** (*Hohlwege*), 6 M. long, on **the right bank** of the Saalach. Near the deserted mill of *Diesbach*, **the stream of that** name forms a pretty waterfall (8 min. to the left **of the road**). The valley then expands, and the Tauern chain **is seen towards the** S.

9½ M. *Saalfelden*, on **the Salzburg and Tyrol Railway, see** *Baedeker's Eastern Alps*.

40. From Munich to Linz by Simbach

148 M. RAILWAY in 4¼-11½ hrs. (fares 16 *M* 80, 10 *M* 90, 6 *M* 50 pf.; by 'Orient Express', first class only, 21 *M* 60 pf.).

From the *Munich Central Station* to the (6 M.) *East Station*, **where the** Rosenheim **line** branches off to **the** right, see p. 221. **To the right, in the distance, are the** Alps, **with** the Wendelstein.

Several unimportant **stations.** 19 M. *Schwaben*, a thriving village (branch-line to *Erding*). Near (47 M.) *Ampfing* Emp. Lewis the Bavarian defeated and took prisoner his rival Frederick of Austria in 1322. **To commemorate** the victory he erected the small church to the left on the railway. — 52 M. **Mühldorf** (1260 ft.; *Post*; **Eberl*, by **the rail.** station, plain), a little **town** on the *Inn*, with 2925 inhab., lies **below** the level of the **line, from which** its towers only are **visible. To** *Rosenheim* and *Plattling*, see R. 43.

Near (60 M.) *Neu-Oetting* (Post) **the** line **crosses the** *Isen* above **its** confluence **with** the Inn.

Alt-Oetting (*Post; Café Wasner***),** 3¾ M. to the E. (diligence in ¾ hr.), **is a** famous pilgrimage-resort, with a miraculous image of the Virgin (in the small church **in** the market), said to have been brought from the East in the 7th century. The abbey-church contains the tomb of Tilly (p. 132); in the treasury are **precious relics** dating from the 8th cent. downwards.

The line approaches the Inn; broad willow-clad valley; to the left, wooded hills. 64 M. *Perach*, prettily situated on the hill to the left. A long embankment on the river-side is next traversed. —

Near (68 M.) *Marktl* the mountains recede, and the train quits the Inn, into which the Salzach falls 3 M. to the S. An omnibus plies thrice daily in 1³/₄ hr. from Marktl to *Burghausen*, on the Salzach, with an interesting old ducal castle. — 73¹/₂ M. *Buch*. — 76 M. **Simbach** *(Alte Post; Rail. Restaurant)*, the last Bavarian station; luggage is examined here by Austrian custom-house officers. The Inn is then crossed.

78 M. **Braunau** *(Ente; Post)*, an old-fashioned town with 3100 inhabitants. The late-Gothic *Church* of the 15th cent., has a fine tower (interior modernized in bad taste). In the **Promenaden-Platz** by the Spitalkirche rises the *Palm Monument, in bronze, designed by Knoll, in memory of John **Palm**, the patriotic bookseller of Nuremberg, who was shot at Braunau by Napoleon's order (comp. p. 102). — Branch-line to *Steindorf*, see *Baedeker's Austria*.

Beyond this the country is pretty and wooded. 84 M. *Minning;* 88 M. *Obernberg-Altheim*. The line ascends; to the left, farther on, we have a fine survey of the Innthal. 90 M. *Geinberg;* 92¹/₂ M. *Gurten*. — 100 M. **Ried** *(Löwe)*, a thriving town (4500 inhab.) on the **Oberach** and *Breitach*, and junction of the Salzkammergut Railway (see *Baedeker's Eastern Alps*). The Schwanthaler-Str. contains the ancestral home of the famous sculptor of that name.

The line again ascends, affording views to the right and left. 104 M. *Peterskirch;* 108 M. *Pram-Haag;* 116 M. *Neumarkt*. Thence to *Wels* and (148 M.) *Linz*, see p. 240 and *Baedeker's Austria*.

41. From Nuremberg to Furth *(and Prague)*.

100 M. RAILWAY to Furth in 3¹/₂-6¹/₂ hrs. (fares 12 ℳ 90, 8 ℳ 60, 5 ℳ 50 pf.), to Prague in 8¹/₂-11¹/₂ hrs.; custom-house examination at Furth.

Nuremberg, see p. 95. The line ascends the left bank of the *Pegnitz* (on the right bank runs the line to Eger viâ Schnabelwaid, p. 109). — 2¹/₂ M. *Mögeldorf* (Restaurant zur Ostbahn); ³/₄ M. from the station the *Schmaussenbuck*, a favourite resort from Nuremberg (p. 109). — 4 M. *Laufamholz*. On the right near (7 M.) *Röthenbach* rises the *Moritzberg* (shady path to the top in 1³/₄ hr., viâ *Rockenbrunn*), which commands the plain of Nuremberg and the valley of the Pegnitz. 10¹/₂ M. *Lauf*, on the *left* bank of the *Pegnitz* (p. 109; Oertel's Restaurant, at the station); 13 M. *Ottensoos;* 15 M. *Henfenfeld*, with a small château. — 17¹/₂ M. Hersbruck (p. 109); the station lies on the *left* bank of the Pegnitz, ¹/₂ M. from the town, and 1¹/₄ M. from the other station (p. 109) on the *right* bank of the Pegnitz, on the N. side of the town.

Near (20 M.) *Pommelsbrunn* (Birner, at the station; *Paulus, Vogel, in the village), a summer-resort, prettily situated at the base of the *Houbirg*, the line quits the Pegnitz-Thal, which here turns to the N. Scenery picturesque. 23 M. *Hartmannshof;* 26 M. *Etzelwang* (N.E., the ruined *Rupprechtstein* and the well-preserved *Schloss*

Neidstein). — 28 M. *Neukirchen*, on the watershed between the Main and the Danube.

FROM NEUKIRCHEN TO WEIDEN (31½ M., railway in 2 hrs.). Stations *Grossalbershof*, *Schönlind*, and (12½ M.) Vilseck, an old town on the *Vils*, with a late-Gothic church. Then *Langenbruck*, *Freiung*, *Rothenbach*, *Weiherhammer*, where the *Heidenab* is crossed, and (31½ M.) *Weiden* (p. 134).

34 M. *Sulzbach* (1394 ft.; **Krone**; pop. 4668), with an old Schloss of the Dukes of Pfalz-Neuburg-Sulzbach, now a house of correction for women. 36 M. *Rosenberg*, with the blast-furnaces of the **Maxhütte** (p. 134); 39½ M. *Altmannshof*. To the right rises the *Erzberg*, with its iron-mines.

41½ M. **Amberg** (1235 ft.; *Pfälzer Hof*; *Mayerhofer's Restaurant*, both near the station), a town on the *Vils*, with 19,100 inhab., has a well-preserved wall and moat, and is encircled by a fine avenue. The large *Jesuits' College* is now occupied by the gymnasium, a seminary, and a brewery. The late-Gothic **Church of St. Martin** (15th cent.), with a tower 295 ft. high, contains a tombstone of Count Palatine Rupert (d. 1393). The *Rathhaus*, with its two fine halls, contains the valuable archives of the town. The large *Prison* has room for 1300 convicts. Guns for the Bavarian army are made at the Gewehrfabrik here. Outside the Vilsthor is a monument to Max Joseph I. The *Mariahilfberg* (1630 ft.), with a pilgrimage-church, affords an extensive prospect (Inn).

45 M. *Hiltersdorf*; 50 M. *Freihöls*; 55 M. *Irrenlohe*. We then cross the *Nab*. 58 M. **Schwandorf** (p. 134), junction of the Eger and Ratisbon line (R. 27). Our line turns to the E., traversing wood and passing several large ponds. 66 M. *Altenschwand*; 70 M. *Bodenwöhr*; 76 M. *Neubäu*; 80½ M. *Roding* (1164 ft.; Kleber, Post), a thriving village on the *Regen*, 1¼ M. to the S.; 82 M. *Pösing*.

88 M. **Cham** (1263 ft.; *Post*; *Vogel*), an old town with 3600 inhab., on the N. margin of the Bavarian Forest (p. 245), is the old capital of the *Chamberich*. Gothic Rathhaus of the 15th cent.; adjoining it the late-Gothic church of St. James (1514).

The old *Chammünster*, 1½ M. to the E. of the town, is a late-Gothic church on Romanesque foundations. Near it is the lofty ruin of *Chamereck*.

FROM CHAM TO LAM. 25 M., railway in 2½ hrs., through the winding valley of the *Regen*. — From (3 M.) *Runding* (Simeth's Brewery), with a ruined castle, a pleasant excursion may be made to the (2 hrs.) *Haidstein* (2450 ft.), a fine point of view, with a chapel and some scanty ruins. The descent may be made via *Ried*, with its gigantic lime-tree, to (1½ hr.) *Kötzting* (see below). — 5½ M. *Chamerau*; 9 M. *Miltach*. Above (11 M.) *Blaibach* the *Schwarze Regen* unites with the *Weisse Regen*. — We follow the valley of the latter via *Pulling* to (13½ M.) Kötzting (1345 ft.; *Decker*; °*Post*; °*Kraus*), a small industrial town at the foot of the steep *Kaitersberg* (3300 ft.). The *Burgstall* (*Hohe Bogen*; see p. 236) is ascended hence via *Rimmbach* in 3½ hrs. Over the *Haidstein* to *Runding* 3½ hrs. (see above). A road leads to the S.E. to *Viechtach* (see p. 246). — 17 M. *Grafenwiesen*; 20 M. *Hohenwarth*, at the base of the *Hohe Bogen* (p. 236); 22½ M. *Arrach*. — 25 M. *Lam*, see p. 247.

We now traverse the deep *Chambthal*. 92 M. *Kothmaissling*; 96 M. *Ahrnschwang*, with an old castle and church.

To the S.W. rises the finely-shaped **Hohe Bogen** (highest point, the *Eckstein*, 3523 ft.), ascended from Ahrnschwang or Furth in 2-2½ hrs. The *Burgstall* (3210 ft.), **the W.** peak, commands **a** fine survey of the valley of the Regen, and **of a** great part of Bohemia and the Upper Palatinate. Amongst the woods **on** the W. spur **lies** the ruin of *Lichteneck* (2438 ft.). From the Burgstall to *Kötzting*, see p. 235. — We may penetrate farther **into** the *Bavarian Forest* by descending from the Eckstein **on** the S.E. side **to the** (25 min.) *Diensthütte* (refreshments), whence we may either descend **to** (¾ hr.) *Hohenwarth* (p. 235), or follow the top of the hill to the (¾ **hr.**) **belvedere** on the *Hohenstein* (path marked in red), and go thence viâ *Kager* **to** (1½ hr.) the high-road, which **leads** to (4½ M.) *Lam* (p. 247).

100 M. Furth (1345 ft.; **Post; Zum Hohenbogen*, at the station; *Waschinger;* breweries of *Utz* and *Altmann; Rail. Restaurant*), a small town with an ancient tower and a ruined castle, the junction of the Bohemian W. Railway (luggage examined).

In the Chambthal, about ½ M. to the E., lies the *Wutzmühle* (*Hôtel-Pension). Fine points of view are the *Aepflet-Kuppe*, 25 min. from **Furth**, and the *Voitenberg-Oed*, 35 min. **farther on** (path marked in white).

Omnibus twice daily in 4¼ hrs. to (15 M.) *Lam* (p. 247; fare 2 ℳ 50 pf.). The road leads by (4 M.) *Eschlkam* (1543 ft.; *Neumaier), a prettily situated summer-resort, and (4¼ M.) *Neukirchen* (**Moreth; Koepl*), at the N.E. base of the *Hohe Bogen* (see above), with a pilgrimage-church.

From Furth to Prague, see *Baedeker's* **Austria**.

42. From Ratisbon to Passau and Linz.
The Danube from Passau to Linz.

140 M. RAILWAY to (74 M.) Passau in 2-4 hrs., to (140 M.) Linz in 5-8 hrs. — STEAMBOAT from **Passau** to Linz daily in summer in 3 hrs. (fares 2 fl. 60, 1 fl. 55 kr.); *up* from **Linz** to Passau, 8 hrs. (fares 1 fl. 60, 1 fl. 20 kr.). The custom-house examination takes place **on** the purchase of tickets in the Rathhaus. The check received is given up on embarking.

To (5 M.) *Obertraubling*, see p. 135. Our line diverges **to the** left from the Munich **railway (R. 27).** Stations *Mangolding, Moosham, Taimering,* **Sünching** (branch-line to *Geiselhöring*, p. 135), *Radldorf*.

25½ M. **Straubing** (1090 ft.; *Schwarzer Adler;* **Post**, R. 1¼-2 ℳ, B. 60 pf., **D.** 2 ℳ; *Kraus*), a very ancient town (pop. 13,850) on the *Danube*, lies in an extensive **and** fertile plain, the granary of Bavaria. The late-Gothic church of **St. James* (1429-1512) contains paintings attributed to *Wohlgemut*, a fine altar with statues of the year 1500, and good stained glass (1442 and 1503). The Romanesque church of *St. Peter*, in the cemetery on the lofty bank of the Danube, passes for the oldest building in the town **and is** supposed to occupy the site of the Roman *Serviodurum*. The Gothic *Gymnasialkirche* (of 1430), formerly the church of the Carmelites, contains the fine monument of Duke Albert II. (d. 1397). **The** *Schloss* (now barracks) was once occupied by Duke Albert III. **with** his wife Agnes Bernauer (p. 114), the beautiful daughter of **a barber** of Augsburg. Her father-in-law Duke Ernest, **exasperated by his** son's mésalliance, cruelly and unjustly caused her to **be** condemned to death and thrown into the Danube from the bridge (1435). Her remains were interred in the churchyard of St. Peter, as recorded

by an inscription on a marble slab in the Agnes Bernauer Chapel (of 1436). The square *Stadt-Thurm* (223 ft.), with its five turrets, was erected by Duke Lewis I. in 1208.

30 M. *Amselfing*; 33½ M. *Strasskirchen*, 4 M. to the S.W. of which are the mineral-baths of *Münchshöfen*; 37 M. *Stephansposching*. On the left the *Natternberg* (1260 ft.), with a ruined castle and a modern château. — 41 M. *Plattling* (1040 ft.), where the line crosses the *Isar*, near its confluence with the Danube, junction for Mühldorf and Eisenstein. (Excursion in the *Bavarian Forest*, see p. 245.)

46½ M. *Langenisarhofen*; 50 M. *Osterhofen*; 54 M. *Girching*; 56½ M. *Pleinting*. The line nears the Danube, and follows it to Passau. On the opposite bank rises the well-preserved ruin of *Hiltgersberg*.

60 M. **Vilshofen** (1007 ft.; *Ochs*; *Bayrischer Hof*), the Roman *Villa Quintanica*, at the confluence of the *Vils* and Danube, has a Gothic church of 1376 — 64 M. *Sandbach*. On a rock to the left, farther on, we observe a recumbent lion, erected to the memory of Maximilian I., the projector of the high-road, which between this point and Passau is in many places hewn through the rock.

69 M. *Schalding*; 71 M. *Heining*. The towers of Passau, the fortress of Oberhaus, and the charming environs of the town now come into view. Luggage is examined at the station.

74 M. **Passau**. — Hotels. *Bayrischer Hof (Pl. a; C, 3), R., L., & A. from 2½, D. 2½ *M*., *Mohr, R., L., & A. from 1½, D. 2 *M*., B. 55 pf., both in the Ludwigs-Str.; *Wenzel zur Sonne (Pl. c; C, 3), corner of Theresiengasse and Untere Sand, near the bridge over the Inn; Zur Eisenbahn, near the rail. station, moderate. — Wine Saloons: *Zum Wilden Mann*, Schrottgasse; *Rathhauskeller, in the Rathhaus (p. 239); *Mühlbauer*; *Cottel*; *Heilige-Geist-Stiftaschenke* (see p. 238; good Austrian wine). — Beer at the *Stadt Wien (Pl. B, 3), Ludwigs-Platz; *Stockbauer-Garten* (Pl. E, 2, 3), with view of the Danube; *Krembauer*, at Anger (Pl. C, 2; p. 239); *Peschlkeller* (Pl. A, 3), near the station, with terrace towards the Danube; *Stockbauerkeller* (Pl. B, 4), *Schmeroldkeller*, *Hellkeller* (Pl. A, 4), beyond the drill-ground; *Innstadt Brewery* (Pl. E, 4). — Post & Telegraph Offices, at the rail. station (Pl. A, 3) and in the old Canonical Court in the Domplatz (Pl. C, 3; p. 238). — Baths in the Danube, left bank; also in the Ilz, right bank, warmer.

Passau (960 ft.), the *Castra Batava* of the Romans, the capital of an episcopal see from 739 to 1803, with 16,600 inhab., lies on a rocky tongue of land formed by the confluence of the *Inn* (319 yds. in breadth) with the Danube (only 264 yds. wide). Numerous houses, chiefly of the 17th and 18th cent., on the banks of the rivers, especially on the Inn, give the town an imposing appearance. The peculiar and picturesque situation of the town at the confluence of the Danube, Inn, and Ilz, and the variety of views commanded by the neighbouring heights, will amply repay a short visit to Passau, one of the most beautiful places on the Danube.

From the station (Pl. A, 3) the Bahnhof-Str. leads to the E. to the Ludwigs-Platz (Pl. B, 3), and thence, somewhat to the left, to the Neumarkt or Ludwig-Str., which, with its E. continuation the

Rindermarkt, is the busiest part of the town. To the right, at the corner of the Heilige-Geist-Str., is the *Votivkirche* in the Romanesque style, erected in 1564 and remodelled in 1864. On the façade are statues of Christ and the Apostles. The interior, which has no aisles, is tastefully decorated. Above the high-altar is a group of the Coronation of the Virgin by *Knabl*. — Adjacent, on the right, is the *Heilige Geistspital*, with a church and the tavern mentioned at p. 237.

Farther on, on the left side of the Rindermarkt, is the *St. Johannes-Spitalkirche* (Pl. C, 2), with numerous wood-carvings, ancient and modern, ranged along the walls, and tombstones in red marble. To the right, higher up, is the *Parish Church of St. Paul* (Pl. C, 2), built in 1678 and skilfully painted in the interior in 1851.

Passing through the **Paulusbogen** adjoining the church, we ascend to the right through the Postgasse to the *Parade-Platz* or *Domplatz* (Pl. C, D, 3). On the E. side, on a height overlooking the town, rises the CATHEDRAL OF ST. STEPHEN, founded perhaps as early as the 5th cent., restored in the Gothic style in the 15th cent., and rebuilt in a florid rococo style by *C. Lorago* after a fire in 1662 (nave completed in 1684, towers in 1695). This is one of the finest German churches of the 17th century. The outside of the choir, transept, and dome date from the 15th cent. restoration, but the interior has been modernized. The fine organ, by Hechenberger (1889), is the largest in Bavaria. On the N. side is the *Domhof*, with interesting restored chapels; on the wall of the cathedral here are numerous old gravestones. The chapel of the *Holy Trinity* (1572), with a large modern carved altar and the names of all the bishops of Passau, contains the monument of the founder, Prince-Bishop Trenbach (d. 1598). The *Heinrichs-Kapelle*, with modern stained-glass windows and gilded carving, dates from 1710. The *Via Dolorosa* or *Kreuzweg Chapel* (1414) has four slender octagonal pillars, and old tombstones of red marble on the walls. The adjacent *Mt. of Olives* or *Oelberg Chapel*, founded in 1288, contains a marble tomb of Count Heinrich III., erected in 1360.

The *Parade-Platz* in front of the cathedral is adorned with a *Statue of Maximilian I.* in bronze. Opposite to it, on the W. side, is the *Post Office*, formerly the *Canons' Residence*, historically interesting as the place where the Treaty of Passau (1552), establishing religious toleration, was concluded between Emp. Charles V. and Elector Maurice of Saxony. See the inscriptions above and adjoining the entrance. The present building dates from 1724.

The choir of the cathedral adjoins the *Residenz-Platz* (Pl. D, 3), in which rise the *Old Bishop's Palace* (now containing the *Amtsgericht* and the *Landgericht*) and the *New Bishop's Palace* (1771), both with rich rococo portals.

A street descends hence to the right to the Inn Bridge (see p. 239). To the left the Schrottgasse leads to the pier of the Danube steamers, passing the *Rathhaus* (Pl. E, 3), rebuilt after a fire in

1662, and considerably enlarged and provided with a tower in 1888-93. The walls and ceiling of the Council Chambers are embellished with paintings from the history of Passau, by *F. Wagner*. Below is the tastefully decorated *Rathhauskeller* (p. 237). Going farther E., we then follow the Braugasse to the right to the *Church of the Holy Cross* (Pl. E, 3), belonging to the dissolved nunnery of Niedernburg, a Romanesque basilica of the beginning of the 13th cent., with low vaulting, lately restored. It is now a school kept by English nuns. The *Maria-Parz Chapel* on the S. side contains the tomb of the Abbess Gisela, Queen of Hungary, and sister of Emp. Henry II. (shown on application).

The Braugasse leads on to the promontory at the E. end of the town, with a few relics of the old castle of *Ort*, where we obtain a fine view of the broad expanse formed by the confluence of the rivers, whose different-coloured waters seem to strive for the mastery.

An iron bridge crosses the **Inn** to the *Innstadt* (Pl. C-E, 4), **the** ancient *Bojodurum*, rebuilt since its destruction by fire in the war of 1809. The church of *St. Severinus* (Pl. C, 4), who was a missionary here in the 5th cent., dates from the Romanesque period but was remodelled **in the** Gothic **style** in 1476. **The** *Parish Church of St. Gertraud* **(Pl. D, 4) was restored in** 1888. Following the Mariahilfgasse **from the bridge and then** ascending **to the** right, outside the town-gate, by **the road leading to the** Waldschloss (see below), we reach ($^1/_4$ hr.) **the pilgrimage-church** of *Mariahilf (1256 ft.; Pl. **E,** 4). Both **on the way to the church** and above it we obtain **charming** surveys **of the town, the confluence** of **the Inn** and Danube, **and the fortress of Oberhaus. The** church, with its richly gilt altar, **attracts numerous worshippers. The** court contains tasteful modern **Stations of the Cross, with coloured** reliefs. From the **vestibule of** the church, **garnished with votive** tablets, a flight of 164 steps descends **to** Innstadt. — **In Austrian** territory, $^1/_2$ M. from Mariahilf, is the *Waldschloss*, a restaurant prettily situated **on the margin** of a wood.

The **Town Park** (Pl. A, 2), on the slopes **of the left** bank of the Danube, $^1/_2$ **M.** to the W. of the Maximilians-Brücke (see below), affords a number **of** shady wood-walks. A **little** higher up is the *Plantage* (beer-saloon), whence **roads** and **paths** lead back to the Danube viâ **the** episcopal château of *Freudenhain* (Pl. A, 1; 1790-92), now a school.

The fortress of ***Oberhaus** (1378 ft.; Pl. E, 2), built by Bishop **Ulric II. in** 1219, **crowns the precipitous,** wooded height of the *Georgsberg*, **on the left bank of the Danube,** opposite Passau. It is **connected by a rampart and walls with the** old fortress of *Niederhaus* (Pl. F, 2), on the tongue between the Ilz and the Danube. The road leaves the town at the upper end, crosses the Danube by the *Maximilians-Brücke*, 240 yds. long, and descends on the left bank **through the small suburb of** *Anger*, **and through a** tunnel in the rock, to the Ilz. The shortest route for pedestrians is by the new *Chain Bridge* at the lower end of the town (3 pf.). On the left, beyond the tunnel, is the Gothic *Salvator-Kirche* (Pl. E, 2), a curious three-storied edifice, with groined vaulting and a series of chapels, erected in 1479-84 on the site of a synagogue and restored in 1861. Modern carved altar, gilded and painted, with good imitations of Adam Krafft's Stations of the Cross at Nuremberg (p. 103).

From the Ilz Bridge (see below) the road ascends to the left to the lower gate of the fortress in $1/_4$ hr. The *Belvedere* on the Katz battery (adm. 50 pf., on Sun. 20 pf.; adjacent the *Lusenhütte Restaurant*) affords a beautiful survey (best in the evening) of the town, of the valleys of the Ilz, the Danube, and the Inn, and of the hills of the Bohemian and Bavarian Forests (see the excellent indicator). A red flag on the fortress indicates that the weather is clear enough for a view of the Berchtesgaden and Salzburg Alps to the S. The tower contains a small collection of objects from the Bavarian Forest. The well which supplies the fortress is 426 ft. deep, and extends down to the level of the Danube. In the middle ages the Oberhaus, now a state-prison, frequently afforded the bishops a refuge from civic broils. In 1809 it was occupied by the French, and the Austrians prepared to besiege it; but they abandoned their intention after their defeat at Ratisbon (p. 119).

Those whose time is limited may take the footpath from *Oberhaus* to the right, by a small house before the old powder-magazine is reached, and descend direct to the Ilz and Danube, or they may follow the telegraph-posts to the left and then descend the steps to the bridge over the Danube. But the traveller who has 2 hrs. to spare should follow the top of the hill from the upper gate of the fortress, passing the old powder-magazine, to (25 min.) *Ries* (*Inn), and descend thence to ($1/_4$ hr.) *Hals (960 ft.; *Hydropathic Establishments*), a village charmingly situated in the valley of the *Ilz*, and commanded by the ruined castle of the same name. There is an old pillory by a corner-house in the market-place. Above the village (finger-post), by the *Hofbauer*, we cross the Ilz (3 pf.), and descend the promenade on the left bank to the ($1/_4$ hr.) *Durchbruch*, a tunnel, 143 yds. in length, hewn in the rock in 1831, through which an arm of the Ilz flows. On the wooded hill above the tunnel is the ruined castle of *Reschenstein*. In clefts of the rocks here is found a beautiful luminous moss. A footway, protected by a balustrade, leads through the tunnel. At the farther end there is a long barrier to intercept the floating timber as it descends from the Bavarian Forest (p. 245). A foot-bridge crosses from the upper end of the tunnel to the *Trifthäuschen* (rfmts.) on the right bank. We return through the Durchbruch, follow the left bank for 8 min., and cross to the steam saw-mill; then follow the right bank to the ($1/_4$ hr.) bridge of Hals. We return by the road on the right bank of the Ilz to ($1^1/_2$ M.) the suspension-bridge of Passau (see above).

At the mouth of the *Ilz* (see above), an important channel for the timber-traffic, a bridge crosses to the *Ilzstadt* (Pl. E, 1, 2), at the base of the *Nonnberg*, inhabited by boatmen and raftsmen. Above it rises the (20 min.) *Klosterberg*, or *Nonnengütl* (Pl. E, 2; visitors generally admitted), a charming point of view, which affords the best survey of the union of the light-gray Inn, the yellowish-green Danube, and the inky Ilz. After having received the waters of the Inn, the Danube becomes a noble stream.

The belvedere on the *Schardenberg (1785 ft.) is another of the numerous fine points near Passau. We cross the bridge over the Inn, and ascend the Linz road to (3 M.) *Gattern*, 1½ M. beyond which a road, slightly descending to the right from the high-road, leads to the tower (adm. 10 pf.) in a few minutes. Restaurant adjacent. A most extensive view is here enjoyed of the Bavarian Mts. and the Alps of the Salzkammergut and Styria, with a picturesque foreground. We may now descend in ¾ hr. to *Wernstein* (p. 242).

From Passau to *Neumarkt (Rott-Thal Railway)*, see p. 244.

From Passau a pleasant excursion may be taken to the S.E. part of the Bavarian Forest (comp. p. 245).

FROM PASSAU TO FREYUNG, 30 M., railway in 3 hrs. The train crosses the Danube above Passau, ascends through wood to (6 M.) *Tiefenbach* (1207 ft.), and then winds down to the pretty valley of the *Ilz*. Stations: *Fischhaus*; *Kalteneck*; 15½ M. *Fürsteneck* (1397 ft.), a prettily situated château, now an inn. We then follow the valley of the *Osterbach*. 19½ M. *Röhmbach* (1692 ft.; *Pfreimter*); 24 M. *Waldkirchen* (*Post; Abel; Meindl); 27 M. *Karlsbach*. — 30 M. Freyung (2170 ft.; *Pröbstl*; *Post*), a busy little town. About ¼ hr. to the N., on a rock towering above the brawling *Sausbach*, is the imposing château of *Wolfstein*, now occupied by the district-authorities; and ½ hr. to the S.W. rises the *Geiersberg* (2592 ft.), a splendid point of view. From Freyung we may proceed to the N., via the *Bierhütte* and *Haslach*, to (2 hrs.) *Hohenau* (2638 ft.; *Moosbauer*). Or we may choose the longer but pleasanter route, which descends by the church of Freyung, crosses the Sausbach, and descends on the right bank, through the *Buchberger Leite*, a romantic rocky gorge, to (1½ M.) the mill of *Buchberg*; we then ascend to the right by *Saulohrn* and *Haslach* to (1½ hr.) Hohenau. From Hohenau roads lead to the S.W. to (4½ M.) *Grafenau* (p. 246), and to the N.W. to (6 M.) *St. Oswald* (p. 247; route to the *Rachelsee* and over the *Rachel* to *Klingenbrunn*, 5 hrs., see p. 247). Ascent of the *Lusen* (p. 247) direct, via the *Schönauer Glashütte*, 3½ hrs. (guide 3 ℳ); descent by *Waldhäuser* to *St. Oswald*, 2½ hrs. (comp. p. 247).

EXCURSION TO THE DREISESSELSTEIN, very attractive (2 days; diligence from Passau to Breitenberg daily in 5½ hrs.; from Waldkirchen in 3 hrs.). We cross the *Ilz* and descend by the Danube to the (3 M.) *Kernmühle*. Here we ascend to the left to (1 hr.) the baths of *Kellberg* (1443 ft.; *Pension, moderate; omnibus to and from Passau on Wed. and Sat.), prettily situated on the hill and commanding a charming view. Thence to the N.W., through the finely situated little town of *Tyrnau* (1560 ft.; Zum Edelfurtner; Enzinger), and by the old road to (2½ hrs.) *Hauzenberg* (1800 ft.; Post; J. Stemplinger; A. Stemplinger), near which rises the *Staffelberg* (2600 ft.), with a belvedere-tower. The road then leads via *Freudensee*, with its ruin and small lake, *Passreut*, and *Krinning*, to (2½ hrs.) *Sonnen* (2676 ft.; *Post*; Metzger), a high and prettily situated village, and thence (picturesque) to (1¾ hr.) *Breitenberg* (see below). Or we may go from the Kernmühle (see above) along the bank of the Danube to *Erlau* and (2½ hrs.) *Obernzell* (see p. 242); then ascend the valley to the left to (3 M.) *Griesbach* (1828 ft.; *Oetzinger), where the road forks. The branch to the left leads to *Hauzenberg* (see above). We take the branch to the right, by (1 hr.) *Wildenranna* and (1¼ hr.) *Wegscheid* (2360 ft.; Fenzl; Haydn), a small town with linen factories, to (3 hrs.) Breitenberg (2316 ft.; *Post*. with fine view from the veranda). The road now descends towards the N. to (¾ hr.) *Klafferstrass*, and ascends slightly to (¾ hr.) *Lackenhäuser* (2668 ft.; Rosenberger). A good path ascends thence in 1½ hr. to the top of the Dreisesselstein (4300 ft.; inn). The summit consists of huge piled-up blocks of granite; admirable view of the Bohemian Forest and the Alps. Still finer from the *Hohenstein* (1365 ft.), ¼ M. distant. From the Dreisesselstein a path on the crest of the hill leads past the *Dreieckmarkstein* (4330 ft.), where the boundaries of Bavaria, Bohemia, and Austria meet, to (1½-1½ hr.) the *Blöckenstein* (4523 ft.), mirrored in the dark waters of the solitary, forest-girt *Blöckenstein-See* (evening light best). On the bank of the lake is a monument to Adalbert Stifter (d. 1868), who has celebrated this spot in his poems. Back to Lackenhäuser in 2 hrs. — From the Dreisesselstein to *Hirschbergen* and *Salznau (Budweis)*, see *Baedeker's Austria*.

A visit to the Bohemian Forest on the *Kubani* is best accomplished by taking the diligence (once daily in 3 hrs.) from Freyung (see p. 241) to (12 M.) *Kuschwarda* (2735 ft.; *Reif; Paullik), a village and summer-resort prettily situated at the foot of the *Schlösslberg*. Hence we proceed to the (1½ hr.) glass-works of *Eleonorenhain* (*Tourists' Inn), whence a visit to the highly interesting primæval forest on the S. slope of the *Kubani* (4468 ft.) may be made in 3 hrs. (there and back). — From Kuschwarda viâ *Böhmisch-Röhren* and *Neuthal* to the *Dreisesselstein* (p. 241), 5 hrs.; guide advisable. — A very attractive trip crosses the *Lusen* to *St. Oswald* in 7 hrs. (guide). The route leads viâ the (2 hrs.) *Alm* (3748 ft.; rfmts.), with a splendid view, to (1¼ hr.) *Mauth* (*Strunz), and then follows a marked path viâ the *Tummelplatz* (rfmts.) to the (2 hrs.) *Lusen-Spitze* (p. 247); descent to *St. Oswald* (p. 247), 1½ hr.

The RAILWAY to Linz passes through a long tunnel, crosses the Inn, and ascends on the right bank of the river. 80 M. **Wernstein**, with an old château, on a height opposite. —83 M. **Schärding** (*Hôt. Altmann; Rail. Restaurant)*, an ancient town with 3600 inhab., picturesquely situated on the Inn, junction of the Salzkammergut Railway (see *Baedeker's Austria*). Near it is the village of *Brunnenthal*, with a chalybeate spring. — The line now ascends the *Pramthal*. 89 M. *Taufkirchen;* 92 M. *Andorf;* 98 M. *Riedau;* 106 M. **Neumarkt** (*Reiss)*, junction of the Simbach-Munich line (R. 40); 113 M. **Grieskirchen**. We now descend (to the right a view of the Alps with the Traunstein) by *Wallern* to (124½ M.) **Wels**, a station on the Linz and Salzburg railway. Thence to (140 M.) *Linz*, see *Baedeker's Austria*.

STEAMBOAT JOURNEY. The steamer, far preferable to the railway, generally leaves Passau at 3 p.m., and reaches Linz in 4 hrs. Luggage examined before embarkation (comp. p. 236).

The scenery of the Danube is grander, but less smiling than that of the Rhine, while the finest points are often rather far apart. The mountains are higher, and the banks are generally fringed with forest, or clothed with luxuriant pasture; but the population is poor and sparse, and there is an almost total absence of the busy traffic which characterises the sister-river.

A beautiful retrospect of the town and environs is enjoyed immediately after starting. Below Passau the right bank belongs to Austria, and the left bank as far as Engelhartszell to Bavaria.

L. *Erlau*.

R. *Schloss Krempelstein*, on an abrupt cliff.

L. (3.30 p.m.) Obernzell or *Hafnerzell* (964 ft.; *Post; Saxinger)*, the last Bavarian village, with large quarries of graphite and manufactories of lead-pencils and fire-proof crucibles. Excursion to the Bavarian Forest, see p. 241.

R. *Viechtenstein*, an old Schloss on the hill, formerly the property of the bishops of Passau and now of Count Pachta. Farther on, below *Grünau*, the *Jochenstein*, jutting far into the river on the left, was the ancient boundary between Bavaria and Austria. The present boundary is a wooded ravine on the left bank, a little lower down.

R. (4 p.m.) Engelhartszell (*Post)*, prettily situated, with the Austrian custom-house (p. 236). Near it is *Engelszell*, once a Cistercian monastery, now owned by Count Pachta.

L. *Ranariedl*, an ancient mountain-castle, still inhabited; at the foot of the hill is the village of *Niederranna*.

R. (4.18 p.m.) *Wesenufer* or *Wesenurfahr*, an old town, with a large wine cellar hewn in the **rock,** formerly owned by the cathedral chapter of Passau.

L. *Marsbach*, with the ancient tower of a mediæval castle.

R. *Waldkirchen*, **a** ruin **on a** pine-clad rock.

L. *Hayenbach*, or the *Kirschbaumer Schloss*, destroyed by Emp. Maximilian I., is seen a second time after a bend in the river.

The channel of the river now contracts to nearly half its former width, and is confined between precipitous wooded hills, 600-1000 ft. in height. This is one of the grandest parts of the river. At —

L. *Obermichl*, a pleasant village, the *Kleine Michl* descends from a wooded ravine into the Danube.

L. *Neuhaus*, **a handsome** château on a lofty wooded height, the property of Herr von Plank. **The** Danube suddenly **emerges** on a broad plain shortly before we reach —

R. (5.30 p.m.) *Aschach* (*Sonne; Adler*), a small town extending picturesquely along the bank, with the château and park of Count Harrach. The Pöstlingberg with its church, near Linz, comes into view; in clear weather the Styrian and Austrian Alps form the background towards the S.; and to the right rises the Traunstein. The view is soon concealed by the numerous islands, overgrown with underwood, between which the river flows. — From this point **to Linz, and** beyond it, the **valley was** the scene **of** many a sanguinary encounter during the revolt of the peasantry **of** Upper Austria. In 1626 Aschach was the headquarters of the insurgents, where, as well **as** at Neuhaus, they had barricaded **the** Danube with chains to prevent the Bavarians from assisting Count **Herberstein, the** Austrian gov**ernor,** who **was** shut **up** at Linz.

[RAILWAY TO WELS, 17½ M., **in** 1½ hr., viâ *Efferding*, *Breitenaich*, and *Haiding*. *Wels*, see *Baedeker's Handbook to Austria*.]

Perched on the hills to the right are the ruined castles of *Stauf* and *Schaumburg*. The latter was once the ancestral seat of a powerful family which held sway over the whole valley between Passau and Linz, but became extinct in 1559.

L. *Landshag*, with **a small château** of Count Harrach.

R. *Brandstatt* **is the** station for *Efferding* (rail. stat., see above), one **of the most ancient** places **in** Upper Austria, mentioned in the Nibelungen-**Lied (21st** Adventure) as the place where Kriemhild passed the night on her journey to the land of the Huns. The village is said formerly to have lain on the Danube, but the tower only is now visible. To the left in the distance rises the Pöstlingberg.

L. *Ottensheim*, with its white walls, **is** conspicuous (rail. stat., see p. 251). Château of Count Coudenhove.

R. *Wilhering*, a Cistercian abbey (1146), with a pleasant garden.

L. *Schloss Buchenau*. Then the *Pöstlingberg*, crowned with its church and fortifications.

R. The *Calvarienberg*, with the *Jägermayr* rising above it. The steamer passes under the handsome new bridge and reaches —

R. (7 p.m.) Linz (see *Baedeker's Austria*).

43. From Rosenheim to Eisenstein by Mühldorf and Plattling. The Bavarian Forest.

133 M. RAILWAY in 8¾ hrs. (fares 17 ℳ 20, 11 ℳ 40, 7 ℳ 40 pf.).

Rosenheim, see p. 222. Soon after starting, the train diverges to **the** right from the Munich railway and runs **to the N.**, across the plain of the **Inn.** 5½ M. *Schechen*; 10 M. *Rott*, with an old Benedictine abbey **on a** hill to the left. The line crosses the valley of the *Attel* on **a** lofty embankment, passing on the right the ancient provostry **of** *Attel*, and at (16 M.) **Wasserburg** reaches the top of a lofty plateau on the left bank of the Inn. The town of Wasserburg (1640 ft.; *Hôtel Schliessleder*; 3700 inhab.), a summer-resort, lies 3 M. to the right, on a peninsula formed by the Inn, and is not visible from the railway.

The train passes the *Soyer See*, or *Kitzsee*, and (19 M.) *Soyen*, and skirts the steep slopes of the *Nasenbach*. Reaching the lofty left bank of the Inn, we now cross the river, flanked here with wooded heights, at *Königswarth*, by means of a viaduct 330 yds. long and 161 ft. high. We next descend on the right bank to (25 M.) *Gars*, opposite which lie the village and monastery of that name. Lower down, on the left bank, is the extensive monastery of *Au*. Beyond (28½ M.) *Jettenbach*, with a château of Count Törring, the river is again crossed. On the wooded table-land lies the station of (32 M.) *Kraiburg* (a village on the right bank of the Inn, 3 M. to the E.). The train quits the forest, passes the church and lunatic asylum of *Ecksberg* on the right, and near (38½ M.) **Mühldorf** (p. 233) reaches the Munich railway.

The train runs to the N. (to the right the railway to Simbach, p. 233), and crosses the *Isen*. Beyond (43 M.) *Rohrbach* it crosses the watershed between the Inn and the *Rott*. — 48 M. *Neumarkt an der Rott* (1470 ft.), with two late-Gothic churches.

From Neumarkt to Passau, 61 M. (branch-railway, 5-5½ hrs.). The line skirts the left bank of the *Rott*. Stations *Hörbering*, *Massing*, *Dietfurt*, (12½ M.) *Eggenfelden*. Beyond (22 M.) *Pfarrkirchen* (1250 ft.) the train crosses the Rott. Stations *Anzenkirchen*, *Birnbach*, *Karpfham*. Then (39 M.) *Pocking*, in the broad valley of the Inn. Next stations *Ruhstorf*, *Sulzbach am Inn*, *Engertsham*, *Höhenstadt* (with sulphur-baths), *Fürstenzell*, *Neustift*. — 61 M. *Passau*, see p. 237.

From *Neumarkt to Landshut*, see p. 136.

Leaving the Rott-Thal 2 M. below Neumarkt, the train runs to the N. through a hilly district to (54½ M.) *Gangkofen*, on the *Bina*, crosses at (58 M.) *Trembach* the watershed between the Rott and the *Vils*, and descends to the Vilsthal. — 63 M. *Frontenhausen*; the village, with an interesting late-Gothic church, lies 1½ M. to the W. We cross the Vils, ascend the opposite bank, cross the profound *Seegraben* by a lofty viaduct, and reach the watershed between the Vils and the *Isar*. 67½ M. *Griesbach*; 72½ M. *Mamming*, where the Isar is crossed; 75 M. *Pilsting*, junction for *Landshut* (p. 136). Then (77½ M.) **Landau**; the town, with 3200 inhab., lies 1 M. to the S., on the right bank of the Isar. — To *Landshut* (and *Munich*), see p. 136.

Below Landau the train enters the broad plain of the Danube. Fine glimpse of the nearer hills of the Bavarian Forest, with the distant *Arber* (p. 247). — 82 M. *Wallersdorf*; 85½ M. *Otzing*; 89 M. **Plattling**, where we cross the Ratisbon and Passau railway (p. 237).

Beyond Plattling the line nears the Danube, passing the isolated *Natternberg* with its ruin on the left, and crosses the river by an iron bridge, 440 yds. long. — 94 M. **Deggendorf** (1090 ft.; *Drei

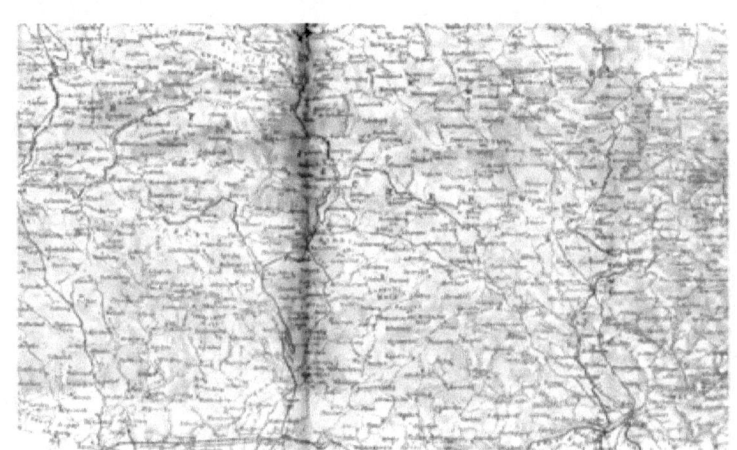

Mohren, R. 1½ ℳ ; *Post; Villa Wittelsbach*, pension 3 ℳ ; *Dasbergerbräu* and *Hallerbräu*, moderate), a pleasant old-fashioned town with thriving trade and manufactures (6200 inhab.). On the outskirts of the town is the *District Lunatic Asylum*.

The *Geiersberg* (1243 ft.), ½ hr. to the N., with a pilgrimage-church, commands a fine view of the valley of the Danube; that from the *Kanzel* (2378 ft.), reached by a marked path in 1½ hr., is more extensive. — Pleasant excursion from Deggendorf by the old post-road, through the valley of the *Höllenbach*, to the (9 M.) beautifully-situated Rusel (2595 ft.; *Inn), formerly a monastery. Thence on foot through the wood to the (½ hr.) *Hausstein (3007 ft.), which commands a magnificent view of the plain of the Danube and the distant Alps (Watzmann, Steinerne Meer, Dachstein, etc.). — The road leads from the Rusel through the valley of the *Ohebach*, past the castle of *Au*, destroyed last century, to (9 M.) *Regen* (see below).

To the W. of Deggendorf (2½ M.; narrow-gauge railway in ¼ hr.) lies Metten (1043 ft.; *Post*), a Benedictine abbey with a celebrated school, founded by Charlemagne in 792. *Schloss Egg (1243 ft.), seat of Count Hohenthal, ¾ M. to the N., has been restored in the mediæval style by Volz.

The railway from Deggendorf to Eisenstein, traversing the *Bavarian Forest*, has had many engineering difficulties to encounter.

The Bavarian Forest is the S. W. portion of the extensive *Bohemian Forest Mountains*, and includes the highest peaks in the range (the Arber 4780 ft., the Rachel 4763 ft.). Nearly one-half of this mountain-region, which is upwards of 1800 sq. M. in area, and lies between the Danube and the Bohemian frontier, extending from Cham and Furth on the N. to below Passau towards the S., is covered with pine and beech-forest, much of which, especially in the less frequented parts (*e.g.* the Rachel and Falkenstein), is still in a primæval condition. At Hals (p. 240), Zwiesel (p. 246), and other places there are traces of glacier-action and moraines, indicating that the mountains were once covered with ice. The beautiful dark forest-tarns also owe their origin to ancient glaciers. The timber-trade and cattle-breeding are the chief resources of the natives, but glass and linen are also manufactured. Snuff, to which they are much addicted, is carried about in little glass bottles made in the district. The paths are good; the inns, though unpretentious, are generally clean and cheap.

The line ascends the W. slopes of the *Kollbach-Thal*, crosses the valley by an embankment, turns to the S., and reaches (100½ M.) *Ulrichsberg* (1319 ft.), ½ hr. above which is the *Ulrichsberg* (1750 ft.; Inn), with a pilgrimage-church and a fine view. The train then skirts the *Kühberg* (to the right a magnificent view of the plain of the Danube, bounded by the Salzburg Alps), passes through a curved tunnel, 530 yds. in length, and ascends the *Graflinger-Thal* in long windings. Then through another tunnel, 630 yds. long, to (109 M.) Gotteszell (1805 ft.; *Bräuhaus*, ¼ hr. from the station), in the *Teisnach-Thal*, with a Cistercian abbey, rebuilt since a fire in 1830.

Interesting excursion (3 hrs.; road) from Gotteszell by *Tafertsried*, *Achslach*, and the forester's house of *Oedwies* (good quarters) to the Hirschenstein (3062 ft.), with an extensive view. To the E. of this point is the (½ hr.) *Rauhe Kolm* or *Klauenstein* (3420 ft.), with a fine view to the S. To the N.W. are the *Glashüttenriegel* and the *Predigtstuhl* (3556 ft.); in a pretty valley at the foot of the latter lies the village of *Engelmar* (2637 ft.; Echinger).

FROM GOTTESZELL TO VIECHTACH, 15½ M., narrow-gauge railway in 1¼ hr. The line runs through the *Teisnach-Thal*. 2½ M. *Ruhmannsfelden* (Post), a large and prettily situated village; 4½ M. *Petersdorf*; 6 M. *Teis-*

nach (Ettl), at the confluence of the **Teisnach** with the *Schwarze Regen* (hence to *Bodenmais* 1½ hr.). The train now follows the valley of the latter stream, passing *Böbrach, Gumpenried*, and (11 M.) *Schönau*. — 15½ M. Viechtach (1323 ft.; *°Neue Post; Obermaier*), a pleasant little town, the seat of the district authorities. To the S. rise the highest summits of the *Pfahl* (see below). An attractive excursion (from Schönau ½ hr., from Viechtach viâ *Blossersberg* and *Bärndorf* 1½ hr.) may be made to the ruin of *Neu-Nussberg* (2276 ft.), the tower of which commands a fine view (Inn). To the S. we may go to (1¼ hr.) *Kollnburg* (Brewery), with a picturesque ruined castle, now used as a church; and thence we may proceed through fine woods, passing *Markbuchen* on the *Predigtstuhl* (p. 245), to (2½ hrs.) the forester's house of *Oedwies* and the *Hirschenstein* (p. 245). — A pleasant road leads to the N.W. from Viechtach to *Pirka, Lammerbach, Wettzell* (Inn), and (9 M.) *Kötzting* (p. 235).

113½ M. *Triefenried* (2120 ft.). The line skirts the forest-clad hills of the *Teufelstisch* (see below), crosses the *Ohebach* by means of a lofty viaduct, and descends on the left bank of the *Schwarze Regen* to (118½ M.) stat. **Regen** (1770 ft.), opposite the small town of that name (*Post; Oswald*; pop. 2200). Diligence daily in 2¼ hrs. to *Bodenmais*, see p. 247.

To the S.E. (¾ hr.) rises *Weissenstein am Pfahl* (2474 ft.), a ruined castle on a jagged quartz rock, with a restored tower commanding a fine view (custodian to the left of the entrance). — The *Pfahl* is a broad seam of quartz and hornblende running from S.E. to N.W. for a distance of 60 M.; it may be conveniently examined in the railway-cutting near the bridge over the Ohe.

From the pleasantly situated village of *Bischofsmais* (2182 ft.; Eder's Brauhaus), 4½ M. to the S. of Regen, attractive excursions may be made to (¾ hr.) *Ober-Breitenau* (3490 ft.), the (¾ hr.) *Teufelstisch* (2960 ft.), and other points. From Bischofsmais to the *Rusel* (p. 245) 1½ hr., to *Deggendorf* (p. 244) 4 hrs.

The train crosses the Regen, recrosses it near *Schweinhütt* by means of a bridge with a span of 236 ft., and regains the right bank at the *Poschinger Saw Mill* near Zwiesel.

125 M. **Zwiesel** (2135 ft.; *Post*, well spoken of; *Deutscher Rhein*, R. 1-1½ *M*; *Bayrischer Wald*), a pleasant little town with 3500 inhab., in a broad basin at the confluence of the *Kleine* and *Grosse Regen*, is a good starting-point for excursions in the Bavarian Forest, but lacks shade and is at a considerable distance from the woods. Near it are the glass-works of *Theresienthal, Ludwigsthal, Ober-Zwieselau*, **Ober-Frauenau**, and *Buchenau*, and numerous saw-mills.

The *Zwieselberg* (2250 ft.), a hill strewn with blocks of granite, ½ hr. to the S., affords a good survey of the environs.

FROM ZWIESEL TO GRAFENAU, 19½ M., narrow-gauge railway in 2 hrs. The line sweeps round the town. 3½ M. *Zwieselau*; 5½ M. *Frauenau*, the station for *Unter-Frauenau* (two inns) and for *Ober-Frauenau* (2358 ft.; 1 M. to the N.E.), the latter with the imposing château of Herr von Poschinger. — Farther on we ascend rapidly through the narrow wooded valley to (10 M.) Klingenbrunn, the station of which lies 3 M. to the N.W. of the village (2693 ft.; *Stangl*). The *Ludwigsstein* (2900 ft.), ¼ hr. to the W. of the village, is a good point of view. Ascent of the *Rachel* from the station, see below. — The train next descends to (12 M.) *Spiegelau* (Inn, poor; ascent of the Rachel, see p. 247) and then runs high on the left side of the narrow gorge of the brawling *Grosse Ohe* to (15 M.) *Gross-Armschlag* and (19½ M.) Grafenau (2004 ft.; *Meindl; Dresely's Brewery; Stangl*). The line is to be continued from this point to (5 M.) *Hohenau* (p. 241) and (5 M.) *Freyung* (p. 241). Near Grafenau are the *Bärnsteiner-*

leite, the narrow wooded ravine of the *Kleine Ohe*, and the ruin of *Bärnstein* (garden-restaurant). Roads lead from Grafenau to (3½ M.) *St. Oswald* (see below) on the N., and to *Tittling* and (26 M.) *Passau* on the S.

The *Rachel (4770 ft.) is best ascended either from *Klingenbrunn* (p. 246; path marked with blue; 2½ hrs.) or from *Spiegelau* (along the Schwarzach; 3 hrs.). The barren summit (refuge-hut; no rfmts.), strewn with blocks of granite, commands a splendid view of the Bohemian Forest and the plain of the Danube, extending in clear weather to the distant Alps. On the S.E. side lies the dark forest-girt *Rachelsee*, 1250 ft. below. It may be reached from the top in ¾ hr. (path indicated by blue marks); and we may then, passing the forester's hut (rfmts.), go by *Guglöd* and *Siebenellen* to (3 hrs.) *St. Oswald* (see below). Or from the Rachel we may follow the frontier-line to the E. (black marks; but as this route is monotonous, it is better to follow the white marks, running on the hillside above the lake and past the chapel, and to descend to the right through the wood and cross the Zwölferlinie, about 5 hrs. in all) to the (4½ hrs.) Lusen (4494 ft.), the granite-strewn summit of which also commands a superb view. Descent by the *Waldhäuser* (3028 ft.; Inn) to (2 hrs.) St. Oswald (2695 ft.; *Schreiner's Bräuhaus*), once a monastery, beautifully situated ('View from the 'gloriette'), whence we may proceed by *Reichenberg* to (1 hr.) *Spiegelau* (p. 246). — The little town of Grafenau (p. 246) lies about 4½ M. to the S.W. of St. Oswald.

A good road leads to the N.W. from Zwiesel to *Klautzenbach* and (2¼ M.) *Rabenstein* (2248 ft.; *Villa Rabenstein*, D. 1¼. pens. 3-4 ℳ, prettily situated), and thence through splendid timber, past a quarry with a small subterranean lake (beautiful rose-coloured quartz) and via *Schöneben* to (8 M.) Bodenmais (2220 ft.; *Post; Dresely's Bräuhaus*, with rooms), pleasantly situated on a hill. (A pleasanter but longer route leads from Rabenstein to Bodenmais via the *Hühnerkobel*, 3110 ft., a hill affording a splendid view of the Arber, Zwiesel, and Rachel.) Opposite Bodenmais rises the red *Silberberg*, composed of a kind of slag, with its indented peak called the *Bischofshaube* ('mitre'; 3136 ft.). Vitriol and red polishing powder are made from the ore obtained here. Rare minerals are also found (good collection at the overseer's house). Diligence to *Regen*, see p. 246.

The *Arber (4780 ft.), the 'King of the Forest', is easily ascended from Bodenmais in 2½-3 hrs. (guide, unnecessary, 4 ℳ; to the Arber and Sommerau 6 ℳ). The path leads through the *Riesloch*, a pretty ravine with small waterfalls. (Attractive digression of ½ hr. from the upper end of this gorge to the *Rechensöldenfelsen*, with pretty views of the valley and of Bodenmais.) On the bare rock-strewn summit of the Arber stand a chapel and the *Arber-Schutzhaus* (Inn, 13 mattresses in 3 rooms, 1 ℳ, clean). A peregrination of the summit-plateau takes about ¾ hr. Superb view of a great part of Bohemia to the E., the Fichtelgebirge to the W., and in clear weather the Alps to the S. On the E. side, far below, lies the sombre *Grosse Arbersee* (3064 ft.; rfmts., dear), surrounded with wood. Descent to the frontier-station *Eisenstein* (see p. 248) either past the lake and through the *Seebachwald* and *Bayrisch-Eisenstein* in 2 hrs., or by the ruined *Oberthurnhof* (good water), the *Brennes-Sattel*, and *Bayrisch-Eisenstein* in 3 hrs.

The excursion to the Arber may be agreeably extended thus. From the (¾ hr.) *Oberthurnhof* (see above) we cross the *Brennes-Sattel* (where the path from Eisenstein comes in on the right) to (1¼ hr.) *Sommerau* (2200 ft.; Brewery) on the *Weisse Regen*, and thence go to the right (poor path) to (½ hr.) *Lohberg* (2125 ft.; *Kellermayer*), a village with a richly decorated Romanesque church, a good centre for excursions (over the *Scheiben-Sattel* to *Eisenstein*, 3 hrs., see p. 248). From Lohberg a road (one-horse carr. to Lam 4 ℳ, incl. fee) leads along the base of the *Osser* (see below) to (3½ M.) Lam (1896 ft.; *Post*, poor), a large village prettily situated on the Weisse Regen, the valley of which ('Lamer Winkel') seems to be closed by the *Hohe Bogen* (p. 236); thence on foot (with guide) across the *Scharreben* (3170 ft.), through beautiful woods, back to (4½ hrs.) Bodenmais. — Railway from Lam to *Kötzting* and *Cham* (2¼ hrs.), see p. 235.

[From Lohberg (see above) to Eisenstein across the Osser, 6-7 hrs., a beautiful walk. A distinct path (indicated by red marks), steep at places, ascends in 2 hrs. to the saddle between the *Little* or *Bavarian Osser* (4075 ft.) on the left, and the *Great* or *Bohemian* Osser (4210 ft.) on the right. The top of either is reached in 10 minutes. The Great Osser (strewn with granite-blocks; open refuge-hut) commands a fine view of the Arber chain; the Little Osser, a good view of the Lam, etc. From the saddle we next follow the bridle-path (direction-boards) to the E. to the (1/2 hr.) *Gütelplatz* (3120 ft.), whither also a route leads direct in 1 1/2 hr. from Lohberg, diverging from the Osser route to the right (guide-post 'Zum Schwarzen See'), and crossing the *Sesselplatz* (3696 ft.). Then through wood (below, to the left, the glass-work *Müllerhütte*) either direct to the **Seewand** (see below) or (better) to the (1 1/2 hr.) *Schwarze See* (3310 ft.; also called *Bistritzer* or *Böhmische See*), 90 acres in area, in a grand solitude. The open pavilion (no rfmts.) on the lake belongs to Prince Hohenzollern-Sigmaringen, who also caused the bridle-path from the Osser to be constructed. From the end of the lake we ascend to the right and follow a path soon diverging to the right to the *Seewand* (4406 ft.; view limited; more extensive from the *Zwergeck*, 10 min. to the N.W.), whence we descend through the *Pichelbach-Thal* to (1 1/4 hr.) *Eisenstein*. Or we may turn to the left at the end of the Schwarze See, cross the watershed between the Elbe and the Danube, and skirt the (1 hr.) gloomy *Teufels-See* or *Girglsee* (3380 ft.); then, passing *Stiegelruck* and *Berghaus*, we descend lastly to *Markt Eisenstein* or to the glass-works of *Elisenthal* (Hotel, with baths) and the (1 1/4 hr.) railway-station of *Eisenstein*. Or, thirdly, from the end of the lake, we may go to the left to the (1/2 hr.) *Seeförster* (Inn, high charges), and then cross the *Spitzberg-Sattel* (3300 ft.; Hôt.-Pens. Rixi, **Pens.** Prokop, both Bohemian; fine view) to the (1 1/2 hr.) station of *Spitzberg* (see below), 1/4 hr. by train from *Eisenstein*.]

Above Zwiesel the train again crosses the Regen, and then the *Kolbersbach* by a lofty viaduct. 128 M. **Ludwigsthal** (2163 ft.), with glass-works. The line ascends the left bank of the Regen, running parallel with the road to Bohemia and passing many glass and smelting houses, and reaches the Bavarian and Bohemian frontier-station (133 M.) **Eisenstein** (2365 ft.; *Rail. Restaurant, R. 1 fl.), where we have a fine view of the Arber to the W. (see above).

To the W. lies the village of (1/2 M.) *Bayrisch-Eisenstein* (2398 ft.; Bräuhaus, with garden, but no beds; *Oberst, rustic). To the N., beyond *Elisenthal* (see above), is the Bohemian Markt-Eisenstein (2540 ft.; *Osser*, with garden; *Post*; *Arber*; *Böhmerwald*), prettily situated at the confluence of the Regen and the *Eisenbach*, with a fine view of the Arber. It is a station on the railway to Pilsen and is frequented as a summer-resort, affording opportunity for many agreeable excursions. — To the (1/2 hr.) *Grosse Tanne* (a fir 6 1/2 ft. in diameter), with descent to the (1/2 hr.) rail. station. — To the (1 1/4 hr.) *Zwieseler Waldhaus* (2283 ft.; *Inn; to Zwiesel 2 hrs.), and thence either to (1 1/2 hr.) the summit of the *Grosse Falkenstein* (4316 ft.), or through fine wood viâ the *Hochberg* to the (1 1/2 hr.) frontier rail. station, or to (1 1/4 hr.) *Ludwigsthal* (see above). — To the (2 hrs.) *Arber-See*, and ascent of the (1 1/2 hr.) *Arber*, with descent to (1 1/2 hr.) *Bodenmais* or (2 hrs.) *Lohberg*, see p. 247. — By railway to *Spitzberg* or *Hammern-Eisenstrass* (see below) and back thence viâ the *Schwarze See* and *Teufels-See* (3 1/2-4 hrs.; see above); or we may ascend the *Osser* (1 1/2 hr.; see above) from Hammern-Eisenstrass. — Ascent of the *Seewand* (2 1/2 hrs.), see above; over the *Scheiben* to (3 hrs.) *Lohberg* (p. 247).

From Eisenstein to Pilsen, 61 M., railway in 3 1/4 hrs. The more important stations are: 3 M. *Böhmisch-Eisenstein* (see above); 5 M. *Spitzberg* (2725 ft.), at the S. end of the *Spitzberg Tunnel* (1 M. long); 10 M. *Hammern-Eisenstrass*, at the S.E. foot of the *Osser* (see above; ascended hence in 1 1/2 hr.) and also the starting-point for a visit to the *Schwarze See* (see above); 15 M. *Grün*; 21 M. *Neuern*; 26 M. *Janowitz*; 31 M. *Klattau*. Comp. Baedeker's *Austria*.

INDEX.

Aach, the 53. 54.
— Linz 55.
Aalen 28.
Abbach 125.
Abensberg 127.
Ablach, the 54.
Abusina 127.
Achalm 46.
Achen 219.
—, the 216. 219.
—, the Grosse 223.
Achenkirch 219.
Achensee 219.
Achenwald 216. 219.
Achslach 245.
Adelholzen 223.
Adelsberg 30.
Adelschlag 132.
Adelsheim 71.
Adlerstein 93.
Adling 221.
Adorf 73.
Aepflet-Kuppe, the 236.
Aeschach 201.
Agatharied 220.
Aggenstein 202.
Ahornthal 94.
Ahrnschwang 235.
Aibling 222.
Aichach 127.
Ailsbach, the 94.
Aisch, the 69.
Aistaig 40.
Aitrang 199.
Alb, the Swabian 42.
—, the Rauhe 32.
St. Alban 197.
Albeck, ruin 40.
Aldingen 40.
Alexandersbad 92.
Alfalter 110.
Algäu, the 199.
Allach 133.
Allensbach 55.
Allersdorf 127.
Alling 125.
Allmannsdorf 57.
Allmannshausen 196.
Allmannshöhe 57.
Allmendingen 53.
Almbach-Klamm 229.
Alpgarten 226.
Alpirsbach 39.

Alpsee, the 200. 201.
Alpspitze 210.
Altbach 30.
Altdorf 118.
Alteburghof 47.
Altenberg 84.
Altenburg 72.
—, castle 80.
Altengronau 85.
Altenmarkt 224.
Altenmuhr 131.
Altenschwand 235.
Altenstadt 33.
Alte Veste 70.
Althegnenberg 134.
Altheim 39. 136. 234.
Althengstett 16.
Altlach 214.
Altmannshof 235.
Altmühl, the 111. 125. 131.
— Thal, the 126.
Alt-Oetting 233.
Altshausen 54. 55.
Altstadt 38. 40.
Altstädter Berg 81.
Alwind 201.
Alzenau 59.
Ambach 196.
Amberg 235.
Ammer, the 197. 207.
Ammerland 194. 196.
Ammersee, the 197.
Ammerthal, the 197. 212.
Ammerwald 212.
— Thal, the 212.
Amorbach 62.
Ampelsbach-Thal 219.
Amper, the 134. 136. 198.
— Thal, the 133.
Ampfing 233.
Amselting 237.
Amstetten 32.
Andechs 197.
Andelsbach, the 55.
Andorf 242.
Anger 216.
Anhausen 54.
Ankathal, the 110.
Annahöhe, the 63.
Ansbach 130. 26.
St. Anton 208.
Arber, the 247.

Arbersee, the 247.
Arch, the 213.
— Bach, the 206.
Argen, the 54.
Arnstein 64.
Arrach 235.
Arzberg 111.
Asamshöhe, the 207.
Asch 73.
Aschach 85. 243.
Aschaffenburg 60.
Aschauer Weiher 229.
Asperg 15.
Assling 221.
Athayingen 54.
Attel, the 221. 243.
—, provostry 213.
Au, castle 245.
—, monastery 244.
Aubing 198.
Auerbach 71.
— (Saxony) 72.
— Thal, the 221.
Aufhausen 194.
Aufkirchen 196. 194.
Augsburg 113.
Aulendorf 34. 54.
Aurach 220.
—, the 69.
Axljoch, the 206.

Baar, the 40.
Babenhausen 23. 61.
Bacher Tobel 200.
Backer-Alp 221.
Backnang 25.
Badersee 209.
Baierbrunn 194.
Baiersdorf 80.
Bairisch-Zell 220.
Balingen 50.
Balteratsried 202.
Bamberg 75.
Bammenthal 22.
Banz 74. 75.
Bärenfang 91.
Bärenthal 53.
Barmsee 210. 215.
Bärndorf 246.
Barnreut 90.
Bärnstein, ruin 247.
Bärnsteiner Leite 246.
St. Bartholomä 231.

St. Bartholomä, Lake of 230.
Bäumenheim 113.
Bavarian Forest, the 236. 241. 245.
Bayerdiessen 197.
Bayersoyen 197.
Bayreuth 86.
Bayrisch-Eisenstein 247. 248.
Bebenhausen 38.
Beckstetten 198.
Beerfelden 23.
Befreiungshalle, the, near Kelheim 126.
Behringersdorf 109.
Behringersmühl 93.
Beihingen 25. 16.
Beilngries 118.
Beimerstetten 32.
Belsener Chapel 48.
Bempflingen 35.
Benediktbeuern 213.
Benediktenwand 213.
Beratzhausen 119.
Berchtesgaden 227.
Berg 12. 136.
—, Schloss 196.
Bergen 223.
Berghaus 218.
Bergrheinfeld 82.
Bergtheim 82.
Bernau 223.
Berneck 89.
Bernhaupten 223.
Bernried 196. 213.
Berolzheim 131.
Bertaburg-Kornberg 31.
Bertholdsheim 128.
Besenbach 213.
Besigheim 19.
Bettelmannshöhle 54.
Bettinger Berg, the 63.
Betzigau 199.
Betzingen 36.
Beuerberg 195.
Beuren 44.
Beurener Fels, the 44.
Beuron, monast. 52.
Beutelsbach 27.
Biberach 34.
Bibersohl 32.
Biberwier 207.
Biburg 127.
Bichelbach 206.
Bichishausen 54.
Bichl 213.
Bichtlingen 55.
Bieringen 38.
Biessenhofen 199.
Bietigheim 15. 25.
Bina, the 244.
Binau 22.

Binder-Mühle 233.
Bindlach 86.
Birgsau 200.
Birkenfeld 18.
Birkensee 134.
Bischofsgrün 90.
Bischofshaube 247.
Bischofsheim 85.
Bischofsmais 246.
Bischofswiesen 227. 229.
Bisingen 50.
Bistritzer See 248.
Blaibach 235.
Blaichach 200.
Blankenberg 73.
Bläsibad 48.
Bläsiberg 48.
Blau, the 32. 52.
Blaubeuren 53.
Blaue Gumpen 210.
Blaueis, the 232.
Blautopf, the 53.
Blenheim 113.
Blindheim 113.
Blindsee 207.
Blöckenau 205.
Blöckenstein, the 241.
— See, the 241.
Blossersberg 246.
Blumenberg, the 132.
Blutenburg 195.
Böbing 197.
Bobingen 198.
Böblingen 39.
Böbrach 246.
Böckl-Weiher 229.
Bocklet 85.
Bodelshausen 48.
Bodenbühl 226.
Bodenlaube 83. 84.
Bodenmais 247. 246.
Bodensee, see Lake of Constance.
Bodenschneid 220.
Bodenwöhr 235.
Bodmann 58.
Bogenhausen 193.
Bohemian Forest, the 242. 245.
Böhlen 72.
Böhmisch-Eisenstein 248.
— Röhren 242.
Böhmische See, the 248.
Böhringen 53.
Bolberg, the 48.
Boll, baths 31.
Böllatfels, the 50.
Bondorf 39.
Bopfingen 29.
Bopser, the 11.
Bornheim 59.
Bosler, the 31.
Boxberg 71.

Brambach 73.
Brandenberger Thal 220.
Brandholz 90.
Brandkopf, the 230.
Brandschrofen, the 205.
Brandstatt 243.
Braunau 234.
Braunenberg, the 28.
Brecherspitze, the 220.
Bregenz 201.
Breitach, the 200. 234.
Breitenaich 243.
Breitenberg 241.
Breitenbrunn 197.
Breiten-Güssbach 75.
Breitenstein 31.
Breitenwang 206. 213.
Bremstall-Wald, the 209.
Brendlorenzen 85.
Brendthal, the 85.
Brennes-Sattel, the 247.
Brentenwand, the 230.
Brenz, the 28. 113.
Brenzkofer Berg, the 52.
Brenztopf, the 28.
Brett, the 230.
Brettach, the 24.
Bretten 14.
Bretzfeld 24.
Brigachthal, the 40.
Brixlegg 220.
Bronnbach 70.
Bronnweiler 47.
Brötzingen 18.
Bruchsal 14.
Bruck on the Amper 198.
Bruckberg 136.
Brückenau 85.
Brühl 57.
Brunnenthal 242.
Brünnling-Alpe 223.
Buch 234.
Buchau 219.
Buchberg 241.
Buchberger Leite 241.
Büchelberg 26.
Buchenau 246.
—, castle 213.
Buchhaus 91.
Buchloe 198.
Budweiss 212.
Bug 80.
Bühl 200.
Bühlerbach, the 25.
Bundesstein, the 92.
Buoch 27
Burgau 133.
Burgberg 25. 28. 200.
—, the 74.
Burgbernheim 130.
Burgfarrnbach 69.
Burgfelden 50.
Burggailenreuth 93. 94.

INDEX. 251

Burghalde **199.**
Burghausen 234.
Burgheim 128.
Burgholz, the **14.**
Burgkunstadt **74.**
Burglengenfeld **134.**
Bürgstadt 62.
Burgstall 25.
—, the 200. 235. 236.
Burgstein, the 46. 92. 131.
Burkardus-Höhle 63.
Burlafingen 133.
Burren, the **31.**
Bürrenhof, the **44.**
Buss-Thurm, the **38.**
Bussen, the 54.
Buttenhausen 54.
Buxheim 54.

Cadolzburg 70.
Calmbach 18.
Calw 16.
Cannstatt 13.
Carolinenfeld, Gross- 221.
Cham **235.**
Chamb-Thal, the **235.**
Chamerau 235.
Chamereck 235.
Charlottenhöhle, the 23.
Chemnitz 72. 73.
Chiemsee, the **222.**
Christlieger, Islet of 230.
Clemenshall 22.
Constance 55. 201.
—, Lake of 56. 201.
Crailsheim 25.
Creglingen 130.
Creussen 110.
Crimmitzschau 72.
Culmbach 74.

Dachau 133.
Dachauer Moos 133. 134. 198.
Dallau 71.
Dambach 70.
Dammbach-Thal 63.
Danube, the 32. 40. 51. 52. 53. 112. 113. 119. 125. 126. 236. etc.
Darching 220.
Darmstadt 61.
Dasing 127
Degerloch 11.
Deggendorf 244.
Deggingen 31.
Deining 118.
Deisenhofen 215.
Derneck, ruin 54.
Dettelbach 69.
Dettingen (on the Main) 60.
— (Swabia) 36. 44. 53.

Dettwang 130.
Deuerling 119.
Diedorf 133.
Diemendorf **197.**
Diepoldsburg **43.** 31.
Diesbach 233.
Diessen 197.
Dietersbach, the 200.
Dietfurt 52. 244.
Dikenreis 34.
Dillingen 113.
Dilsberg 72.
Dingolfing 136.
Dinkelsbühl 112.
Dinkelscherben **133.**
Distelhausen 70.
Ditzenbach 31.
Ditzingen 16.
Dobel 19.
Döbraberg, the **73.**
Dolderthal, the **47.**
Dollnstein 131.
Dombühl 26. 112.
Donauheuneburg **54.**
Donaumoos, the **127.**
Donaustauf 124.
Donauwörth 112.
Donzdorf 31.
Doos 70. 81. **93. 94.**
Dorfen 194.
Dorfgütingen 112.
Dorfprozelten 62.
Dörnigheim-Hochstadt 59.
Dosbach, the **112.**
Dottenheim **69.**
Drei Brüder **91.**
Dreieckmarkstein **241.**
Dreifaltigkeitsberg 124.
Dreifürstenstein 48.
Drei Quellen, the **93.**
Dreisesselstein 244.
Dreistelzenberg 85.
Durach 202.
Durlach 18.
Durlesbach 34.
Dürnbuch 127.
Dürreberg 203.
Dürrenzimmern **111.**
Düsselbach 110.
Dusslingen **48.**
Dutzendteich **118. 109.**

Ebelsbach 82.
Eben 219.
Ebenhausen 83. **85.** 194.
Ebenhofen 202.
Ebensfeld 75.
Eberbach 22. **71.**
Eberhartsberg 81.
Ebermannstadt 93.
Ebersbach 30.
Ebingen 50.

Ebnisee 25.
Echaz, the 36. **47.**
Eckarts 85.
Eckartshausen 25.
Eckbauer 209.
Eckenberg 208.
Eckersdorf 88.
Ecksberg 244.
Eckstein 236.
Ed, the **221.**
Edelfingen 70.
Edelsberg 202.
Edelstein 58.
Edelweisslahnerkopf 232.
Efferding 243.
Eger 73. **111.**
—, the 29. 91. 111. 134.
Egern 218.
Egg, château 245.
Eggen 199.
Eggenfelden 244.
Egglkofen 136.
Eggmühl **135.**
Eggolsheim 80.
Egloffstein 81. 93.
Eglosheim 16.
Ehingen 38. 53.
Ehningen 39.
Ehrenberg 22.
Ehrenberger Klause 206.
Ehrenfels, **château 51.**
—, Old, **ruin 54.**
Ehrwald 210.
Ehrwalder Schanze 210.
Eibsee 209.
Eichhofen 119.
Eichicht 74.
Eicholzheim 71.
Eichstätt 132.
Eining 127.
Einkorn 25.
Einödsbach 200.
Einsingen 34.
Eisenbach, the **248.**
Eisenstein 248.
Eislingen 31. **43.**
Elchingen 133.
Eleonorenhain 242.
Elisabethenburg 27.
Elisenthal 248.
Ellingen 131.
Ellrichshausen 26.
Ellwangen 26.
Elm 63.
Elmau 209. **218.**
Elmauer Gries 212.
Elsawa-Thal, the 63.
Elsenz, the **22.** 72.
Elster 73.
—, the Weisse 72.
— Thal, the 72.
Eltersdorf 81.
Eltmann 82.

252 INDEX.

Elz, the 22. 71.
Empfing, baths 224.
Emskirchen 69.
Endersbach 27.
Endorf 222.
Endsthal 230.
Engelhardsberg 93.
Engelhartszell 242.
Engelhof 43.
Engelmannsreuth 110.
Engelmar 245.
Engelsberg, monastery 62.
Engelsburg 89.
Engelszell, monastery 242.
Engen 41.
Engstlatt 50.
Eningen 46.
Enter-Rottach 218.
Enz, the 15. 17. 18. 19.
Enzberg 17.
Enzenau 216.
Enzenstetten 203.
Enzisweiler 201.
Enzklösterle 19.
Epfendorf 40.
Epfenhausen 198.
Epprechtstein 91. 134.
Erbach 23. 34.
Erding 233.
Eremitage, château 88.
Ergenzingen 39.
Ergoldsbach 135.
Erkenbrechtsweiler 44.
Erlangen 80.
Erlau 241. 242.
Erlenbach 60.
Ermetzhofen 123.
Erms, the 36. 44.
Erpfingen 47.
Ertingen 54.
Erzberg, the 235.
Erzherzog-Johann-Klause 220.
Eschau 63.
Eschelbronn 71.
Eschenau 24.
Eschenbach 31. 110. 131.
Eschenlohe 207.
Eschlkam 236.
Essendorf 34.
Essing, Alt and Neu 126.
Essingen 28.
Essleben 82.
Esslingen 29.
Esterberg-Bauer 210.
Ettal 211.
Ettaler Mandl, the 211.
Etterzhausen 119.
Etwashausen 69.
Etzelwang 234.
Etzerschlössl 229.
Eubigheim 71.

Euerdorf 64.
Eurasburg 195.
Eussenheim 64.
Eutingen 17. 39.
Eyach 38.
—, the 50.
Eyachhörnle 50.
Eyachmühl 19.
Eybach 31.
Eybachthal, the 31.

Falepp 220.
—, the Rothe 220.
—, the Weisse 218.
Falkenstein, ruin, near Sigmaringen 52.
— (Saxony) 72.
—, the 202. 223.
— — (Königs-See) 230.
—, the Grosse 248.
Fall 216.
Fallmühle 202.
Falls-Gefrees 74.
Falterbach Waterfall 200.
Falzköpfl, the 232.
Falznerweiher 109.
Fantaisie, château 83.
Farchant 208.
Faukenbach, the 208.
Faukenschlucht 208.
Faulenbach 203.
—, the 40.
Faurndau 30.
Fechenbach 62.
Federsee 54.
Feilberg 199.
Feldafing 196.
Feldmoching 136.
Feldstätten 53.
Fellbach 27.
Ferchenbach, the 210.
Ferchen-See 209. 211.
Fern Pass 207.
Fernstein 207.
Fessenheim 112.
Feucht 118.
Feuchtwangen 112.
Feuerbach 17.
Feuerbacher Heide 11.
Feuerpalfen 231.
Fichtelberg 110.
Fichtelnab, the 110. 134.
Fichtenberg 25.
Fichtelgebirge, the 89.
Fieberbrunn 216.
Filder, the 39.
Fils, the 30. 31.
Filseck, château 30.
Fischburg-Thal 45.
Fischen 197. 200.
Fischhausen 220.
Fischingen 40.
Fischunkel-Alp 231.

Fleck 216.
Flochberg, the 29.
Floriansberg, the 36.
Forchheim 80.
Fornsbach 25.
Förstersböhle 94.
Förtschendorf 74.
Francon. Switzerland 92.
Frankfort 59.
Franzensbad 73.
Frauenau 246.
Fraueninsel 222.
Freiberg-See 200.
Freihöls 235.
Freilassing 224.
Freising 136.
Freiung 235.
Fremdingen 112.
Freudenberg 62.
Freudensee 241.
Freudenstadt 39.
Frenndschafts-Höhlen 53.
Freystadt 118.
Freyung 241.
Fridingen 52.
Friedberg 127. 133.
Friedrichshafen 35.
Friedrichshall 22.
Frommern 50.
Fronau 232.
Frondeck 38.
Frontenhausen 244.
Fuchseck 31.
Fuchsenstein 227.
Fuchsstadt 64.
Funtensee-Tauern 230.
Fürstenau 23.
Fürsteneck 241.
Fürstenfeld 198.
Fürstenfeldbruck 198.
Fürstenhöhe 51.
Furth 236.
Fürth 69. 81.
Füssen 203.

Gabelbach 133.
Gacht, Pass 206.
Gachtspitz 206.
Gädheim 82.
Gaildorf 25.
Gailenkirchen 24.
Gailenreuther Höhle 94.
Gaimersheim 132.
Gaimühle 23.
Gaisalpe 218.
Gaishöhe, the 63.
Galgenberg 109.
Gamburg 70.
Gamertingen 50.
Gangkofen 244.
Garatshausen 196.
Garmisch 208.

Gars 214.
Gärtringen 39.
Gaschwitz 72.
Gasseldorf 93.
Gattern 241.
Gäu, the 39.
Gausmannsweiler 25.
Gauting 195.
Gebhardsberg 201.
Gebrochen - Gutenstein 51.
Gefrees 74. 89.
Geiersberg, the 211. 215.
Geinberg 234.
Geiselhöring 135. 236.
Geisenhausen 135.
Geislingen 31. 43.
Geislinger Steig, the 32.
Geitau 220.
Gelber Felsen 43.
Gemünden 63.
Genderkingen 128.
Genkingen 47.
Gennach, the 198.
St. Georgen 86. 88.
Georgenau 44.
Georgensgmünd 111.
Georgsberg 239.
Gera 72.
Gerbershöhle 54.
Gerhausen, castle 53.
Gerlachsheim 70.
Gern 229.
Gernsbach 39.
Gernspitz 206.
Gernthal 216.
Gerold 210.
Geroldsgrün 73.
Geroldshausen 70.
Gersthofen 113.
Gessertshausen 133.
Geyerkopf 212.
Geyersberg, the 63.
Giech, castle 75.
Giengen 28.
Giessenbach, the 211.
St. Gilgenberg 88.
Gimpel, the 206.
Gindel-Alp 218.
Gindelalmschneid 218.
Gingen 31.
Girching 237.
Girgelstein 92.
Girglsee, the 218.
Glasenmühle 90.
Glashütte 218.
Glashütten 89.
Glashüttenriegel 245.
Glasthal, the 54.
Glauchau 72.
Glon, the 133.
Glonn 221.
— Thal, the 221.

Gmain 227.
Gmund 217.
Gmundbrücke 227. 231.
Gmünd (Swabia) 28.
Gögging 127.
Göggingen 55. 118.
Göhlstein 230.
Goldmühl 90.
Goldmühlthal 90.
Goldshöfe 28. 26.
Göll, the Hohe 230.
Göltzschthal, the 72.
Gomadingen 47.
Gompelscheuer 19.
Gondelsheim 14.
Gönningen 47.
Göppingen 30. 43.
Gosberg 93.
Gössenheim 64.
Gossmannsdorf 128.
Gössnitz 72.
Gössweinstein 94.
Gottes - Zell, monast. 28. 215.
Gottfrieding 136.
Gottmadingen 41.
Gotzen-Alp 231.
Grabenstetten 43.
Gräblensberg 50.
Grafenau 246.
Gräfenberg 81.
Grafeneck, castle 47. 54.
Grafenherberg Alp 221.
Grafenwiesen 235.
Grafing 221.
Graflinger-Thal, the 245.
Grassemann 90.
Graswang 212.
Grat, the 50.
—, the Schwarze 54.
Greifenberg 198.
Greifenstein, the 46.
Greiz 72.
Griesbach 241. 244.
Griesen 212.
Grieskirchen 242.
Grönhard 131.
Gronsdorf 126.
Groschlattengrün 134.
Grossaltdorf 25.
Gross-Armschlag 246.
— Auheim 59.
— Carolinenfeld 221.
— Gmain 225.
Grossgründlach 81.
Gross-Heppach 27.
Grosshesselohe 193. 215.
Grossheubach 62.
Gross-Krotzenburg 59.
— Sachsenheim 15.
— Umstadt 23.
Grötzingen 18.

Grün 248.
Grünau 242.
Grunbach 27.
Grünbach, the 70.
Grüner Felsen 45.
Grünenburg 31.
Grünenwörth 62.
Grünsee-Tauern 230.
Grünsfeld 70.
Grünsiein 89.
Grünten 199. 200.
Grünwald 194.
Gruttenstein, castle 225. 227.
Gschwänd, the 213.
Gschwandner Bauer 209.
Guckhüll 93.
Guffert, the 219.
Guglöd 247.
Gumpe, the 229.
Gumpenried 246.
Gundelfingen 54. 113.
Gundelsdorf 74.
Gundelshausen 125.
Gundelsheim 22.
Gundershofen 53.
Gündlkofen 136.
Gündringen 17.
Günz, the 133.
Günzach 199.
Günzburg 133.
Gunzenhausen 111. 131.
Gurgler-Thal 207.
Gurten 234.
Güssbach 75.
Gussmanns-Höhle 43.
Gutenberg 43.
— Stalactite Grotto 43.
Gutenstein 51. 52.
Güterstein 45.
Guttenberg 22.

Haag 234.
Haar 221.
Haberstein 92.
Haderfleck 127.
Hafenlohr 62. 63.
Hafenlohr, the 63.
Hafnerzell 242.
Hagel-Hütte 216.
Hagelstadt 135.
Hagenbüchach 69.
Hagenmühle 109.
Hahnenkamm, the 60.
Haidhausen 157. 221.
Haidhof 134.
Haiding 243.
Haidstein 235.
Haigerloch 38.
Hainberg, the 73.
Hain-Säulen, the 62.
Hainstadt 23.
Hall (Swabia) 24.

INDEX.

Hallstadt 75.
Hallthurm 227.
Hals 240.
Hammelburg 63.
Hammern - Eisenstrass 248.
Hammerau 224.
Hanau 59.
Hangende Stein, the 48.
Hausgörgl-Berg, the 109.
Harbatzhofen 200.
Harburg 112.
Hard, the 110.
Harsdorf 86.
Hartenstein 110.
Hartershofen 128.
Harthwald, the 85.
Hartmannshof 234.
Haselbach 85.
Hasenberg 12. 39.
Haslach 241.
Haspelmoor 134.
Hassfurt 82.
Hasslach, the 74.
— Thal, the 74.
Hassmersheim 22.
Hattingen 41.
Hausach 39.
Hausen (Franconia) 84.
— (Swabia) 52.
Hausener Felsen 31.
Hausham 220.
Hausstein, the 245.
Hauzenberg 241.
Hayenbach, ruin 243.
Hechendorf 207.
Hechingen 48.
Heersberg, the 50.
Hegau, the 41.
Heidelberg 72.
Heidelsheim 14.
Heidenab, the 89. 110. 134. 235.
Heidenheim 28.
Heidenlöcher 53.
Heidingsfeld 128. 70.
Heigenbrücken 62.
Heilbronn 20.
Heilbrunn, baths 216.
Heilbrunnen 36.
Heiligenberg 58.
Heilsbronn 26.
Heimenstein 31.
Heimgarten 207. 214.
Heining 237.
Heinsheim 22.
Heiterwang 206.
Helfenstein, ruin 31.
Hellenstein, ruin 28.
Hellmitzheim 69.
Helmbrechts 73.
Henfenfeld 234.
Heppenloch, the 43.

Herbertingen 54.
Herblingen 41.
Herbrechtingen 28.
Hergatz 200.
Herlasgrün 72.
Hermaringen 28.
Herrenalb 19.
Herrenberg 39.
Herrenchiemsee 222.
Herreninsel 222.
Herrlingen 52.
Herrnbergtheim 128.
Hersbruck 109. 234.
Hersching 197.
Herzogberg 230.
Herzogstand 214.
Heslach 11. 39.
Hesselberg 111.
Hessenthal 24. 25.
Hetzbach 23.
Heubach 23. 28.
Heuberg 40.
Heuchelberg 15.
Heuchelberger Warte 19.
Heudorf 54.
Heunensäulen 82.
Hienheim 127.
Hilgerberg 229.
Hiltersdorf 235.
Hiltgersberg, ruin 237.
Himmelkron 74.
Himmelschroffen 200.
Hinter-Graseck 209.
— Riss 216.
Hintersee, the 232.
Hirsau 18.
Hirschaid 80.
Hirschbachthal, the 110.
Hirschberg, the 218.
— Haus 218.
Hirschbergen 242.
Hirschbichel 233.
Hirschenstein, the 245.
Hirschhorn 71.
Hirschlanden 71.
Hobbach 63.
Hochalpe, the 218.
Hochberg 54.
—, the 44. 248.
Hochdorf 17. 39.
Hochfelln 223.
Hochhausen 22. 70.
Hochkalter, the 232.
Hochkopf 214.
Hochriss 223.
Hochschloss 197.
Höchst 23.
Hochstadt 59. 74.
Höchstädt 113.
Hochstauffen 224. 226.
Hochzoll 127. 133.
Hof 73. 134.
Hofalpe, the 223.

Höfen 18.
Hofheim 82.
Höfle 209.
Hofmannsruhe 230.
Högelberg 224.
Hohe Bogen, the 236.
— Fricken 208.
Hohenaschau, château 223.
Hohen-Gerhausen 53.
Hohenasperg 15.
Hohenau 241.
Hohen-Baldern, castle 29.
Hohenberg, the 40.
Hohenburg, château 216.
Hohen-Gundelfingen 113.
Hohengutenberg, ruin 43.
Höhenhain 194.
Hohenheim 14.
Hohenhöwen 41.
Hohenkarpfen 40.
Hohenkrähen 41.
Hohennagold 17.
Hohenneuffen 44.
Hohenrechberg, ruin 42.
Hohenschäftlarn 194.
Hohenschwangau 203.
—, castle 204.
Hohenstadt 109.
Höhenstadt 244.
Hohenstaufen 42.
Hohenstein, the (Bavaria) 93. 236. 241.
— (Swabia) 31.
—, ruin 110.
Hohenstoffeln 41.
Hohentwiel, ruin 41.
Hohen-Urach, ruin 45. 44.
Hohenwaldeck, ruin 220.
Hohenwarth 235.
Hohenwittlingen 44.
Hohenzollern, castle 48.
Hohe Licht 200.
— Wacht, the 93.
— Warte, the 63. 88.
Hohlefels 63.
Hohlohthurm, the 19.
Hohlwege (Defile) 233.
Hoierberg, the 201.
Hoiren 201.
Holenbrunn 92. 134.
Holledau 127.
Höllenbach, the 245.
Höllenthal, the 73.
— Klamm 210.
Höllriegelskreut 193. 194.
Hölltobel 200.
Holzkirchen 215.
Holzpoint Alp 218.
Homburg, ruin 62. 64.
Honau 46.
Honauer Steige 46.
Honburg, ruin 41.

INDEX. 255

Hopfenbach, the 126.
Hopfensee, the 203.
Hopferau 202. 203.
Hoppingen 112.
Horb 39. 38.
Hornberg, castle 22.
Hörnle, **the** 36. **44.** 207.
Hösbach 62.
Houbirg, **the** 234.
Hradschin, castle 72.
Huglfing 207.
Hühnerkobel, **the 247.**
Hülben 44.
Hummerstein 93.
Hundersingen 54.
Hunding-Hütte 212.
Hundsruck 50.
Hürben 28.
Hürbethal, **the 28.**
Hütten 53.

Icking **194.**
Igersheim **26.**
Igling 198.
St. Ilgen 14.
Ilkahöhe 196.
Iller, the 32. 34. 199. etc.
Illereichen 33.
Illertissen 33.
Illingen 15.
Ilm, the 127. **133.**
Ilsank 234.
Ilz, **the** 240. **241.**
Ilzstadt 240.
Immendingen 41.
Immenreuth 110.
Immenstadt 199.
Immenstadter Horn 199.
Imnau 38.
Imst **207.**
Indelhausen 54.
Ingolstadt 132. 127.
Inn, the 222. **233.** 237. 243.
Inner-Thiersee 221.
Inningen 198.
Innsbruck 219. 221.
Inzell 223.
Inzigkofen 51.
Ipf, the 29. **111.**
Iphofen 69.
Ipsheim 69.
Irrenlohe 134. 235.
Irrsee, monastery **198.**
Irschenhausen 194.
Isar, the 135. 136. 144. 215. 237. 244.
Isareck 136.
Isen, the 233. **244.**
Isenburg, castle 58.
Isny 54.

Jachenau 216.
Jägerkamp 220.

Jägermayr, the 243.
Jägersburg, the 80.
Jagst, the 22. 25. 71.
Jagstfeld 21.
Jakobsthal 60. **62.**
Janowitz 248.
Jenbach 219.
Jenner, the 230.
Jettenbach 244.
Jettenberg 232.
Jettingen 133.
St. **Jobst** 109.
Jochenstein, the **242.**
Jochplatte 214.
St. **Johann** 45.
Johannesberg **61.**
—, the 196.
Johannisbad **198.**
Jordanbad 34.
Josephslust 55.
Josephs-Thal 220.
Jossa 63. 85.
Jugend, the 205.
Jungingen 50.
Jusiberg 36.
Justingen, ruin 53.

Kager **236.**
Kahl **59.**
Kahlgrund **59.**
Kailbach 23.
Kainzen-Bad 210.
Kaiserbrunnen 213.
Kaiserklause 220.
Kaiserwacht 219.
Kaiseringen 50.
Kaitersberg 235.
Kälberau 60.
Kalte Keller, the 230.
Kaltenbrunn 19. 210. 217.
Kaltenburg, ruin 28.
Kammerlinghorn 233.
Kampenwand 223.
Kapfenburg 29.
Kappel 202.
Kapps-Höhle, **the 95.**
Karches 91.
Karlsbach 241.
Karlsbad (near Mergentheim) 71.
Karlsburg 64.
Karlshöhle, the **47.**
Karlslinde 44. 36.
Karlstadt 64.
Karlstein, ruin **226.**
Kasbach-Thal 219.
Karwendel-Gebirge 210.
— Spitze 211.
Katzenbuckel, **the 22.**
Katzenkopf 215.
Kaufbeuren 199.
Kaufering 198.
Kaunerwand 231.

Kelheim 125.
Kellberg 241.
Kemnath-Neustadt 89.
Kempten 199.
Kentheim 16. 19.
Kernmühle 241.
Kessel, the 230.
Kesselberg, the **214.**
Kieferthal 221.
Kienberg 223.
Kieritzsch 72.
Kilchberg 38.
Kinzig, the 39. **59.**
Kirchahorn 89.
Kirchberg 26.
—, baths 226. **225.** 227.
Kirchdorf 202.
Kirchehrnbach 93.
Kirchenbirkig 95.
Kirchenlaibach 89. **110.**
Kirchenlamitz 134.
Kirchentellinsfurt **36.**
Kirchheim 14. 19. 70.
— **unter** Teck 43.
Kirchleite, the 89.
Kirchseeon 221.
Kirnach, the 71.
Kirnachthal, the **71.**
Kirschbaumer **Schloss** 243.
Kislau **14.**
Kissingen 83.
Kisslegg 54.
Kitzingen **69.**
Kitzsee, **the** 244.
Klafferstrass 241.
Klais 210. 215.
Klardorf 134.
Klattau 248.
Klauenstein, the 245.
Klausenberg, the 136.
Klaushöhe, the 84.
Klautzenbach 247.
Klein-Auheim 23.
Kleinblankenbach 60.
Klein-Engstingen 47.
Kleinhesselohe 198.
Kleinheubach 61.
Klein-Hohenheim 14.
— Komburg 24.
— Ostheim 60.
— Steinheim 59.
— Umstadt 23.
Kleinwallstadt 61.
Klesheim 224.
Klingenberg 61.
Klingenbrunn 246.
Klingenstein 52.
Klosterberg, the 240. 60.
Klosterhof 225.
Klumpermühle 95.
Knäufelspitze 230.
Kniebis 39.

Kniepass 206. 226.
Knittlingen 15.
Kochel 213. 216.
Kochelsee 213.
Kochendorf 21.
Kocher, the 21. 24. 25. etc.
Kofel, the 212.
Kögel-Alp 219.
Köfering 135.
Kohlgrub 207.
Kohlhiesl 229.
Kohlstetten 47.
Kolbermoor 222.
Kolbersbach, the 218.
Kollbachthal, the 245.
Kollenberg 62.
Kollnburg 216.
Komburg, abbey 24.
Köngen 35.
König 23.
Königs-Alpe 218.
Königsbach, the 230.
Königsberg 82.
Königsbronn 28.
Königsbrunnen, the 28.
Königsdorf 195.
Königsegg, castle 55.
Königshofen 71.
Königs-See 230.
Königswarth 211.
Konstanzer Ach, the 199.
— Thal, the 200.
Kornberg, the Grosse 73.
Kornthal 16.
Kornwestheim 16.
Kössein, the 110. 134.
Kösseine, the 92. 110.
Kothbach Fall 202.
Kothmaissling 235.
Kötzting 235.
Krähenbad, the 39.
Krähenberg, the 23.
Kraiburg 244.
Kraichgau, the 15.
Krankenheil, baths 216.
Kranzberg 211.
Krauchenwies 54.
Krausenbach 63.
Krebsstein 43.
Krekelmoos 206. 213.
Krempelstein, castle 242
Kreuth 218.
—, Wildbad 218.
Kreuz, the 92.
Kreuzberg, the 85.
Kreuzlingen 57.
Kreuzwertheim 63.
Krinning 211.
Kronach 74.
Kronheim 111.
Kronwinkel 136.
Krottenkopf 209.
Krottensee 110.

Krün 215.
Kubani 242.
Kuchalb 31.
Kuchen 31.
Kuchler Loch 230.
Kufstein 221.
Kugelberg 47.
Kübberg 245.
Kuhflucht 203.
Kühlenfels 95.
Kühlenfelser-Thal 95.
Kulmbach 74.
Kupfer 24.
Kuppenburg 93.
Küps 74.
Kuschwarda 242.

Laber 119.
—, the 118.
—, the Grosse 135.
—, the Kleine 135.
—, the Schwarze 119. 125.
Labyrinthenberg 73.
Lackenhäuser 211.
Laiz 51.
Lam 217.
Lamboiwald, the 59.
Lammerbach 216.
Landau 244.
Landestrost, castle 133.
Landl 221.
Landsberg 198.
Landshag 243.
Landshut 135.
—, castle 135.
Langacker 223.
Langenargen 35.
Langenau 28.
Langenauer-Thal 73.
Langenbach 136.
Langenbruck 235.
Langenbrücken 14.
Langenbrunn 52
Langenenslingen 51.
Langenfeld 69.
Langenisarhofen 237.
Langenprozelten 63.
Langenschemmern 34.
Langentheilen 110.
Langenzenn 69.
Lange Thal, the 93.
Langlau 111.
Längsee 221.
Langstadt 23.
Langweid 113.
Latten-Gebirge 221. 232.
Lauchert, the 54.
Lauchheim 29.
Lauda 70.
Laudenbach 26. 61. 64.
Lauenstein 74.
Lauer, the 85.

Lauf 109. 234.
Laufach 62.
Laufamholz 234.
Laufen an der Eyach 50.
Laufenmühle 53.
Lauffen 19.
Lauingen 113.
Laupheim 34.
Lauter 224.
—, the Grosse 47. 53.
Lauterach 53.
Lautereck 25.
Lautern 53.
Lanter-See 209. 211.
Lauterthal, the Grosse 53.
Lautlingen 50.
Lech, the 114. 127. 123. 133. 198. etc.
Lechfeld, the 198.
Lehberger, the 217.
Lehesten 74.
Lehrberg 130.
Leinleiter Thal 93
Leipheim 133.
Leiten 211. 219.
Leitzach-Thal 220.
Lemberg, the 40.
Lengenwang 202.
Lenggries 216.
Lenninger Thal, the 43.
Leogang Steinberge 233.
Leonberg 16.
Leonhardstein 218.
Leoni 196. 194.
Lermoos 203.
Leutasch-Klamm 211.
— Valley 211.
Leuterschach 202.
Leutershausen 26.
Leutkirch 54.
Lichtenau 63.
Lichteneck, ruin 236.
Lichtenfels 74.
Lichtenstein, château 46.
Lichtenstern 24.
Liebenstein 19.
Liebenzell 18.
Lierheim 112.
Lindau 201.
Lindenhart 110.
Lindenhof, the 201.
Linder 212.
Linderhof, castle 212.
Lindich, château 48.
Linz 234. 242. 243.
Listsee 226.
Lochenstein, the 50.
Lochhausen 134.
Löchle-Thal 90.
Lockstein 223.
Lofer 226.

Loferer Alpe 226.
— Hochthal 226.
— Steinberge 226.
Lohbach Fall 218.
Lohberg 247.
Lohhof 136.
Lohr 62.
Lohrbach-Thal 60. 62.
Loisach, the 194. 207. 212.
Lonsee 32.
Loquitz-Thal 74.
Lorch 27.
St. Loretto 200.
Lossburg 39.
Löwenstein 23.
Lübnitz, the 89.
— Thal, the 74.
Ludwigsbad-Wipfeld 82.
Ludwigsburg 15.
Ludwigs-Canal, the 75. 111. 125.
Ludwigshafen 201.
Ludwigshall 22.
Ludwigshöhe, the 109.
Ludwigshöhle, the 94.
Ludwigs-Insel, the 209.
Ludwigsquelle 90.
Ludwigsstadt 74.
Ludwigsstein 246.
Ludwigsthal 246. 248.
— (Danube) 52.
Ludwigsthurm 60. 61.
Luhe 134.
Luisenburg, the 92.
Lukas-Terrasse, the 208.
Lupfen, the 40.
Lusen, the 242. 247.
Lustheim, château 229.
Lustnau 36.
Luxburg, the 92.
Mädchenfels, the 46.
Mädelegabel 200.
Mägdeberg 44.
Maihingen 112.
Main, the 59. 74. 90. 123.
Main, the Rothe 74. 110. etc.
—, the Weisse 74. 86. 89.
Mainau, Island of 57.
Mainberg 82.
Mainbernheim 69.
Mainkur 59.
Mainleus 74.
Mainroth 74.
Mairhalde, the 31.
Maisach 134.
Maisenburg, ruin 54.
Mamming 244.
Manching 127.
Mangfall, the 217. 220.
Mangolding 236.
Mangoldstein, fortress 112.

Mantler Wald 89.
Marbach (Baden) 40.
— (Würtemberg) 25. 47. 54.
Marblinger Höhe 221.
Markt-Bibart 128.
St. Maria-Einsiedel 194.
Mariahilfberg 118. 235.
Maria-Plain 224.
Marienberg, fortress (Würzburg) 68.
—, the (Algän) 199.
Marienbrücke 205.
Markbuchen 246.
Markelfingen 55.
Markelsheim 26.
Markt 113.
Markt-Bibart 69.
Marktbreit 128.
Markt-Einersheim 69.
Markt-Eisenstein 248.
Marktgölitz 74.
Marktheidenfeld 62.
Marktl 234.
Marktleuthen 134.
Marktoffingen 112.
Markt-Redwitz 110. 134.
— Schorgast 74.
Marktzeuln 74.
Marquartstein 223.
Marsbach, castle 243.
Martinlamitz 134.
Marxen-Höhe 229.
Marxgrün 73.
Mätze, the 92.
Maubach 25.
Mauer 22.
Maulach 25.
Maulbronn 15.
Maurach 249.
St. Maurus 52.
Maushain 119.
Mauth 242.
Mauthhäusl 226.
Maximilianshöhle 110.
Maximilianshütte 134. 223.
Mayence 61.
Meckenbeuren 35.
Meckesheim 22. 71. 72.
Meersburg 57. 201.
Mehltheuer 73.
Mehrstetten 53.
Meiningen 86.
Meitingen 113.
Mellrichstadt 85.
Memmingen 33. 198.
Mengen 54.
Menningen 55.
Menterschwaige 193.
Mergelstetten 28.
Mergentheim 70. 26.
Mering 133.
Merlbach 194.

Mertingen 113.
Mespelbrunn 63.
Messelstein 31.
Messkirch 55.
Metten 245.
Metzingen 36.
Michaelsberg 19. 126.
Michelbach 60.
Michelfeld 110.
Michelsberg, the (near Hersbruck) 109.
— — (Swabia) 31.
— — (on the Neckar) 22.
Michelstadt 23.
Miesbach 220.
Miltach 235.
Miltenberg 62.
Mindel, the 133.
Mindelheim 198.
Minneburg 22.
Minning 234.
Mirskofen 135.
Mistelgau 89.
Mittag, the 199.
Mittelberg 199.
Mittel-Graseck 209.
Mitten 201.
Mittenwald 210.
Mitterkaser-Alpe 232.
Mittersendling 215.
Mitterteich 73.
Mochenwangen 34.
Möckmühl 22. 71.
Mödishofen 133.
Mögeldorf 109. 234.
Mögglingen 28.
Möhringen 41.
Molkenbauer 226.
Mömbris 60.
Mondfeld 62.
Monrepos, château 16.
Montfort, château 35.
Moosach 221.
Moosburg 136.
Moosham 236.
Mooswacht 233.
Moritzberg, the 234.
Mosbach 71.
Mössingen 48.
Möttingen 112.
Müdesheim 64.
Muggendorf 93.
Mühl 206. 213.
Mühlacker 15.
Mühlbach 111.
Mühlberg, the 52.
Mühldorf 233. 244.
Mühlen 38.
Mühlfeld 197.
Mühlhausen (Swabia) 44.
— (Franconia) 64.
Mühlheim 52. 59.
Mühlingen 55.

258 INDEX.

Mühlthal 195.
Müller am Joch 214.
Müllerhütte 248.
Müllnerhorn 224.
Mümling, the 23.
— Grumbach 23.
Münchberg 73.
Münchshöfen 237.
Münchsmünster 127.
Munderkingen 53.
Munich 137.
  Academy of Art 152.
  — of Science 190.
  Allerheiligenhofkirche 148.
  Alte Hof, the 152.
  — Residenz, the 145.
  Anatomical Institute 191.
  St. Annakirche 156.
  Antiquarium 179.
  Arcades 148.
  Archives 151.
  Arco-Zinneberg, Palace 157.
  Arsenals 187. 192.
  Art-Industrial School 180.
  — Union 149.
  Au 192.
  Auer Kirche 192.
  Basilica 187.
  Baths 140.
  Bavaria 191.
  St. Benno's 186.
  Blind Asylum 151.
  Botanic Garden 187.
  Brienner-Strasse 157.
  Bronze Foundry 186.
  Cabinet of Coins 190.
  — of Drawings 172.
  — of Engravings 172.
  — of Vases 173.
  Cattle Market 191.
  Cemeteries 180. 191. 192. 193.
  Clinical Institutes 191.
  Coach Houses, Royal 148.
  Collection, Palæontological 190.
  —, Prehistoric 190.
  — of Minerals 190.
  — of Phys. and Opt. Instruments 190.
  —, Zoological-Zootomical 190.
  Corn Hall 192.
  Court Chapel 148.
  Crystal Palace 187.
  English Chapel 144. 150.
  — Garden 193.

Munich:
  Ethnograph. Museum 149.
  Exhibitions of Art 142.
  — of Exports 190.
  Exhibition Building 184.
  Feldherrnhalle 149.
  Festsaalbau 147.
  Fischbrunnen 189.
  Frauenkirche 189.
  GasteigPromenades 157.
  Georgianum 151.
  Giesing Church 192.
  Glass-Painting 142.
  Glyptothek 180.
  Government Buildings 152.
  Gynæcological Institute 191.
  Haidhausen 157.
  Hall of Fame 191.
  Herzog-Max-Burg 188.
  Hofbräuhaus 138. 152.
  Hofgarten 148.
  Holy Ghost, Church of the 192.
  Hospital, General 191.
  Hygienic Institute 191.
  Isarthor 192.
  St. John's 157.
  Justice, Courts of 190.
  Karlsthor 190.
  Kaulbach-Museum 150.
  Königsbau 147.
  Kunstgewerbehaus 188.
  Landtagsgebäude 188.
  Leopoldstrasse 152.
  Library 150.
  Loggie 171.
  Lotzbeck Collection 158.
  Ludwigsbrücke 192.
  Ludwigskirche 151.
  Ludwigstrasse 149.
  Luitpold-Terrace 157.
  Maillinger Collection 192.
  Mariahilfkirche 192.
  Marien-Platz 188.
  St. Mark's 157.
  Market, Provision 192.
  Marstall 148.
  Mary, Column of 188.
  Maternity Hospital 191.
  St. Matthew's 191.
  Maximilianeum 156.
  Maximiliansplatz 188.
  Maximilianstrasse 152.
  Max-Joseph-Platz 145.
  Max-Joseph-School 151.
  St. Michael's 190.
  Military Museum 187.

Munich:
  Mint, the 152.
  Municipal Hist. Museum 192.
  National Museum 153.
  Nat. Hist. Collection 190.
  Nibelungen Frescoes 147.
  Nymphenburg 194.
  Obelisk 157.
  Observatory 193.
  Odeon 150.
  Ophthalmic Institute 191.
  Palace, Royal 145.
  — of PrinceRegentLuitpold 150.
  — of Duke Max 150.
  Panoramas 143. 180. 191.
  Pathological Institute 191.
  St. Peter's 189.
  Pharmacological Institute 191.
  Physiological Institute 191.
  Pinakothek, New 173.
  —, Old 158.
  Plaster Casts, Museum of 149.
  Polytechnic School 180.
  Porcelain Paintings 174.
  Post Office 152. 140.
  Priests' Seminary 151.
  Prinz-Regenten-Strasse 149.
  Promenade-Platz 188.
  Propylæa 184.
  Protest. Church 192.
  Railway Station 137. 191.
  Rathhaus, New 189.
  —, Old 189.
  Reiche Capelle 146.
  ReichenbachBridge 192.
  Reisingerianum 191.
  Residenz, Alte 145.
  Ruhmeshalle 191.
  Schack Gallery 184.
  Schwanthaler Museum 191.
  Sendlingerthor-Platz 191.
  Siegesthor 152.
  Slaughter House 191.
  Statue of Deroy 152.
  — of Ehrhardt 156.
  — of Fraunhofer 152.
  — of Gabelsberger 188.
  — of Gärtner 192.
  — of Gluck 188.

INDEX. 259

MUNICH
Statue of Goethe 190.
— of Klenze 192.
— of Kreittmayr 188.
— of King Max Joseph 145.
— King Maximilian II. 156.
— of Elector Maxim. I. 157.
— of Elector Max Emanuel 188.
— of Lewis I. **149**.
— of Liebig **188**.
— of Nussbaum **191**.
— of Orlando di Lasso 188.
— of Rumford 152.
— of Schelling 152.
— **of** Schiller 157.
— **of** Senefelder 191.
— **of** Westenrieder 188.
Synagogue 190.
Thal, the 192.
Theatine Church 149.
Theatres 141. 148. 191. 192.
Theresienwiese 191.
Treasury 146.
University 151.
War Office 150.
Wittelsbach **Fountain** 188.
— Palace 157.
Münnerstadt 85.
Münsing 194.
Münsingen 47.
Murgthal, the 39.
Murnau 207.
Murr, the 25.
Murrhardt 25.
Musau 206.
Mylau 72.

Nab, the 110. 119. **134. 235.**
Nabburg 134.
Nagold 17.
Nagold, the 16. 17.
Naiderach-Thal, the 212.
Naila 73.
Nannhofen 134.
Nase, the 214.
Nasenbach, the 244.
Nassereit 207.
Natternberg, the 237. 244.
Nebelhöhle, the 47.
Nebelhorn 200.
Nebringen 39.
Neckar, **the** 12. 21. 71. etc.
Neckarburken **71**.
Neckarelz 22. **71**.

Neckargemünd 22. 72.
Neckargerach 22.
Neckarhausen 40. **71**.
Neckarsteinach 71.
Neckarsulm 21.
Neckarthailfingen 35.
Neckarzimmern 22.
Neidenstein 71.
Neidingen 52.
Neidstein 235.
Nellenburg, ruin 55.
Nellmersbach 25.
Nendingen 52.
Nenzingen 55.
Nersingen 133.
Nesselgraben 226.
Nesselwang 202.
Netzschkau 72.
Neubäu 235.
Neuberg 71. **73.**
Neuburg 128.
—, abbey 72.
Neudeck, ruin 93.
Neudenau 22. 71.
Neudorf 63.
Neuenburg 18.
Neuenmarkt 74. **86.**
Neuenreuth 110.
Neuenstein 24.
Neuern 248.
Neu-Essing 126.
Neufahrn 135. 136.
Neuffen 44.
Neufra 40.
Neuhaus, castle (on the Danube) 243.
— (Bavaria) 110. **220.**
— (Baths) 85.
Neuhausen 41.
Neu-Kelheim 126.
Neukirchen 235. 236.
Neumark 72.
Neumarkt (Austria) 234. 242.
— (on the Rott) 244.
— (on the Sulz) 118.
Neundorf 72.
Neu-Nussberg, ruin 246.
— Oetting 233.
— Offingen 133. 113.
Neureut 218.
Neu-Schwanstein, castle 204.
Neusorg 110.
Neustadt an der Aisch 69.
— am Main 62.
— (Franconia) 85. 89.
— (in the Odenwald) 23.
— an der Donau 127.
— (near Stuttgart) 24.
— an der Waldnab 134.
Neustädtle 24.
Neuthal 242.

Neu-**Ulm** 32. 33. 133.
St. Nicola 135.
Niederaschau 223.
Niederbiegen 34.
Niederhaus, Fort 239.
Niederlauer 85.
Niedernau 38.
Niederpöcking 195.
Niederranna 242.
Nieder-Sonthofer See 199.
Niederstetten 26.
Nieder-Stotzingen 28.
Niefern 17
Non 226.
Nonnberg, the 240.
Nonnengütl 240.
Nonsberg, ruin 54.
Nordendorf 113.
Nordheim 19.
Nördlingen 111.
Nufringen 39.
Nuremberg 95.
Ægidien-Platz 105.
St. Ægidius, Church of 105.
Archives 102.
Behaim's House 100.
— Monument 105.
Bratwurst-Glöcklein 95. 102.
Breweries 109.
Bridges 98.
Bronze-Foundry 103.
Burg 103.
St. Catharine's Church 104.
Cemeteries 103. 104.
Deutsche Haus, the 104.
Dürer's House 102.
— **Statue** 102.
St. Elizabeth's Church 104.
Eucharius Chapel 106.
Exhibitions 96. 105.
Eysser's House 105.
Fortifications 98.
Frauenkirche 99.
Frauenthor 98.
Freiung 103.
Gänsemännchen 100.
Germanic Museum 106.
Gewerbe-Museum 105.
Grübel Fountain 105.
Gymnasium 105.
Hallerthor 104.
Harbour 104.
Heiligegeist-Kirche 105.
— Spital 105.
Heiligkreuz-Kapelle 104.
Heinzel Fountain 105.

17*

260 INDEX.

Nuremberg:
Holzschuher Chapel 103.
Industrial Museum 105.
— Art, Royal School of 106.
St. Jakob's Church 104.
St. John's Church 103.
Kaiserburg 103.
Koberger's House 105.
Krafft's House 105.
— Stations 103.
Landauer Monastery 106.
Law Courts 102.
St. Lawrence, church 99.
Library 102.
Manufactories 103. 109.
Marienkirche 99.
St. Maurice 102.
Maxfeld 109.
Melanchthon's Statue 105.
St. Moritzkapelle 102.
Museum 99.
Nassauer Haus 99.
Nat. Hist. Museum 106.
Neuthor 104.
Olives, Mt. of 103.
St. Ottmar's Chapel 103.
Palm's House 102.
Paumgärtner's House 105.
Peller's House 105.
Pentagonal Tower 103.
Petersen's House 106.
Picture Gallery, Municipal 101.
Pirkheimer's House 100.
Post Office 96. 105.
Private Houses 105. 106.
Rail. Station 98.
Rathhaus 100.
Rosenau 109.
Rotermundt Collection 102.
Rupprecht's House 106.
Sachs's House 105.
— Statue 105.
St. Sebaldus 101.
Schöne Brunnen 100.
Schütt, Island of 105.
Shops 96.
Spitalkirche 105.
Spittler Thor, the 101.
Stadtpark 109.
Stadtwage 102.
Synagogue 105.
Tetzel Chapel 106.

Nuremberg:
Theatre 96. 104.
Thiergärtner-Thor 103.
Topler's House 106.
Towers 103. 104.
Tucher'sches Landhaus 106.
Tugendbrunnen 99.
Vischer's House 104.
Walpurgis Chapel 103.
Warriors' Monument 99.
Weisser Thurm 104.
Nuremberg Switzerland 110.
Nürtingen 35. 44.
Nusshard, the 91.
Nusshausen 126.
Nymphenburg 194. 133. 134.

Oberach, the 234.
Ober-Ammergau 211.
Oberau 126. 207.
Oberaudorf 221.
Ober-Böhringen 31.
— Breitenau 246.
Oberdachstetten 130.
Oberdorf 199. 202.
Ober-Eichstädt 132.
— Frauenau 246.
— Grainau 209.
Obergünzburg 199.
Oberhaid 82.
Oberhaus, fort 239.
Oberhausen 46. 113. 133.
Ober-Herrlingen, castle 53.
Oberholzheim 34.
Ober-Kirchberg 33.
Oberkochen 28.
Oberkotzau 73. 134.
Ober-Langenstadt 74.
Oberlenningen 43.
Obermarchthal 54.
Obermichl 243.
Ober-Mieming 207.
Obernach 215.
Obernau 61.
Obernberg 234.
Obernburg 61.
Oberndorf 40. 125.
— Schweinfurt 82.
Obernesselgraben 226.
Obernzell 242.
Oberrad 59.
Oberrain, baths 226.
Oberreitnau 200.
Oberschmeien 51.
Obersee, the 231.
Ober-Siegsdorf 223.
Oberstaufen 200.
Oberstdorf 200.

Oberstimm 133.
Ober-Theres 82.
Oberthurnhof 247.
Obertraubling 135. 236.
Obertürkheim 29.
Oberwappenöst 110.
Ober-Warngau 215.
— Weissbach 233.
Oberwerrn 83.
Oberzeismering 196.
Oberzell (near Friedrichshafen) 35.
— (on the Main) 64.
Ober-Zwieselau 246.
Obsteig 207.
Ochenbruck 118.
Ochsenfurt 128.
Ochsenkopf, the 90.
Ochsenwang 31. 43.
Odenwald, the 22.
Oedwies 245.
Oehringen 24.
Oelsnitz 72.
—, the 89.
Oethlingen 43.
Oetting, Alt and Neu 233.
Oettingen 111.
Offenau 22.
Offenbach 59.
Offenhausen 47.
Offenhausen 47.
Offingen 133.
Ohe, the Grosse 246.
—, the Kleine 247.
Ohebach, the 245. 246.
Ohlstadt 207.
Ohrn, the 24.
Olching 134.
Olgahöhle 47.
Oppenau 39.
Oppenweiler 25.
Osser, the 248.
Osterbühl 212.
Osterburken 22. 71.
Osterhofen 220. 237.
Ostermünchen 221.
Ostersee, the 218.
St. Oswald 242. 247.
Oswald-Hütte 216.
Oswaldshöhle 93.
Ottendorf 25.
Ottensheim 243.
Ottensoos 234.
Ottobeuren 34.
Otzing 244.
Owen 43.
Oy 202.
Oythal, the 200.

Paar, the 127.
Padinger Alpe 226.
Pähl 197.
St. Pancras, Chapel of 226.

INDEX. 261

Pappenheim 131.
Parksteiner Wald 89.
Parksteinhütten 89.
Parsberg 119.
Partenkirchen **208.**
Partenstein 62.
Partnachklamm 208.
Partnach Valley 208.
Pasing 134. 195. 198.
Passau 237.
Passrent 211.
Pegnitz 110.
—, the 70. 98. 109. **231.**
Peissenberg 197.
Penzberg 213.
Perach 233.
Pertisau 219.
Petersberg 130.
Petersdorf 245.
Petershausen 133.
Petershöhle, the **52.**
Peterskirch 234.
Peterstirne 82.
Pfaffenhofen 133.
Pfaffenstein, the 93.
Pfahl, the 246.
Pfahlbronn 27.
Pfahlrain, the 127.
Pfänder, the 201.
Pfarrkirchen 244.
Pfinz, the 18.
Pflach 206.
Pflaumloch 29.
Pflieglhof, the 217.
Pflummern 51.
Pforzen 198.
Pforzheim 17.
Pfreimd 134.
Pfronten 202.
Pfullendorf 55.
Pfullingen 46.
Pfünz 132.
Philippsruhe, château 59.
Pichelbach-Thal 248.
Piding 224.
Pilsting 136. 244.
Pinswang 206.
Pinzberg 92.
Pipping 195.
Pirk 72.
Pirka 246.
Plain, castle 225.
Planegg 195.
Plansee, the Great 213.
—, **the** Little 206. 213.
Plassenburg 74.
Platnersberg, Schloss 109.
Plattling 237. 244.
Plauen 72.
Pleinfeld 111. 131.
Pleinting 237.
Plettenberg 50.
Plochingen 30. 43.

Plüderhausen **27.**
Plumser Joch 216.
Pocking 244.
Pöllat, the 205.
Polling 207.
Pommelsbrunn 234.
Pommersfelden, château 80.
Ponholz 134.
Poppenhausen **83.**
Pösing 235.
Possenhofen 195. **196.**
Postbauer 118.
Pöstlingberg, the **243.**
Pottenstein 95.
Prag, the 17.
Prague 236.
Pram-Haag 234.
Pramthal, the 212.
Predigtstuhl, the 245.
Pressath 89.
Pretzfeld 93.
Prien 222. 223.
— Thal, the 222. 223.
Primthal, the 40.
Probstzella 74.
Prüfening 119. 125.
Prunn 126.
Pullach 194.
Pulling 235.
Püttlach-Thal, the 95.

Quakenschloss, the 94.
St. Quirin 217.

Rabeneck, castle 94.
Rabenecker Thal, the 94.
Rabenstein, castle (Franconia) 94.
— (Bavar. Forest) 247.
— (on the Altmühl) 126.
— Cavern 94.
Rachel, the 247.
Rachelsee, the 247.
Radersdorf 127.
Radldorf 236.
Radolfzell 55.
Rain 128.
Rainer Alpe 218.
Rainthal, the 210.
Raitersaich 26.
Ramsau 232.
—, the 207. 231.
Ramsauer Ache, the 227. 229.
Ranariedl 242.
Randeck **31.**
Ranna 110.
Rappenau **22.**
Raschenberg, ruin 224.
Rathsberg, the 81.
Ratibor, château 111.
Ratisbon 119.

Rauberburg, **ruin 31. 43.**
Rauberhof 31.
Rauhe Alb, the 32.
Rauhe Kulm, the 89. 245.
Ravensburg 34.
Rechberg, the 42.
Rechenau 221.
Rechensoldenfelsen 247.
Rechtenbach 63.
Rechtenstein 54.
Rednitz, the 26. 69. **111.**
Redwitz 74.
Regen 246.
—, **the** 119. 134. 235.
—, **the** Grosse 246.
—, **the** Kleine 246.
—, the Schwarze 235. 246.
—, the Weisse 235. 247.
Regensburg, see Ratisbon.
Regenstauf 134.
Regnitz, the 70. **75. 81.**
Rehau 73.
Reichelsdorf 111.
Reichenau 55.
Reichenbach (Saxony) 72.
— **(W**urtemberg) 19. 30.
Reichenberg (Bavaria) 70. **247.**
— (Wurtemberg) 25.
Reichenhall 224.
— Kirchberg 227.
Reichenschwand 109.
Reichenstein, ruin 53.
Reichersbeuern 215.
Reichertshausen 133.
Reichertshofen 133.
Reicholzheim 70.
Reinertshof 203.
Reisensburg, castle 133.
Reistenhausen 62.
Reitalpgebirge 224. 226.
Reiter-Alpe 232.
Reith 211.
Reitofen 229.
Remsthal, the 24. 27.
Renningen 16.
Rentershofener **Damm** 200.
Rentwertshausen 86.
Reschenstein, ruin 240.
Retzbach 64.
Reussenstein 31.
Reuth 73. 134.
Reutlingen 36.
Reutte 206.
Rezat, the Franconian 26. 111. 130.
—, **the** Swabian 111.
Rhine, **the** 41. 56.
—, Falls of the 41.

Rhön Mts., the 85.
Ried 197. 213. 234. 235.
Riedau 242.
Rieden 207.
Riedenburg 126.
Riedernberg, the 48.
Riederstein, the 218.
Riedlingen 54.
Ries 240.
—, the 112.
Riesenburg, **the (Franconia)** 94.
Riesloch, the 247.
Riesserbauer 208.
Rietenau 25.
Rietheim 40.
Rigi, the Kleine **57**.
Riglasreuth 110.
Ringberg, the 125.
— Sattel 218.
Risserkogl, **the 218**.
Rissthal, the **31. 216**.
Risstissen 34.
Ristfeichtkogl 224. **226**.
Ritschenhausen 86.
Rockenbrunn 234.
Rodach, the 74.
Rodenbach 62.
Roding 235.
Roggenthal, the 32.
Röhmbach 241.
Rohr 127.
Rohrbach 244.
Rohrbrunn 63.
Rohrenfeld 127.
Röhrmoos 133.
Roigheim 71.
Romanshorn 201.
Rorschach 201.
Röschenauer Höhe 194.
Rosenbach 130.
Rosenberg 71. 74. 235.
Rosenburg 126.
Rosenheim 222.
Rosenmüller's Höhle 93.
Rosenstein, château (near Stuttgart) 13.
—, the (near **Aalen**) 28.
Rösla, the 91.
Röslau 91. 134.
—, the 110. 134.
Rossbach 73.
Rossberg 54.
—, the Dettinger 44.
—, **the** (near Lichtenstein) 47.
Rösslau, the 91.
Rossrücken 213.
Rossschläg-Pass **206**.
Rossstall 26.
Rosthäusl 229.
Rostwald 229.
Roth 111.

Roth am See 26.
Röthenbach (near Nuremberg) 234. 235.
— (near Lindau) 200.
— (Swabia) 18. 19.
Rothenburg, ruin 109.
—, the (near Cannstatt) 29.
—, the (near Neckarelz) 22.
Rothenburg on the Tauber 123.
Rothenfels 62.
—, the 199.
Rothenkirchen 74.
Rothenstadt 134.
Roththal, the 25.
Röthswand 231.
Rothwand 220.
Rott 243.
—, the 244.
Rottach 218.
—, Falls of the 218.
Rottenacker 53.
Rottenbuch 197. 212.
Rottenburg 38.
Rottendorf 81. 69.
Rottershausen 85.
Rottmannshöhe 196.
Rottweil 40.
Rucken, the 53.
Rückersdorf 109.
Ruderatshofen 199.
Rudolfstein, the 91.
Ruhmannsfelden 245.
Rummbach 235.
Rumpenheim 59.
Runderberg 44.
Runding 235.
Rupprechtstegen 110.
Rupprechtstein 234.
Rusel, the 53.
Rusenschloss 53.
Rutschenhof 45.

Saal 125.
Saalach, the 224.
Saale, the 73. 91. 224.
—, the Franconian 63. 83.
Saaleck 64.
Saalfeld 74.
Saalfelden 233.
Sachenbach 216.
Sachsen 26.
Sachsenhausen 59.
Sagereckwand 230.
Salem 59.
Sallet-Alp 231.
Salmendinger Chapel 48.
Salzach, the 224.
Salzberg, the Upper 229.
Salzbüchsel, castle 225.
Salzburg 224.

Salzburg, ruin 43. 85.
Salzgau, the 15.
Salznau 242.
Sandbach 237.
Sanderau 128.
Sandsee, castle 111.
Sassau, Islet of 215.
Sattel 43.
Sattelbogen, the 44.
Sauerlach 215.
Sauldorf 55.
Saulgau 54.
Saulgrub 207. 212.
Säuling 205. 206.
Saulohrn 241.
Sausbach, the 241.
Schachen 201.
— **Alp**, the 210.
Schachenbad 201.
Schafberg 50.
Schaffhausen 41.
Schafhausen 16.
Schaftlach 215.
Schäftlarn 194.
Schalksburg 50.
Schalding 237.
Schalmei-Schlucht 208.
Schambachthal, the 126.
Schappach 232.
Schardenberg 241.
Schärding 242.
Scharfenberg, ruin 31.
Scharfeneck, ruin 80.
Scharitzkehl-Alp 230.
Scharling 218.
Scharnhausen 14.
Scharnitz 211.
Scharreben 247.
Schaumburg, ruin 243.
Schechen 243.
Scheer **54.**
Schefflenz 71.
Scheiben, the 248.
Schelklingen 53.
Schellenberg 112.
Schellneck 126.
Schemmerberg 84.
Schenkenzell 39.
Schierenhof 28.
Schildenstein 218.
Schillerhöhe, the 11. 25.
Schiller-Höhle 44.
Schillingsfürst 130.
Schillingsloch 44.
Schiltach 39.
Schimborn 60.
Schinder 218.
Schirnding 111.
Schlachters 200.
Schlath 31.
Schlattan 209.
Schlattstall 43.
Schlehdorf 214.

INDEX.

Schleissheim 136. 194.
Schleiz 73.
Schlicke 205.
Schlierach-Thal 220.
Schlierbach 72.
Schliersee 220.
Schlossberg, the 206. 222.
Schlösslberg, the 242.
Schlössibichi 229.
Schlott 127.
Schluxenwirth 206.
Schmachtenberg 82.
Schmalsee 210.
Schmaussenbuck 109. 234.
Schmeie, the 50.
Schmeienthal 50.
Schmelz, the 209.
Schm**iechen** 53.
Schmiechthal 53.
Schmutter, the 113. 133.
Schnabelwaid 110.
Schnaith 27.
Schnaitheim 28.
Schnaittach 109.
Schnaizlreut 226.
Schneeberg. the (Fichtelgebirge) 91.
Schnelldorf 26.
Schöllenbach 23.
Schöllkrippen 60.
Schömberg 19.
Schönau (Franconia) 63. 85.
— (Bavaria) 229. 246.
Schönauer Glashütte, the 241.
Schönberg 73.
Schönbichl 202.
Sch**ö**nbornsprudel, **the** 84.
Schönbuchwald, the 39.
Schönbühl, castle 27.
Schondorf 198.
Schöneben 247.
Schönenberg 26.
Schönfeldspitze 230.
Schönfels, château 72.
Schongau 198.
Schönhof 94.
Schönsteinhöhle 93.
Schönthal 61.
Schonungen 82.
Schopfloch 31. 39. 112.
Schoreberg, ruin 63.
Schorndorf 27.
Schottenhof 126.
Schotter-Thal, the 94.
Schrainbach, the **231**.
— Fall, the 226.
Schreckee 221.
Schrezheim 26.
Schrobenhausen **127**.

Schröcke 43.
Schrozberg 26.
Schullerloch, the 126.
Schülzburg, ruin 54.
Schurwald, the 27.
Sch**ussen**, the 34.
Schussenried 34.
Schutterthal, the 95.
Schützensteig, the **205**.
Schwabach 111.
Schwabelweis 124.
Schwaben 233.
Schwabhausen 198.
Schwabing 152.
Schwäbisch-Gmünd **28**.
— Hall 24.
Schwabmünchen 198.
Schwaigen 136.
Schwaighof 218.
Schwaikheim 24.
Schwakenreute 55.
Schwanberg, the 69.
Schwandorf 134. 235.
Schwanegg, château 193.
Schwansee 203.
Schwanstein, castle 204.
Schwarzachthal 118.
Schwarzbach, the 232.
— Thal 71.
Schwarzbachwacht 232.
Schwarzberg-Klamm 226.
Schwarzenbach 73. 89.
Schwarzenberg, the 203.
Schwarzenbronn 130.
Schwarzenbruck 118.
Schwarzenfels 85.
Schwarze See 243.
Schwarzhanskarkopf 206.
Schweigern 71.
Schweinau 26.
Schweinfurt 82.
Schweinhausen 34.
Schweinhütt 246.
Schweinsberg 21.
Schwenningen 40.
Schwimmschule 136.
Sebastiansweiler 48.
Seckach 71.
Seebachwald 247.
Seebruck 223.
See**burg 45**.
Seeburger **Thal 44**.
Seefeld 211.
Seeg 202.
Seegraben, the **244**.
Seehausen **207**.
Seeon 223.
Seeshaupt 196. 213.
Seespitz 219.
Seethal 45.
Seewald, the 35.
Seewand, the 243.
Seisenberg-Klamm 233.

Selb **73**.
Seligenstadt 23. 81.
Senden 33.
Sennfeld 71.
Sentenhart 55.
Seubersdorf 119.
Se**ulbitz** 73.
Seussen 111.
Seybothenreuth 89.
Sibyllenloch 43.
Siebenellen 247.
Siegelsdorf 69.
Siglingen 71.
Sigmaringen **51**.
Sigmaringendorf 54.
Sigmundsburg, ruin 207.
Silberberg, the 247.
Simbach 234.
Simmsee, the 222.
Singen 41.
Sinn, **the 85**.
Sinnberg, the 85.
Sinnthal, the 63.
Sinzheim 22.
Sinzing 125.
Sodenthal 61. 63.
Söflingen 52.
Söhnstetten 32.
Söldenköpfl 231.
Solitude, the 14.
Solnhofen 131.
Sommerau 247.
Sondelfingen 36.
Sonnen 241.
Sonnenhügel 197.
Sonntagshorn 224. 226.
Sontheim 28. 198.
Sonthofen 200.
Sophienhöhle 94.
Soyen 244.
— Lake 197.
Soyer See 244.
Spaichingen 40.
Spalt 111.
Sparneck 73.
Sperberseck 43.
Spessart Mts., the 63.
Spezgarder Tobel 58.
Spiegelau 246.
Spielmannsau **200**.
Spitzberg 248.
— Sattel, the 248.
Spitzenberg, the 31.
Spitzing-See 218. 220.
Springen 53.
Stadelhorn 232.
Stadt am Hof 124.
Stadtprozelten 62.
Staffelbach 82.
Staffelberg 75. **241**.
Staffelsberg 84.
Staffelsee 207.
Staffelstein 75.

264 INDEX.

Stahringen **55**.
Stallau 216.
Staltach 213.
Stammbach 73.
Starnberg 195.
—, **Lake of** 195.
Starzel, the 38.
Starzeln 50.
Staubfall 226. 232.
Stauf, ruin (near Linz on the Danube) 243.
— (near Ratisbon) 124.
Staufen (Swabia) 31.
Staufenberg, ruin 39.
Staufeneck, ruin 31.
Stauffeneck, ruin 224.
Stauffengebirge 226.
Steben 73.
Steckelburg, ruin 63.
Stegen 198.
Steigberg, the 48.
Steigerwald, the 128.
Steigkoppe, the 60. 62.
Steilenfälle, the 210.
Stein (Fichtelgebirge) 89.
— (near Nuremberg) 26.
— **an der Trann** 224.
Steinach (Bavaria) 74. 202.
— (on the Main) 128.
—, **the** 90.
— **Thal, the** 17. 74.
Steinbach (near Hall) 24.
— (on the Main) 60.
— (near Michelstadt) 23.
— (Franconia) 74.
— (in the Murrthal) 25.
— (near Tölz) 216.
Steinberg, on the Main 64.
Steindorf 234.
Steinenbach 54.
Steinheim 59. 28. **113**.
Steinlachthal, the 48.
Steinmühle 73.
Steinrain 135.
Steinsee, the 221.
Steinwiesen 73.
Stemenhausen 74.
Stempfermühle 93.
Stephanskirchen 222.
Stephansposching 237.
Stepperg 128.
Stetten 48.
Stettfeld 82.
Steusslingen, ruin 53.
Stiegelruck 248.
Stillach, the 200.
Stock 222.
Stockach 55.
—, **the** 55.
Stockau 89.
Stockheim 74.
Stöffelberg, the 47.
Stoffelsberg, the 199.

Storzingen 50.
Strassberg 50.
Strasskirchen 237.
Straubing 236.
Streitberg 93.
Streitburg 93.
Streu, **the** 85.
Stromberg, the 15.
Strub, the 229.
Stuben 218.
— **Alp, the** 218.
Stuiben, the 199.
— **Falls** 206. 213.
Stuttgart 1.
Sülchenkirche, the 38.
Sulz am Neckar 40.
—, **Bad** 197.
—, **the** 118.
Sulzbach 25. 61. 235.
— **Waterfall** 197.
Sulzberg 202.
Sulzberglehen, the 229.
Sulzbrunn 202.
Sulzdorf 25.
Sulzerain 13.
Sulzthal, the 118.
Sünching 236.
Süssen 31.
Swabian Alb, the 42.

Tabor-Kapelle 223.
Tachenstein 126.
Tafertsried 245.
Taglaching 221.
Taimering 236.
Tanner-Alp, the 221.
— Mühle, the 221.
Tannheim 206.
Tapfheim 113.
Tatzelwurm 221.
Taubenberg, the 220.
Taubensee, the 232.
Tauber, the 70.
Tauberbischofsheim 70.
Tauberfeld 132.
Tauern, the 206. 213.
Taufkirchen 242.
Teck, the 31.
—, **ruin** 43.
Tegelberg, the 205.
— **Alp, the** 205.
Tegelstein 201.
Tegernheim 124.
Tegernsee 217.
Teinach 16.
—, **baths** 16.
Teisendorf 224.
Teisnach 225.
— **Thal, the** 245.
Telfs 207.
Tettnang 35.
Teufelsfelsen, the 125.
Teufelsgraben, **the** 215.

Teufelshörner, the 231.
Teufelsloch 95.
Teufelsmauer, the 127.
Teufelssee, the 248.
Teufelstisch 246.
Thaldorf 126. 127.
Thalfingen 28.
Thalham 220.
Thalhausen **40**.
Thalhof 54.
Thalkirchdorf 200.
Thalkirchen 194. 221.
Thalmühle **17**. 41.
Thalsteusslingen 53.
Thamm 15.
Thaneller, **the 206**.
Thäusser Bad 24.
Thayingen 41.
Theres 82.
Theresienklause, the 229.
Theresienstein, the 73.
Theresienthal 246.
Thierberg, the 50.
Thiergarten 52.
Thiergartenberg, the **44**.
Thiersee, the 221.
Thierseer Ache, the 221.
Thiersee-Thal, the 221.
Thonbrunn 73.
Thörlen, the 210.
Thumsee, the 226.
Thüngen 64.
Thüngersheim 64.
Tiefenbach 200. **211**.
Tiefenbronn 17.
Tirschenreuth 134.
Tittling 247.
Titt**moning** 224.
Todte Mann, the 230.
Tölz 215.
Trabitz 89.
Traifelberg, the **46**.
Trappensee 21.
Trauf, the 50.
Traun, the 223.
—, **the Rothe** 223.
Traunstein 223.
Traunthal, monastery 126.
Trausnitz, castle 135.
Trebgast 86.
Trembach 244.
Trennfeld 62.
Trettach, the 200.
Treuchtlingen **131**.
Triefenried 246.
Triefenstein 62.
Triesdorf 131.
Trimberg 64.
Tristram Ravine, the 227.
Trochtelfingen 29.
Trubachthal, the 93.
Trudering 221.

INDEX. 265

Tübingen 136.
Tüchersfeld 95.
Turkenfeld 198.
Türkheim 198.
Tuttlingen 41.
Tutzing 196.
Tyrnau 241.

Ueberkingen 31.
Ueberlingen 58. 201.
Ueberlinger See 57.
Uebersee 223.
Uffenheim 128.
Uffing 207.
Uhenfels 45.
Uhingen 30.
Uhlandshöhe, the 11.
Uhlbach 29.
Ulm 32.
Ulrichsberg 245.
—, the 245.
Ummendorf 34.
Umpfer, the 71.
— Thal, the 71.
Umratshausen 223.
Unken 226.
Unlingen 54.
Unnütz, the 219.
Unter-Ammergau 197. 212.
Unterauer Alp, the 214.
Unterbalbach 70.
Unterböbingen 28.
Unterbodenlaube 84.
Unterboihingen 35. 43.
Unterbuchen 195.
Unter-Elchingen 28.
— Frauenau 246.
— Grainau 209.
— Griesheim 71.
Unterhausen 46. 128.
Unterkochen 28.
Unter-Leinleiter 93.
Unterlenningen 43.
Unterloquitz 74.
Unterlötzen 206.
Untermarchthal 53.
Unter-Peissenberg 197.
Unterreichenbach 18.
Unterrodach 73.
Untersberg, the 224.
Unterschüpf 71.
Unter-See, the 55.
— Steinach 74.
Unterthölau 134.
Untertürkheim 29.
Unterwilzingen 53.
Urach 44.
—, Waterfall of 45.
Uracher Bleiche 44.
— Thal 44.
Urbach 27.
Urbanlehen 229.

Urfeld 214.
Urspring, nunnery 53.
— Thal, the 221.
Ursulaberg, the 46.
Utting 197.

Vach 81.
Vaihingen 15. 39.
Veitsberg, the 75.
Veitsburg, the 35.
Veitsböchheim 64.
Velden 110.
Veldenstein 110.
Vereins-Alpe 211.
Viechtach 246.
Viechtenstein, castle 212.
Vier Linden, the 207.
Vierzehnheiligen 75.
Villingen 40.
Vils 202.
—, the (Danube) 202. 235. 237. 244.
Vilsbiburg 136.
Vilseck 235.
Vilshofen 237.
Vohburg 127.
Vohenstrauss 134.
Voigtland, the 72.
Voitenberg-Oed, the 236.
Voitersreuth 73.
Volkersberg 85.
Vollmerz 63.
Volsbach 89.
Vorbach 110.
Vorderbrand 229. 230.
Vordereck 229.
Vorder-Graseck 208. 209.
— Hohenschwangau, castle 204.
Vorderkaser-Klamm, the 226.
— Riss 216.
— Thiersee, the 221.
Vorra 110.

Wagenbrech-See, the 210.
Wahlwies 55.
Waiblingen 27.
Waibstadt 71.
Waidbach, the 227.
Waidmannsgesess 94.
Waischenfeld 94.
Waizinger Alp 220.
Walchen, the 216. 219.
Walchensee 214.
Waldburg, castle (Swabia) 35. 39.
— — (Franconia) 82.
Waldeck 17.
Waldenburg 24.
Waldershof 110.
Waldhausen 27.
Waldhäuser 247.

Waldbaushof, the 50.
Waldkirchen 211. 243.
Wald-Leiningen 62.
Waldnab, the 134.
Waldsassen 73.
Waldsee 54.
Waldstein, castle 91.
—, the Grosse 73. 91.
Waldthurn 134.
Walhalla, the 124.
Walhallastrasse 124. 134.
Wallern 242.
Wallersdorf 214.
Wallerstein 111. 112.
Wallgau 215. 216.
Walmberg, the 218.
Walser Schänzle 200.
Waltenhofen 199.
Wangen 29.
Wannenberg, the 62.
Warmensteinach 90.
Wartberg, the 19. 21.
Warthausen 34.
Wartstein, ruin 54.
—, the 232.
Wasach 200.
Wäschenbeuern 27.
Wäscher-Schlössle 27.
Wasseralfingen 28.
Wasserberg, the 31.
Wasserburg (Lake of Constance) 201.
— (on the Inn) 213.
Wasserstetten 54.
Watzmann, the 232.
— Anger, the 232.
— Grube, the 232.
— Hocheck, the 232.
Wassertrüdingen 111.
Wechsel-Alp 218.
Wegfurt 85.
Wegscheid 216. 244.
Wehrstein 40.
Weibertreu, ruin 23.
Weichering 127.
Weiden 134. 235.
Weigolshausen 64. 82.
Weihenstephan 136.
Weiherhammer 235.
Weikersheim 26.
Weil 14.
Weilbach 62.
Weilderstadt 16.
Weiler 38. 54.
Weilerburg 38.
Weilheim 197.
Weinbauer, the 197.
Weinberg-Kapelle 220.
Weingarten (Swabia) 34.
Weinsberg 23.
Weischlitz 72.
Weissach, the 25. 218.
Weissbach 202. 223.

INDEX.

Weissbach, the 225. 226. 227. 233.
— Thal 223.
Weissenburg am Sand 131.
Weissenhorn 38.
Weissensee, the 202. 207.
Weissenstadt 91.
Weissenstein 18. 32.
— am Pfahl 246.
Weisshaus 206.
Weissmainfelsen 90.
Weissmainquelle 90.
Weitenburg, castle 38.
Weizern-Hopferau 202. 203.
Wellenburg, the 198.
Wels 234. 242. 243.
Welschingen 41.
Weltenburg, Abbey 126.
Welzheimer Wald 27.
Wemding 112.
Wemholz, the 229.
Wendelstein 118. 221.
— Alp, the Upper 221.
— **Haus**, the 221.
Wendthal, the 32.
Werdau 72.
Werenwag, château 52.
Wernberg 134.
Werneck 64. 82.
Wernfeld 64.
Wernstein 242.
Wernthal, the 64.
Wertach, the 113. 133 202.
Wertheim 63.
Wesenufer, or
Wesenurfahr 243.
Westerhof, the 217.
Westerstetten 32.
Westhausen 29.
Westheim 133.
Wettelsheim 131.
Wetterau 59.
Wetterstein-Alp 210.
— **Chain** 206.
Wettzell 246.
Weyarn 220.
Wichsenstein, the 93.
Wichtelshöhlen, the 84.
Wicklesgreuth 26.
Wiebelsbach 23.
Wiedergeltingen 198.
Wielandstein, the 43.
Wiesau 134.
Wiesensteig 31. **43.**
Wiesent, the 80.
— Thal, the 92.

Wiesenthau **93.**
Wiesloch 14.
Wilburgstetten 112.
Wildbad (Wurtemberg) **18.**
— (Bavaria) **129. 130.**
— Kreuth 218.
Wildberg 17.
Wildenranna 211.
Wildenstein, **castle** (on the Danube) 52.
— (Spessart) 63.
Wildflecken 85.
Wildpoldsried 199.
Wildsee, the 19. 211.
Wilferdingen 18.
Wilfersreut 90.
Wilhelma, the 13.
Wilhelmsbad 59.
Wilhelmsburg, the 32.
Wilhelmsfelsen, the 44.
Wilhelmsglück 24. 25.
Wilhelmshall 40.
Wilhering, abbey 243.
Wilibaldsburg 132.
Willsbach 23.
Wilzhofen 197.
Wimbach-Klamm 231.
Wimpfen 22.
Wimsener Höhe, the 54.
Windisch-Eschenbach 134.
— **Gailenreuth** 93.
Windloch, the **110.**
Windsfeld 131.
Windsheim 69.
Winkel 216.
Winnenden 24.
Winnenthal, château 24.
Winterbach 27.
Winterhausen 123.
Winterschneidbach 131.
Wipfeld 82.
Wirsberg 74.
Wittelsbach, ruin **127.**
Witthoh, the 41.
Wittighausen 70.
Witzenhöhle, the 93.
Wölchingen 71.
Wolfach 39.
Wolfegg 54.
Wolfert, the **53.**
Wolfratshausen 194.
Wolfstein 118. 136. **241.**
Wolfsthal 53.
Wolnzach 133.
Wörnitz, **the 111. 112.**

Wörnitzstein 112.
Wörth 61. **136.**
Wunderburg 80.
Wundersböhle, the 93.
Wunsiedel 91. 134.
Würm, the (Bavaria) 133. **134.** 198.
— — (**Wurtemb.**) 17.
— Thal, **the** (Bavaria) 195.
Wurmesau 207. 212.
Wurmlingen 40.
Wurmlinger Capelle 38.
Würmsee 195.
Würzburg **64.**
Wutzlhofen **134.**
Wutzmühle, the 236.

Zapfendorf **75.**
Zaupenberg 94.
Zavelstein 16. 19.
Zeil 82.
Zeitlofs 85.
Zell **in** the Odenwald 23.
— (Fichtelgebirge) 91.
— (**on** the Main) 64.
Zeller **Horn**, the 48.
Zellerhörnle, the 50.
St. Zeno 225.
Zielfingen 54.
Zimmern 70.
Zinneberg, **château 221.**
Zipfelhäusl, **the 231.**
Zirl 211.
Zizenhausen 55.
Zollern 48.
Zollhaus 202.
Zoolith Cavern 91.
Zoppatenbach, the 90.
Zorneding 221.
Zucbering 127.
Zuffenhausen 16.
Zugspitze, the 206.
Zumhaus 26.
Zusam, the 133.
Zusameck 133.
Züttlingen 71.
Zwergeck, the 248.
Zwickau 72.
Zwiefalten 54.
Zwiefaltendorf 54.
Zwiesel 246.
—, the 226.
— Alp 226.
Zwieselau 246.
Zwieselberg, the 206. 246.
Zwingenberg 22.
Zwingsteg 200.

Leipsic: Printed by Breitkopf & Härtel.

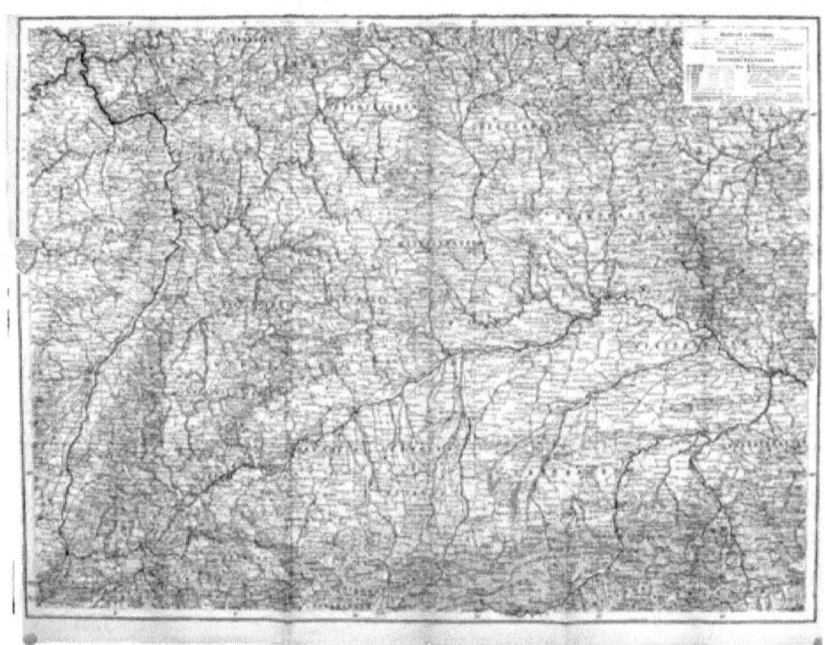

nobe
loa
gru

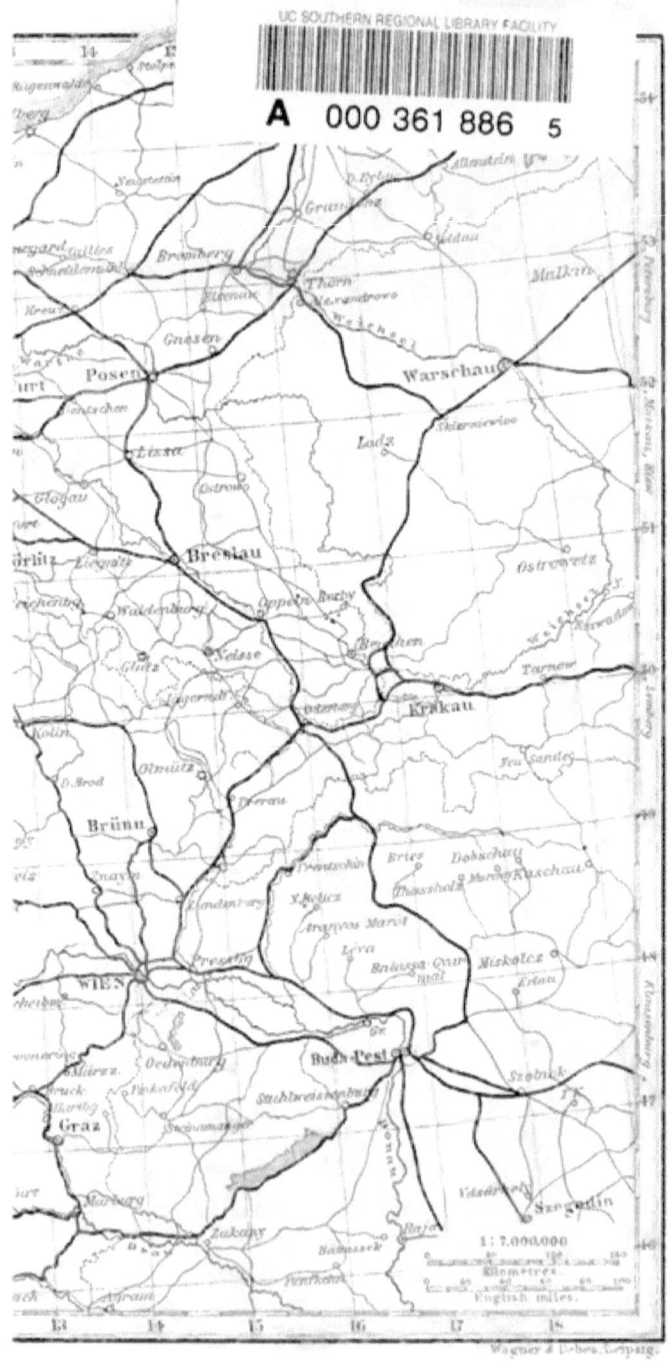

www.ingramcontent.com/pod-product-compliance
Lightning Source LLC
Chambersburg PA
CBHW030320240426
43673CB00040B/1223